Nazi Juggernaut in the Basque Country and Catalonia

Conference Papers Series No. 14

Nazi Juggernaut
in the Basque Country and Catalonia

Edited by Xabier Irujo and Queralt Solé

Center for Basque Studies
University of Nevada, Reno
2018

This book was published with generous financial support from the Basque Government.

Nazi Juggernaut in the Basque Country and Catalonia
Conference Papers Series No. 14
Series editor: Sandra Ott

Center for Basque Studies
University of Nevada, Reno
1664 North Virginia St.
Reno NV 89577-2322 USA

http://basque.unr.edu
Editors: Xabier Irujo and Queralt Solé

Library of Congress Cataloging-in-Publication Data

Names: Irujo Ametzaga, Xabier, editor. | Sole, Queralt, editor.
Title: Nazi Juggernaut in the Basque Country and Catalonia / Editors,
    Xabier Irujo, Queralt Sole.
Description: Reno : Center for Basque Studies Press, [2019] |
    Series: Basque government conference papers series ; no. 14 | Includes
    bibliographical references and index.
Identifiers: LCCN 2019001083 | ISBN 9781949805055 (pbk. : alk. paper) |
    ISBN 1949805050 (pbk. : alk. paper)
Subjects: LCSH: Nazis--Spain--History--20th century. | País Vasco
    --History--20th century. | Catalonia--History--20th
  century. | Germany--Relations--Spain. | Spain--Relations--Germany.
Classification: LCC DP302.B53 N39 2019 | DDC 946.081/343--dc23

Contents

Introduction

Xabier Irujo and Hilari Raguer i Sunyer

During the morning of July 17, there was a revolt by officials in the garrison of the Spanish army in Melilla. Immediately thereafter, there was a military revolt by military units in Ceuta and Tetouan, which was at the time the capital of the Protectorate of Morocco. With that, war was declared on the legitimate government of the Spanish Republic in which the Italian and German regimes would be involved.

Following the death of General José Sanjurjo in a plane crash, leadership of the military revolt soon passed over to Generals Emilio Mola (in charge of the army in the north) and Francisco Franco (in charge of the army in the south, with forces stationed mainly in the Spanish colony of Morocco). Franco needed to transport his troops from Africa to the Iberian Peninsula across the Strait of Gibraltar. He could not transport his units by ship because most of the Spanish navy had remained loyal to the republican government, so that his only option was to transport the contingent of nearly thirty thousand men by plane. But Franco did not have any planes, so just four days after the coup d'état, the rebel leader contacted the German ambassador to ask for planes and military assistance for the rebels.

The request was not well received by the German ministry for foreign affairs but Adolph P. Langenheim and Johannes Bernhardt, members of the Auslands-Organisation der NSDAP (Foreign Organization of the National Socialist German Workers Party), a Nazi party cell in Morocco, offered to take General Franco's request for military aid to the German government. Langenheim and Bernhardt contacted their direct superior, Ernst W. Bohle, in charge of international relations for the Nazi party, who, ignoring the position of the ministry for foreign affairs, headed by Konstantin von Neurath, contacted Rudolf Hess, Hitler's representative in the Nazi party, and he organized a meeting between Franco's delegate and Hitler.

These events were hurried and took place without much planning. On July 22, Franco ordered Captain Francisco Arranz to fly from Tetouan to Berlin to negotiate the sending of Junker Ju52 transport planes with Hitler, but when Arranz arrived in Berlin on July 25, Hitler was not there. The Führer was in Bayreuth, attending a performance of Wagner's opera *Siegfried*, directed by Wilhelm Furtwängler at the Villa Wahnfried. The third act of *Siegfried* represents the heroine Brünnhilde enclosed in a magic ring of fire by Wotan (Odin), from which she can only escape by receiving a kiss from a hero. There is only one requirement, namely that this hero should not be a coward; only a man who knows no fear can break the magic ring of fire and awaken and marry the heroine. Siegfried reaches the place and plays his horn loudly, thereby breaking the spell that had kept the ring of fire, within which Brünnhilde is enclosed, going. Siegfried kisses Brünnhilde, who wakes up from a sleep that has kept her prisoner for seventeen years.

Arranz's request reached Hitler at 10:00 pm, following the performance, and the idea moved Hitler so much that he excitedly accepted the idea of aiding the rebels, even against the opinion of the ministry for foreign affairs, a large number of Reich ministers, and most high-raking officials of state. Germany would be Spain's Siegfried and Spain would be Germany's Brünnhilde. And the contract, negotiated in record time, was termed Operation Feuerzauber (Operation Magic Fire, recalling Wagner's magic ring of fire).

Hermann Göring ordered Lieutenant General Helmuth Wilberg, at the time the head of the Luftwaffe War Academy in Berlin, to take charge of creating and organizing an aerial unit for Franco titled Special Staff W (for Wilberg), which he did in two days. On July 27, ten days after the military uprising in Morocco, six Heinkel He51 fighter planes and eighty-six men (pilots and mechanics) were dispatched on the steamship *Usaramo*, which set sail from Hamburg on July 27 and arrived in Cadiz on August 5, 1936. The ground staff serving the aircraft was recruited from among the personnel at the Döberitz air base. Together with the six Heinkel He51s, led by Colonel Von Scheele, twenty Junker Ju52s were also sent that landed in Tetouan on July 28, 1936. These initial Junker bombers and their crew members were under the control of Lieutenant Rudolf von Moreau, who some months later would take part in the bombing of Gernika.

Germany was now participating in the war in support of the rebels and Mussolini had, likewise, ordered the sending of troops and arms to the insurgents. However, there was never any official declaration of war against the Republic by either of the two regimes. Quite the contrary, because both subscribed, alongside twenty-seven European governments, to the Non-Intervention Pact of August 1936, by which these countries would remain neutral in the conflict and would not send troops or arms to either side in the war. And that war was baptized emphatically by the Non-Intervention Committee as a "Spanish Civil War" and for three years European governments contended that neither Germany nor Italy were sending troops in favor of the insurgents. These events drove the British journalist Claud Cockburn to outline his famous phrase: "Believe nothing until it has been officially denied."

The reaction of most Basque and Catalan political parties was likewise immediate. On the morning of July 19, Manuel Irujo and Josemari Lasarte announced on the radio that the Basque Nationalist Party opposed the military coup led by the rebel soldiers. They likewise announced that their support for the legitimate government of the Spanish Republic did not mean that they would abandon their political principles, that is, their aspiration to create an independent Basque republic. The Catalan political forces behaved in a similar way and, after the formation of the Basque government in October 1936, both the Catalan and Basque governments, led by Presidents Lluís Companys and Jose A. Agirre respectively, confronted the insurgents politically and militarily.

By virtue of the limitations imposed by the Non-Intervention Committee, the military unit sent by the German regime was named the Condor Legion. In line with the needs and ideas of Hermann Göring, at that time minister of aviation in Nazi Germany, thus unit was made up almost entirely of Luftwaffe units and by April 1937 the German government had sent a total of 157 machines to Franco: fifty-one bombers, fifty-seven fighter planes, thirty-nine reconnaissance planes, nine seaplanes, and a transport plane. Of these 157, on April 17, 1937 the legion had, in the aerodromes of Gasteiz and Burgos, destined for the Basque Front, a total of eighty-two machines: thirty bombers, thirty-four fighters, seventeen for reconnaissance, and one liaison.

The military campaign on Basque soil was marked from the beginning by terror bombings. The first bombing took place on Wednesday, July 22, 1936, just five days after the uprising. On that occasion two Breguet Br.19 planes appeared over Otxandio. As Gabriel Otalora, a witness to the bombing, stated, the town was in the middle of its annual festival when, at 9:00 a.m., these two planes appeared, flying quite low, given that they were almost touching the church steeple. They made several rounds of the town. The pilots waved to people who, engrossed, gazed at and hailed them. By their gestures they attracted a large number of children that, as had been the case on previous days, were expecting sheets of paper to rain down on them, shouting *"papelak die!, papelak die!"* (Flyers! Flyers!). After making several rounds at 70 meters in height, they bombed and machine-gunned the town center. While the children had no idea what the war meant or what a terror bombing consisted of, at that stage the pilots were conscious of the fact that the victims were civilians because they could see them perfectly well. They did so for twenty-five minutes, carrying out repeated sweeps, machine-gunning and dropping all the bombs they had.

José Antonio Maurolagoitia, the doctor in Otxandio, was one of the first to arrive at the scene:

> I went out toward Andicona Square. The rooves were not damaged, nor the electricity lines destroyed. It was something more serious and more awful; it was human pain. People torn to pieces, children mutilated, women decapitated. It was the cries of the townspeople, in Basque, pleading with me to treat them; it was the torrent of blood that ran toward the water of the small well set in the middle of the square. I asked others for help, which was given me immediately and tirelessly. With sheets, with strips of sheets, I began to carry out urgent treatment. There were some, many, that, unfortunately, did not need anything. They had perished mown down by the brutal shrapnel of many bombs dropped twice. Other boys and girls, their limbs dangling, appealed to me in Basque phrases that I still have impressed in my heart."[1]

That morning, sixty-one people died in Otxandio. The immense majority of them were civilians, and sixteen of the dead were under ten years old. Personal tragedies were those of war. Every member of the

---

1   "La histórica villa vasca es bombardeada por los sediciosos," *Euzkadi*, July 24, 1936, 2.

Aldai Kapanaga family died that July 22; together with Bixente and Feliciana, their children Juan, Francisco Javier, and Irene died. Aged nine, seven, and five, the brothers Sabin, Iñaki, and Justo Lasuen died in the bombing. Jon and Miren Lasuen, cousins of the former, lost their two brothers and their father. Nikolasa Belakortu and Tomas Aspe left six children orphaned. Sabina Oianguren was widowed. The reporter for the daily *Euzkadi* stated that Sabina had lost her sight. She had lost her husband, Emeterio Garces, and four of her five children: Pedro, Juan Manuel, Teodoro, and Maria Jesus. The oldest was thirteen.

This was just the beginning of a nine-year war. The results of the bombing operations were startling: more than 1,200 bombings in one year of war, most of them aimed at open cities, most of the victims civilians. In the spring of 1937, within this context of aerial warfare, the bombing of Gernika took place. From the spring of 1937 onward, likewise, Catalonia would suffer a huge number of bombings, with a balance that is still difficult to quantify, although far more than the 1,200 records offered by the Basque case.

During the course of the bombing of Gernika more than two thousand people lost their lives, most of them civilians, many of them children. Faced with the dimension that the terror bombing campaign was taking on and, in the face of the impossibility of protecting children from aerial bombings, the Basque government organized the massive evacuation abroad of Basque children. In May 1937, Bilbao, the main city of the Basques, took in 150,000 refugees that had fled zones occupied by the rebels, among them tens of thousands of children. Just three days after the bombing of Gernika the French prime minister, Léon Blum, and the minister of foreign affairs, Yvon Delbos, agreed to receive 100,000 Basque refugees, which goes to show that everyone took the threats of the rebel leadership and its terror strategy very seriously. Barely ten days after the bombing, the number of refugees in Bilbao had risen to 250,000 according to the American consul in Bilbao, William E. Chapman.[2] In total, at least 32,000 children under the age of sixteen had to be evacuated between early May and mid-August 1937, in the face of the infant mortality that the terror bombing campaign was generating in the Basque Country. It was the largest evacuation of children in European history. They were called "the children of Gernika" and most of them would never return home.

---

2   Xabier Irujo, *Gernika: 26 de abril de 1937* (Barcelona: Crítica, 2017), 91.

With the occupation of Bilbao in June 1937 and the fall of the Basque Country as a whole into the hands of the insurgents at the end of August 1937, the Basque government took up residence in Catalonia. While the first bombings of urban centers in Catalonia took place in late 1936 and early 1937, there was a spectacular increase in the number of bombings and Catalan towns attacked from early 1938 on. This would continue to be constant until the end of the war. In total, the rebel air force in Catalonia had 388 bombers operating continuously. Among the most destructive aerial attacks suffered, one might cite those of Lleida and Granollers, or the bombings of Barcelona in March 1938. From Christmas Day 1938 on, the date on which the final offensive against Catalonia started, aerial bombings intensified once more and with them the number of civilian deaths.

At the close of 1938, the collapse of Republican forces was obvious, and in March 1939 the last troops and large streams of refugees sought refuge in the French Republic: it was an exodus of refugees made up of more than five hundred thousand people of all ages. Many of them crossed the border only to be housed in a "reception" camp, surrounded by barbed wire, in camps like those in Argelés-sur-Mer, in which the refugees were interned out in the open, on a sandy promontory.

Defeated in the Basque Country and Catalonia, and knowing that World War II would soon break out, the Basque and Catalan governments set up in exile, in French territory. When, on September 3, 1939, the United Kingdom and the French Republic declared war on Germany, the Basque government-in-exile in Paris came on board, allying with the Allied side. In fact, in September 1939 the Basque government was already at war with Nazi Germany, Fascist Italy, and Falangist Spain: on January 24, 1939 Lehendakari Agirre wrote in his official capacity to the prime minister of the French state, Édouard Daladier, communicating to him that, the global conflict having broken out, the Basque government would position itself against the totalitarian forces and on the side of the democracies. The international policy of the Basque government left no room for any other solution, whether moral, ideological, political, strategic, or even from the perspective of

TELEGRAMMA IN PARTENZA N. 3088

MINISTERO
DEGLI
AFFARI ESTERI

Uff. "S"

Oggetto

Per corriere
In cifra

Indirizzato a Generale BERTI

V I T O R I A

Roma, li 14-12-1937-XVI 19 ... ore ...   Spedito da

(Testo) Leggo Suo rapporto in data 10 da Vitoria circa immi-
nente attacco alt Aviazione delle Baleari sarà rinforzata et
avrà compito di terrorizzare le retrovie rosse et specie i
centri urbani alt Preparare bene i legionari in modo che il
loro attacco sia decisivo et curare i loro rifornimenti in
viveri caldi e munizioni alt V.E. è autorizzata a far sape-
re che si tratta dell'ultima battaglia per le ragioni che
V.E. espone alt Molto bene la designazione di Frusci e.
Roatta per tenere i collegamenti con gli spagnoli alt Est
inteso che i comandi devono tutti dico tutti essere sul campo dell'azione alt Est essenziale che il tempo permetta al-
l'aviazione nazionale di agire a massa; chi si difende può
farne a meno non chi attacca alt Sono sicuro che le nostre
divisioni saranno all'altezza del loro compito e avranno il
mordente di Malaga e di Santander (.)

MUSSOLINI

In this telegram from Mussolini to General Berti, the Duce states categorically that the first task of the air force bombardment is to terrorize the rearguard and bomb urban centers. Source: Archivo del Ministerio degli Affari Esteri.

so-called political realism, condemned repeatedly in Jose A. Agirre's correspondence with Manuel Irujo.[3]

This position refusing neutrality was crystallized in the directives for foreign policy in the *Planned Project for the Government of Euzkadi* signed by the Basque government in Paris on April 12, 1940, two months before the occupation of the city of light:

> The Basque government ratifies its commitment made in Gernika on October 7, 1936, by which Euzkadi "will strengthen the links that unite it with the peoples that maintain democratic forms of government and especially with those others in which important Basque collectivities live." With the European war declared, these norms must be developed and settled as follows: (a) the Basque government rejects spiritual neutrality in a conflict in which the liberty of men and people is defended, against tyranny and force. Its position is of spiritual belligerence and maximum material support in favor of the democratic nations in their struggle against the totalitarian dictatorships; (b) the Basque government condemns the German-Russian pact and all acts and demonstrations of this nature that have occurred or may occur against the liberty of peoples; (c) the Basque government ratifies its protest published on the occasion of the signing of the Anti-Comintern Pact by General Franco, rejecting any representation or jurisdiction of the current government of Spain over the Basques.[4]

In effect, intervention meant a position of open hostility to any totalitarian power and maximum material support for the democratic nations in their struggle against totalitarian dictatorships.

The *drôle de guerre* or "phony war" on the Western Front ended on May 10, 1940 when the Wehrmacht invaded Western Europe. The Northern Basque Country (Iparralde) and Northern Catalonia (Catalunya Nord) were occupied and on July 24 that year the Reich imposed on France the so-called demarcation line that divided Iparralde in two: Lapurdi and Navarre remained under direct German control while Zuberoa was under the administration of Vichy France led by Philippe

---

3   "Prologue," in Iñaki Goiogana, Josu Legarreta, and Xabier Irujo, *Un nuevo 31. Ideología y estrategia del Gobierno de Euzkadi durante la Segunda Guerra Mundial a través de la correspondencia de José Antonio Aguirre y Manuel Irujo* (Bilbo: Sabino Arana, Bilbo, 2007).

4   *Proyecto de programa para el Gobierno de Euzkadi*, Paris, April 12, 1940.

Pétain. Catalunya Nord likewise remained under the collaborationist Vichy administration. A four-year period of terror thus began for the inhabitants of these zones.

The policy of the Francoist state from 1939 on would be one of lining up with the Axis powers but maintaining a neutral policy. The Spanish regime signed the Anti-Comintern Pact on March 27, 1939 and declared itself a "non-belligerent" state on June 12 the same year in the context of World War II. Franco gave numerous demonstrations of support for the German war effort, such as the interview between Ramón Serrano Suñer and Joachim von Ribbentrop on September 16, 1940; the interview between Heinrich Himmler and General Franco in Madrid on September 20 and 24; and the meeting between Franco and Hitler in Hendaia on the following October 23 and the meeting between Franco and Benito Mussolini in Bordiguera on February 12, 1941. Franco would send the Spanish Division 250,[5] the Wehrmacht's *Einheit spanischer Freiwilliger*, known as the *Blaue Division* or Blue Division, to the Russian Front between June 24, 1941 and 1943.[6]

In this context of rapprochement between the German and Spanish regimes, Himmler visited Montserrat in search of the Holy Grail. On October 19, Himmler, accompanied by General Karl Wolff and other SS dignitaries, arrived in the Basque Country by train via Hendaia. Passing through Donostia, Altsasu, and Burgos, he would arrive in the early morning of October 20 at the Estación del Norte in Madrid, where he would meet with authorities of the regime. Three days later he went to Barcelona, staying in the Ritz Hotel in the Catalan capital. There, a lavish banquet was held in his honor, attended by ninety representatives of the regime, the cost of which rose to 13,275 pesetas of the time, around 155,000 euros at the current exchange rate.[7] Following the obligatory parades, Himmler held meetings with Franco and the minister of foreign affairs, Ramón Serrano Suñer (the former's brother-in-law), with whom he studied the preliminaries of Operation Felix (the planned attack and capture of Gibraltar) and the creation of a joint Hispano-German intelligence service that would operate in Latin America with the aim of bringing some countries there into the Axis, among them Mexico, Brazil, and Argentina. During that visit the collaboration of the two police forces and reciprocal extraditions were

---

5   Around 46,000 Spanish soldiers would be sent to the Russian Front.
6   "Prologue," in Goiogana, Legarreta, and Irujo, *Un nuevo 31.*
7   "Himmler, Montserrat y el Santo Grial: la factura de una visita desagradable," *El Confidencial*, April 10, 2017.

also set up. Thus, José Finat, director general of security in the Francoist regime, obtained the extradition of the president of Catalonia, Lluis Companys, and a former government minister in the Republic, Julián Zugazagoitia. Both of them were executed by firing squad.

Once the meetings with the members of the Francoist regime were finalized, Himmler decided to visit Montserrat in the belief that Montserrat was the Monsalvat in Richard Wagner's opera *Parsifal.* As the historian Hilari Raguer points out, more than the Holy Grail, Himmler was looking for documentation about it, hence his request to consult the archives concerning the location of the covenant cup. Abbot Antoni M. Marcet and Prior Aureli M. Escarré did not come out to greet him because, through German Benedictines, they had learned of the persecution the Catholic Church had suffered at the hands of the National Socialist regime. Three monks that spoke German attended to him, among them Father Andreu M. Ripol.

> Visiting the museum of prehistory that we had then in the lobby, before an Iberian sepulture discovered on the mountain, with a very tall framework, Himmler said: "This man, so tall, was Aryan. The Catalans are Aryans." Ripol responded: "We Catalans are not Aryans, nor of any race, but a mixture of several because Catalonia has been, since time immemorial, a crossroads of invasions and migrations." In the bible museum, before a model that reproduced the temple in Jerusalem, Himmler clapped his hands to summon his whole entourage, scattered among different display cabinets, and, pointing to the temple, said: "*Die erste Bank!*" [The first bank!]. He said that Jesus was Aryan, and that is why the Jews killed him.[8]

In line with the policy of strategic, economic, and diplomatic agreements between the German and Spanish regimes, and as a consequence of the conversations held during Himmler's visit to Franco, on November 30, 1940 Heinrich Müller, head of the Gestapo, negotiated with Franco the capture and imprisonment of all "Spanish reds" up to fifty-five years of age that had worked for the French army in German concentration camps. This measure, agreed with the Spanish police, had already started to be applied in August 1940 and led to the detention, torture, and death of many Basque, Catalan, and Spanish exiles in Nazi concertation camps like Mauthausen, Gussen, and Auschwitz, as well as

---

8   Letter from Hilari Raguer to Xabier Irujo, Montserrat, Friday, December 1, 2018.

in work camps.[9] Specifically, as regards forced labor, on March 23, 1942 Hitler issued Directive No. 40 that demanded the creation of an "Atlantic Wall." The Todt Organization supplied supervisors and a workforce, as well as organizing supplies, machinery, and transport to complement the workers and equipment of the construction companies. The Vichy regime imposed a system of obligatory labor, conscripting six hundred thousand French workers. As regards the Basque coast, at the end of June 1944, 194 defensive buildings of different kinds had been constructed and 16 more were being built. To this it is necessary to add machine-gun nests, bunkers, monitoring posts, and other buildings established in the interior and grouped into five points of support (Adour-Nord, Adour-Soud, Anglet-Ouest, Biarritz, and Marine-Schule-Biarritz). In order to carry out these works, a workforce of between 1,100 and 1,500 laborers was needed from different sources, mainly prisoners of war (such as the soldiers conscripted from Stalag 222 in Beyris) and local labor of different backgrounds.[10]

Naturally, the communities of Basque and Catalan Jews in Iparralde and Catalunya Nord suffered German repression and the severity of the collaborationist Vichy regime. Initially, Franz Rademacher, an SS official in the foreign ministry headed by Joachim von Ribbentrop, drew up the so-called Madagascar Plan in June 1940, formulated in a report titled "The Jewish Question" in the Peace Treaty, written in July that year. In accordance with this plan, the Jewish population of Europe would be transferred to camps located in Western Europe such as Gurs, and from there deported to the island of Madagascar. In October 1940, around 6,500 German Jews were transferred to the Gurs concentration camp situated in the Basque Country and administered by the Vichy regime. Most of the Jewish population in the Basque Country and Catalonia disappeared during the period of German domination.

Much has been said of the protection offered by Franco to some Jews, especially Sephardic Jews, but it would be best to mute such praise. It is undeniable that antisemitism was one component of the Francoist ideology. In different European countries (Germany, Poland, and also France) the impoverished middle classes were accusing Jews of having gotten rich at their expense. In the new social context,

---

9   Xabier Irujo, *Expelled from the Motherland: The Government of President Jose Antonio Agirre in Exile (1937–1960)* (Reno: Center for Basque Studies Press, University of Nevada, Reno, 2012), 213–14.

10   Xabier Irujo, *Genocidio en Euskal Herria (1936–1945)* (Iruñea: Nabarralde, 2015), 202–4.

a collection of articles by Henry Ford under the provocative title *The International Jew* was very successful. Ford retracted the work, but a translation into Spanish appeared in Leipzig in 1924–1925, which was received so well that it went through further publications in Barcelona in 1930, 1932, 1934, 1936, and 1940. Onésimo Redondo, leader of the JONS (Juntas de Ofensiva Nacional Sindicalista, Councils of the National-Syndicalist Offensive), a national-syndicalist party, incorporated antisemitism into Spanish fascism. After 1936 some journalists would accuse international Judaism of having started the war of 1936. The Antisectarias publishing house distributed the apocryphal *Protocols of the Elders of Zion* in Spanish as *Protocolos de los Sabios de Sión* (Valladolid, 1938). In 1938 it published a collection of articles by Pío Baroja under the title *Comunistas, judíos y demás ralea* (Communists, Jews, and other breeds). Pemán, in his *Poema de la Bestia y El Ángel* (Poem of the beast and the angel, Zaragoza, 1938), which sought to gloss the Apocalypse applying it to the supposed crusade, identified the infernal beast with the synagogue, yet praised the Moors that had come to fight for Franco, for God, and for Spain. Serrano Suñer, in a 1938 discourse against the campaign of the French Committee for Peace based in Paris, accused its president, Jacques Maritain, of being Jewish and a falsely converted Christian (Maritain was not Jewish, although his wife Raïssa was): "The wisdom of Jacques Maritain has accents that remind one of the elders of Israel and he has the false ways of Jewish democrats. We know that he is at risk of receiving, or having already received, the homage of the lodges and of the synagogues, and we have the right to doubt the sincerity of his conversion and denounce before the Catholic world this tremendous danger of treachery."[11]

Three documents in the Central Police Archive help to illustrate the antisemitism of the Francoist regime. On April 5, 1943 the German consul in Donostia asked the civil governor in Gipuzkoa to hand over a German Jew as if he were an object: "I would be grateful to V.E. if he would be so kind as to arrange for the detainee at my disposal to be handed in to Delegate Mr. Denker, so that he may be taken to Hendaia. He is Leon Hoffmann, born in St. Johann on January 9, 1902. The aforementioned Hoffman lacking any documents, it would be appreciated if the exit visa could be included in this very letter."

11   Hilari Raguer, *La Unió Democràtica de Catalunya i el seu temps (1931–1939)* (Montserrat: L'Abadia de Montserrat, Montserrat, 1976), 450.

Along the same lines, on May 5, 1941 the director general of security, José Finat, the Count of Mayalde, sent a circular out to all the civil governors that began thus: "The need to understand in a specific and decisive way the places and persons that, at any given moment, could be an obstacle to or means of action against the postulates that underpin the New State requires that special attention be paid to Jews resident in our Fatherland, collecting, in due form, as many details and antecedents to allow us to know the ideology of each of them and their potential to act, within and outside national territory." He specified that people who were the object of such monitoring would have to be, "mainly those of Spanish extraction, designated with the name of Sephardic Jews, given that through their adaptation to the environment and similarity to our temperament they possess greater guarantees of hiding their origin and even getting by unnoticed without any possibility of restricting the scope of easy unsettling schemes." The governors would have to send to the General Office for Security "individual reports on the Israelites, national and foreign, residing in that province," in which the following would be specified:

> all the details to allow us to determine the personal and politico-social affiliations of each of them, as well as their livelihoods, commercial activities, current situation, degree of danger, police considerations, and the nature or prominence that in sects or political or labor union bodies they may have achieved and, in the event of being absent, the place in which it is assumed they are to be found and the means of subsistence of the family members they left behind, as well as any other things that emerge in the investigation so that their antecedents are complete, adding, with regard to natives of other countries, their original nationality, place of origin, and motive for stay in Spain.

Finally, he asked for a "general impression surrounding the importance of activities of a Jewish nature in the province and of institutions of all types he may have constituted and the means at his disposal."

As a result, perhaps, of the previous circular, from the main police headquarters in Barcelona information was sent to the General Office for Security, on June 30, 1944, regarding a young Jewish woman from Barcelona, aged twenty-three and called Sinaí, in the following terms: "She has no nationality and no known political affiliation, nor has she held any political or sect positions. She lives at the expense of her father

. . . and she was given residence authorization. It is assumed she is as dangerous as the Jewish race itself to which she belongs (Sephardic)."

Parallel to the persecution of Jews in zones occupied by the Nazis or controlled by Vichy forces, the persecution of Basque and Catalan political dissidents by the German, (Vichy) French, and Spanish secret police, acting in a coordinated way, led to a new massive exodus of Basque and Catalan refugees toward the Americas. Two of these refugees were Presidents Lluis Companys and Jose A. Agirre. Companys would be arrested on August 13, 1940 by German agents and handed over to the Spanish authorities on August 29. On October 15 that same year he would be executed by firing squad. Meanwhile, the German offensive took the president of the Basque government, Jose A. Agirre, by surprise on the beaches of Dunkirk. Pursued by the German police and without the option of fleeing to Paris, he decided to hide in Berlin. He lived in the Reich capital for several months at a short distance from the Gestapo headquarters. With the help of the Panamanian consul in Belgium, Germán G. Jaén, Agirre managed to obtain a false identity and between May 1940 and October 1941 he lived as a fugitive in the heart of Nazi Germany, until he managed to take a ship from Sweden and flee to the Americas, where he would remain until the end of the war.

Many other Basque and Catalan agents would be detained, tortured, and, occasionally, executed in an extrajudicial manner. Many of them were anonymous and to this day we lack accurate statistics on the number of victims. Some managed to escape, such as the Catalan Manuel Pérez Vila, who had to hide in a coffin in which there was a body to escape sure death before a firing squad. Exiled in Venezuela, he became the first director of the Boulton Foundation. Pedro Grases and Bingen Ametzaga, both exiled, would work some years later under his leadership.[12]

No patriotic militia functioning under the protection of the German regime operated in the Basque Country or Catalonia, nor a foreign section of the Nazi party (*Ausland Organisation, Volksdeutsche Bewegung, Sicherheits und Hilfsdienst*), or paramilitary organizations like the Hitler Youth (*Hitler Jugend*). There were, however, several resistance groups, independent of one another, such as the Basque government's resistance networks, the French Resistance networks operating in

---

12 Letter from Arantzazu Anmetzaga to Xabier Irujo, Altzuza, Sunday, November 25, 2018.

the Basque Country, the resistance networks of left-wing republican parties such as the Maquis, and other autonomous forces. In Zuberoa, for example, members of the Basque resistance liberated the territory, without the participation of any Allied force.

Simultaneously, in the face of Agirre's disappearance and the execution of Companys, the leaders of the Basque and Catalan resistance movements in London organized the Basque and Catalan National Councils. These councils would represent their respective governments as long as the continent remained occupied. On January 18, 1941, the Consejo Nacional de Euzkadi and the Consell Nacional de Catalunya signed a joint declaration in London, the first public demonstration of the intentions of the Basque and Catalan governments-in-exile. Likewise, the recently founded Basque National Council in London launched negotiations with the British government and De Gaulle's Free French Council. With conversations with the British government directed via the Consejo Nacional de Euzkadi by mutual agreement, the following agreement was agreed on in writing, which includes de facto and literally the British proposal to recognize an independent Basque state in the event that the Spanish state would enter the war on the side of the totalitarian powers. The form of collaboration between the Basque National Council and the British government would be founded on four points:

1. H.M. Government sympathises with the cause of the Basque peoples, in their claim for liberty and independence.

2. In the event of hostilities breaking out between the British and Spanish Governments, H.M. Government will immediately recognise the Basque National Council as the Provisional Basque Government.

3. In the event of a British victory, H.M. Government will undertake to do everything in their power to secure the constitution and security of a Basque State.

4. The delimitation of frontiers is a matter for settlement later on.[13]

Thereafter, the Basque National Council negotiated an agreement on military collaboration with the Free French. In accordance with that stipulated in the agreement of May 17, 1941, on September 12, 1941 both councils agreed, following a long period of negotiations of almost

---

13   Letter from José Ignacio Lizaso to Ramón Sota, London, July 9, 1941.

three months, an initial set of regulations for a Basque military unit that would form part of the general framework of Free French troops; on October 22, these regulations were agreed on by both parties.[14] The signed document was titled *Reglamento del Tercer Batallón de Fusileros Marinos* (Regulations for the Third Battalion of Marine Fusiliers).

Yet, notwithstanding these agreements, it would not be until the bombing of Pearl Harbor and the intervention of the United States in the war that the Basque government acted in a decisive way in the Allied war effort. In May 1942 the Basque government-in-exile and the U.S. government agreed to collaborate on espionage matters in Latin America and the Philippine Islands. Thus, the first Pan-American organization of Basque secret services was created that would act in a coordinated way with the Office of Strategic Services or American intelligence. By virtue of this agreement, Basque agents collaborated with OSS agents and the operations were financed by the Americans. The Basque agents operated under direct Basque orders in Europe, although fundamentally in South and Central America and also in the Philippines. The objective of the operations was counterespionage: to inform on and dissolve Nazi and Fascist spy networks in Europe and Latin America.

Following years of resistance, struggle, and terror, following the landing of Allied forces in Normandy in the summer of 1944, a swift Allied victory seemed certain. The consequence of negotiations between the Basque National Council and the Free French would be the subsequent creation of the Gernika Battalion, a Basque military unit that would participate in some of the last battles to liberate the territory south of the River Garonne, and the active participation of Basque contingents in the liberation of Iparralde (resistance and services) and of Les Landes. Until March 4, 1945, German forces led by Colonel Walter Sonntag and later by Colonel Oberst Prahl had 25,000 troops, 461 canons, 528 bunkers, and almost 800,000 mines on the Médoc Front in southwest France. De Gaulle had designated General Edgard de Larminat as commander of the French Western Forces in October 1944, and Larminat ordered Jean de Milleret (known by his nom de guerre of "Carnot"), the chief of the Carnot Brigade, to attack German positions in Pointe-de-Grave. In the attack, the Gernika Battalion, led

---

14 Letter from Manuel Irujo to Francisco Javier Landaburu, London, September 20, 1944.

by Major Kepa Ordoki, fought within the mixed Moroccan and foreign regiment, led by Major Chodzko.[15]

On April 14, 1945, fighting broke out in Pointe-de-Grave, at the far northern end of the Médoc Peninsula, at the mouth of the Gironde Estuary. The fighting lasted seven days. The Gernika Battalion, attacking from the south, liberated the towns of Lesparre, Saint-Vivien, and Soulac, in its arch northward. In total, four hundred men in the Carnot Brigade were killed and around a thousand injured. There were 680 German deaths and the Allies took 3,320 prisoners, including 80 officials. The Gernika Battalion lost four men: Antonio Mugika (from Donostia); Félix Iglesias Mina (from Atarrabia); Juan J. Sasia (from Alonsotegi), and Antonio Lizarralde (from Durango). The attack ended with the liberation of the Isle of Oléron as part of Operation Jupiter, and the liberation of La Rochelle, La Pallice, and the Isle of Ré. On April 22, 1945, De Gaulle honored the Gernika Battalion with these words: "Major, France will never forget the efforts and sacrifices made by the Basques in the liberation of our land."[16]

On August 29, 1945 the French authorities ordered a general demobilization, but Ernest Pezet, a member of the Liga Internacional de Amigos de los Vascos (International League of Friends of the Basques, LIAB), in reply to a request from the Basque government, asked the French authorities to delay the demobilization: "We would like to retain a small nucleus of military forces, in order to create around this a body responsible for protecting citizens, for security, and for maintaining order in our country in the event of a change of the current regime and the taking of power on the part of the democratic forces." On September 24, 1945 the vice president of the Basque government, Jesús M. Leizaola, wrote to De Gaulle, but without any effect: the Gernika Battalion was dissolved at the beginning of the summer of 1945.[17]

Following the end of the war, and in view of Basque and Catalan support, as well as the support given by Spanish republican forces to the Allies, the signatory countries of the Declaration of the United Nations, principally the United States, the United Kingdom, and the Soviet Union, decided to keep the Francoist regime outside the United Nations, due to the support shown by the Spanish regime to the Axis. Article 4 of the Charter established that entry into the United Nations

---

15 Irujo, *Expelled from the Motherland*, 131–32.
16 Ibid.
17 Ibid.

Organization (UNO) was open to all states that loved peace and that accepted the obligations contained in the Charter and that, in the judgement of the organization, were capable of and were disposed to carrying out these obligations by which, at the request of the Mexican delegation in the heart of the commission and the conference in San Francisco, this article excluded the Spanish state, born out of a coup d'état backed by the Axis powers and transgressive of practically all the basic human rights. And, while the Charter did not establish that a dictatorship could not be part of the UNO, given that two of them formed part of the security council no less, on February 9, 1946, at 10:30 a.m., in the Central Hall of Westminster, in London, Roberto Jiménez, representative of the Panamanian government in the United Nations assembly, presented a discussion proposal for the "Spanish Case."

The Panama proposal had to be approved by the assembly. As a consequence, document A/64, which, following a brief debate, would be approved by the assembly in its twenty-sixth session, was based on three points:

1. The General Assembly recalls that the San Francisco conference adopted a resolution according to which paragraph 2 of Article 4 of Chapter II of the United Nations Charter "cannot apply to States whose regimes have been installed with the help of armed forces of countries which have fought against the United Nations so long as these regimes are in power."

2. The General Assembly recalls that at the Potsdam Conference the Governments of the United Kingdom, the United States of America and the Soviet Union stated that they would not support a request for admission to the United Nations of the present Spanish Government "which, having been founded with the support of the Axis powers, in view of its origins, its nature, its record and its close association with the aggressor States, does not possess the necessary qualifications to justify its admission."

3. The General Assembly, in endorsing these two statements, recommends that the Members of the United Nations should act in accordance with the letter and the spirit of

these statements on the conduct of their future relations with Spain.[18]

The governments of Ecuador, Costa Rica, Cuba, Peru, and Uruguay decided, after parliamentary sessions in their respective countries, to withdraw their ambassadors from Madrid and break off diplomatic relations with the Spanish government. For their part, dictatorships such as El Salvador and Nicaragua, took an opposing stand to these measures through their representatives.

The resolution of the United Nations assembly was followed by a whole series of resolutions and declarations. The first of those was a declaration by the U.S. Department of State on the Spanish question on March 4, 1946:

> The governments of France, the United Kingdom, and the United States of America have exchanged views with regard to the present Spanish Government and their relations with that regime. It is agreed that so long as General Franco continues in control of Spain, the Spanish people cannot anticipate full and cordial association with those nations of the world which have, by common effort, brought defeat to German Nazism and Italian Fascism, which aided the present Spanish regime in its rise to power and after which the regime was patterned.

> There is no intention of interfering in the internal affairs of Spain. The Spanish people themselves must in the long run work out their own destiny. In spite of the present regime's repressive measures against orderly efforts of the Spanish people to organize and give expression to their political aspirations, the three Governments are hopeful that the Spanish people will not again be subjected to the horrors and bitterness of civil strife.

> On the contrary, it is hoped that leading patriotic and liberal-minded Spaniards may soon find means to bring about a peaceful withdrawal of Franco, the abolition of the Falange, and the establishment of an interim or caretaker government under which the Spanish people may have an opportunity freely to determine

---

18   Hans Kelsen, *The Law of the United Nations: A Critical Analysis of its Fundamental Problems: With Supplement* (New Jersey: The Lawbook Exchange Ltd., 2000), 77. See likewise, *El problema de España ante el mundo internacional. Resolución aprobada por la 1ª Asamblea General de Naciones Unidas. Texto y discusión de la misma,* (London: República de España, Ministerio de Estado, Londres, 1946), 13.

the type of government they wish to have and to choose their leaders. Political amnesty, return of exiled Spaniards, freedom of assembly and political association and provision for free public elections are essential. An interim government which would be and would remain dedicated to these ends should receive the recognition and support of all freedom-loving peoples.

Such recognition would include full diplomatic relations and the taking of such practical measures to assist in the solution of Spain's economic problems as may be practicable in the circumstances prevailing. Such measures are not now possible. The question of the maintenance or termination by the Governments of France the United Kingdom, and the United States of diplomatic relations with the present Spanish regime is a matter to be decided in the light of events and after taking into account the efforts of the Spanish people to achieve their own freedom.[19]

By virtue of resolution 4 (1946) of April 29, 1946, and in accordance with the provisions of article 35 of the Charter, the assembly asked the security council to declare that the situation in the Spanish state had produced disagreement of an international nature and put peace and international security at risk. As a consequence, the security council, "taking into account the unanimous moral condemnation that the Security Council has pronounced about the Franco regime" and the resolutions that have been passed about the regime at the san Francisco conference and in the first period of sessions in the general assembly of the United Nations, as well as the opinions expressed by members of the security council about the Francoist regime, decided to carry out new investigations with the goal of determining if, in effect, the situation in the Spanish state implied a risk for peace and international security and, that being the case, to determine what practical measures the United Nations could adopt. With this aim, the security council appointed a subcommittee made up of five members entrusted with examining the declarations made before the council in relation to the Spanish state, handing in the corresponding report to the security council before the end of May. The decision was approved at the thirty-ninth session held

---

19   Press Release by the Department of State on March 4, 1946. In Paul Preston, Michael Partridge, and Denis Smyth, Denis, eds., *British Documents on Foreign Affairs—Reports and Papers from the Foreign Office Confidential Print: From 1945 through 1950,* Europe, part 4, vol. 3 (Bethesda, MD: University Publications of America, 2000), 464.

on April 29, 1946, by ten votes to zero with one abstention (the USSR). The council decided likewise that the subcommittee created by virtue of its resolution 4 (1946) would be made up of representatives from Australia, Brazil, China, France, and Poland and that the representative from Australia would be its president.

By virtue of resolution 7 (1946) of June 26, 1946, the security council, in light of the investigations carried out by the subcommittee, confirmed at the forty-ninth session that it "fully confirmed the facts which led to the condemnation of the Franco regime by the Potsdam and San Francisco Conferences, by the General Assembly at the first part of its first session and by the Security Council by resolution of the date mentioned above [resolution 4 (1946)]," by which it decided to monitor continually the situation in the Spanish state and maintain the question on the list of pending issues with the aim of taking, at any moment, the necessary measures in order to maintain peace and international security. The thirty-fifth and thirty-six plenary sessions of the general assembly, on October 24, 1946, examined once more the question of the Spanish regime, underscoring once again the fact that, despite the defeat of the German, Italian, and Japanese regimes, the ideologically fascist government had not undergone any change. It was clear to the assembly that while General Franco's regime continued to govern, it would constitute a serious cause for mistrust and disagreement among the founders of the United Nations. As a result, the assembly concluded that, "those that have given us victory and peace should know likewise how to find the means to restore freedom and democratic government in the Spanish state."20

And, finally, by virtue of resolution 10 (1946), of November 4, 1946, approved unanimously at the seventy-ninth session, the security council decided to remove from the list of issues submitted for its consideration the point relating to the existing situation in the Spanish state, placing at the disposition of the general assembly all the documents and acts pertinent to the case. As a consequence, during the course of the fifty-ninth session, held on December 12, 1946, the general assembly of the United Nations passed Resolution 39 (I), by which a series of sanctions were imposed on the Spanish state:

---

20 Irujo, *Genocidio en Euskal Herria*, 282.

Relations of Members of the United Nations with Spain.

The peoples of the United Nations, at San Francisco, Potsdam and London, condemned the Franco regime in Spain and decided that, as long as that regime remains, Spain may not be admitted to the United Nations.

The General Assembly, in its resolution of 9 February 1946, recommended that the Members of the United Nations should act in accordance with the letter and the spirit of the declarations of San Francisco and Potsdam.

The peoples of the United Nations assure the Spanish people of their enduring sympathy and of the cordial welcome awaiting them when circumstances enable them to be admitted to the United Nations.

The General Assembly recalls that, in May and June 1946, the Security Council conducted an investigation of the possible further action to be taken by the United Nations. The Sub-Committee of the Security Council charged with the investigation found unanimously: |1|

> "(a) In origin, nature, structure and general conduct, the Franco regime is a fascist regime patterned on, and established largely as a result of aid received from, Hitler's Nazi Germany and Mussolini's Fascist Italy.

> "(b) During the long struggle of the United Nations against Hitler and Mussolini, Franco, despite continued Allied protests, gave very substantial aid to the enemy Powers. First, for example, from 1941 to 1945, the Blue Infantry Division, the Spanish Legion of Volunteers and the Salvador Air Squadron fought against Soviet Russia on the Eastern front. Second, in the summer of 1940, Spain seized Tangier in breach of international statute, and as a result of Spain maintaining a large army in Spanish Morocco large numbers of Allied troops were immobilized in North Africa.

> "(c) Incontrovertible documentary evidence establishes that Franco was a guilty party with Hitler and Mussolini in the conspiracy to wage war against those countries which eventually in the course of the world war became

banded together as the United Nations. It was part of the conspiracy that Franco's full belligerency should be postponed until a time to be mutually agreed upon."

The General Assembly,

Convinced that the Franco Fascist Government of Spain, which was imposed by force upon the Spanish people with the aid of the Axis Powers and which gave material assistance to the Axis Powers in the war, does not represent theSpanish people, and by its continued control of Spain is making impossible the participation of the Spanish people with the peoples of the United Nations in international affairs;

Recommends that the Franco Government of Spain be debarred from membership in international agencies established by or brought into relationship with the United Nations, and from participation in conferences or other activities which may be arranged by the United Nations or by these agencies, until a new and acceptable government is formed in Spain.

The General Assembly,

Further, desiring to secure the participation of all peace-loving peoples, including the people of Spain, in the community of nations,

Recommends that if, within a reasonable time, there is not established a government which derives its authority from the consent of the governed, committed to respect freedom of speech, religion and assembly and to the prompt holding of an election in which the Spanish people, free from force and intimidation and regardless of party, may express their will, the Security Council consider the adequate measures to be taken in order to remedy the situation;

Recommends that all Members of the United Nations immediately recall from Madrid their Ambassadors and Ministers plenipotentiary accredited there.

The General Assembly further recommends that the States Members of the Organization report to the Secretary-General and to the next session of the Assembly what action they have taken in accordance with this recommendation.[21]

The document could not be more categorical. The United Nations commended the Franco regime on account of its links with the Axis forces, which implied that it was complicit in all the atrocities committed by the governments that made them up and that the seriousness of the atrocities committed by those in charge was fully comparable to that of those being judged, sentenced, and, where applicable, executed at Nuremberg and in the other trials that were taking place in relation to the atrocities committed during the course of the war in Europe.

But the pressure exerted by the United Nations did not have the expected result, and General Franco was never forced to leave power. He remained head of the Spanish state until his death, so that the Basque and Catalan peoples, as well as the Spanish people, would have to suffer three long decades of dictatorship between 1945 and 1975.

During his visit to Montserrat, the monks took Himmler to the image of Mare de Déu, known as La Moreneta, the patron saint of Catalonia. Finding himself facing the statue, Himmler said to Wolff: "We will finish with all these superstitions…" Father Ripol, who heard him, responded: "There have been many attempts and no one has ever been able to."[22] That was how it was, for almost ten years of war and forty of the Francoist dictatorship, with the Basque and Catalan peoples still defending their historic rights, and their identity as peoples. And the culture of both nations continued to flourish.

---

21   Preston, Partridge, and Smyth, Denis, eds., *British Documents on Foreign Affairs*, Europe, Part 4, vol. 1, 330.
22   Letter from Hilari Raguer to Xabier Irujo, Montserrat, Friday, December 1, 2018.

BIBLIOGRAPHY

El problema de España ante el mundo internacional. Resolución aprobada por la 1ª Asamblea General de Naciones Unidas. Texto y discusión de la misma. London: República de España, Ministerio de Estado, Londres, 1946.

Irujo, Xabier. *Expelled from the Motherland: The Government of President Jose Antonio Agirre in Exile (1937–1960).* Reno: Center for Basque Studies Press, University of Nevada, Reno, 2012.

———. *Genocidio en Euskal Herria (1936–1945).* Iruñea: Nabarralde, 2015.

———. *Gernika: 26 de abril de 1937.* Barcelona: Crítica, 2017.

Kelsen, Hans. *The Law of the United Nations: A Critical Analysis of its Fundamental Problems: With Supplement.* New Jersey: The Lawbook Exchange Ltd., 2000.

Preston, Paul, Michael Partridge, and Denis Smyth, Denis, eds., *British Documents on Foreign Affairs—Reports and Papers from the Foreign Office Confidential Print: From 1945 through 1950.* Europe, part 4, volumes 1 and 3. Bethesda, MD: University Publications of America, 2000.

"Prologue." In Iñaki Goiogana, Josu Legarreta, and Xabier Irujo. *Un nuevo 31. Ideología y estrategia del Gobierno de Euzkadi durante la Segunda Guerra Mundial a través de la correspondencia de José Antonio Aguirre y Manuel Irujo.* Bilbo: Sabino Arana, Bilbo, 2007.

Chapter 1

Terror Bombing Campaign in Euskal Herria

Xabier Irujo

In the words of Göring, throughout World War I and up to 1936, the land army had illegitimately occupied a powerful place at the heart of the German armed forces. However, in applying a four-year plan during his time as aviation minister and, following a generous injection of funding for the air force between 1936 and 1940, the Luftwaffe would become, by the spring of 1939, "the most powerful of the three branches of the German armed forces (land, sea, and air)," even managing to "occupy first place."[1] Göring calculated that, by 1940–1941, the Luftwaffe would have 14,000 machines organized into 1,000 flying squadrons, each of them with nine aircraft, three in reserve and two for training new pilots.[2] This goal would be achieved at different stages with an expected budget of 40 million marks (300 million lira) in 1939: until April 1, 1937 the German air force would have 250 flying squadrons with a total of 3,500 aircraft; by the spring of 1938, that number would double to 500 flying squadrons and 7,000 aircraft and, in 1940, the Luftwaffe would be prepared to confront "the next war" with a total of 1,000 flying squadrons and 14,000 planes.[3]

As Ángel Viñas points out, General Franco never negotiated with Hitler about the nature and composition of the military support

---

1   *Promemoria per S. E. Il Capo di Stato Maiore Generale*, Rome, February 1, 1937. NARA, RG 242. *Foreign Records Seized Collection: Collection of Italian Military Records, 1935–1943*, Microfilm Publication T821, R. 214, 3–5.
2   Xabier Irujo, *El Gernika de Richthofen. Un ensayo de bombardeo de terror* (Gernika: Gernikako Bakearen Museoa Fundazioa; Gernika-Lumoko Udala, 2012), 67–68.
3   Ibid.

he was going to receive but, rather, he adjusted to what he was given by the future Axis powers as regards men and material.[4] Nevertheless, when Hitler had to decide on the nature and dimension of the military support for the Spanish rebels, Göring, who had recently been appointed director of the four-year plan and who enjoyed the full trust of the Führer, quickly organized a contingent made up almost exclusively of Luftwaffe units, the Condor Legion, with one basic idea in mind: to demonstrate that "the next war will be won in the air" and that, as a result, the air force represented the best and most destructive weapon of the emerging German empire. Göring understood that victory in a future war would be gained by means of a "determined offensive action" (*"tempestiva azione ofensiva"*) led and carried out by the air force, so that the office overseeing the four-year plan had to implement an ambitious plan to produce bombers.[5] More specifically, according to the general, between 75 and 78 percent of the Luftwaffe units had to be bombers.[6]

In sum, in 1936 Göring was determined to convince Hitler that the air force would play a decisive role in the future war and that if he had the necessary bomber planes, the air force itself could bring about victory. In this sense, Franco's war favored him enormously in that it offered him the possibility to try out on the ground his theories on aerial warfare and his aircraft. William E. Chapman, the U.S. consul in Bilbao, observed that, with international involvement, the war had effectively become a field of experimentation that offered better opportunities than other places to try out the machinery of warfare.[7]

This explains on the one hand why Hitler sent the Condor Legion to Franco, a fully aerial unit with a small and accessory support by sea and land units, and it explains likewise why General Hugo Sperrle appointed Wolfram von Richthofen chief of staff of this unit in January 1937. Richthofen had been sent by Major Hellmuth Felmy, chief of the air office in the Reichswehr, to study the aerial warfare concepts of Giulio Douhet, author of the famous treatise *Il dominio dell'aria* (The

---

4   Ángel Viñas, "Negociaciones sobre el apoyo nazi-fascista a Franco," unpublished ms.
5   *Notizie di carattere militare*, February 1, 1937, *Foreign Records Seized Collection: Collection of Italian Military Records, 1935–1943*, Microfilm Publication T821, R. 214, 7.
6   *Promemoria per S. E. Il Capo di Stato Maiore Generale*, Rome, February 1, 1937, NARA, RG 242, *Foreign Records Seized Collection: Collection of Italian Military Records, 1935–1943*. Microfilm Publication T821, R. 214, 3–5.
7   Memorandum of the consul of the United States in Bilbao, William E. Chapman, to ambassador Claude G. Bowers. Donibane Lohitzune, June 14, 1937. NARA, Bilbao Consulate General Records (1936–1946). Box 4, 1937.

command of the air).[8] In his work, Douhet defended the idea that a future war would be determined by the use of aerial power. Aviation, according to him, should execute fast, decisive, and devastating action, which should not allow for either material reconstruction or moral recovery by the enemy. Achieving the desired "paralyzing effect" over the enemy would be obtained by using massive and indiscriminate aerial bombing.[9] Richthofen was made chief of staff with the dual mission of demonstrating in the field that it was possible to win a war "from the air" and perfecting bombing and land-based attacking techniques. And with that aim he arrived at the Basque Front at the end of March 1937.

From the first moments of the military insurrection in July 1936, the Spanish rebel leadership perceived that the demolition of the Spanish republican order and the establishment of a solid social and political base on which to build a new dictatorial order would require implementing a terror strategy. General Emilio Mola thus announced, on July 19, 1936, to the mayors around Pamplona, "terror must be spread ... the feeling of control must be given, eliminating without any scruples or hesitation anyone who does not think like us."[10] But generating terror was only a necessary condition, not in itself sufficient. Mola understood that this terror had to be administered, as a social poison, through time, with the goal of defeating and subjecting people to the new order. For all these reason, at the beginning of the conflict the general claimed that "in this warlike trance I have already decided on all-out war. To any soldiers who have not joined our Movement, thrown them out and take away their pay checks. To those who have taken up arms against us, against the army, execute them. I see my father in the opposing ranks, I execute him."[11]

Mola's ideas were shared by almost all the leaders of the insurgent side and their allies. Colonel Wolfram von Richthofen, chief of staff of the Condor Legion, understood that military aviation should not be limited to bombing the front lines and assisting troops on the battlefield (tactical bombings), but should be concentrated on destroying the

---

8   Giulio Douhet, *Il dominio dell'aria: probabili aspetti della guerra futura e gli ultimi* (Milan: A. Mondadori, 1932).
9   Wesley Craven and James L. Cate, eds., *Army Air Forces in World War II* (Washington D.C.: Office of Air Force History, 1948), 81.
10   Juan Iturralde, pseud. of Juan Jose Usabiaga Irazustabarrena, *El catolicismo y la cruzada de Franco*, vol. 2 (Vienne: EGI Indarra, 1960), 88. See also José María Maldonado, *El frente de Aragón: la Guerra Civil en Aragón (1936–1938)* (N.p.: Mira Editores, 2007), 28.
11   Alberto Reig Tapia, *Ideología e historia: sobre la represión franquista y la guerra civil* (Madrid: Akal, 1986), 146.

means of communication and cutting off the movements of troops and war material between the rearguard and the front, destroying the supply sources of food and the arms industry in the rearguard (strategic bombings), and, fundamentally, destroying the morale of the enemy by means of bombing the civilian population (terror bombings).[12] The rebel leaders very soon understood that the destructive power of aerial bombings was limited but that their psychological power was immense and that the terror bombings constituted the best tool to spread terror and break the morale of the republican population and troops. General Vincenzo Velardi, head of the Italian air force, stated in a report of April 13, 1937, that, "the moral effect [of aerial attacks] has shown to be very great."[13] Two days after taking Bilbao and in view of the excellent military results that the terror bombing campaign had yielded in the Basque Country, Mussolini sent a telegram to Bastico ordering him not to let up against the enemy, that they should be bombed until being completely demoralized.[14]

The rebel side did not even entertain any idea of respecting population centers without any military or strategic interest so that the decision to bomb urban centers indiscriminately took shape in practice, without any intervention of strategic planning, on July 22, 1936, four days after the coup d'état, when two Breguet Br.19s bombed Otxandio. The result was monstrous, with a balance of sixty-one people dead in half an hour, forty-five of them civilians, nine soldiers, and no data on the remaining seven.[15] In other words, at least 73.77 percent of the victims were civilians, including twenty-four children, 39 percent of the total. Sixteen of the dead were under ten years old (26 percent).[16] The reporter for the daily *Euzkadi* stated that Sabina Oianguren had lost her sight. Later, he found out that she had lost her husband, Emeterio Garces, and four of her five children: Pedro, Juan Manuel, Teodoro, and Maria Jesus. The oldest was thirteen.[17]

---

12   Richthofen, Diary, March 24 and 26, 1937, in Klaus A. Maier, *Guernica. La intervención alemana en España y el "caso Guernica"* (Madrid: Sedmay, 1976), 52–53. See also *Informe sobre las experiencias de la Legión Cóndor acerca de la acción de los pilotos de combate de Knauer*, 185.

13   Vincenzo Velardi, "Promemoria per S. E. Il Sottosegretario di Stato," Gasteiz, April 23, 1937, 6. USAM, Prot. M.2325.

14   Telegram from Benito Mussolini to General Ettore Bastico, Rome, June 21, 1937, AMAE, Gabinetto del Ministro (1923–1943), Busta 7 (Uffizio Spagna Leg. 44, No 1.250).

15   Zigor Olabarria, *Gerra Zibila Otxandion* (Donostia: Eusko Ikaskuntza, 2011), 79 and 81.

16   Xabier Irujo, *Gernika: 26 de abril de 1937* (Barcelona: Crítica, 2017), 106.

17   Xabier Irujo, "El bombardeo de Otxandio según el general Salas," *Deia*, July 18,

By article 25 of the Hague Convention of 1907, in the course of a war aerial forces had to respect hospitals, infirmaries, and any centers in which there were sick or wounded people.[18] Nevertheless, the result of indiscriminate bombings during the initial months of the conflict prompted the rebel leadership to transgress the laws of warfare and promote indiscriminate bombings. In fact, on Saturday, October 24, 1936, General Queipo de Llano threatened to bomb hospitals[19] and only a few days later aerial attacks were recorded on diverse Basque hospital centers such as that of October 25 against the military hospital in Markina, on which, despite displaying clearly the symbol of the Red Cross, rebel planes dropped five bombs.[20] The field hospital in Elorrio, that in Durango, and San Luis Hospital in Bilbao were likewise attacked by the Francoist air force. With good reason, Imanol Agirre, a child of barely ten years of age in 1937, after surviving the bombing of Gernika, stated that in the course of a rebel aerial attack it was safer to take shelter in an arms factor than in a hospital.[21]

This campaign of indiscriminate bombing was announced publicly by Mola in announcing from Valladolid on November 18, 1936, that such raids would be carried out with whatever violence military requirements demanded and without prior warning:

> Basques and Santander people: Irun and San Sebastian having been conquered by my troops, I am going to give the order immediately for operations to continue in Bizkaia and Santander ... from a time onward on the 25th of the present month, there will be freedom of action to proceed against the tactical and strategic objectives with the violence required by military needs. From that date on, no aerial bombing will be announced. In order to make a decision sufficient time will be given.[22]

2015, 18–19.

18 Annex to the convention on regulations for laws and customs of war. Sections I and II, chapter 1 on means of hurting the enemy, places, and bombings.

19 "Los facciosos bombardean, a sabiendas, los hospitals," *El Liberal* 36, no. 12,429, October 28, 1936, 2.

20 "La guerra en los frentes de Guipúzcoa," *El Noticiero Bilbaino* 62, no. 21,376, October 28, 1936, 1.

21 Yvonne Cloud (Yvonne Kapp) and Richard Ellis, *The Basque Children in England: An Account of their Life at North Stoneham Camp* (London: Victor Gollancz Ltd., 1937), 56–57.

22 War pamphlet dropped from planes over Bizkaia. In José María Iribarren, *Mola: datos para una biografía y para la historia del Alzamiento Nacional* (Zaragoza: Librería General, 1938), 231.

And Richthofen came to an agreement with Colonel Juan Vigón, chief of staff of the Navarrese brigades under the leadership of General Solchaga, that German, Italian, and Spanish aerial units would attack from the air enemy positions, local reserves, and other sectors "without any consideration for the civilian population."[23]

One month later, nine Junker Ju52 bombers escorted by twelve Heinkel He52 attack aircraft attacked the urban area of Bilbao. The enemy aircraft appeared at 4:00 p.m. over Bilbao, dropping their load of explosive and incendiary bombs on the old quarter and the Matiko neighborhood. The bombing of Bilbao caused major damage. Homes located at numbers 28 and 29 Iturribide Street were attacked by several bombs, the former collapsing and the latter suffering major damage. Three bombs likewise caused damage to the outside laundry spot, from the ruins of which two women were rescued alive.[24] Fortunately, most of the inhabitants of these buildings had sought refuge in nearby tunnels, so that a catastrophe was avoided.[25]

The eight fighter aircraft stationed in Lamiako went out to meet the attackers and engaged in aerial combat over Bilbao itself, during the course of which three rebel planes were shot down. One of the flaming planes fell and landed in Larraskitu, another in Alonsotegui and the third in Enekuri, on the outskirts of Bilbao, where one of the republican fighters was also shot down.[26] The Basque defense department confirmed that:

> the battle was exciting and perfectly visible to many of the general public. One could immediately see the efficiency of our planes, as a powerful, tri-motor enemy who had pursued one of our fighters courageously, fell in flames, while its crew employed their parachutes. The burned out fascist plane landed near the Arráiz pines, close to the hamlet of 'Arana' behind the Torre Urízar neighborhood, precisely where the 'captains' fell to earth with balloons filled with smoke that rose in the bullring. One of the pilots landed in the Arana thicket and the other two must have fallen on Mount Cobetas. Three more aviators descended with their parachutes in various other places. The

23 Maier, *Guernica*, 52.
24 "Los de ayer lunes [January 4]," *El Noticiero Bilbaino* 62, no. 21,434, January 5, 1937, 1.
25 "Los daños causados," *Euzkadi* 25, no. 7,495, January 5, 1937, 1.
26 "Los partes oficiales," *Euzkadi* 25, No. 7,495, January 5, 1937, 3. And "Parte oficial del ministerio de marina y aire," *El Liberal* 37, no. 12,487, January 5, 1937, 3.

pilot that was killed, ranked second lieutenant in the German air force, was called Adolf Herrmann, a fitter by trade, born in Gelrenkirshen (Germany) and resident in Berlin. He was twenty-seven years old.[27]

The press highlighted the origins of the planes and pilots: "all the planes were German, piloted by crew of that same nationality, and according to the list held by the Government, five of whom perished inside the planes."[28]

The rebel air headquarters, inaccurate and lacking detail, limited itself to reporting that, "nine Junker planes bombed Bilbao's thermo-electric power plant and port. . . . In the Bilbao attack two red fighters and one of our Junkers were destroyed."[29] No reference to the Iturribide laundry spot.

It was not the first time that Bilbao had been bombed. On the morning of September 25, 1936, seven planes dropped bombs on Bilbao over an hour and a half period, and another four continued for an hour in the afternoon. At least five hits were registered in the vicinity of the San Luis hospital. In line with the logic of terror bombings, Mola sent the Basque authorities an ultimatum, demanding the unconditional surrender of the Basque troops before midnight on September 25, 1936, the alternative being attacks by air, land, and sea, which was not answered.[30] That same day rebel planes dropped four bombs on Durango, hitting the Ezkurdi pilota court, the Doctor Marcos Unamunazaga orchard, and the railroad station. The bomb that hit the pilota court killed everyone gathered there. While twelve fatalities and numerous casualties were recorded, Joxe Iturria remembered doing three trips in his truck, transporting bodies from the pilota court to the cemetery, a fact that would total more than thirty bodies, according to his estimations.[31] The following day, September 26, 1936, six planes grouped in pairs again

27 "Los de ayer lunes [4 de enero]," *El Noticiero Bilbaino* 62, no. 21,434, January 5, 1937, 1.
28 "Parte oficial del País Vasco," *El Liberal* 37, no. 12,487, January 5, 1937, 3. And "Partes del consejero de defensa del gobierno de Euzkadi," *El Noticiero Bilbaino* 62, no. 21,434, January 5, 1937, 1. See also "Detalles del emocionante combate aéreo librado ayer en Vizcaya," *El Noticiero Bilbaino* 62, no. 21,434, January 5, 1937, 1.
29 Parte de la jefatura del aire del estado mayor, sección de información, Salamanca, January 4, 1937.
30 Xabier Irujo, *Gernika 1937: The Market Day Massacre* (Reno: University of Nevada Press, 2015), 26.
31 Interview with Joxe Iturria, Lesaka, May 17 and 21, June 7, and July 30, 2013. See also Joxe Iturria, *Memorias de Guerra* (Gernika: Gernika-Lumoko udala, 2013), 67–68.

bombed Bilbao for three hours. According to data from the district court of Bilbao and Getxo, from the department of statistics at Bilbao city hall and the Basque Department of Health, the attacks on Bilbao and Areeta over these three days killed 96 people and injured 650.[32]

However, Bilbao would be bombed many more times. In fact, it is difficult to find a town in Bizkaia that was not repeatedly struck. Bilbao and Legutio suffered fifty-six aerial attacks. Markina and Zornotza were bombed forty times, Zigoiti thirty-three, Mungia thirty-two, Bermeo twenty-nine, Galdakao twenty-seven, Eibar, Otxandio, and Larrabetzu twenty-five, Irun and Leioa twenty-three, Elorrio, Lemoa, and Barakaldo twenty-two, Arrasate and its municipality in Santa Marina, Udala, and Kurtze Txiki were bombed on twenty-one occasions, Durango, Sondika, and Donostia eighteen (eight of which were naval attacks), Lezama and Zeanuri fifteen, Dima and Getxo fourteen, Ubide fourteen, Arrigorriaga Lekeitio, Ugao-Miravalles, and Zuia thirteen, Abadiño twelve, the áreas of Bergara, Ondarroa, Elgoibar, and Mañaria eleven, and so on. An endless number of towns were bombed fewer than ten times, making a grand total of more than a thousand bombing operations on Basque soil in one year.[33]

Between the rebels bombing Bilbao for the first time on September 25 and January 1937, 160 bomb shelters were built.[34] Later on this number increased to 269[35] but was clearly still not enough. The spring 1937 campaign began with a magnificent display of rebel aviation on the Bizkaia Front and the month of April was extremely bloody: more than 250 bombing operations were registered then, with more than 300 registered in the following month of May. The cost in human lives was also frightening; in April 1937 alone, figures from the Basque government accounted for 2,445 killed and 1,601 injured in the aerial bombings.[36] Those directly responsible for these raids were perfectly aware of the effects of these attacks on the civilian population; in fact, Richthofen promptly came to study the aftermath on areas at

---

32 *Euzko Deya* I, no. 4, Paris, December 10, 1936.
33 Xabier Irujo, "Bonbaketa kanpaina Enkarterrin," in Javier Barrio et al., eds., *Itxaropena iñoiz ez da galtzen. Encartaciones. 1937. Los últimos meses de la guerra civil en Euskadi* (Bilbo: Enkarterriko Museoa, 2017), 97–98.
34 "Bilbao cuenta hoy con 160 refugios," *Euzkadi* 25, no. 7,495, January 5, 1937, 5.
35 Tania González, "Bilbao bajo las bombas: Análisis espacial de los refugios antiaéreos de la ciudad en época republicana (1936–1937)," undergraduate thesis, University of Barcelona, 2017, 4, 17.
36 *Relación de víctimas causadas por la aviación facciosa en sus incursiones del mes de abril de 1937*, IRARGI, Euskadiko Dokumentu Ondarearen Zentroa / Centro de Patrimonio Documental de Euskadi, Doc. GE-0037-03.

the front once the rebel troops had occupied them. In this way, after studying the ruins in Otxandio on April 4, he wrote in his diary: "I went to Ochandiano. Wonderful results of bombing and fighters [Heinkel He51s and Messerschmitt Bf.109s] and of the A/8 [Heinkel He70 and Heinkel He45 of the reconnaissance squadrons]. Dead and mutilated bodies everywhere, heavy trucks, carrying part of their ammunition exploded. Ochandiano annihilated, with many dead."[37]

The epitome of horror occurred in Gernika, a military experiment to measure the destructive capacity of the incendiary bombs and bombing techniques developed by Richthofen between December 1936 and April 1937. The bombing was carried out on Monday, April 26, 1937, market day when the town was crowded with civilians, the majority having come from Bilbao on trains organized by the Basque government to relieve the hunger caused by the Bilbao blockade.[38] This great concentration of civilians provided the opportunity to practice machine gunning from ground attack aircraft, a fact confirmed by Hans J. Wandel during his trial, when he stated that all pilots were given the order to "shoot from the air whenever they saw movement."[39] In addition, civilian refugees in Bilbao, around a quarter of million people in late-April 1937, were not familiar with or simply did not completely know any techniques to avoid an aerial attack like they were going to suffer that day in Gernika.

Interrogations of prisoners of war and civilians who had survived the bombings allowed Richthofen, during his visits to sites bombed on the Basque Front between March 31 and April 25, 1937, to get a clear idea of the layout and nature of the shelters constructed by the Basque authorities, as well as the protocols of the emergency services in the event of a bombing (generally speaking, the ringing of church bells, and remaining there until the relevant signals were given). Further still, the rebel leader was perfectly aware of the layout of different points of interest in the town since, by means of inside informants, they had obtained very detailed plans of the locality.[40]

---

37 Entry in diary of Richthofen, April 4, 1937. Maier, *Guernica*, 104.
38 Irujo, *Gernika: 26 de abril de 1937*, 65–69.
39 "Los aviones que bombardearon Guernica y que actúan en el frente vasco son alemanes, conducidos por pilotos de la misma nacionalidad," *Ahora*, Sunday, May 30, 1937, 8. See also "Un informe sensacional de Mr. Mackinnon, jefe del departamento de investigaciones aeronáuticas de la marina inglesa, sobre el bombardeo de Gernika," *El Sol*, Sunday, May 30, 1937, cover. Hemeroteca Municipal de Madrid (HMM).
40 *Guernica. Con la situación aproximada de sus fábricas de guerra*. In Various Authors, *Sustrai Erreak 2, Guernica 1937* (Gernika-Lumo: Aldaba-Gernikazarra, 2012), 267.

One circumstance to bear in mind was the geographical position of Gernika, a town some six miles from the coast. Faced with an absence of radars or other more sophisticated monitoring methods, the detection systems for planes were limited to organizing mountaintop lookout posts from which, on seeing any planes, visual signals were transmitted to the church bells of the town, from which the bells were understood. Given the low nature of the Basque sky, and the amount of daily bombing operations registered, the lookouts saw planes approaching continuously, so that there tended to be an excessive number of warnings, most of which did not result in any aerial attacks. As Trinidad Rementeria observed, this meant that many people did not bother to go to the shelters.[41] However, if the attack was carried out from the sea, the lookouts stationed on the peak of Mount Kosnoaga in Gernika, 885 feet in height, would not be able to make out the planes until it was too late, since a plane going at a cruising speed of 125–150 miles per hour would take between two and a half and three minutes to cross the six miles that separated downtown Gernika from the coast. This was not sufficient time to reach a shelter, since people would be trapped by surprise, without any shelter.

And, in effect, the report of Captain Stefano Castellani, head of three Savoia-Marchetti SM.79 bombers in the 280 Squadron stationed in Soria, which attacked Gernika, mentions a "surprise act from the sea." Yet Castellani's report includes a good number of errors and as such, lacks credibility.[42] In fact, all the witnesses confirm that they saw the first planes coming from the east, from inland, at 4:20 p.m. This was particularly surprising, given that not only has it been documented that the first plane to attack Gernika (very probably a ground attack Heinkel He51) came from the east, but that it went around the towns several times before dropping its six bombs right in the center of the town and machine-gunning the population for several minutes at an approximate altitude of 130 feet.[43]

The raison d'être of this first attack was, precisely, to attract refugees. No one knew at that moment that Gernika was going to be

---

41 Testimony of Trinidad Rementeria, in William Smallwood, *El día en que Gernika fue bombardeada* (Gernika: Gernikako Bakearen Museoa Fundazioa / Gernika-Lumoko Udala, 2013), 33.

42 Irujo, *Gernika: 26 de abril de 1937*, 58n351.

43 Testimony of Jose Ramon Urtiaga, in Smallwood, *El día en que Gernika fue bombardeada*, 50. See also the testimonies of Pedro Gezuraga, Aurelio Artetxe, Iñaki Rezabal, and Faustino Pastor in William Smallwood, *The Day Guernica Was Bombed: A Story Told by Witnesses and Survivors* (Gernika-Lumo: Gernikako Bakearen Museoa Fundazioa / Fundación Museo de la Paz de Gernika, 2012), 44, 51, 55–56.

the target of one of the most devastating war bombings in the Basque Country and, for that same reason, they did not know that the shelters were going to become traps in which hundreds of people were going to lose their lives. That first Heinkel He51 was not, then, as some authors have suggested, an "indicator," that is, a reconnaissance plane whose mission was to make sure that there were no anti-air batteries in the town that may danger the bombers that would arrive later, because, as noted, the rebel leadership had plenty of information about the town and its resources. The mission of this first plane was, on the other hand, to make people go to the shelters in which they would be surprised when the first wave of heaving bombings would attack Gernika, one hour and a half later.

After this first attack, a second wave made up of three bombers (most likely two Heinkel He111s and a Dornier Do17), headed by Lieutenant Rudolf von Moureau, attacked Gernika likewise from the east. The three planes dropped their load on the city center, following the water channel line through the town and destroying the channel at the Iturriburu crossroads, leaving Gernika without running water. The witness González Echegaray claimed emphatically that the Dornier Do17 flew three and even four times over Gernika.[44] Immediately afterward, a squad of between three and six Savoia-Marchetti SM.79s led by the aforementioned Captain Castellani from the Soria air base bombed Gernika.[45] All the bombs fell right on the city center.

The raison d'être that this first attack was carried out in three successive waves was threefold. First, the water channel in the town had been destroyed, thereby impeding the efforts of firefighters and the use of water by other municipal emergency services. Second, the population had been pocketed in shelters since all those people that could find protection in one of the more than eleven shelters in the town had done so, crowded in there. Third, the emergency services (firefighters, medical staff, and soldiers and other members of the municipal administration) were now in the downtown area, carrying out urgent tasks by attending to the wounded, looking for and transporting the first bodies, and extinguishing fires. They would all be surprised by a second wave of bombing right there in downtown, exposed.

---

44 González Echegaray, interview by Jesús Salas, no date, AHEA, A-2124.
45 Xavier Juncosa documents the participation of a bomber squadron made up of three Savoia-Marchetti SM.79 bombers commanded by Paolo Moci, to which Castellani's report refers, so there could be a total of six or more bombers. Xavier Juncosa, *El País*, 8 de agosto de 1999.

For most of the people that had gone to Gernika that day, the bombing was over. The Heinkel He51 had dropped its six 10-kilo bombs on the urban center, followed by the approximately ten tons dropped by the Moreau squadron and the five or ten tons of bombs of the Italian 280 Squadron (depending on whether they were three or six planes). A total of between ten and fifteen tons of bombs on the small urban center of Gernika had caused enormous destruction and many deaths in a short span of barely forty minutes. This already seemed excessive in itself for a town that lacked any strategic or military importance. Indeed, all the bombs had targeted civilians, and none of them had destroyed any objective of military interest.

At the moment in which the last Italian bombers abandoned the town once the first forty minutes of the attack were over, Richthofen sent fighter and assault plane squadrons over Gernika at about 4:40 p.m. There were twenty-one Heinkel He51s, seven Messerschmitt Bf.109s, ten Fiat Cr.32s, and seven Heinkel He45s in the Gasteiz aerodrome in April 1937. To these one should add the Italian fighter planes in the Logroño bases and the Spanish Northern Air Force units in Lasarte, whose participation, although documented, remains uncertain. Their task was to generate a ring of fire around the town and machine-gun from the air anyone who sought to flee Gernika in any direction. In a matter of minutes, there was a concentration of twelve planes from the first Heinkel He51 J/88 Fighter Squadron, made up of Messerschmitt Bf.109s led by Lieutenant Günther Lützow, who, it seems, did not take part personally in the attack because he was off sick. Likewise, at least thirteen Italian Fiat Cr.32 fighters based in the Gasteiz aerodrome took part, under the orders of Captain Mario Viola[46] and Lieutenant Corrado Ricci; besides an indeterminate number of fighters from Logroño.[47] The light planes were in the Gasteiz aerodrome, barely twenty-minutes flying time from Gernika, so they could easily return to base, refuel, and return to Gernika within an hour.

For thirty minutes the fighter aircraft flew in circles around Gernika, machine-gunning down civilians who were attempting to escape the town, but without attacking the downtown area. The people

---

46   Mario Viola used the pseudonym Mario Viotti, Elenco nominativo del personale dell'Aviazione Legionaria del continente, 15. USAM, Gabinetto del Ministro, Busta 88, Fasc. 7.

47   Velardi's report mentions the activity of fifty-seven Fiat Cr.32 fighters flying on the Basque and Aragon Fronts that same day, completing a total of eighty-two flying hours. USAM, Busta 71, Fascicolo 9, y Diario Storico, USAM, Busta 68, Fascicolo 98.

in charge of the relief work were not necessarily aware that the bombing was happening as they were busy with emergency work and could not see the fighters flying over the downtown area. The fighters and ground attack aircraft flew in "chains" of three, each of which had a specific task over the course of aerial strafing (trench machine-gunning method). The first mission of the three was to observe and detect the target and, on doing so, it "dropped" to a height that in Gernika would be less than 3,000 feet and then pike at an angle of about 60° until descending to a height of 165 feet, machine-gunning its victims at a speed of between 90 and 125 miles per hour and firing 40 bullets of 7.9 millimeters per second with its two MG17 machine guns. In general, civilians reacted in terror and ran away. At that time, the second device of the chain, which followed the first after a fairly long time interval of a few seconds, struck and had a safe target since civilians usually did not expect a new attack. Finally, the third device picked off the survivors by machine-gunning them for the third time and, descending to just 500 feet, dropped one or several 10-kilogram bombs before ascending once more.[48] The first of the three Heinkel He51s had already regained altitude, and the chain turned and struck again repeatedly in rows of three, without breaking the formation. The Messerschmitt Bf.109 fighters and the Fiat Cr.32s as well as the Heinkel He45 and Heinkel He70 reconnaissance aircraft acted in the same way.

Many civilians lost their lives in the course of aerial bombardments because, unaware of the tactics of flight and the nature of the war itself, they did not even conceive that someone would want to kill them from a plane. Such is the anonymous testimony of a woman from Ajangiz:

> I heard the plane crashing down behind me and without looking back I threw myself headlong into a ditch and yelled at the woman who was walking with her donkey on the road alongside me to do the same. The moment I lay down I heard the machine guns of the plane and the bullets that were hitting the ground around me. When the plane had gone, I looked at the woman who was standing next to her donkey looking puzzled at the plane. "What is that bird trying to do to us?" she shouted. I watched the plane climb and turn sharply. It was coming back. It began to dive toward us and I shouted at the woman again. Then I buried my face in the ditch and covered my head with

---

48 *Informe sobre pilotos alemanes e italianos.* APC, Documentos Militares Guerra Civil (1937–1939), n.º 52.

my hands. I heard the machine guns and was afraid to move even after the plane was gone for fear of discovering that I had been shot. But I was uninjured and the plane left for Mendata. I climbed back to the road and my fear was confirmed when I saw the woman lying in a large pool of blood with her donkey still alive at her side.[49]

After thirty minutes of aerial machine-gunning and one hour and ten minutes since the bombing began, the twenty-one Junker Ju52 heavy bombers from the Burgos air base burst into the Gernika sky from the sea, taking advantage of the surprise effect that this offered them. They attacked Gernika successively, flying in a closed wedge and in groups of three, all available devices of the K / 88 bomber squadrons of the Condor Legion, specifically, the seven apparatuses of the first bomber squadron under the command of Lieutenant Karl von Knauer, at least seven aircraft of the second squadron led by Lieutenant Hans Henning von Beust, and at least seven other aircraft from the third squadron of Captain Erhart Krafft von Dellmensingen.[50]

Joachim von Richthofen wrote that "250 kilo German breaker projectiles were used in the individual and successive launch mode [*Reihenwurf*]. After crossing the entire house, the detonation takes place at ground level, producing funnels about 0.75 meters deep. The house collapses completely, including its outer walls. The neighboring buildings show considerable cracks in them. Incendiary bombs were also used."[51] This is obviously false, given that we have photographs that were even published by the German press at the time—so that it is not possible to claim ignorance or secrecy—in which we observe craters of the characteristics indicated in this chapter previously, that is, closer to four meters (thirteen feet) deep and about eleven meters (thirty-five feet) in diameter. In fact, the technique used in Gernika was the Koppelwurf launch, which in this particular case involved dropping a total of approximately 31 tons of bombs in several successive flyovers during a period of no more than thirty minutes, flying low (at a height of between 600 and 800 meters) and at low speed, on an area of land (the corral) limited to the urban center of Gernika (0.134 km2 or an

---

49 Anonymous testimony of a woman from Ajangiz, in Smallwood, *El día en que Gernika fue bombardeada*, 44.
50 Irujo, *Gernika: 26 de abril de 1937*, 75–77.
51 Report on the effect of bombs on Spanish cities (Bizkaia Front) by Colonel Joachim von Richthofen, May 28, 1937. *Heft 2, Führung, Abschnitte IV bis VI*, legajo RL 7/57b.

irregular polygon of 340m x 700 m) where there was a concentration of between 10,000 and 12,000 people, mostly civilians.

After the first round of the Junkers, the cocktail of explosive 250 kilo bombs and incendiary devices generated a great fire, and the whole of the downtown area of Gernika began to burn. The Junker Ju52s carried the bombs in ESAC-250 holders and the airman in charge of the launch operated a lever that could automatically drop all the bombs arranged in the hold at the same time, in less than a second. Nevertheless, despite the fact that the bombers took at least 15 seconds to cross the half mile separating the north and south of the town, enough time to drop the full load of bombs, numerous witnesses observed the Junker Ju52s perform several flyovers above Gernika. Such is the case of Aurelio Artetxe, who saw how "the first wave of bombers turned around and came back to make another pass. At that moment we looked up and saw fighters flying in a circle over the village higher up. Then the bombers flew over us again. The gudaris kept firing. Afterward, the second wave returned to fly over us again. I soon lost count. The bombers passed over the town repeatedly. In addition, more waves came from the south. The sky seemed full of planes."[52]

The reason for this was a direct order from Richthofen. As reported by Captain Erhart Krafft von Dellmensingen,[53] commander of the Junker Ju52 third squadron, these aircraft could carry about 1,500 kilos of explosive bombs and up to 1,728 kilos of incendiary bombs in the ESAC-250, but the total amount of cargo of these transport aircraft was 3080 kg.[54] As a result, Richthofen ordered his men to load boxes of incendiary bombs in the central aisle of the plane to be thrown by hand through one of the side doors by an airman placed specifically for that purpose in the aforementioned aisle.[55] Each plane would launch between 41 boxes (or thousand kilos of cargo) and 55 boxes (1375 kg), for which they needed to make several passes over the urban center of Gernika. Witnesses like Josefa Bilbao saw how they threw what

---

52 Testimony of Aurelio Artetxe, in Smallwood, *El día en que Gernika fue bombardeada*, 70.

53 *Auswertung Rügen*. Heft 2, Führung, Abschnitte IV bis VI, legajo RL 7/57b. Ángel Viñas cites the references by the page number in the original text that starts in legajo 7/57 a. Ángel Viñas, "Epílogo," in Herbert Southworth, *La destrucción de Guernica* (Granada: Comares, 2013), 644.

54 *L'Aviazione Tedesca al 10 gennaio 1936*. NARA, RG 242. *Foreign Records Seized Collection. Collection of Italian Military Records, 1935–1943*. Microfilm Publication T821, R. 214, 66-133.

55 Jesús Salas, *Guernica* (Madrid: Rialp, 1987), 282.

appeared to be empty ammunition boxes through the doors of aircraft.[56] This was confirmed by other witnesses such as Imanol Agirre and the gudari Martín Morante Berreteaga.

After two or even three flyovers for about 20 to 25 minutes on the target, Gernika had literally disappeared and the flames would take up to three days to be extinguished. This was what José Ramon Segues experienced:

> For an hour or so, they bombarded the town with very powerful explosive bombs. Then they started throwing incendiary devices. They launched thousands. They fell like rain. From where we were, they looked like silver pencils falling through the air. Then they made a sound like shh, shh, shh when they exploded, sending up bright geysers of white flames. Then the white flames went out. But everywhere there were yellowish flames. Through the dust and the smoke those flames seemed like the flames of hundreds of burning candles. Gradually, some of the fires grew larger. More and more smoke covered the village. Toward the end of the bombing everything was dark even though it was still daylight.[57]

Joachim von Richthofen noted in his report on the bombing that, "in the first attack, first of all incendiary bombs were used that caused numerous fires on the roofs of the buildings. This weakened their structure. In the following attacks, 250 kilos of breaking projectiles were used that destroyed the water pipes, which prevented the fire extinguishing systems from working."[58] Richthofen also lied when he stated in this same report that Junker Ju52s "caused a degree of destruction of the village close to 75 percent, with a launch volume of 31,000 kilos of bombs from a height of between 600 and 800 meters."[59] The actual fact is that the total cost of the bombing was that 85.22 percent of the buildings of the town were totally demolished and an index of destruction that diversely affected 99 percent of the constructions in the town. Only 1 percent of the buildings were undamaged, including the armament factory.

---

56   Testimony of Josefa Bilbao, in Smallwood, *El día en que Gernika fue bombardeada*, 82.
57   Testimony of Jose Ramon Segues, in ibid., 94.
58   Report on the effect of bombs on Spanish cities (Bizkaia Front) by Colonel Joachim von Richthofen, May 28, 1937. *Heft 2, Führung, Abschnitte IV bis VI*, legajo RL 7/57b.
59   Ibid.

After the attack of the three squadrons of Junker Ju52s, the survivors who had not been trapped or buried in the shelters, like the 450 or 500 people in the Andra Mari shelter, of whom hardly any survived, had no other choice than to flee from the urban center. In order to prevent these people from escaping the ring of fire, the twelve Heinkel He51s of the J / 88 squadron led by Harro Harder took off from Gasteiz around 5:00 p.m. with the mission to machine-gun the survivors. They were accompanied by the fighter squadron composed of five Fiat Cr.32s under the command of Captain Mario Viola and the fighter squadron composed of about seven Messerschmitt Bf.109s of Lieutenant Günther Lützow. Up to that point, 100 minutes of bombing had elapsed, and the fighters would machine-gun the survivors for another hundred minutes. As Captain Elosegi recorded,

> Heinkel He51 fighter planes had entered into action and where the smoke cleared and opened a gap of visibility, they threw themselves into machine-gunning all living beings. Approximately one hour had elapsed since the bombing began [in fact closer to 100 minutes had elapsed, just over an hour and a half], when I ended up in the Plaza del Ferial, in the heart of Guernica. The town had suffered terribly and the fire was raging. Numerous houses were fueling the flames and many others had been torn apart from top to bottom, with only the main walls left standing. However, there were still some intact houses that, miraculously, were still standing, like a tragic lottery win, despite the enormous shocks they had suffered. The Plaza del Ferial painted an impressive picture of death and desolation.[60]

Civilians, unaware of the destructive power of aviation, were easy prey for the fighters:

> My wife was downstairs and saw Kattalin running down the road. She was carrying a large roll of wire. Just then a plane flew low above the house. He was firing his machine guns at her. My wife shouted, "Get in here before you kill us all." I ran down. Kattalin just came through the door. She was sweaty and excited. "Those planes tried to kill me," she exclaimed. Then she told us how they had plummeted toward her and shot at her when she was walking along the train tracks south of Gernika.

---

60 Joseba Elosegi, *Quiero morir por algo* (Barcelona: Plaza y Janés, 1977), 131.

She was like a madwoman and my wife offered her a glass of brandy to calm her down. But she could not drink.

There was fear and nervousness in her eyes. She repeated, "I have to go home and cut grass for the cows." We tried to dissuade her from this idea but it was useless. She left and we wished her luck. Then about ten minutes later, the planes returned. They plummeted and shot everything that moved. One of the planes surprised us when we were at the entrance of the house. He descended over the roof, firing his machine guns. When he left, the leaves of the trees still fell to the ground. Then we learned that Kattalin had gone to the bakery, left her roll of wire, and asked them to deliver it to her at home along with the bread the next day. Then she walked along the road and had just reached the junction of the cemetery road when a plane came along firing its machine guns. Later someone found her lying at the beginning of the cemetery road, just below the embankment. She was dead. Her body was riddled with bullets. One had entered her head from behind and come out just above her eye.[61]

At around 7:40 p.m. the last fighters abandoned Gernika. The aerial attack technique, known as shuttle bombing, had generated a cycle in four phases of bombing-machine-gunning-bombing- machine-gunning that assured the constant presence of fighter aircraft and bombers over the objective for three and a half hours. And, as Richthofen and Colonels Erwin Jaenecke and Wilhelm Meise recorded, the experiment was, "a complete technical success of our 250 bombs and the EC-B1s [B-1E incendiaries]."[62] Richthofen added that, "a small part of the population had perished in shelters that received impacts" and that when, four days later on April 30, he went to study the effect of the bombing, it was "still" possible to see the holes caused by the 250-kilo bombs, which he classified as "totally incredible." The bombing left, in a record time of three and a half hours, 85 percent of the buildings in the locality totally destroyed (a total of 271 edifices), 99 percent of Gernika affected, and more than two thousand deaths, of whom between 450 and 500 were buried alive in the Andra Mari shelter, suffering an agonizing death.

---

61 Testimony of Mikel Barazpe (pseudonym), in Smallwood, *El día en que Gernika fue bombardeada*, 46.
62 Diary entry of Richthofen, March 27, 1937; Service trip report by Colonel Jaenecke, May 18, 1937; Service trip report by Colonel Meise, March 21, 1937, in Maier, *Guernica*, 128, 180, 181.

And Richthofen pointed out in a letter signed on May 25, 1937, in what was apparently a macabre irony: "In Gernika, despite everything, I behaved very badly, for sure!"[63]

Apart from the quantitative dimension of the destruction obtained, the attack reached a level of precision difficult to exceed. From the observation of aerial photographs taken on the days following the bombing one can deduce that the destruction affected exclusively the urban area of the historic center of the locality. Bearing in mind that the width of a railroad track (including the edges) is no more than 50 feet, one can observe that the bombing was scrupulously precise: barely 30 feet from the railroad toward the urban center everything was destroyed, while 30 feet beyond this same railroad in the other direction the industrial area suffered not the slightest impact. Such is the distance that separates the train station from one side of the tracks, which was totally destroyed, to the industrial area on the other side, which was not touched. If we look at San Juan and Portu kalea streets, which at that time would have been no more than 50 feet wide, we observe that they also separate surgically the part totally destroyed (from these streets inward toward the center of Gernika)

Aerial photograph in which the surgical nature of the bombardment is observed. Photo Archive of the Ufficio Storico della Regia Aeronautica Militare in Rome (Riproduzioni varie, busta 44, fasc.1).

63 Maier, *Guernica*, 128.

from that which suffered barely any harm (from these streets outward from the town). Finally, Asilo Calzada Street also divided surgically the part affected by the bombs from that which was untouched. In this case one can even observe how the trees in the area west of the Pasileku still had their leaves after the bombing while those situated to the east were totally scorched.

The town was closed to examine the ruins and the effects of the bombing by order of General Emilio Mola.[64] As Pilar Beitia recorded, a group of Germans took photographs of the ruins and shot a movie from the Olazabal family home, *Arizetxea*.[65] As had happened previously, the survivors were interrogated. In particular, the gudari Sabin Apraiz was interrogated by two colonels, three lieutenant colonels, and two majors about the bombing of Gernika.[66] This time was likewise dedicated cleaning up any evidence of the bombing of Gernika, and bomb fragments and projectiles that had not exploded as well as other material evidence were removed with the aim of substantiating the lie, ordered by General Franco that same day, April 27, 1937, that Gernika had not been bombed but reduced to ashes by the Basques themselves.[67] Apart from Richthofen and Sperrle themselves, the presence of Generals Mola and Cabanellas in the ruins of Gernika is documented, and they all had an opportunity to study the results of the bombing.[68] Many photographs were taken, both on the ground and in the air, during the days in which research into the effects of the bombing was carried out. Some of these photographs, such as those taken by Richthofen's chauffeur, are mere war memories, but very probably the photographs impressed Hitler.

The city was blocked for twenty-four hours at least, which would have allowed ground troops to advance and occupy the ruins of this locality without barely any opposition. A demonstration that the strength of war would fall on air forces. This was not untrue, since

---

64 Instructions of the general of the Northern Army, Emilio Mola, to the general chief of staff of the Black Arrows, General Sandro Piazzoni, in Deba. Instrucciones sobre Operaciones, Gasteiz, April 28, 1937. AGMA, Caja 2585, Carpeta 42/1. See also USSME, F. 18.

65 Humberto Unzueta, "Las víctimas del bombardeo. La documentación básica," *Aldaba Gernika-Lumoko Aldizkaria* 86 (March–April) 1997, 43.

66 Interview of Sabin Apraiz by William Smallwood, 1972. WSA, File Gernika, E. Sabin Apraiz, 1972.

67 Operazioni di Bilbao. Salamanca, April 27, 1937. There is a copy of this document in the Centro de Documentación del Bombardeo de Gernika (GBDZ).

68 Irujo, *Gernika: 26 de abril de 1937*, 62.

World War II ended with the dropping of the atomic bomb on a civilian population. Nevertheless, no one advanced on Gernika, because it was simply an experiment of war. And after visiting the ruins of the town, Richthofen finished the entry in his diary for April 30 with a laconic comment: "Otherwise, peace in Gernika."[69]

But Gernika, although especially bloody in that it was a military experiment, was just one of the thousands of bombings that the rebel air force carried out on Basque soil between July 1936 and August 1937. The aerial war in the Basque Country began just four days after the uprising and it is possible to divide it into three successive offensives (summer and fall of 1936 and spring of 1937) that were, in turn, very different as regards aerial warfare, their resources, and the impact they had on the civilian population.

The summer offensive began abruptly with the terror bombing of Otxandio immediately following the military uprising in Morocco. This offensive focused essentially on taking and controlling Gipuzkoa, since most of the bombings were recorded in this territory, specifically in the context of the Battle of Irun and the capture of Donostia by rebel troops on September 12, 1936. In this period a total of 91 bombing operations were recorded, which implied 8 percent of the total bombing operations registered in the conflict. The disproportion between rebel and republican forces was clear from the outset, which explains that of these 91 bombings in the summer offensive, 71 or 78 percent of the total were from the rebel side.

A bombing operation is an aerial attack against an objective (mountain positions, an urban center, or another aerial objective) on a specific day. This was the case of the bombing of Mount Bizkargi on May 15, 1937. Between 7:45 and 9:45 a.m., squadrons of Italian Fiat Cr.32 fighters from the Northern Air Force in Group 1-G-15-17 machine-gunned and bombed with light bombs positions on Mount Bizkargi[70] and, later, squadrons of J/88 attack aircraft in the Condor Legion attacked for a second time at a low level infantry concentrations stationed on that mountain.[71] In the afternoon, leaving their bases at 4:00 p.m., the two squadrons in Group 1-G-15-17 of the Northern Air Force bombed the area for the first time, and after refueling in their respective bases, they carried out another bombing in the same places.

---

69   Maier, *Guernica*, 128.
70   POFAN, No. 350, May 15, 1937.
71   LCIJA, Gasteiz, May 15, 1937.

Both services were carried out under the protection of the Italian fighter squadron and all the units returned to their airport base at 7:00 p.m., having dropped ten tons of explosives.[72] These six services (or ground attack missions), carried out by machines of the three air forces present in the theater of operations, constituted one single bombing operation so the total number of services and bombings is substantially greater than one thousand and is probably more than several thousand.

After the capture of Donostia, the fall-winter campaign began that was prolonged until March 31, 1937, although there were hardly any bombings between January and March that year due to the bad weather. In this phase of the war in which the republican forces carried out the offensive on Legutio, there were 291 bombing operations, which implied 19 percent of the total bombings registered during the war in the Basque Country. As had occurred during the summer offensive, the aerial supremacy of the rebel forces was obvious, with 63 percent of the total bombing operations.

The spring offensive began on March 31, 1937, and on August 18 that same year the last bombing on Basque soil took place. With a total of 718 bombing operations, 73 percent of the total, it was the bloodiest phase of the war. With scarcely no republican aerial intervention, 97 percent of the bombing operations during this phase were carried out by the rebel side.

From what has been said thus far, it can be deduced that the number of bombing operations increased dramatically through the war and that most of the bombings took place when the Condor Legion transferred to the Basque Front at the end of March 1937. From an average of two daily bombing operations in August 1937, the rate shot up to three daily bombing operations in October and to practically double, four a day, in December that year. In April and May 1937 the rate rose to an average of ten daily bombing operations.

As regards the relation of bombings by side, the number of rebel bombing operations rose constantly until reaching a peak in the spring, since practically all the bombing operations from March 1937 on were carried out by the rebel side. In the case of bombing operations carried out by republican leadership the progression was inverse, that is, with two maximum peaks in the months of October and December 1936 in which 44 and 39 bombing operations were registered respectively within

72   POFAN, No. 350, May 15, 1937.

the context of the Legutio offensive, 57 percent of the total operations of the republican side for the war as a whole.

In general terms, air dominance was in rebel hands throughout the war, although it was especially evident from the spring of 1937 on, and in light of the data we possess, we can point out that participation of Luftwaffe aerial units, with records of up to ten daily bombing operations in May 1937, the activity of these units was decisive in determining the course of the war. It is likewise evident that most of these operations were terror bombings on localities far from the warfront and, in light of the quantity of localities bombed we can likewise state that most municipalities in Bizkaia suffered repeated indiscriminate aerial attacks. In general terms and circumscribing the quantitative analysis to the spring of 1937, between March 31 and August 18, 1937, the seven districts in Bizkaia suffered repeated aerial attacks and 92 of the 112 municipalities in Bizkaia were bombed (82 percent), many of them on repeated occasions. In particular, all the municipalities in Greater Bilbao and Enkarterri and practically all of those in Arratia-Nerbioi suffered bombings and, as noted, 33 of those suffered more than ten bombing operations.

At the end of this bombing campaign Göring managed to convince Hitler that aviation would play a key role in the future world war and that if he had the necessary bombing apparatuses, the air force on its own could determine victory. And Göring likewise obtained Hitler's favor, becoming in a short time the successor to the Führer and one of the richest men in the Reich after being appointed by Hitler as director of the four-year plans and gaining control of exports and imports between Germany and the Spanish state.[73] And, in line with the destructive power of aviation and its role in the course of the Spanish war, Hitler would later contend:

> One thing is quite certain. People speak of an intervention from Heaven which decided the civil war in favor of Franco; perhaps so—but it was not an intervention on the part of the madam styled the Mother of God, who has recently been honored with a Field Marshal's baton, but the intervention of the German General [Wolfram] von Richthofen and the bombs his squadrons rained from the heavens that decided the issue.[74]

---

73   On Göring's manoeuvers in relation to his salary, properties, and rents, see Irujo, *Gernika: 26 de abril de 1937*, 37–52.

74   Adolf Hitler, *Hitler's Table Talk, 1941–1944: His Private Conversations* (New York:

And he added that Franco should erect a monument to the Junker Ju52s, to which he owed victory.[75]

BIBLIOGRAPHY

Barrio, Javier et al., eds. *Itxaropena iñoiz ez da galtzen. Encartaciones. 1937. Los últimos meses de la guerra civil en Euskadi.* Bilbo: Enkarterriko Museoa, 2017.

Cloud, Yvonne (Yvonne Kapp), and Richard Ellis. *The Basque Children in England: An Account of their Life at North Stoneham Camp.* London: Victor Gollancz Ltd., 1937.

Craven, Wesley, and James L. Cate, eds. *Army Air Forces in World War II.* Washington D.C.: Office of Air Force History, 1948.

Douhet, Giulio. *Il dominio dell'aria: probabili aspetti della guerra futura e gli ultimi.* Milan: A. Mondadori, 1932.

Elosegi, Joseba. *Quiero morir por algo.* Barcelona: Plaza y Janés, 1977.

Gaskin, Margaret. *Blitz: The Story of December 29, 1940.* Orando, FL: Houghton Mifflin Harcourt, Orlando, 2006.

González, Tanioa. "Bilbao bajo las bombas: Análisis espacial de los refugios antiaéreos de la ciudad en época republicana (1936–1937)." Undergraduate thesis, University of Barcelona, 2017.

Hitler, Adolf. *Hitler's Table Talk, 1941–1944: His Private Conversations.* New York: Enigma Books, 1951.

Iribarren, José María. *Mola: datos para una biografía y para la historia del Alzamiento Nacional.* Zaragoza: Librería General, 1938.

Irjo, Xabier. *El Gernika de Richthofen. Un ensayo de bombardeo de terror.* Gernika: Gernikako Bakearen Museoa Fundazioa; Gernika-Lumoko Udala, 2012.

———. *Gernika 1937: The Market Day Massacre.* Reno: University of Nevada Press, 2015.

———. *Gernika: 26 de abril de 1937.* Barcelona: Crítica, 2017.

Enigma Books, 1951), 569.
75   Paul Preston, *Franco: A Biography* (New York: Basic Books/Harper Collins, 1994), 161.

Iturralde, Juan [pseudonym for Juan Jose Usabiaga Irazustabarrena]. *El catolicismo y la cruzada de Franco*. Vienne: EGI Indarra, 1960.

Iturria, Joxe. *Memorias de Guerra*. Gernika: Gernika-Lumoko udala, 2013.

Maier, Klaus A. *Guernica. La intervención alemana en España y el "caso Guernica"*. Madrid: Sedmay, 1976.

Maldonado, José María. *El frente de Aragón: la Guerra Civil en Aragón (1936–1938)*. N.p.: Mira Editores, 2007.

Olabarria, Zigor. *Gerra Zibila Otxandion*. Donostia: Eusko Ikaskuntza, 2011.

Preston, Paul. *Franco: A Biography*. New York: Basic Books/Harper Collins, 1994.

Reig Tapia, Alberto. *Ideología e historia: sobre la represión franquista y la guerra civil*. Madrid: Akal, 1986.

Salas, Jesús. *Guernica*. Madrid: Rialp, 1987.

Smallwood, William. *The Day Guernica Was Bombed: A Story Told by Witnesses and Survivors*. Gernika-Lumo: Gernikako Bakearen Museoa Fundazioa / Fundación Museo de la Paz de Gernika, 2012.

———. *El día en que Gernika fue bombardeada*. Gernika: Gernikako Bakearen Museoa Fundazioa / Gernika-Lumoko Udala, 2013.

Unzueta, Humberto. "Las víctimas del bombardeo. La documentación básica." *Aldaba. Gernika-Lumoko Aldizkaria* 86 (March–April) 1997: 43.

Various Authors. *Sustrai Erreak 2, Guernica 1937*. Gernika-Lumo: Aldaba-Gernikazarra, 2012.

Chapter 2

Himmler's Shadows over Euskal Herria

Ingo Niebel

"Si no se reconocen las cosas, no se pueden superar nunca"

(If things are not recognized, they cannot ever be overcome)

Paco Etxeberria, forensic pathologist and director of

the study on torture and mistreatment in the Basque Country, 2017.

Repression has been a constant factor in Basque history and politics since Basques lost their self-government in 1876 as a consequence of their defeat in the third Carlist War (the second one that took place in Euskal Herria).[1] Since then there is no family in the Basque Country that has not suffered different kinds of state-run violence that in itself generated other forms of violent actions, above all after the occupation of the four southern Basque provinces by the troops of the fascist dictator

---

1   When this essay was finished in December 2017, the government of the Autonomous Basque Community (in the Kingdom of Spain) published its report on torture and mistreatment in the Basque Country (1960–2014). http://www.irekia.euskadi. eus/uploads/attachments/10773/RESUMEN_EJECUTIVO_-_Investigacion_ tortura-malos_tratos_18-12-2017.pdf (last accessed December 22, 2017). The Basque Institute of Criminology documented 4,113 cases of torture and mistreatment, 73 percent of which took place after the death of the dictator Francisco Franco. Though the study refers to the "País Vasco" (Basque Country), the investigation excludes the cases of torture that occurred in Navarre because the latter constitutes its own Foral Community inside the Spanish state. For more individual reports related to the different Basque regions see Euskal Memoria Fundazioa, ed. *No les bastó Gernika. Euskal Herria 1960–2010* (Andoain: Euskal Memoria Fundazioa, 2010). Seven provinces constitute Euskal Herria. Three of them—Lapurdi, Behenafarroa, and Zuberoa—are part of the French republic. Basques call them Iparralde, the northern part. The other four—Araba and Bizkaia, Gipuzkoa and Nafarroa—make up Hegoalde, the southern part, located in the Spanish state.

Francisco Franco in the period 1936–1937 during the Spanish Civil War. The plotter general was able to conquer the autonomous Euzkadi, the so called Basque republic, thanks to the military intervention of Nazi Germany and Fascist Italy. The airplanes of the German Condor Legion cracked the Basque defense lines and enabled the occupation of the city of Bilbo (Bilbao), the industrial and economic center and seat of the government of Euzkadi, headed by the democratically elected president José Antonio Agirre. The occupation started a new period of Spanish repression beginning with the execution of significant politicians, soldiers, and intellectuals, following the liquidation of the Basque autonomy status, the prohibition of political parties, the Basque flag or *ikurriña*, and the Basque language, Euskara.[2]

In its oppression of Basque society, the Francoist regime was able to count on the assistance of the Nazi Reich of the Führer and Reichschancellor Adolf Hitler. There are pictures of Reichsleader SS and Chief of the German Police, Heinrich Himmler, receiving protocolar honors in the Basque city of Donostia (San Sebastián) on his trip to Madrid, where met Franco in person. To them are added those which show the meeting that Hitler and Franco held in the northern Basque city of Hendaia. All together, they create a better impression of that collaboration than it was in reality.[3]

In this chapter I will try to create a scholarly base for more research on how Germans and Spaniards worked together in police matters. I will focus especially on the SS-controlled Sicherheitspolizei und Sicherheitsdienst (security police and security service, Sipo-SD) due to reasons of space and time. Later, I will explain why I prefer the abbreviation Sipo-SD than the more popular term, Gestapo. Then my second goal is to connect the historical events that occurred in the Basque Country with the state of the art of the international academic research on the Sipo-SD. Lastly, I decided to approach the work of Sipo-SD in both parts of Euskal Herria, the Spanish-controlled south (Hegoalde) and the French-administrated north (Iparralde), following the path Xabier Irujo cleared with his study on the genocide in Euskal

---

2   Xabier Irujo, *Genocidio en Euskal Herria 1936–1945* (Iruñea: Nabarralde, 2015) offers a more complete vision on how repression of the Basques worked on both sides of the Pyrenean border.

3   Sometimes history does not provide the desired facts to sustain certain impressions. For instance, in *Defending the Rock: How Gibraltar Defeated Hitler* (London: Faber & Faber, 2017), Nicholas Rankin resumes all the problems Hitler had in 1940–1941 to convince Franco to join him in the war. On the other hand, there is no doubt that on lower levels collaboration worked better for both sides.

Herria (1936–1945). My decision is based on the fact that, for example, the escape route that Allied pilots used on their way out of German occupied Europe did not end at the *muga*, as Basques call the border between the Spanish and the French states, but at the British Consulate General in Bilbo. Moreover, the members of the Basque Intelligence Service that worked for the British Secret Intelligence Service (SIS, MI6) and the US Office of Strategic Services (OSS) ignored fully the existence of that border. Even the Germans considered it at best a hurdle on their way to move agents, intelligence, or raw materials into or out of Spain. Anyone who wants to understand how Basque intelligence and resistance worked during the period 1936–1945 should know how the German repression worked on both sides of the *muga* in collaboration with and sometimes against the Spanish and the French.

Addressing these three aims does not allow me more space and time to also take into consideration other German intelligence police organizations such as the military intelligence service, the Abwehr, or the little known and underestimated Zollgrenzschutz (customs border protection, ZGS), among others. Even the description of the SD, acting as a foreign intelligence service, which it was only partly, falls short. This is due to the absence of any research on the Francoist repression system that matches international studies on the SS police and intelligence apparatus. Completely excluded remain, for the same reasons, individual biographies of people and their operations. The difference between secret organizations such as the Sipo-SD and the Abwehr becomes blurred on the operational level at which, often, one of their assets used to serve several masters at the same time. That is normal on the battlefields of secret wars but it makes academic research more complicated.

IT IS NOT (ONLY) "GESTAPO," BUT SIPO-SD

Nowadays, it is common to use the German acronym "Gestapo" as a reference point for all kinds of Nazi repression, torture, and crimes against humanity. Nazism sells. Yet from a scholarly and also political point of view it is incorrect to focus only on the Geheime Staatspolizei (secret state police) because this was only one police organization, when in fact several were involved in the German repression and extermination policy. The reason for this focus on the Gestapo is that after the German defeat, a very common defense strategy of the people involved in Nazi crimes was to blame Hitler, the chain of command, or, if it matched, the Gestapo, for what they did.

When World War II ended, members of the German repression apparatus sought individual exit strategies that would help them to escape prosecution for the crimes committed by National Socialism in the name of the German people. Soldiers in the armed forces, the Wehrmacht, tended to blame the SS for every mass murder in and outside the concentration and extermination camps. Members of Himmler's so-called black order tried to appear either as normal soldiers, who served only in the elitist Waffen-SS and its crack divisions or as "normal intelligence agents" when in fact they belonged to the SS Sicherheitsdienst (security service, SD). According to the legend they fabricated, they had nothing to do with police work that, according to them, was carried out only by the Gestapo. In the same way, officers of the Kriminalpolizei (criminal investigation police, Kripo) argued that they were distinct from the Gestapo and yet both bodies constituted, since 1936, the Sicherheitspolizei (security police, Sipo), commanded at the time by Reinhard Heydrich, Himmler's right-hand man and also head of the SD.

Yet in April 1945, the G-2 Counter Intelligence Sub-Division of the Supreme Headquarters Allied Expeditionary Force (SHAEF) knew that Sipo-SD was one and the same organization. In its detailed handbook, titled *The German Police*, the CI specialists state, taking into consideration the structural differences and internal rivalry between the Gestapo, Kripo, and the SD: "Nevertheless, the predominant fact is that at present the three services together constitute a single striking force forged by and wielded by the leading Nazi clique as an instrument to strengthen and perpetuate their [sic] power."[4]

Maybe the approaching Cold War or an interest in employing former Nazi police and intelligence assets made the British SIS and its wartime US partner, the OSS, forget with whom they were dealing. Neither the successor to the OSS, the Central Intelligence Agency (CIA), nor the British secret service (MI5) had any problem in hiring former Gestapo officials such as Klaus Barbie, known as the "butcher of Lyon," or Horst Kopkow, head of the counterespionage section and as such responsible for the killing of British agents.[5]

---

4   Supreme Headquarters Allied Expeditionary Force (SHAEF), *The German Police* (London: N.p., 1945), 45.
5   Richard Breitmann, *U.S. Intelligence and the Nazis* (Cambridge: Cambridge

This may explain why, on the cover sheet of a recently declassified CIA document, an unidentified person makes this handwritten remark: "Document contains a fairly complete roster of Sicherheitspolizei (Sipo) and Sicherheitsdienst (SD) personnel stationed in France, as well as some Gestapo names."[6] Moreover, it specifies that "Gestapo officers and offices have been listed as such, but it should not be taken that they necessarily belong to the Sipo & SD unless additional evidence is available."

This assertion contradicts the SHAEF handbook. Perhaps it should be considered a smokescreen behind which the CIA and some concerned politicians tried to hide any path that would lead investigators to the skeletons some SS war criminals had left in the closet of US foreign policy. The policy of plausible deniability and turning a blind eye to the war crimes of former Sipo-SD officers was also common in the previous Federal Republic of Germany (FRG, also known as West Germany), which since its founding in 1949 opted for forgetting the Nazi past and looking forward rather than to the past. This was one reason why only in the late 1950s did the German justice system first file a lawsuit against a former police officer accused of mass killings in Eastern Europe. In late 1960s, trials involving personnel accused of involvement in the extermination camps of Auschwitz and Majdanek drew public attention to both the SS guards and to their victims. This may explain why the Sipo-SD complex only became a topic of academic interest again relatively late.

In 1996 Ulrich Herbert published his extensive biography on Werner Best, the Nazi ideologue who used his skills as a lawyer to give a legal basis to Himmler's repression apparatus.[7] He became the *Konzepteur* (conceiver) of the Reichssicherheitshauptamt (Reich security main office, RSHA) and also of the extermination policy, while Alfred

---

University Press, 2005).

6   "Sipo and SD Kommandos in France: Personnel and Chief Groups of Agents," doc. no. 519cd819993294098d515d10, Nazi War Crimes Disclosure Act, Central Intelligence Agency Library. At: https://www.cia.gov/library/readingroom/docs/GERMAN%20INTELLIGENCE%20SERVICE%20%28WWII%29%2C%20%20VOL.%201_0001.pdf (last accessed May 24, 2017). The CIA does not give any information on the date of the document. The information could have been gathered between the spring of 1942 and fall of 1943. It seems to be very typical for an intelligence agency to not add the date or the source of documents. It seems that once the responsible officer has considered the information source reliable, it is hidden.

7   Ulrich Herbert, *Best. Biographische Studien über Radikalismus, Weltanschauung und Vernunft. 1903–1989* (Bonn: J. H. W. Dietz, 1996).

Eichmann was its *organisator*. Despite these responsibilities, Best never had to face trial in the FRG.

In a similar way to Herbert, the US scholar George C. Browder also examines the symbiosis of the Gestapo, Kripo, and the SD. He starts from the idea that,

> Historians have long agreed that a key element of Himmler's system was the fusion of the SS, a "revolutionary" instrument of force from the NS Movement, with the legitimate police force of the state. Himmler intended an eventual, complete fusion of SS and police and, therefore, of Sipo and SD. Although this never happened de jure, it was clearly a de facto reality by the 1939 creation of the Reichssicherheitshauplamt. From its inception in 1936, Sipo and SD was a de facto entity for shaping the attitudes and actions of its members, police and SS alike.[8]

And Browder comes to the conclusion that, "The special union that Sipo and SD represented offers insights into how its members came to play the roles that they did. Especially since so many of its members came from the so-called better elements of society, there is a need for better explanations than a takeover by sadists or authoritarian personalities."[9]

The studies by Herbert and Browder influenced Michael Wildt in his analysis of the formation of the Sipo-SD officer corps.[10] His research in turn served as a basis for Bernhard Brunner in his examination of the crimes that Germans, and especially members of the RSHA, committed in France and how the FRG justice prosecuted them.[11] Claudia Moisel completes this line of research, comparing how the French and West German judicial systems treated German war criminals.[12]

The result of these and other studies, together with a wider sensibility on the part of policymakers as regards the unsolved Nazi issue, led the German federal chancellery and the office of the federal president, the highest ministries, police, and intelligence agencies in the country, to commission historians to investigate the influence of former

---

8   George C. Browder, *Foundations of the Nazi Police State: The Foundation of Sipo and SD* (Lexington: The University Press of Kentucky, 1990), 8.
9   Ibid., 249.
10   Michael Wildt, *Generation des Unbedingten. Das Führungskorps des Reichssicherheitshauptamtes* (Hamburg: Hamburger Edition, 2003).
11   Bernhard Brunner, *Der Frankreich-Komplex. Die nationalsozialistischen Verbrechen in Frankreich und die Justiz der Bundesrepublik Deutschland* (Göttingen: Wallstein Verlag, 2004).
12   Claudia Moisel, *Frankreich und die deutschen Kriegsverbrecher. Politik und Praxis der Strafverfolgung nach dem Zweiten Weltkrieg* (Göttingen: Wallstein Verlag, 2004).

Nazi members when the corresponding institutions were established in 1949.[13]

French historians address the issue quite differently. In a very general way, Dominique Lormier refers to the *La Gestapo et les Français* (2013).[14] His publication is based mainly on French documents and he lists a lot of names of Sipo-SD personnel, including those that were deployed in the Basque Country. His information coincides with copies of original French documents that can be consulted online.[15] It seems that the cited reports were written in the late 1940s, after the end of World War II. They document the atrocities committed by the occupying Germans, who were mainly members of the Sipo-SD. The latter are identified by their family names and their ranks. In some cases the orthography of the German family names should be revised. Generally speaking, no further information on the careers of the Sipo-SD officers is given.

Like Lormier, the French journalist Dominique Sigaud also uses the abbreviation "SD-Gestapo" in her book *Le Piège des loups* (2012), documenting nearly all the places in which the Sipo-SD were housed during the occupation.[16] Sigaud provides an overview of the structure of the Sipo-SD in that part of the Basque Country but further research is required, especially on the officers, their professional background, and on what happened to them after the defeat. This would complement similar studies on the middle and lower Sipo-SD leaders, but it would also require more comprehensive investigation in German archives that exceeds the limits of this chapter.[17]

---

13 On the German domestic intelligence service, see Constantin Goschler and Michael Wala, *'Keine neue Gestapo'. Das Bundesamt für Verfassungsschutz und die NS-Vergangenheit* (Hamburg: Rowohlt, 2015). These authors do not use the term Sipo-SD but instead distinguish between the Gestapo, the SS, and the SD.

14 Dominique Lormier, *La Gestapo et les Français* (Paris: Pygmalion, 2013). This book is mentioned here because it is one of the more recent works on this issue. Currently, Lormier is involved in a legal struggle after several Basque historians accused him of having committed plagiarism regarding the work of the late Manex Goyhenetche. On this issue: http://www.sudouest.fr/2016/12/02/pays-basque-un-collectif-d-historiens-denonce-un-plagiat-2588681-4018.php; http://www.naiz.eus/eu/actualidad/noticia/20171208/goyhenetcheren-plagiatzaileek-ez-dute-epailearen-agindua-bete (last accessed December 21, 2017).

15 See "Gestapo à Hendaye," at http://margoytia.fr/2015/12/29/gestapo-a-hendaye/ (last accessed November 24, 2017).

16 Dominque Sigaud, *Le piège des loups: Les 175 maisons de la Gestapo en France* (Paris: Stock, 2012).

17 See Andrey Angrick, "Verlängerter Arm des Reichssicherheitshauptamtes: Das mittlere und untere Führungspersonal lokaler Mordkommandos von Sicherheitspolizei und SD 'im Osten'." In *Siftung Topographie des Terrors. Gestapo, SS und Reichssicherheitshauptamt in der Wilhelm- und Prinz-Albert-Strasse. Eine*

HIMMLER'S REPRESSION APPARATUS

In inverse proportion to the decline of military influence in the Nazi Reich, the SS in general, and in particular the RSHA, grew in power and authority. The Reich's main security office was built on seven offices, or *Amt* (in singular), every one identified by a Roman numeral. Offices I and II dealt with personal and legal matters, while Amt III, VI, and VII belonged to the SD. The first of these focused on domestic espionage, that is, in Germany or the countries under German control; the second gathered intelligence abroad or sabotaged foreign interests; and the third collected all kinds of information that could be important for the safety of Nazism. For instance, the RSHA based the policy of the final solution on studies that the highly educated academics of Amt VII had conducted on target groups abroad before Hitler started to conquer Europe. Amt IV organized the Gestapo, which defined its mission as investigating and fighting the enemy that threatened the cohesion of the Nazi Reich. Its main goal was to act as a preventive police force, identifying and arresting potential enemies before they became a real threat. Traditional criminal police work was done by the Kripo, organized in Amt V. Although the Gestapo and Kripo were labeled as Sipo, they remained autonomous organizations under the command of the Chef der Sicherheitspolizei und des SD, who also headed the RSHA. Both were rivals of their comrades in the SD, who generally had a more ideological or political and less of a professional police background. Heydrich was the first Chief of the Sipo-SD, but after he died as a result of the injuries sustained in an ambush by Czech resistance members in 1942, Ernst Kaltenbrunner succeeded him in the post until the Nazi defeat in 1945.

Both acted under the dual command of Himmler, who was on the one hand their Reich Leader SS and on the other the chief of the German police (since 1936). As such, he also commandeered the ordinary police, the Ordnungspolizei. The latter was organized in another Hauptamt (main office) that did not belong to the RSHA but was equal to it. Together with seven other main offices they formed an SS empire that included as its military branch the Waffen-SS and as a financial source the exploitation of the prisoners held in the concentration camps, run by the SS exclusively. Finally, Himmler also acquired control over the development of so-called wonder weapons and the rocket

---

Dokumentation, 2nd rev. ed. (Berlin: Siftung Topographie des Terrors, 2010).

scientists who worked on them. In 1943, Hitler named him head of the Schutzstaffeln (SS) as Reich minister of the interior, too, and one year later even commander-in-chief of the reserve army. In February 1944, moreover, he gave him control over the military intelligence service, the Abwehr, which had been the strongest rival of the RSHA. It then became integrated in this SS structure as Amt Mil.

Before Himmler took over the Abwehr, his repression apparatus had 50,648 officers, agents, and clerks on its payroll; 31,374 of them in Amt IV working for the Gestapo, 12,792 for the Kripo, and 6,482 for the SD offices.[18] Their lethal effectiveness in repressing resistance in Germany and the occupied countries was also based on the fact that the RSHA used to create task forces, made up of officers from all its offices and other police and SS units, if the Wehrmacht did not want or could not give a helping hand. The other reason was that the RSHA had standardized its work, starting with the bureaucratic organization. In general, its dependences abroad had the same structure as the central department in Berlin. In order to avoid misunderstandings, they did not have offices but rather Abteilungen (departments), which had the same Roman numerals as their parent Amt in the RSHA.

The image of a monolithic state, focused on the Führer, should not be overestimated because, from the second level down, the other Nazi leaders used to create their own domains in an attempt to get more influence and outstrip their competitors. This explains how Himmler and Heydrich, for example, managed to convert the embryonic SS—originally a small group of bodyguards inside the larger Nazi militia or brown shirts known as the Sturmabteilungen (assault detachments, SA) —into a state within a state. To achieve this aim they eliminated several rivals, starting with the murder in 1934, on Hitler's orders, of their superior, the SA-Chief Ernst Röhm.

Until the end of the war, the construction of the SS as a Staatsschutzkorps (state protection corps) was a permanent struggle for power inside the Nazi movement. It was even a struggle against the dominant National Socialist German Worker's Party (Nationalsozialistische Deutsche Arbeiterpartei, NSDAP) and other organizations within the German state; an attempt to take over the entire police force and smaller police corps and intelligence structures in other ministries; and, last but not least, the military intelligence.

---

18 Angrick, "Verlängerter Arm des Reichssicherheitshauptamtes," 358.

The Sipo-SD in Hegoalde

German-Spanish police cooperation during and after the Spanish Civil War started with an initiative by the rightwing government in Madrid at the end of 1933.[19] In March 1934, the Gestapo responded by asking the German foreign ministry to mediate in the matter. The plan did not move forward, however, until 1935, after the German secret state police had signed an agreement with Hungary and Poland. Heydrich was interested in establishing a direct channel of communication between his Gestapo and its foreign partners. The aim was to exchange intelligence on communism, sidelining the foreign ministry. In Spain, the German embassy proceeded as requested by Heydrich but also involved the German military intelligence service, the Abwehr, and its chief, Admiral Wilhelm Canaris. The plan itself became complicated because the German diplomacy involved someone from the shadowy world of intelligence rather than regular diplomats and the formal channels of negotiating with the Spanish ministry of state. Even though the February 1936 general elections in Spain brought a leftist coalition into power, two months later Himmler and Heydrich communicated to the Spanish foreign ministry that they wished to send an agent to Spain to investigate communism and its methods on the ground. He would act under diplomatic protection and be a member of the German embassy in Spain. Naturally, Berlin did not communicate this fact to the Spanish government.

In May 1936, Paul Winzer, a German police officer, arrived in the Spanish capital. A law school dropout from the Universities of Breslau and Berlin, he had decided to enter the police service in 1934. Two years before, he had also joined the Nazi party and then in 1933 the SS. Winzer started his police career in the ranks of the Kripo and transferred later to the Gestapo. Moreover, he had also studied Spanish at university. When he arrived on Spanish soil, he held the rank of a SS lieutenant, also serving in the SD. In Madrid, Winzer had to adapt to the everyday work routine of life in the diplomatic corps. There, he also shared his own information with that which diplomats used to get from more open sources. The documents we have indicate that neither he nor the German chargé d'affaires, Hans Hermann Völckers, were

---

19   For further details see Angel Viñas, *La Alemania nazi y el 18 de julio* (Madrid: Alianza Editorial, 1977), 246–55.

involved in planning the plot for the military rebellion that took place on July 17 and 18, 1936.

In fact, the military uprising caught Winzer by surprise. At that moment he was in Barcelona, and undercover of course, where he wanted to observe the People's Olympiad, an alternative event in protest at the official Olympiad to be held in Nazi Germany. When the fighting between defenders of the Republic and the plotters broke out in the Catalan capital, the Gestapo agent managed to escape on an Italian vessel to its home country and from there back to Berlin.

Later, when the German Reich decided to recognize officially General Francisco Franco's rebel military junta as Spain's government, Winzer returned as a member of the new diplomatic staff. He belonged to a group of Nazis who had their own political agenda and stood in contrast to the professional diplomats selected by the foreign ministry. This internal rivalry may explain how the Gestapo achieved the desired police agreement with the junta in March 1937, passing over the norms of the German embassy. And this agreement was extended in July 1937. It is important to stress that this was just an agreement between two official institutions, the German police and Spain's security, public order, and borders services, headed by Himmler and General Severiano Martínez Anido, respectively. The fact that this agreement was not signed on a governmental level (neither Himmler nor Martínez Anido were ministers at that moment) would later cause trouble on both sides because the foreign ministries were not involved, although it was within their sphere of operations to decide on the extraditions of foreign citizens. And that is exactly the point of which the Sipo-SD and Franco's police security services reached agreement – exchanging intelligence and making extraditions free of any legal procedure and the involvement of third parties.

It is known that the Sipo-SD interrogated and even repatriated Germans who had fought in the international brigades on the Republican side against Franco. That issue requires more scholarly research in Germany as well as in Spain. This kind of police collaboration was under Winzer's control. There is also documentary evidence that he placed his agents in German consulates where they checked, together with the diplomats there, the applications of German citizens who came for example to renew their passports. When the civil war ended in 1939, the Bilbo consulate also became responsible for the Germans that the Spaniards had imprisoned in the concentration camp at Miranda del

Ebro. The huge amount of correspondence by the people involved—including Austrians, Czechs, and Poles who had become "German" after the Reich annexed or occupied their countries—survived World War II. However, the extent of German, and especially Winser's, involvement in running the concentration camp at Miranda de Ebro remains unclear.

Yet Himmler and Heydrich also used the Geheime Feldpolizei (secret field police, GFP) as a backdoor to get onto Spanish soil and into contact with the Francoist intelligence services.[20] The GFP was the executive branch of the Abwehr. Canaris' military intelligence service used it as a police force that investigated every kind of crime within the armed forces, especially those related to sabotage and espionage. That is not the only reason why the GFP can be considered as the Wehrmacht's Gestapo, because the armed forces could also call in police officers to serve in the ranks of the GFP. This was on the one hand a logical decision for improving the GFP's police work, and on the other a little ploy intended to make Himmler's life as SS leader and chief of the German police a little bit harder.

In any case, a dozen Sipo-SD officers (mainly with a Gestapo background) served in the Gestapo detachment of the Condor Legion, Hitler's expeditionary force that helped Franco to win the war. They were attached to the military hierarchy and not to Winzer. The quality of their work, then, depended on the goodwill of the Abwehr officers who were in charge of the intelligence structure within that German expeditionary corps. The main goal of the Condor Legion GFP was to protect it from espionage. When the unit returned to Germany in May 1939, the GFP handed over their files to Winzer.

At present, we do not know whether the GFP or the Gestapo acted on Iberian soil against the Basque government of José Antonio Agirre. According to other German sources, this would seem to have been the main duty of the Abwehr, which acted from both outside and within the Condor Legion.

---

20   Klaus Gessner, *Geheime Feldpolizei. Zur Funktion und Organisation des geheimpolizeilichen Exekutivorgans der faschistischen Wehrmacht* (Berlin, GDR: Militärverlag der DDR, 1986), 19–27.

THE CASE OF JAKOB GAPP

One of Winzer's main duties was the surveillance of German citizens and their prosecution if they acted against the Reich. One interesting case in the Basque Country is that of Jakob Gapp.[21] He was an Austrian clergyman who belonged to the Catholic Society of Mary. He fled from his homeland when he got into trouble with the new pro-Nazi authorities because he dared to criticize Nazism. First he went to Bordeaux and, later, in May 1939, to the Marianist Colegio Católico de SantaMaría in Donostia. His congregation then sent him to Andalusia, where Gapp had a very difficult time. First he had to adapt to the hot climate and then to the Andalusian way of life that was so different from his own. Another factor was that he could not talk to his brothers about how Nazism persecuted all the Christians who did not bow to Nazi ideology or come to an arrangement with the new pagans wearing the insignia of their brown shirts, skulls, swastikas and SS runes. After improving his skills in Spanish, Gapp returned to Donostia in 1939, but his personal situation did not improve because he did not avoid any fight when it came to defending his faith against Nazism, even in front of his students. His behavior caused more and more problems so he decided to quit his job at the Marianist Colegio and to work as a private teacher for a wealthy Spanish-Austrian family in the Basque fishing port of Lekeitio (Lequeitio), where he also taught in the college of the Order of the Blessed Virgin Mary of Mercy there. In the summer of 1941 he was back in Donostia but his brothers sent him to Valencia. In that southern town Gapp continued criticizing Nazism and the social inequality he had confronted when he had taught students from rich families. Ultimately, the Gestapo became aware of Gapp, and two of its agents or collaborators got in contact with the clergyman. One of them posed as a German Jew in exile who wanted to convert to Catholicism, seeking to be taught by Gapp. The final chapter in that charade was to thank Gapp by inviting him on a trip to the Basque Country. The Austrian ignored all warnings and joined the tour that ended at the frontier post in Hendaia, where he walked straight into a trap the Sipo-SD had prepared for him.

Himmler's henchmen escorted him to Berlin, where the Volksgerichtshof, the people's court, sentenced him to death. Jakob Gapp was

---

21   Josef Levit, *Jakop Gapp. Zeuge seines Glaubens* (Innsbruck-Wien: Tyrolia-Verlag, 1988).

beheaded on August 13, 1943. He had to bear the costs of his execution, and the authorities handed his dead body over to the anatomical-biological institute at the University of Berlin for research purposes, on the condition that it could not be delivered to his family. The Gapp case shows how the Sipo-SD used its presence on both sides of the Basque border for its purposes.[22]

GERMANS IN AGIRRE'S HEADQUARTERS IN PARIS

It was possibly the Abwehr department III that handled counterespionage, or the Sipo-SD cell in Paris, which contributed to the arrest of the Basque espionage network on Spanish soil. In January 1943, Spanish police arrested Luis Álava and some thirty people who were connected to his clandestine organization that provided the Basque government in exile with intelligence from inside the Francoist state. It is clear that the information that led to the fall of the "Álava Network" was found in the Basque government's headquarters at 11 Marceau Avenue in Paris. Basque contemporaries and historians point to the Germans as responsible for seizing Agirre's headquarters.[23] From an academic point of view the issue is more complicated. Of course, if the Germans had not conquered Paris, certain documents would not have been seized and certain persons would not have been handed over to the Francoists, imprisoned, and executed. Following research into the arrest of Catalonia's president, Lluis Companys, in France and his deportation to Spain in August 1940, we know that the initiative for that operation stemmed from the Spanish police officer and Falangist Pedro Urraca, based at the Spanish embassy in Paris. He asked the German military authorities for permission to seize the offices of the Spanish Republicans, Catalans, and Basques that they had used in the French capital. At that time the Sipo-SD had no authority to act officially in the occupied zone. In fact, Himmler's and Heydrich's men found themselves in a legal twilight zone because the Oberkommando der Wehrmacht (high command of the armed forces, OKW) and the Oberkommando des Heeres (high command of the army, OKH) had decided that only

---

22 Xabier Irujo mentions the case of the Basque Lekaroz brothers who became victims of a cross-border operation by German and Spanish police agents. See *Genocidio en Euskal Herria 1936–1945*, 209.

23 Juan Carlos Jiménez de Aberásturi and Rafael Moreno Izquierdo, *Al servicio del extranjero. Historia del servicio vasco de información (1936–1943)* (Madrid: A. Machado Libros, 2009), 214.

the military, and not the SS, would carry out police work there. Despite using the Sipo-SD cells, as had happened before during the annexation of Austria, Czechoslovakia, and Poland, the Abwehr, its GFP, and the military police (the Feldgendarmerie) would guarantee public safety in collaboration with the French police.

Finally, the Sipo-SD managed to convince the Wehrmacht to tolerate its small task forces that had arrived in Paris wearing GFP uniforms. They were commanded by the SS lieutenant colonel Helmut Knochen. This SD officer became the Beauftragter, the representative of the Chief of the Sipo-SD in France. Yet the Sipo-SD was only able establish bases in Bordeaux and two other French cities, and it had to ask the army's permission for any operation it sought to undertake. Its policing work was limited to monitoring Jews, communists, and emigrants, and it reported to the police department of the military administration staff.

Currently, no German documents explain how Urraca, the Abwehr department III, and the Sipo-SD worked together (or against each other) during this early stage of the war. From the Companys case we know that Urraca had to have involved his superior, the director general of state security in the ministry of state, the Count of Mayalde, José Finat, for getting Germans approval to deport the Catalan president from prison in Paris to Spain. In order to do so, several calls would have been necessary between Finat, the head of Abwehr III counterintelligence in Paris, and perhaps the RSHA in Berlin. Unfortunately, any German documents (if at all they existed) that show the circumstances of Urraca's operations against the Republican, Basque, and Catalan exiles, have disappeared or were destroyed.[24]

By the end of the summer of 1940, the OKH had built up its military administration in France, controlled from Paris by the Militärbefehlshaber Frankreich (the German military high command in France, MBF). The demarcation line divided the French Republic in an occupied and unoccupied zone. It also split the northern Basque Country into two parts.[25] The occupied zone belonged to German army district B, with its headquarters in Angers, while the unoccupied zone was governed by the French government, based in Vichy. It was

---

24   By now, the absence of any such documents shows that the Germans—whether the military, the SS, the Nazi party, or the foreign ministry—were not especially interested in the Basques. On the contrary, the Abwehr collaborated very closely with the Bretons.

25   For more details, see chapter 5 on the Atlantikwall in this book.

strictly forbidden to cross the demarcation line without permission and beyond the border points. Police work in Iparralde was carried out by the smaller Feldgendarmerie units no. 732, deployed in Donibane Garazi (Saint-Jean-Pied-de-Port); no. 524 in Miarritze (Biarritz); and no. 659 in Baiona (Bayonne). The GFP-group 14, with its headquarters in Bordeaux, operated a Kommissariat (police station) in Miarritze, where the Abwehr was also present, and an outpost in Hendaia.[26] Officially, there were no Sipo-SD officers acting in Iparralde.

The former *gudari* (Basque nationalist militiaman), Joseba Elosegi, was stopped twice by the German military police. He encountered "A soldier with a spectacular collar over his chest that justified his rank and service asked me for my identity documents," remembers the member of the Basque intelligence service. His description indicates that a military police officer stopped him because only Feldgendarmerie soldiers wore a great silver gorget with a heavy chain around the neck.[27]

Little is known about how far exactly the Wehrmacht was involved in the repression of Basque society in Iparralde. The military was at least responsible logistically, in August 1940, for sending a first batch of 927 Spanish Republicans from Angoulême to the concentration camp of Mauthausen in Austria. And there is documentary evidence that the Sipo-SD organized training courses for Francoist police agents in Berlin.

THE SIPO-SD TAKE CONTROL OF IPARRALDE

In the spring of 1942, Himmler and Heydrich finally achieved their major goal when they took control of all German police structures in occupied France. The Wehrmacht had to recognize its weakness in fighting the French Resistance, a weakness that increased after Hitler began the invasion of the Soviet Union on June 22, 1941. As a consequence of this new assault on a sovereign country, his former ally in the East, Joseph Stalin, gave the Communist Party of France a free hand to attack the German occupiers. Until that moment, the French communists were restricted from taking any action by the German-Soviet Non-Aggression Pact, signed in 1939. On August 21, 1941, however, the first occupying German soldier, Alfred Moser, was shot dead in Paris,

---

26 "Eisnatzgliederung vom 31.5.1942," in Kurt Mehner, ed., *Die geheimen Tagesbericht der deutschen Wehrmachtführung im Zweiten Weltkrieg 1939–1945*, vol. 4, *1.11.1941– 31.05.1942* (Osnabrück: Biblio Verlag, 1992).
27 Joseba Elosegi, *Quiero morir por algo*, 2nd ed. (Barcelona: Plaza & Janes, 1977), 249.

and two further officers were killed in subsequent attacks. Hitler ordered an extreme retaliation: one hundred hostages had to be executed. The numbers then grew in proportion to the increasing number of attacks. The MBF, Otto von Stülpnagel, tried to satisfy both his superiors in Berlin and French society by selecting Jews and foreigners to be killed or deported. In the end, though, he chose to resign and to hand over his post to a relative, Heinrich von Stülpnagel.

Himmler and Heydrich decided to reorganize their chain of command in the occupied zone. They introduced the figure of the higher SS and police leader to head the order police and the Sipo-SD, and then selected SS Major General Carl Oberg for that post. He had served previously in Poland, where he had been responsible for the persecution of the Jewish population and the detention of Polish forced laborers. His personal assistant became the former head of the Sipo-SD Bordeaux base, Herbert Martin Hagen.

SS Colonel Knochen remained the second in command, although the name of his post was changed from Beauftragter (representative) to Befehlshaber (commander) of the Sipo-SD (BdS). The internal structural organization of the Sipo-SD in Paris remained untouched, but it grew in its geographical extension and in numbers. The new personnel came from the GFP groups deployed in France. Their members had to relinquish the Wehrmacht uniform and dress instead in the field gray and the skull of the Sipo-SD. In this way, the number of Sipo-SD officers grew from 300 to 2,400.[28] These measures did not affect the Feldgendarmerie, which stayed under army control.

Parallel to the internal reorganization, Knochen set up a new territorial structure. In January 1943 he had established seventeen Kommandeure der Sipo-SD (commanders of the Sipo-SD, KdS) who became the German counterparts to the French regional *préfects*. Every KdS had at his disposal between fifty and one hundred Sipo-SD officers and an unknown number of informants. They served not only in the KdS headquarters but also in so-called Aussenkommandos (external units) and Aussenposten (outposts). Sometimes, when it was necessary to carry out a special task, the BdS or KdS gathered the required men in an Einsatzkommando (task force, EK). That method made police work flexible, but also difficult to reconstruct later who made up such a unit.

---

28 Brunner, *Der Frankreich-Komplex*, 53.

Regarding the territory of Euskal Herria, the new Sipo-SD structure remained as arbitrary as before. The KdS Bordeaux took over the former GFP outposts in the occupied zone. On November 8, 1942, the Wehrmacht invaded the non-occupied zone. The KdS Toulouse then became responsible for the Aussenkommando Pau and for the rest of the Basque border region. In 1943, the RSHA decided that the KdS positions should be occupied only by its own people and no longer by the military administration or the GFP.

In the costal Basque area, the KdS Bordeaux commanded the Grenzkommissariat in Hendaia. It included, according to French post-war sources, ten officers, eight police officers, four interpreters, eight clerks, and ten enlisted men. Its first head was the SS lieutenant and criminal secretary Jahn. In 1943, he was succeeded by SS First Lieu-tenant Kutschmann, who was also responsible for the highly sensitive section IV N that had informants on both sides of the *muga*.[29] From its headquarters—the La Gobette villa in Ondarraitz-Hendaye-Plage—the Sipo-SD controlled two further outposts, one in Kanbo (Cambo-les-Bains) and another in Donibane Garazi.

The Sipo-SD base in Kanbo was headed by Franz Warthona. With him served the interpreter Frédéric Wessels and the clerk Émile Gierth.[30] Before returning to Hendaia, they resided in three differ-ent villas: Les Lauriers (1942), Bi Ainarak (sic) (1943), and Behartia (1944). Donibane Garazi became important to the Sipo-SD and the Wehrmacht because of its railroad station and its location as a border point at the demarcation line. The Germans occupied the old citadel there and converted it into another prison.[31]

In Baiona SS First Lieutenant Hubner was in charge of the Sipo-SD Aussenkommando, based at the Mont-Carmel villa in Maréchal-Soult Avenue.[32] SS Lieutenant Franz Wiedemann headed section IV N, which worked together with French citizens such as André Bassahon. Like Kutschmann, he also held the rank of Kriminalsekretär (criminal secretary, KS), which identified both as members of the Kripo. This detail again proves that the criminal police was part of the Sipo and

---

29 The spelling of his family name may be not correct because there are other versions in the French documents such as Kutzmann or Kustchmann. (The latter seems to be definitively wrong.)

30 "Frédéric" may be the French translation of the German "Friedrich." This example shows once again the difficulties that different spellings present for identifying Sipo-SD members.

31 Sigaud, *Le piège des loups*, 110.

32 Ibid., 107.

as such responsible for its actions. They used the Château-Neuf Prison in Baiona Handia (Grand-Bayonne) for interning people, arrested for being Jewish. The other prisoners were held in the citadel of Baiona.

Another Sipo-SD external unit was based in Miarritze. It used the Hotel Édouard VII for questioning arrested people. A former boardinghouse, Maison Blanche, situated at 6 Dominique Morin Drive, served as a detention center.[33] According to French information, that Aussenkommando was particularly special because its SD foreign intelligence department reported directly to the KdS Bordeaux or the BdS in Paris. It was run by SS Lieutenants Jung and "Werner." The latter may have been an alias for someone who posed as a merchant doing business with Latin America. Their mission was to keep in touch with the SD offices in Lisbon and Madrid.

If necessary, in its work the Sipo-SD could rely on the assistance of both the Wehrmacht, especially the Feldgendarmerie, and the customs border protection units. It also counted on the cooperation of the French police and administration, above all, when a policy of deporting Jews from the Basque area to Bordeaux began. When the war turned against the Nazi Reich, some members of the military police, like the Austrian sergeant Felix Löffler, helped some French citizens to escape from an Sipo-SD round-up.[34] But he was not the sole German to do so, as the case of the Sipo-SD officer and interpreter Gustav Hammer demonstrates: "During the occupation, Hammer enjoyed his dual power to harm and to help local citizens. Often ruthless, he was responsible for numerous arrests and deportations. Yet he often addressed people in familiar terms and sometimes strategically 'turned a blind eye' to acts of resistance," notes the ethnologist Sandra Ott.[35] The behavior of these two members of the German repression system should not be compared only with each other but also to that of their several thousand fellow countrymen and women who fought and died with the French Résistance.

On the other side of the *muga*, the Germans were aided by their Spanish counterparts, even though sometimes bribes were required to

---

33   Ibid, 106–07.

34   Mixtel Esteban, *Regards sur la Seconde Guerre mondiale en Pays basque* (Baiona: Elkar, 2007), 96–97.

35   Sandra Ott, "The Enemy as Insider: German POWs as Trial Witnesses in the Basses-Pyrénées, 1944–1946," in *War, Exile, Justice, and Everyday Life, 1936–1946*, ed. Sandra Ott (Reno: Center for Basque Studies, University of Nevada, Reno 2011), 315.

gain such help. Likewise, the British and US intelligence services also bribed the Spanish when Basque smugglers brought Allied pilots across the Bidasoa River into Hegoalde on their secret route to the British consulate general in Bilbo.

The fight against the different resistance networks and the young French people who evaded obligatory work service (*Service du Travail Obligatoire*, STO) were further concerns for the Sipo-SD. In 1943, Himmler's police and intelligence agents started to dismantle the Comète escape organization that operated an escape channel from Belgium through France up to the Basque border. In March 1943 the Sipo-SD carried out a round-up of local members of the network. The coordinator in the Baiona-Angelu (Anglet) area was Édouard Dassié, aka "Jean," aided by his wife Marthe and their daughter Lucienne. The Sipo-SD arrested and deported all of them, and only Lucienne would survive. For different reasons, the Germans deported around 1,500 people from the Basque Country between 1940 and 1944, and only 900 would return.

The nightmare of German occupation ended on August 22, 1944 when the remaining agents of the Sipo-SD, the customs border protection, and the Feldgendarmerie left Iparralde in a convoy heading eastward, back to the German Reich. Some of their comrades went south instead, in one car and two motorcycles with sidecars, into Spain. Yet they did not reach the border because the Résistence stopped them at a roadblock. In the ensuing fight, three Germans were killed and an unknown number injured and arrested. Among their belongings the French found "a list of Gestapo members who escaped to Spain in the days before."[36] As Sigaud concludes, "When the German left, some résistance members entered the SD offices and burned the remaining archives. In this way, a history was cleansed from trace that could have been very compromising for some of them."[37]

HIMMLER'S MEN WHO DID NOT LEAVE SPAIN

On May 8, 1945, World War II officially ended in Europe. Hitler had already committed suicide on April 30, and Himmler would follow him on May 23. By then, the last chief of the Sipo-SD, Kaltenbrunner, was

---

36   Esteban, *Regards sur la Seconde Guerre mondiale en Pays basque*, 164.
37   Sigaud, *Le piège des loups*, 107.

in American custody and the head of the Gestapo, Müller, had gone underground. His SD counterpart, Schellenberg, and other "intelligence agents" of his, such as the "war hero" Otto Skorzeny, managed to become key witnesses for the International Military Tribunal (IMT) that was preparing to judge the major Nazi war criminals. On October 1, 1946, the IMT sentenced twelve of the twenty-four accused to death. Among them was Kaltenbrunner, who would be hanged on October 16. The judgment declared the Gestapo and the SD "criminal organizations."

Far away from the courtyard in Nuremberg, in Bilbao, the situation was quite different. While all over Europe former Sipo-SD officers were trying to hide and keep a low profile, in Francoist Spain they did not care so much about being discrete. For that reason they came on the radar of the US intelligence. On May 23, 1946, just one year after Himmler's death, an unknown OSS agent in Spain wrote, from Bilbao, a "Report on Germans" detailing a "Kidnapping of a German by the German Gestapo."[38] The author was serious about the German acronym because he used it again in his first sentence: "Last Saturday, at half-past six in the evening LOESCH was kidnaped by order of the Gestapo."[39]

The report is about the secret collaboration of Spaniards and Germans in the area between Santander and Bilbao. They channeled large amounts of money secretly, which was meant to sustain German citizens either in the internment camps or in the underground. Among the latter were aviators who had crashed their Heinkel He 111 bomber plane, with the Belgian SS Colonel Léon Degrelle on board, on the beach in Donostia on May 8, 1945. The OSS informant uses the acronym because a member of this clandestine Nazi Falangist network was Father Lange, who, in his words, "belongs to the Gestapo in Spain." In fact, that clergyman of German origin appears frequently in intel-

---

38 "Reports on Germans: Kidnaping of a German by the German Gestapo," Bilbao, May 23, 1946, Nazi War Crimes Disclosure Act, Central Intelligence Agency Library, at OSS - SSU - CIG EARLY CIA DOCUMENTS VOL. 4_0006.pdf (last accessed December 15, 2017).

39 This person, Loesch (or Lösch), could not be identified. Although historians should be pleased that the CIA opens its archive for research, the agency sometimes publishes every document as one pdf file, instead of digitizing the entire folder as both the US and the British National Archives used to do. Another problem is that the documents are scanned in black and white but not in color like the British National Archives do. Therefore, information can be lost if distinct colors were used in documents, as was typical in Germany, for instance. The excessive use of the term "Gestapo" makes one speculate about what the acronym could have meant to the anonymous OSS agent. Was it common to use it to refer to a secret group of active Nazis/Germans? Or was it just a term that the unknown writer used to spark the interest of superiors and hence gain a rise in importance and in salary, if he was only an informant for the OSS?

ligences records as a collaborator of several German and Spanish secret services in the Basque region. His full name, at least in Spanish, was Agustin María Lange.[40] He used to operate out of the Bizkaian town of Balmaseda (Valmaseda). The cited OSS report shows how, after the defeat of the Nazi Reich, the collaboration between the former Sipo-SD structure and Spaniards transformed into illegal activity based on money laundering, corruption, kidnapping, torture, blackmailing, and other felonies.

Hitler and Himmler had gone, but their middle and lower henchmen were still active. On December 23, 1946, the German magazine *Der Spiegel* reported that the German colony was surprised that, "the entire staff of the Gestapo in Madrid, made up of Mr. Vey, Singer, and Mosig, had arrived completely safe and sound in the Spanish capital."[41] Mosig took a plane to Latin America and in the meantime, "ex Gestapo chief Georg Vey went cheerfully for a drive in his own car through Madrid." It is said that his longstanding predecessor, Paul Winzer, died on September 27, 1944, when a US fighter pilot intercepted the civil Focke Wulf 200 Condor plane he was traveling in and shot it down over Dijon, France. It was a regular Lufthansa flight on route from or to Barcelona.[42]

Quite different was the situation of former Sipo-SD personnel in France. There, Oberg, Knochen, and others had to face trial and were sentenced to long prison sentences but were freed when their time in pre-trial custody was taken into consideration. Others, like Hagen, were sentenced in absentia or only decades later in Germany because they were found guilty of deporting Jews from France.

It is generally established that Franco's dictatorship ended either with his death on November 20, 1975 or when, on December 6, 1978, the majority of the Spanish (but not the Basque) voters ratified

---

40   Elixabete Castresana, "Balmaseda descifra las claves de su propia trama de espías," *Deia*, March 19, 2017, at http://m.deia.com/2017/03/19/bizkaia/margen-izquierda-encartaciones/balmaseda-descifra-las-claves-de-su-propia-trama-de-espias   (last accessed December 15, 2017).

41   "Komm zurück nach Spanien," *Der Spiegel*, December 23, 1946, 11–13.

42   It is not clear if the Lufthansa flight was heading to Stuttgart or to Barcelona when it was intercepted. In general, there is no doubt that Winzer died on that day but Eduardo Martín de Pozuelo and Iñaki Ellakuría mention a letter, dated February 2, 1945 (!) and attributed to Winzer, which was found by the OSS. The contradiction cannot be solved because the authors do not reveal the exact source; only that their book is based on OSS records released by the US National Archives. See *La guerra ignorada. Los espías españoles que combatieron a los Nazis* (Barcelona: Debate, 2008), 210.

the new constitution that transformed the fascist state into a constitutional monarchy. Although the dates mark the beginning of a political and legal conversion from one system to another, it is open to question whether that process did not ende some years later, for instance, after the failed military coup that took place on February 23, 1981, or when the Spanish Socialist Workers' Party (Partido Socialista Obrero Español, PSOE) came to power for the first time since the civil war, on December 2, 1982. There is no doubt that political and constitutional circumstances in Spain changed between 1975 and 1982, but this did not affect certain structures. The oligarchy and the Catholic Church preserved their privileges as did the military and the police forces. The latter continued fighting ETA and every person or group they thought sympathetic to the clandestine organization. In that struggle, they adopted both new antiterrorist measures, developed in West Germany for example, and counterinsurgency methods put into practice in Latin America. There is evidence that Spanish police and intelligence officers were trained by Argentinian *compañeros*, whose violations of human rights were notorious; but the alleged international "fight against communism" obviously justified all means.[43] That also included the use of clandestine paramilitary groups that acted outside the law in all imaginable manners against supposed enemies. All these practices were imported into Spain. The passive voice has to be used, at least in an academic paper, because it is difficult to get hard evidence, meaning documents that prove who was responsible for that "dirty war" against Basque and other dissidents.

On June 8, 1980 there was an explosion in the town hall of Elgeta, Gipuzkoa. The attack was carried out by an underground fascist group, the Batallón Vasco Español (Spanish Basque Battalion, BVE). On the forty-fourth anniversary of Franco's plot, July 18, 1980, the BVE threw an improvised explosive device into a Basque bar full of people. They were lucky that the device did not explode. Had that technical failure not have occurred, it could have caused a huge massacre. The authors of both crimes were never arrested or brought to justice.

The people involved in the BVE structure were part of a wider network that connected intelligence agencies like the CIA to NATO's "stay-behind" operations of armed resistance, codenamed Operation Gladio, and European neofascists and old Nazis. In that context, three

---

43 Danilo Albin, "El Gobierno de Aznar ocultó datos sobre militares y policías adiestrados por Videla," *Público*, December 10, 2017, at http://www.publico.es/politica/dictadura-argentina-gobierno-aznar-oculto-datos-militares-policias-adiestrados-videla.html (last accessed December 14, 2017).

significant names emerge: the SS officers Otto Skorzeny, Léon Degrelle, and Klaus Barbie. Skorzeny, a specialist in commando raids and other SD operations, and the Walloon Degrelle, the former commander of the Belgian SS division, were linked to the BVE, the Guerrilleros de Cristo Rey (Warriors of Christ the King, a paramilitary fascist group), and the neofascist Spanish organization CEDADE (Círculo Español de Amigos de Europa, Spanish Circle of Friends of Europe). The latter connected Skorzeny to the "butcher of Lyon," Klaus Barbie. He had worked closely with the Italian neofascist Steffano delle Chiaie, who was involved in the activities of the BVE against Basques.[44] When the Italian terrorist had to escape from Europe because the Italian justice was catching up with him, he joined Barbie in Bolivia, from where they participated in covert operations in Latin America as part of the sinister Operation Condor.

It is difficult to prove how much they were involved in the Elgeta attacks because the Spanish police never investigated these and other crimes. Only in December 2017 did the mayor of that Gipuzkoan town bring the matter of the two bombings and some other crimes committed by Francoists between 1936 and 1977 to justice. A judge has considered the charges well-founded and started the appropriate investigation. But Skorzeny and Barbie, both deceased, are not the only German (neo)Nazis suspected to have continued the activities of the ex Sipo-SD under other circumstances and with different means against Basques. The murder of the leftist congressman Josu Muguruza on November 20, 1989 in the Hotel Alcalá in Madrid occurred in the presence of an eyewitness of German origin connected to the Spanish security forces. He was at the time running a business built by his father, who had worked for the military intelligence service, the Abwehr, during World War II. That coincidence, if it was one, shows again that there seems to be a certain continuity of structures and people related to that very special world populated by intelligence agencies and their contacts.

---

44 For Delle Chiaie and Barbie see Magnus Linklater, Isabel Hilton, and Neal Ascherson, *The Nazi Legacy: Klaus Barbie and the International Fascist Connection* (New York: Holt, Rineheart and Winston, 1984), 227. On NATO and Operation Gladio see Daniele Ganser, *NATO's Secret Armies: Operation GLADIO and Terrorism in Western Europe* (London: Routledge, 2004). Skorzeny published several books of his memories, recounting a past that diverged widely from the historical truth and, of course, without mentioning the crimes he committed before and after World War II. In 2016 the Israeli daily *Haaretz* uncovered the fact that Hitler's favorite SS man had even worked as a hitman for the Mossad. In the summer of 2017 the German sensationalist newspaper *Bild* reported that it had access to Skorzeny's personal documents. In fact, some of his correspondence had been put out to auction in 2011.

Some Suggestions on how to Deal with the Legacy of Himmler's Men in the Iberian Peninsula

The abovementioned cases of the BVE bring researchers back to the shadowy parallel universe of secret services, their agents and governments, organized crime, neofascism, and secret military structures, and all this despite little documented evidence for sustaining this or that theory. This is the terrain in which so-called conspiracy theories like to flourish.[45] With any doubt, Skorzeny and his Nazi and Falangist *Kameraden* or comrades, who acted in charge of one or more intelligence agencies or were driven by personal interests, conspired against the law, the state, and the individual rights of the people they targeted. Therefore, uncovering their conspiracies requires theories that must be proved with facts. Problems occur when some people adapt facts to their theory, because in doing so it that is when they become "conspiracy" theories. Instead of that, a theory should be adapted to the facts and not the other way round.

The above mentioned study on torture and mistreatment and research into the Francoist genocide against Basque society requires a fresh start, going back to sources that may explain the origins of the repression system. This *ad fontes* method requires that researechers have free access to all archives, including those of the military, police, and secret services. That step also requires investigation into which records were already destroyed after the dictator died. Research on German-Spanish collaboration in police and intelligences matters, in particular, demands access to the archives of the public administration, the secret services, the armed forces, and the police corps.

In the current political situation, in which the Spanish state is becoming more repressive because of its conflict with Catalonia, is it too much to ask that it opens the gates to those secrets? In the meantime, such inquiry has to be carried out by others: for example, by representatives of the Argentinian justice system that is gathering information and testimonies on Francoist crimes and by historians and journalists who have access to sources beyond those in Spain alone.

---

45 I do not like the term "conspiracy theory" and its semantic derivations because its literal translation, which ignores the wider significance of "conspiracy" in US criminal law, has become—especially in Germany—some sort of insult directed in general against anyone who questions an official version of a delicate political issue.

Beyond that obstacle, and focusing only on the Sipo-SD personnel who served in the Basque Country and its bordering regions, we can observe that little is known about their lower and middle commanders, but we do know a lot about their superiors. Connecting with the ongoing analysis of their comrades who served in the Sipo-SD killing squads in the former Soviet Union, it would be worth scrutinizing the biographies and activities of people assigned to the KdS Bordeaux and KdS Toulouse. The French archives house relevant information that, after an academic research, could provide new insights into how the Sipo-SD repression system worked in thsoe two areas in southwestern Europe. And then the result could be compared to the presence of Himmler's men in other European regions.

A further consequence for Basque history would be that *les allemands* and *los alemanes* would cease to be some unidentified individuals who acted in a mass and somehow anonymous way against civilians. That could be a first to step to a broader goal: namely, identifying the offenders means also honoring their victims who did not suffer or even pass away because some unidentified group intervened, but rather because of the decisions of specific individuals.

Honoring victims can be completed only by naming their offenders, the people who were empowered to assault them and who created the repression system. All this work is fundamental because it reveals actors, methods, and structure that must be changed if the higher goal is a long-term peace, based on truth, reparation, and justice.

BIBLIOGRAPHY

Angrick, Andrey. "Verlängerter Arm des Reichssicherheitshauptamtes: Das mittlere und untere Führungspersonal lokaler Mordkommandos von Sicherheitspolizei und SD 'im Osten'." In *Siftung Topographie des Terrors. Gestapo, SS und Reichssicherheitshauptamt in der Wilhelm- und Prinz-Albert-Strasse. Eine Dokumentation.* 2nd revised edition. Berlin: Siftung Topographie des Terrors, 2010.

Breitmann, Richard. *U.S. Intelligence and the Nazis.* Cambridge: Cambridge University Press, 2005.

Browder, George C. *Foundations of the Nazi Police State: The Foundation of Sipo and SD.* Lexington: The University Press of Kentucky, 1990.

Brunner, Bernhard. *Der Frankreich-Komplex. Die nationalsozialistischen Verbrechen in Frankreich und die Justiz der Bundesrepublik Deutschland.* Göttingen: Wallstein Verlag, 2004.

Elosegi, Joseba. *Quiero morir por algo.* 2nd edition. Barcelona: Plaza & Janes, 1977.

Esteban, Mitxel. *Regards sur la Seconde Guerre mondiale en Pays basque.* Baiona: Elkar, 2007.

Euskal Memoria Fundazioa. *No les bastó Gernika. Euskal Herria 1960–2010.* Andoain: Euskal Memoria Fundazioa, 2010.

Ganser, Daniele. *NATO's Secret Armies: Operation GLADIO and Terrorism in Western Europe.* London: Routledge, 2004.

Gessner, Klaus. *Geheime Feldpolizei. Zur Funktion und Organisation des geheimpolizeilichen Exekutivorgans der faschistischen Wehrmacht.* Berlin, GDR: Militärverlag der DDR, 1986.

Goschler, Constantin, and Michael Wala. *'Keine neue Gestapo'. Das Bundesamt für Verfassungsschutz und die NS-Vergangenheit.* Hamburg: Rowohlt, 2015.

Herbert, Ulrich. *Best. Biographische Studien über Radikalismus, Weltanschauung und Vernunft. 1903–1989.* Bonn: J. H. W. Dietz, 1996.

Irujo, Xabier. *Genocidio en Euskal Herria 1936–1945.* Iruñea: Nabarralde, 2015.

Jiménez de Aberásturi, Juan Carlos, and Rafael Moreno Izquierdo. *Al servicio del extranjero. Historia del servicio vasco de información (1936–1943).* Madrid: A. Machado Libros, 2009.

Levit, Josef. *Jakop Gapp. Zeuge seines Glaubens.* Innsbruck and Wien: Tyrolia; Verlag, 1988.

Linklater, Magnus, Isabel Hilton, and Neal Ascherson. *The Nazi Legacy: Klaus Barbie and the International Fascist Connection.* New York: Holt, Rineheart and Winston, 1984.

Lormier, Dominique. *La Gestapo et les Français.* Paris: Pygmalion, 2013.

Martín de Pozuelo, Eduardo, and Iñaki Ellakuría. *La guerra ignorada. Los espías españoles que combatieron a los nazis.* Barcelona: Debate, 2008.

Mehner, Kurt, ed. *Die geheimen Tagesbericht der deutschen Wehrmachtfüh-rung im Zweiten Weltkrieg 1939–1945*. Volume 4. *1.11.1941–31.05.1942*. Osnabrück: Biblio Verlag, 1992.

Moisel, Claudia. *Frankreich und die deutschen Kriegsverbrecher. Politik und Praxis der Strafverfolgung nach dem Zweiten Weltkrieg*. Göttingen: Wallstein Verlag, 2004.

Ott, Sandra, ed. *War, Exile, Justice, and Everyday Life, 1936–1946*. Reno: Center for Basque Studies, University of Nevada, Reno, 2011.

———. "The Enemy as Insider: German POWs as Trial Witnesses in the Basses-Pyrénées, 1944–1946." In *War, Exile, Justice, and Everyday Life, 1936–1946*, edited by Sandra Ott. Reno: Center for Basque Studies, University of Nevada, Reno, 2011.

Preston, Paul. *El holocausto español. Odio y exterminio en la Guerra Civil y después*. Translated by Catalina Martínez Muñoz and Eugenia Vázquez Nacarino. Barcelona: Random, 2011.

Rankin, Nicholas. *Defending the Rock: How Gibraltar Defeated Hitler*. London: Faber & Faber, 2017.

Siftung Topographie des Terrors. Gestapo, SS und Reichssicherheitshauptamt in der Wilhelm- und Prinz-Albert-Strasse. Eine Dokumentation. 2nd revised edition. Berlin: Siftung Topographie des Terrors, 2010.

Sigaud, Dominique. *Le piège des loups: Les 175 maisons de la Gestapo en France*. Paris: Stock, 2012.

Supreme Headquarters Allied Expeditionary Force (SHAEF). *The German Police*. London: N.p., 1945.

Viñas, Angel. *La Alemania nazi y el 18 de julio*. Madrid: Alianza Editorial, 1977.

Wildt, Michael. *Generation des Unbedingten. Das Führungskorps des Reichssicherheitshauptamtes*. Hamburg: Hamburger Edition, 2003.

Chapter 3

The Basque Children and the Bombing of Gernika: An Event that Shaped their Lives

Susana Sabín-Fernández

During the Spanish Civil War, depending on the evolutions of the fronts, hundreds of thousands of civilians fled their homes in the Basque Country looking for safety. From the beginning of 1937, the particularly brutal Francoist offensive on the Northern Front generated a vast migration of noncombatants retreating toward Bilbao. Ultimately, the sustained bombing of civilians in small towns produced a massive child exodus never seen before. By September 1937 approximately 32,000 children had been evacuated abroad as a temporary measure. Many of them never returned to their homeland.

More than three quarters of a century on, while some believe it has been so long since these events took place that it is now time to forget, many still consider that the tragic story of these children being taken away from a war-torn country has not been dealt with properly. In order to heal old open wounds, and also to ensure that lessons from the past are learned, it is crucial to bring to light what, how, and why it happened, and the consequences it brought about.

As a warning call we only need to look at one of the most critical problems facing the modern world, namely the refugee crises, more specifically those related to unaccompanied child refugees. Since the 1930s we have seen abundant examples that followed this first massive child exodus. It announced the beginning of a disturbing series of the kind that continue today, from the children of the *Kindertransport* to, most recently, the young Syrian refugees.

Armed conflict, hunger, and fear of persecution often remove children from their roots, to place them in alien contexts in which they are tested to their limits, having to deal with a number of psychological and practical barriers and stressors; these start with the fracture of everyday life that happened when war shattered their familiar world, and are followed by the separation trauma and settlement issues.

It is argued here that the two key issues that led to the child evacuations in the Basque Country were food rationing and air raids against civilians.

The lack of food, and illnesses due to the unhygienic conditions inherent in a war, were in this case aggravated by the fact that the areas occupied by the insurgents were the main food producing regions; therefore hunger was an added problem for loyalists to the Spanish Republic in general. This became a major struggle in the spring of 1937, as Bilbao was rapidly running short of supplies.

As the *nacionales*[1] were making advances from the north-east, there was a vast influx of refugees toward Bilbao, thus many more people to feed, which put pressure on the already scarce provisions left. Moreover, acquiring additional supplies was virtually impossible. The insurgents had isolated the northern provinces from the adjacent territories of the Republic and severed the railroad line; hence, importing food by land was not an option.

Furthermore, Franco was preventing cargo ships from supplying any Republican ports on the Cantabrian coast, and most importantly, there was an international embargo that the foreign powers justified for reasons of neutrality and nonintervention. This situation undoubtedly favored the rebels, as they counted on far superior stockpiles of food and also the help of both the Germans and Italians, thus it was in fact a one-sided embargo.

In order to understand the indecisive positions adopted by the foreign governments we need to examine the topic in the larger diplomatic context and remember that the Spanish Civil War broke out within the divided Europe of the 1930s. Europe was still recovering

---

1   The term used to identify Franco's faction as opposed to the *Nacionalistas* (nationalists) from the Basque Country (who did not support Franco but the Republican elected government).

from World War I; it was battered by a big economic crisis and social unrest; relations between countries were fractious; and policies of appeasement prevailed as Hitler was perceived as a considerable threat. Within such an unstable arena, governments certainly feared their involvement in the confrontation could lead to a much dreaded second major war. Consequently, in order to stay as far away from the conflict as possible and to contain it to Spain alone, a Nonintervention Agreement, proposed originally by the French and British governments, was signed by twenty-seven countries at the end of August 1936.

It must be noted that not all the countries signed up to the same conditions and some were not as restricted in their actions as others. Furthermore, according to the Nonintervention Agreement, supplying food was not prohibited. As a result, the naval blockade became a major issue of enormous controversy with regard to international law.

There was much confusion when applying the regulations. For instance, during the second week of April there were a number of incidents that caused both much debate and disagreement within the British government, and also precarious tensions with the insurgents. These incidents concerned British private merchant ships, that is, not government sponsored, which transported food supplies. Thus, they were in violation of neither the Nonintervention Agreement nor the Merchant Shipping Act of December 1936, which prohibited British ships from ferrying war equipment to Spain. The skippers did not know for certain whether they could, or moreover, should, try to reach Bilbao or not, due to the contradictory messages they received from one warring side and the other. When they decided to deliver their cargo, the British Royal Navy had to become involved and defend them from the rebel threat at sea.

The second decisive factor that singled out the Basques as being treated particularly viciously, and that gained international sympathy toward them especially after the destruction of Gernika, was the fact that they were being subjected to ferocious air raids against the civil population.

The *villa foral* of Gernika as a symbol of "Basqueness" epitomizes the cradle of Basque history and culture, thus its importance as a point of reference for the collective Basque identity. Hence, when the German Condor Legion targeted it during a busy market day, destroying the town, killing nearly 2,000 people—by June 1937 the Basque government had already reported 1,654 deaths—and leaving behind a large number of injured, this was not a mere random act of war but one conscientiously planned and executed.

There were neither military targets nor aerial defenses in Gernika, and although this was not the first but only one of a series of saturation bombings over Basque towns, it became the one event that galvanized much of the debate regarding the Spanish Civil War within the international community.

Soon after the war started in 1936, a variety of international political parties, labor unions, and organizations had established committees to provide humanitarian aid and to relieve the children of the harsh consequences of the war, but the officially planned large clusters of evacuations did not start until 1937.

As a result of the atrocity of Gernika on April 26, 1937, and also due to prior threats made at the beginning of April by the insurgent General Mola that he would raze Bizkaia to the ground unless it surrendered, panic spread and everyone feared that the rebel attacks against civilians would continue. This intensified the avalanches of refugees toward Bilbao.

The effects of the attack were horrifying and the global resonance it triggered was enormous. It was clearly a violation of basic military rules and human rights regarding not targeting civilians. Its purpose was to terrorize and to demoralize the civil population. For the German Air Force it was also the perfect training site to test under realistic conditions new battle strategies and equipment that it would use later on in World War II.

This tremendous display of power and such a devastating type of warfare was new within the European context and it has been argued that it was the first time that an air force deliberately attacked a nonmilitary target of a white population.

As a direct consequence there was an upsurge in international public opinion, which revitalized the interest in the Spanish Civil War. There had previously been a great deal of literature concerning the ferocity of the fighting, but much of it was about the atrocities committed by both sides. Gernika prompted a wider passionate debate, and stirred general perceptions of the war. Not only was the world shocked by the events, but people also wanted to know the truth about who had done it.

The perpetrators, that is, the German Condor Legion in support of Franco, did not acknowledge their responsibility for the bombing of Gernika. Despite the testimony to the contrary of numerous witnesses, which included foreign journalists, Franco maintained that it had been carried out by the Basque military forces in retreat. He also played down the number of casualties.

The information released after the event was highly controversial; but George Steer, the war correspondent for *The Times* stationed in Spain during the conflict who was visiting the front east of Bilbao at the time of the massacre, confirmed that when he returned to Gernika immediately after the assault, he found German ammunition on the ground.[2] On the morning of April 28, *The Times* published Steer's detailed account, whose accuracy was corroborated by the British consul in Bilbao, Ralph Stevenson. Steer's article was read everywhere in the UK and further afield. As a result, the foreign states reconsidered their stance and started to relax their noninterventionist attitudes.

Subsequently, the Basque government made a distress call to the international community to save the Basque children by offering them asylum, as these were deemed the most vulnerable members of society. The slogan, which reached all the territories still held by the Republican government and further beyond, was ¡Salvad a los niños! (Save the children!).

There had been previous thoughts and attempts to ship children off to safer areas. By December 1936 there were already talks about the possibility of child evacuations, but there were practically no demands, and, moreover, attempts to evacuate children had found resistance within the Basque government. However, after the bombing of Bilbao on January 4, 1937 and the consequent reaction that left more than 200 prisoners of war killed, in less than two weeks the number of requests increased to more than 1,500. Plans for removing the children and noncombatants were progressing rapidly.

By March 1937 the republicans were quickly losing ground and it was only a matter of time before the Basque Country would fall, so the plans to spare the children from the adversities of the end of the war were now firm and irrevocable.

---

2   George Lowther Steer, *The Tree of Gernika: A Field Study of Modern War* (1938; London: Faber and Faber Ltd., 2009).

In March 1937, ten days before the bombing of Durango, a first expedition took 450 children to France. They traveled in two British destroyers to Donibane Lohizune (Saint-Jean-de-Luz , on the southwest coast) to end up in the refugee home *La Maison Heureuse*, on the island of Oleron (west coast).

It was only after this first trial venture, and particularly immediately after the air attacks of Durango and Gernika that followed, that the Basque government and a number of institutions and organizations intensified their efforts to draw children away from harm. The borderline between the civilian and the combatant had been blurred and now the civilians had become war casualties. There was no regard for children, women, or the elderly, and towns were being subjected to aerial saturation bombardment, newly developed incendiary shells, and strafing of the fleeing population.

In this context the parents were in a constant state of anxiety and increasingly worried for the safety of their children. In addition to the lack of food, they feared the relentless threat coming from the air as they heard of the Francoist advances. Moreover, parents also wanted to prevent the reprisal, reeducation of their children in a new fascist regime, imprisonment, or even death that would indeed occur once the north had been defeated by Franco's troops. Furthermore, the separation was seen as a mere temporary measure, as it was widely believed that the war would finish shortly.

For all those reasons the families were now ready, and keener than any time before, to follow the official recommendations and procedures in order to send their children away. Families trusted the government was recommending the best possible action for their children's safety.

Each voyage was announced in the local press, in which parents could read all the relevant information, such as the country of destination, acceptance criteria, and other requirements. Once they knew they met these criteria and the children were fit for admission, including medical clearance of their health condition, they decided whether to register them or not. This was a voluntary choice.

A key person devotedly committed to the evacuation of children to the UK was the Labour MP Leah Manning, an energetic campaigner who was in Bilbao liaising with the Basque government at the time of the bombing of Gernika. She highlighted the meticulously careful and fair way the evacuations were managed and the records of each evacuee were kept by the *Asistencia social* (Social welfare), which was the department in charge.[3] However, it is worth noting that sometimes the parents were so desperate to procure a passage for their children that they lied about the children's ages, their own political affiliation, or any other details if they could not sign them up for a particular voyage because they did not strictly meet the criteria; for instance, for reasons such as imposed quotas.

For the evacuations within the Spanish territory the Basque government had the support of the Republican Government and the *Generalitat* (Catalan Autonomous Government). The international help included both governmental and nongovernmental institutions, such as the Red Cross, and a large number of bodies and committees that were set up at local and international level in order to assist the initiatives. Sometimes these were *ad hoc* committees created with the specific purpose of providing relief to refugees. They had different affiliations, if they had any at all, such as to political groups, labor unions, and religious or humanitarian aid groups. There were also many others who as individuals provided a generous and inestimable assistance once the children arrived in the host countries.

Although the Basque government now had the full support of the parents for the evacuation effort, they still encountered resistance from the foreign governments they approached.

The committees started to take care for the children normally at the point of origin. In their expeditions these children were accompanied by a limited number of adults, which generally included teachers, assistants, a small medical team, and sometimes a few priests.

Once they arrived at the country of destination, keeping siblings together was always a priority, although this condition could not be met all the time. Sometimes the unaccompanied children passed a quarantine period at a refugee camp, from which they were either dispersed in groups to other collective child refugee places, called *colonias* (colonies), or individually placed with families. The new locations might have been where the first period of their lives as exiles started; or a temporary residence before returning home; or simply a reception or first transit step to other countries.

Until the fall of Bilbao the ships departed from Santurtzi (Bizkaia), the nearest port. Then they navigated from Santander. There are no

---

3   See http://www.basquechildren.org/ (last accessed September 5, 2017).

sufficient reliable data of how many ships were used and the number of voyages they made transporting children; therefore, while some informal sources quote about thirty ships that made around seventy trips, this remains a topic to be explored in more depth by researchers.

With regard to quantitative data on the children shipped out, authors usually provide approximate estimates, as there is a remarkable difficulty in obtaining exact figures. These estimates tend to play down the real numbers.

Those specializing in the topic under consideration usually agree on an average of 32,000 children being sent abroad by the end of August 1937. According to the archives of the Departamento de Asistencia Social of the Basque government, in March 1938 the records show that 31,104 children had been sent away.

There is a general belief that between 1936 and 1939 there were between 150,000 and 200,000 Basque refugees; therefore a child exodus of 32,000 represents a large proportion of the total Basque exiled population, probably 18 percent. This increases to 20 percent when we compare it to the total child population, that is, those between five and fourteen years old, from Bizkaia and Gipuzkoa in the 1930 census, which was the last one recorded before the outbreak of the war.

There are four important points that need to be made with regard to these figures.

First, they refer to organized evacuations, as for instance about 20,000 are accounted for as officially sent to France, but in 1939 there were about 68,000 refugee children there. Moreover, in June 1937 there was the one and only organized official expedition to Mexico of 456 children, but out of the 20,000 Republican refugees hosted in that country, 4,000 were children.

This takes us to the second point, which relates to the enormous difficulties in providing exact figures. We must remember that there was constant movement and relocation of refugees both at home and in the destination country. Sometimes this host country was only a temporary place of asylum, from which the children traveled to yet another country. This was the case of many children who were originally taken to France, but from there to Belgium, Mexico, Denmark, and other countries. There are also cases of children being sent back to the country of transit after a while. For example, after a short period in Denmark the group of children who had gone there via France were taken back to a *colonia* near Paris. Likewise, within the host country they were often relocated if, for instance, the *colonia* was closed, or unsuitable conditions were discovered, and so on. Were all children correctly accounted for?

To answer to that question it would have required a comprehensive register to have been kept recording the total amount of refugees placed at all possible locations simultaneously. However, as Alicia Alted Vigil points out,[4] from 1939 on and due to the constant repatriations, there was a continuous fluctuation of the refugee numbers. There was no coexistence of all of them as refugees at any one time; by the time some fled their homes, some of the others had already returned.

A third aspect that impedes tracking the data is that during the war, and still during the decades of Franco's dictatorship that followed, many of the primary sources were destroyed or withheld from the general public and scholars. The research community only had access to the records seized by Franco and stored in the National Historical Archives in Salamanca and Madrid from the late 1980s on. There was also a significant collection of documents related to the Spanish Civil War, Nazi Germany, and Fascist Italy withheld at the Secret Archives of the Vatican that was only made available to the public as recently as September 18, 2006.

Finally, we need to bear in mind the human factor and the reliability of manual record keeping, particularly within such an extremely complex and disorderly context as the one under scrutiny. Not only was it a mammoth task to keep accurate records in a country at war inundated by constant floods of refugees, but also at the country of destination the clerks had to register unfamiliar names to which they were not accustomed. Thus, human error due to language barriers, confusion about foreign names, lack of consistency regarding the names of the locations and care homes where the children were taken, and so on, cannot be ignored.[5]

So far we have discussed some central aspects related to the problems faced by all the concerned parties in the processes of thinking about, organizing, urging, and accomplishing the evacuations; but what

---

4   Alicia Alted Vigil, "Las consecuencias de la Guerra Civil española en los niños de la República: de la dispersión al exilio," *Espacio, Tiempo y Forma*, Serie V, *H.ª Contemporánea* 9 (1996), 217.

5   For example, my own aunt whose name was "Manola" Fernández Learra and was evacuated to the UK on the ship *Habana* appears as "Manuel" Fernández Learra in all the records consulted, which gives the impression she was a boy, not a girl.

were the underlying problems and the decisions made by the individual countries that hosted the children?

We have highlighted that this was the first massive child evacuation in modern history, which means there were no previous courses of action that served as a prototype. No country had either a previous model to follow or past mistakes from which to learn. It was also a story of politics, diplomacy, statecraft, ambiguity, and contradictions that generated many tensions between the authorities and civil society in the western democracies and continued to be a tense topic in the public forum until the end of the war.

On the basis of noninterventionist positions, governments tried to discourage and to stop the evacuations, conveying the message that they would not favor one side over the other; conversely, there was a considerable movement of volunteers who played a vital role by putting enough pressure on the decision-makers so that the evacuations were finally at the very least tolerated, if not officially dealt with, by the reluctant governments.

Among the host countries, France took the largest number of children, followed by Belgium and the UK. Lesser numbers went to the USSR, Mexico, Switzerland, Denmark, and Holland. Norway and Sweden did not take any children but subsidized collective child refugee homes for them in France, as well as a variety of projects. The United States, despite significant efforts on the part of various political leaders, intellectuals, and civil society to give asylum to a considerable number of children, eventually rejected the proposal.

Predictably, France was the major recipient of refugees, and accounts indicate that in the final year of the war there were about 170,000 noncombatant refugees there. Its proximity made it the first choice of state to be approached, since it was Spain's neighbor to the north. Not only was it the closest geographically, with the two countries sharing an extensive border, but they also shared many secular traditions, both historical and sociocultural; furthermore, they had strong links well established over a long period of time due to the fact that Euskal Herria (the Basque Country) is a stateless nation made up of seven provinces, of which three are within the French Republic, thus there was a Basque population who were French citizens; finally, it was also the most alike at a political level, as the French Popular Front coalition had recently won the elections in 1936, three months after its Spanish counterpart.

The Prime Minister Léon Blum's initial response to the Republican government's petition to grant asylum to as many children as possible was positive and he agreed to help, but both French civil society and the political class were deeply divided with regard to this matter. While socialists and communists were committed to accept them, there were large sectors of the population and the establishment that fiercely opposed the idea, adducing the need to stay neutral. They claimed that helping the child refugees would compromise France's neutrality. There was also pressure for nonintervention from abroad. Finally, the government succumbed to the high level of both domestic and foreign pressure, and the agreed offer was withdrawn.

However, France, including its colonies in North Africa, had been receiving large numbers of refugees from the beginning of the war and this continued throughout the conflict. It was overwhelmed by the size of the torrents of refugees, which was an unexpected phenomenon, and it is generally acknowledged that between 20,000 and 22,000 children went to France as part of the official organized evacuations.

By comparison, Belgium was not considered a priority country to be approached. In contrast to France, this relatively unknown nation had a considerably lower political profile. Moreover, its suitability was uncertain as it did not share a border with Spain, but it did with Germany. However, its case is unique in the sense that, after France, it gave asylum to the largest number of refugee children. The French Republic received more children than all the other countries combined, but the small and distant Belgium was the second most deceptive country with regard to numbers.

Other distinctive particularities include the fact that, as Dorothy Legarreta points out, among the nonsocialist countries, Belgium was the only one that provided actual government assistance and only there "did they enjoy the fruits of close cooperation between the trade unions, the Socialist and Communist political organizations and the Catholic hierarchy."[6] Many sources, both in the academic literature as well as also those who have presented an account of their own personal experiences in public events[7] or for oral history projects, have consistently highlighted the fact that, as a result, there was a high level of care and

---

6   Dorothy Legarreta, "Hospitality to the Basque Refugee Children in Belgium," *Belgisch Tijdschrift voor Nieuwste Geschiedenis* 1–2 (1987), 276.
7   See Idi Ezkerra, *Gerrako euskal umeentzako omenaldia/homenaje a los niños y niñas de la guerra vascos*, DVD (Bilbao: Idi Ezkerra, 2009).

handling of the unaccompanied child refugees operations not seen in other destinations. The collective realization of how desperate the need for aid was prevailed above everything else, and thus the political dispute did not reach the bitter tone it did in other countries.

Nevertheless, initially the Belgian office had been beset by strong internal divisions on the issue of accepting child refugees and thus helping the Spanish Republic. The government, which maintained an independent stance from that of the other Western powers during the increasingly menacing position of Hitler's Germany in the 1930s, was shaped by a stable coalition of socialists, Catholics, and liberals. The aspiration for neutrality was behind the demands of some sectors to officially adhere to rigorous refusal to take sides regarding the Spanish Civil War. This was the root of the controversy over the issue. Ironically both sides of the debate were defended by socialist leaders, namely, Emile Vandervelde, who rallied to give asylum, and his opponent Henri Spaak, who opposed the idea. The final decision was to remain neutral, following the traditional Belgian position on political issues.

Nonetheless, agents from the entire social spectrum were on a mission to make the evacuations happen. A variety of groups such as socialists, labor unions, many catholic sectors lead by the very committed Cardinal Van Roey, the Communist Secours Rouge (Red relief), and the Belgian Red Cross continued to negotiate a temporary solution for the children and to encourage families to accept them in their homes. Subsequently, despite its initial decision, the government became involved and creatively secured funding for the host families through the national family allowance, that is, the Benefit Fund for Family Allotments of 1930. This scheme allowed authorities to contribute to the maintenance of the children but not directly, as they were actually supporting not the children but the host families, who were Belgian citizens.

Eventually a minimum of 5,000 Spanish children were given asylum.[8] While most minors were Basque—according to different sources, between 3,200 and 3,500 of the total—there were also many who came from other regions. These children were first evacuated from Spain to France, where some spent some time in camps before continuing their trips to Belgium by train. There they were placed in private homes or in some cases taken to a *colonia*. With regard to the Basque children, the

---

8   Alonso Carballés, Jesús Javier, "La acogida de los niños en Bélgica, la expresión de una solidaridad familiar," in El Exilio de los Niños, eds. Alicia, González, Roger & Millán, María José (Madrid: Sinsentido, 2003): 86

department of *Asistencia Social* of the Basque government collaborated to organize the evacuation. For example, some children were taken to the *Home Belgo-Basque de Marchin-lez-Huy* in the Liège region as a result of a joint operation with *Asistencia Social*.

The British case was a typical example of the conflicting ideological sides that fought for control of the complex situations generated by the Spanish Civil War at an international level. But before we move on to discuss the intricacies and the paradoxes of the British case, attention must be drawn to a notable fact that distinguishes the UK situation from that of other countries.

After many struggles over the issue of whether to provide humanitarian aid or not and despite vehement opposition, eventually there was one and only one official evacuation, which to this day remains the largest ever single arrival of child refugees in England. This means that all the Basque children who were granted asylum in Britain, that is, nearly 3,900, left their homeland behind at the same time, on May 21, 1937, to make their journey together in a single expedition aboard the same ship, the 10,800-ton transatlantic steamer *Habana*. As a result they became a rather cohesive group that was easily identifiable, still known today as the *Niños Vascos* (Basque Children).

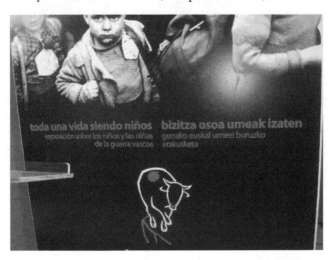

*Poster advertising a week of commemorative events in hon-
or of the evacuee children, Bilbao, June 2008.*

Among the foreign governments the Basque government approached in the hope that it would accept child refugees, that of the UK was one of the most divided on the issue. Many in the UK interpreted the action as a means of intervention that shrewdly deceived the official policies of British leaders, who had advocated strict adherence to the Nonintervention Agreement. In fact, the UK and France were the main driving forces behind the treaty, as indicated above. Conversely, another characteristic that singled out this country was its intense maritime participation in a great deal of controversial issues and incidents regarding intervention.

Paradoxically, despite the officially sanctioned neutrality, throughout the conflict the British Royal Navy rescued and transported people in need to safety across both the Mediterranean Sea and the Bay of Biscay. *HMS Shropshire*, a vessel repeatedly assigned to evacuation operations in the Mediterranean, was a noteworthy example. In addition to this, there was a long shipping trade tradition between the Basque Country and Britain that traders were keen to continue. Hence there was a ubiquitous presence of British ships at sea, exceedingly condemned by Franco's *nacionales*. On occasion, the level of confrontation between the British and the insurgent Spanish fleets reached such a critical point that the unequivocally more powerful British navy had to threaten the use of massive force in order to avoid major clashes.

Meanwhile, negotiations regarding child evacuations were taking place, led by the National Joint Committee for Spanish Relief (NJCSR), which was created in December 1937 and officially presented on January 6, 1937. Although the NJCSR was introduced as nonpolitical and aimed exclusively at humanitarian aid work, its chair was, ironically, the Duchess of Atholl. She was a progressive Conservative MP, thus her stance clashed with the noninterventionist attitude of her own political party. It is also significant that the public launch of the committee was at a meeting held at the House of Commons, at which the official position maintained was to keep as distant as possible from the Spanish affairs.

Discussions went ahead, yet, despite the work of the NJCSR and the insistent requests from the Basque government regarding evacuation and also medical and food supplies—which were firmly supported by the British Consul in Bilbao, Ralph Stevenson—for a few months the official response was either negative or insistent. However, after news of the widespread devastation that was occurring in the Basque

Country began to circulate, public pressure increased and on April 30, 1937, immediately after receiving reports of the destruction of Gernika, the reluctant authorities capitulated and conceded to acknowledging a limited evacuation of 2,000 child refugees between the ages of 5 and 12.

In order to maintain an official noninterventionist position publically, a number of prerequisites were stipulated. First, the selection of children needed to be open to all political affiliations with no favoritisms or inclination toward any political party. Second, any kind of governmental assistance was absolutely precluded. And third, at no time would the government would have any financial responsibility for the children (including maintenance, meaning they would have to be self-supporting) or any responsibility regarding custody matters. From then on the Basque Children's Committee, created on May 15, 1937 under the umbrella of the NJCSR, would be in charge of the operation and the welfare of the children. [9]

Group of Niños Vascos at the annual reunion meal, London, May 22, 2011.

9   Adrian Bell, *Only for Three Months: The Basque Children in Exile* (Norwich: Mousehold Press, 1996).

Finally, on May 23, 1937 about 3,861 Basque children aged between 5 and 15, escorted by a group of teachers, *señoritas* (assistants), priests, two doctors, and Leah Manning arrived at Southampton Water on an overcrowded ship that was built to carry less than 1,000 passengers but evidently exceeded this number during the evacuation. Upon arrival, all the children underwent a medical examination, after which they were taken to a nearby refugee camp as a temporary measure. From there they were dispersed to the *colonias* that were set up to host groups of children throughout the UK, and were always fully subsidized by private means and managed by nongovernmental committees and local groups.

While France, Belgium, and the UK took the largest contingents of Basque children, other European countries were also recipients to a lesser degree. Switzerland, Denmark, and the Netherlands received smaller numbers of children, and Sweden and Norway funded various projects in other countries.

Politically neutral and stable Switzerland was renowned for its positive attitude toward humanitarian activities and social intervention in the face of armed conflict, which signaled it out as a potentially good candidate to be approached; however, it was also subject to the pressure of those sectors that strived for nonintervention with regard to the Spanish Civil War. For this reason the federal government at first forbade its citizens to become involved in any kind of support. However, after initial internal disagreements and a few months of complicated negotiations, it finally approved the idea of providing humanitarian help under the promise of joint action among a good range of groups. Thus in February 1937 the Swiss Committee to Aid Spanish Children (later renamed Swiss Aid) was formally created, and included a mixture of charitable, voluntary, and pacifist organizations. Two prominent Swiss figures worth noticing for their commitment to facilitating aid to Spanish refugees were Rodolfo Olgiati, who became the secretary of the Swiss Committee, and Elisabeth Eidenbenz, who in 1939 founded the Maternité Suisse d'Elne (Mothers of Elne) in France.

An initial plan to evacuate 500 children to Switzerland was unsuccessful, due in large part to some restrictions imposed by the Republican government, but eventually a considerable number of children reached the country. For these missions, the organizers frequently counted on French collaboration. Regarding numbers, there are vast discrepancies according to different sources, which oscillate between

450 and more than 800. According to one study, there were 245 Basque children among them.[10]

A lesser known episode is the evacuation of children to Denmark, which was a member of a Quaker-founded organization, the International Commission for the Assistance of Child Refugees (created in Geneva in 1937), along with the UK, Norway, Sweden, Belgium, Switzerland, and France, among others. This country provided aid through its Committee for Children's Spanish Sojourn in Denmark, also created in 1937 as a response to the *salvad a los niños* plea.

The initial idea of the committee was to give asylum to approximately 300 children and it raised funds to subsidize the initiative and relocate the children among Danish families. However, the anticipated support did not come about and only 122 were received.[11] Despite the low number, the campaign was very popular and enjoyed the support of influential people such as the King of Denmark and also some businesses. Additionally, the press became very involved, contributing with daily news that persistently praised the great courage of the children.

The evacuees traveled on a British ship escorted by two French vessels from the Spanish port of El Musel in Asturias, via Bordeaux, to Paris, where they spent a few weeks. There negotiations took place to take them to Denmark, where they arrived in two separate contingents made up of children from the Basque Country, Cantabria, and Asturias. The first 70 children arrived on September 22, 1937 and the second group of 52 a week later. They were not accommodated with families, but in two *colonias*, one in Ordrup near Copenhagen and the other in Odense. After a while they were relocated to Vejstrup. For a short period of time there was also a *colonia* subsidized by the Danish in Catalonia.

After a few months the child refugees' presence in the country became a controversial issue, as it added tension to the already problematic relations between Denmark and Hitler's Germany; and moreover in a context of the escalating prospect of war. In the end, a year after their arrival the children were sent on a return trip back to France, where they stayed at a *colonia* near Paris that Denmark funded until the outbreak of World War II.

---

10 Sebastián Farré, "Política y propaganda: niños refugiados en Suiza durante la Guerra Civil," in *El Exilio de los Niños*, ed. Alicia Alted Vigil, Roger González, and María José Millán (Madrid: Sinsentido, 2003), 116.

11 Iñaki Ibisate, *Elogio al horizonte*, documentary film (TPA, 2009).

So far we have examined the European countries that hosted children despite the friction there resulting from the tension between humanitarian need and political expediency, and the often great discrepancy between state interests and the public agenda.

The USSR was initially indisposed to become involved, but the strong support that Nazi Germany and Fascist Italy gave to the *nacionales* from the commencement of the war in some way compelled Stalin's regime, and to a certain degree the Mexican government, to defend the Republican cause. What makes the USSR and Mexico rather unique in comparison to other destinations is the fact that the decision to concede asylum was not contested domestically. Moreover, the respective governments did not mask that decision under a humanitarian flag, which was evidently an important contributing factor to take the children, but were consistently open about their pro-Republican position and overtly subsidized the housing of the children.

However, sending "Catholic" children to the "communist" Soviet Union was not an ideal option for the Basque government, and it was in fact an argument used by the insurgents in their attempts to discredit the loyalist government and its legitimate intentions at the international level. As a result, when the Basque authorities decided that saving as many children as possible was a priority above all other considerations, and also pressurized by the Basque socialist and communist parties into making that decision, they agreed to evacuate children to the Soviet Union. As a prerequisite, the parents had to sign an official form confirming their wish to send them to that destination.

Between March 1937 and October 1938 a total of more than 3,000 children were shipped in four voyages from Spanish ports in the Mediterranean and the Cantabrian coast to Leningrad. The largest volume of children traveled on the second expedition, which carried 1,495 mostly Basque children from the port of Santurtzi; and on the third, which left the northern port of El Musel with 1,100 children from Asturias, the Basque Country, and Santander.[12] The children were housed in the *Casas infantiles para niños españoles* (Children's homes for Spanish children).

The expedition of 456 children to Mexico started as two groups, one traveling from Madrid to Valencia and the other from Barcelona,

---

12   Alted Vigil, "Las consecuencias de la Guerra Civil española en los niños de la República," 215.

including Catalan children but also those Basques and Asturians who had sought refuge and lived in *colonias* in Catalonia from the early stages of the war. Both groups gathered in Barcelona to continue their journey to Bordeaux by train, where they boarded the ship *Mexique* that would take them to Veracruz in Mexico on June 7, 1937.[13] Among the thousands of Spanish refugees that Mexico received, including approximately 4,000 children, this official evacuation was particularly welcomed by the locals[14] and the children came to be known as the *Niños de Morelia* (Children of Morelia).

In addition to the countries analyzed so far, which to some extent and for longer or shorter periods of time all granted asylum, others that were approached did not. The Netherlands allegedly received 100 or 195 children (depending on the sources consulted) but it is also maintained that this country's participation was merely to pay for the care of the children in a *colonia* in France. This remains the least known operation and the lack of scholarly work on it certainly calls for further investigation.

Norway and Sweden, despite their sympathy for the Republican side, did not take children on the grounds of their official allegiance to neutrality. However, for humanitarian, political, and religious reasons, and largely due to their pacifist values, they contributed in other ways to the welfare of the children. The president of the International Commission for the Assistance of Spanish Child Refugees was the Norwegian judge Michael Hansson, and one of its vice presidents was the Swede Bertil Ohlin. Meanwhile, the Norwegian Christian Lous Lange was the president of the Union Internationale de Secours aux Enfants (International Save the Children Union) in Geneva. Clearly, then, there were high-profile Scandinavian figures decidedly involved in organizing aid for the refugee children.

These countries cooperated with the French and Spanish Republican and Basque governments in order to carry out a great number of initiatives. For instance, they maintained *colonias* in France and on the Spanish Mediterranean coast. They also collaborated with expeditions to the Americas, and generally contributed with funds, medical

---

13 Ibid., 216.
14 Juan Pablo Villaseñor, *Los niños de Morelia*, documentary film (Mexico City: Arte 7/Hermanos Films, 2004).

staff and equipment, medicines, social work volunteers, clothing, food supplies, and even took children on vacation to Norway.[15]

Lastly, another country convulsed by the horrors that were taking place in Spain was the United States. The echo of the mayhem in Gernika was such that the debate about the Spanish war took a renewed prominence and fervent discussions regarding neutrality ensued at all levels. There was a great deal of controversy, as the entire spectrum of the American society as well as the political class were deeply polarized on the issue.

In response to the *salvad a los niños* request, a number of intellectuals and liberals created the Board of Guardians for Basque Refugee Children in May 1937. Their idea was to ferry a group of 500 children to New York by the end of June to be distributed mostly among participating Basque families. Some of them would in theory be housed in a preschool run by Basque priests, teachers, and nurses. This initiative had great support including that of well-known public personalities such as Eleanor Roosevelt, the honorary president of the board, and Albert Einstein as an advisor.

Front page of the newspaper La Gaceta del Norte, *Bilbao, December 1937.*

---

15   Rose Duroux, "La ayuda de Noruega y Suecia," in *El Exilio de los Niños*, ed. Alted Vigil, González, and Millán, 126–43.

Indeed, the public reaction was so positive that 2,700 Basque families offered to take in children, resulting in the board suggesting granting asylum to 2,000 instead of 500.

Eventually, however, some dominant pro-Francoist sectors, particularly the Catholic circle in Boston lead by the Cardinal William H. O'Connell, fought so ferociously against the initiative that they managed to halt the project.[16] Congress finally voted against it, but this was not the end of the story, as humanitarian aid continued by other means; one was to collect money for the relief of Basque refugee children and send it to the International Red Cross in Bilbao.

Just as the processes surrounding the evacuations were beset by diverse political problems and subsequent profound internal and international tensions, so this was definitely the case with regard to the repatriations that followed. Franco never ceased to put pressure on the host countries to return the children, because keeping them away was irrefutable proof of the horrors occurring in Spain. By 1937, he had already established a Delegación Extraordinaria de Repatriación de Menores (Special Delegation for the Repatriation of Minors), whose function was to guarantee the return of the children. However, the majority of the relatives and some governments, most obviously those of the USSR and Mexico, refused to participate in the scheme because they neither recognized the Francoist government nor considered that the conditions for a safe return were met. Ironically, those states that had left the responsibility for the children entirely in the hands of volunteers and nongovernmental agencies as a result were not in a position to make any decisions in this regard. Alted Vigil states that, by 1949, out of 32,037 expatriated children, 20,266 had been repatriated.[17]

These children did not participate directly in the war but they were still a fundamental part of the conflict. Specifically, they were used in the political arena to serve the interests of all the parties concerned at such a deeply unsettled time in history as the interwar period. Their fate varied a great deal. Those who returned frequently found it difficult to adapt to a new society that often appeared alien and hostile, not only because they belonged to the defeated faction, but also because they were by now very different; they had been "contaminated" with

16   For further details, see Xabier Irujo and Susana Sabín-Fernández, "Forbidden Haven to Basque Refugee Children," *AEMI Journal* 13–14 (September 2016), 47–69.

17   Alted Vigil, "Las consecuencias de la Guerra Civil española en los niños de la República," 218

foreign ideas, foreign cultures, and were considered foreigners in their homeland. They looked at things in a completely different way. Many bonds had been broken.

Life was not easy for those who remained in the host countries either. As exiles, they experienced homesickness, disorientation, and feelings of both insecurity and not belonging. They also had to adapt to a new culture and learn a language while trying to keep their own identity. Moreover, they soon found themselves immersed in yet another great conflict, World War II. Despite Franco's declaration of neutrality in the war, his previous alliance with Hitler was too recent to be forgotten. Thus, paradoxically, while the children were exiles because their families opposed Franco's regime, abroad they were often considered "alien enemies," even those who lost their Spanish nationality and passports.[18] At home these children were the state's adversaries, but in their host lands they endured the stigma of belonging to a state that was the very reason why they had been uprooted so early in their lives.

Undoubtedly they would all carry an unforgettable mark for the rest of their lives.

Carmen Fernández Learra, an evacuee child to the UK standing by a commemorative plaque, Southampton, May 2008.

---

18   Steve Bowles, *The Guernica Children*, DVD (London: Eye Witness Productions Ltd., 2005).

BIBLIOGRAPHY

Alonso Carballés, Jesús Javier. "La acogida de los niños en Bélgica, la expresión de una solidaridad familiar." In *El Exilio de los Niños*, edited by Alicia Alted Vigil, Roger González, and María José Millán. Madrid: Sinsentido, 2003.

Alted Vigil, Alicia. "Las consecuencias de la Guerra Civil española en los niños de la República: de la dispersión al exilio." *Espacio, Tiempo y Forma*, Serie V, *H.ª Contemporánea* 9 (1996): 207–28.

Alted Vigil, Alicia, Roger González, and María José Millán, eds. *El Exilio de los Niños*. Madrid: Sinsentido, 2003.

Arrien, Gregorio. *¡Salvad a los niños! Historia del exilio vasco en Gran Bretaña, 1937–1940*. Bilbao: Sabino Arana Fundazioa, 2014.

Bell, Adrian. *Only for Three Months: The Basque Children in Exile*. Norwich: Mousehold Press, 1996.

Duroux, Rose. "La ayuda de Noruega y Suecia." In *El Exilio de los Niños*, edited by Alicia Alted Vigil, Roger González, and María José Millán. Madrid: Sinsentido, 2003.

Farré, Sebastián. "Política y propaganda: niños refugiados en Suiza durante la Guerra Civil." In *El Exilio de los Niños*, edited by Alicia Alted Vigil, Roger González, and María José Millán. Madrid: Sinsentido, 2003.

Irujo, Xabier, and Susana Sabín-Fernández. "Forbidden Haven to Basque Refugee Children." *AEMI Journal* 13–14 (September 2016): 47–69.

Legarreta, Dorothy. *The Guernica Generation: Basque Refugee Children of the Spanish Civil War*. Reno: University of Nevada Press, 1984.

———. "Hospitality to the Basque Refugee Children in Belgium." *Belgisch Tijdschrift voor Nieuwste Geschiedenis* 1–2 (1987): 275–88.

Sabín-Fernández, Susana. *The 'Niños Vascos': Memory and Memorialisation of the Basque Refugee Children of the Spanish Civil War in the UK*. Vitoria-Gasteiz: Eusko Jaurlaritzaren Argitalpen Zerbitzu Nagusia-Servicio Central de Publicaciones del Gobierno Vasco, 2011.

Steer, George Lowther. *The Tree of Gernika: A Field Study of Modern War*. 1939. London: Faber and Faber Ltd., 2009.

FILMOGRAPHY

Bowles, Steve. *The Guernica Children*. DVD. London: Eye Witness Productions Ltd., 2005.

Ibisate, Iñaki. *Elogio al horizonte*. Documentary film. TPA, 2009.

Idi Ezkerra. *Gerrako euskal umeentzako omenaldia/homenaje a los niños y niñas de la guerra vascos*. DVD. Bilbao: Idi Ezkerra, 2009.

Villaseñor, Juan Pablo. *Los niños de Morelia*. Documentary film. Mexico City: Arte 7/Hermanos Films, 2004.

OTHER SOURCES

http://www.basquechildren.org/ (last accessed September 5, 2017).

Chapter 4

The German Occupation of the Northern Basque Country (1940–1944)

Sandra Ott

Drawing upon fieldwork, archival research, and a range of secondary sources, this chapter explores the experience of German occupation and its impact on citizens in the northern Basque Country (Iparralde). Part one provides a sociopolitical and historical context for understanding the German occupation in the historic territories of Lapurdi, Behe-Nafarroa, and Xiberoa.[1] Part two highlights key policies implemented by the Nazi and Vichy regimes that deeply affected people living in Iparralde at the time. It also explores changing attitudes toward Philippe Pétain, the Vichy regime, and the German occupiers. Part three traces the rise of resistance in Iparralde, and examines the role played by Basque clandestine guides who helped fugitives escape into Spain. This section also partially recounts the tragedy of one hamlet deeply affected by German violence and then traces the process of liberation and post-liberation judgments in the region. Part four identifies some reasons why the experience of German occupation, and its impact, varied from one community to another.

---

1   At the time, Iparralde and Béarn were in the department of the Basses-Pyrénées (now known as the Pyrénées-Atlantiques).

I

The 1930s and 1940s brought tumultuous times to the people of Iparralde. Socioeconomic and political divisiveness began well before the Germans ever arrived. In the late 1930s, conservatism and Catholicism shaped the political culture of the region. Having served the department of the Basses-Pyrénées in the French Chamber of Deputies from 1914 until 1939, Jean Ybarnegaray dominated the political scene. He adamantly opposed Communism, Basque nationalism, and the presence of southern Basques on French territory. Like other ultra-conservative elites, Ybarnegaray favored a Francoist victory in Spain.

In the wake of the German bombardment of Irun and Donostia (San Sebastián) in the late summer of 1936, around ten thousand refugees crossed into Iparralde on the coast, "perhaps as many as 9,000 on the evening of August 31, 1936, alone."[2] In Miarritze (Biarritz) and Baiona (Bayonne) local authorities created "reception centers" and organized fundraising events to help the refugees.[3] When Bilbo (Bilbao) fell to the Francoists in June 1937, an estimated 160,000 exiled Republicans flooded into the Basses-Pyrénées. As one departmental deputy complained to the French minister of foreign affairs, "France must not become the dumping ground of Europe."[4] An abandoned hospital in Baiona became a refugee center, which by June 1937 held some 1,150 exiled Republicans. The coastal communities of Bidart, Hendaia (Hendaye), and Getaria (Guéthary) housed an additional 560 refugees.[5] From April through June 1938, the Battle of Aragón sent a further 24,000 Republican refugees into the department.

The crisis intensified in the wake of the final exodus (the *Retirada*) in 1939 of around 500,000 exiled Republicans into southern France after the fall of Catalonia.[6] French authorities responded to the crisis by establishing camps like Gurs. On the Basque coast, the mayor

---

2   James Jacob, *Hills of Conflict: Basque Nationalism in France* (Reno: University of Nevada Press, 1994), 92.

3   Claire Arnould, "l'acceuil des réfugiés en Béarn et en Soule de 1936 à1940," in *Les espagnoles et la guerrre civile*, ed. Michel Papy (Biarritz: Atlantica, 1999), 339.

4   Jacob, *Hills of Conflict*, 93.

5   John C. Guse, "Polo Beyris: A Forgotten Internment Camp in France, 1939–1947," *Journal of Contemporary History*, February 2018, Online First DOI: 10.1177/0022009417712113, 6. For information on the refugees in Getaria, Bidart, and Hendaia, see file 4M 254 Police, Archives départementales des Pyrénées-Atlantiques (hereafter ADPA, Pau).

6   Guse, "Polo Beyris: A Forgotten Internment Camp in France, 1939–1947," 7.

of Baiona opened the former polo grounds in Beyris on February 6, 1939, to shelter some six hundred Catalan refugees.[7] Even as left-wing deputies defended the refugees' right of asylum, critics like Ybarnegaray railed against their presence and the sociopolitical, economic, and health problems that, in his opinion, they caused.[8]

Supporters of the Spanish Republic mainly lived on the Basque coast and in inland industrial towns such as Hazparne (Hasparren) and Maule (Mauléon), where sandal factory owners had recruited seasonal Spanish and Navarrese workers from the end of the nineteenth century until the 1920s. During the Spanish Civil War, exiled Spanish Republicans often sought refuge in the Spanish and Navarrese neighborhoods of these communities. In Maule, most people in "the Spanish quartier" felt an intense solidarity with the refugees.[9] The most visible members of that neighborhood were militant Communist, southern Basque workers who clashed regularly with their conservative, Catholic, anti-Communist Basque employers. Differences in class, politics, and ethnicity often deeply divided them.[10]

On March 31, 1939, Francisco Franco signed a five-year treaty of friendship with Nazi Germany. On April 1, he announced the end of the civil war. On August 29, 1939, Hitler signed pact of non-aggression with the Soviet Union. Germany invaded Poland on September 1. Two days later, France and Great Britain declared war on Germany. On September 4, Franco declared Spain's neutrality in the burgeoning international conflict.

On May 10, 1940, the Germans invaded Belgium, Holland, and Luxembourg. Terrifying air raids triggered a chaotic, southbound exodus of civilians who entered northern France to escape Hitler's advancing troops.[11] During May and June, two million Belgians flooded into Paris. The massive German advance displaced an estimated eight million people, of whom some 6,200,000 were French.[12] One young Jewish

---

7   Manuel Castiella, *Un siècle à Bayonne* (Anglet: Atlantica, 2003), 259; Guse, "Polo Beyris: A Forgotten Internment Camp in France, 1939-1947," 7. Polo Beyris was one of the few "reception centers" in Iparralde.
8   Geneviève Dreyfus-Armand, *L'exile des Républicains espagnols en France* (Paris: Albin Michel, 1999), 53.
9   Madalon Rodrigo Nicolau, personal communication, Maule, April 21, 2005.
10   See Sandra Ott, *War, Judgment, and Memory in the Basque Borderlands, 1914–1945* (Reno: University of Nevada Press, 2008), esp. chaps. 4 and 5 for more detailed information on divisiveness in Maule during the 1930s.
11   Hanna Diamond, *Fleeing Hitler, France 1940* (Oxford: Oxford University Press, 2007), 27.
12   Ibid., 150.

woman, Tereska Szwarc Torrès, and her family set off from Paris for the Basque fishing community of Donibane Lohitzune (St-Jean-de-Luz). In her memoir, Tereska describes the lovely weather, the picturesque fishing boats bobbing on the sea, and her relaxing walks along the beach. The war seemed very far away indeed. Two weeks later, however, the atmosphere changed dramatically when exhausted British and Polish soldiers filled the streets. People began to panic. Friends urged Tereska to leave France, as it became an increasingly dangerous place for Jews. Her family struggled to decide where to go next. By the evening of June 25, 1940, posters in Donibane Lohitzune warned citizens that the Germans would soon arrive. The Franco-German armistice treaty went into effect that same day, which Marshal Pétain declared a national day of mourning.[13] In Donibane Lohitzune, shops closed. People lowered flags to half-mast. The German navy arrived that night.[14] France's disastrous defeat and the harsh terms of the armistice left more than one and a half million French soldiers in German prisoner of war camps. Most would remain in captivity until the end of the war.[15]

The armistice agreement divided France into an occupied zone that included the entire Atlantic coast and most of northern France and an unoccupied zone that covered most of southern France. The line of demarcation split Iparralde in two and extended one hundred fifty kilometers (ninety-three miles) across the department from the northern tip of Xiberoa near the Béarnais town of Sauveterre across Behe-Nafarroa to Donibane Garazi (St-Jean-Pied-de-Port) at its southwestern tip. The Germans continuously occupied Lapurdi and most of Behe-Nafarroa from June 1940 until August 1944. The rest of Behe-Nafarroa and Xiberoa fell within the unoccupied or Vichy zone until Hitler occupied all of France in November 1942. As one Xiberoan resister wrote in his memoirs: "Even in January 1941, those of us living in Maule feel a certain sense of euphoria. We are in the so-called free zone. From those living in the occupied zone [of Iparralde], we hear that the Germans behave correctly."[16] Owing to the sparsely populated terrain and dispersed rural settlements in the interior of Iparralde, the line of demarcation proved to be quite porous, despite attempts by both

---

13   Ibid., 109.
14   Tereska Szwarc Torrès, *Une Française libre: journal, 1939–1945* (Lonrai: Éditions Phébus, 2000), 50.
15   Julian Jackson, *France, The Dark Years 1940–1944* (Oxford: Oxford University Press, 2001), 127, 169.
16   Béguerie, *Témoignage*, unpublished memoir, Sohüta, Xiberoa, copy obtained by the author from the Béguerie family.

Vichy and German authorities to control access to the two zones. The Vichy regime allocated only 480 gendarmes and former soldiers from the French Armistice Army to patrol the line. In total, they had only nine bicycles and one vehicle at their disposal.[17] The Germans also created "forbidden" and "reserved" zones along the Franco-Spanish border, in northeastern and southeastern France, and along the Atlantic coast.

The Germans established significant military and intelligence bases in Baiona and Miarritze. German troops occupied Baiona on June 27, 1940. The *Feldkommandanteur* established headquarters in Miarritze on the same day. The 31st Corps of the Wehrmacht (German Army) and the 1st division of the German infantry also requisitioned residences there, including the former private residence of the Empress Eugenie, wife of Napoleon III. The German Army's military intelligence service (*Abwehrstelle* or AST) occupied an elegant villa on the other side of the street. The German secret field police (*Geheime Feldpolizei* or GFP) stationed themselves in another villa nearby. The Germans had already created espionage networks in the southern Basque Country, notably in Donostia and Bilbo, which they now utilized extensively.[18] The German Air Force commandeered the airport at Parme outside Miarritze to train Luftwaffe pilots.[19]

The Basque coast had strategic military importance for the Germans. Hendaia and its railroad bridge served as the key frontier post that linked the Third Reich to Francoist Spain, where the Germans planned various military operations and supply routes. The port of Baiona was also strategically key to German defense strategies, especially in relation to their naval operations in Bordeaux. According to the Chief of Staff of the German First Army, "Bordeaux was an important strategic point of the first order. It was regarded as our central citadel behind the Biscay front." As he observed, the German Navy was eager to secure its submarine bases in Bordeaux, La Rochelle, and St-Nazaire at the mouth of the Loire and to protect the harbor of Baiona as a port through which the German Navy planned to receive shipments of much needed ore from

---

17 Louis Poullenot, *Basses-Pyrénées, occupation, liberation 1940–1945* (Biarritz: J&D Éditions, 1995), 23. The Franco-German armistice permitted the Vichy-controlled French army to retain one hundred thousand soldiers in order to maintain order in the unoccupied zone.

18 See Juan Carlos Jiménez de Aberásturi and Rafael Moreno Izquierdo, *Al servicio del extranjero: historia del servicio vasco de información (1936–1943)* (Madrid: A. Machado Libros, 2009).

19 Francis Sallaberry, *Quand Hitler bétonnait la côte basque* (Bayonne: Harriet, 1988), 14, 35.

northern Spain. The Germans also constructed a network of batteries around the harbor of Donibane-Lohitzune. They also built extensive installations on either side of Miarritze, "where absolutely bomb-proof shelters were built for local combat and artillery commanders, flanking batteries and infantry units . . . and a second network of coastal batteries were grouped around the harbor gateway of Bayonne . . . to offer support against possible enemy attack over Spanish territory."[20]

II

On July 10, 1940, the French National Assembly granted Marshal Philippe Pétain full powers. On the same day, a leading newspaper in Baiona urged "the suppression of parliamentary democracy and the class struggle" under the banner of "The New Europe." Its editor extolled the virtues of accepting Germany's invitation to join Hitler's "great movement," National Socialism.[21] In July, the Vichy regime began to enact exclusionary laws against the Jews. In August 1940, freemasons became the targets of Vichy repression in Baiona and Pau, where Vichy authorities requisitioned and auctioned off all property that belonged to masonic lodges.[22]

On September 27, 1940, a German ordinance forbade Jews in the unoccupied zone to return to occupied territory. The spoliation of Jewish property by the Germans had begun as early as June 1940, with a focus on artwork.[23] Ordinances issued on September 27 and October 18, 1940, required the registration of all Jews and all Jewish-owned businesses by the French (rather than the German) authorities in the sub-prefecture of Baiona. The first of the Jewish Statutes, implemented on October 3, excluded French Jews from employment in public service.[24]

On October 20, 1940, the Reich leader of the SS and chief of the German police, Heinrich Himmler, traveled to the Basque coast to

---

20 General Kurt Gallencamp, responsible for the coastal sector from the Loire to the Spanish border (April 1, 1942–August 10, 1944), interviewed by Artillery General Anton Freiherr von Bechtolsheim in his report, "The Atlantic Wall from the Loire to the Spanish Border," Karlsruhe, October 16, 1952. U.S. Army European Command, Box 0028, Accession no. 66026, File C-022, Hoover Institute Archives, Stanford University, CA.
21 *Le Sud-Ouest La Presse*, no. 7695, July 10, 1940, Musée Basque, Baiona.
22 Josette Pontet, ed., *Histoire de Bayonne* (Toulouse: Éditions Privat, 1991), 275–76.
23 Shannon Fogg, *Stealing Home: Looting, Restitution, and Reconstructing Jewish Lives in France, 1942–1947* (Oxford: Oxford University Press, 2017), 21.
24 Jackson, *France The Dark Years, 1940–1944*, 150–51.

finalize security arrangements for an important visitor. On October 23, accompanied by Göring, Hitler traveled in a special train to the seaside Basque town of Hendaia, with a brief stop in the Baiona train station, where German nurses offered the Fuhrer bouquets of flowers and German soldiers took photos to immortalize the event.[25] In Hendaia, Hitler held his only meeting with Francisco Franco who, contrary to Hitler's expectations and to his great annoyance, decided not to enter the war as an ally of the Axis.[26]

As happened elsewhere in France, French propaganda services (under German control) glorified Pétain and tried to rally citizens around him as France's "savior." On August 20, 1940, Pétain united veterans of World War I and the Franco-German war of 1939–1940 by creating the French Legion of Combatants (Légion Française des Combattants). Its leaders fervently supported Pétain but were also often anti-German. In the Basses-Pyrénées, a similar form of Pétainism existed among both veterans and the Basque clergy, who gave Masses and said prayers to promote Pétain's wellbeing.[27] Vichy authorities honored him at public commemorative ceremonies, military music concerts, folkloric festivals, at conferences, and on radio broadcasts. Postcards and posters featuring the Marshal's portrait were widely distributed among the local population.[28]

In December 1940, the sub-prefect in Baiona designated thirty provisional administrators of Jewish-owned businesses whose remit was to suppress "all Jewish influence" on the French economy through the sale or requisition of Jewish property. Under the direction of the Office of Jewish Affairs in the sub-Prefecture and the scrutiny of the *Feldkommandanteur* in Miarritze, the spoliation of Jewish property in Baiona was carried out efficiently and rapidly. Provisional administrators received information from the police, the town hall, and the sub-prefecture of Baiona. Within six months, 90 percent of Jewish-owned

25 Mixel Esteban, *Regards sur la Seconde Guerre Mondiale en pays basque* (Donostia: Elkar, 2007), 44.
26 Stanley G. Payne, *Franco and Hitler: Spain, Germany, and World War II* (New Haven: Yale University Press, 2008), 90–94.
27 As Richard Vinen points out in *The Unfree French: Life under the Occupation* (New Haven: Yale University Press, 2006), 79, there were different kinds of Pétainists, e.g. veterans in the French Legion of Combatants embraced a "conservative and patriotic form of Pétainism," whereas its more youthful offshoot, the Service d'Ordre Légionnaire (SOL), represented a far more politically radical kind of Pétainism.
28 Poullenot, *Basses-Pyrénées, occupation, liberation 1940–1945*, 42. During fieldwork in Xiberoa in 2004–2006, local people who admired the Marshal showed me postcards with Pétain's portrait.

enterprises in the city had been liquidated or expropriated by provisional administrators.[29]

According to the collaborationist press in Baiona, Vichy and Pétain still enjoyed the support of many people on the Basque coast in 1941. In May, Vichy's representative in Paris and close ally of Pierre Laval, Fernand de Brinon, presided over a bullfight that the French authorities had specially arranged for him in Baiona. In June, the Vichy authorities appointed Marcel Ribeton as mayor of Baiona along with nineteen councilmembers, who all expressed their admiration for, confidence in, and dedication to Marshal Pétain as France's chief of state. The mayor organized large regional assemblies of young men and women in Baiona to "fight against prostitution and the lowering of moral standards." They extolled the virtues of the family and emphasized the role it should play not only in population growth but also in the local economy. In the summer of 1941, Georges Scapini, the blind veteran of World War I who was responsible for Vichy's Diplomatic Service for Prisoners of War, also visited Baiona and the French POWs held in the nearby camp at Polo Beyris.[30]

In order to rally support for Pétain, Vichy authorities organized his visit to Pau, where an estimated ninety thousand people gathered to welcome him in October 1941. Seven trains and three buses transported supporters from the surrounding countryside. (It is not known how many among them were Basque.)[31] Pétain's principal minister at that time, Admiral Darlan, accompanied him. The Prefect, Jean Ybarnegaray (by then a minister in Pétain's cabinet), and various other regional dignitaries greeted the delegation. The Vicar General of Pau, Canon Daguzan, was among them. Daguzan allied himself with the controversial Bishop of Baiona, Monseigneur Vansteenberghe.

Although the Catholic Church remained largely silent on the "Jewish problem" during the first two years of the Occupation, Monseigneur Vansteenberghe and Canon Daguzan deeply opposed the German occupation and the anti-Semitic measures taken by the Vichy and Nazi regimes. When the Germans arrived in Baiona in June 1940, the bishop refused to celebrate Mass for them in the cathedral.[32] In De-

---

29 Martine Bacqué, "Un aspect de la collaboration: la spoliation des juifs de Bayonne," in *Vichy et la collaboration dans les Basses-Pyrénées*, ed. Laurent Jalabert and Stéphane Le Bras (Pau: Éditions Cairn, 2015), 27–28.
30 Pontet, ed., *Histoire de Bayonne*, 276.
31 Poullenot, *Basses-Pyrénées, occupation, liberation 1940–1945*, 113.
32 Pontet, ed., *Histoire de Bayonne*, 277.

cember 1940, he did, however, call his parishioners to support Marshal Pétain, "whose noble character compels everyone to respect him."[33] The bishop, like so many older veterans of World War I, was Pétainist, yet anti-Vichy (owing to the Franco-German collaborationism embraced by Laval) and anti-German. When German censors severely restricted the bishop's publications in the diocese, Vansteenberghe turned to Canon Daguzan to publish an anti-German bulletin in Pau, which was then still unoccupied. In December 1941, the regional head of Vichy censorship issued a "secret" report on the bishop's "anti-German" and "anti-collaborationist" attitude.[34]

Despite the outward expression of support for Pétain during his tour of the southwest, his popularity began to wane across France by the end of 1941. People began to realize that he had failed to obtain any of the significant concessions from the Germans that he had promised to secure. German troops remained on French soil. Most French prisoners of war remained in Germany.[35] Food shortages contributed to the general discontent. In Basses-Pyrénées, the citizens of Pau and Orthez in Béarn and the people of Baiona and Biarritz experienced the shortages most keenly.[36]

In early January 1942, the situation of the Jews in Baiona worsened. As one Jewish architect observed: "We live in fear of tomorrow, anxiously opening the newspaper every day to see if a new measure had been taken against us . . . We wonder whether the day after tomorrow will find us in a concentration camp or under deportation."[37] On the Basque coast, French administrators and the Germans collaborated together to resolve the "Jewish question." The mayor of Miarritze undertook a detailed census of 103 Jews in his town and neighboring Angelu (Anglet) just a few weeks before the massive roundup of Jews in Paris at the Vél d'Hiv on July 14, 1942. Thirty-two Jews were arrested

---

33 Sylvaine Guinle-Lorinet, "Collaborer ou resister: l' Église du diocèse de Bayonne pendant la Seconde Guerre mondiale," in *Vichy et la collaboration dans les Basses-Pyrénées*, ed. Laurent Jalabert and Stéphane Le Bras (Pau: Éditions Cairn, 2015), 18. The author is quoting Philippe Fabas, "Vansteenberghe Edmond," *Dictionnaire des évêques de France au XXe siècle* (Paris: Éditions du Cerf, 2010), 236.

34 Archives Départementales of the Pyrénées-Atlantiques, hereafter ADPA, dossier 30W52, document 2/71, "secret report," no. 432, Pau, December 3, 1941, from the regional director of Vichy censorship to the head of the Vichy press and censorship services.

35 Vinen, *The Unfree French*, 56.

36 Poullenot, *Basses-Pyrénées, occupation, liberation 1940–1945*, 39.

37 Mixel Esteban, "Les Juifs du Pays basque: De l'exclusion de la citoyenneté à la "solution finale," in *Exodes, Exils et Internements dans les Basses-Pyrénées (1936–1945)*, ed. Laurent Jalabert (Pau: Éditions Cairn, 2014), 91.

in Baiona and Miarritze on the night of July 15, 1942, transferred to Mérignac, and on to Auschwitz. In October 1942, the sub-prefecture of Baiona undertook a second roundup of another thirty-two Jews.[38] The Bishop of Baiona, Vansteenberghe, and other Catholic leaders in the department condemned the anti-Semitic policies of Vichy and the local authorities.[39]

By 1942, the war had taken a great toll on the German economy. The Third Reich urgently needed French workers. Pressed by the Nazis for a solution, Pétain's Deputy Prime Minister, Pierre Laval, created the Relief (*Relève*) scheme in June 1942. The *Relève* promised that one French prisoner of war would be released for every three skilled French workers who volunteered to go to Germany. The scheme failed miserably, with an estimated total number of French volunteers at 49,000.[40] In Lapurdi and Behe-Nafarroa, only around 250 people signed up. Another 400 volunteered from Xiberoa and Béarn. But of the estimated 650 contracts issued for the *Relève* in the department, very few were Basques or Béarnais. The vast majority of volunteers were manual laborers with foreign nationalities. Twenty percent were female.[41]

Under pressure from Hitler's Plenipotentiary for Labor, Fritz Sauckel, to send 250,000 French workers to Germany, Laval took the first steps toward obligatory work service (*Service du Travail Obligatoire* or STO) in September 1942. The law, sometimes referred to as "the second relief scheme," required French men from eighteen to fifty years old, and single women aged twenty-one to thirty-five, to participate. The authorities called up an estimated 916 men and women in Xiberoa and Béarn, of whom 341 actually went to work in Germany, while 419 evaded conscription.[42] An estimated 290 citizens from occupied Iparralde answered the call and 351 evaded it.

November 1942 brought the total occupation of France. In Upper Xiberoa, German customs officers requisitioned houses and herding huts in borderland communes such as Santazi (Ste-Engrâce). German authorities declared the borderlands "a forbidden frontier zone." The German Security Service (*Sicherheitsdienst* or SD) established a commissariat in Pau under the direction of SS Lieutenant Otto Doberschütz.

---

38 Ibid., 92–93.
39 Ibid., 94.
40 Nicholas Atkin, *The French at War, 1934–1944* (Harlow: Pearson Education, 2001), 67.
41 Poullenot, *Basses-Pyrénées, occupation, liberation 1940–1945*, 110.
42 Ibid., 111–12.

He had previously overseen the repression of Jews by the German se-curity police and intelligence service (Kommando of the Sipo-SD) in the Bordeaux region.[43] Once based in Pau, Doberschütz oversaw three auxiliary SD posts, one of which was in Xiberoa. In December 1942, the SD established a garrison of fifty-eight soldiers and customs officers in the Xiberoan market town of Sustary. Their mission was to arrest Jews and other fugitives, to gather information about the intelligence and trans-Pyrenean escape networks, and to repress resisters, who were not yet fully organized in Xiberoa.[44]

Vichy implemented the second stage of the STO in February 1943. This law required those French citizens born during 1920–1922 to sign up for a two-year period of work in Germany. Those who defaulted faced prison sentences of three to five years and fines ranging from 200 to 100,000 francs. In Xiberoa and Béarn, the authorities called up 5,138 citizens for the STO between March and September 1943. Only 1,425 went to work in Germany. An additional 665 undertook work for the Germans in France. An estimated 1,045 evaded conscription.[45] Around 1,300 men from occupied Iparralde worked in Germany under the STO, with some 862 evading conscription. The total number of citizens from Iparralde and Béarn who volunteered to work in Germany or answered the STO call is around 4,006. With a departmental population of 413,411 at the time, less than one percent worked for the enemy. An estimated 2,677 citizens in the department evaded the "relief" systems and the STO altogether.[46] Although around 650,000 French workers went to work in Germany as either volunteers or conscripts, the STO led to an intensification of public disillusionment with Vichy across France. It also swelled the ranks of rebel groups (*maquis*) as young STO evaders took to the hills to join the Resistance.[47]

The introduction of STO in February 1943 coincided with the arrival of 500 German troops and an SS division (*Das Reich*) in Xiberoa's capital, Maule. Both factors greatly increased opposition to Vichy and generated support for the Resistance. Given that the STO required all men born between 1920 and 1922 to register for the scheme, it also sharpened class-based and political tensions in the town. Unlike the poor and underprivileged factory workers, the sons of factory owners

---

43   René Terrisse, *Bordeaux, 1940–1944* (Paris: Perrin, 1993), 110.
44   See Ott, *War, Judgment, and Memory in the Basque Borderlands, 1914–1945*, 94.
45   Poullenot, *Basses-Pyrénées, occupation, liberation 1940–1945*, 114.
46   Ibid., 117.
47   Vinen, *The Unfree French*, 250.

obtained dispensations or found secure hiding places thanks to their fathers' influence and wealth. Two hundred men from Maule went to Germany as STO workers in the spring of 1943. Nearly all of them were factory workers of Spanish or Navarrese origin. As one police inspector observed, many workers felt that the STO was part of "some grand scheme aimed at neutralizing their class and seeking to punish them for political beliefs they held before the war began."[48]

People in Maule responded to the arrival of the Germans with a mixture of resentment, resignation, and curiosity. As one police inspector observed, such curiosity was "perhaps unhealthy, but understandable, given that such a sensational display [of military equipment] seemed like the arrival of a circus to people with little experience of the world."[49] In those first few months of occupation, the mayor and his staff established nonconfrontational relations with German officers and sought to ensure that the Germans treated civilians and their property with respect.[50] In his weekly report on local public opinion about Vichy, the Germans, and the Resistance, the same police inspector noted that the townspeople seemed to worry as much about the STO as about the Germans. "The deportation of so many young Frenchmen to Germany sows anguish in parents' hearts," he wrote, "and many young men are thinking about fleeing toward the Spanish frontier, that is to say, towards the unknown."[51]

On February 19, 1943, Radio-Vatican condemned the STO. Bishop Vansteenberghe of Baiona vigorously protested against the measure and on March 14, 1943, addressed a group of young draftees in the cathedral. He equated the STO with deportation and "enslavement." His attack drew sharp criticism from the collaborationist press and provoked the Germans to search his residence. The bishop met a brutal end that December. It is not known whether the Germans were involved.[52] Mgr. Vansteenberghe posthumously received the Medal of the Resistance in January 1946.[53]

---

48 See Ott, *War, Judgment, and Memory in the Basque Borderlands, 1914–1945*, 95.
49 ADPA, 37W15, CA2965, CD101, Inspector Carbou to the sub-prefect, March 23, 1943.
50 Arnaud Aguer, bi-monthly installments of his wartime memoirs published in the local newspaper, *Le Miroir de la Soule*, in 1960. The material is available to the public only with the permission of the editor of that newspaper.
51 ADPA, 37W15, CA2965, CD101, note 10 in the file, Inspector Carbou to the sub-prefect, March 23, 1943.
52 Guinle-Lorinet, "Collaborer ou resister," 20.
53 Ibid., 19.

III

As historians of the Occupation have long recognized, "resistance" is a highly ambiguous term and took a wide range of forms, from providing food parcels for resisters to sabotaging railroad lines. In Iparralde the concentrated and prolonged presence of Germans on the Basque coast made organized resistance very difficult and particularly dangerous there. Nevertheless, and despite numerous betrayals and arrests, escape networks such as the Comet Line made valuable contributions to the Resistance. From 1941 until June 1944, the Comet Line took some 688 Allied pilots from Belgium and northern France to the Basque coast. A young Belgian nurse, Andrée de Jonghe, led the celebrated escape network and often accompanied the pilots as they crossed the Pyrenean foothills and the Bidasoa River into the southern Basque Country with the help of local Basque guides.[54]

Despite their location in the occupied zone, the Benedictine monks of the Abbaye de Belloc likewise helped thousands of refugees—mainly Jews and Allied pilots. From the early days of the Occupation in 1940, the monks collaborated with two escape networks that operated from Hazparne. The monks sheltered fugitives and, with the help of Basque clandestine guides, organized their passage to the frontier at Itsasu (Itxassou) and on to the Benedictines at Lazkao (Lazkano) in Gipuzkoa. The Germans arrested the three monks central to the operation in December 1943. One was released; the other two endured deportation to Buchenwald and then Dachau. The Allies liberated them on April 29, 1945.[55]

The trans-Pyrenean escape networks that operated in Iparralde relied heavily on clandestine Basque guides and the many citizens who helped them. In Upper Xiberoa, Santazi served as a popular route over the Pyrenees. Santazi lay within a "forbidden zone," in which German patrols regularly searched for Jews and other fugitives who sought local shelter. During fieldwork in the 1970s and 1980s, elderly people often recalled the fear displayed by Jewish men, women, and children

---

54 See Juan Carlos Jiménez de Aberasturi, *En passant la Bidassoa: Le réseau Comète au pays basque (1941–1944)* (Biarritz: Éditions J&D, 1996).

55 For an account of one monk's experiences, see the memoir of Grégoire Joannateguy, published in Basque as *Alemaniara deportatua: Büchenwald 1944, Dachau 1945* (Donostia: Elkar, 2003). See also Esteban, *Regards sur la Seconde Guerre Mondiale en pays basque,* chap. 7, on "Les moines résistants de Belloc," 99–107. The French version of the memoir, *Récit de ma déportation en Allemagne: Buchenwald 1944, Dachau 1945* by Père Grégoire, is available from the monks at the Abbaye de Belloc.

as they waited for a local shepherd to collect them for the next stage of their perilous journey across the mountains.[56] Basque shepherds who worked as clandestine guides also faced extreme danger, not only as a prime target of German patrols but also as a victim of denunciation.[57] In 1976, I discovered the tragic case of one Santazi guide while working on birth, death, and marriage records. Tomas H. was twenty-two years old when he and a young neighbor attempted to take a group of Jews, Allied pilots, and evaders of the STO into Spain. Acting on a local denunciation, a German patrol arrested the group. The two young shepherds perished in Buchenwald. The community struggled to overcome these losses and the divisiveness of betrayal. Traditional rural Basque values (such as mutual aid, cooperation, and trust), institutionalized relations between "first neighbors," and the ritual exchange of blessed bread by such neighbors enabled them to do so.[58]

An estimated 212 men and sixteen women served honorably as clandestine guides in Iparralde.[59] During fieldwork in the 1980s and in 2004, I recorded the experiences of several former guides—men and women—who typically underplayed their wartime bravery, courage, and humanitarianism.[60] One of them, Rufino Jauregui, took refuge in Kanbo (Cambo-les-Bains) in 1936 during the Spanish Civil War and became a highly successful trans-Pyrenean smuggler. Kanbo came under German occupation in June 1940. In 1941, an hotelier asked Rufino to take some of his guests across the frontier. In the years of foreign occupation that followed, Rufino mainly passed Jewish, Canadian, and British clients and then became involved in the escape network Alsace, which passed men wishing to join the Free French Forces in North Africa.[61] By his own reckoning, Rufino took around nine hundred people across the Pyrenees into Spain during the Occupation.[62]

---

56 F. Eyheralt, G. Harriguileheguy, X. Mohorade, personal communications, on numerous occasions in 1976–1977 and during the 1980s, Santazi.
57 See Gisèle Lougarot, *Dans l'ombre des passeurs* (Donostia: Elkar, 2004) and Sandra Ott, *Living with the Enemy* (Cambridge, UK: Cambridge University Press, 2017), 162–63, 173–74, for accounts of these guides' wartime experiences.
58 For an account of the tragedy, see Sandra Ott, "Gift-Giving and the Management of Justice among Borderland Basques during the Occupation (1942–1944) and the Liberation," *The Proceedings of the Western Society for French History* (October 2007), 266–81.
59 Poullenot, *Basses-Pyrénées, occupation, libération 1940–1945*, 136.
60 In 2004, I spent several days recording and filming, with the help of Eusko-Ikaskuntza, the clandestine guide, Rufino Jauregui. The film is now in his family archives in Ezpeleta (Espelette).
61 See the section on Rufino Jauregui in Dominique Halty, *Cambo sous l'occupation allemande, 1940–1944* (Cambo: Imprimerie San Juan, 1985), 122–36.
62 Rufino Jauregui, Ezpeleta, personal communication, June 13, 2004. He gave the

Owing to the much more sparsely inhabited terrain and less concentrated German presence, the people of Xiberoa and rural Béarn were far better placed to engage in organized resistance than their coastal counterparts. The two largest resistance groups that operated there were Sector IV of de Gaulle's Secret Army (*Armée Secrète*) and a company of the right-wing *Corps-Franc Pommiès* (CFP) that initially supported General Giraud, de Gaulle's arch rival. The Secret Army was established in the Basses-Pyrénées in late September 1941.[63] In January 1943, the main southern resistance groups—Combat, the Secret Army, and the Communist *Francs-Tireurs et Partisans* (FTP)—merged to form a unified resistance movement known as the MUR (*Mouvements Unis de la Résistance*). Following disagreements with Combat and Secret Army leaders over strategic matters in late 1942, André Pommiès created his own resistance group, the *Corps-Franc Pommiès* (CFP), in seven departments of southern France.[64] Closely linked to the Resistance Organization of the Army (*Organisation de Résistance de l'Armée* or ORA), the CFP created a Xiberoan company in June 1943 and asked a local factory owner and reserve officer, Pierre Béguerie, to lead it. He recruited more than a hundred conservative, anti-Communist men—many of whom were Xiberoans—with former military experience. Many recruits remained loyal to Pétain but opposed Vichy's policy of Franco-German collaboration.

In May 1944, the departmental head of the Secret Army asked a local Xiberoan, Clement de Jaureguiberry, to take charge of Sector IV, which included disparate *maquis* groups of *Francs-Tireurs et Partisans* (FTP).[65] Three Secret Army *maquis* operated in Xiberoa: in Maule, the rural hamlets of Larzabale (Larceveau) and Larrabile (Larrebieu), and the mountainous zones of Arbaila (Arbailles) and Upper Xiberoa.

Bitter rivalry over military strategy and politics deeply divided the local leaders of the CFP and Secret Army.[66] In Xiberoa, the Secret Army differed considerably from the CFP in several respects. Unlike the CFP, Secret Army recruits were mainly local civilians—some of southern Basque descent but largely Xiberoans—rather than career

---

same estimate to Halty in *Cambo sous l'occupation allemande*, 134.

63 Poullenot, *Basses-Pyrénées, occupation, liberation 1940–1945*, 178. Combat was the largest, most organized non-Communist resistance movement in southern France.

64 General Céroni, *Le Corps-Franc Pommiès*, vol. 1 (Toulouse: Éditions du Grand-Rond, 1980), 41, 46.

65 Poullenot, *Basses-Pyrénées, occupation, liberation 1940–1945*, 188.

66 For a detailed exploration of these two resistance groups, see Ott, *War, Judgment, and Memory in the Basque Borderlands, 1914–1945*, 107–13.

military men from elsewhere in France. Secret Army resisters were also often politically left-wing and working class, while CFP men tended to be conservative, Catholic, and middle class. Unlike the CFP, the Xiberoan Secret Army included women. While the CFP's mission entailed military action against the occupiers, the Secret Army sought to avoid military aggression until D-Day and de Gaulle's command to begin the insurrection. The Secret Army's leader wished to prevent German retaliations against the local population, whereas his CFP counterpart in 1944 (an outsider to the region) encouraged acts of sabotage and skirmishes with the enemy that often endangered citizens. Organized resistance in Xiberoa intensified as D-Day approached in June 1944. Hitler's First Army sent nearly 5,000 troops into southwestern France.[67] The 276th German infantry moved within forty miles north of Maule. The regional Secret Army leader urged resisters to refrain from combat near civilians.

As happened elsewhere in France, resistance against the Germans intensified after D-Day on June 6. On the same day, a unit of Das Reich joined the German battalion based in Mont-de-Marsan. On June 27, their combined forces pursued CFP resisters in the Xiberoan hamlet of Ospitaleku. The attack became one of the greatest resistance tragedies in Iparralde. Between five and six hundred German soldiers descended upon the hamlet. Through informers, the Germans knew that several households sheltered CFP resisters. During the massive raid several civilians died. The Germans burned down buildings, destroyed livestock, and rounded up the terrified villagers. They deported six men to Mauthausen and three women to Ravensbrück. Of the nine civilians, only two survived the camps: a mother and her daughter, liberated by the Allies in April 1945.[68]

In Iparralde, the experience of liberation varied from one community to another. In Maule, the process of liberation began with a highly controversial skirmish between the Germans and aggressive CFP resisters on the outskirts of town on August 10, 1944. In retaliation for the ambush, a German airplane bombed Maule on August 12. Tensions increased not only between the German battalion leader and the FFI commander, who held German prisoners of war; tension also escalated between rival leaders of the CFP and Secret Army (who also headed the

---

67 Dominique Lormier, *Le corps franc Pommiès* (Toulouse: Grancher, 1990), 33.
68 For a detailed account of the raid, see Ott, *War, Judgment, and Memory in the Basque Borderlands, 1914–1945*, 114–30.

FFI). In the end, the Allied landing in Provence—rather than military combat—prompted the Germans to leave Maule abruptly on August 15.

One hundred sixty-three well-armed Germans still held nearby Sustary, a town deeply divided by political and personal animosities. After protracted negotiations with the FFI leader, the German commander of Sustary surrendered on August 23. The FFI took 250 German prisoners of war to Gurs, which already held some 3,000 captives—roughly half of whom were suspected collaborators.[69] As one observer of the Occupation noted, "the liberation opened a Pandora's box of jealousy, rancor, acrimony, covetous desire, resentment, contemptible acts, and vengeance" in some communities.[70] Sustary was one of them. Unlike Santazi, where the foundations of rural Basque culture remained strong, the "first neighbor" relationship had fallen into disuse in Sustary. Suspicion eroded the trust that neighbors had traditionally enjoyed. One particular woman sowed wartime extensive discord that divided the town long after the war ended.[71]

The departure of the Germans occurred on a much larger scale on the coast. Twenty-four thousand German Army soldiers left Baiona and headed for Bordeaux on August 22. Although the convoy included some elite troops, the soldiers were mainly very young recruits and reservists. Among local citizens, emotions were mixed in Baiona: relief and joy that the Germans were gone alongside anxiety and impatience over continuing food shortages.[72] In Miarritze on the same day, an FFI company of Secret Army men took twenty-nine German prisoners without exchanging fire. A huge crowd gathered in carnival mood. The celebrations began before the last German cavalcade had left town.[73] The new prefect promised that the purge would be carried out relentlessly but also vowed to temper it with "the greatest respect for the human person."[74] On August 23, Germans in nearby Angelu fought against resisters for two hours, leaving two Germans dead and one resister seriously wounded, before they surrendered to the FFI.[75] In the days that followed a few women on the Basque coast and in the interior had their heads shaved for "horizontal collaboration." In

---

69 Ibid., 165.
70 Jean Touyarot, *l'Hôtel des ombres* (Paris: Seuil, 2011), 236–37.
71 For a detailed account, see Ott, *War, Judgment, and Memory in the Basque Borderlands, 1914–1945*, 162–65.
72 Pontet, ed., *Histoire de Bayonne*, 278.
73 Esteban, *Regards sur la Seconde Guerre Mondiale en pays basque*, 164, 166.
74 *La IVIéme République* (Pau), no. 2, August 24, 1944.
75 *La Résistance Républicaine* (Baiona), no. 8342, August 24, 1944.

some communities, citizens eager for revenge pillaged the properties of suspected collaborators.[76]

The head of the departmental liberation committee urged people to behave in a dignified, disciplined manner, as the authorities initiated an orderly purge of the police and the judiciary in the autumn of 1944. The purge of suspected collaborators among the citizenry of Iparralde took much longer. The court of justice in Pau heard their cases from October 16, 1944, and until late 1948, by which time the court had rendered 649 verdicts.[77]

IV

In conclusion, the experience of German occupation in Iparralde varied according to a range of factors: location, access to food, the density and duration of the Germans' presence, the presence or absence of organized resistance, the socioeconomic and political fabric of a community, and the durability or demise of key features in rural Basque culture.

Location made a difference in several respects: those who came under total occupation from June 1940 felt the impact of a concentrated German presence far more deeply than Xiberoans did. Even after November 1940, Xiberoans never experienced the sheer number and long duration of German troops that coastal people endured. Location also affected accessibility to food. Those living in rural communities close to the border fared the best. Proximity to the Franco-German frontier likewise brought closer and usually more prolonged contact with Spanish and southern Basques, during and after the Spanish Civil War and the Occupation.

The people of Iparralde also had quite variable experiences with the Germans in their midst. In most coastal communities, where the German presence was particularly dense for four years, ignoring the enemy was nearly as impossible as resisting them in organized fashion. Most people on the coast had regular contact with Germans, but daily contact does not always entail the formation of relationships. Archival research thus far has revealed only a few cases in which local people in coastal Lapurdi established close, amicable relations with particular

---

76 Ott, *War, Judgment, and Memory in the Basque Borderlands, 1914–1945*, 89.
77 See Ott, *Living with the Enemy*, for a detailed account of the Occupation and post-liberation trials of suspected collaborators.

Germans. (Not all were Basque.) This may be due to the shorter duration of Germans' assignments in coastal communities, where troops moved regularly and often, in comparison to those in Xiberoa. In towns such as Sustary, multilingual German officers often stayed one year or more in the same small community and thus had opportunities to become well acquainted (if only rarely amicably) with local people.

Whether as an active member or an occasional supporter, experience with organized resistance occurred mainly in Xiberoa. Although members of rival resistance groups all fought for the same ultimate cause, their leaders quarreled bitterly. Preexisting animosities, based upon class, ethnic difference, religion, and political convictions, fueled wartime and post-liberation divisiveness among ordinary citizens. Maule, in particular, provides a lens through to understand this phenomenon.

The Basque culture also had an impact upon the ways in which people experienced the Occupation. The rural house, the highly structured institution of "first neighbors," and traditional Basque values of mutual aid, trust, and cooperation are the foundations of this robust culture. As I have shown elsewhere, rural communities like Santazi had strongly knit neighborhood bonds and ritual practices that strengthened ties between households and the wider community. Communities with high social solidarity typically endured the Occupation and post-liberation tensions and traumas far better than towns like Sustary, where deep internal divisiveness existed before the Germans ever arrived.[78]

BIBLIOGRAPHY

Archives Départementales of the Pyrénées-Atlantiques (ADPA), dossiers 30W52; 37W15.

Arnould, Claire. "l'acceuil des réfugiés en Béarn et en Soule de 1936 à1940." In *Les espagnoles et la guerrre civile*, edited by Michel Papy. Biarritz: Atlantica, 1999.

Atkin, Nicholas. *The French at War 1934–1944*. Harlow: Pearson Education, 2001.

Bacqué, Martine. "Un aspect de la collaboration: la spoliation des juifs de Bayonne." In *Vichy et la collaboration dans les Basses-Pyrénées*,

---

78   See Ott, *War, Judgment, and Memory in the Basque Borderlands, 1914–1945*.

edited by Laurent Jalabert and Stéphane Le Bras. Pau: Éditions Cairn, 2015.

Béguerie, Pierre. *Témoignage.* Unpublished memoir, Sohüta, Xiberoa, n.d.

Castiella, Manuel. *Un siècle à Bayonne.* Anglet: Atlantica, 2003.

Céroni, Marcel. *Le Corps Franc Pommiès.* Volume 1.Toulouse: Éditions de Grand-Rond, 1980.

Diamond, Hanna. *Fleeing Hitler, France 1940.* Oxford: Oxford University Press, 2007.

Dreyfus-Armand, Geneviève. *L'exile des Rèpublicains espagnols en France.* Paris: Albin Michel, 1999.

Esteban, Mixel. *Regards sur la Seconde Guerre Mondiale en pays basque.* Donostia: Elkar, 2007.

———. "Les Juifs du Pays basque: De l'exclusion de la citoyenneté à la "solution finale." In *Exodes, Exils et Internements dans les Basses-Pyrénées (1936–1945),* edited by Laurent Jalabert. Pau: Éditions Cairn, 2014.

Fogg, Shannon. *Stealing Home: Looting, Restitution, and Reconstructing Jewish Lives in France, 1942–1947.* Oxford: Oxford University Press, 2017.

Guinle-Lorinet, Sylvaine. "Collaborer ou resister: l'Église du diocèse de Bayonne pendant la Seconde Guerre mondiale." In *Vichy et la collaboration dans les Basses-Pyrénées,* edited by Laurent Jalabert and Stéphane Le Bras. Pau: Éditions Cairn, 2015.

Guse, John C. 2018. "Polo Beyris: A Forgotten Internment Camp in France, 1939-1947." *Journal of Contemporary History* (February 2018). Online First DOI: 10.1177/0022009417712113.

Halty, Dominique. *Cambo sous l' Occupation Allemande.* Cambo: Imprimerie San Juan, 1985.

Hoover Institute Archives, Stanford University, CA. "The Atlantic Wall from the Loire to the Spanish Border," Karlsruhe, October 16, 1952. U.S. Army European Command, Box 0028, Accession no. 66026, File C-022.

Jackson, Julian. *France: The Dark Years 1940–1944.* Oxford: Oxford University Press, 2001.

Jacob, James. *Hills of Conflict: Basque Nationalism in France*. Reno: University of Nevada Press, 1994.

Jiménez de Aberasturi, Juan Carlos. *En passant la Bidassoa: Le réseau Comète au pays basque (1941–1944)*. Biarritz: Éditions J & D, 1996.

Jiménez de Aberásturi, Juan Carlos, and Rafael Moreno Izquierdo. *Al servicio del extranjero: historia del servicio vasco de información (1936–1943)*. Madrid: A. Machado Libros, 2009.

Joannateguy, Grégoire. *Alemaniara deportatua: Büchenwald 1944, Dachau 1945*. Donostia: Elkar, 2003.

Kedward, H. R. *In Search of the Maquis: Rural Resistance in Southern France, 1942–1944*. Oxford: Oxford University Press, 1994.

La IViéme République (Pau), no. 2, August 24, 1944.

La Résistance Républicaine (Baiona), no. 8342, August 24, 1944.

Lormier, Dominique. *Le corps franc Pommiès*. Toulouse: Grancher, 1990.

Lougarot, Gisèle. *Dans l'ombre des passeurs*. Donostia: Elkar, 2004.

Ott, Sandra. "Gift-Giving and the Management of Justice among Borderland Basques during the Occupation (1942–1944) and the Liberation." *The Proceedings of the Western Society for French History* (October 2007): 266–281.

———. *War, Judgment, and Memory in the Basque Borderlands, 1914–1945*. Reno: University of Nevada Press, 2008.

———. *Living with the Enemy: German Occupation, Collaboration and Justice in the Western Pyrenees, 1940–1948*. Cambridge, UK: Cambridge University Press, 2017.

Payne, Stanley G. *Franco and Hitler: Spain, Germany, and World War II*. New Haven: Yale University Press, 2008.

Pontet, Josette, ed. *Histoire de Bayonne*. Toulouse: Éditions Privat, 1991.

Poullenot, Louis. *Basses-Pyrénées, occupation, liberation 1940–1945*. Biarritz: J&D Éditions, 1995.

Sallaberry, Francis. *Quand Hitler bétonnait la côte basque*. Bayonne: Harriet, 1988.

Szwarc Torrès, Tereska. *Une Française libre: journal, 1939–1945*. Lonrai: Éditions Phébus, 2000.

Terrisse, René. *Bordeaux, 1940–1944.* Paris: Perrin, 1993.

Touyarot, Jean. *l'Hôtel des ombres.* Paris: Seuil, 2011.

Vinen, Richard. *The Unfree French: Life under the Occupation.* New Haven: Yale University Press, 2006.

Chapter 5

Myrmidon and Atlantikwall, or the Military Importance of Iparralde

Ingo Niebel

"Things are only as important as the importance you give them."
(Unknown author)

On April 5, 1942 at 5:45 a.m. flares shot out from an unidentified vessel illuminating the Basque port of Donibane Lohizune (Saint-Jean-de-Luz) and waking up the German sentry. The German battery situated on the eastern shore of the bay spotted an enemy ship. Alarm spread throughout the communication network of the German armed forces, the Wehrmacht. Soldiers got up and ran to their positions, manning trenches, bunkers, and guns. The batteries of the coastal artillery received the order to open fire on the target. German troops based in the Bay of Biscay feared a new British raid like that of only a week earlier, on March 28, 1942, when several commando units blew up an essential part of the naval base at Saint-Nazaire. When the Germans started shooting at the British vessel they did not know that this was not the beginning, but the end of an aborted secret mission that several hundred British commandos and royal marines should have carried out against several targets in the port of Baiona (Bayonne), situated some 26 km (16 miles) north of Donibane Lohizune.

On that spring day, the war had come across the sea, and was knocking on that entrance door to Euskal Herria (the Basque Country).

After almost two years, the German occupiers considered Iparralde, the northern part of the Basque Country, as something akin to a large military resort in which their units could recover from fighting in other war hotspots that their Reichschancellor and Führer of the National Socialist German Workers' Party (Nationalsozialistische Deutsche Arbeiterpartei, NSDAP), Adolf Hitler, started on September 1, 1939 by invading Poland. After occupying Denmark and Norway, Luxembourg, Belgium, the Netherlands, and France in the first half of 1940, in Western Europe only the United Kingdom, with Prime Minister Winston Churchill at the head of government, resisted the Wehrmacht. In February 1941, the military conflict spread to North Africa, where Hitler sought, through deployment of his expeditionary corps, to prevent his Italian ally, Benito Mussolini, from being defeated by the British Eighth Army. After conquering the Balkans in the spring of 1941, on June 22 Nazi Germany invaded its former ally, the socialist Soviet Union. The German Blitzkrieg military tactic was halted by fresh and well trained Siberian divisions and frozen by a harsh Russian winter in the proximity of Moscow. Thus any German soldiers who could serve at a post in occupied France, especially in Iparralde, were lucky.

Today, historians disagree over the strategic importance the Basque coast had for German military planning. Francis Sallaberry concludes that the installation of at least ten artillery batteries with a caliber larger than 75 millimeters shows an "enormous density along a coastline of 30 kilometers [19 miles] without having any major strategic interest."[1] On the contrary, Mitxel Esteban states that the "Basque coast had become a strategic military site facing a sea dominated by the Royal Navy."[2]

Both are right because the military value of Euskal Herria depended on the importance the Germans or British gave to it. Therefore, it is necessary to put the fortification of the Basque coast in a wider historical and academic context. This chapter is based on the information Francis Sallaberry publishes on the location and technical specification of German weapons and bunkers on the Basque coast during the war. My objective is to explain why that part of Iparralde was given military

---

1   Francis Sallaberry, "La Wehrmacht sur la Côte Basque, de 1940 à 1944," *Oihenart* 14 (1997), 219. In all his work Sallaberry shows a lot of interesting details but he does not identify the sources he used, although he does specify the French archives he consulted. His bibliographies tend to be superficial and incomplete, as he does not mention either the authors' first names, nor the place or the year of publication.
2   Mitxel Esteban, *Regards sur la Seconde Guerre mondiale en Pays basque* (Baiona: Elkar, 2007), 133.

importance by both the Germans and the British at specific times during World War II. This requires linking the findings of Basque research on the issue with that carried out in Germany.

Many publications on the so-called Atlantikwall, which was in effect nothing but a pure Nazi propaganda term, prioritize its technical and military aspects, ignoring the fact that this fortification could be built only by the thousands of forced workers. In the Irargi archive (now the Basque national archive) I found some documents by a Basque, Leonardo Salazar, who had been forced to work by the Germans on the construction of that fortification project. To be sure, there were other forced laborers who did the same work in poorer conditions than him, but that is not the issue here: Salazar's case reminds us that all that such construction work and the entire Nazi weapon production could exist only because the Nazi regime had the power to force millions of people to work for it in factories and on constructions sites.

This chapter is only one pixel of the larger picture drawn of the Basque Country during World War II. It is linked to my other research on the Sipo-SD in Chapter 2 of this book.

Taking Hendaia

The *drôle de guerre* or "Phoney War" on the western front was over by May 10, 1940, when the Wehrmacht invaded Luxembourg and Belgium, the Netherlands, and France. The operation Gelb (yellow) finished on June 4, 1940, when the German army conquered the port of Dunkirk in northern France; and this after the Royal Navy had managed to evacuate most of the British Expeditionary Force (BEF) before it had to surrender to the invaders. On June 5, 1940, the supreme command of the German armed forces, the OKW (Oberkommando der Wehrmacht), started operation Rot (red), which envisaged fighting the French army until its complete capitulation. The Wehrmacht achieved that goal seventeen days later when the French government had to sign the armistice with the Reich.

Three days later, on June 25, the first German units reached the *muga*, as the Basques call the Franco-Spanish border that divides Euskal Herria between the two states. From that moment on, German military personnel would stand on guard at the international bridge that connects the towns of Hendaia (Hendaye) and Irun (Irún), on the western shore of the Bidasoa River. Demoted to a mere walk-on part, the remaining French border officers could observe how, at this frontier post, the German military authorities and diplomats celebrated their victory with the head of the Spanish sixth military region at Burgos, with Captain General José López-Pinto and other Francoist representatives, on June 29, 1940.

With the end of hostilities, the new German military authorities started to establish their own administration that would work together with the French civil administrative structures, with the latter reporting to the French government at Vichy. Then, on July 24, the Reich imposed the so called demarcation line on French territory. It divided the French territory into an occupied and an unoccupied zone, the latter ruled by the World War I hero, Marshal François Pétain. This partition also split Iparralde into two zones. The demarcation line ran along the national route no. 133 (now D 933), starting at the little frontier village of Arnegi (Arnéguy), then passing through Donibane Garazi (Saint-Jean-Pied-de-Port) to Ozaraine (Osserain), from where it continued to the French town of Sauveterre-de-Béarn. In the second half of 1940, its control was assigned to several German military units and to the SS Totenkopf (death's head) division, which belonged to the Seventh German Army.

At this stage of the war, the Germans only used the existing fortifications that they took over from the defeated and dismantled French Army. The German navy, the Kriegsmarine, became responsible for the administration and protection of the ports.

Due to the fact that the next campaign would be a landing on British soil, the OKW concentrated all its efforts at the northern shores of France and Belgium facing the United Kingdom. The operation was called Seelöwe (Sea Lion) and was due to be launched from Calais, Dunkirk, and other ports on the continental coast. While the German army were reorganizing their troops and gathering the shipping space needed for the next invasion of a democratic country, the German air force attacked the British mainland on a daily basis, trying to bring the airspace under its control. This was the main premise that the landing operation could start. But once again, the high commander of the Luftwaffe, Reichsmarschall Hermann Göring, made promises he could not keep. At the end of August, the Royal Air Force was still operative while the German air force had suffered heavy losses of their fighter and bomber pilots and planes.

In that situation, Hitler declined to execute Operation Seelöwe but he maintained the preparations at the coast just to keep pressure on the United Kingdom. In the meantime, he had sent a group of specialists to Spain on a mission to explore the conditions for an attack on Gibraltar. The conquest of the Rock would permit the Germans to control the entrance and exit of the Mediterranean Sea. The strategic goal was to prevent the British from transporting reinforcements from their Asian and African colonies through the Suez Canal in Egypt and the Mediterranean to their homeland. After the loss of Gibraltar, they would have to use the longer passage across the Atlantic, where German submarines would be waiting for them.

FELIX, A MILITARY OPERATION THAT MADE IPARRALDE IMPORTANT

In the fall of 1940, Hendaia was the unique border post that connected the Nazi Reich to Francoist Spain geographically and especially by its railroad bridge. Since the wars that had led to the foundation of the second German Empire in the nineteenth century, the Prussian-German General Staff considered the transport of troops by train essential. But in order to enter Spain, the OKW and the high command of the army, Oberkommando des Heeres (OKH), had no other choice than Hendaia because the other two main railroad stations on the Franco-Spanish border, at Canfranc in the center of the Pyrenees and Perpignan on the Mediterranean coast, were under control of the Vichy government.

Regarding the strength of the forces that would be needed for the operation, the Wehrmacht planned to bring two army corps into Spain, one for the attack, and the other as backup for the former. All other units and the supplies needed for the operation had to be concentrated in southwestern France before they could be brought to the border.

The next logistical problem was that the Spanish railroad system was not compatible with its French counterpart so that the trains could be loaded only at Irun. Spain's weak railroad infrastructure presented another challenge to the German logistics officers because the Spanish trains had only half the transport capacity the Germans used to calculate with. Then the railroad bridge from Hendaia to Irun would have to be reinforced because of its poor condition.

Hence the military planners decided that the two army corps would have to cross Spain by their own means. From Irun to Algeciras in the south of Spain, facing Gibraltar, they would have to overcome a distance of 1,200 km (745 miles). The Germans would have to bring with them all kinds of supplies because the country was still suffering from the consequences of the Spanish Civil War (1936–1939). Though the dictator, General Francisco Franco, was in charge, thanks to the aid he received from Nazi Germany and Fascist Italy after his military coup against the Spanish Republic on July 17–18, 1936, he could not deprive his population of basic foods and fuel without risking an uprising. Therefore, the OKW and OKH had to plan also how to get the required stocks of food, ammunition, fuel, and spare parts into Spain and where to store all that material. All this had to be done secretly, of course, because the attack on the Rock would have to be a surprise mission. Once Operation Felix was underway, further supplies would be transported by sea from southwestern French and Italian ports to harbors in Andalusia and Catalonia.

This is why the Operation Felix made Euskal Herria strategically important to the German planners. The port of Baiona was well equipped enough for transporting heavy material by sea to Pasaia (Pasajes) and Bilbo (Bilbao), the main harbors in Hegoalde, the southern part of the Basque Country. But the ports in the area and the German navy lacked the capacity to transport two entire army corps via this way to the area of operations. Therefore, mechanized units and infantry would have to cross the *muga* by land. The poor road network presented another obstacle to this plan.

According to a contemporaneous German military map, they were not too many options for entering Spanish territory and the army and the air force demanded, if possible, their own routes for their chains of supply.[3] The mountainous geography of that border region allowed the Germans only two ways for entering from Iparralde to

---

3   Bundesarchiv (German federal archive, hereafter BArch), RHD 21/577. The body responsible for the kind of "plagiarism" in creating the map was the Department of Military Cartography and Engineering of the German General Staff of the Army. In 1940, it copied the 1938 Michélin road map drawn at a scale of 1:200.000. The following description of the routes the Germans might have chosen for crossing the *muga* is based on this source. Other routes in, from Bilbo for instance, could not be investigated because there was no immediate access to any contemporaneous maps. The names of the roads given in parentheses here are taken from a current road map. See *Errepide mapa 1:200.000* (Bilbo: Sua, 2015). In order to analyze the German plan, however, it is essential to use a map dating from the 1930s, because the road network in Euskal Herria today has changed noticeably since 1980.

Hegoalde. From Hendaia, some light units could cross the somewhat weak international bridge into Irun, although such movements would compromise the secrecy of the operation. Alternatively, they could use French highway, the *rue national* no. 10, which, at Behobia (Behobie), became the Spanish *nacional* no. 1. Now on the western shore of the Bidasoa River, the German units could then proceed along a secondary route (the current N 121-A) to Bera (Vera de Bidasoa) and from there to Berroeta. At this point the German columns would meet with their Kameraden (comrades) who had entered Hegoalde from inland point of the Dantxarinea (Dancharinea) pass. That border post was connected to Donibane Lohizune by the secondary routes no. D 4 and the N 618, passing through Sara (Sare)and Azkaine (Ascain), and would have created another bottleneck. The alternative was to us the D 20 from Kanbo (Cambo-les-Bains) and Ezpeleta (Espelette) to Dantxarinea. This route (the current N-121 b) would bring the troops to Elizondo and to Berroeta in Hegoalde. From this point on there was only one secondary road to Iruñea (Pamplona). And the march through that mountainous area would require gathering units and refilling vehicles in the capital of Navarre, the ancient kingdom on Basque soil, before they headed southward on the *nacional* 2 highway.

The third border post at Arnegi was not a real option because the secondary route on the continental side of the mountains became "a difficult or dangerous road" on the stretch from Luzaide (Valcarlos) to Zubiri (the current N-135) in Navarre. If the troops and supplies were to land at Bilbo, meanwhile, they would have to take two highways, the *nacional* 21 via Vitoria-Gasteiz and then the *nacional* 22 to Burgos. The German plans do not reveal how secrecy could have been maintained when several thousand soldiers with heavy weapons had a 1,200 km-march ahead of them.

From the military point of view, the weakest points in all these plans were the potential bottleneck at Hendaia and Irun and the fact that only the port of Baiona could be used for Operation Felix. Hence, the main preoccupation of the OKW was how to protect the two border towns against any attacks from air and sea, as stated in a document of November 27, 1940.[4] Due to the secrecy of the operation, the German

4   Hans-Günther Seraphim. "'Felix' und 'Isabella'. Dokumente zu Hitlers Planungen betr. Spanien und Portugal aus den Jahren 1940/1941," *Die Welt als Geschichte* 1 (1955), 54. As the title of this article indicates, Seraphim published German documents relating to the two potential German military operations. Their value is that he completely transcribes the German documents. In 1955, most of the

military could not involve its Spanish partner nor could it build new gun emplacements without risking British air reconnaissance learning about it. Therefore, the OKW and OKH had to think twice about which military measures they should take to enforce the protection of their operation. They thus concluded that, "The positioning of two naval railroad batteries with the support of the army's railroad engineers can be done now because in this area there are still existing naval batteries and that is why any additional installation of further batteries will not expose Felix."[5] At that moment, one 164 mm artillery battery was positioned at Bokale (Boucau), two further 75 mm caliber-ones at the mouth of the Aturri (Adour) River, protecting the entrance to Baiona, and in Zokoa (Socoa), on the western tip of the Bay of Donibane Lohizune. Then, when they finally arrived on July 18, 1941, two 240 mm naval railroad batteries would be placed on the opposite side of the bay.[6]

The OKW and OKH had almost finished their plans when, in December 1940, Hitler put an end to Operation Felix "because the political preconditions are no longer given." Despite all diplomatic efforts, which included a personal meeting with Hitler at Hendaia on October 23, 1940, the Caudillo refused to join the war with the Führer and the Duce. In effect, he could not afford either the military or the political price of such a decision because Spain was in too weak of a position. In any event, the British secret intelligence service (MI6) had also bribed enough Spanish generals and businessmen, whose influence prevented Franco from making that call.[7] At the close of 1940, then, the population of Iparralde had avoided becoming embroiled in a hotspot of war and for the Germans, the strategic importance of the Basque Country had decreased.

German military and political records were still withheld by the Allies and could not be consulted by historians.

5   Ibid., 57
6   Francis Sallaberry, *Aquitaine allemande. Bordeaux - Girond - Landes - Pays Basque* (Biarritz: J&D Editions, 1995), 26.
7   Richard Norton-Taylor, "MI6 Spent $200m Bribing Spaniards in Second World War," *The Guardian*, May 23, 2013, at https://www.theguardian.com/uk/2013/may/23/mi6-spain-200m-bribes-ww2 (last accessed October 8, 2017). For more details on Gibraltar and how the British managed to defend that very important military base, see Nichols Rankin, *Defending the Rock: How Gibraltar Defeated Hitler* (London: Faber & Faber, 2017).

Barbarossa: Another Operation Gives Birth to Isabella

During the first half of 1941, the OKW focused on planning the invasion of the Soviet Union, code-named Operation Barbarossa. That required withdrawing crack divisions, such as SS Totenkopf, from southwestern France and replacing them with lower-strength military units. That is why Iparralde became an area in which young soldiers were trained to become fighter pilots or artillerymen.

Almost six months after he decided to stop Operation Felix, Hitler thought again of Spain, as well as Portugal. The Führer feared that when he attacked his socialist ally comrade Josef Stalin, Prime Minister Churchill would order an invasion of the two fascist states on the Iberian Peninsula, thereby creating a second front at the rearguard of the Nazi Reich. Obviously, Hitler still considered Franco as a very weak partner in military terms. He therefore ordered the OKW to prepare a military operation whose mission would be to expel any potential British expeditionary corps from both countries and to take possession of the Atlantic ports. On May 1, 1941, the OKW passed the Führer's order on to the high commands of the army and the air force.

Once again, from a military point of view Iparralde became important to Germany because it was the sole place from which the Wehrmacht could cross the border into the Spanish state. For that purpose, the Paris-based German high command in the West (Oberbefehlshaber West, Ob West) had to mobilize the sixth, seventh, and eighth armies from its occupying forces. The mission was code-named Operation Isabella on May 9, 1941, and consisted of a plan to occupy the plateau of Old Castile between Valladolid and Madrid. Minor rapid deployed forces would then take the northern coast from Vigo to Santander.[8] The order issued that day does not mention the occupation of Hegoalde. Obviously, it considered the conquest so easy that no special order was required.

Although the mission had changed, German military planners were still dealing with the same logistical problems as the year before because, in the words of the OKH, "foods and fuel in Spain may not be taken from the country."[9] And Iparralde remained a potential bottleneck for any German military action aimed at the Iberian Peninsula. Franco

8   Seraphim, "'Felix' und 'Isabella'," 72.
9   Ibid., 76.

and the majority of his potentially bribed generals were not keen on openly joining Hitler in the war, but at least the OKW received permission to construct an auxiliary railroad bridge at Irun.[10]

In September 1941, the OKW stopped all plans for Spain because Hitler agreed with his foreign affairs minister, Joachim von Ribbentrop, that "political and military relations with Spain may not be interrupted until the next spring, but, on the contrary, they must extended." The supreme command of the armed forces added that, "Military actions on the Iberian Peninsula, though, are unwelcome, until the campaign in the East is concluded—at the earliest in the spring of 1942—and sufficient German forces are available."

The British did not land either on the Spanish or Portuguese coast, and the Germans refrained from making the political situation any more difficult for their Spanish *compañeros* by reducing their active military planning south of the Pyrenean border. Once again, then, Iparralde's military importance for both sides was reduced.

OPERATION MYRMIDON:
A SECRET OPERATION AGAINST IPARRALDE

"When the enemy is at ease, be able to weary him," explains the ancient Chinese philosopher and military strategist Sun Tzu in his famous book *The Art of War*. Perhaps British Prime Minister Winston Churchill was remembering this lesson when he created the Special Operations Executive (SOE) in July 1940—to use guerrilla warfare behind German lines in occupied Europe—and when he ordered the first commando raids against targets on the Norwegian coast after the Wehrmacht had conquered that Scandinavian country.[11]

In the spring of 1942, London was planning new missions to be carried out by its different special forces. As noted, in late March these forces attacked the naval base of Saint-Nazaire. Their mission was to destroy the only port on the Atlantic coast the Kriegsmarine could use for repairing its battleship *Tirpitz*, if necessary. The strategic goal

---

10   Ibid., 77.
11   Kenneth Macksey, *Commando Strike: The Story of Amphibious Raiding in World War II* (London: Secker & Warburg, 1985), 86. Nicholas Rankin unravels another aspect of the secret military and intelligence warfare in *Ian Flemming's Commandos: The Story of 30 Assault Unit in WWII* (London: Faber & Faber, 2011).

was to prevent Berlin from sending the second of two *Bismarck*-class battleships into the Atlantic to attack Allied convoys. Although British losses in the mission, termed Operation Chariot, were high—with 162 soldiers killed in action, and a further 200 taken as prisoners of war (POWs)—the raid was successful in completely destroying the targeted installation. In fact, thereafter, the Kriegsmarine never dared send the *Tirpitz* to this part of the Atlantic. Shortly after the success at Saint-Nazaire, the commander of combined operations, Lord Louis Mountbatten, planned further amphibious operations because the Germans clearly still underestimated the threat of this kind of warfare, "and lived, at the start of 1942, in a state of false security."[12]

In this context, Operation Myrmidon was born. According to its final plan, 400 men of No. 1 and No. 6 Commandos would land at Baiona and attack several targets on land. On April 2, 1942, a small flotilla left the port of Falmouth in southwest England. Two vessels, the *Queen Emma* and *Princess Beatrix*, transported the 400 commandos, and they were escorted by five Royal Navy destroyers. The mission consisted of a plan for No. 1 Commando to first take out the two batteries at the mouth of the Aturri River. Then No. 6 Commando would enter the port and sabotage the cargo vessels docked there, the bridges, the powder magazine, and any factories on its way.[13] The mission also included two intelligence officers who would decide which of the German prisoners should be taken to England for further interrogation about German plans. Depending on circumstances, shipping in the Bay of Donibane Lohizune would also be destroyed, if possible. The mission was scheduled to last only five hours. The main goal of Operation Myrmidon was to damage the only port close to the Spanish border at which the Germans could unload the iron ore they imported from Bilbo. The amphibious landing operation would also exert psychological pressure on the Francoists. Despite some technical problems with an engine on the *Princess Beatrix*, the group reached its operational area nearly on time.

---

12 Macksey, *Commando Strike*, 82.
13 Sallaberry, *Aquitaine allemande*, 145; Macksey only briefly mentions Operation Myrmidon. He does, however, discuss a second mission, Operation National, aimed at striking Donibane Lohizune, which he describes as the reedition of the aborted first mission. See *Commando Strike*, 86–87, 109. French authors like Sallaberry maintain that there were two plans for Operation Myrmidon. The first envisaged the landing of 3,000 soldiers with armed vehicles and artillery. They would attack not only targets at Baiona but along the entire cost of Iparralde down to Miarritze (Biarritz) and even Donibane Lohizune. That mission was scheduled to last seventeen hours but it was scaled down to a smaller operation, Myrmidon II, which took place on April 5, 1942. The disagreement among authors on this topic requires further investigation.

Shortly after midnight the commandos launched their assault landing craft (ALC). These small boats were made of hardwood planks and clad with armor plates. Each of them could ferry thirty-one soldiers, an infantry platoon. Fully loaded, they could speed up to 7 kph (4 mph) but they would lay very deep in the water. This became a problem when the dozen ALC were ready to approach their targets. That was when the Gulf of Biscay taught them why sailors had so much respect for these tricky waters. The fully loaded ALC could not get over either the increasing swell from northwest or an unidentified sandbar caused by the Aturri River. One ALC ran aground and the soldiers therein had to be evacuated. As a result, the commanding officer of the two commando units, Lieutenant Colonel Will Glendinning, decided to abort the raid and called all ALC back.

The commanding officer of the whole operation, Captain Maxwell-Hyslop, then ordered two destroyers to Donibane Lohizune. There, HMS *Calpe* shot flares over the coast that woke up the German soldiers stationed in the town. Together with HMS *Badsworth*, she approached the bay and discovered that there were no ships there. Then she fired some 102 mm rounds toward the coast without causing too much damage. The Germans flashed a spotlight in the Zokoa lighthouse and the two British warships turned around and retreated, laying down an artificial smokescreen in their wake. Four 155 mm guns at Zokoa opened fire as did four 75 mm guns in the fortress. From the same place, 20 mm anti-air guns fired some rounds at the flares, thinking that an aircraft could have dropped them. No single shot hit the British ships. The flotilla was able to escape and headed westward parallel to the coast of Hegoalde. There were no losses, and only one damaged ALC was left behind. It sunk some 10 nmi north of Donibane Lohizune and, on April 6, an auxiliary minesweeper of the Kriegsmarine tried to tow it back to Baiona. At 1:00 pm the German command in the area informed the other posts that no further enemy appearances were expected and gave the all-clear. Only in the afternoon did several reconnaissance planes discover the flotilla some 60 nmi north of Santander, Spain, heading west, too far for the Luftwaffe to attack them.[14] According to the records I have consulted, the German military authorities suspected that there had been a raid on the way but they were never aware that the real target of that operation had been Baiona, not Donibane Lohizune.

---

14   BArch, RM 6/III/252.

IPARRALDE: THE APPENDIX OF THE ATLANTIKWALL

The failed Operation Myirmidon had consequences for Iparralde because similar operations against other German targets followed and yet, on December 14, 1941, Hitler had declared that he wanted the entire West European coastline, from the Cap of the North in Scandinavia to Hendaia, to be fortified. His twin strategic goal was to prevent any landing along the coastline and to free up German soldiers from protecting the coasts because he needed more and more human resources for the increasing numbers of operational theaters in which the Wehrmacht was engaged. At this stage of the war, the priority of this new fortification was Norway, followed by the area between Brest and the Gironde in France. In the summer of 1942 Hitler ordered that the coast in the West had to be fortified. On August 13, 1942, he claimed that a "Fortress Europe" had to be built, with 15,000 bunkers of different types to be constructed through May 1, 1943. By that date, however, only 40 percent of the constructions were finished. After invading the former unoccupied zone of Vichy France, in November 1942, another line of coastal fortifications was erected along the Mediterranean, the so called Südwall (south wall). It is calculated that the Germans used 17 million tons of concrete and 1.2 million tons of steel for the 12,000 bunkers and gun emplacements. The most important sites were at Pas de Calais, the narrowest point of the Channel, because Hitler and the OKW thought that any Allied landing would take place there.

Needless to say, the armed forces fought among themselves over which construction should have priority. And there was another internal quarrel between the army engineers and the Nazi's civil and military engineering group, the Todt Organization (Organisation Todt, OT), about who should be responsible for the constructions work. Before the war, the OT had built not only highways but also major fortifications in the Reich such as the Westwall, named the Siegfried Line by the Allies, on the western border of the German mainland. Finally, the OT won the fight but military specialists, engineers, and geologists also explored the Basque coast and its hinterland, searching for places where they could build bunkers or underground depots and facilities. They also studied the possibility of flooding, if necessary, certain areas. In the meantime, they created new gun emplacements along the coast between Hendaia and Zokoa and based an antiaircraft training school in Miarritze (Biarritz)-Beaurivage.

FROM ISABELLA TO GISELA

The several British amphibious operations in the first half of 1942 led the German military and its commander-in-chief to believe, once more, that the Allies might land an expeditionary force in Spain. In their opinion, the best place for such an operation would be somewhere in the south. On May 29, 1942, Hitler issued Führer directive no. 42, which meant that, in the event of this happening, the Wehrmacht had to take the ports of northern Spain and the mountain passes of the Pyrenees. The operation was code-named Ilona. In fact, it was an update of Operation Isabella. Once again, the high command in the West (Ob West) would send some of its divisions into Spain. In the first phase of Operation Ilona, two tank divisions would race nonstop from Hendaia to Bilbo and Vitoria-Gasteiz. At the same time, two infantry divisions would enter Hegoalde across the Pyrenean passes and head for Iruñea, covering the south flank of Panzer divisions. In a second step, the army units would establish a defense line from Santander along the Ebro River to Zaragoza. The Kriegsmarine would protect and administer the ports of the north, while the Luftwaffe would cover the German advance from the air and reconnoiter enemy forces.

But at that point the fortunes of war decided to change and appeared to favor the Germans. In July 1942, in a North African theater, General Field Marshal Erwin Rommel and his Afrika Korps reached El Alamein, the last major obstacle on the way to Egypt's capital of Alexandria. The defeat of the British Eighth Army and German occupation of the Suez Canal seemed to be only a matter of time. Meanwhile, on the Eastern Front, the German Sixth Army was heading for Stalingrad in the Soviet Union. Taking that strategic city would open up the way to the Caspian oilfields. And what is more, another British landing operation at Dieppe, Belgium, turned into a disaster. As such, Operation Ilona was shelved, although it was given the new codename Gisela after an SS officer reported to his superiors that he had lost confidential documents related to Ilona in a traffic accident.

In November 1942, however, the fortunes of war began to favor the Soviets and the Western Allies. At that moment, the Red Army broke through German lines and trapped the Sixth Army in Stalingrad. Meanwhile, as part of Operation Torch, Allied troops landed in North Africa and sandwiched the German Afrika Korps. Therefore Hitler feared again that his enemies might repeat their success in the form of an extended Operation Torch on Spanish soil, opening up a second front in Europe; an idea on which Stalin insisted. Consequently, Operation Gisela was immediately resurrected and its importance upgraded.

By the new plan, the 715th Infantry Division, based in Iparralde, would occupy Donostia and Bilbao before advancing to take the Galician port of Vigo. Further divisions would follow to protect the north flank. From southern France, now occupied by the Wehrmacht, other units would then enter Catalonia and head westward to take Zaragoza and Valladolid. The Ob West made plans for its units to act as an occupation army in Spain although it thought that Spain would remain friendly to German troops. The OKW approved this plans completely. In late January 1943 Operation, Gisela was ready, but Hitler still needed to be convinced. He then ordered the Ob West that all units involved in the plan should be ready for immediate action because he believed strongly that the Allied landing in Spain was only a matter of days away. The army obeyed its master's voice, acting as ordered, but their enemies did not behave as predicted by the Führer. Finally, in June 1943, he deactivated Operation Gisela and ordered two reinforced regiments to take up defense positions on the Franco-Spanish border. The new operation was code-named Nuremberg.

From the spring of 1943 on, Hitler had to focus on other theaters of the war. In early February he lost his Sixth Army in Stalingrad and in May the German Afrika Korps surrendered to the Allies in Tunisia. Hitler then appointed the latter's former commander, General Field Marshal Rommel, as inspector of French coastal fortifications in November. On February 9, 1944, the former "Desert Fox" visited the artillery emplacements on the Basque coast. There are some pictures showing how German units would convert even the drains of Basque cities into machine gun nests in case of an Allied landing.

Rommel was an expert in mobile war but not in fortification. He carried out Hitler's order and strengthened the so called Atlantikwall by reinforcing the defense position. The main weak point of the Atlantikwall lay in its conception because, according to the German military thinking, it was enough that it would be strong enough to stop any landing forces on the beaches and to repel them back into the channel. This was a plan A without having a plan B in the event that the Allies might break through the fortification line. Rommel argued with the other generals on that very point. Yet neither the OKW nor the OKH discussed the notion of imposing a doctrine that responded to both the potential military threat and the decreasing strength of the Wehrmacht. That would have meant confronting Hitler with the need to give up establishing fixed and fortified lines and to go over to a more mobile warfare. The Führer detested this idea and insisted that everybody had to remain in their position, which had to be defended to the bitter end.

Trapped in this sort of military thinking, Rommel introduced the so called Haltelinie (stop line) some three to five kilometers (two to three miles) behind the coastal fortifications. Experts like him realized that this defense system was too weak to contain an enemy landing in the coastal area. That is, once the Atlantikwall was breached, there would be no further fortification in France capable of stopping an advancing enemy until it would reach the Westwall (Siegfried Line) on the German border.

FORCED LABOR

The fact that the Wehrmacht needed every man to raise new troops obliged the OT to contract foreign workers, if they were considered friendly to Germany, or to forcibly conscript those who did not want to work for the Reich voluntarily. The (male) Spanish refugees in France were in a special situation. On the hand, they feared extradition to Francoist Spain, where prison or even execution awaited them. On the other, they could be arrested by the Germans for being Rotspanier (Red Spaniards) and transported as such to a concentration camp. The SS used to hire Spanish inmates as slave labor in industry and employ them on major construction sites inside the Greater German Reich. The alternative for the so called Rotspanier would have been to desert to the Maquis resistance or to volunteer for the OT.

Occasionally, the German authorities did not give them any opportunity to choose. That was the case of the Basque refugee Leandro Salazar. The Gestapo arrested him together with sixty-four others in different roundups that took place in Hendaia, Kanbo, and Donibane Lohizune on November 1, 2, 4, and 10, 1943.[15] Finally, thirty-nine of them were released but six were deported to Buchenwald concentration camp in Germany, and twenty sent to the OT. Salazar belonged to the last group that was obliged to work for the Siemens-Bauunion (SBU)

---

15 Irargi, Colección Bidasoa C 8/7.

at Baiona. The firm belonged to the Siemens trust. Since its founding in 1921, it had gained experience in several large-scale construction projects such as the subways in Berlin and Athens, for example. From its office in Baiona, on rue Thiers, the OT organized construction work along the Basque coast. Its recruiting office was in the Hotel Régina in Miarritze,[16] and it was run by chief engineer Hans Werner. Salazar and the other nineteen Basques belonged to the 152,000 forced laborers in France who had to construct German fortifications on both the Atlantic and Mediterranean coasts.[17] In August 1944, some fifteen thousand people worked on the coastal construction sites of the Atlantikwall throughout the Aquitaine region. They included eight thousand Spaniards and at least one thousand African POWs. The rest were conscripted French citizens. Two thousand of them had to serve in the Basque Country. In Baiona, one thousand men worked for the Wehrmacht.[18] Salazar was dismissed from his paid work on January 18, 1944. The reasons are unknown. Some historians mention that the German units in Iparralde had little interest in completing the construction of new bunkers because that could mean they would be redeployed to the frontline. Therefore they slowed down the construction.

In the summer of 1944, the Wehrmacht possessed the following positions on the Basque coast. Each of them was gathered in a so-called Stützpunktgruppe (group of positions).[19]

The Saint Anne Stützpunktgruppe covered the coastal stretch from the *muga* to Hendaia. It consisted of six "resistance nests" and two artillery positions. In the former, there were six Russian guns located in bunkers that were camouflaged as Basque farms. The railroad battery was considered the second Stützpunkt.

Saint Jean de Luz Stützpunktgruppe comprised the area from Donibane Lohizune to Getaria (Guéthary). In total, it had three positions and forty-three bunkers. The first Stützpunkt had three antiaircraft guns, the second was substantially better armed and was made up of the other railroad battery that was manned by 550 soldiers. They lived

---

16 Esteban, *Regards sur la Seconde Guerre mondiale en Pays basque*, 130.
17 Manfred. Philipp Holzmann: Geschichte eines Bauunternehmens, 1849 - 1999. München: Beck, 1999, 253.
18 All numbers based on Peter Gaida, *Der Atlantikwall in Aquitanien. Baumeister und Zwangsarbeiter im Dienste Hitlers* (N.p.: N.p., 2014), 195. The term can be translated as a "group of positions" and these were subdivided into "Stützpunkt" (position), meaning mainly artillery emplacement, and "Widerstandsnester" (resistance nests), equipped with lighter weapons such as machine guns.
19 Ibid., 202–4.

in several bunkers that were also camouflaged as Basque farms. The third position was located in an old fortress and armed with one gun. From the land side, the port was protected by several "resistance nests" positioned at the main entrances to Donibane Lohizune.

Bayonne Stützpunktgruppe was made up of five positions and 139 bunkers located between Bidarte (Bidart), Miarritze, and up to Baiona. Two positions protected the beach of Bidart and Miarritze. In Miarritze another position was located in the garden of the luxury hotel that served as a military hospital. It was part of a complex bunker system of caves in the rocks on the Basque coast. The fourth positions had twelve bunkers constructed in the same way on the cliffs of Angelu (Anglet). The last two Stützpunkte were artillery batteries stationed on both shores of the mouth of the Aturri River.

NORMANDY, NOT IPARRALDE

The Allied military planners decided to land in Europe on the beaches of Normandy, not in Iparralde. Thus, June 6, 1944, became D-Day and the date when the liberation of Europa from the Nazi yoke started. Once again, the Basque Country and its northern part escaped devastation, although it did suffer an Allied air raid against Miarritze on March 27, 1944. At least 115 civilians died in the bombing, as well as several dozen German military personnel.[20] The D-Day landings demonstrated that, even at the better fortified places, there was never really an Atlantikwall as such; rather, it was a string of defenses full of holes that at some points had some stronger little knots, as a German general had recognized already in 1943.[21]

As a consequence, the Allied forces built a bridgehead and then started their offensive to liberate France. The second landing, this time on the Mediterranean coast, forced the OKW to withdraw its units that risked being sandwiched. On August 17, 1944, the general order to retreat was given. Four days later, the troops sabotaged and destroyed their installations and depots on the Basque coast. The next day, around twenty-four thousand German soldiers left Iparralde, rushing back to the Reich. They left behind twenty-nine of their Kameraden, who were

---

20   Esteban, *Regards sur la Seconde Guerre mondiale en Pays basque*, 137.
21   Gaida, *Die „Festung Europa"*, at http://www.petergaida.de/Atlantikwall/deutsch/festung.htm (last accessed October 10, 2017).

taken prisoner by French resistance forces. Thus, August 22 became the very special liberation day of Iparralde. Some of the Atlantikwall bunkers on the Basque coast are still visible and stand as silent proof of the time when the German and British military considered this part of Euskal Herria important.[22]

BIBLIOGRAPHY

Burdick, Charles. "Planungen für das Einrücken deutscher Kräfte in Spanien in den Jahren 1942-1943. Die Unternehmen „Ilona" und „Gisela"." *Wehrwissenschaftliche Rundschau* 13 (1963): 164–78.

Esteban, Mitxel. *Regards sur la Seconde Guerre mondiale en Pays basque*. Baiona: Elkar, 2007.

Gaida, Peter. *Der Atlantikwall in Aquitanien. Baumeister und Zwangsarbeiter im Dienste Hitlers*. N.p: N.p., 2014. At: https://books.google. de/books?id=DIq2BgAAQBAJ&printsec=frontcover&hl=de &source=gbs_ViewAPI&redir_esc=y#v=onepage&q&f=false.

———.*Die „Festung Europa"*. At http://www.petergaida.de/Atlantikwall/ deutsch/festung.htm (last accessed October 10, 2017).

Heber, Thorsten. "Der Atlantikwall 1940-1945. Die Befestigung der Küsten West- und Nordeuropas im Spannungsfedl nationalsozialistischer Kriegsführung und Ideologie." PhD. Diss. University of Düsseldorf, 2003. At https://docserv.uni-duesseldorf.de/ servlets/DocumentServlet?id=2613.

Macksey, Kenneth. *Commando Strike: The Story of Amphibious Raiding in World War II*. London: Secker & Warburg, 1985.

Norton-Taylor, Richard. "MI6 Spent $200m Bribing Spaniards in Second World War." *The Guardian*, May 23, 2013. At https:// www.theguardian.com/uk/2013/may/23/mi6-spain-200m-bribes-ww2 (last accessed October 8, 2017).

Pinat, André. "L'opération Myrmidon des 4 et 5 avril 1942 à l'entrée du port de Bayonne." In *Passé, présent et avenir du port de Bayonne: congrès des 16–17 avril 1999*. Bayonne: Société des Sciences, Lettres et Arts de Bayonne, 2000.

---

22 "Die Wehrmacht sur la côte basque de 1940 à 1944," at http://wehrmacht64. canalblog.com/archives/2017/01/27/34860915.html (last accessed October 13, 2017).

Pohl, Manfred. *Philipp Holzmann: Geschichte eines Bauunternehmens, 1849–1999*. München: Beck, 1999.

Rankin, Nicholas. *Ian Flemming's Commandos: The Story of 30 Assault Unit in WWII*. London: Faber & Faber, 2011.

———. *Defending the Rock: How Gibraltar Defeated Hitler*. London: Faber & Faber, 2017.

Sallaberry, Francis. *Aquitaine allemande. Bordeaux - Girond - Landes - Pays Basque*. Biarritz: J&D Editions, 1995.

———. "La Wehrmacht sur la Côte Basque, de 1940 à 1944." *Oihenart* 14 (1997): 217–20.

Seraphim, Hans-Günther. "'Felix' und 'Isabella'. Dokumente zu Hitlers Planungen betr. Spanien und Portugal aus den Jahren 1940/1941." *Die Welt als Geschichte* 1 (1955): 45–86.

Chapter 6

Anti-Semitic Practices in the Service of Nazi Genocidal Plans in the Basque Country

Mixel Esteban

Baiona (Bayonne), January 11, 1944. French officials of the Vichy government were organizing a roundup of Jews in the southwest. Like previous roundups, it was conducted in close collaboration with the Nazi occupiers. But this one was a little different. It marked a new step in the policy of collaboration, since this time, the arrests were to open the door to joint action on the ground by the German armed forces and French law enforcement. The roundup affected Bordeaux and the department of the Gironde, with dozens of arrests of men, women, and children, and more discreetly Baiona and Biarritz, where seventeen individuals were arrested in their homes. They were among the last Jews still present on the Basque coast. It is difficult to say whether the arrests were met by indifference among the neighbors, the wider population, or the numerous Resistance networks in the region. In effect, on issues concerning the Jews during this period, there is little archival material to be found shedding light on the state of local public opinion. Still, it is possible to ask about the circumstances in which the policy of Jewish exclusion leading to genocide took shape: how did the genocide of the Jews develop in the Basque Country, a region without visible public anti-Semitism before the war?

It was during the night of January 10 to 11 that seventeen individuals were arrested. The majority were families originally from Turkey who had arrived in France in the 1920s and settled in Biarritz and Baiona, where they ran boarding houses and businesses. The children were all French, born in France. Shortly after their arrest, the Jews of Baiona and Biarritz were incarcerated in Baiona's Château-Neuf, a barracks converted into an auxiliary jail and placed under French administration. Among the seventeen individuals rounded up in the two cities, ten were members of the same family. They were all "handed over"[1] to the German Feldgendarmerie on January 12, to be transferred by train to Bordeaux. There, they joined Jewish families held in the city's synagogue, turned into a detention center for the occasion. The roundup in Bordeaux and the surrounding region was more significant, affecting around two hundred individuals. They were combined with other Jews arrested earlier, in December 1943, and quickly sent to the camp at Drancy, a group of several sites around Paris transformed into a detention center and guarded by French gendarmes under SS command. They left Drancy, an antechamber of the death camps, on January 20, 1944, departing from the nearby Bobigny-Drancy train station packed into the cattle cars of sadly infamous convoy no. 66. The convoy included 1,153 individuals arrested between September 1943 and January 1944 in fifty-one French departments. Its destination was the Auschwitz-Birkenau extermination camp in southern Poland, where it arrived on January 23, 1944. Immediately, 862 men, women, and children among the deportees were selected for the gas chambers. The others, judged capable of work, were brought to another part of the camp to be dispersed among different *kommandos* for forced labor in nearby factories.

The two administrations, the German Nazi regime and the Vichy French government, jointly carried out the operation of January 11, 1944. Maurice Papon, the prefect of the Gironde, directed the action in the southwest in collaboration with the Vichy government, and Aloïs Brunner, a Nazi officer assigned in June 1943 to relaunch the "final solution" in France, was in charge of directing the German operations. The roundup was part of the policy of collaboration launched by Philippe Pétain in October 1940 following the Montoire meeting,[2] but it also fell within the framework of police agreements between the French and German authorities beginning in the summer of 1942 and the Vel' d'Hiv roundup of July 16 and 17, 1942. Between 1941 and 1944, 76,000 Jewish men, women, and children were victims of deportation in France. The number is striking, but we know that many more Jews would

---

1   AD64, Maison d'Arrêt de Bayonne – Château Neuf - 1338W45.
2   Meeting in Montoire between Adolf Hitler and French head of state Philippe Pétain, October 24, 1940.

have been deported from France without the solidarity of Frenchmen and Frenchwomen in hiding families or the alertness of Jewish families themselves who fled and went into hiding. It is estimated that 240,000 Jews survived in France in this way.[3] Beyond the national figures and well-known events in France, the implementation of anti-Semitic policies in the region of Baiona allows us to understand how deportation became banal, at least for the French officials on the ground who were responsible for implementing the collaboration policy. The deportation of children and teenagers—of the seventeen Jews who were rounded up, eight were between the ages of four and eighteen—undoubtedly constituted the culmination of a quite rapid process that began in late 1940 with simple policies of family exclusion that aroused no known reaction in the society of the time.

INSTITUTIONAL COLLABORATION IN THE SERVICE OF THE GENOCIDE OF THE JEWS

Maurice Halfon was five years old in 1944. Today, he is an American. A resident of the United States, he returned to his native city of Baiona for the first time in August 2015, seventy-one years after he left it. He came back with his son and daughter-in-law in order to introduce them to his history and to the places where he spent his unusual childhood: the childhood of Jewish children in France. In total, 11,600 French children were arrested, imprisoned, deported, and exterminated. Maurice Halfon was saved, like 85 percent of Jewish children in France. He is the sole surviving witness of the roundup of January 11, 1944, in Baiona. As he remembers it:

> It was night, and I think that they knocked very hard on the door. I remember noise in the stairway, shouts also. I was sick. Did I have something contagious? Someone must have asked that I stay there. They said yes. My mother certainly entrusted me to our neighbor Marie Cazaux. She lived above us. She was a seamstress. From that day on, I stayed with her, until the end of the war in 1945. She treated me as her child. I became a different boy. I went to the school in the center of Baiona, the public school, in order to blend in better among the other

---

3   Serge Klarsfeld, *Mémorial de la déportation des Juifs de France* (Paris: Association des Fils et Filles des Déportés Juifs de France, 2012), xvii.

children. I often asked where my parents were, without getting any answer. I didn't know that I was a Jew. Therefore I didn't tell anyone else.[4]

Then the Germans withdrew from Baiona in August 1944. Halfon's uncle, David Bally, who had survived the roundup, returned from Auschwitz-Birkenau at the end of June 1945.[5]

In Baiona, David Bally was one of the rare Jews who had survived the camps. He was greatly weakened and now had to rebuild his life. He sent his nephew Maurice to the United States in 1947, to live with some cousins. "I've never understood why he sent me to them, to a foreign country, where I became a refugee, then an American," Halfon said:

> but maybe it was better for a young child without parents, lost in a Europe that had suffered from the war and where the Jews had suffered. He never told me, despite my letters. He, David, had lost his wife, his daughter, relatives like my parents, including my mother, who was his sister-in-law. Except for me, they were all arrested on the night of January 11 and the following morning, then deported, men, women, and children, to Auschwitz. Only David Bally (thirty-eight years old) and a young cousin, Liliane Badour (nineteen years old), returned.

The majority of the women and all of the children were murdered as soon as convoy no. 66 arrived at Auschwitz. The two survivors were kept alive to perform forced labor at the same camp.

"Visiting this city of Baiona and finding the building and the streets where we lived, I'm sad. It nags at me that I survived, and it's always the same question that haunts me: why was I saved when all the others died?" This question of a psychoanalytical order, affecting the victims of genocide and violence, brings us back to a historical problem, one for which it is still complicated to find an answer: why and how did the genocide of the Jews affect in this way a region like Baiona and the Basque Country, where it was said after the war that the region had been "protected" and that "the Jews suffered very little there"? The answer is complicated because it means researching the microhistory of genocide: the criminal and his accomplice always have an interest in concealing

---

4   Marie Cazaux was declared "Righteous among the Nations" by Yad Vashem on August 18, 2015. In the department of the Basses-Pyrénées (Pyrénées-Atlantiques), there are one hundred and eleven Righteous, five of them in the Basque Country.
5   David Bally, "Matricule 172625: Ceci est mon histoire, récit d'un rescapé des camps," Archives de la famille Bally, Baiona, 2008.

their actions and so in concealing all the evidence for them, while the victim is often living in the silence of trauma. And when the witness says nothing, and time does its work, nothing is left but the institutional archives, where we have been able to confirm a lack of information on the organization of the roundups and arrests carried out by the French police and the gendarmes of the Baiona region. What has to be done is to cross-reference witness accounts, official archives, family archives, contemporary press accounts, and so on. In Pierre Laborie's words on the subject of historical research about this period, "memory is silence." It is "a shifting terrain, a fleeing object, with all the flux and the slipperiness of meaning suggested by those two images."[6]

Moreover, can Maurice Halfon remember that much, more or less accurately, from when he was five, and can he still preserve those memories at the age of seventy-six? The question of the testimony of those involved, those who are still alive, who were all young at the time, becomes ever more complicated as time passes. Even if the facts are authenticated, the details are often absent. And the details are sometimes essential for the historian: who ultimately participated in the roundup of the Halfon family? The Germans, the French, both?

In his writings, David Bally says that "six giants, two [French] gendarmes, three SS soldiers, and an SS officer," arrived at his house at two in the morning on the occasion of the roundup.[7] At the regional level, the documents used in the 1997 trial of the former general secretary of the prefecture of the Gironde, Maurice Papon, demonstrate that the roundup was jointly organized by the Germans and the Vichy police. Maurice Papon was likewise in charge of tracking down and arresting Jews in the region of Baiona. The Jews rounded up in the Baiona region were brought to the Château-Neuf, an annex of the Baiona jail placed under the authority of the French prison system. The only known documents relating to the arrests are the prison registers recording the intake and discharge of each person arrested, indicating the reason for their arrest on the prison lists: they were all declared "Jews." It is thus clear that the documents referring to the organization of the roundup are not very numerous. As a consequence, we must turn to the operational modes of the anti-Semitic policy implemented in the Basque Country during this period in order to try to understand the institutional practices involved.

---

6   Pierre Laborie, *Les Français des années troubles* (Paris: Desclée de Brouwer, 2001), 57–58.
7   Bally, "Matricule 172625."

THE NECESSARY GRADUALISM OF STATE ANTI-SEMITIC POLICY

Even as the works of Serge Klarsfeld and more recently of Robert Paxton[8] have laid out in detail the course of the persecution of the Jews in France, whether foreigners or French natives, the authors have above all described the extensive involvement of the Vichy government and its administration in the implementation of anti-Semitic policies. These policies were simultaneously regulated and methodical: regulated by their official status as state anti-Semitism, methodical for the sake of greater effectiveness. From the beginning of the occupation, the new Vichy regime started by consciously taking advantage of the despair of defeat and the trust placed in Philippe Pétain, the hero of the Great War who became head of state. Public opinion was thus led to put up with daily difficulties, notably in connection with the displacement of refugees in the spring of 1940. Focused for the moment on other matters, this public opinion would very quickly become a subject of interest for the new regime, particularly after the promulgation of what was in effect an entire body of anti-Semitic law and its implementation on the ground. Where the institutionalization of anti-Semitic policy and the method of dealing with the "Jewish question" were concerned, the government would take a gradual approach based in the first instance on exclusion.[9] At Baiona and Biarritz, then, it is easy to understand that it was a matter of managing public opinion, which was decidedly Catholic and humanist, since after all, even though the regime did not get its legitimacy from the ballot box, it still had to try to win support for, or at least a certain indifference to, its planned measures concerning the Jews.

It was ultimately the response by the head of government, Pierre Laval, to a Basque, Jean Ybarnegaray, the brand-new minister of families and youth in July 1940, that revealed the already refined strategy associated with this future anti-Semitic policy. Faced with the ardor of this former parliamentary deputy from Lower Navarre, a far-right xenophobe who was proposing the imposition of quotas or bans on the practice of the professions "targeting individuals of foreign origin" in

---

8   Robert Owen Paxton, *La France de Vichy 1940-1944*, Points Histoire (Paris: Seuil, 1999).

9   Mixel Esteban, "Les Juifs du Pays Basque: De l'exclusion de la citoyenneté à la 'solution finale'," in *Exodes, exils et internements dans les Basses-Pyrénées (1936-1945)*, ed. Laurent Jalabert (Cairn, 2014), 70-97.

France, including Jews,[10] Pierre Laval explained to him that it was better to take the time needed to develop a structured anti-foreigner policy.[11]

The "Statute on the Jews" that was being drawn up was a new body of law, divorced from the values of the French Republic and based on the exclusion of part of the population, denying Jews the fundamental rights of citizenship. The initial provisions excluded Jews from certain jobs, just as Jean Ybarnegaray had proposed for all foreigners in France. Jews who were foreigners, that is, certainly fell within the scope of Ybarnegaray's proposal, but for Pierre Laval and the government, it was above all French Jews who were to be excluded first of all from public employment, the army, management positions, the leadership of press outlets, and the liberal professions.[12] This policy of exclusion was based on the idea of separating the population according to "racial" origin and, through exclusion, transforming Jews into foreigners in their own country, "Israelites" in the Vichy government's terminology. In the Basque Country, the idea was readily implemented by the portion of the political elite represented by the far-right parliamentary deputy Jean Ybarnegaray, enabling us to suppose that some portion of the population was favorable to the ideas of their deputy or of prominent local figures with anti-Semitic views. Already during the period between 1937 and 1939, the very popular Ybarnegaray, who founded the Fédération Française de Pelote Basque (French Jai-Alai Federation) and was a personal friend of the head of the Croix-de-Feu (Fiery Cross), a French nationalist league, Col. François de La Rocque, had been attacking "foreigners." A leader of the far-right Parti Social Français (French Social Party) in Paris, Jean Ybarnegaray had already taken a position with regard to refugees from the Spanish Civil War, as had a number of other prominent figures in the Basque Country. After the fall of the French Popular Front, a political and administrative regime of exclusion targeted Spanish republican refugees, whom Jean Ybarnegaray referred

---

10 Letter from the office of the president of the council of ministers of the Vichy government to Jean Ybarnegaray, minister of families and youth, July 1940, concerning measures to be taken "targeting individuals of foreign origin" practicing professions in France. "Observations sur deux projets de loi soumis à la signature du Chef de l'État," August 17, 1940, Paris. AN F60 46, 197/SG.

11 Tal Bruttmann, *Au Bureau des Affaires juives: L'administration française et l'application de la législation antisémite 1940-1944*, L'espace de l'histoire (La Découverte, 2006), 23-28.

12 Exclusion of Ruben Auguste Posso from his position as clerk of the Bayonne Commercial Court, correspondence of April 1941, Archives Mémorial de la Shoah/CDJC, Paris, fonds CGQJ, April 15 and 25, 1941, CXIV-10.

to disdainfully as "Reds" or "Basque and Catalan separatists" in the daily newspaper *La Gazette de Biarritz* in the spring of 1940.[13]

Other prominent figures developed xenophobic ideas that became clichés in the local press. The emergence of reception camps transformed into internment centers, in the Béarnaise village of Gurs and in the Polo-Beyris district of Baiona, validated a practice of exclusion. The rejection and surveillance of German refugees fleeing Nazism, who were officially considered suspicious beginning in September 1939, would illustrate the banalization of the discourse. Among these refugees, a majority of Jews had fled German-speaking countries and regions since the Nazis came to power in 1933, and others came from the countries of Eastern Europe, where they were fleeing pogroms. In these troubled times, the treatment of foreign Jews was ultimately not a perceptible concern for public opinion, if the local press and the gendarmes' reports are to be believed,[14] and the first collaboration agreements in October 1940 concerned the Jewish population of foreign origin, specifically the transfer of German Jews from the Reich's western *Länder* and Eastern European Jewish refugees in France (18,185 internees, men, women, and children) to the Gurs camp.[15] They joined "suspicious" foreign Jews already there, especially German Jews and anti-Nazi refugees in France, detained in Gurs since the spring of 1940.

The authorities' first efforts were devoted to anti-Semitic propaganda activities, which would continue throughout the period of the occupation.[16] The far right knew its subject here, since it had been engaged in propaganda before the war. However, the prewar

---

13 Article by Deputy Jean Ybarnegaray on the refugees from the war in Spain, in the daily newspaper *La Gazette de Biarritz*, May 27, 1940, ADPA Pôle archives de Bayonne.

14 Archives de la gendarmerie, Service Historique de la Défense, Fort de Vincennes, confidential notes from the Biarritz brigade, GD64.

15 Claude Laharie, "Les camps des Basses-Pyrénées pendant la Deuxième Guerre mondiale (1939-1945): les différentes formes de l'enfermement," in *Exodes, exils et internements dans les Basses-Pyrénées (1936-1945)*, ed. Laurent Jalabert (Cairn, 2014), 51.

16 "To the delicate nose of the average Frenchman, laws against the Jews always carry a nauseating whiff of wars of religion . . . It is time to demonstrate that what is at issue between them and us is something entirely different from different ways of honoring their god or differences of detail in baptismal rites, but rather above all an opposition of races, and that we should refrain from interbreeding with the same care with which the whites of the United States, Aryans or not, protect themselves from an intermixture of black blood." "La question juive," *La Gazette de Biarritz* daily newspaper, January 15, 1944. Mixel Esteban, "Les Juifs du Pays Basque: De l'exclusion de la citoyenneté à la 'solution finale'," in *Exodes, exils et internements dans les Basses-Pyrénées (1936-1945)*, ed. Laurent Jalabert (Cairn, 2014), 94-95.

press archives and those of the locally authorized press rarely show evidence of anti-Semitic propaganda efforts. The strategy developed by the Vichy government and its local administrative arms was based more on a method that appeared simultaneously gradual and discreet, with the consequent objective of seeking to win the support of public opinion or at least avoid a public reaction. Anti-Semitic measures were thus put into place gradually, in stages, following the German and especially the French ordinances. In this way, from 1940 to 1944, the phase of exclusions was succeeded by that of arrests and then by that of deportations. This gradualism required methodical implementation by officials on the ground, relying on the new anti-Semitic laws and sometimes on administrative zeal, to judge by the exchanges between the subprefecture and the Commissariat Général aux Questions Juives (CGQJ, General Commission on Jewish Questions). Where measures affecting families were concerned, an individualization of approach is evident. Hence when the policy of spoliating Jewish property was launched, it too was implemented with regard to certain families and in a gradual fashion. The absence of publicity and communication in connection with the implementation of concrete anti-Semitic measures at the local level constituted an element of discretion with regard to public opinion, in a small geographical area and among a population where people knew one another. The question of time is also relevant. We see rapid phases of the implementation of anti-Semitic measures starting in the first months of the occupation, followed by slower phases occupied with the economic implications of the sale or spoliation of "Jewish property."

IDENTIFY JEWS, LOCATE THEM, LIST THEM, EXCLUDE THEM FROM SOCIETY

More than three months after their arrival in the Basque Country on June 27, 1940, the occupiers implemented the anti-Semitic measures of the German ordinance of September 27, 1940. This ordinance defined the concept of "Jewish race"[17] and prescribed a census of Jews in the

---

17 "Those individuals are recognized as Jews who belong or belonged to the Jewish religion or who have more than two Jewish grandparents (grandfathers and grandmothers). Those grandparents are considered Jews who belong or belonged to the Jewish religion." German ordinance of September 27, 1940, Article 1.

occupied zone by the French prefectural[18] administration. It targeted "Jewish enterprises" that were to be "Aryanized," ordering signs to be posted at businesses, workshops, corporations, and banks where the owners, directors, leaseholders, or shareholders were identified as Jews.[19] Starting in October 1940, signs appeared in the shop windows of many shopkeepers and artisans with the words "Jewish enterprise"in German and French. The occupiers fleshed out their interest in "Jewish property"in another ordinance[20] that placed "Jewish enterprises"under the trusteeship of a "managing administrator"charged with "dejudification." The point was to set up a procedure for liquidating the enterprise for resale, an essential element of "economic Aryanization" known today as "spoliation."This ordinance was implemented in the occupied zone: Baiona, the Basque coast, and part of the rural Basque Country, as far as the line of demarcation passing through Saint-Jean-Pied-de-Port and Saint-Palais. The objective was to deprive families of their resources and bring their daily needs under surveillance, all while making daily life difficult for Jews.

On the basis of its own anti-Semitic legislation, under development since the summer of 1940, Vichy aimed to replace the Germans in the management of "Jewish property" and established a specific administrative body for this purpose in December 1940, the Service de Contrôle des Administrateurs Provisoires (SCAP, Inspection Service for Provisional Administrators). This was the first stage in the creation of a true "ministry of anti-Semitism," the CGQJ, to which the liquidation of "Jewish property"was central from its establishment on March 29, 1941. The CGQJ had a special police force, the Police aux Questions Juives (Police for Jewish Questions), charged with implementing anti-Semitic measures. In Baiona, its intervention took the form of regular inspections of shops declared "Jewish" or in which Jews were employed. Les Dames de France, a department store in Baiona, was a target of these inspections: the subprefecture sent police there multiple times between May and August 1941 for the purpose of verifying with the director whether there were any "Israelites among

---

18 "All Jewish individuals are to present themselves by October 20, 1940, before the subprefect of the district in which they are domiciled or habitually reside, to be registered in a special register. The declaration by the head of a family will be valid for the entire family." German ordinance of September 27, 1940, Article 3.

19 "Every business of which the owner or operator is Jewish is to be designated as a Jewish enterprise by a special sign in German and French." German ordinance of September 27, 1940, Article 4.

20 German ordinance of October 18, 1940.

the senior staff" and confirming that two "Israelite" employees had "no interaction with customers and suppliers."[21] A kind of competition emerged between the German and French authorities with regard to the spoliation of Jewish property. After all, the handling of Jewish affairs became a central element of sovereignty for Vichy, since Vichy's anti-Semitic policies were implemented throughout the whole French territory.[22] It was a matter of economic self-interest, given that sales of Jewish property and tapping the amounts seized from bank accounts under guardianship enabled the payment of the war debt assessed by victorious Germany.

The Spoliation of "Jewish Property" as a First Instrument of Social Exclusion

Initially, anti-Semitic measures were oriented toward spoliation. Between January 1941 and August 1944, we consequently see intense activity aimed at liquidating "Jewish property" under the authority of the CGQJ. In collaboration with the subprefecture of Baiona, the CGQJ handled more than five hundred property cases in the Basque Country and the southern part of the department of Landes. The administration established a network of private provisional administrators charged with managing the seized property and preparing real-estate sales. While the first property administrators were active collaborationists, the complex tasks involved soon required the involvement of legal experts and real-estate professionals: notaries, real-estate agents, lawyers, and architects.[23] In a lackluster economic environment, spoliations represented an economic opportunity for them. They also implicated the banking establishments in which Jewish families' accounts were frozen and placed under the sole supervision and management of the property administrator, who assigned the account owners a monthly allowance for food and personal expenses and used the rest to repay the war "debt" to Germany, the

---

21 Letters from the director of Les Dames de France to his superiors in Bordeaux, May and August 1941, Archives familiales Dalmeyda-Suares.

22 France was divided into two parts, Occupied France in the north and along a long stretch of the Atlantic coast and the French-administered or non-occupied zone in the center and southeast. This partition was no longer effective after November 11, 1942, when German troops entered the southern zone.

23 Marie-Thérèse Chabord and Jean Pouëssel, *Inventaire des archives Commissariat Général aux Questions Juives et du service de restitution des biens des victimes des lois et mesures de spoliation*, Centre Historique des Archives Nationales, Sous Série AJ38 (Paris: Centre historique des Archives nationales, 1998).

basis for which had been established following the French defeat of May and June 1940.

The Baiona subprefect, René Schmitt, thus launched the first "Aryanization" proceedings in the fall of 1940. These were measures of economic exclusion, and hence necessarily of social exclusion as well. One example of "economic Aryanization"—now called "spoliation"—may serve as a good illustration of the method employed.

Isaac Édouard Gommez-Vaëz owned a jewelry store at 13 Rue Port-Neuf in the center of Baiona. He had his shop on the ground floor and lived with his family on the floor above. He descended from a so-called Portuguese-Jewish family, members of the ancient Sephardic community of the Middle Ages who fled the kingdoms of Castile and Portugal in the fifteenth century to settle prominently in Baiona. A small businessman, he and his wife Samuelle had succeeded in acquiring some property with which to ensure their family's future. The building in Rue Port-Neuf had been acquired during the 1920s. Without excess, the family lived there before the war. Without history, they stayed out of political life. They lived their Judaism peacefully and quietly. Were they even aware of any danger in 1940? Certainly, Jewish refugees from the East brought disquieting reports. But how could they imagine that in France, French citizens could be persecuted?

Nevertheless, after the "Jewish enterprise" signs and the first censuses of Jewish families in Baiona, which this Baiona family could not fail to know about, it was from a "managing administrator" appointed by the subprefect that the Gommez-Vaëz family learned that their business and their building were to be the object of an "Aryanization" proceeding. On December 27, 1940, Gaston P. was named managing administrator of the "Jewish" building belonging to the Gommez-Vaëz family. His mission was to liquidate the jewelry store and put the five-story building up for sale.[24] On December 30, 1940, the same day he took up his position, he visited the Jewish family to "invite them to move out," as he wrote in his narrative record of his actions as administrator.[25] In the larger context of anti-Semitic spoliations, this one might have seemed almost banal.[26] However, the personal history of Gaston P.

---

24 Affaire Gommez-Vaëz c/P., ADPA, Pôle archives de Bayonne, 17S17, 1940–1953.
25 Ibid.
26 Several hundred case files exist concerning the "Aryanization" of "Jewish property," including businesses, workshops, corporations, farms, land, and houses, in the Basque Country between 1940 and 1944. See Chabord and Pouëssel, *Inventaire des*

and his family illustrates what was at stake in the initial stages of anti-Semitic policy, based at the time on a form of "activism." The father of the "managing administrator," Armand P., was the Gommez-Vaëz family's neighbor. He had a bookstore and stationary shop on the same street, Rue Pont-Neuf. But above all, he was the local representative of the Parti Populaire Français (PPF, French Popular Party), an anti-Semitic far-right organization founded by Jacques Doriot. This party stood out in the summer of 1940 for threatening Jews and smashing shop windows in multiple cities, with the occupiers' approval. Nothing of the sort happened in Baiona, but the PPF had local activists.

The Gommez-Vaëz family experienced a brutal change in its way of life. Zealously implementing the economic Aryanization procedure, Gaston P. launched the liquidation. Starting on January 4, 1941, the administrator took charge of putting the business's stock up for sale, buying the jewelry himself. The family was ordered to move out four days before this first forced "transaction." But that was not to be the end of the matter. The family's affairs would come to illustrate the tug-of-war between the Vichy French administration and the German authorities on the subject of the management of "Jewish property." Now that it was to be sold, the building was finally requisitioned by the Germans, and then the ground floor became the location of the PPF headquarters. It was not put up for sale until February 10, 1944, and an unexpected event ultimately subverted the spoliation ordinance. On the night of February 17 to 18, 1944, a bomb destroyed the PPF office, causing significant damage to the building. The action was claimed by the Francs-Tireurs et Partisans (FTP, Sharpshooters and Partisans) of Boucau and Tarnos. The attack took place simultaneously with the bombing of other offices of pro-Vichy and collaborationist organizations in Baiona. The Gommez-Vaëz family no longer lived in the building. Having been spoliated and expelled, they left Baiona, where they no longer felt safe. In October 1941, they took "shelter"[27] in Marseilles before finding refuge in a small village in the Aveyron, Saint-Rome-de-Tarn, where they lived with a baker, always hiding their Jewish identity. This forced displacement ultimately saved them.

---

archives Commissariat Général aux Questions Juives.
27 Affaire Gommez-Vaëz c/P., ADPA, Pôle archives de Bayonne, 17S17, 1940-1953.

From Institutionalized Denunciation to Deportation

In Baiona, the local representative of the state, the subprefect, and his hierarchical superiors reaching up to the level of the regional prefect in Bordeaux were charged with implementing Vichy's ordinances, but also those of the German authorities. Always advancing with a prudent regard for public opinion—assessed throughout the occupation by departmental prefects and subprefects in the form of "general observations" sent to Vichy—the government moved to implement the first "Statute on the Jews" on October 3, 1940. This statute defined the "Jewish race."[28] It targeted the entire population of Jewish religion and culture. At first, neither institutional nor family archives show evidence of much reaction within the Baiona Jewish community. Only the young Marcel Suares engaged in individual sabotage activities in the port of Baiona prior to joining the Free French in London in January 1943, and then fighting with the French *maquis,* with whom he was embedded by parachute jump.[29] Grand Rabbi Ernest Ginsburger is also said to have preached anti-Nazi sermons within the community. The Grand Rabbi of Baiona was arrested and deported in March 1942 and died in Auschwitz on February 14, 1943. With his arrest, Baiona lost a significant figure, a spokesman known beyond the Jewish community, and notably among veterans of World War I, in which he had participated.

Finally, perhaps the reactions to the Vichy government that appeared that year were signs of a deteriorating situation. These reactions were expressed by a dozen prominent Jews brought together by Benjamin Gomez, a leading figure in the world of modern architecture between the wars. In early 1942, the group wrote a collective letter to head of state Philippe Pétain, sent by way of Vichy's ambassador to the Vatican, Léon Bérard. Bérard was a former president of the Basses-Pyrénées departmental legislature and a former senator. He was in regular contact with Marshal Pétain and his cabinet. In effect, Léon Bérard's task in Rome was to assess the resonance of French anti-Semitic measures at the Holy See and in Catholic circles. In their letter, veterans of World War I, heads of sports leagues, businessmen, company directors, and the

---

28   "For purposes of this law, an individual is regarded as a Jew if he is descended from three grandparents of the Jewish race, or from two grandparents of the same race if his spouse is also Jewish." Article 1 of the Statute on the Jews of the Vichy government. Proposed text of the Statute on the Jews annotated by Philippe Pétain before adoption of the definitive text at the meeting of the Council of Ministers on October 1, 1940, Coll. Mémorial de la Shoah/CDJC, Paris.

29   Archives familiales Dalmeyda Suares.

former president of the Baiona Chamber of Commerce and Industry, all removed from their positions by the anti-Semitic measures, expressed great confusion, denouncing this mockery of their citizenship: "The Jews are grievously injured in their dignity and their interests. They are subject to a ban on engaging in any kind of business and holding any job that involves interaction with the public, to the freezing of their bank accounts, to the imposition of a fine of a million francs, to a regime of semi-captivity with curfew at eight p.m. and forced residence."[30] In effect, the racial measures restricted Jewish daily life. Shopping, for example, was limited to an hour a day.[31] The Jewish leaders' letter received no reply.

In early 1942, the situation grew worse, Benjamin Gomez affirmed. He wrote at the time to an architect friend in Bordeaux: "We live in fear of tomorrow, anxiously opening our newspaper every day to see whether a new measure has been taken, aggravating the previous ones. We ask ourselves whether tomorrow won't be the gauntlet with all the humiliations and vexations that will come with it, whether the day after tomorrow won't be the concentration camp, deportation . . ." Describing a deteriorating situation, Benjamin Gomez thus attested to a stage in the implementation—gradual and methodical, as we have seen—of the government's anti-Semitic policy. And his letter had the force of a premonition, given that Aktion Reinhard had begun in Poland in the fall of 1941 with the methodical extermination of the Jews of Eastern Europe.

In France, the approach was more gradual, but it led to the extermination of a portion of the Jewish population, with the same objective, confirmed on January 20, 1942, by the Wannsee Conference in Berlin, at which the Reich's Nazi leaders planned the "final solution of the Jewish question." In France, consequently, the occupiers decreed the wearing of the "yellow star" in June 1942. Vichy rejected the star on its territory, in order not to offend public opinion, but it required the notation "Jew" on the identification cards and ration cards of all Jews in France. The Jewish population in the Baiona region was thus subjected to a double restriction, the star and the identification card or ration coupon indicating "Jew." With these new restrictions, Jews became identifiable in public space, a change that brought in its train

---

30 Archives familiales de Benjamin Gomez, ADPA Pôle archives de Bayonne.
31 Letter from Robert Pinède, delegate of the Union Générale des Juifs de France (UGIF, General Union of the Jews of France), to the organization in Paris, October 31, 1942. Mémorial de la Shoah/CDJC, Paris, fonds CGQJ, CDXXIV–15.

a differentiation between populations and the banalization of anti-Semitic measures.

Month by month, the situation thus grew worse, culminating in a new stage starting in 1942: the organization of roundups. This anti-Semitic policy might translate at the municipal level into meticulous surveillance (especially by Vichy-appointed mayors), the compilation of lists, the identification of Jews in public space, and spoliations, in which the numerous proceedings affected families individually. Denunciations were common, but they remained at the same time and above all an institutional matter. In Biarritz, Mayor Henri Cazalis—appointed by the Vichy regime in 1941—thus addressed to the commandant of the Feldkommandatur in his municipality a report on four Jewish individuals under surveillance by the Biarritz municipal police. The letter contained numerous details about the civil status, parentage, movements, and localization of these "Jews." It was dated June 25, 1942, a few days before the July roundups in France. It was based on the anti-Semitic legal measures and correspondingly alluded to the organization of a census: "I write to inform you that a census of the Jews of Biarritz and Anglet has just been carried out."[32] In this context, some individuals with "presumably"[33] Jewish names had to prove their Catholic origin by presenting their grandparents' baptismal certificates at city hall, since the definition of a Jew was based on family ancestry according to the Statute on the Jews promulgated by Vichy.

In 1941, in various municipalities in which Jewish families lived, detailed records of their identity, nationality, address, real property, and even personal property and effects were drawn up by the mayors' offices for the use of the CGQJ.[34] Over the next several months and especially following the new Statute on the Jews of June 2, 1941, "individuals who are Jews according to the law"[35] were to register—under pain of prosecution—at the prefectures and subprefectures, submitting in the process an account of their property. The mayors' offices drew up lists on the basis of this information and took good care to verify the details,

---

32   Letter from the mayor of Biarritz, Henri Cazalis, to the head of the Biarritz Feldkommandantur, June 25, 1942. Archives municipales de Biarritz, letter book, 1942, 277, Dépôt Biarritz, ADPA Pôle archives de Bayonne.

33   This idea of presumption is found in the "List of Jews of Biarritz," in which the 103 individuals identified as Jews include "individuals presumed to be Jews." Archives municipales de Biarritz, Dépôt Biarritz 4H31, ADPA Pôle archives de Bayonne.

34   "Liste des Juifs de Biarritz," concerning 103 individuals identified as "Jews." Archives municipales de Biarritz, Dépôt Biarritz, ADPA Pôle archives de Bayonne.

35   Law of June 2, 1941, replacing the law of October 3, 1940, concerning the status of the Jews and prescribing a census of the Jews.

as indicated by the investigative work described by the Biarritz mayor in his missive to the German authorities.

The gradual implementation of measures of economic and social exclusion, coupled with the identification, localization, and surveillance of Jews, would facilitate the new stage of roundups starting in 1942. On the eve of the great roundup of the Vel' d'Hiv in Paris, thirty-two "Israelites" from the Baiona region, seventeen men and fifteen women, were arrested during the night of July 15, 1942, thanks to collaboration between the occupiers and the Baiona subprefecture. They were immediately transferred to the Mérignac internment camp near Bordeaux. "They took all the foreign Jews younger than forty-five, as well as all the French and foreign Jews younger than forty-five who were in prison, the majority of them detained at the demarcation line," wrote Robert Pinède, a local representative of the Union Générale des Juifs de France (UGIF, General Union of the Jews of France), in a letter to a friend.[36] "I had the opportunity," he continued, "to get to know the majority of the latter, and I was present for the train's departure. Among them was Élisabeth Poliakoff, a Russian woman whose poor mother is now alone in Biarritz. There's still one poor foreign woman who was taken ill and is being treated at the hospital in Baiona. Her two young children were left with her, but once she recovers, I think that she will have to leave and we will have to look after the children." After arriving at the Mérignac camp late in the afternoon on July 16, the Jews arrested in Baiona and Biarritz joined a convoy of more than 170 Jews at the Bordeaux train station. Their destination was Drancy. From there, crowded into boxcars, they left on July 19, 1942, in convoy no. 7 headed to the extermination camp at Auschwitz.

The collaboration between the Nazis and the French administration intensified during 1942. On October 19, the Baiona subprefect drew up a report on a new roundup affecting around thirty other people, all foreign Jews: Poles, Russians, Germans, Latvians, Austrians, refugees from before the war. Vichy targeted foreigners first in order to avoid public reaction. Precisely one reaction is known, but it was a significant one, that of the bishop of Baiona, Msgr. Edmond Vansteenberghe. On September 20, 1942, in the diocesan bulletin, he took a position opposing the Vichy government, notwithstanding his support of Vichy in previous writings on the subject of the family. "Under the pretext of a new order and of

---

36   Letter from Robert Pinède to Maurice Lévy, July 24, 1942. Archives familiales Pinède, Bayonne.

[national] revolution, the worst enterprises of hate . . . are accepted, justified, exalted, [although] the human person is inviolable and sacred." He specified with regard to "the state," meaning Vichy, that "injustice is still injustice, wherever it comes from and whoever its victims are."[37] The German authorities, whose general staff was located in Biarritz, banned the diocesan bulletin after the article appeared. The bishop's intervention was part of a protest movement by a number of French bishops launched in August 1942 by Toulouse archbishop Jules Saliège.

The Baiona bishop's position aroused a reaction from French collaborationist movements, but nothing from the Vichy regime, which paid close attention to the state of Catholic public opinion. These facts are essential, in our view, in order to gain a better understanding of the reason for the distinction in the treatment of foreign and French Jews when it came to arrests in the Baiona region, even if the question of the Jews' nationality was not always clearly posed by the Vichy government as it handed the Jews of France over to the Germans. In effect, French Jews, like the children of foreign parents, remained in great danger, as shown by the roundup of January 11, 1944, in which children were targeted alongside adults. It is thus appropriate to ask, in view of public reactions addressed to Vichy, whether the modes of deportation changed during 1942, with a strategy aimed at initially targeting the foreign Jewish population in Baiona. This point remains to be clarified, but we have been able to confirm that subsequent deportations from Baiona tended to affect foreign families or individuals, generally isolated ones. The small number of families of Turkish origin in Baiona and Biarritz, previously left in peace due to the diplomatic ties between Germany and neutral Turkey (the non-aggression pact of June 1941), were thus, as we have seen, the privileged target in January 1944.

But in order to explain the salvation of the great majority of France's Jewish population, we cannot focus on Vichy's political choices. As we now know, a large proportion of the Jews of France benefited from the protection of numerous Frenchmen and Frenchwomen, but circumstances or their own initiative also favored the "protection" of Jews by themselves. In the end, the Basque Country's geographical situation may thus explain, here at least, the safety of part of Baiona's Jewish community. The Basque Country was in effect a heavily militarized sector, with the confirmed risk of an Allied landing on the coast and two

---

37   Edmond Vansteenberghe, *Bulletin Diocésain* (Bayonne), no. 37 (September 20, 1942): 1–2. Archives de l'évêché de Bayonne.

borders under guard, that of the Pyrénées and that of the demarcation line. These geo-strategic aspects undoubtedly had an influence on the Jewish community's life: at the beginning of May 1943, on the orders of the German authorities, the Jewish population was in large part "evacuated," forced to leave the "banned coastal zone," a militarized space extending along the entire French coast. These families were thus assigned to live in the "southern" zone, occupied beginning on November 11, 1942, essentially in Zuberoa (Soule) and Béarn. A number of families, the Pinède family among them, in fact left the department of the Basses-Pyrénées.[38] Although the Jews were supposed to present themselves to the German security services, the Sicherheitspolizei SD, or the gendarmes upon arriving in their assigned municipality, some managed to be "forgotten." But the times were not always favorable to isolated families, outside the networks that arranged passage or escape to Spain. Wandering in search of a peaceful location, Robert Pinède's family, three adults and three children, thus happened to settle in the department of Haute-Vienne, believing that they had found rest in Oradour-sur-Glane. History decided otherwise when the village's population, including a number of displaced Jews living there, was massacred by the SS armored division Das Reich on June 10, 1944. Only the Pinède children escaped by hiding.

The German troops left Baiona on August 24, 1944. Few of the deported Jews returned. Baiona's hidden Jews returned home, as did those who had been assigned to live elsewhere and sometimes forgotten. But it was then necessary to open proceedings in the courts in order to recover ownership of spoliated property. Some days after the Germans' departure, the Gommez-Vaëz family reclaimed possession of their building in Rue Port-Neuf and their destroyed shop. The damaged building had not been sold, but the merchandise had disappeared. Like other families, they filed a legal claim to have their dispossession annulled and demand reimbursement for their spoliated moveable property. They sued the P. family for the restitution of the value of the merchandise and the repair of the jewelry store. Armand P., for his part, had been killed in broad daylight by unknown assailants on a road on Baiona's northern outskirts in late August 1944, shortly after the Germans' departure. He was a victim of the "wild purification," extrajudicial executions carried out during the first weeks after Liberation. Confronted by the

---

38 Evacuation ordered issued by the Biarritz Feldkommandantur, communicated by the Baiona subprefecture for implementation prior to May 8, 1943. Archives familiales Pinède, Baiona.

Gommez-Vaëz family, however, Armand P.'s wife and his son Gaston did not yield, and the consequent legal appeals were not exhausted until 1953, when the Jewish family finally won their case after nine years of proceedings. These proceedings were the fruit in the first instance of a desire for justice, both for the Gommez-Vaëz family and for other Jewish families, along with a will to see the restitution of the essential point: the status of citizen in a reborn French Republic.

Maurice Halfon himself no longer has property in Baiona, but he maintains family ties with David Bally's second wife and their children. He is still trying to understand why his life as a child and that of his family were turned upside down to such a degree. His incomprehension reminds the historian, the teacher, of a question posed by highschool students: "Sir, why such inhumanity?" And the teacher's reply: "I can explain many things in history to you, but racism and murder are more difficult."

BIBLIOGRAPHY

Chabord, Marie-Thérèse, and Jean Pouëssel. *Inventaire des archives Commissariat Général aux Questions Juives et du service de restitution des biens des victimes des lois et mesures de spoliation.* Centre Historique des Archives Nationales, Sous Série AJ38. Paris: Centre historique des Archives nationales, 1998.

Klarsfeld, Serge. *Mémorial de la déportation des Juifs de France.* Paris: Association des Fils et Filles des Déportés Juifs de France, 2012.

Laborie, Pierre. *Les Français des années troubles.* Paris: Desclée de Brouwer, 2001.

1 – Cover of an anti-Semitic propaganda tract.
Fond d'archives Mixel Esteban.

COMMISSARIAT GÉNÉRAL AUX QUESTIONS JUIVES

VENTE DE BIEN JUIF
par soumission, sous plis cachetés

IMMEUBLE DE RAPPORT
sis à **BAYONNE**
13, rue Port-Neuf

Mise à prix : **400.000** francs

La vente aura lieu à la Sous-Préfecture de Bayonne,
à une date qui sera ultérieurement fixée.

DÉSIGNATION DU BIEN A VENDRE :

Une Maison construite en maçonnerie, élevée d'un rez-de-chaussée et de cinq étages et grenier sous combles.

Superficie : 0 are, 60 centiares.

Le rez-de-chaussée comprend : un magasin avec agencement moderne.
Le premier étage comprend : 3 pièces, 1 dégagement, 1 w.-c.
Le deuxième étage comprend : 2 pièces, 1 dégagement, 1 w.-c.
Le troisième étage comprend : 3 pièces, 1 dégagement, 1 w.-c.
Le quatrième étage comprend : 3 pièces.
Le cinquième étage comprend : 1 grenier sous-pente, 1 grenier sous combles.

L'immeuble ne comportant pas d'entrée au rez-de-chaussée, il est desservi jusqu'au premier étage par l'entrée et l'escalier de la maison voisine qui appartient à Madame Jeanne-Marie DARANATZ, épouse de Monsieur Gabriel HIRIART. L'acquéreur devra s'entendre avec cette dernière qui a obtenu un jugement faisant cesser cette servitude. Dans le cas où toute entente serait impossible, il devrra réintégrer dans l'immeuble les canalisations d'eau, gaz et électricité qui passent actuellement par l'entrée DARANATZ.

RAPPORT BRUT ANNUEL. L'immeuble n'est pas loué mais certaines de ses parties sont occupées et donnent un revenu brut annuel de 7.200 francs.

Cette propriété appartient à l'israélite : M. Edouard GOMMEZ-VAEZ.

CONDITIONS POUR SOUMISSIONNER :

Les personnes intéressées par l'achat du dit bien désirant soumissionner, devront en aviser l'Administrateur Provisoire pour le 10 Mars 1944, dernier délai, sous peine de forclusion, en lui envoyant une déclaration certifiant qu'elles sont aryennes au sens des lois françaises et ordonnances allemandes, et qu'il n'existe entr'elles et le propriétaire israélite aucune entente occulte.

Pour tous renseignements, s'adresser à M. Joseph FOURNIOL, Administrateur provisoire, 8, rue des Gouverneurs à Bayonne.

Fait à Bayonne, le 10 Février 1944.

2 – Sign indicating that a spoliated property is being put up for sale, the Gommez-Vaëz family's building at 13 Rue Port-Neuf in Bayonne. ADPA Pôle archives de Bayonne.

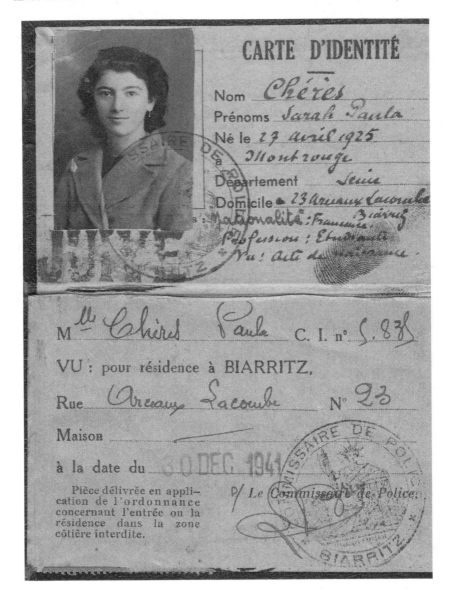

3 – Identification card, dated December 30, 1941, belonging to Sarah Paula Chérès, detained in the Biarritz roundup of January 11, 1944, and murdered at Auschwitz on January 23, 1944, at the age of eighteen. Archives familiales Bally, Baiona.

*4 – Members of the Serez (or Chérès) family, rounded up on
January 11, 1944, and deported to Auschwitz.
The children were four, twelve, and eighteen years old.
Archives familiales Bally, Baiona.*

5 – A battery in service on an Anglet beach.
Archives municipales de Bayonne, fonds Aubert, undated.

6 – German tourists on the Grande Plage of Biarritz.
Archives municipales de Bayonne, fonds Aubert, undated.

Chapter 7

The Basque Intelligence Services in the Americas

Iñaki Goiogana

THE BASQUES, BELLIGERENTS

On June 30, 1937, shortly before abandoning the peninsular Basque Country and heading into exile, in the western Basque town of Turtzioz, the *lehendakari* (president) of the Basque government, José Antonio Agirre, made a public farewell statement. The document was intended to be a proclamation of what had been the guiding principles of Basque government activity in contrast to what the new Francoist regime was applying in its place. At the same time, this brief manifesto emphasized several ideas that had underpinned past Basque government activity and that would form the strong foundations on which the Basque executive operated during forty years of exile.

On the one hand, in his message, Agirre confirmed a military but not a moral defeat: "I have arrived at the borders of Euzkadi [the Basque Country].... While its territory may have been conquered, the soul of the Basque people has not; nor will it ever be." On the other, he reaffirmed his intention to come back and the objectives for that moment of return: "We will recover the land of our people in order to restore our ridiculed language, our insulted laws, our stolen freedom," given that fascism was not the solution. Finally, in this farewell document, the lehendakari also reaffirmed the legitimacy of the institution over which he presided, "because it interprets the feeling of a people, which has not been beaten, but temporarily browbeaten and insulted. And the affection of our compatriots will accompany it until victory day."[1]

In the cited text mention was also made of foreign intervention in the civil war, which, in Agirre's opinion, had facilitated Franco's victory in the conflict. Meanwhile, the lehendakari reclaimed the aid of "friendly peoples" in order the aforementioned wishes.

As long as the civil war continued, the struggle would center on Spanish terrain, but once the Republic was defeated on April 1, 1939, and a democratic system was replaced by Francoism, the theater of operations would be transferred to another scenario, initially that of Europe, and thereafter onto a global scale.

In the opinion of the Basque leaders and, especially, Agirre, there was no major change from one war to another. Ultimately, World War II was just the continuation at a global level of a struggle that had begun in July 1936 with the uprising of Spain's Army of Africa. And this continuation of the struggle, which began in 1936, made the Basque cause fully belligerent in the war.

Agirre repeated these ideas in a public statement of April 16, 1939, in response to the adhesion in late March that same year of Francoist Spain to the so-called Anti-Comintern Pact. This had originally been signed on November 25, 1936, by the German Reich and the Japanese Empire, with the aim of isolating the Soviet Union; an international agreement to which Italy subscribed one year later, on November 6, 1937.

In that note, Agirre, speaking on behalf of the vast majority of Basques, denied any legitimacy whatsoever to the Spanish dictator Francisco Franco when it came to representing Euskadi and, therefore, in signing any pact. The lehendakari understood that the Anti-Comintern Pact, like any other similar treaty to which the Generalísimo may subscribe, "constituted acts of vassalage with totalitarian powers, transforming fundamentally democratic peoples like the Basque people into forced instruments at the service of the Italo-German plan against the democracies, especially Great Britain and France."[2]

---

1   Manifiesto de Trucíos, June 30, 1937, at https://es.wikisource.org/wiki/Manifiesto_de_Trucios.
2   "Ante los pactos del General Franco. Una nota del Presidente Aguirre," *Euzko Deya*

The lehendakari recalled that Italo-German forces had fought against Basques and that Euskadi, at the time of publishing the note, was "the vanguard point of the totalitarian axis of military elements." For all those reasons, the Basques, according to Agirre, rejected all forms of dictatorship and reaffirmed their struggle "exclusively in favor of national freedom and on the basis of universal principles inherent to human dignity." Furthermore, Agirre contended that the will of the Basque people was "to continue being loyal to the democratic peoples, defenders of the postulates for which [it had] fought."[3]

Some months later, in September 1939, at the official start of hostilities in Europe on account of the invasion of Poland by Germany and in a much more delicate situation than April that same year, the lehendakari again repeated the commitment of the Basque government to the democracies represented by the United Kingdom and the French Republic. On this occasion, Agirre said the following: "The intransigent spirit of totalitarianism, of domination, has provoked a war against the spirit of freedom, of human personality, and the independence of peoples. The freedom of men and of peoples is defended by France, England, and their allies. Basques cannot accept any spiritual neutrality in such a struggle. The triumph of Hitler would be the slavery of all peoples, including ours. The victory of the Allies would be the victory of our spirit and of our cause."[4]

Following the same line of argument, the lehendakari, in a document sent to the representative for Gipuzkoa and political head of the Basque intelligence services, José María Lasarte, titled "The international situation in relation to the interests of Euzkadi," he outlined the international panorama and how the Basque leaders were perceived in Paris "after very interesting conversations and consultations." In the cover letter to the document, Agirre clearly affirmed that, with the outbreak of hostilities in Europe and the declaration of war on the part of Great Britain and France against Germany, they were entering into "a new era in our history."[5]

156, April 16, 1939.

3   Ibid.

4   Declaraciones de José Antonio Aguirre incluidas en una carta circular de Javier de Gortazar, September 15, 1939, GE-42-9.

5   *Dossier de instrucciones de José Antonio Aguirre para José María Lasarte*, including: "Carta de José Antonio Aguirre a José María Lasarte," "Informe de José Antonio Aguirre sobre la situación internacional en relación con los vascos," "Informe de José Antonio Aguirre sobre la situación legal de los exiliados vascos en Francia," "Instrucciones de José Antonio Aguirre para la Oficina del Censo," and "Instrucciones de José Antonio Aguirre para comunicarlas al interior," September

As regards the panorama that would open up as a result of the recently initiated conflict in relation to Basque interests, the Basque president contemplated two possible scenarios: a first, in which Germany, following resounding victories in the East, would offer peace, forcing France and the United Kingdom into a corner over a refusal of the offer and thereby prolonging the war. In this scenario, the lehendakari viewed Italy and Spain as mere secondary players following in the wake of the Reich. Agirre continued with his analysis, contending that the democratic powers were steadfastly determined to not accept any offers of unilateral peace. In this case, the lehendakari asked rhetorically what position Italy and Spain would adopt, a question he answered by saying that both countries, sooner or later, would enter (or perhaps not) the war, but that whatever the case, they would support Germany. This was an ambiguous position that did no favors at all to the democratic powers. Agirre predicted that, "if they were to go to war rashly, which should not be ruled out, their destruction would be obvious." The second scenario predicted by Agirre was a war in which Spain and Italy would remain neutral. For this eventuality, Agirre predicted a significant internal change that would destabilize the Franco regime.

According to the lehendakari, the ongoing struggle was not for the Danzing corridor or any other military target. It was, "a struggle of civilizations and of totally distinct concepts," in which, with the triumph of "totalitarianism, freedom would suffer a long-term eclipse, since the methods of force would impose, even against the will of peoples, their brutal methods." On the contrary, "the triumph of democracies would, naturally, change the face of more or less totalitarian systems in the world and their fall would be inevitable."

In the face of all this, the lehendakari argued that the Basque position could only be that of "energy and underscoring, increasingly clearly, our personality." The lehendakari attested the document, declaring that, "our role will depend on how well we situate ourselves and how well we keep our personality in the spotlight. No one hears those that do not speak."

These three solemn declarations by Lehendakari Agirre, published at three critical moments of national and international crisis—the loss of

---

11, 1939, in Iñaki Goiogana, Xabier Irujo, and Josu Legarreta Josu, eds., *Un nuevo 31. Ideología y estrategia del Gobierno de Euzkadi durante la Segunda Guerra Mundial a través de la correspondencia de José Antonio Aguirre y Manuel Irujo* (Bilbao: Sabino Arana Fundazioa, 2007), 110–23.

Euskadi to the Francoists, the latter's adhesion to the Anti-Comintern bloc, and the outbreak of what would be World War II—and his analysis of the international situation sent to Lasarte, demonstrate that was total congruence between the Basque government's ideas and the values defended by the western democratic powers. But it did not escape the Basque president's attention that the adhesion he proclaimed would have to be demonstrated in acts, not just in manifestos.

THE BASQUE INTELLIGENCE SERVICES

This is why the Basque autonomous administration made a great financial effort to maintain, so that they were not a burden for the French state, the thousands of Basque exiles. With this aim in mind, the Basque government counted on a network of refuges, schools, and health centers in order to attend to the most urgent needs of its people. Furthermore, it was a Basque government rule that the people it administered should not be the cause of any scandal in the land that had welcomed them and that the Basque exile population complied with everything the French authorities demanded of them.

Yet even this was not sufficient. Not being a nuisance or the cause of any scandal was the minimum that the country welcoming them in could expect in order to be tolerant of the exiles. That is why the Basque government always sought something similar to be indispensable in the eyes of the western powers: that is, to be a necessary and useful agent and not, at most, a bump on a log or a nuisance in the concert of nations.

To some extent, the Basque government managed to achieve this role of actor in the theater of operations, or at least that a Basque institutional presence would be accepted by the democratic powers (however minimally), through its intelligence services and the reports they were able to send, mainly to the French authorities and via them to the British, before the fall of France during May and June of 1940.

Among other sources that speak about the activities of the Basque intelligence serves, we have a report drawn up with the aim of informing Auguste Champetier de Ribes, senator for the Basses-Pyrénées, undersecretary of state for foreign affairs, and member of the Liga Internacional de Amigos de los Vascos (International League of

Friends of the Basques, LIAB), about the activities of the services for the French government.[6] The report, dated September 1939, was drawn up at an especially sensitive moment for the French authorities. World War II had been declared and Spain's position was unclear, although, following the signing of the Anti-Comintern Pact by Franco, only the worst was to be expected on the Pyrenean front, especially by France.

This report begins by stating:

> For more than two years Basque groups taking refuge in France have established an intelligence service both in the Basque Country and in Spain. Numerous relations were established with the competent bodies in the French army with this mission, but from April 27, 1939 on there has been both a daily and steadily organized link and relationship between the Basque bodies and the French authorities.[7]

The intelligence services the aforementioned report refers to had been created at the start of the civil war, before even the Basque government was established, by the Partido Nacionalista Vasco (Basque Nationalist Party, PNV) with the goal of creating a link between Bilbao and Lapurdi. Following the creation of the autonomous executive in October 1936, these services came under the authority of the Basque government and continued to carry out their function as a point of union between the exterior and interior of Euskadi.

When the Basque territory fell into Francoist hands, with the so called Pact of Santoña, the subsequent rendition of the Basque army, and the imprisonment of *gudaris* (Basque soldiers) and Basque nationalist leaders in El Dueso prison, the recently exiled Basque leaders were faced with a serious problem of communication between the authorities living freely abroad and those leaders that had decided to take their chance with the incarcerated soldiers.

José María Lasarte contacted Bittori Etxeberria, an old member of the women's nationalist organization Emakume Abertzale Batza (Women's patriotic section, EAB) in Baztan (Navarre). Because of her political activism, at the outbreak of the civil war she had been sent to Pamplona-Iruñea, but later, after returning to her home town, she had helped numerous politically persecuted people flee across the Spanish-

---

6   *Informe sobre actividades de los Servicios para Auguste Champetier de Ribes* (September 1939), in Goiogana, Irujo, and Legarreta, eds., *Un nuevo 31*, 139–45.
7   Ibid., 139.

French border. He got in contact with her to find out about some way to create a channel of communication between the exiled authorities and the Basque nationalist leaders that had handed themselves in alongside the gudaris, because he believed it to be his responsibility to do so and in order to organize the resistance from within. In a short space of time Etxeberria was able to create a network of women who vowed to carry out the work requested by Lasarte, thereby establishing a flexible means of communication that demonstrated its efficiency.

This budding network, formed mainly by women, did not just serve as a means of exchanging political information between the two wings of the Basque leadership. On account of the handing over of Basque prisoners by Italian volunteer troops to the Spanish, in contravention of the Pact of Santoña, and the immediate beginning of summary trials against the prisoners (with the subsequent death penalties and executions), the Basque executive soon learned about the harsh reality of the prisons. Agirre's government, having been informed quickly and precisely about the repression taking place in the prisons, and making use of this information, was able to make official complaints and demand clemency to the international civil and ecclesiastical authorities so that they may requests for pardons to the Francoist agencies.[8]

This budding communication network between the different parties and humanitarian aid for the prisoners developed in a short space of time to the point of becoming a true intelligence network, as well as functioning as a clandestine structure for the interior-based PNV in the Basque Country itself. In this sense, in the abovementioned report drawn up for Champetier de Ribes it is stated that work was carried out in the area of military information, confidential studies of a political, economic, and religious nature, and daily examinations of the media (the radio and written press).[9]

---

8   On the Basque intelligence service see Juan Carlos Jiménez de Aberasturi Corta, *De la derrota a la esperanza: Políticas vascas durante la Segunda Guerra Mundial (1937–1947)* (Oñati: IVAP, 1999), 141–73; Josu Chueca, "Emakumeak erresistentziaren haziak," in *Emakumeak hitza eta bizitza. 90 urte Emakume Abertzale Batza*, ed. Begoña Bilbao Bilbao, Gurutze Ezkurdia Arteaga, Karmele Perez Urraza, and Josu Chueca Intxausti (Bilbao: Euskal Herriko Unibertsitatea Argitalpen Zerbitzua, 2012), 123–40; and Juan Carlos Jiménez de Aberasturi Corta and Rafael Moreno Izquierdo, *Al servicio del extranjero. Historia del servicio vasco de información de la Guerra Civil al exilio (1936–1943)* (Madrid: Antonio Machado Libros, 2009), 119–235.

9   *Informe sobre actividades*, 140.

As regards the military information gathered by the service, in the report it is stated that questionnaires sent by the French authorities on specific topics were filled out. Additionally, the Basque service sent reports to the French spy network on troop movements in Euskadi and the border area, the location of troops in the Spanish army, fortification works being carried out in the Pyrenees, data on the arms industry output, data on the location of and activity in aerodromes as well as plans and activities relating to Italian and German planes and arms sent to Spain.

As well as drawing up reports requested by the French services, in September 1937 and with some of the information received the Basque intelligence service—often termed Mimosas after the name of the lodge in Baiona (Bayonne) that housed its headquarters—began to prepare a weekly information bulletin that was expanded in January 1939 with supplements on religious and political information. These confidential reports continued to be drawn up without interruption until at least March 1940.

With regard to the diffusion of these bulletins, in July 1938 Lasarte informed Antonio Irala, the lehendakari's secretary, that fifty copies were being distributed to the leading figures in the Basque government and several of its delegations, the exiled Spanish ministries of government, agriculture, state, and defense, as well as Manuel Azaña (president of the Spanish Republic), Manuel Irujo, Indalecio Prieto, Julián Zugazagoitia, the Spanish consulate in Hendaia (Hendaye), and the PNV leadership, together with some copies kept in the archives in Mimosas.[10] In this statement, the reports sent to the French were not mentioned.

OFFERS TO THE FRENCH AND BRITISH

With the outbreak of World War II, the French and British governments began to show interest in new services offered by the Basques in different areas to those explored to that point: namely, propaganda work in favor of the Allies to be carried out in Latin America.

An unsigned report that was not addressed to anyone, but whose author was probably Pablo Azkue (the former director of the

---

10   Letter from José María Lasarte to Antonio Irala, July 13, 1938, Archivo del Nacionalismo Vasco, Sabino Arana Fundazioa, Bilbao, DP-1.544-03.

daily newspaper *Euzkadi*) and sent most likely to the Euzkadi Buru Batzar (EBB, the national executive of the PNV), dated January 22, 1940, deals with these offers to the French and British governments. According to this report, an extensive project was initially prepared although this was not presented to the French government; instead, it received a more specific plan. By the time an offer of cooperation in Latin America was sent to the French, in late 1939, another proposal was sent to the British. The Ministry of Information in the UK took an interest in this latter plan and sent its person in charge of British propaganda in Latin America to Paris to meet with the lehendakari.

At first, the French replied to the Basque offer by saying it would be better to postpone any discussions for the time being, claiming political reasons related to Franco-Spanish diplomatic relations. On the contrary, Kenneth G. Grubb, the British delegate who visited the lehendakari in Paris, was very satisfied both in regards to the meeting with Agirre and the offer of cooperation. He said he endorsed the idea, although his superiors in the British Ministry of Information had the final word.

According to another report, dated February 29, 1940, on the visit of Francisco Basterretxea to the offices of the PNV journal *Euzko-Enda*, the French had still not accepted the Basque offer although there were high hopes for a change in their position. Meanwhile, the British had accepted the offer and by this time, José Ignacio Lizaso and Manuel Irujo, the Basque government delegate and the former minister in Spain's republican government resident in England respectively, began to cooperate with the British Ministry of Information by writing articles in the press releases by the ministry aimed at Latin America.[11]

In the spring of 1940 the situation in which Basque exiles were living in the French state had changed substantially since the end of the war in Spain. While still not good, it was in no way like the chaos resulting from the fall of Catalonia. One way or another, many of the exiles had adapted to the new situation of exile. The refuges and health centers, such as that of Le Rosarie, which the Basque government had established on French soil between the fall of Bilbao in the summer of

11   *Los vascos peninsulares en servicio de Francia*, September 19, 1939, Report on a visit by Antonio Irala to Euzko-Enda, January 22, 1940; *Visita de D. Francisco Basterrechea a "Euzko-Enda"*, February 29, 1940, Archivo del Nacionalismo Vasco, Sabino Arana Fundazioa, Bilbao, PNV-362-3. On the visit of Kenneth G. Grubb to Paris and the Basque offer to cooperate with the British, see Archivo Histórico de Euskadi, GE-44-5 and GE-247.

1937 and the winter of 1939, were emptying. Moreover, those Basques interned in concentration camps, which had been set up by the French state to take in male republican exiles without anywhere else to go, were finding jobs mainly in the French arms industry. This industry had been saturated with work as a consequence of the outbreak of war in Europe and the demand for labor in the wake of young men in France being conscripted to fight. Moreover, some hundreds of Basques had managed to get passages in order to emigrate to the Latin American republics, and the Basque government itself had sent out instructions for anyone who did not have reasonable motives for fearing Francoist repression to return home. For all of that, while there were still thousands of people who depended on aid given out by Agirre's executive to live in exile, many were able to survive on their own and were not a strain on the Basque treasury.[12]

Parallel to the improving general situation of the exiles, and at the behest of the PNV, the Basque government adapted its political objectives to the new situation of exile and the (at first potential and later effective) war in Europe. The Basque Nationalist Party understood that, with the end of the civil war, a new period of conflict was beginning. During this time, on the one hand, the Basque parties would have to formalize a national declaration, with those of a state allegiance breaking away from their original Spanish parties; and, on the other, the PNV asked Agirre's executive to dedicate its time to the work of national policy, reducing as much as possible spending on budgetary items destined to aid the refugees. This request for a national declaration and to adapt the work of the Basque government to more political than aid tasks consumed Agirre's time for several months in 1939 and 1940. In the end, though, he was able to reach an agreement with the Basque socialists, the main targets of the appeal for a national declaration, in early May 1940.[13]

On May 8, 1940, just hours before Agirre would leave for Belgium on vacation with his family in the Flemish town of De Panne-La Panne, the lehendakari met with a delegation of the Comité Central Socialista de Euzkadi (Central Socialist Committee of Euzkadi, CCSE) to finalize the remaining details of a draft government plan on which the future Basque administration would be based. Within this draft plan,

---

12   Gregorio Arrien and Iñaki Goiogana, *El primer exilio de los vascos. Cataluña 1936–1939* (Bilbao: Fundación Sabino Arana and Fundació Ramon Trias Fargas, 2002), 389–532.

13   Ibid., 553–98.

in the section on fundamental principles, it was stated that the Basque government would develop all future activity based on the following principles:

(a) On the existence and recognition of Euzkadi as the Basque national entity.

(b) On Basque solidarity and fraternity both among individuals and among the regions of Alaba, Gipuzkoa, Nabarra, and Bizkaya [the original spellings in the document], the territories to which the Basque will, expressed in plebiscite, historical solidarity, and the current Basque purpose extended.

(c) On the gaining of Basque freedom to the extent and proportion determined by the free will of Basques.[14]

On the basis of these principles, within the foreign policy regulations, the plan resolved that the Basque government would tighten the bonds that linked it to peoples who maintained democratic forms of government and, once war was declared, the rules to be followed should be developed and established on the basis that: "(a) The Basque government rejects spiritual neutrality in a conflict in which the freedom of men and peoples is defined as being against tyranny and force. Its position is one of spiritual belligerence and maximum material support in favor of the democratic nations in their struggle against totalitarian dictatorships." Points (b) and (c) then went on to condemn the Nazi-Soviet Pact and ratified the abovementioned public protest at the Anti-Comintern Pact.[15]

The signing of this document, containing a national declaration and a governmental program for the Basque executive agreed to by Socialist representatives and the lehendakari, was postponed until Agirre's return from Belgium, following his vacation. But that opportunity never arose due to German's invasion of Holland, Belgium, and Luxembourg beginning on May 10, 1940, which, within a month and a half, led to the fall of France and the subsequent Franco-German armistice on June 22 that same year.

---

14 *Proyecto de programa para el Gobierno de Euzkadi*, April 12, 1940, in Goiogana, Irujo, and Legarreta, eds., *Un nuevo 31*, 210–11.
15 Ibid., 211.

THE FALL OF FRANCE

The Allied disaster, saved in part by the evacuation of British troops from Dunkirk, did not just result in the fall of France into German hands, but it also caused chaos among the Basque exiled community and, more specifically, its government. The lehendakari was stuck in Belgium, unable to return to Paris, and the rest of the ministers, with the exception of Ramón María Aldasoro who was at the time in Buenos Aires, together with other leaders and functionaries, had to flee as best they could from the French capital. Some of them managed to reach a precarious safety in the south of France and in Iparralde (the northern Basque Country). Others, meanwhile, found equally provisional refuge in what was beginning to be termed the free zone, French territory administered by the collaborationist Vichy government, especially in Marseille.

The French collapse also impacted on the activity of the Basque intelligence services. The occupation of Paris by the Germans was of enormous benefit to Spanish agents belonging to the Commission for the Recuperation of Material in France in seizing the holdings of the Spanish Republic in the country.

Thus, among the buildings broken into by Francoist agents in order to seize the possessions there was the headquarters of the Basque government's Paris delegation, the de facto central headquarters of the Basque administration. All the Basque government presidency documentation as stored in the building, located at 11 Marceau Avenue. The person in charge of it, Secundino Urrutia, received—on an incorrect date, but around May 20—the order to box it up sufficiently well for its evacuation. The packages prepared by Urrutia (six metal filing cabinets, three wooden boxes, one wicker basket, and twenty-one packets) left the Paris headquarters on June 5 but never arrived at their destination, the Brittany home of the French representative Ernest Pezet. According to urrutia, the Basque presidential archive fell into the hands of Spanish agents on account of the chaos that governed Paris in the days prior to German occupation and the betrayal of some Basque exile.[16]

---

16   Reports by Secundino Urrutia on the evacuation of the presidency archive of the Basque government, titled *Asunto archivo*, June 15, 1940 and July 20, 1941 and Inventory of the archive of the presidency archive of the Basque government, Archivo del Nacionalismo Vasco, Sabino Arana Fundazioa, Bilbao, PNV-100-6.

Celestino Urrutia, as well as packaging the archive, made an inventory of the documentation he was looking after and we therefore know that the metal filing cabinet number one contained Agirre's correspondence with Lasarte between 1937 and 1940, a sealed envelope with secret information from Lasarte, as well as information of a military nature on the German and Italian intervention in Spain, and so on. Among these papers, Spanish agents came across a report titled "Interior service," dated March 15, 1939, in which the necessary work carried out by the domestic network of the Basque intelligence service to the date of the report was outlined in some detail.[17] With this report in their hands and, after identifying the agents of the so-called interior service camouflaged by pseudonyms, in December 1940 and January 1941 the Spanish police was able to arrest the members of this clandestine network, with all of its members succumbing to arrest.[18]

TO THE AMERICAS

While Spanish agents were searching the seized headquarters of the Paris delegation, the lehendakari was in Belgium without being able to return to France or embark on the British military evacuation in Dunkirk and thereby flee to the United Kingdom. With such escape routes closed to him, Agirre's only option was to, first, go into hiding in Belgium and, later, in January 1941, attempt to reach freedom by crossing Germany. Finally, together with his family, he managed to board a ship in Sweden heading for Rio de Janeiro on July 31, 1941, arriving on August 26 that same year.[19]

In setting out on this journey via occupied Europe, it is highly likely that the lehendakari intended to settle in Buenos Aires, rather than New York, as was actually the case. This was because, among other reasons,

---

17　This domestic service was also known as the Álava Network (Red Álava), after Luis Álava Sautu, the main person in charge.

18　Trial 103.590/1940 against Luis Álava and others, AHGD, 1929-4 and 1930-1. The members of the interior service or Álava Network were tried in 1941 and all but one of them sentenced to death on the charge of "supporting rebellion." However, because the legal compliance auditor disagreed with the decision, the supreme court tried them again in 1942, this time sentencing them to different prison terms, except the main leader of the network, Luis Álava, who was sentenced to death and executed on May 6, 1943 in Madrid.

19　On Agirre's escape to the Americas, see José Antonio de Aguirre, *Escape via Berlin: Eluding Franco in Hitler's Europe* (Reno: University of Nevada Press, 1991) and José Antonio Agirre Lekube, *Diario 1941–1942* (Bilbao: Sabino Arana Fundazioa, 2010).

of the large population in Argentina of Basque extraction as well as the warmer political welcome extended to him. This was evident as revealed in the Argentinian government's decree of January 20, 1940, enacted by President Roberto M. Ortiz Lizardi, facilitating Basque immigration into the country.[20] The hypothesis of the Argentinian option as a final destination for Agirre's journey is confirmed by a July 11, 1941 entry in his diary of the odyssey through the Reich and Sweden. That day, the lehendakari noted: "Today we had a geography lesson describing the Gothenburg-New York-Buenos Aires-Euzkadi itinerary, which is the one we're planning to follow if God does not determine otherwise."[21]

However, Manuel Ynchausti's work on behalf of Agirre both with the academic authorities at Columbia University in New York and the US State Department resulted in the former hiring the lehendakari as a history lecturer, thereby enabling him to give classes. The lehendakari understood that, "this appointment will put me in an advantageous situation for my necessary work and travel on behalf of our cause." Indeed, the lectureship offered him an unbeatable calling card, according to Agirre.[22]

On arriving in New York on November 6, 1941, Agirre met with both colleagues and old friends who, since 1938 but especially since the outbreak of hostilities in Europe, had not been idle. Manuel Ynchausti and Manu de la Sota, making the most of old acquaintances and other contacts, had established relations with governmental and paragovernmental agencies as well as maintained contact with the British secret services, established in the US partly in order to gather information and partly to influence American public opinion in favor of intervening in the war, thereby abandoning isolationism, the latter a policy that enjoyed widespread support in the country.

FIRST THE BRITISH:
THE BRITISH SECURITY COORDINATION (BSC)

In effect, while the Americans allowed Agirre to enter the country as an exile and university professor, permission that the US government of the time did not grant very easily, the first people to show an interest in

---

20 Arrien and Goiogana, *El primer exilio*, 521–26.
21 Agirre Lekube, *Diario 1941–1942*, 97.
22 Ibid., 133.

the Basques were the British. Thus, in his diary entry for November 24, 1941, the lehendakari noted: "I received the delegation of English heads of the South American service. They all left satisfied with their letters of introduction to all our delegates. Later, I was visited by the English representative here who deals primarily with the Iberian Peninsula service."[23] It was not the first visit. The British had already visited him a few days earlier, on November 20, one of them being the aforementioned individual in charge of Spanish matters who, according to Agirre, sought the union of Spaniards since "the attitude regarding Franco is changing radically."[24]

Already with these visits and the topics discussed therein the British were defining their interests and the areas of influence at that time in which the Basques could be of use to them: on the one hand, Latin America, and on the other, Spain. In both theaters of operations the assistance sought by the British agents centered on the search for information and propaganda efforts.

This early British interest in the Americas can be explained by the isolation the United Kingdom found itself in at that moment in the war. In short, France was defeated, the Soviet Union neutral and allied to Germany through the Molotov-Ribbentrop Pact of August 1939, the UK had been in a resounding retreat in the face of the Nazi advance since June 1940, and the US was still neutral. All the United Kingdom had to stand up the Nazi threat was its empire and American empathy.

In the face of this situation, in May 1940, having just assumed the office of prime minister and realizing that only the entry of the United States in the conflict could change the course of the war, Winston Churchill entrusted a personal friend, the Canadian William Stephenson, with establishing an intelligence agency in the US to work in favor of British interests. Stephenson accepted the assignment and installed himself in Rockefeller Center in Nueva York, from where he created and established the residency of the British Security Coordination (BSC), the British agency with which the Basques in the Americas first initiated contact.

The BSC was made up of four main sections: secret intelligence, headed by Bill Ross-Smith; special operations, under Ingram Fraser;

---

23 Ibid., 164.
24 Ibid., 161.

economic intelligence, commanded by John Pepper; and propaganda and political struggle, led by Cedric Belfrage. The Basques, at one time or another during the war, carried out services for all four divisions of the BSC, but they were especially active in working with Ross-Smith's section.

The relationship between Agirre and his British colleagues was so close that they even became personal friends. Proof of this can be seen in a text by Alberto Onaindia, the canon of Valladolid from Markina (Bizkaia) and a close colleague of the lehendakari during the civil war. Following a meeting in Europe with Ross-Smith, who had presented him with a letter of introduction from the lehendakari, Onaindia wrote to Agirre on May 27, 1943: "We received a visit from your great friend Mr. A.M. Ross-Smith. He spoke to us compellingly, fondly, with clear admiration for you . . . I have had several chats with him. We agreed on all the issues that we are both interested in."[25]

The stated objectives of the division headed by Ross-Smith were to monitor official Spanish representatives in the US and the Americas as a whole; getting a hold of Spanish diplomatic codes in order to see what Franco's plans and communications were; monitoring Spanish diplomatic representatives as well as members of the Falange and other suspicious individuals; monitoring and spying on Axis supporters; the monitoring of shipping; the investigation and monitoring of businesses; and propaganda in favor of the Allies.[26]

Among his tasks, Ross-Smith's principal mission was to avoid at all costs the Axis powers gaining influence in Latin America for their own purposes. One method for restricting this Axis influence in the Latin American republics was to monitor transatlantic shipping, especially those ships sailing under the flags of neutral countries, and among them, especially, Spanish and Portuguese ships.[27] Insofar that many of these ships belonged to Basque shipping lines and a lot of their crewmembers were also Basque, the involvement of the Basque intelligence services was fundamental for the BSC.

---

25 Letter of presentation for A.M. Ross-Smith, sent by José Antonio Agirre to Alberto Onaindia, April 19, 1943 and Letter from Alberto Onaindia to José Antonio Agirre, May 27, 1943, both in the Instituto Labayru, Fondo Onaindia, Onaindia 32-3.

26 Jiménez de Aberasturi Corta and Moreno Izquierdo, *Al servicio del extranjero*, 453–54.

27 Ibid., 458.

Monitoring these ships, from their ports of embarkation to those of arrival, and not forgetting their en route passage, sought to know the precise location of all suspect shipping, obtain the most detailed list possible of passengers and crew, and halt any espionage- or contraband-related activity.[28] And Ross-Smith was fully successful his mission. By May 1941, he had observers reporting back to him on 145 ships and by mid-1943, the Allied intelligence services always had one or two informers on every Spanish and Portuguese vessel crossing the Atlantic.[29]

As well as the crew, passage, and cargo of the ships, allied agents were also very interested in a document that also traveled on them. In effect, Spanish vessels carried sealed envelopes that their captains were only supposed to open in the event they received a previously agreed on radio or *avurnave* (an acronym for *aviso urgente a los navegantes* or "urgent warning to navigators") warning. The envelopes contained an order by which the ships' captains were ordered to change course and head immediately, according to where they were in the Atlantic, to either a Spanish or a Norwegian or Latin American port, preferably in Argentina in the latter case. The objective of the message was for as many Spanish ships as possible to reach safety and avoid falling into Allied hands, since this special *avurnave* was designed to be broadcast three days prior to the official entry of Spain into the war on the Axis side.

The British intelligence services knew of the existence of these secret orders but they needed to find out their exact content in order to be able to alert the Royal Navy in time. In his diary entry for December 18, 1941, Agirre noted: "Today a bold deed was done, one that is a great help to the British Admiralty. Finally, one of our ship's captains—Etxabe from Somorrostro—has turned over the envelope with secret instructions from Franco's officials to the captains in wartime and in the event that Spain enters the conflict, as she is sure to do."[30]

However, others would have to repeat what Etxabe did because the warning by prior agreement to open the secret envelopes was changed periodically, so that the corresponding information would also have to be updated constantly, and this was the case. Some pages later in the same diary, Agirre noted that one Captain Cobeaga had informed them of

28 Ibid., 458.
29 Ibid., 474–75.
30 Agirre Lekube, *Diario 1941–1942*, 175.

just such a change in the *avurnave*. In the same entry, Agirre remarked that, "the English and American services have set about capturing the new instructions. Each of them wants to get there first, but the Captain won't do it, only to the person I indicate."[31]

Moreover, in order to be fully informed about Franco's plans in Latin America, the British intelligence service planned to get hold of the statistics records used by Spanish embassies. And in the cases of the Spanish diplomatic legations in Washington DC and Caracas, Basque participation was vital. Thus, in both cases British agents made use of Basque employees in the official Spanish representations in order to be able to access these records and copy ledgers without being found out.[32]

Another activity of interest to the Allies and involving Axis agents in the transatlantic crossings was the contraband of raw materials likely to be used in the arms industry. These materials included, among other things, platinum and diamonds. One case in which there was significant diamond trafficking that Basque agents also got involved in was that of Venezuela, the second ranked diamond exporter in Latin America after Bolivia. This case was important, moreover, because the black market diamond trade was controlled by José Antonio Sangróniz, the Spanish ambassador in the country. The involvement of the ambassador's chauffeur was particularly important in the operation. He was Basque and persuaded to take part in the investigations carried out by Allied agents by the lehendakari himself in August 1942, when Agirre stopped off in the Caribbean country during his Latin America tour.

Such acts of "audacity," as Agirre termed them, and the more day-to-day monitoring indicate that Basque-Allied relations were good. As such, on December 18, 1942 Agirre wrote to Telesforo Monzón, offering a short evaluation of the clandestine activity in the Americas: "The head of the Steer Company visited me to thank me for another important task carried out in Ramón's house. There is complete trust as I expected and out of this there will be worthy rewards. Even previously, through Garate's work, we also received truly splendid congratulations." The term "Steer Company" used by the lehendakari here referred to the British, citing the name of the Anglo-South African journalist George L.

---

31 Ibid., 230.
32 Iñaki Anasagasti and Koldo San Sebastián, *Nuestro hombre en Bilbao. Los nacionalistas vascos que espiaron para los Aliados en la Segunda Guerra Mundial y en los comienzos de la Guerra Fría (1939–1960)* (Madrid: Catarata, 2016), 78–79.

Steer, author of *The Tree of Gernika: A Field Study of Modern War* (1938); the expression "Ramón's house" was a pseudonym for Argentina, where the Basque delegate was Ramón María Aldasoro; and "Garate" was a reference to Venezuela, where the delegate was José María Garate.[33]

Yet the British were not just interested in direct activity. They also wagered on propaganda in the Latin American countries and in this activity, they also saw in the Basques well prepared and appropriate organization and people to influence public opinion in favor of Allied interests. In Agirre's words:

> I was in New York with the head of liaison between the English and American propaganda services. A well-oriented man, he received me with all friendliness. We talked for an hour and a half about our problem, the Spanish problem, the South American problem, everything related to propaganda. . . . I came away with a very good impression. He gives the problem of Spain the disturbing character that we assign to it.[34]

Agirre noted this in his diary entry of April 1, 1942, after meeting with H. Mackintosh, a member of the British Press Service. This was an office created by the Ministry of Information in the United Kingdom in October 1940 and located in Rockefeller Center, New York, in order to channel British information to the US press. A week after this diary entry, Agirre wrote that he was finalizing a report for the British agent. However, he had come across a problem in the propaganda to be aimed at Spain: namely, the British were not up to the task of considering the national problems within the Spanish state.

Yet propaganda aimed the peninsula was not the only topic discussed by MacKintosh and Agirre. They must also have spoken about the information destined for Latin America, as the lehendakari commented to Onaindia in May 1942: "There have been moments in which we thought our participation would be imminent—although with much organization—in a significant campaign whose mission was to crush all those who still believe in crusades, the illusion and myth of saviors of faith and order."[35]

---

33 Letter from José Antonio Agirre to Telesforo Monzón, December 18, 1942, Onaindia 32-2.
34 Agirre Lekube, *Diario 1941–1942*, 215.
35 Letter from José Antonio Agirre to Alberto Onaindia, May 7, 1942, Onaindia 31-8.

However, this British propaganda in Latin America never materialized. The entrance of the United States into the war following the bombing of Pearl Harbor on December 7, 1941 altered the whole situation in the Americas. In short, the British were displaced in the initiative, which passed directly into US hands. The United States maintained the Americas as its exclusive sphere of influence, a decision that the British had no other option but to accept. As Agirre said, "the Monroe Doctrine has invaded even this terrain."[36]

In contrast, on the other side of the Atlantic the Basque government delegation in London and especially Onaindia were cooperating with the Ministry of Information and with the British Broadcasting Corporation (BBC) in propaganda efforts aimed at Spain and Latin America. In the concrete case of the canon of Valladolid, between September 1940 and July 1948 he published more than four hundred news reports for publication in the Latin American press or for radio broadcast on the continent. Furthermore, he published just as many reports again for the BBC and aimed at Spain and Latin America, and he cooperated with European Christian Democrat Catholic institutions and bodies exiled in London as well as official and semi-official news agencies for which he also published dozens of articles designed to support the Allied war effort.[37]

Onaindia summarized his work in London to the lehendakari in October 1941, saying: "I write for the Ministry of Information here, I've done translations, I've translated a book of Polish propaganda from English into Spanish, another pamphlet by the Czechs, etc., I write weekly and I now even speak and write for the BBC. I've already given six talks." In May 1943 this priest from Markina added to the previous summary, stating:

> I work here in the Newman Association, International Christian Democratic Union, Inter Allied Catholic Information Group, and People and Freedom. The first of these works admirably in the field of university graduates. In the future it will be a liaison point for many continentals. I established the second. There are representatives from eleven nations. On the 25th of

---

36   Ibid. See also Alberto Onaindia, *Experiencias del exilio. Capítulos de mi vida II* (Buenos Aires: Editorial Vasca Ekin, 1974), 65.
37   Luis Monferrer Catalán, *Odisea en Albion. Los republicanos españoles exiliados en Gran Bretaña (1936–1977)* (Madrid: Ediciones de la Torre, Madrid, 2007), 397–434; Alberto Onaindia, *Obras completas de Alberto Onaindia*, vol. 1 (Bilbao: La Gran Enciclopedia Vasca, 1980), 9–47.

this month we held our annual meeting. It was very good. It has been somewhat lethargic, but there are better prospects in store. The third entity is related directly to the Ministry of Information here and to a Belgian, Monsieur Cauwelaert, who is there and who you know. I am not a member, but they have called me to team up because they know me from other bodies and because I know Spanish. The fourth is Don Sturzo's work. All of these bodies have already expelled the last pro-Franco vestiges and we know each other fully.[38]

THE LEHENDAKARI'S MEN

On Agirre's arrival in New York in November 1941, the Basque institutional framework in exile had been reduced significantly on account of the fall of France into German hands and the confusion that followed the French disaster. Most of the ministers and high-ranking members of the Basque administration, together with numerous refugees, had found refuge to varying degrees of safety in Paris, Aquitaine, Iparralde, Marseille, and certain Pyrenean localities; and many of them were desperate to escape to the Americas. Only the delegations in London, and the men based therein, Buenos Aires, and New York remained safe from the repressive activity of the Spanish fascists or the Axis powers. In London there was Manuel Irujo, who, in the face of the lehendakari's disappearance in May 1940 and in order to fill the void, created the National Council of Euzkadi, a body that was dissolved when Agirre arrived in the Americas.

The Basque delegate in Argentina, Ramón María Aldasoro, was based in Buenos Aires. He had arrived there to carry out a propaganda tour among the Basques in the country and, after fulfilling the mission in a few months, was due to return to Paris. However, the abrupt end of the civil war made his work among the Basque community and the official authorities in Argentina more important than returning to Europe and he ended up residing in Buenos Aires as the delegate there. Although of a republican affiliation, Aldasoro was the only Basque political figure resident in the Americas with some kind of connection to the lehendakari.

---

38 Letters from Alberto Onaindia to José Antoniol Agirre, October 25, 1941 and May 27, 1943, Onaindia 31-5 and Onaindia 32-3, respectively.

For his part, during his initial months in New York, Agirre only counted on the help of Manuel Ynchausti and Manu de la Sota, individuals the Basque president trusted fully that were very well placed to establish connections with organizations and functionaries in the US administration and its affiliates, but that were not politicians in the strict sense. Prior to Agirre's arrival, both Sota and Ynchausti had led the New York delegation on account of the particular circumstances they found themselves in rather than their political importance. Ynchausti had left France before the outbreak of hostilities in Europe with the idea of reaching the Philippines in order to attend to his business interests there. On the way, he stopped off in the United States also on a private matter and with the intention of establishing an American section of the LIAB. This was an association created in 1938 by Ynchausti himself with the mission to develop allies to the Basque cause and represent Basques interests abroad, at a time when the Franco regime was impeding the Basque government from having any legal protection in the face of the cravings of the new Spanish state. With World War II breaking out, Ynchausti prolonged his stay in New York and, later, the US declaration of war against Japan made his journey to the Philippines unfeasible. For his part, Manu de la Sota arrived in the Americas in his role as director of the Euzkadi soccer team, created by the Basque government as a propaganda tool that toured several European and Latin American countries between 1937 and 1939 playing games against local teams. When this sports embassy was dissolved, Sota went to New York to replace Antón Irala, who like Aldasoro in Argentina had arrived in the US on a propaganda mission. And, also like the republican politician, Sota had to take on responsibility for delegation there when Irala was recalled by Agirre in the face of the imminent Republican collapse at the end of 1938.

In these circumstances, at the start of his exile in New York, Agirre found himself missing his closest allies, the people who had worked with and for him since his appointment as lehendakari in October 1936. The first of these to arrive in the Americas was the minister of government, Telesforo Monzón, who after eleven chaotic months aboard the steamships *Alsina* and *Quanza*, disembarked in Veracruz on November 18, 1941, settling in Mexico. Julio Jauregi, José María Lasarte, Antón Irala, and Pedro Basaldua did not endure such a complicated journey, but they did face difficulties in getting exit permits from France, especially in the cases of Jauregi and Lasarte. As an example of the importance that Agirre gave to having these figures at his side, one only need look at the following summary the lehendakari communicated to Monzón on the paperwork being undertaken in New York to enable these high-ranking figures in the Basque administration to leave: "We've done the paperwork for José Mari Lasarte and Jauregi. Through Archbishop Spellman for the Vichy nuncio, through some good English friends for the American embassy in Vichy, and directly with the French through their consular representative here being a man willing to do so."[39]

Once in the Americas, Monzón, Jauregi, Lasarte, Basaldua, and Irala became the lehendakari's men. In August 1942, before heading off on a visit to several Central and South American countries, Agirre convened them to instruct them on the different individual tasks he was assigning them. Thus, Irala, who had held the post of secretary general to the presidency since the creation of the Basque government, continued to be the lehendakari's right-hand man and remained with Agirre in New York. Monzón and Jauregi were appointed to the Mexican delegation on account of its importance in the context of the exiled Spanish republican community in Mexico City, with the mission of liaising with expatriate Spanish, Catalan, and Galician leaders. Lasarte and Basaldua were assigned to the Southern Cone, and especially Argentina; the former to take charge of the Basque intelligence service in that region and the latter to try and influence Latin American Christian Democratic groups and parties, especially those in Chile, Argentina, and Uruguay.[40]

COOPERATION WITH THE AMERICANS: ESPIONAGE AND PROPAGANDA

The contacts between the Basque and American authorities, as noted, date from even prior to Agirre's arrival in New York. However, these conversations—as in the case of the relations with the British and even the French before the outbreak of World War II—met with serious resistance on the part of those in charge of the US State Department. The Allied foreign affairs ministries had agreed on a mission to keep Franco out of the conflict and they understood that any explicit aid to

---

39 Letter from José Antonio Agirre to Telesforo Monzón, February 21, 1942, Archivo del Nacionalismo Vasco, Sabino Arana Fundazioa, Bilbao, AN-EBB-117-02.
40 Letter from Antón Irala to Alberto Onaindia, September 11, 1942, Onaindia 32-1; see also Anasagasti and San Sebastián, *Nuestro hombre en Bilbao*, 75 and 80.

the Basque government in its public activity, dealing with the Basques, would be seen by Spain as a hostile act that would turn the dictatorship against the democratic countries. That is why Agirre, in his different attempts to negotiate with the British and Americans, met opposition from the two governments. Nevertheless, this refusal on the part of the British Foreign Office and the US State Department to deal with the Basques was not total in the American case. In their contacts, the Basques did find certain sections of the Roosevelt administration that did not turn down cooperation with the Basque government.

Making the most of personal friends and acquaintances, Manu de la Sota dealt with people who were very close to the US administration. And Manuel Ynchausti was equally well connected. They were able to rescue Agirre in his journey across Nazi-dominated Europe and bring him to New York thanks to their friends. Among these people was a personal friend of Sota, Gregory Thomas, who in 1942 joined the Office of Strategic Services (OSS), the US intelligence agency. Thomas's help, together with participation in organizations like the American Emergency Rescue and organizations financed or led by Nelson Rockefeller, both official and private, were behind Sota's and Ynchausti's efforts in New York. These contacts were not broken with the rescue of the lehendakari. The continued long after his arrival in New York and had significant consequences.[41]

In effect, between January 7, 1941 and May 28, 1942, Agirre's diary is full of entries he made since his arrival in the US about contacts with American agents. But through the end of the diary the notes on these meetings speak about the difficulties in reaching any sort of agreement. Reports on a potential US-Basque cooperation, which at the request of American officials and functionaries were drawn up by the Basque delegation in New York, invariably fell on deaf ears; "diplomacy," as Agirre used to say, implied that it was better to not bother the Spanish dictator than act directly against him.

This negative view of a partnership with the Basques began to change in May 1942, when the lehendakari was able to get the attention of the US vice president, Henry A. Wallace, a high-level and prominent progressive political figure. Moreover, Wallace knew Latin America, taking a great deal of interest in the continent, and he was convinced

---

41 Koldo San Sebastián, "Y Aguirre salió de Berlín," *Deia*, June 13, 2016.

that Spain was exerting influence among Catholic sectors in the region, with this being used to channel pro-Axis ideas there.

Besides Wallace, Nelson Rockefeller also met Agirre. Rockefeller was a non-isolationist Republican with many business interests in Latin America—among them one could mention oil concessions in Venezuela—and he headed a US government body, the Office of the Coordinator of Inter-American Affairs (OCIAA), which dealt principally with Latin America. Agirre met Rockefeller through two intermediaries: Max Ascoli, an Italian intellectual who had fled his home country on account of his ideas and because he was Jewish, and an employee in the Rockefeller Foundation; and Enrique Sánchez de Lozada, a Bolivian member of the Rockefeller Committee on International Affairs who also had ties with Vice-President Wallace.[42]

Parallel to these contacts with official US bodies, the members of the New York Basque delegation were also beginning to meet with exiled European Catholics resident in the United States. These meetings were convened by the Catholic Association for International Peace, funded in 1927 by Monsignor John Augustine Ryan and headed at this time by Raymond A. McGowan. As Agirre wrote in his diary on January 23, 1942, the goal of these encounters was "to set up a Catholic bloc to study the reconstruction of the world, and principally of Europe."[43] A few weeks after this entry, in a letter to Don Sturzo, the lehendakari defined more of what he expected from these meetings with other Catholics: "I attend meetings in Washington in which very practical work can be done if there is the will to do so. If that is not so, it will just be a waste of time, enthusiasm, and authority." This was because, Agirre continued to the priest leader of Italian Christian Democracy, "unfortunately the attitude of a great deal of Catholics at the present moment constitutes a difficult problem for the future. If we don't take the lead at this time, it will be difficult to get it during those transcendental moments in which a new world is built. I think for that reason that our action must be brave and audacious."[44]

These meetings were also attended by personalities of the level of Heinrich Brüning and the abovementioned Sturzo, the last democratic German chancellor before Adolf Hitler came to occupy the position and

---

42 Agirre Lekube, *Diario 1941–1942*, 200, 201, and 211.
43 Ibid., 190.
44 Letter from José Antonio Aguirre to Luigi Surzo, March 19, 1942, in *Luigi Sturzo e gli amici spagnoli. Carteggi (1924–1951)*, ed. Alfonso Botti (Soveria Mannelli: Rubbetino, 2012), 539.

the founder of the Italian Partito Popolare (Popular Party), respectively; Paul Van Zeeland, the former Belgian prime minister; the Catholic thinkers Raïsa and Jacques Maritain; Frans Van Cauwelaert, president of the Belgian Chamber of Representatives, leader of the (Flemish Catholic) People's Party, and the most prominent political figure among the exiled Belgians in the United States; as well as other American and Quebecois figures, all of them Catholic democrats worried by the growing influence of traditionalist Catholic ideas in Latin America and also concerned about the future of Europe after the war.[45]

The contacts made at these meetings, held every month in Washington DC, resulted in Basque participation in several propaganda schemes. One of the least known plans was, perhaps, that which linked exiled Basques and Belgians, not just in the Americas, but also in the United Kingdom.

In England Cauwelaert founded the Inter Allied Catholic Information Group, a small propaganda organization that focused on commissioning press articles from writers in the Allied countries to be disseminated in Latin America as well, as well as studying topics such as the position and role of the church after the war, the question of young people in relation to education and propaganda, social and labor union issues, the German situation, and the Jewish question.[46] Onaindia, despite not being a citizen of an Allied country, cooperated with this group created by the former president of the Belgian senate.

Concurrently with the canon's activities in London, toward the end of 1942 in New York Luis Navascues and Jon Bilbao, two Basque exiles that were cooperating with the New York delegation, began working for Belgium's Office for Latin America. Among the publications of this office, one should mention *La Revista Belga* (The Belgian Review), of which Navascues was editor-in-chief and Bilbao his deputy. This journal published articles by, among others, the lehendakari himself and Manu de la Sota. One should also note that the exiled Catalan Jaume Miravitlles formed part of the journal's editorial board. The journal and the office published a book by Cauwelaert, titled *Ensayo sobre las pequeñas naciones* (Essay on small nations), which was translated into

---

45   See Iñaki Goiogana, "José Antonio Aguirre, de lehendakari en París a profesor de la Columbia University en Nueva York," in *Exilio y universidad (1936–1955). Presencias y realidades*, ed. José Ángel Ascunce, Mónica Jato, and María Luisa San Miguel (Donostia-San Sebastián: Saturraran, 2008), 599–657.
46   Letter from the Groupe Catholique Inter-Allies d'Information to Alberto Onaindia, December 24, 1942, Onaindia 32-2.

Spanish by Navascues at Agirre's request. Following the liberation of Belgium, *La Revista Belga* ceased publication and was substituted by *Ambos Mundos* (Both worlds), which was also edited by Navascues and Bilbao.[47] The goal of this office was, through publications of all kinds and as well as cooperating with the Belgian Resistance, to counteract totalitarian influence in Catholic circles in Latin America. As part of this objective, in a speech before an audience made up of exiled Catholic democrats in London in September 1942, Cauwelaert called for the establishment of a Catholic front against totalitarianism.[48]

Some months earlier, at the beginning of 1942, a group of Catholic Quebecois intellectuals at the University of Laval suggested to coreligionist exiles in North America publishing a manifesto in order to state publicly the Catholic position on the global conflict. The first version of the manifesto, published by the French-Canadians, was unpopular among the more progressive members of the group that was meeting in Washington DC under the auspices of the Catholic Association for International Peace. This was due to its conservative content and the text was rejected by Maritain and his friends Vincent Ducatillon, Yves Simon, and Paul Vignaux. When Sturzo received the text for his signature he also criticized it on the grounds that it lacked any perspective on fascism, it omitted any criticism of exaggerated nationalisms, it could be construed that the signatories did not openly defend democracy, and other minor aspects. Finally, the text, amended by Sturzo, was made public with the signatures of forty-three religious, intellectual, and political figures. According to Maritain, through the manifesto, titled *Devant la crise mondiale. Manifeste de catholiques européens séjournant en Amérique* (In face of the world crisis: Manifesto of European Catholics staying in America), a number of Catholic representatives affirmed their total opposition to Nazi-Fascist totalitarianism. The alphabetical order in which the signatories of the text were listed was headed by the signature of Agirre.[49]

Among the Christian Democrat and Catholic propaganda activities carried out by Basques opposed to the conservative view

47 Koldo San Sebastián, "J.A. Agirre: Democracia cristiana y europeísmo en EEUU," *Hermes* 34 (June 2010), 72–79.
48 Letter from Alberto Onaindia to Frans Van Cauwelaert, September 16, 1942, Onaindia 34-2.
49 Goiogana, "José Antonio Aguirre, de lehendakari en París," 599–657; see also the original text: J.A. Aguirre, Charles Boyer, et al., *Devant la crise mondiale. Manifeste de catholique européens séjournant en Amérique* (New York: Édition de la Maison Française, Inc., 1942).

liable to be used by the Axis powers in order to gain adherents in Latin America, perhaps the best known campaign was that of the tour of several countries on the continent undertaken by the lehendakari between August 15 and October 24, 1942.

The overwhelming German victories during the second half of 1940 had encouraged Spanish leaders to dream and Spain's Ministry of Foreign Affairs began to use the Hispano-American Cultural Association with the aim of diffusing their imperial ideas in Latin America. The aforementioned association, as well as sending out a message of anti-liberal Catholic Hispanic identity, also exhibited a radical combative tone. As such, the discourse of this cultural body under the authority of the Ministry of Foreign Affairs identified the enemies of Hispanic identity as materialism, liberal democracy, communism, Judaism, freemasonry, the black legend, indigenous identity, and so on, bluntly naming the adversary that condensed all these threats to the Hispanic stock: the United States.[50]

With the entry of the United States into the war, especially, this Spanish imperialist offensive, which was termed Spanish cultural imperialism by the Americans, became a potential threat. It was a threat supported not just by US diplomatic reports, but also by the news coming out of the FBI that indicated that Germany and Italy were operating in Latin America through feelings of friendship and affinity on the continent toward France and, especially, Spain.[51]

This attempt to insert Spanish propaganda via diplomatic and Catholic channels in Latin America and the suspicion it engendered among the US authorities helped open certain doors within the Roosevelt administration to the Basque government. The change of hands regarding intelligence and propaganda work from the British to the Americans together with the demonstration to the Allied authorities of the value of Basques for this work, as well as their untarnished Catholicism, ability to communicate in Spanish, and widespread community in Latin America meant that some US agencies were coming round to the idea of using the Basque route to oppose Spanish cultural imperialism.

On May 5, 1942, on the advice of the British, Allen Dulles, head of the New York office of the Coordinator of Information (COI), the

---

50   Rosa Pardo Sanz, ¡Con Franco hacia el Imperio! La política exterior española en América Latina, 1939–1945 (Madrid: Universidad Nacional de Educación a Distancia, 1994), 165–66.
51   Ibid.

name of the US wartime intelligence service at that time, and Gregory Thomas, another COI head with responsibility for Spain and a friend of Sota, met with Agirre. On this contact, the lehendakari wrote: "An interesting and very important conversation. In the end, we'll probably be able to coordinate our services with theirs and do useful work."[52] And, in effect, that was the case: "The Americans informed us that our joint work should start quickly. . . . President Roosevelt's Donoban [sic] Committee is the organization that we've seen working most effectively up to now."[53]

The Donovan Committee cited by the lehendakari referred to the previously mentioned COI, created in July 1941 by Roosevelt to coordinate the different intelligence agencies working for the US government. Some months later, internal conflicts within the COI led President Roosevelt to split up the agency. Thus, on June 13, 1942 the Office of Strategic Services (OSS) was created, which assumed the functions of the COI, leaving all other tasks, purely propaganda work, to the Office of War Information (OWI). The person charged with first setting up the COI and later the OSS, as well as heading them from the outset, was William Joseph Donovan, hence the lehendakari's denomination.

One of the first outcomes of this American-Basque cooperation was the abovementioned tour, carried out by the Basque president between August 15 and October 24, 1942 through ten Latin American countries. On the trip Agirre gave twenty-three lectures, mainly at university facilities, but without avoiding other venues such as theaters when college classrooms were not large enough for the public demand. Besides these cultural talks, the lehendakari was honored by numerous bodies and received by official organizations and political figures, including among them even several presidents of Latin American republics. In many of these talks and receptions Agirre's message was, moreover, broadcast by local radio stations. The press followed the trip closely as well as the lehendakari's lectures.

On each occasion, according to the audience Agirre was addressing, the lehendakari tackled different topics. Thus, when talking to an audience of locals he chose cultural themes that, rooted in Basque

---

52 Agirre Lekube, *Diario 1941–1942*, 225. See also David Mota Zurdo, *Un sueño americano. El Gobierno Vasco en el exilio y Estados Unidos (1937–1979)* (Oñati: IVAP, 2016), 131.
53 Agirre Lekube, *Diario 1941–1942*, 231.

history, would be connected to the present they were experiencing in order to later address subjects like "The meaning of freedom, democracy, my experiences in totalitarian countries, the sincerity of the Allied war aims, the need to locate Catholicism beside freedom, the legality and logic of an alliance with the USSR, and the principles of just cause, etc."[54] These were all tackled from a Catholic and democratic point of view.

When talking to Basques, Agirre discussed themes relate to freedom, rousing them in unison. As for Galicians and Catalans, Agirre spoke to them about the unity between both nations and Euskadi. Finally, Agirre also had the opportunity to speak to exiled Spanish republicans in the way he spoke during a tribute to him at the Republican Center of Buenos Aires; here, addressing those exiled Spaniards, he stated that the Iberian Peninsula was a multinational territory and supported the idea that the solution to its problems rested on a "democratic, social [program] and one of freedom and independence for the Iberian nationalities, within a federal or confederal political system."[55]

In a report sent by the New York Basque delegation to the US authorities on the lehendakari's trip, as well as reporting his impressions of the domestic political situation and attitudes to the war in the countries he passed through, among his conclusions was the observation that, "there is no greater problem for democracy and an Allied triumph in South America than the definitive incorporation of Latin American Catholics the side of freedom." For this reason, there was an urgent need to develop propaganda "carried out by those who, free of the accusation of being extremist in their politics or proselytizing in religious matters" would be able to connect Catholic religious sentiment with a feeling of liberty and democracy. In his conclusions, Agirre affirmed that the trip had been a success in his capacity as a Catholic, a democrat, and a Basque; that is, for encompassing those characteristics that he deemed necessary to carry out the mission.[56]

The trip, which was officially a tour of a Basque, Catholic, and democratic nature as well as being a visit by a professor at an prestigious American university, was entrusted to Agirre by the OSS with the backing of Rockefeller's OCIAA; and with the visit, its organizers were trying to show that it was possible to be Catholic and at the same

---

54   *Informe sobre la gira suramericana de José Antonio Aguirre*, September 4, 1942, in Goiogana, Irujo, and Legarreta, eds., *Un nuevo 31*, 513–24.
55   Ibid., 514.
56   Ibid., 523.

time democratic and pro-Ally. In this sense of Christian Democrat propaganda, the Basque president's tour was a success, although the work of the Basque intelligence services was much more extensive.

As noted above, Pedro Basaldua was earmarked for Argentina. He had been the lehendakari's personal secretary since the creation of the Basque government through the fall of Paris and, before that time, during the Second Spanish Republic. He was, moreover, an active figure in the field of Christian Democracy within the PNV, becoming the head of the social page of the party's newspaper *Euzkadi* as well as a writer on social affairs. In Argentina, Basaldua became one of the principal figures behind diffusing the idea of Christian Democracy in the Southern Cone. For example, one could say that Basaldua and Basque religious figures, whether exiled or not, that were resident in Argentina played a key role in work such as publishing the journal *Orden Cristiano* (Christian Order), an important Catholic anti-fascist publication. Through their work in such dissemination, the former secretary to the lehendakari was a major catalyst for the activities of different groups that followed this current within Catholic thought.[57]

Citing the report on the tour sent by the New York delegation to the US authorities, I noted above that the lehendakari spread a message of Basque unity among his compatriots. Indeed, Agirre used the trip to prepare his followers for the times to come. According to the Basque president, Allied victory would bring in its wake the overthrow of Franco and the resulting return to democracy, thereby leading to a situation similar to that of 1931 with the establishment of the republic. For that to come about, the lehendakari thought it vital to be prepared for that future historic date that Agirre believed to be close. It was inconceivable to consider the possibility that a new constituent moment like that of 1931 would catch them, like it did at that time, off-guard. Basque unity, alongside the unity of action with Galicians and Catalans, was essential in order to be able to influence the future political configuration of the Spanish state; and he made every effort to promote this idea during his wartime stay in the Americas.

But in order to do all this it was also necessary to receive help from the Allied countries, and especially the United States. Thus, the

---

57 José Zanca, "Agitadores jesucristianos. Los católicos personalistas del antifascismo al antiperonismo," paper presented at the conference "Los opositores al peronismo," Universidad Nacional de General San Martín, 2010. At https://es.scribd.com/document/297312091/Agitadores-jesucristianos-Jose-Zanca.

goal of Basque intervention in Catholic-democrat propaganda activities, besides disseminating ideas they believed in, was to gain friends that, in a future democratic Europe, could be of use to the Basques. Yet for all that, this was not enough.

As pointed out earlier, since the start of the conflict, the Basque government considered itself a belligerent while offering to take an active part in the war, contributing to the Allied war effort with whatever resources it possessed. This is what Agirre came to do and suggested on arriving in the Americas: namely, putting at the disposal of the Allies, and in this case the US, his intelligence service. In other words, the idea was to contribute as much as possible during the war in order to deserve receiving the help of the victors after the conflict. Thus, the lehendakari's trip to Latin America also had a secret objective: that of coordination between the Basque intelligence services and the US agencies.

Indeed, since the Americans had assumed the Americas as an exclusive sphere of operations, thereby displacing the British from involvement, Agirre had no choice (although it was indeed what he wanted) than to deal with the COI and the OSS. Likewise, he had to deal with the FBI, since in the distribution of powers among the different US security and intelligence agencies it was decided that this federal law enforcement body would be responsible for intelligence in Latin America. During his tour, then, Agirre took the opportunity to meet with local delegates and heads of the Basque intelligence services, and especially with Lasarte, in order to organize and coordinate their work with that of the Americans.

In principle, the work of the Basque informants in conjunction with the Americans did not differ so much from what they had done for the British. However, as the Allies gradually gained the upper hand over the Axis powers in the war, so Spanish and Nazi-Fascist propaganda activities declined together with their threat, whether real or perceived. Yet at the same time the Americans began to consider to some extent at least another no less important threat: communism.

The efforts of the Soviets during the war and the desire of the most marginal classes to achieve better living conditions meant that sympathy for communist parties had grown all over the world, including in Latin America. And, with this growing sympathy for communists, so among the Americans there was increasing mistrust of progressive forces. These need not necessarily be communist, although they were the main focus, on account of their global activity and especially in the Americas. People began to feel the first winds of a coming storm that would be called the Cold War.

The Basque services working with the Americans thus had new objectives, without relinquishing their anti-Nazi-Fascist activities, struggle against Spanish collaboration with the Axis powers, and observation of maritime traffic: namely, Basque agents also began to investigate communists in Latin America.[58]

With the work of the Basque intelligence services in Latin America well established, the next stage in Basque-Allied cooperation took place after the Normandy landings in June 1944 and the beginning of the liberation of Western Europe. From that summer on, there was a feeling among Basque exiles that a return to a democratic Euskadi following the Allied victory was close at hand.

In November 1944, Antón Irala left his position as coordinator of the Basque intelligence services in Latin America and moved to France with the aim of organizing an information network between the Pyrenees, France, and Belgium, within a cooperation plan between the OSS and the Basques. Irala's mission, despite old and renewed mistrust on the part of Allied diplomacy to not upset Franco, was to lay the necessary foundations for the work of liberating Euskadi.[59]

Avoiding chaos and anarchy as well as assuring control of the territory were for the Basque government essential. Only with this goal in mind can one understand the cooperation of the Basque intelligence services; the creation of the Gernika Battalion and its participation in the liberation of the remaining territory under German occupation in the Medoc region of southwestern France; and Operation Airedale, which consisted of a group of gudaris being selected and trained as special commandos by the US military for a future intervention in Euskadi following the potential overthrow of the Spanish dictatorship. Yet the Cold War and "diplomacy," as Agirre would term it, prevented the lehendakari's plans from being realized. And on the contrary, Franco would survive three decades more than the dictators who helped him become head of the Spanish state.

---

58 Mota Zurdo, *Un sueño americano*, 168.
59 Ibid., 171–72.

CONCLUSION

The Basque government, and Basque nationalism more generally, did not give up after Euskadi was occupied by the Francoists. They understood this as a temporary defeat and they prepared for a return to their homeland. This return would take place after the defeat of the fascist dictatorships within a global struggle. Basques would fight in this war on the side of the democratic powers and they would have to contribute everything at their disposal for the common effort of defeating fascism. The Basque government created an intelligence service with several objectives. The first was humanitarian: helping prisoners; the second political: putting exiled figures in touch with imprisoned leaders as well as soldiers that had surrendered; and third, for reasons of intelligence gathering, in order to obtain military and political information that could be of use to the Allied governments and armed forces in their struggle against fascism.

This whole clandestine organization was put at the disposal of the Allies in their military efforts and it operated initially in the Basque Country, Spain, and France, and later in the Americas. In the Americas, as well as the task of monitoring Falangist, Fascist, and Nazi activities, the Basque intelligence services also cooperated in propaganda deeds by disseminating Catholic and democratic ideas associated with Christian Democracy.

The Basque government, and Basque nationalism more generally, contributed everything they had during World War II, hoping in exchange for Allied help to defeat the Francoist regime. Yet the Cold War that began soon after the end of World War II meant that the Allies came to prefer certain dictatorships in the Iberian Peninsula over democratic systems like those longed for by people like the lehendakari of the Basque government, José Antonio Agirre.

BIBLIOGRAPHY

Aguirre, José Antonio de. *Escape via Berlin: Eluding Franco in Hitler's Europe*. Reno: University of Nevada Press, 1991.

———. *Diario 1941–1942*. Bilbao: Sabino Arana Fundazioa, 2010.

Aguirre, J.A., Charles Boyer, et al. *Devant la crise mondiale. Manifeste de catholique européens séjournant en Amérique.* New York: Édition de la Maison Française, Inc., 1942.

Anasagasti, Iñaki, and Koldo San Sebastián. *Nuestro hombre en Bilbao. Los nacionalistas vascos que espiaron para los Aliados en la Segunda Guerra Mundial y en los comienzos de la Guerra Fría (1939–1960).* Madrid: Catarata, 2016.

Arrien, Gregorio, and Iñaki Goiogana. *El primer exilio de los vascos. Cataluña 1936–1939.* Bilbao: Fundación Sabino Arana and Fundació Ramon Trias Fargas, 2002.

Botti, Alfonso, ed. *Luigi Sturzo e gli amici spagnoli. Carteggi (1924–1951).* Soveria Mannelli: Rubbetino, 2012.

Chueca, Josu. "Emakumeak erresistentziaren haziak." In *Emakumeak hitza eta bizitza. 90 urte Emakume Abertzale Batza,* edited by Begoña Bilbao Bilbao, Gurutze Ezkurdia Arteaga, Karmele Perez Urraza, and Josu Chueca Intxausti. Bilbao: Euskal Herriko Unibertsitatea Argitalpen Zerbitzua, 2012.

Goiogana, Iñaki. "José Antonio Aguirre, de lehendakari en París a profesor de la Columbia University en Nueva York." In *Exilio y universidad (1936–1955). Presencias y realidades,* edited by José Ángel Ascunce, Mónica Jato, and María Luisa San Miguel. Donostia-San Sebastián: Saturraran, 2008.

Goiogana, Iñaki, Xabier Irujo, and Josu Legarreta Josu, eds. *Un nuevo 31. Ideología y estrategia del Gobierno de Euzkadi durante la Segunda Guerra Mundial a través de la correspondencia de José Antonio Aguirre y Manuel Irujo.* Bilbao: Sabino Arana Fundazioa, 2007.

Jiménez de Aberasturi Corta, Juan Carlos. *De la derrota a la esperanza: Políticas vascas durante la Segunda Guerra Mundial (1937–1947).* Oñati: IVAP, 1999.

Jiménez de Aberasturi Corta, Juan Carlos, and Rafael Moreno Izquierdo. *Al servicio del extranjero. Historia del servicio vasco de información de la Guerra Civil al exilio (1936–1943).* Madrid: Antonio Machado Libros, 2009.

Monferrer Catalán, Luis. *Odisea en Albion. Los republicanos españoles exiliados en Gran Bretaña (1936–1977).* Madrid: Ediciones de la Torre, Madrid, 2007.

Mota Zurdo, David. *Un sueño americano. El Gobierno Vasco en el exilio y Estados Unidos (1937–1979)*. Oñati: IVAP, 2016.

Onaindia, Alberto. *Experiencias del exilio. Capítulos de mi vida II.* Buenos Aires: Editorial Vasca Ekin, 1974.

———. *Obras completas de Alberto Onaindia*. Volume 1. Bilbao: La Gran Enciclopedia Vasca, 1980.

Pardo Sanz, Rosa. ¡Con Franco hacia el Imperio! La política exterior española en América Latina, 1939–1945. Madrid: Universidad Nacional de Educación a Distancia, 1994.

San Sebastián, Koldo. "J.A. Agirre: Democracia cristiana y europeísmo en EEUU." *Hermes* 34 (June 2010): 72–79.

———. "Y Aguirre salió de Berlín." *Deia*, June 13, 2016.

Steer, George L. *The Tree of Gernika: A Field Study of Modern War*. London: Hodder and Stoughton, 1938.

Zanca, José. "Agitadores jesucristianos. Los católicos personalistas del antifascismo al antiperonismo." Paper presented at the conference "Los opositores al peronismo," Universidad Nacional de General San Martín, 2010. At https://es.scribd.com/document/297312091/Agitadores-jesucristianos-Jose-Zanca.

Chapter 8

Basques in the Liberation of Europe: The Gernika Battalion

Iñaki Fernandez

The end of the Spanish Civil War in 1939 sent the Basque government into exile. After initially establishing itself in Paris, it was forced to flee again following the German invasion of France in 1940. From the beginning of World War II, the Basque authorities took a very clear position on the side of the belligerent democracies against the Axis forces, by offering their services to the Allies. This collaboration primarily revolved around the transmission of information gathered by the Basque intelligence services and by numerous Basques employed on the construction of the Atlantic Wall.

However, that engagement, by its very nature, required discretion, but the Basque government sought clear and official acknowledgement on the part of the Allies. In effect, the new world conflict could lead to the fall of the dictator Franco. The Basque representatives thus wished to reclaim as soon as possible the legitimacy granted them by the 1936 Statute of Autonomy,[1] in order to be able to take the reins in the territory of Euskadi should the opportunity present itself. This was the origin of the idea of a battalion that would demonstrate to the world

---

1   The Southern Basque Country obtained a statute of autonomy on October 7, 1936, after the outbreak of the Spanish Civil War on July 18. In theory, the Basque government's powers extended over the provinces of Bizkaia, Gipuzkoa, and Araba, even if in reality, given Franco's military conquests, its powers were mostly exercised in Bizkaia (the last territory to fall into the hands of Franco's supporters).

Basque involvement in the war and would give them greater weight in the probable reorganization of Europe after victory over the Axis.

FIRST ATTEMPT TO CREATE A BASQUE BATTALION IN LONDON

President Jose Antonio Agirre was unreachable.[2] Therefore, it was the representatives of the National Council of Euzkadi[3] who made the first contacts in London with Gen. Charles de Gaulle's "Free France."

Following lengthy negotiations between the fall of 1940 and the summer of 1941, the decision was made on May 17, 1941 to create a military unit within the Forces Françaises Libres (FFL, Free French Forces) made up solely of personnel of Basque origin. However, General de Gaulle was merely a guest of the British government and had to compromise with his hosts: Franco had not brought Spain into World War II, and the British were treating him with kid gloves in order to keep him from modifying his position. The agreement between Free France and the National Council of Euzkadi thus had to remain secret, by order of the Foreign Office, so as not to irritate Franco's regime.

The Third Marine Battalion was created in the course of the second half of 1941, but the Basque authorities had difficulty recruiting for it in view of the obstacles repeatedly posed by the British government, which ultimately forced the battalion's dissolution in the spring of 1942.

This first experience, which we could characterize as a failure, would serve as a precedent for renewed negotiations with the Free French authorities, once the latter were on French territory and hence had their hands free beginning in 1944.

---

2   Following the German occupation of Belgium and France in May 1940, Agirre, who was wanted by the Gestapo, the French police, and Franco's forces, went into hiding in Berlin, eventually reaching the United States on July 31, 1941, after which he took up residence in New York.

3   After the German invasion and *lehendakari* Agirre's flight, the Basque government's only remaining operational delegation was the one in London. In order to fill this power vacuum, Manuel de Irujo (a prominent leader of the Partido Nacionalista Vasco [PNV, Basque Nationalist Party] and a former minister of the Spanish republican government during the Spanish Civil War), in exile in London, decided to create the National Council of Euzkadi, which was founded on July 11, 1940, and ceased to exist in early 1942, once the *lehendakari* was again in a position to take the reins.

THE CREATION OF THE GERNIKA BATTALION DURING THE LIBERATION OF FRANCE

In these new negotiations in 1944, the Basque representatives relied on the Statute of Autonomy of 1936 and stressed their competence in matters of public order. In effect, if Allied victory led to the fall of Franco's regime, the Basque government would need to ensure the maintenance of order in its territory, and for this purpose, it needed to have an equipped and trained unit at its disposal.

However, another argument certainly carried more weight with the French authorities. Dozens of Basques were fighting the Nazis as part of the Spanish *maquis* present in thirty-one departments in southern France. In effect, the Unión Nacional Española (UNE, Spanish National Union) had been created on December 7, 1942, on the initiative of the Partido Comunista de España (PCE, Communist Party of Spain), with the idea of imitating the national fronts created by the European Communist parties after Germany's attack on the USSR.[4] The idea was to bring all Franco's opponents together around the establishment of a government of national unity aimed at reestablishing democratic freedoms in Spain. However, the UNE and its armed wing, the Agrupación Guerrillera Española (AGE, Spanish Guerrilla Group), with around ten thousand fighters, were entirely controlled by the PCE. In the fall of 1944, the UNE planned a major offensive with the aim of entering Spain by way of the Pyrenees and sparking a massive popular uprising that would overthrow Franco's regime. However, the invasion of the Val d'Aran in October 1944 ended up being a failure that forced the guerrilla general staff to change strategy in favor of the infiltration of small groups of fighters across the border. At the time, however, de Gaulle's priority and that of the Allies remained the fight against Nazi Germany: the guerrillas' movements in the Pyrenees and the border incidents with Spain that these operations might provoke were consequently an irritant to the French authorities. As a result, the opportunity to remove dozens of Basques from Communist influence while provoking tensions and weakening the UNE certainly told in favor of the decision to create a unit of Basque fighters within the French army.

---

4   Geneviève Deyfus-Armand, *L'exil des républicains espagnols en France: De la guerre civile à la mort de Franco* (Paris: Albin Michel, 1999).

The separation between this group of Basques and the UNE took place in two stages. First, in the fall of 1944, the Basque government entrusted to Kepa Ordoki,[5] a veteran of the Spanish Civil War, the task of gathering all willing guerrillas among the Spanish *maquis* into a unit made up solely of Basques, without informing the UNE's leaders that the goal was subsequently to take them away and place them under the orders of the French army. Moreover, the guerrilla chiefs looked favorably on this unit's birth:

> The Basque Brigade that Ordoki was organizing in Angelu [Anglet] was going to be a very useful element for acting in Euskadi. Since they were Basques, it would be easier for them to get the support of the *baserritarras.* . . . I'd already said to Luis Fernández, the commander of the Guerrilla Group, when we threw out the Spanish consul and installed ourselves in his headquarters, Villa Castilla, in Pau, "Look, I don't want anything to happen to me like when we entered Lérida, when we had to get out under fire because we didn't have anybody who knew Catalan."[6]

In a second phase, however, this unit, which took the name of the Gernika Battalion, left the Sauveterre camp in Béarn in December to head to the Bordeaux region and place itself under the French government's authority. In effect, all the guerrilla and resistance groups were normally supposed to be dissolved on January 1, 1945 (a date ultimately pushed back to March 31, 1945). The Basque government, led by the Partido Nacionalista Vasco (PNV, Basque Nationalist Party), wanted to avoid the battalion's dissolution at all costs: "All the Spanish bodies have armed forces. If the Basque government does not form this brigade, it will find itself in a situation of inferiority in relation to

---

5   Ordoki was a native of Irun and a mason before the war. A member of Acción Nacionalista Vasca (ANV, Basque Nationalist Action), part of the *abertzale* or Basque nationalist movement, he took to the streets, like many others, as soon as news of the military rebellion began to spread through the media, on July 18, 1936. He participated in the battle of San Marcial and then in the defense of Gipuzkoa and Bizkaia, notably serving as captain of the Second Company of the San Andres Battalion of the Euzko Gudarostea, the Basque government's army. Taken prisoner in Santoña in 1937 and sentenced to death by Franco's regime, he succeeded in escaping on July 22, 1939. He crossed the border and was involved with the French resistance when the Basque government entrusted him with the mission of creating a Basque unit.

6   Account of Victorio Vicuña, commander of the Tenth Guerrilla Brigade, in Mikel Rodriguez, *Memoria de los vascos en la Segunda Guerra Mundial: De la Brigada Vasca al Batallón Gernika* (Navarre: Pamiela, 2002), 130.

the other bodies. . . . This brigade has to be autonomous, that is, with Basque characteristics and not Spanish ones."[7]

The transfer of Ordoki's group to Bordeaux enabled it to get out from under the UNE's ascendancy and negotiate its survival directly with the French authorities. The large majority of the unit's men decided to follow Kepa Ordoki in leaving the AGE. Their fate would thus be decided independently from that of the remaining guerrillas, who considered the Basques deserters:

> Then, the Basque Brigade deserted overnight. They were in Sauveterre in Béarn, and they disappeared, taking weapons and trucks with them. Ordoki and the nationalists had done a sapper's job and took to their heels. The political instructor, Esparza, and some others stayed, but they were unable to convince the majority. They ought to have said something, like men, cleanly and clearly, but they took off like thieves, relying on the darkness of night to go to Bordeaux and place themselves at the orders of Colonel Druilhe.[8]

The Basque government submitted to the French authorities a document titled "Bases pour l'organisation d'une unité militaire basque" (Foundations for the organization of a Basque military unit).[9] It was a document of eighteen articles drawn up by the Basque government's Paris delegation in late 1944, according to which recruitment, on a voluntary basis, would be conducted by a commission of the Basque government made up of Jesús Maria Leizaola and Eliodoro de la Torre. It was thus the Basque government that submitted candidates to the French authorities. Article 3 stipulated that the *gudaris*[10] would enlist directly and individually in the French army for the duration of the war. One of Leizaola's[11] objectives was to have a military or police force in the event that Franco was forced out of power. Article 16 stipulated that "if the Government of Euzkadi is restored in the Peninsular Basque

---

7   Minutes of a meeting held on February 24, 1945, between PNV leaders and battalion members belonging to the same party, Sabino Arana Fundazioa archives, file P.N.V-N.A.C- E.B.B 153.

8   Victorio Vicuña, in Rodriguez, *Memoria de los vascos en la Segunda Guerra Mundial,* 154.

9   Sabino Arana Fundazioa archives, file P.N.V-K76, C2.

10   The term *gudari* designates a "soldier" in Basque. It was used especially by the members of the Euzko Gudarostea (Basque Army) during the Spanish Civil War, as well as by the Basques who fought in World War II in the name of the Basque government-in-exile.

11   Vice-president of the Basque government.

Country prior to the end of hostilities against Germany, the French Government undertakes to release the volunteers of the U.M.B. [Unité Militaire Basque, Basque Military Unit] from their military enlistments and place them, with their arms, at the disposal of the duly constituted Basque Government."

When the battalion's members signed their individual enlistment papers in February 1945, however, this document had still not been ratified by the authorities, and those *gudaris* who had no intention of finding themselves enlisted in the army without the certainty that the Basque government had concluded an agreement with France refused to turn in their papers, which were held by Kepa Ordoki pending receipt of a formal order from his government to turn them over to the French military authorities.

Alongside veterans of the Spanish Civil War, numerous young men joined the battalion. In effect, on the paylist drawn up by the French army in April 1945, at the time of the fighting at Pointe-de-Grave discussed below, out of 153 *gudaris* whose date of birth is known, 68 were under twenty-four years old. They were consequently no older than fifteen when the Basque troops surrendered at Santoña in August 1937, following the invasion of the entire Southern Basque Country by Franco's forces. Even if it is possible that some of them, despite their extreme youth, might have participated in the fighting, it is equally reasonable to suppose that others who were sixteen or seventeen at the time did not. Thus, between a third and a half of the Gernika Battalion's *gudaris* were not fighters hardened by years at war and in the *maquis*, but young men completely without experience. Many had crossed the border between 1944 and 1945, fleeing the oppressive conditions of life imposed on the conquered by Franco's regime, and were interned in various camps in France, including the Gurs camp in Béarn. Thanks to an agreement with the French authorities, the Basque government's Baiona (Bayonne) delegation was able to arrange their release on condition that they enlist in the battalion.

Except for an appeal by Leizaola in *Lehendakari* Agirre's name in the PNV's newspaper, *Euzko-Deya*, the Basque Country's various political parties were not asked to order their members to join the battalion, as had been the case when the Basque army was formed during the Spanish Civil War. The PNV's leaders had taken good care to get the other parties represented in the Basque government involved in the project, in order to strengthen their position in negotiations with the Allies. In effect, for all the difficulty of keeping the various parties united around the Basque government, that unity conferred on the Basque government a credibility that the Spanish republican authorities in exile, ravaged by internal quarrels, were hard put to it to obtain. This necessary unity, however, nevertheless did not erase the distrust among the various parties. Thus, even if it was necessary to recruit soldiers from different parties, the PNV did not seem to have any desire for an overly wide appeal, in order to maintain its ideological hegemony over the battalion. Moreover, the correspondence exchanged between the various parties reveals a certain withholding of information on the part of the PNV and a very superficial engagement by the non-*abertzale* (Basque nationalist) parties.

The recruitment criteria did not fail to incorporate the social prejudices of the time. According to the *gudari* Paco de Eizagirre, born into a well-off family in Tolosa, in exile since the start of the Spanish Civil War, and moving in aristocratic French circles,

> I spoke with the Nationalist Party. Nothing would ever have been done without consultation with people who were like my family. Then Doroteo de Ziaurriz, the president of Euzkadi Buru Batzar, Don Secundino Rezola, and Juan Manuel Epalza told me that the Basque Battalion was being formed, but that due to my conditions of education, I would be better off not going. People had been brought in from many places, from the *maquis,* etc.[12]

Immediately after arriving at the Bouscat camp, the battalion received a visit from the Bordeaux high command, and shortly afterward, each *gudari* received his arms and uniform. Since they were officially part of the Forces Françaises de l'Intérieur (F.F.I., French Forces of the Interior), the Basques were paid by France. They received uniforms left over from Pétain's youth camps, which came in two kinds: blue pants and shirts or green pants and shirts. In order to avoid confusion, the *gudaris* received blue sheets and green pants. They wore an *ikurriña* (Basque flag) with the word "Euzkadi" on their sleeves and berets or English helmets on their heads, and they also received mountain boots.

According to the *gudari* Manuel Bueno,[13] from the first weeks onward, some Spanish Civil War veterans complained about the lack of

---

12 Paco de Eizagirre, in Rodriguez, *Memoria de los vascos en la Segunda Guerra Mundial,* 157.
13 Manuel Bueno, in ibid., 169.

discipline and training of the younger men in the battalion and preferred to leave and join the Foreign Legion. After a brief course of military instruction, the battalion was transferred to the Macau training camp north of Bordeaux around March 15.

The French wanted to know whether they would be able to recruit enough men to be able to form a complete battalion, but it seems that a month before going into combat, there were not many more than 120 men in the unit. In effect, this was the number of copies of *Euzko-Deya* ordered by Kepa Ordoki over the course of the month of January 1945.[14] Recruitment did not occur with the speed Ordoki desired; he promised General Carnot that within two or three weeks, their effective force could reach three hundred men. He consequently urged Pepe Mitxelena, in charge of the Basque government's intelligence services, to accelerate the release of Basques detained in French camps in order to incorporate them into the battalion: "we have to get there, no matter what it costs, if we don't want to appear ridiculous."[15] Nevertheless, the battalion's effective force at the time of the fighting in Pointe-de-Grave in April of the same year was only 185 men.

THE POINTE-DE-GRAVE POCKET: THE FORCES PRESENT

On March 25, the Foreign Moroccan Mixed Regiment (Régiment Mixte Marocain Etranger, R.M.M.E.), to which the Gernika Battalion was attached, was created within the Carnot Brigade. This regiment was composed of three battalions: the Sixteenth Battalion of Foreign Volunteers (Gernika Battalion and Libertad Battalion), the Moroccan Battalion, and the Mixed Battalion.

Since the Basque unit had not attained the required number of soldiers, it formed a battalion with a group named "Libertad" (Freedom), in which Spanish anarchists were the majority. Nevertheless, in reality, these two companies were quite distinct and were never confused either in official documents or on the ground, to the Basques' great satisfaction.

On March 21, the Gernika Battalion received orders to proceed to relieve the Second Battalion of the Second Lot Infantry Regiment.

---

14 Letter from Kepa Ordoki to Pepe Mitxelena, March 21, 1945, Sabino Arana Fundazioa archives, file P.N.V-K 76 C2.
15 Ibid.

The relief was carried out the next day, with the result that the R.M.M.E. was billeted along the front south of Montalivet.

The *gudaris* conducted nocturnal forward reconnaissance in enemy territory two or three hundred meters from their positions. It was on one of these reconnaissance missions that the battalion suffered its first casualty, on April 2, 1945. The soldier Prudencio Orbiz Uranga, a native of Villabona (Gipuzkoa), the married father of a child, died probably in consequence of a grenade explosion.

As Allied forces neared Berlin, and the capitulation of the Third Reich appeared imminent, the Gernika Battalion was to go into combat to liberate Pointe-de-Grave in southwestern France. In effect, three large pockets of German resistance had existed in that region since October 1944 and had been neglected by the French general staff in favor of the German front and victory over Berlin. Nevertheless, a number of resistance groups now integrated into the F.F.I. were billeted around these pockets. The most significant of them was that of La Rochelle-La Pallice and its hinterland, the islands of Ré and Oléron, defended by 16,000 German soldiers dispersed among 200 fortifications. The Royan pocket had 5,000 soldiers and 218 fortified gun emplacements, and in Pointe-de-Grave, 4,500 Germans were billeted in 110 blockhouses that formed a functioning fortification system, completing the Atlantic Wall and surrounded by pine forests planted with mines. This position, which extended along both sides of the Gironde estuary, entirely blocked river access to Bordeaux. The Carnot Brigade (of which the Gernika Battalion was part), was assigned to liberate this last pocket of resistance.

According to the interrogation record[16] of Helmut Melzer, a German soldier in the Fifteenth Company of the Festa Battalion that surrendered on April 10, 1945, four days before the fighting, the Germans were divided into three battalions, the Narvick Kriegsmarine battalion with 1,400 men, Marine Battalion 1059 with 900 men, and the Festa LXXX Battalion with 600 men, plus an auxiliary naval artillery detachment with 1,000 men.

The official report on the operations[17] draws a picture of well-armed, well-equipped, and trained troops, almost all of them veterans under arms since 1940. Their morale was supposedly unwavering, given that it was upheld by the prestige of their commander, Colonel Sontag.

---

16 Personal archive of Andres Prieto.
17 Archives du SHAT (Service Historique de l'Armée de Terre), Vincennes.

In reality, the men were indeed hardened combatants, but they had been fighting on different fronts for five years, and the majority of them were tired. Moreover, Colonel Sontag died several days before the fighting, when a grenade that he was handling exploded. The same prisoner declared, "The officers themselves are starting to be discouraged. They are holding on without conviction, the troops are weary of the war, many of them have nothing left in Germany, they don't see that they have anything left to defend. Many of them are kept in place by fear of reprisals in the part of Germany that is still unoccupied."[18] The Festa Battalion was supposed to protect the ten-kilometer long anti-tank ditch, an indispensable element in Pointe-de-Grave's defenses. This was one of the battalions that the Basque unit found blocking its path. According to the German prisoner, the men had orders to fight to the death. Nevertheless, he characterized their military value as mediocre, since the majority were worn down by the Russian campaign. Moreover, around a third of the soldiers were foreigners, and not all of them were trustworthy, so that an officer had even reportedly declared, "I would have to fire eighteen rounds behind me if I wanted to fire twenty at the enemy."

The French feared the German artillery, which they estimated at around ninety guns, solidly installed in what were most often concrete emplacements and provided with plentiful ammunition. Where provisions were concerned, the German troops were well supplied, according to the French general staff's official account, by requisitioning livestock from the pocket's civilian population. Nevertheless, the Basque battalion's *gudaris* affirmed that they found all kinds of Spanish products in the German fortifications. "The German sheds and blockhouses were full of Spanish canned goods and foodstuffs: Spanish tins of sardines, Spanish cans of tuna, Spanish tea cookies [*galletas María*], Spanish alcohol, Spanish cotton, iodine, bandages ... All Spanish! Franco was supplying them with everything!"[19]

In the event, the reduction of the various pockets of German resistance along the Atlantic necessitated the creation of a new military command, the Forces Françaises de l'Ouest (F.F.O., French Forces of the West) under General de Larminat, appointed by de Gaulle on October 14, 1944. Since the regular army was busy on the German

---

18 Ibid.
19 Pantxo Echeverria, in Rodriguez, *Memoria de los vascos en la Segunda Guerra Mundial*, 206.

front, the personnel of the F.F.O. were recruited from the F.F.I. The French forces at Pointe-de-Grave were placed under the command of Colonel de Milleret, also known as Carnot. From October 1944 to April 1945, Larminat's soldiers (numerically inferior to their opponents) had the mission of holding a front of around a hundred kilometers, without having the resources to fight a battle in the field. During this period, they took up defensive positions. The F.F.I. were satisfactorily equipped with light arms, albeit of disparate kinds, since a large part of their equipment was made up of foreign weapons, requiring the use of a variety of ammunition. Where heavy weapons were concerned, the French infantry was in a very inferior position, able to bring only thirty-one guns to bear in the Médoc region, against ninety German guns. Nevertheless, the F.F.O.'s chief trump card remained their overwhelming air and naval superiority.

On the eve of the fighting, the French forces at Pointe-de-Grave, who had seen their numbers increase since October 1944 (notably with the arrival of the Gernika Battalion), were supplemented by reinforcements placed at their disposal for the duration of operations. As a result, Col. Jean de Milleret, charged with destroying the Pointe-de-Grave pocket, had around 11,000 men with which to carry out his mission. Before the battle, the forces were divided into three tactical groups. The western group, under the orders of Lieutenant-Colonel Reverdy, included the R.M.M.E. (1,000 men), of which the Gernika Battalion was part, the Second Lot Infantry Regiment (1,800 men), and the Thirty-Eighth Infantry Regiment (2,000 men).

APRIL 1945: A WEEK OF INTENSE FIGHTING FOR THE GERNIKA BATTALION

The Médoc operation was launched on April 14, 1945. It was the baptism of fire for the Gernika Battalion.

At 7:30 a.m., the 196th Artillery Regiment of the Carnot Brigade opened fire on the German positions; the guns fired more than 1,200 rounds in two hours. The Gernika Battalion was charged with taking a German position known as Hill 40 and located between Vendays and Montalivet, between the dunes and pine forests planted with mines. According to the *gudari* Luis Fernandez, Ordoki, the commanding officer, gave a speech before the attack, which was to take place at 3:35

p.m.: "The hour has come to fight, to defeat the enemy, to make the people of France know that the Basques know how to fight and die for freedom. You veterans, guide the young men to victory. Avenge the young men of Euskadi. These are the same Germans who dealt out death at Durango and Gernika: do not forget that France will be proud of your example. *Gora Euskadi Askatuta!* [Long live the Free Basque Country!]." The French deminer did not arrive until about 3:00 p.m., with a mine detector and white ribbons that would show the *gudaris* the path to follow. The battalion's left flank was covered by the Moroccan Battalion, and their right flank by the Libertad Battalion. The German position was around eight hundred meters (just under nine hundred yards) distant, but the only path along which the battalion, divided into sections, could advance was a fire belt around ten meters (eleven yards) wide, entirely mined and in full view of the enemy. The *gudaris* were therefore forced to advance in single file, following the white ribbons placed by the deminer. They moved forward in this way for about an hour, at which point the lead column opened fire in the direction of the German fortifications. The Germans replied with artillery shells, mortars, and machine guns. "Fire rains down on us; a series of explosions; the pine trees bursting into splinters; the first dead and wounded, including the deminer, his head blown to pulp, followed by other *gudaris*; we find ourselves without a deminer, no one to do the job, the mine detector destroyed."[20] The battalion was no longer able to advance, and the situation of the two other units guarding its flanks was even worse; the general staff then gave the order to fall back. The Gernika Battalion's retreat was covered by two men from the Libertad Battalion who came to their assistance with their machine gun (the Basques' machine gun was being repaired). One of these Spanish soldiers was severely wounded and would lose an arm as a consequence of his wounds. This first day of fighting left some thirty *gudaris* wounded and four dead. Pantxo Etxeberria was one of the battalion's stretcher-bearers:

> We carried a Mauser rifle and a folding canvas stretcher. In the fighting at Hill 40, there were quite a few wounded and three dead [It was not until the following day that Antonio Lizarralde died of his wounds] among our *gudaris*. The Germans were very well fortified and knew all too well where we were coming from; they were waiting for us and met us with crossfire. Then there were the mines, which were a real danger because, when

---

20 Campaign journal of the *gudari* Luis Fernandez.

you least expected it, you could go flying with your body blown to bits. The Germans did not stop firing, and it became very difficult to evacuate the wounded. We got to them by crawling, and we took them out of there as well as we could, dragging the stretcher along the ground until we were a little further away, and then we stood up and starting running, carrying the wounded man.[21]

The initial orders were reaffirmed for the next day, April 15, but the Germans had withdrawn from Hill 40 after the fierce attack the day before, and the Gernika Battalion forged a path through woods set on fire by the aerial bombardment and reached the Montalivet road, carrying out the previous day's mission. They were then supposed to advance toward Soulac, passing between the dunes and the Atlantic Ocean. Allied air and naval forces never stopped bombing the German positions, and the infantry advanced rapidly, taking prisoners all along its route. The Basques received orders to attack the blockhouses built on the dunes. They had already been bombed and were either buried in the sand or thoroughly battered. Some blockhouses surrendered without even a fight, but others offered fierce resistance. In the latter case, it was a matter of approaching unseen and throwing grenades into the interior in order to force the surrender of the besieged. Those Germans who were especially reluctant to fall into French hands, fearing that they would be subject to extortion, surrendered to the Basques thinking that they were British, since they confused the *ikurriña* with the Union Jack.

> We felt that in fighting against Germany, we were fighting against Franco. But that doesn't mean that we had hatred for the Germans. I remember that we took some prisoners on the front line. There were boys among them, because at that time, Germany had kids of fourteen as soldiers. And the French had given us orders: "Whatever you take, they're to be cleaned out." That was the French order, which Ordoki refused to follow. We sent the adult prisoners off to the French, who weren't going around with kid gloves. But we kept the kids with us. Supposing they were a bunch of poor unfortunates, like us, as we were mixed up in this mess! I don't know whether it was Ordoki's idea or whose it was, but we kept them, we dressed them in one guy's jacket and another guy's pants, and we had them for days.

---

21 Pantxo Echeverria, in Rodriguez, *Memoria de los vascos en la Segunda Guerra Mundial*, 205.

We gave them Basque names like 'Sabino Arana'. But here as everywhere, there are people who can't keep their mouths shut, so one day the French came and took them away.[22]

After three days of marching, the battalion finally arrived in Soulac on April 18, and the anti-tank ditch that had been bombarded by four hundred planes was finally crossed:

> The Germans are resisting like demons, with the energy of despair; they don't want to lose the territory they have left, whatever their casualties. The Germans have a fortress near Soulac. We're very near Soulac. French, Moroccans, and foreigners. The road is plowed up like a potato field; the water bottles are red with blood . . . at nightfall, Soulac was liberated; the Germans have fallen back toward Pointe-de-Grave; they can't go any farther; around ten-thirty, the German artillery bombarded what was left of Soulac; we withdrew toward the beach. We're digging trenches to protect ourselves from the German machine guns.[23]

The Germans no longer held more than a very small triangle of land including Verdon and Pointe-de-Grave.

Ordoki recalled that the French general staff entrusted him with the mission of reducing fortification Y33:

> The Germans were barricaded inside an enormous fortification next to the rail line. They sent the Leclerc Division, supported by the tanks. But the Nazis were well organized; they fired their guns and mowed down the French tanks. The whole forest surrounding them was ablaze. The battalion had to fall back. They then sent another battalion made up of men from the French colonies, but they were unable to advance very far. Our liaison with the general staff (all the battalions had one), Eusebio Mitxelena, informed me that I was to appear immediately. There, they informed me that we were to attack. They would not accept any retreat without having suffered at least 70 percent casualties, and no prisoners need be taken that day.[24]

The battalion advanced along the rail line amid the pine forests, the only easily accessible and demined access route, but one that was in

---

22 Jesus Blanco, in Rodriguez, *Memoria de los vascos en la Segunda Guerra Mundial*, 211.
23 Campaign journal of Luis Fernandez.
24 Account of Kepa Ordoki, in Carlos Blasco, *Dialogos de guerra en Euskadi 1936* (Usurbil: N.p., 1983).

full view of the enemy, while an armored division forged a path along a parallel road. Groups of Germans surrendered all along the road. Suddenly, as the battalion was approaching the fortress, the German bombardment stopped. Luis Fernandez made out a white rag: the German colonel who was in command of the fortification had just committed suicide, the garrison was surrendering, and the Basques took possession of the German colors. Carlos Iguiñiz raised the *ikurriña* over the blockhouse. The next day, April 20, 1945, the fighting ended for the Gernika Battalion's *gudaris*, after a week of bitter combat.

Point-de-Grave was officially liberated at 1:00 p.m. Colonel de Milleret raised the French flag over the Pointe lighthouse, and the French soldiers sang the Marseillaise.

The Carnot Brigade's casualties came to 400 dead and 1,000 wounded, while 600 dead, 80 missing, and 3,320 prisoners were reported on the German side.

For its part, the Gernika Battalion mourned five dead, four of whom had been killed in the fighting at Pointe de Grave: Prudencio Orbiz Uranga, thirty-three years old, a native of Villabona, killed by an explosion on April 2; and Juan Jose Jausoro Sasia, twenty-nine, born in Alonsotegi; Felix Iglesias Mina, thirty-two, born in Atarrabia; and Antonio Múgica Arrizbalaga, twenty, born in Donostia, all killed in the fighting at Hill 40 on April 14, 1945. In addition, Antonio Lizarralde Garamendi, thirty-seven, born in Durango, died the following day of his wounds.

On April 22, 1945, two days after the end of the fighting, General de Gaulle landed at the Grayan aerodrome at around 4:00 p.m., accompanied by General de Larminat, the commander of the F.F.O. They were welcomed by Colonel de Milleret, the commander of the French forces at Pointe-de-Grave. De Gaulle reviewed the troops. Passing before the *ikurriña* carried by Lt. Carlos Iguiñiz, he saluted it at length. It was on this occasion, according to Kepa Ordoki, that the general addressed to him these famous words: "Commander, France will never forget the efforts and the sacrifices made by the Basques for the liberation of our soil."

The battalion paraded with the Carnot Brigade in Bordeaux on April 26 and before *lehendakari* Agirre on May 1, while the wounded were cared for in the hospitals of the Bordeaux region or in Biarritz.

This participation in the fight for France's liberation, of quite modest significance in the end (a week of combat when Germany was on the point of being defeated), nevertheless possessed great symbolic weight. The Basques had officially and visibly participated in the fight against Nazism, even if in reality the battalion was only the tip of an iceberg made up of the hundreds and hundreds of Basques who assisted the Allies, often much more discreetly.

AFTER THE GERMAN CAPITULATION: PART OF THE U.S. ARMY

As soon as the war was over, starting in May 1945, the Basque government launched a new plan prepared with the American authorities. While the future of the battalion as a whole was still unknown, some of the unit's members would receive military instruction provided by the U.S. Army and secretly negotiated by *lehendakari* Agirre. The battalion's *gudaris* would be joined by men who had just crossed into France as a consequence of the raids against the Euzko-Naya organization in the Southern Basque Country.

Euzko-Naya was a PNV project that began in 1940 with the complicity of the Western intelligence services. The aim was to create an organized force under the PNV's direct control in Euskadi, recreating an army structure with former officers and soldiers of the Euzko Gudarostea (the Basque army during the Spanish Civil War), which would obtain the support of the local population and prevent the Communists from taking power in the event that the end of World War II led to the fall of Franco's regime in Spain. In November 1944, the Bizkaian part of this organization was dismantled by Franco's police.

Thus, in parallel the Gernika Battalion, still under Kepa Ordoki's orders, 114 men received military instruction of the very highest quality in extreme secrecy, at a château belonging to the Rothschild family in Cernay-la-Ville, near Rambouillet. The plan was to train around a thousand Basque soldiers in several waves. Of the 114 soldiers in the first group, 35 were members of Euzko-Naya, and a few others were Basques who had been in the British Isles or were part of the French resistance and had been chosen directly by the PNV. Around 70 came from the Gernika Battalion and were selected by Ordoki.

Appointed to lead them was Primitivo Abad Gorostiza, a trusted PNV activist, the former captain of the Gorbeia Company of the Arana Goiri Battalion during the Spanish Civil War, and formerly in charge of Euzko-Naya in Bizkaia before its dismantlement by Franco's police. The majority of the men were members of or sympathetic to the PNV, but there were some anarchists, socialists, and ANV *abertzales*. The Americans' only condition was that there be no Communists among them.

These "Mexican"[25] *gudaris* received the same training as American rangers. On June 8, 1945, Primitivo Abad sent a report on the first part of their stay to Jose Antonio Agirre, detailing the instruction received during the first month: they benefited from extensive training in all aspects of the most modern weapons, including the explosives and assault rifles used by the American and British armies. They took courses in mapping, orienteering, and military tactics; they learned to attack, defend, and counterattack in small-unit formations; they trained to besiege and capture fortifications and to avoid minefields. They were also taught to use and make explosives, along with point shooting. In sum, everything that an elite American soldier should master. Physical exercise (fighting, swimming, rowing, and so on) took up a large part of the day.

The *gudaris* followed strict military discipline and were equipped, fed, and paid by the American army. They expressed satisfaction with their training, even if they complained about the regime of seclusion to which they were subjected as a consequence of their mission's secret nature.

The soldiers did not know or at least did not recall their instructors' identities and referred to them by nicknames derived from their specialties: the captain was called "Plastic" because he was specialized in explosives, the mapping instructor was "Sphéra" (Globe), the self-defense specialist was "El Cuchillo" (The Knife), and another instructor was given the name "Okay," for obvious reasons. Nevertheless, the name of the mission's commander, alias "Plastic," is known, since he remained in contact with Primitivo Abad later on: Captain Bassett.

The Basques were organized in different sections, and Abad affirms that the first section, which he led himself, was on the point of leaving for Germany in American uniforms as an occupying force[26]

---

25   Since the French government was not officially informed of this military training received by the Basques on its territory, the *gudaris* were officially listed as soldiers of Mexican origin in U.S. Army service.
26   Interview with Primitivo Abad, April 7, 2003.

when geopolitical considerations that extended far beyond the Basque problem put an end to this collaboration with the American army. In effect, the end of World War II marked the beginning of a new opposition, already latent during the conflict, that was not yet called the Cold War but that had as a consequence a reorientation of American policy with regard to Franco's opponents of all stripes, even those who were openly anti-Communist. The USSR and Communism become the new specter haunting the United States, and Franco, suddenly more respectable, was considered a lesser evil, a rampart against the Communists who might incite a new revolution in Spain.

Consequently, on July 8, the American officers announced that training was suspended: the *gudaris* were required to hand in their uniforms and weapons and leave the château. It was an immense disappointment for the *gudaris* and for the entire Basque government, especially *lehendakari* Jose Antonio Agirre.

DECLINE AND DEMOBILIZATION

After the abrupt end to their training in Cernay-la-Ville, the *gudaris* wanted to rejoin the Gernika Battalion, which had continued to function under Kepa Ordoki's orders, but which had experienced quite a few changes since the end of the fighting and was struggling to survive.

After a period of rest during May, the Foreign Moroccan Mixed Regiment had been dissolved, and as a result, the army commissariat had stopped paying their salaries. Between the men who had left for Cernay-la-Ville and those who deserted due to the new situation, the battalion had lost around a hundred men. On the other hand, new young men continued to arrive from the Southern Basque Country, and the Basque government urged them to join the military unit in order to justify its continued existence to the French authorities; however, since these new arrivals had not signed any enlistment papers with the army, their situation had not been regularized. At the end of May, the battalion numbered around a hundred and twenty men, only a third of whom had participated in the fighting at Pointe-de-Grave. Deserters therefore went unreported in order to continue collecting their rations.

On June 18, Leizaola and de la Torre[27] had obtained a meeting with General Druilhe, the commander of the Eighteenth Military Region. The Basque delegates insisted on the need to maintain the military unit in order to be able to train and have the capacity to intervene in the event of Franco's fall. They thus continued to believe that the battalion might constitute the nucleus of a future Basque police force. Since the Basques refused to enlist in the Foreign Legion, as the French officers proposed, they finally agreed to form, provisionally, a company of foreign sappers.

Moreover, the presence of the Basque *gudaris* in the neighborhood of Baiona was becoming more and more problematic: on the one hand, the Spanish authorities were starting to complain about the presence of uniformed *gudaris* near the border, and on the other, the battalion's precarious economic situation meant that the men were very poorly clothed and their appearance was becoming more and more detrimental to the Basque government's image. As a result, on June 7, the battalion was transferred near Lormont to form the Seventh and Eighth Companies of the Fourteenth Infantry Group of Foreign Sappers. After a period during which the French again authorized recruitment, they halted the incorporation of new arrivals over the course of the summer.

It was in this context that the *gudaris* trained by the Americans joined the battalion in mid-July, and that the battalion was transferred to the Luchey-Mérignac camp. The building was in ruins, and there was no running water. The battalion was charged with making repairs and managing the camp.

The soldiers who had gotten to know the American army's discipline were depressed by the atmosphere that reigned in the battalion. In effect, with the goal of rapidly swelling their numbers, the Basque government had lowered its recruitment standards. Consequently, young men were enrolled who had no political awareness and created discipline problems: thefts, brawls, excessive alcohol consumption. We should also not forget that World War II was definitively over in Europe and the possibility of the fall of Franco's regime was growing more distant by the day. It was difficult to maintain morale in these conditions, and some of the *gudaris* were questioning the usefulness of maintaining the battalion. The Communist and socialist parties began to demand its dissolution, since they did not understand why all the foreign units had been dissolved except the Basque one. The consideration that the

---

27   Respectively vice-president and economy minister of the Basque government.

battalion might potentially be used against them by the PNV in a struggle for power in the Basque Country in the event (more and more improbable) of Franco's fall also played a role in their determination.

In a letter of August 19, 1945,[28] Abad complained to Luis Zarrabeitia, a member of the PNV leadership, that these parties had begun to proselytize among the younger *gudaris*, provoking tensions and disputes that had been avoided one way or another until then. According to Abad, again, some men were making anti-Basque statements and had a hostile attitude toward their officers, violating the battalion's rules and mocking its discipline.

In these conditions, the battalion, which had reached an effective roster of 260 soldiers, was no longer able to benefit from the Basque government's trust, since the majority of the *gudaris* no longer met the ideological, physical, or moral criteria for a police force or intervention force. Abad consequently tried to maintain the unity and discipline of a restricted group of around fifty soldiers selected for their efforts among the soldiers trained at Cernay-la-Ville, whom he believed he could save from the battalion's "shipwreck" to continue to operate in the Basque government's service even after the military unit's demobilization.

Finally, despite the Basque authorities' insistence, the demobilization order arrived on September 1, 1945, and the *gudaris* were gradually returned to civilian life.

Conclusion

After demobilization, Abad maintained around fifty men divided into several groups along the length of the Basque border. They survived by working as woodcutters or as agricultural workers on the nearby farms. Although their economic situation was extremely precarious, they smuggled men and material (essentially propaganda) across the border in both directions, through the Basque mountains. The last of these groups is said to have remained in operation until the early 1950s.[29]

Except for the men we have just mentioned, the other *gudaris* scattered after the demobilization: some enlisted in the Foreign Legion

---

28 Letter from Abad to Zarrabeitia, August 19, 1945, Sabino Arana Fundazioa archives, P.N.V. K72 C2.
29 Interview with Primitivo Abad, April 7, 2003.

and met again in Indochina, others tried their luck in South America, others settled in France, and others returned to the Southern Basque Country, where they often suffered from the regime's repression.

The epic story of the Gernika Battalion portrays in miniature those years of immense hope and terrible disappointment in which the Basques, like so many others, were no more than pawns sacrificed to higher geopolitical interests by the great democratic powers of the postwar period.

BIBLIOGRAPHY

Blasco, Carlos. *Dialogos de guerra en Euskadi 1936.* Usurbil: N.p., 1983.

Jiménez de Aberasturi, Juan Carlos. *Los vascos en la II Guerra Mundial: El Consejo Nacional Vasco de Londres (1940–1944).* San Sebastián: Eusko Ikaskuntza, 1991.

———. "Los vascos en la II Guerra Mundial: De la derrota a la esperanza." *Oihenart* 14 (1997): 57–84.

Larronde, Jean Claude. *Le Bataillon Gernika, Gernika Batallun euskalduna: Les combats de la Pointe-de-Grave.* Bayonne: Bidasoa, Institut d'Histoire Contemporaine, 1995.

Lormier, Dominique. *Le livre d'or de la Résistance dans le Sud-Ouest.* Bordeaux: Sud-Ouest Éditions, 2011.

Rodríguez, Mikel. "La lucha antifranquista de posguerra: El caso de los 'comandos' vascos." *Vasconia* 31 (2001): 275–304.

———. *Maquis: La guerrilla vasca 1938–1962.* Tafalla: Txalaparta, 2001.

———. *Memoria de los vascos en la Segunda Guerra mundial: De la Brigada Vasca al Batallon Gernika.* Iruña: Pamiela, 2002.

Chapter 9

The Nazis, a Contested Site of Memory in Twenty-First-Century Basque Fiction[1]

Mari Jose Olaziregi

It has been widely accepted that the Holocaust in general, and the Nazi as a character in particular, has become a kind of universal trope for political trauma and genocide discourses, allowing for the emergence of other memories that stand for the ethical human need for recognition and restitution for the pain caused by a troubled past. My brief chapter will try to analyze some representations of Nazis in twenty-first-century Basque literature in order to reflect on the tension that such representation establishes with the memory not only of the German occupation, but also of other political conflicts in the Basque Country, such as the Spanish Civil War and the terrorism of ETA.

As you can see, my point of departure here is an assumption of the importance that transnationalizing the memory of the Holocaust has had, both in the audiovisual media—through TV series like *Holocaust* (1978) and films like *Schindler's List* (1993)—and institutionalized commemorative acts such as the designation in 2005, on the part of the UN General Assembly, of January 27 as International Holocaust Remembrance Day. I am referring to a memory boom that, as noted by

---

1   This article was written as part of the following projects: IT 1047-16 (Basque Government), US 17/10 (University of the Basque Country), and FFI2017-84342-P (MINECO). Translated by Cameron Watson.

Andreas Huyssen,[2] began in the 1990s and that is, in reality, a consequence of the culture of amnesia that we experience in our media-driven neoliberal society. In this context, we should differentiate between artistic recreations of the past that function as "prosthetic memory"[3] and that free us from thinking for ourselves; and recreations of the past that invite critical reflection on that past and encourage "memory work"[4] on our part. I would say that the recovery of the past addressed by Basque literature is of the reflexive type and it seeks to regain and create what is, in my opinion and following Maurice Halbwachs,[5] a past that has been denied or silenced. The social aspect of any act of remembrance, the influence that the group exerts in its creation, means also that the memory we are creating and recreating in the Basque context is fluid, and in keeping with the needs and impetus of the group at each given historical moment.

Clearly one of the most noteworthy aspects of Basque literature in recent decades has been its invoking of crucial historical events in order to create literary universes that give voice to the suffering of protagonists often silenced by and distanced from the official historiography. One could say that, from 1990 onward, the Basque Country has also experienced a memory boom in works that have attempted to rewrite—on the part of the postmemory generation and drawing on our conflictive past—episodes like the Spanish Civil War, the Nazi occupation of the French Basque Country, and the radicalization of Basque nationalism with the emergence of ETA terrorism. I am, of course, speaking about a current Basque literature that is eclectic in its influences and typologies, a literature that feels postmodern in its questioning of the limits between reality and fiction, and likes rewriting genres such as that of history. The limited number of narratives in the 1980s that explored the Civil War or the French occupation was transformed in 1990s with a literary output whose main focus has been since then the rememoration of our conflictive past. Although the Spanish Civil War and the terrorism of ETA are, by far, the main conflicts addressed, the transnational memory of the Holocaust and the presence of the Nazis

---

2   Andreas Huyssen, *Twilight Memories: Marking Time in a Culture of Amnesia* (New York: Routledge, 1995).

3   Alison Landsberg, *Prosthetic Memory: The Transformation of American Remembrance in the Age of Mass Culture* (New York: Columbia University Press, 2004).

4   Elizabeth Jelin, *State Repression and the Labors of Memory*, trans. Judy Rein and Marcial Godoy-Anativia (Minneapolis: University of Minnesota Press, 2003).

5   Maurice Halbwachs, *On Collective Memory*, ed., trans., and intro. Lewis A. Coser (Chicago: University of Chicago Press, 1992), 191–235.

in twentieth-century Basque fiction has allowed our literature to address local conflicts thanks to a *multidirectional* memory that centers around the character of the Nazi. In this sense, I agree with Daniel Levy and Nathan Sznaider when they affirm that cosmopolitanization and Europeanization have successfully influenced national narratives.[6] This is a cross-border and diasporic memory that incorporates not just the Nazi occupation of the Northern Basque Country, but experiences crucial to the construction of the Basque collective identity, such as exile (following both the Civil War and the terrorist threat) and emigration. I am referring, then, to a hybrid multidirectional memory constructed on the basis of "dynamic transfers that take place between diverse places and times during the act of remembrance."[7]

In truth, the presence of Nazi characters in contemporary Basque fiction is very clear, especially since 2000. This coincides with the translation strategy of Basque publishing houses like Alberdania, which in the first decade of the new century published the works of authors like Hiren Saleem, Lydia Flem, and Primo Levi in Basque. There were also subsidized translations, within the Universal Literature collection sponsored by an agreement between the Basque government and the Translators' Association EIZIE, of canonical stories by Jewish writers like Isaac Bashevis Singer, and translations of paradigmatic texts such as *The Diary of Anne Frank*, translated by Josu Zabaleta for the Erein publishing house in 2004. This translation policy attempted to incorporate into the Basque literary universe Holocaust remembrance, a global memory that was paralleled in works created by Basque writers. That is the case of Alberto Ladrón Arana's *Eguzki beltzaren sekretua* (The secret of the black sun, 2004), a spy thriller set in Nazi Germany; and of the novella *Anbroxio* (2002), by the French Basque writer Eneko Bidegain (2002), which tells the story of wartime memories recounted to the protagonist, Kattalin, by her grandfather, a young man from Itsasu in Lapurdi who was arrested by the Germans and freed six months later, so that he was able to look after his family. The vigilance the *kommandantur* of Hendaia exercises over him results in the discovery of his clandestine cross-border activities and he is sent to the Buchenwald concentration camp, from where he will manage to get out alive. This

---

6   Daniel Levy and Nathan Sznaider, "Memory Unbound: The Holocaust and the Formation of Cosmopolitan Memory," *European Journal of Social Theory* 5, no. 1 (2002), 87–106.
7   Michael Rothberg, *Multidirectional Memory: Remembering the Holocaust in the Age of Decolonization* (Stanford: Stanford University Press, 2009), 11.

is an interesting story insofar that it narrates the suffering of a whole generation of French Basques during the occupation. And it advocates the transmission—whether intergenerational via communicative memory or by means of literary creations that make up cultural memory—of a past that should also form part of the Basque collective identity. For its part, the novel *Ihes betea* (2006; in Spanish, *Línea de fuga*, translated by Jorge Giménez Bech, 2007) by Anjel Lertxundi, one of the most prolific and established contemporary Basque writers, takes us back to the start of World War II in Germany and narrates the story of the involuntary flight across a Europe at war of an enthusiastic member of the Hitler Youth who discovers, by chance, that he was born Jewish. The Basque settings of Hendaia and Hondarribia will be the destination for the young Werner, a Nazi who must learn about and accept his identity and put himself in the shoes of the oppressed. With this literary argument, Lertxundi suggests the inevitability of hybridity, both in terms of identity and politics, as the acceptance of that diversity that should dwell within us. Still more innovative was, without doubt, *Belarraren ahoa* (2004; *Blade of Light*, translated by Kristin Addis, 2005), by another canonical prizewinning Basque author, Harkaitz Cano: an uchronia in which Hitler has won World War II and conquered Europe, at which point he decides to take Manhattan as part of a larger attempt to capture North America. His journey takes him to New York, and with him on his ship travels Charles Chaplin, who has been captured and punished for his film *The Great Dictator*. In a second narrative, we read about a stowaway who in 1886 travels to New York hidden inside the crown of the Statue of Liberty. This stowaway's destiny will cross paths with Chaplin's and help him escape his torturers. The hypothesis of the Nazi conquest is gripping and has been used in novels such as Philip Roth's *The Plot against America* and Philip K. Dick's *The Man in the High Castle*. The novel finds its narrative counterpoint in Cano's powerful poetic prose, which is full of lyricism and yet finds room for metanarrative passages that question the function of art. It could be said that the text is a metaphor of freedom—both individual and collective—and that it suggests that reality has several layers, and several readings.

Other Basque narratives, like the trilogy *Hilen bizimoldea* (Lifestyles of dead) by Xabier Montoia, have turned to other international conflicts, with novels like *Hezurrik gabeko hilak* (The boneless dead, 1999) about World War I; *Blackout* (2004), which focuses on World War II; and *Elektrika* (Electricity, 2005), which explores the memory of the

Algerian War. In this trilogy, different members of the French-Basque Etxegoien family reflect on the cruelty of wars and the sense of loss that has prevailed across different generations of Basques.

As we can see, Basque literature has also incorporated works and arguments about the Holocaust. But the truth is that the Nazi presence in Basque-language fiction goes further, and has been constant, especially in recent decades. One could argue, without a shadow of doubt, that we are witness to a trope related to evil and to dwindling Basque hopes during the Spanish Civil War. There are few novels about the Civil War that do not include Nazis collaborating with the Francoist fascists, as in the case of the young adult novel *Memorias de una vaca* (Memories of a cow, 1991), by Bernardo Atxaga; or Nazis in everyday life in cities like Vitoria-Gasteiz, in which German pilots who will later bomb Gernika experience illicit love stories, in short stories like "Ikatza bezain beltz" (As black as coal) in *Gasteizko hondartzak* (Beaches of Gasteiz, 1997), by Xabier Montoia, and so on. The fictional Nazi presence in novels like *Ohe bat ozeano erdian* (A bed in the middle of the ocean, 2001), by Mikel Hernandez Abaitua, allows for a reflection on the transmission of blame by perpetrators to their children;[8] and on the victimization processes that result in creating future aggressors.[9] This is a clear feature of Basque novellas that reflect on the radicalization of Basque nationalism and the beginnings of terrorism; a reflection that situates the causes of this process in the loss and repression that followed the bombing of Gernika by Nazi forces and the subsequent rendition of the Basque army in Santoña, a port in Cantabria to which many Basques fled in the aftermath of the fall of Bilbao in 1937. *The Accordionist's Son* (translated by Margaret Jull Costa, 2009), by Bernardo Atxaga, for example, clearly suggests a continuation from the Civil War to young ETA members in the 1960s and 1970s.

Whatever the case, I think that if one had to select fictional works in which remembrance of the occupation and the Holocaust as a cosmopolitan memory have served to channel national memories and incorporate them into the Basque collective identity, the three novels I will now discuss are paradigmatic.

---

8   Mikel Hernandez Abaitua, *Ohe bat ozeano erdian* (Donostia: Erein, 2001), 123.
9   Xabier Montoia, *Elektrika* (Zarautz: Susa, 2005), 181.

The Navarrese writer Aingeru Epalza's *Tigre ehizan* (Chasing tigers, 1996) won the prestigious Euskadi Prize and has been translated into Spanish, Catalan, and French. The drama of exile, its alienation and fear, pounds through the novel, a drama that Epaltza himself experienced in the flesh since the autobiographical background of the novel is evident. The protagonists are Martin and his son Martintxu, both exiled, the former in Venezuela, and the latter, with the rest of the family, in Larresoro, a French-Basque locality that they flee to in order to escape the Civil War and that is later occupied by the Nazis. Chance will mean that both, on August 7, 1944, have to hunt a tiger, a puma in the case of the father and a German tank, known colloquially as the "tiger," in the case of the son. The heteroglossic use of the Bizkaian and Lapurdian dialects in the book give color and intensity to the narration of anguish that this family experiences, separated by wars; an anguish that is symbolized by the tiger that the protagonists must hunt. Killing the tiger signifies overcoming the fear and its paralyzing effects for these exiles who take on ghostly features in their hideouts.

For its part, *Hobe isilik* (Best be quiet, 2013) is the first novel by the journalist Garbiñe Ubeda. The plot is, to some extent, typical of novels in which sibling relationships encourage the search for a missing family member, a search that, according to the political scientist Judith Shklar, is governed by a sense of family loyalty.[10] Bakartxo is the narrator of a story that, from the start, takes as its textual recipient José Bermejo Zabaleta, a Navarrese anarchist railroad worker who goes missing after World War II. It is a question of clearing up a major family mystery, of that mystery accepted by generations of the family that continue to admire old family photos in which José appears as the revolutionary anarchist he was, but in which the outlook of the photos, his presence therein, makes up that *punctum*, as Roland Barthes would say, which like a menacing arrow still reminds the family members of his fatal outcome: "he will disappear."[11] Yet what really troubles the novel is the spectral presence of that grandfather, that ghost who appears before the granddaughter and reminds us of the mystery, the moral crime perpetrated in the past and that remains unpunished. In the same way as in other contemporary Basque novels, like *Twist* (2011) by Harkaitz

---

10   Cited by Sebastiaan Faber, "La literatura como acto afiliativo: la nueva novela de la Guerra Civil (2000–2007)," in *Contornos de la narrativa española actual (2000–2010). Un diálogo entre creadores y críticos,* eds. Palmar Álvarez-Blanco et al. (Madrid: Iberoamericana, 2011), 103.
11   Roland Barthes, *La cámara lucida. Nota sobre fotografía* (Barcelona: Paidós, 1989), 52.

Cano—an example of transnational memory on account of the link the work establishes between the disappeared due to the dirty war in Spain and the disappeared in different Latin American dictatorships during the last century—Ubeda's novel topologizes, within that ghostly body that appears suddenly, resistance toward forgetting the crime perpetrated in the past. One must speak about the ghost, even to or with the ghost, states Jacques Derrida in *Specters of Marx*, and that is, precisely, what the protagonist of the novel does in a story of great emotional and affective density in which sweating, chills, and emotions, which bring with them an ethical evaluation like hatred, rage, or pain, are wrapped up in a dreamlike atmosphere. The discovery of the grandfather's double life, of his conscious abandonment of his Basque family in order to start a new life with his new French family, reveals to Bakartxo an unforeseen and painful reality.

Finally, mention should be made of a canonical author, Kirmen Uribe, an author of major international standing (his first novella, *Bilbao-New York-Bilbao*, has already been translated into fifteen languages), and whose work, especially in his last three novels, has been marked by the esthetic reworking of political exile. Characteristics like fragmentation, metanarrative reflection on writing and the function of art, and *docufiction*, popular in current European narrative and which delves into our past, as well as autofiction, a return to the real, characterize Uribe's novels, novels that enjoy taking inspiration from the heroic biographies of anonymous beings. Besides those mentioned, the Spanish Civil War and the exile of thousands of Basques, together with Franco's repression that followed and the resistance to the Nazi regime, influence the universe of his novels. *Mussche* (2012), for example, is inspired by the life of Carmen Cundín, one of the thousands of children who were exiled following the bombardment of Gernika and who was taken in by the writer from Ghent, Robert Mussche, who, in the end, became a leading member of the anti-Nazi resistance and died as such. The goal of highlighting the kind-hearted, generous attitude of people like Mussche, of constructing a memory of anonymous human beings marked by crucial decision-making moments at some point in their lives, drives Uribe's writing. For its part, *Elkarrekin esnatzeko ordua* (The hour of waking together, 2016; in Spanish, *La hora de despertarnos juntos*, translated by Jose Maria Isasi Urdangarin, 2016) is, without doubt, this author's most ambitious novel. It is a novel that is also inspired, through the life of the Letamendia-Urresti family, by the drama of Basque exile and Francoist repression that followed the Civil War. The charisma of the first Basque *lehendakari* (president), José Antonio Agirre, his Christian Democratic inspiration, his incredible escape through Berlin from Nazi Europe, as well as the frenetic activity that the Basque government he presided over in exile in order to overthrow fascism and construct a Europe of nations, would define the destiny full of sacrifices and broken dreams of the protagonists Chomin and Karmele.

By way of conclusion, I would say that, as I have tried to show in this brief chapter, the global memory of the Holocaust and the Nazi occupation of Europe during the last century in places like the French Basque Country has permitted, via that "cosmopolitan empathy" that Ulrich Beck alludes to,[12] the elaboration in Basque fictional works of a multidirectional memory. This allows for the incorporation into the Basque collective identity of an enriching of our most troubled past in a dialogue with a transnational memory.

BIBLIOGRAPHY

Atxaga, Bernardo. Memorias de una vaca. Iruñea: Pamiela, 1991.

———. The Accordionist's Son. Translated by Margaret Jull Costa. New York: Graywolf, 2009.

Barthes, Roland. La cámara lucida. Nota sobre fotografía. Barcelona: Paidós, 1989.

Beck, Ulrich. The Cosmopolitan Vision . Cambridge: Polity Press, 2006.

Bidegain, Eneko. Anbroxio. Donostia: Elkar, 2002.

Cano, Harkaitz. Twist. Zarautz, Susa, 2012. In Spanish: Twist. Translated by Gerardo Markuleta. Barcelona: Seix Barral, 2013.

———. Belarraren ahoa. Zarautz: Susa, 2004. In English: Blade of Light. Translated by Kristin Addis. Reno: Center for Basque Studies, University of Nevada, Reno, 2006.

Derrida, Jacques. Specters of Marx: The State of the Debt, the Work of Mourning, and the New International. Translated by Peggy Kamuf. Introduction by Bernd Magnus and Stephen Cullenberg. New York: Routledge, 1994.

---

12   Ulrich Beck, *The Cosmopolitan Vision* (Cambridge: Polity Press, 2006), 5–6.

Epaltza, Aingeru, Tigre ehizan. Donostia: Elkar, 1996. In French: Á la chasse au tigre: roman. Translated by Elena Touyarou-Phagaburu. Anglet: Aubéron, 1999.

Faber, Sebastiaan. "La literatura como acto afiliativo: la nueva novela de la Guerra Civil (2000–2007)." In Contornos de la narrativa española actual (2000–2010). Un diálogo entre creadores y críticos, edited by Palmar Álvarez-Blanco et al. Madrid: Iberoamericana, 2011.

Halbwachs, Maurice. On Collective Memory. Edited, Translated, and Introduction by Lewis A. Coser. Chicago: University of Chicago Press, 1992.

Hernandez Abaitua, Mikel. Ohe bat ozeano erdian. Donostia: Erein, 2001.

Huyssen, Andreas. Twilight Memories: Marking Time in a Culture of Amnesia. New York: Routledge, 1995.

Jelin, Elizabeth. State Repression and the Labors of Memory. Translated by Judy Rein and Marcial Godoy-Anativia. Minneapolis: University of Minnesota Press, 2003.

Ladrón Arana, Alberto. Eguzki beltzaren sekretua. Donostia: Elkar, 2004.

Landsberg, Alison. Prosthetic Memory: The Transformation of American Remembrance in the Age of Mass Culture. New York: Columbia University Press, 2004.

Lertxundi, Anjel. Ihes betea. Irun: Alberdania, 2006. In Spanish: Línea de fuga. Translated by Jorge Giménez Bech. Irun: Alberdania, 2007.

Levy, Daniel, and Nathan Sznaider. "Memory Unbound: The Holocaust and the Formation of Cosmopolitan Memory." European Journal of Social Theory 5, no. 1 (2002): 87–106.

Montoia, Xabier. Gasteizko hondartzak. Zarautz: Susa, 1997.

———. Blackout. Zarautz: Susa, 2004.

———. Elektrika. Zarautz: Susa, 2005.

———. Hezurrik gabeko hilak. Zarautz: Susa, 1999.

Rothberg, Michael. Multidirectional Memory: Remembering the Holocaust in the Age of Decolonization. Stanford: Stanford University Press, 2009.

Ubeda, Garbiñe. Hobe isilik. Donostia: Elkar, 2013.

Uribe, Kirmen. Mussche. Zarautz: Susa, 2012. In Spanish: Lo que mueve el mundo. Translated by Gerardo Markuleta. Barcelona: Seix Barral, 2013.

———. Elkarrekin esnatzeko ordua. Zarautz: Susa, 2016. In Spanish: La hora de despertarnos juntos. Translated by Jose Maria Isasi Urdangarin. Barcelona: Seix Barral, 2016.

Chapter 10

Jon Mirande and the Ideological Question of National Socialism[1]

Aurélie Arcocha-Scarcia

With an Appendix:

Jon Mirande Ayphasorho's Journey from Spengler to Nazism

Txomin Peillen

Jon Mirande (1925–1972), who was born and died in Paris, came from a family of Zuberoan origin that had settled in Paris. His parents had three children, the oldest of whom, Yvonne, died at the age of eight months. Simone, his second sister, was raised until the age of eight in her mother's family home, Chaho, in the village of Sohüta (Chéraute) in Zuberoa (Soule), where she learned Basque. Jon, who at the time spoke only French, did not meet her until he was five.[2]

---

1   "In Basque texts he uses only the first name Jon, not Jean," according to Txomin Peillen, in Jon Mirande, *Jon Mirande, olerkaria (Jon Mirande poète parisien)* (Bilbao: Euskaltzaindia 2012), xix. The same is true of Txomin Peillen himself, who signs his name as Txomin and not Dominique, as he has specified to me. I have respected this choice in my chapter. I thank Txomin Peillen (Université de Pau et des Pays de l'Adour) and Gwendal Denis (Université Rennes 2) for their valuable help during the writing of this chapter.
2   Peillen, in Mirande, *Jon Mirande, olerkaria*, 1–44.

Jon Mirande learned Basque as an adult and wrote his first poem in that language at the age of twenty-two.[3] At the same time, he was "a great and good letter-writer who corresponded with researchers from across Europe, often in their own language." In effect, he knew a dozen languages to different degrees, something that also led him to translate poetry and narrative texts written in a variety of foreign languages into Basque. Professionally, he was a bureaucrat;[4] working at the French Finance Ministry.[5] He did so "following competitive examination" in 1944, "right before the end of the war," after earning a senior high school diploma in philosophy in 1943.[6] This job, at which he worked solely in order to support himself, nevertheless left him intervals of free time in which to study languages and philosophy.

Following his mother's death on March 14, 1958, Mirande suffered from periods of severe depression and even had to undergo "violent treatments"[7] at the Pitié Salpêtrière Hospital in Paris and at a psychiatric clinic in Châteaulin, near Quimper, where he was treated for melancholic depression. His condition grew even worse after his father's death on February 16, 1967. The fact that he had to leave, not long afterward, the public-housing apartment in the Rue Davout where he had grown up and lived with his family since the early 1930s, and where he had his "bedroom-library," was the final blow that broke him psychologically. The public-housing authority (Office Public d'Habitations à Loyer Modéré, OPHLM) offered him another apartment "on the fifth floor overlooking the courtyard at 7 Rue Jules Dumien." He lived there for four years until he committed suicide, apparently on December 28, 1972, according to the coroner.[8]

Txomin Peillen was bound to Jon Mirande by an indestructible friendship that a fundamental political opposition on the question of National Socialism and fascism never succeeded in shaking.[9] Peillen says

---

3   Ibid., xv.
4   "All his life, Mirande was a simple bureaucrat of the lowest rank," *Jon Mirande, olerkaria*, 9.
5   He worked first at 13 Rue du Général Beuret, then in the Foreign Finance department, which was located at the time in "the Richelieu wing of the Palais du Louvre, with windows looking onto the Rue de Rivoli . . . Today this wing is attached to the museum," Mirande, *Jon Mirande, olerkaria*, 10.
6   Mirande, *Jon Mirande, olerkaria*, 9.
7   Ibid., 11.
8   Ibid., 4–5, 12–13.
9   Txomin Peillen has specified that these crucial ideological divergences led him to distance himself from Jon Mirande for a number of years: "It has to be acknowledged that this intelligent man, seized by a passion for the far right, had absurd ideas and lived in a state of contradiction. We had a period of five years of coldness in our

of him that he was "a true *poète maudit* as a consequence of declaring himself a member of the far right and, although he was spiritually inclined, proclaiming himself an opponent of Christianity."[10]

If Jon Mirande willingly identified himself as a "National Socialist" or a "fascist" in his correspondence and his opinion articles, he took good care, on the other hand, to emphasize that he was not an activist poet in the style of the Communist poet Gabriel Aresti and that poetry's function for him was above all a playful one: "Nevertheless, I think that there is a difference, and not a small one, between Aresti and myself. Aresti sees in poetry something grand, transcendent; according to him, the poet has a mission for which he is accountable to the people. For me, on the other hand, poetry is a game, a word game; it need not be taken seriously."[11]

Putting the same idea in different terms, he also reaffirmed that his poetry did not have the messianic charge (Fry) that Gabriel Aresti's poetry might:[12] "I am ready for every war ... but when I am composing verses, it's something else that I have in mind."[13] The following statement

---

relationship after he began to reproach me for being neither a fascist nor a Nazi and to wish that I was not a democrat, since he wanted to censor an article that he had asked me for, because in the article I strongly criticized Hitler and his totalitarian conception of culture. I never saw either the journal or the article." Peillen, in Mirande, *Jon Mirande, olerkaria*, 176.

10   This quotation, the themes of which have been reaffirmed by Txomin Peillen in 2017 (see the appendix below), appears in more complete form in the 2012 Basque-French bilingual edition of Mirande's works, in which it continues: "he was an innovator in a Basque Country that had long been subjected to a puritanical Catholic clergy, a country that would swing to the opposite extreme with the revolutionary Marxism that we are familiar with. In his time, he never found his place as a writer, nor did he find Basques who shared his political ideas, although his extremist ideas appeared only rarely in his literary writings, just in his letters. His 1953 collection of poems did not appear until 1976, after his death in 1972." The most detailed biography of Jon Mirande to date is found in the 2012 edition of his works just mentioned. Particularly relevant are the prologue in Basque and French by Txomin Peillen ("Ce que je sais de Jon Mirande" [What I know about Jon Mirande]), and the "Biographie de Jean Mirande Ayphassorho" (Biography of Jean Mirande Ayphassorho) established in collaboration by "Alain and Christian Angelié, his nephews, and José Pablo Aristorena" (the name of this paratext's translator is not specified).

11   "Halaz ere uste dut ba dela diferentzia bat ez ttipia Arestiren ta ene artean: Arestik zerbait handi, zerbait goien ikusten du poesian: harentzat poetak mandatu bat ba omen du, jendeari esan beharra. Niretzat, berriz, poesia joku bat da, hitz-joku bat da: ez da serioski hartu behar." Jon Mirande, *Jon Miranderen gutunak (1948–1972)*, ed. Patri Urkizu (Donostia-Saint-Sebastián: Susa, 1995), 176.

12   See Aurélie Arcocha-Scarcia (A. Arkoxta), "Imaginaire et poésie dans *Maldan behera* de Gabriel Aresti (1933–1975)," *ASJU* 27, no. 1 (1993), 3–240.

13   "guduka guztietara gerthu nago ... bainan, neurrthizketan dihardudalarik, bertzerik dut gogoan." Quoted in Aiora Jaka, "Miranderen itzulpen argitarabe batzuk," *Senez* 39 (2010), 251.

by Antonio Arrue, who corresponded with Mirande during the years 1963–1964, points in much the same direction: "Mirande is above all an enemy of that poetry and that literature in general that is today called 'committed' [*comprometida*]. He wrote to us just recently saying that a poet should not in any way be an 'activist' [*engagé*]. For the rest, his understanding is that a poet should flee both preaching and social issues and should seek to cultivate poetry.[14] Txomin Peillen thinks that Mirande's "extremist ideas appeared only rarely in his literary writings, just in his letters;"[15] while for Emilio Lopez Adan "his literary production is saturated with ideology."[16]

The goal of this chapter is to open new avenues for research in connection with Mirande's works (processes of creation and translation, peritextuality, and epitextuality). For various reasons, it is impossible at present to take a synthetic view of this author's varied works. Scholarly studies of Mirande, focused in different directions, are lacking. The very first (thematic) dissertation on his work was defended in November 2018,[17] and an analytical classification of the totality of Jon Mirande's correspondence and his various works published in French, English, German, Breton, and so on is beyond the scope of what can be envisioned at the moment.

Our study addresses only one aspect of this task, the consideration of Jon Mirande's works in relation to National Socialism. In the following lines, we will first examine certain general aspects of Jon Mirande's thought. Subsequently, tracing certain clues left in his known correspondence and in his published articles, as well as the indications given by Txomin Peillen in the appendix (see below), we will pause briefly over some selected texts and translations by Mirande that have clear ideological content. This aspect will be complemented by a brief investigation into his known and published opinion articles and the known and published fragments of his correspondence, in Basque and in French. In the appendix, Txomin Peillen provides an unpublished perspective

---

14 Jaka, "Miranderen itzulpen argitarabe batzuk," 251.
15 Peillen, in Mirande, *Jon Mirande, olerkaria*, xiii.
16 "Mirande's 'revolt' has been turned into a myth. From the perspective of political ideology, it is clear that there are far-right conventions that he used in order to rattle the conformism of his day. In sum, his literary production is saturated with ideology, he is a far-right writer, and that is how he saw himself." Emilio Lopez Adan, "Jon Mirande, eskuin muturreko idazlea," *Mirande arazo*, spec. issue, *Jakin* 106 (1998), 45.
17 Amaia Elizalde, "*Haur besoetakoa* (1970), la modernité littéraire niée de l'écrivain Jon Mirande," PhD diss., Bordeaux Montaigne University, 2018.

on the issue, under the title "Jon Mirande Ayphasorho's Journey from Spengler to Nazism."

A COMPLEX, MULTIFACETED AUTHOR AND TRANSLATOR

Mirande was familiar with the Greek and Latin classics, as his texts show, but also with Gothic, Dutch, Breton, Welsh, Cornish, Gaelic,[18] as well as, of course, English, German, and Spanish. He translated into Basque authors whose works he had read in their original language (Hugo von Hofmannsthal, Friedrich von Schiller, Franz Kafka, John Keats, Federico García Lorca, Saul Tchernikhovsky, and others).

Nevertheless, it was especially "English [and] Scots" poets "and Irish prose authors" who were the focus of his admiration.[19] Translating enabled him to have access to other imaginaries, to add dynamism to his creativity in Basque,[20] and above all, to breathe oxygen into a Basque literary language that had become frozen, in his judgment, cut off from the great aesthetic and ideological movements that had marked the Western world, and Europe in particular, since romanticism. Mirande laid claim to the dark, tragic side of romanticism, in the style of Edgar Allan Poe. He counted himself among the *vascones inquieti* and wanted to be the bard of a "romantic Basquitude" (*euskaltasun erromantiko*) that had nothing to do with well-meaning moderation.[21]

Mirande patiently constructed a poetic corpus, publishing fragments of this body of work in various journals, but he did not manage to see the collection of his poetry, titled *24 Poèmes* (Twenty-four poems), published in his lifetime.[22] At the same time, he had great difficulty finding a publishing house that would agree to publish his "story," *Aur besoetakoa* (The foster daughter). In a letter addressed to Txomin Peillen on February 1, 1959, he said that he was in the middle of "making a clean copy" of the text that he had mentioned to him previously, which

---

18 Txomin Peillen, "Jon Miranderen bizia," in *Jon Mirande-ren idazlan hautatuak. Gero.* Euskal liburuak, Literatura (Bilbao: Ediciones Mensajero, 1976), 20; Txomin Peillen, "Jon Mirande, penseur basque," in *Le Devenir Européen, organe ethniste-socialiste de doctrine et d'information: Spécial Euskadi: Hommage à Jon Mirande* (Nantes: Y. Jeanne, 1974), 11.
19 Mirande, *Jon Mirande, olerkaria*, 169.
20 Jaka, "Miranderen itzulpen argitarabe batzuk," 253.
21 Mirande, *Jon Mirande, olerkaria*, 166–67.
22 Xabier Olarra, intro., Jon Mirande, *24 poema*, facsim. ed. (online), Susa literatura, at http://www.susa-literatura.eus/emailuak/mirande/.

was practically finished at the time of the letter. He specified that it was "about a very 'special' subject: a love story that recounts the romantic relationship between a thirty-year-old man and an eleven-year-old little girl [Mirande intentionally wrote *nexka* (little girl), not *neska* (girl).], in other words, a Basque version of *Lolita* (even if, unfortunately, I have not had the opportunity to read Nabokov's work)."[23] The publisher Lur brought the book out in 1970 thanks to the efforts of the Communist poet and editor Gabriel Aresti.[24]

EXTREME AND CONFLICTUAL POSITIONS

A number of works and studies have been devoted to Jon Mirande's philosophical and political thought, particularly *Mirande eta kristautasuna* (Mirande and Christianity),[25] which addresses topics such as fascism and Nazism, rejection of Christianity, paganism, morality, the legitimacy of violence, and the influence of Spengler and Nietzsche. Other aspects, such as Mirande's Holocaust revisionism or Holocaust denial,[26] have also been discussed; along with his racist ideas, his homophobia, and his misogyny.[27] On the latter, Peillen has had occasion to characterize it in milder terms:

> Feminist exegetes of his poetry look for misogyny there, since he talks about prostitutes and homosexuals, and in his novel *Haur besoetakoa* the hero, a pedophile, prefers a precocious slip of a girl to a chaste bourgeois fiancée. These exegetes have certainly

---

23 "eta gaia oso berezia: maitasun - kondaira bat, 30 urteko gizon baten eta 11 urteko nexka baten elkar maitatzea kondatzen duena, ots, euskerazko Lolita bat (naiz [*sic*] ez dudan zoritxarrez V. Nabokov'en lanegiña irakurri ahal izan)." Mirande, *Jon Miranderen gutunak (1948–1972)*, ed. Urkizu, 152.

24 In standard Basque, *Haur besoetakoa*. "Two years before his death, and after the end of the nightmares of frustrated hope, his friend—although his opposite in political ideas—Gabriel Aresti succeeded in overcoming the concerns and fears of his coeditors, and Jon Mirande had the pleasure of seeing his novel published with the title spelled slightly differently, *Haur besoetakoa*, with 'h'. In addition, the novel, which was initially written in literary Gipuzkoan, was corrected by the author into a form very similar to '*euskara batua*' or 'unified Basque,' but it was too late, because— except for his participation in the humor magazine *Igela* between 1962 and 1964— he had ceased writing in what was for him the language of Marxist-Leninists or of frustrated clerical censors." Txomin Peillen, "Jon Mirande Aiphasorho y su novela 'La ahijada'," *Revista de lenguas y literaturas catalana, gallega y vasca* 2 (1992), 105–6.

25 Joxe Azurmendi Otaegi, *Mirande eta kristautasuna* (San Sebastián: Caja de Ahorros Provincial de Guipúzcoa, 1978).

26 While Lopez Adan speaks about Holocaust denial where Mirande is concerned, Peillen believes that he was more of a revisionist (see the appendix).

27 Lopez Adan, "Jon Mirande, eskuin muturreko idazlea," 45, 52, 57.

not read how the poet shows empathy for these prostitutes, who endure the cold of the street and the coarseness of their customers (cf. "Un samedi soir" and "Merry Christmas").[28]

In order to understand Mirande's position on the question of racism, and especially anti-Semitism, it is first of all necessary to admit that these are not "marginal or folkloric"[29] issues in his works and to pause a moment over the terms "National Socialism" and "fascism." Thus, even if Nazism is "habitually classified under the category of fascism," and even if Mirande sometimes claims the label of "fascist" for himself,[30] National Socialism has quite distinctive characteristics.

Certain points, like the topic of Europe, which is very much present in Mirande's works, can be linked to the National Socialist racial question. If Mirande does not preach the "Basque race," it is in order to better introduce the "Basque people" into the "great family of 'white races'" and so adapt himself to the emphases of Hitler's ideology ("The racial question is the key to world history"[31]):

There is no Basque race, certainly, but there is a Basque people historically made up of individuals belonging in a certain proportion to the various races of the overarching white or Europoid race, and to those races only. It is not my intention to investigate which European race the "primitive" Basques might claim, that is, to which race the majority of those individuals belonged who first introduced the Basque language to this corner of Europe. . . . Let us be content to admit that the Basques, like the other European peoples, are members of the great family of 'white races': this is the first and surest indicator of our fundamental Europeanness.[32]

Setting as one's goal the defense of "Basque culture" should thus consist in becoming conscious of this European culture, so threatened today by the aggressive nationalism of the Blacks

---

28 Peillen, in Mirande, *Jon Mirande, olerkaria*, 176.

29 "Mirande's Nazism is not marginal or folkloric," Lopez Adan, "Jon Mirande, eskuin muturreko idazlea," 46.

30 Mirande, *Jon Miranderen gutunak (1948–1972)*, ed. Urkizu, 177.

31 Adolf Hitler, *Ma Doctrine*, Les grandes études politiques et sociales (Paris: Librairie Arthème Fayard, 1938), 91.

32 Jon Mirande, in Jose María Larrea, *Miranderen lan kritikoak* (Iruña: Pamiela, 1985), 98.

and the Yellows—Nietzsche's anguished appeal is addressed to us as well: let us be good Europeans![33]

According to Lopez Adan, Mirande ideologically positions the Basques at the center of a "mythicized Aryan" history, constructing out of whole cloth the image of a "proud, strong, and cruel people [the Basques], of the master race," which was nothing but the "transposition of Nazi-Germanic mythology," without historical foundation.[34] Lopez Adan also believes that Mirande's appropriation of paganism, as well as his references to Celticism and Druidism, corollaries to his rejection of Christianity, should be read through the same ideological filter:

> By origin, the Basques would supposedly be among the first peoples; they would be members of the mage peoples who had a pagan and magical vision of the world; . . . the multitude of Celtic references, including Mirande's obsession with dressing up as a druid, should be studied from this perspective, in my view. Christianity would supposedly be an "Afro-Semitic doctrine," and the paganism of the peoples of the East would have been upheld by the "Celts and the Germanic peoples." In this way, it is easy to slip from religion into racism.[35]

The fact that Mirande depicted enemy figures in the guise of Frenchmen in 1948, in the aftermath of the war, as in "Hiru buruak" (The three heads), with an epigraph in Breton[36] by Roparz Hemon (Louis-Paul Némo), sentenced to civic disability in 1946, seems to obey the same logic, at the same time that it seems to echo Hitler's ideas:

> It is necessary to finally realize this clearly: the mortal enemy, the pitiless enemy of the German people is and remains France. The question of knowing who has governed France is of little importance . . . the final goal of their foreign policy will always be to take control of the Rhine border and fortify France's position along that river, striving in every way possible to keep Germany disunited and dismembered.[37]

---

33 Jon Mirande, "Culture et Folk-lore, 25 janvier 1961," in *Le Devenir Européen, organe ethniste-socialiste de doctrine et d'information: Spécial Euskadi: Hommage à Jon Mirande* (Nantes: Y. Jeanne, 1974), 20.

34 Lopez Adan, "Jon Mirande, eskuin muturreko idazlea," 49.

35 Ibid., 51.

36 "À notre rêve bleu qui s'en est allé loin" (To our blue dream that has departed far away), French translation in Jon Mirande, *Jon Mirande orhoituz (1925–1972): Antologia*, ed. Patri Urkizu, KM Kulturunea (Donostia: Gipuzkoako Foru Aldundia-Diputación Foral de Gipuzkoa, 1997), 39.

37 Hitler, *Ma Doctrine*, 250–51.

This also raises the question of the status and origin of the Nietzsche texts that Mirande read. Did Mirande read Nietzsche unfiltered or by way of his reception among the National Socialists?[38] Arthur Goldschmidt points out the fascination Nietzsche exercised over the Nazis and the deformations of his original texts carried out by his own sister, Elisabeth Förster-Nietzsche:

> Nazi writers like Ernst Bertram, Hermann Cysarz, and Alfred Baümler, assisted in this regard by Nietzsche's own sister, knowingly distorted all of Nietzsche's thought, which was arbitrarily simplified and expurgated. They isolated and incessantly quoted certain passages, such as the chapter "On war and warriors," . . . carefully detached from their context and stripped of their symbolic meaning . . . It was necessary to wait until 1976 and the Colli-Montinari edition to see that *The Will to Power* and *The Innocence of Becoming* were only some projected titles among others.[39]

Pierre Milza likewise takes another look at those themes, dear to National Socialism and to fascism, that might have led both Nazi and fascist ideologies to read Nietzsche's Zarathustra: cult of the body, rootedness in the earth-Fatherland, heroism, and sacrifice:

> The exaltation of a vigorous and healthy body ("there is more wisdom in your body than in the proudest reason"), "faithfulness to the earth," the cult of a dangerous life ("man is a rope stretched between the Beast and the Superhuman"), . . . heroism that infinitely surpasses ephemeral individuality and is affirmed in the destruction or the sacrifice of the self: such are the themes from which numerous theoreticians of National Socialism and fascism drew inspiration. And along with them the idea of a world to change and to mark for the ages: "Let your highest happiness," Zarathustra says, "be imprinting the mark of your hand on the ages to come, as on a soft sponge. You must engrave your will on the millennia as on a metal more resistant than bronze."[40]

---

38 Arno Münster, *Nietzsche et le nazisme*, Collection Philosophie, épistémologie (Paris: Éd. Kimé, 1998).

39 G. Arthur Goldschmidt, "Commentaires," in Friedrich Nietzsche, *Ainsi parlait Zarathoustra* (Paris: Librairie Générale Française, 1983), 482–83.

40 Pierre Milza, *Les fascismes: Notre siècle* (Paris: Imprimerie nationale, 1985), 14–15.

FIVE TEXTS BY JON MIRANDE WITH AFFINITY TO NATIONAL SOCIALISM

We have selected the following five texts, presented here in alphabetical order, by consulting four principal sources: The indications given by Txomin Peillen in the appendix; the indicative paratexts added by Jon Mirande himself; for "Iru buruak" (The three heads), Patri Urkizu's 1997 anthology; and the historical details provided by Gwendal Denis (see the note in the appendix and *Ar Stourmer* in the bibliography).

"BA NIN ADISKIDE BAT (ICH HATT' EINEN KAMERADEN)"

This text, which appeared in Basque in the 1984 Larrea edition with the title "Ba nin adiskide bat" (I had a friend) and the parenthetical German subtitle "Ich hatt' einen Kamaraden" (I had a comrade), is mentioned by Peillen in the appendix with the following commentary: "A 1914 German soldier's poem, 'Ich hatte einen Kameraden', excellently translated into Basque [by Mirande] as 'Banin adiskide bat', has also been characterized as a Nazi work: it is a soldier's lament for a comrade's death." This military song, titled "Der gute Kamerad" (The good comrade), is more often referred to by the first line of the first stanza, "Ich hatt' einen Kameraden," as here.

"ERESI" (1952)[41]

Mirande's sonnet with this title speaks in epic tones of the exaltation of warrior values, of combat, and of blood poured out in defense of the "beloved old earth." The hero, rooted in his fatherland, forms part of a vital cycle of death and rebirth (metempsychosis), embedded in a pagan dramaturgy[42] and perhaps looking back in part to Greek ideas of palingenesis or rebirth. The wheeling suns (or revolving days) of the

---

41 Txomin Peillen translates the title of the poem "Eresi" as "Chanson de geste," in Mirande, *Jon Mirande, olerkaria*, 49. In *Les proverbes basques* (1657), the poet Arnault Oihenart (1592–1668) defined *eresi* as "an account, [an] old song that contains a story or narration."

42 Cf. Txomin Peillen's note in Mirande, *Jon Mirande, olerkaria*, 49.: "The divine idol in Basque mythology is the mother goddess Ama Lur" ("Lurra, Amalur edo Mari jainkosa da").

last stanza bring the poem to a grandiose conclusion, in the style of Wagnerian opera.[43]

Composed in ten-syllable lines grouped into two quatrains and two tercets with alternating ABAB rhyme or assonance, this text is not in fact an imitation in the strict sense of a medieval *chanson de geste*, the epic poetic account of some heroic deed or *gesta*. It is not even certain that the title "Eresi" meant "chanson de geste" for Mirande. Rather, if "Eresi" is not a translation or an imitation (always possible, since scholarship about the process of creation of certain of Mirande's compositions is still in a state of extreme flux at present), the title may simply highlight the text's status: it is a *chanson* or "song" (one that we might characterize here as warlike).

"GOIZTAR TXORIEK KANTA BEZATE (MIRANDE-TAR JON-EK ITZULIA)" (1951)[44]

With regard to this short six-line poem, which bears the title "Goiztar txoriek kanta bezate" (That the morning birds sing) and the parenthetical indication "Mirande-tar Jon-ek itzulia" (Translated by Jon Mirande), and which is preceded by a brief introduction, in the appendix Peillen says that, "he wrote a poem on the burial of a *Breiz Atao* collaborator, 'Goiztar txoriek'."[45]

If we pursue Peillen's hint, we can identify this "Breiz Atao" mentioned without further details in the appendix: Léon Jasson, sentenced to death on July 17, 1946. The text was published in 1984 in the Larrea edition of Mirande's works. It consists of an introductory paratext in Basque, composed by Mirande, that leaves no doubt about its political affiliation, and a six-line poem that is a Basque translation of a composition written by Léon Jasson in prison,[46] on the eve of his execution:

---

43 Like the pan-Germanists (Milza, *Les fascismes*, 18), Mirande professed a true passion for Wagner. Cf. also Mirande's letter to Jon Loustau of March 9, 1948: "I also like the musicians you mention, and Wagner as well. I am transported by *Tannhäuser, Parsifal*," in Mirande, *Jon Miranderen gutunak (1948–1972)*, ed. Patri Urkizu, 24. The contents of his record collection are telling: *The Twilight of the Gods, The Flying Dutchman, Tannhäuser, The Valkyrie, Lohengrin, Tristan and Isolde*, and others are included, sometimes interpreted by different symphony orchestras. See Mirande, *Jon Mirande, olerkaria*, 188–89.

44 This poem appeared in the journal *Eusko Gogoa* in 1951. Mirande, *Jon Mirande orhoituz*, ed. Urkizu, 124.

45 Jon Mirande, *Poemak 1950–1966*, ed. Txema Larrea (Donostia: Erein, 1984), 65.

46 Mirande gives no details about the character of Léon Jasson's original text or about

Here is a version in Basque of a Breton poem. The author wrote it in the prison of Roazan in Brittany. A young Breton fighter, he fought to liberate his fatherland in the last war.

He served as a member of the Bezen Parrot [*sic*, Bezen Perrot or the Perrot Formation was a Breton nationalist force that collaborated with the Nazis during World War II]. This military unit, the first in four hundred years, was named for a Breton priest, Yann-Vari Perrot Aba, whom the hated members of the "French" resistance assassinated for having been a Breton patriot. The French seized Jasson and then sentenced him to death. He wrote this poem on the eve of his death.[47]

"Iru buruak" (1948)

This brief prose text, the title of which translates as "The three heads," is not mentioned by Peillen in the appendix. It was published for the first time by Patri Urkizu in his 1997 anthology *Jon Mirande orhoituz (1925-1972)*. Urkizu indicates in a note that it was found in the archives of the Basque writer Andima Ibinagabeitia at the Sanctuary of Estibalitz and that it was "completed" (*ondua*) in 1948. It raises questions both for the mention of Roparz Hemon (Louis-Paul Némo), who was "sentenced to civic disability in 1946" and "went into exile in Ireland the following year" (Denis in the appendix) and who is cited in connection with a Breton phrase translated into Basque in a note,[48] "Urrun igesi joandako gure amets urdiñai" (To our blue dreams that have departed far away), and for the narrative it presents. The protagonist of the story is Kurt, who "has the beauty of a young Nordic god."[49] Kurt is a member of the SS, as the story specifies. The entire story is a torture scene. The three "heads" are those of three "Frenchmen" (*iru Prantzitar-buru*), whom the reader imagines are members of the French Resistance. The three torture victims have been butchered but kept alive. Following the

---

its textual itinerary.

47 Jasson "subsequently enlisted in an SS division, fighting the Allies in the Bastogne region . . . arrested by the Americans and turned over to the French authorities, he was sentenced to death and shot in Rennes on July 17, 1946." Mirande, *Poemak 1950–1966*, ed. Larrea, 65.

48 Mirande, *Jon Mirande orhoituz*, ed. Urkizu. Urkizu does not identify the author of the translation from Breton into Basque.

49 "Kurt, ipar-jainko gazte bat iduri ederrez," Mirande, *Jon Mirande orhoituz*, ed. Urkizu, 39.

sentence of death carried out on the "plain of torments" (*zigor-zelaia*), Kurt, helped at one point by his SS friend Ernst, has the idea of burying them standing up, with their heads above ground. Afterward, Kurt remains alone to perform the meticulous beheading, by axe, of each of the victims, all while singing them sailors' laments "that speak of love and shipwrecks."[50] It is a scene of final torture in which Kurt, the SS man, acts to extend his pleasure, which increases in the same measure as the atrocious suffering of those tortured. The entire story is marked by barbarism, cruelty, and criminal sadism.

"Oroituz" (1950)[51]

With regard to "Oroituz" (In remembrance), which has the subtitle, or in some editions the title, "Godu abestia" (Song of the Goths), Peillen wonders in a note whether it might not be "a reminiscence of an old song of Germanic origin, since it is equally known as the 'Song of the Goths'."[52] In translating this note from Basque into French, and then in the appendix here, Peillen adds crucial information:

> "Godu abestia" as a subtitle leaves room to suppose that this poem was inspired by a "Gothic song," not to say the German Wessel-Lied.[53]
>
> One of his 1950 poems, "Oroituz," . . . seems to have been inspired by the Horst-Wessel-Lied . . . The only German army war poem, it seems to me, is "Oroituz," "In memoriam," subtitled "Godu abestia."

---

50 "Abestu zizkien itxaslari-eresiak, Ipar-itxaso'ko eresi zâr batzu, maitasunaz ta ontzi-ondamenez mintzo ziranak," Mirande, *Jon Mirande orhoituz*, ed. Urkizu, 40.

51 The French translation of this poem that Peillen offers here in the appendix is the same as the one he published in his 2012 edition of Mirande's works, except for the last line of the fourth stanza, which contains a variant: "Quand reverrons-nous briller le soleil de Midi?" (When will we again see the Midi sun shine?), Mirande, *Jon Mirande, olerkaria*, 52, or "Quand notre Midi brillera t-il?" (When will our Midi shine?) (appendix).

52 Peillen, in Mirande, *Jon Mirande, olerkaria*, 52; Peillen specifies that the subtitle is indeed "Godu abestia" and not "Gudu abestia." See Txomin Peillen "Jon Miranderen ordeinua bere lekuan," *Mirande arazo*, spec. issue, *Jakin* 106 (1998), 12. He believes that it should be translated as "Song of the Goths" and that the translation "Song of war" is incorrect. We might add that in that case, Felipe Juaristi's Spanish translation of the title, "Canto de guerra" [Song of war], would be equally incorrect from this perspective. See Juaristi's edition in Jon Mirande, *Claroscuros, Ilhun-argiak*, trans. Felipe Juaristi (Leioa: UPV-EHU, 1992), 112.

53 Peillen, in Mirande, *Jon Mirande, olerkaria*, 52.

An examination of the text of the Horst-Wessel-Lied in German and in French translation reveals beyond dispute that Peillen is correct and that "Godu abestia" is the German song's Basque hypertext.[54] The historical trajectory of this song, which would become the SA's official anthem and then the national anthem after Hitler's rise to power in 1933, is complex. In effect, the Nazi activist Horst Wessel, assassinated by the Communists in 1930, himself used a hypotext that he adapted: a poem by the German Communist writer Willi Bredel. We add that the Horst-Wessel-Lied has been banned in Germany since 1945.

Composed in 1809 by the German romantic poet Ludwig Uhland, then set to music by Friedrich Silcher in 1826, it was one of the songs sung by the armed forces of the Third Reich. Notably, it was sung at Rommel's funeral on October 18, 1944, four days after Hitler forced him to commit suicide.

Let us state in conclusion that this is only a first glance at this subject. Evidently, other texts and translations by Mirande more or less distantly connected to National Socialism might have been mentioned, such as, for example, "Ez diteke nor-nai izan pagano" (Not everyone can be a pagan, 1960),[55] the Basque translation of a Flemish poem by René de Clerq that Jon Mirande also translated from Flemish into Breton and published in the sixth issue of the journal *Ar Stourmer* in 1962. Peillen likewise mentions this text in the appendix. Another possibility would be "Euskaldun gudu-zalduntza baten beharriaz" (On the necessity of a warrior [or 'Gothic'] Basque nobility).[56]

Texts that appeared in other languages, only a portion of which are known, might also have been added. Along the same lines, Mirande is supposed to have written a poem in honor of the Nazi Eichmann that he mentioned in his correspondence with Ibinagabeitia in 1962.[57] What happened to this poem, which Itxaro Borda—understandably indignant—searched for in vain, without managing to find it?[58] Might it not be a hypertext in the form of a translation/adaptation—as often in Mirande's work—of one of the poems in honor of Eichmann that

---

54 We will analyze the connections between the two texts in detail in a subsequent study.
55 See also, among others, Mirande, *Poemak 1950–1966*, ed. Larrea, 155. Mirande's Basque translation appeared in *Egan* in 1960, Mirande, *Jon Mirande orhoituz*, ed. Urkizu, 130.
56 Mirande, *Jon Mirande orhoituz*, ed. Urkizu.
57 Mirande, *Jon Miranderen gutunak (1948–1972)*, ed. Urkizu, 205.
58 Itxaro Borda, "Jon Miranderen heziketaz," *Jon Mirande: gogoeta itxi gabea*, spec. issue, *Hegats* 50 (2012), 19.

appeared in Breton in one of the six 1962 issues of the neo-Nazi journal *Ar Stourmer,* to which Mirande contributed and on the editorial committee of which he served?

IDEAS PROCLAIMED IN THE PRESS AND IN CORRESPONDENCE

Before continuing, let us note once again that numerous texts and translations by Mirande that were published in a variety of languages are unknown, and the same is true for the totality of his correspondence. For example, Mirande's writings that appeared in Breton in *Ar Stourmer's* six issues are not included in current bibliographies related to Mirande, which is why we have judged it useful to inventory them (see the bibliography below). This journal can be consulted today on the internet.

Over and over and without mincing words, Mirande declares himself a "National Socialist;"[59] or in the contracted form of the compound, a "Nazi,"[60] and not a "fascist," as in a five-page letter in French dated November 1949 and composed at his home at 106 Boulevard Davout, in Paris's 20ème arrondissement. The letter has at the end his address, with his name spelled as "Jon" (not "Jean") Mirande, followed by his signature in the center of the page, flanked on the left by two Nazi swastikas or *Hakenkreuz,* connected by a calligraphic design, oriented clockwise, and of slightly different sizes. The recipients of the letter were the editors of the quarterly journal *Gernika,*[61] characterized as "orthodox nationalists." The journal's leadership prudently chose the path of censorship and published only part of the fifth page. The paragraphs that I transcribe below from a good-quality photocopy[62] are significant for our subject. But the readers did not read them, since they are absent from the reply that *Gernika's* leadership ultimately made (the underlining was Mirande's):

59　See Centre National de Ressources Textuelles et Lexicales: "*national-socialiste* [National Socialist]: translation of the German *Nationalsozialist,* a noun composed of *national,* 'national', and *Sozialist,* 'socialist'. Nationalsozialistische Deutsche Arbeiterpartei (National Socialist German Workers' Party) is the name given in 1920, at the time of its foundation, to this movement led by Hitler (see *nazi* [Nazi])."

60　Ibid., "*nazi, -ie* [Nazi]: German word, informal contraction of **Na**tionalsozialist (see *national-socialisme* [National Socialism]). Cf. L. Spitzer, 'La Vie du mot *nazi* en français,' *Fr. mod.* 2 (1934): 263-69. Number of corpus occurrences: 127."

61　The journal *Gernika* was founded in 1945 in Donibane Lohizune (Saint-Jean-de-Luz) by republican exiles from the 1936–1939 Spanish Civil War. Between 1951 and 1953, it was published in Buenos Aires.

62　In contrast, the photographic reproduction of the letter's five manuscript pages in Larrea, *Miranderen lan kritikoak,* 13–17, is practically illegible. The letter is not transcribed in the edition.

Anti-Francoism [underlined but not capitalized in the original]. I hate Franco the Spaniard, the enemy of our ethnicity, but I would equally hate any Spanish head of state, republican or monarchist, and I should say that the majority of émigré Spanish republicans seemed perfectly repugnant beings to me; when I see the Basque standard waving alongside the purple-yellow-red [the colors of the flag of the Spanish Republic: red, gold, purple] dishcloth, I want to go off and vomit.

At the same time, I should say that my anti-Francoism is not anti-fascism (in parentheses, by the way, I am not a fascist but a National Socialist; it is quite clear that you lump all that together). . . .

It is true that twice, Basques trained by France, in a war in which they were sinking madly into the abyss, got themselves killed by soldiers in green uniforms; this is an additional reason to hate France, not Germany.

This was also the thinking of the majority of the Basques where we are from who "collaborated" when they could with the occupiers, SS or others (comparing occupiers to occupiers, I preferred them to the current ones; they had better manners). The resistance, in my region, was primarily the work of émigré Spanish republicans, whom the country's natives justly considered riffraff.

You now impose hatred of Soviet Russia on us. I am not a Communist, since I am a Nazi, but I attest that Stalinism does not lead to the destruction of minority cultures.[63]

---

63   "L'anti-franquisme. Je hais Franco l'Espagnol, ennemi de notre ethnie, mais je haïrais tout autant n'importe quel chef de l'état espagnol, républicain ou monarchiste et je dois dire que la plupart des républicains espagnols émigrés me paraissent des êtres parfaitement répugnants; quand je vois l'étendard basque flotter côte à côte avec le torchon violet-jaune-rouge, j'ai envie d'aller vomir.

"D'autre part, je dois dire que mon anti-franquisme n'est pas de l'anti-fascisme (entre-parenthèses, je ne suis d'ailleurs pas fasciste, mais national-socialiste, il est bien évident que vous mettez tout cela dans le même panier). . . .

"Il est vrai que par deux fois, des Basques entraînés par la France dans une guerre dont ils se fichaient dans le fonds éperdument, se sont fait tuer par des soldats aux uniformes verts; c'est une raison supplémentaire de haïr la France, et non l'Allemagne.

"C'est d'ailleurs ce que pensaient la plupart des Basques de chez nous qui ont 'collaboré', lorsqu'ils le pouvaient avec les occupants SS ou autres (occupants pour occupants, je préférais ceux-là aux actuels, ils étaient plus propres). La résistance, dans ma région, a surtout été le fait de républicains espagnols émigrés, que les naturels du

According to Jose María Larrea, it was Isidoro Fagoaga who replied to Mirande in the name of the editorial board, in these terms (bold text in the original):[64]

> Nevertheless, it is good for you to know that it is possible to be a Basque, even a patriotic Basque, and nevertheless vomit that mixture of Christian Democracy, Jewry [*youtrerie*], **and Freemasonry that is Basque nationalism at present. I do not know whether you will do me the honor of publishing my letter or do me the favor of a reply. As you see, Mr. Jon Mirande, we are doing both: we are reproducing what can be reproduced, and we are replying. We are replying above all in the name of our collaborators, our Basque poets, so unjustly attacked by you.** [bolded in quote]. . . We hesitated a long time before deciding to reply to your letter. At base, we believe that you might thank us for it. If we had published it in full, as you desired, you would have been in prison a long time ago, and so would I.[65]

Jon Mirande spoke euphemistically about the totalitarian regime of "Hitler's Germany" and downplayed the forced exile of German writers: "There was more freedom of expression in Hitler's Germany than in our own country; and whatever the case may be, the German writers banned in their country could write in exile (like Mann, Freud, and many others)."[66]

Likewise, embarrassed by an article to be published by Txomin Peillen, too anti-Hitler for his taste, he did not hesitate to retouch the manuscript or to write these words to him: "Nevertheless, your last paragraph against Hitler is too harsh in my view. It seems to me that it

---

pays considéraient à juste titre comme de la racaille.

"Vous nous imposez maintenant la haine de la Russie soviétique. Je ne suis pas communiste, puisque nazi, mais je constate que le stalinisme ne conduit pas à la destruction des cultures minoritaires."

64 Jon Mirande, in Larrea, *Miranderen lan kritikoak*, 11–12.
65 As regards the word *youtrerie*, see Centre National de Ressources Textuelles et Lexicales, cnrtl.fr, "*youtrerie*, feminine noun, obsolete, pejorative (with a very strong racist connotation). Gathering of Jews. 'In sum, behold Meyer, and all the *youtrerie* falling all over him to congratulate him' (Goncourt, *Journal*, 1886, 568).—[jutʀ əri].—1st attestation 1878, 'gathering of Jews; avarice, usury' (Rigaud, *Dict. jargon paris.*); from *youtre*, suffix -*erie**." www.cnrtl.fr/etymologie/youtrerie. Cf. also op. cit., "*youtre*: Racist insult referring to a Jew." At www.cnrtl.fr/definition/youtre.
66 "Mintzatzeko libertate geiago ba zegoen Hitler'en Alemanian gure errian baño; eta dena dela orduan beren errian debekatuta zeuden aleman idazleek erbestean idatz zezaketen (Mann, Freud eta beste askok egin duten bezela)." Mirande, *Jon Mirande orhoituz*, ed. Urkizu, 162.

is unjust to be entirely opposed; this is why I have deleted his name and have given your text a more general scope."[67] He also did not hesitate to use the Hitler salute or to take up the worst anti-Semitic calls for murder.[68]

In 1961, Mirande would adopt a similar position in two other articles in French that appeared in the Basque nationalist weekly *Enbata*, published in Baiona (Bayonne). Titled "Race, Peuple et Nation (I)" (Race, people, and nation I) and "Race, Peuple et Nation (II)" (Race, people, and nation II), they appeared in the journal's fifth and sixth issues. In these articles, Mirande returned to the Hitler-inspired racist theses he had already proclaimed in the 1949 letter discussed above. They generated an enormous scandal among the Basque nationalists—labeled "Christian Democrats" by Mirande—who expressed their views in this weekly.[69] Mirande then replied to them in another incendiary article with the evocative title "Je refuse ce nationalisme-là!" (I refuse that nationalism!), published in *Courrier des lecteurs*:

> Has this leading member of the Basque Nationalist Party ever read Gobineau? On the other hand, it hardly matters. This intellectual bad faith is common currency among the Christian Democrats and has nothing that should surprise me. What does deeply displease me, in contrast, is precisely the importance given to Christian Democrats' opinions in your journal. . . . why not then also allow the expression in Basque publications of the points of view of those who are fascists, monarchists, or National Socialists?
>
> Let us be content to admit that the Basques, like the other European peoples, are members of the great family of white races . . . This admission implies a racism that can and should be part of Basque nationalism. . . . there is . . . reason to obstruct any hybridization with races that do not belong to the Basque people's anthropological stock, that is, extra-European races (evidently,

---

67 "Halaz ere, zure azken parrafoa gogorregi iruditu zait Hitler-en kontra; etsai gehiegi baitu gaixo Führer horrek, bai eta faxisten artean ere. Ez zait irudi zuzen denik hari kontra baizik ez aritzea, eta horrengatik haren izena kendu dut, et azure textua generalago bihurtu dut. Baina, jakina, nahi duzun bezala egizu." Mirande, *Jon Mirande orhoituz*, ed. Urkizu, 173.

68 Mirande, *Jon Mirande orhoituz*, ed. Urkizu, 31.

69 Notably, the Basque-language playwright and priest Pierre Larzabal, the journal's editorial writer and director Jacques Abeberry, and the Basque-language poet and columnist Jean-Louis Davant, all fiercely anti-Nazi and anti-fascist.

I am using the word 'European' here in an anthropological
sense and not a geographical one: the descendants of European
immigrants in North or South America who have remained
pure from any mixture with the autochthons are Europeans,
while on the other hand, there are in Europe itself quite a few
halfbreeds who are not purely European ... These extra-European
halfbreeds would be disastrous from a double perspective. First
of all, they would sooner or later bring about the destruction of
the Basques as a people ... At the same time, from a perspective
that is no longer uniquely Basque, but pan-European, they would
be detrimental in favoring the appearance on our continent of
individuals of inferior value than pure Whites ... if we at least
admit an inequality among the great human races, according to
a hierarchy ascending from the Blacks to the Yellows and from
them to the Whites ... Granted, a Basque-Indian halfbreed,
for example, might be very nice and even have learned to speak
Basque as well as Axular; this does not prevent it from being
the case that by the sole fact of his mixed blood, he cannot be
an authentic Basque and would not be accepted as such in our
ethnic community if he happened to manifest that ambition.[70]

Besides Arthur de Gobineau, whom Mirande mentioned several
times, his racial theories may have been directly or indirectly inspired by
Mein Kampf, of which he owned a German edition published in Munich
in 1941.[71] He could also have read other editions in German or even in
French, since a translation had been available since 1934 under the title
Mein Kampf-Mon Combat (unabridged translation, Nouvelles Éditions
Latines, with a preface). In the 1938 French version published by Fayard
under the title *Ma Doctrine* [My doctrine], expurgated according to the
methodology proposed by Hitler himself[72] and authorized by him, we
come across passages like this one:

Nature habitually takes care and corrects the effect of mixtures
that alter the purity of the human races. She does not favor
halfbreeds. The first fruits of these hybridizations are harshly

---

70 Jon Mirande, in Larrea, *Miranderen lan kritikoak*, 103, 98–101.
71 Mirande, *Jon Mirande, olerkaria*, 15.
72 "By this method, the result will be obtained that a thesis in conformity with
   Germany's interests on the question of national minorities in Europe will be
   presented for publication in the various countries in such a way as to be adapted to
   different points of view." Adolf Hitler, *Mein Kampf*, with a preface, Histoire du XXe
   siècle (2015), at aufildelapensee.blog.

impacted, sometimes to the third, fourth, and fifth generation. What constituted the value of the primitive element is denied to them; beyond that, the lack of unity in their blood has as a consequence a disharmony of wills and vital energies.[73]

Hitler accorded crucial importance to the question of "mixtures" or "hybridizations" that "alter the purity of the human races." It is easy to find the same racist obsessions in Mirande.

Where Mirande's dream geography and its greater European context is concerned, it appears that his utopia of a "Basque state" founded on race was directly influenced by Hitler's same theses and the geographical vision of the National Socialist "Great Germanic Reich." Multiple articles and texts by Mirande point in this direction:

> In the absence of a Basque state that could take legislative measures designed to protect this anthropological side of our nationality, it is therefore necessary for every aware Basque to impose on himself a self-discipline that causes him to flee any marriage and generally any hybridization (at least any susceptible of bearing fruit) with individuals not belonging to truly Basque races. This may sometimes be difficult, even painful, but we must persuade ourselves that as members of a people, our chromosomes are more important than our feelings.[74]

CONCLUSION

To be clear, we have no intention of reducing Jon Mirande's poetic and narrative works to his ideological ties with National Socialism, an ideology from which he also sometimes maintained a certain distance, as his writings show. Nevertheless, there is a demonstrated need to explore this question in greater depth in the future, through broader scholarly research in a variety of foreign archives. Mirande was a very discreet, not to say secretive, man who led a quite compartmented life. He wrote a great deal to various correspondents scattered throughout Europe, and he visited them when he could, in Germany (notably in Bavaria), in England, in Ireland, in Belgium, and elsewhere. These

---

73 Hitler, *Ma Doctrine*, 154.
74 Jon Mirande, in Larrea, *Miranderen lan kritikoak*, 99.

aspects of Mirande are unknown and would shed fuller light on his trajectory and works.

Appendix

Jon Mirande Ayphasorho's Journey from Spengler to Nazism[75]

Txomin Peillen (April 17, 2017)

Jon Mirande's first intellectual model was his philosophy teacher at the Lycée Arago in 1942. From that early instruction, he retained only the ideas of Oswald Spengler's *The Decline of the West* and a "rejection of populism" inspired by Friedrich Nietzsche (a translation of the elitist poem "Aus hohen Bergen" [From high mountains] that would become an ideal of life: the "meritocracy" that would always compel him to decline to seek a university sheepskin). This ideal was reinforced by his parents' poverty, and he soon entered the Finance Ministry[76] as a clerk in 1943 [*sic*], following competitive examination.

Within his thought, contradictory ideas and behaviors coexisted. While he rapidly joined the far right, beginning in 1947, he violently, and despite everything, rejected the Catholicism of his childhood, and along the same lines, he considered "Marxist materialism" an enemy and the cause of the decline of the West.

---

75   We have added some notes to Txomin Peillen's text in order to provide the reader more precise guidance.

76   And not the War Ministry. See Francis Favereau, "Goulven Pennaod, Jon Mirande et la Bretagne," *Lapurdum* (2000), 294. In reality, Mirande must have begun working at the Finance Ministry in 1944, according to an earlier account by Peillen, who states that "Jean obtained a senior high school diploma in philosophy in 1943 and began to work at the Finance Ministry a year later, right before the end of the war, without wanting to pursue further studies. . . . All his life, Mirande was a simple bureaucrat of the lowest rank, with the corresponding salary." Peillen, in Mirande, *Jon Mirande, olerkaria*, 38

For Mirande, spirituality could not be the monopoly of dogmatic religions. He expressed his beliefs in a very concise article that appeared in *Ar Stourmer* no. 6:

> I believe in the soul—since it is necessary to give it its vulgar name—that is, I am convinced that a psychical part exists in every being and that this *psukhê* is not, as the mechanistic materialists say, a simple epiphenomenon of matter (of the brain in man and the other animals), but rather on the contrary that in its deepest way of being, it is distinct from common physico-chemical phenomena. In my view, this has been proven, one way or another, by parapsychological research. One could say, to a certain extent, that the soul in the strict sense is the only reality. Yes, I would even go so far as to believe sometimes that my own soul is the only and unique reality.

At the same time, Mirande was interested in Basque mythology, such as Ortzi's drum, the Basque *laminas* (nature spirits), and Celtic mythology (the poem "A un dieu de pierre" [To a god of stone],[77] and like Jung, he thought that these beliefs were the reflection of each people's archetypes.

He believed that Christianity was the source of part of Western Greco-Roman thought, and he pointed out that the Church inflicted as many martyrdoms as it suffered, writing a poem on the hundred Basque witches burned at the stake by French royal justice, "Sanguis martyrum" (Blood of the martyrs):[78]

Mon bon pays pacifique	My good, peaceful country
Rempli de blanches églises,	Full of white churches,
Cher pays choisi	Dear country, chosen
Par le dieu venu d'Orient,	By the god come from the East,
Ton ciel est pur, les fumées	Your heaven is pure, the smoke
Le vent du Sud les a chassées,	Has been driven away by the south wind,
Sans écho dans notre mémoire	Without an echo in our memory

---

77   Mirande, *Jon Mirande, olerkaria*, 122, 132, 120.
78   Ibid., 111.

Vos gémissements se sont tus ...	Your moans have been silenced ...
Vos lamentations mes sœurs	Your lamentations, my sisters,
Réduites en cendres sur les places,	Reduced to ashes in the town squares,
Vous sorcières du Pays Basque	You witches of the Basque Country
Que les hommes en noir ont brûlées	Burned by the men in black

He twice expressed his rejection of Christianity, in 1947 in his sonnet on suicide and in 1951 in his poem "A mon ex-dieu" (To my ex-god).[79]

Mirande was not the only one in Pétain's France to think until 1943 that Nazism was the only serious obstacle to Soviet expansion. All the same, few took the step of fighting alongside the Germans. The Breton nationalists of *Breiz Atao*, a Breton nationalist journal, joined them in the Yann Vari Perrot Battalion, in the hope of obtaining autonomy for Brittany and legal status for their language and culture; some even enlisted in the Waffen SS, including Yves Jeanne, who along with Goulvenn Pennaod performed the Hitler salute before Mirande's coffin. It was through them that Mirande, who wanted to learn Breton, would meet the most committed Nazi of them all, their puppet, the brilliant Celtic scholar Goulvenn 'Pennaod'. This Breton nationalist or 'Nazi-alist' escaped the firing squad to which the other members of the *Breiz Atao* group were sentenced because he was too young and had only distributed propaganda and weapons; he was sentenced to two years in prison and five years of civic disability. In order to recover his civic rights, he enlisted in the army and parachuted into Diên-Biên-Phu in the First Indochina War. He is one of the characters in Saint Loup's novel *Les nostalgiques* (The nostalgics). Later on, Captain Pennaod was a clandestine activist in the Organisation Armée Secréte (OAS, Secret Armed Organization), a right-wing paramilitary group.

Unfortunately for the Breton language, the majority of the writers who had just unified it went through a period of involvement with the *Breiz Atao* group, either politically or militarily: Perrot and

---

79   Ibid., 47, 109.

Jasson were shot, Per Denez was reduced to silence, while Olivier Mordrel and Roparz Hemon took refuge in Ireland.[80]

Mirande, who was one of those people who never did military service, and who did not know how to use a weapon (just a library paper knife), preached the "violence" that he discovered in the behavior of the SS and in *Mein Kampf;* this love and admiration for Hitler's violence was regularly fostered by Pennaod, who encouraged him to drink during his depressive phases. In effect, Mirande was bipolar and, during his manic phases, he associated with moderate Basque nationalists, with royalists, and in a different context with the L.V.F. (Légion des Volontaires Français, Legion of French Volunteers), veterans of the Charlemagne Division, Frenchmen who fought for the Germans in World War II.

Mirande's violence was essentially verbal, but initially, in 1948, he tried in vain to organize a Basque armed struggle against the two states that had divided Basque territory between them. This is clear in two letters he sent to a young engineer of regionalist and democratic ideas in 1948. One of his 1950 poems, "Oroituz" (In remembrance),[81] seems to have been inspired by the Horst-Wessel-Lied. And he wrote a poem on the burial of a *Breiz Atao* collaborator, "Goiztar txoriek."[82]

It is more in his articles that we can find an echo of Nazi and anti-Semitic theories, and especially his praise of violence and his rejection of pacifism, which were limited to thunderous verbal declarations, Hitler salutes, tall tales, and scandals. In order to provoke

---

80 In an email dated October 12, 2018, Gwendal Denis modifies Peillen's account, providing additional information and corrections concerning the individuals mentioned: "This passage is surprising, to say the least: Perrot was never part of *Breiz Atao* (BA), but he did participate in the 1941 meeting about the new spelling. He was assassinated by the resistance in 1943. Jasson was part of BA, but he did not take part in the agreement on the new spelling (he did not speak Breton). He was sentenced to death and shot in July 1946. Per Denez was never part of BA, and he was also not a signatory of the agreement. In 1941, he was twenty years old and was in Cambo being treated for tuberculosis. Mordrel was sentenced to death in absentia in 1946 and took refuge in Argentina in 1948, not in Ireland. He was part of BA, but he was not among the signatories of the agreement on the new spelling. Roparz Hemon, who was a signatory of the agreement, was never attached to BA. Sentenced to civic disability in 1946, he went into exile in Ireland the following year."

81 Mirande, *Jon Mirande, olerkaria*, 52.

82 Mirande, *Poemak 1950–1966*, ed. Larrea, 65. The collaborator was León Jasson, whom Peillen mentions a few lines earlier. A member of the pro-Nazi paramilitary unit Bezen Perrot, Jasson subsequently enlisted in an SS unit and was shot on July 17, 1946. The poem Mirande translated was written by Jasson in prison on the eve of his execution, July 16, 1946 (see above).

his democratic visitors, he played recordings of Third Reich SS songs and speeches by Hitler, Goebbels, Goering, and Lutze.

He wrote no articles describing Nazi theories and practices.

Not a Holocaust denier, he acknowledged the Holocaust of the Jews, but he was a revisionist, disputing the numbers on the basis of an article published by an American Jew that stated that only (!!!) two million Jews had been eliminated.

He openly declared himself to be anti-Jewish due to Jewish "control" over the press. His anti-capitalism and his disdain for money were perhaps a consequence of these ideas.

He translated from Dutch a poem by the neo-pagan René de Clerq, "Niet lederen kan heiden zijn," that has been characterized as a Nazi work, but the text has nothing to do with that ideology.

N'importe qui ne peut être païen	Not Everyone Can Be a Pagan
N'importe qui ne peut être païen,	Not everyone can be a pagan.
Pour cela il faut être vaillant	For that, he must be brave,
Aimer le soleil et le vin	Love the sun and wine,
Sentir la volonté dans ses veines.	Feel his will in his veins.
N'importe qui ne peut dans le sein de la terre	Not everyone can be in the earth's bosom
Trouver tous ses désirs	Find all his desires
Tant qu'il vit et va sans peur	To the extent that he comes and goes without fear,
Sans se lasser jusqu'à la mort.	Without rest until death.
Il peut oui pour ses terriens ingrats	He is able to hear, on behalf of his ungrateful fellow residents on the earth,
La terre qui les aime comme une mère	The earth that loves them like a mother.
Le païen existe en restant vivant	A pagan exists by staying alive

Dans la plénitude de la beauté.	In the fullness of beauty.
Au petit matin s'envole l'alouette	The lark takes wing at dawn,
En chantant et son ciel est juste	Singing, and his heaven is just,
Beau et juste élevé	Beautiful, and just raised on high.
Tous les autres cieux ne sont que mensonge.	All the other heavens are no more than lies.
Tous les autres sont illusion	All the others are illusions.
Seule cette voûte étoilée	Only this starry vault
Transborde les étoiles anciennes:	Carries across the ancient stars:
La beauté fleurit en moi.⁽ʾ⁾	Beauty flowers in me.

A 1914 German soldier's poem, "Ich hatte einen Kamareden," excellently translated into Basque as "Banin adiskide bat," has also been characterized as a Nazi work: it is a soldier's lament for a comrade's death, with no mention of "impure blood" that "waters our furrows" (see above).

The only German army war poem, it seems to me, is "Oroituz," "In memoriam," subtitled "Godu abestia," "The song of the Goths."[83]

Oroituz

Les noirs chevaux hennissaient,	The black horses neighed,
Les hautes plaines alentour brûlaient,	The high plains blazed on all sides,
Nous prenions notre repos	We took our repose
Réjouis par les plaintes des veuves.	Rejoicing in widows' laments.
Tous les vautours envieux observaient	All the envious vultures looked on

---

83 Mirande, *Jon Mirande, olerkaria*, 52.

Pour se gaver de charogne humaine;	In order to glut themselves on human carrion;
Dans les fougères les ventres des filles forcées	Amid the ferns the bellies of forced girls
Pleuraient du sang par leur plaie;	Wept blood from their wound;
La fertile nuit écoulait son froid poison	The fertile night poured out its poisonous cold,
Bonheur pour nos cœurs endoloris	Good fortune for our grieved hearts,
Souvenir de générations passées.	The remembrance of past generations.
Camarades! Dans les jardins de la mort	Comrades! In the gardens of death
Nous errions au clair de lune,	We wandered beneath the light of the moon.
Quand notre Midi brillera t-il?	When will our Midi shine?

Racist, yes. He thought that hybridization with non-European races would bring with it a disappearance of European culture; a more justified version of the same disquiet is what gives rise to the fear of European decline caused by the ideology of the Islamic State.

Where Mirande's contact with the National Front is concerned, it lasted for two meetings, the first when Goulvenn Pennaod introduced him to Jean Marie Le Pen on the occasion of the Alliance Bretonne's award of a literary prize to Jean Markale.[84] He subsequently attended a National Front meeting at which the discourse was different; populism and Jacobinism disgusted him, and he tore up on his way out the card that he had taken upon entering, especially since he also found nothing about a plan for armed struggle.

He preferred to meet with the nostalgic neo-Nazi groups that the novelist Saint Loup describes in *Les Hérétiques* (The heretics) and

---

84 See the photo in *La ahijada*, 31 and 33.

Les Nostalgiques (The nostalgics), or else with far-right writers like Alain de Benoist.

Mirande's anti-Soviet views were highly nuanced. He wrote about Basque democrats and the Cold War in the journal *Gernika*: "Now you impose on us hatred of Soviet Russia. As a Nazi, I am not a Communist, but I attest that Stalinism does not lead to the destruction of minority cultures, which in the time of the tsars, unlike in today's Russia, were persecuted and condemned to disappear in short order, and which currently enjoy national status."

In the course of Jon Mirande's journey, there were three of us who failed in the attempt to drag him away from his demons: Jon Etxaide, a great friend of Mirande and a Catholic writer in Donostia-San Sebastián (Gipuzkoa); Andima Ibinagabeitia, a Bizkaian nationalist writer; and myself, Txomin Peillen of Paris, an atheist. Mirande sometimes characterized me as a biological materialist, and he thought that I was "too much of an aesthete" to appreciate philosophy. Illness and Nazi comrades were stronger than we were. Ill as he was, he tried to commit suicide in 1947 and 1955, and he succeeded in 1972.

BIBLIOGRAPHY

Ar stourmer gouenn ha glenn, gwad ha glad! 1962, no. 1. Genver-c'hwevrer, Savigny-sur-Orge, . . . Paris.

———. 1962, no. 2. Meurzh-ebrel, Savigny-sur-Orge, . . . Paris.

———. 1962, no. 3. Mae-mezheven, Savigny-sur-Orge, . . . Paris.

———. 1962, nos. 4/5. Gourzheren-Heneoal, Savigny-sur-Orge,... Paris.

———. 1962, no. 6. Du-Kevarzu, Savigny-sur-Orge, . . . Paris. At bibliotheque.idbe-bzh.org/recherche-enklask.php?l=fr.

Arcocha-Scarcia, Aurélie (Arkoxta, A.). "Imaginaire et poésie dans *Maldan behera* de Gabriel Aresti (1933–1975)." *ASJU* 27, no. 1 (1993): 3–240.

———. "Mirande eta thanatos: heriotz heroikoa." In *Jon Mirande orhoituz (1925–1972): Antologia*, edited by Patri Urkizu. Donostia-San Sebastián: Gipuzkoako Foru Aldundia, Koldo Mitxelena Kulturunea, 1997.

———. "La mirada malévola de la luna en la 'ahijada' de Jon Mirande (1925–1972)." In *Breve historia feminista de la literatura española*, edited by Iris M. Zavala, volume 6, *Breve historia feminista de la literatura española (en lengua catalana, gallega y vasca)*. Barcelona: Anthropos Editorial, 2000.

Azurmendi Otaegi, Joxe. *Mirande eta kristautasuna*. San Sebastián: Caja de Ahorros Provincial de Guipúzcoa, 1978.

Borda, Itxaro. "Jon Miranderen heziketaz." *Jon Mirande: gogoeta itxi gabea*, special issue, *Hegats* 50 (2012): 9–29.

Elizalde, Amaia. "*Haur besoetakoa* (1970), la modernité littéraire niée de l'écrivain Jon Mirande." PhD diss., Bordeaux Montaigne University, 2018.

Favereau, Francis. "Goulven Pennaod, Jon Mirande et la Bretagne." *Lapurdum* (2000): 293–305.

Gero. Jon Mirande-ren idazlan hautatuak. Gero euskal liburuak, Literatura. Bilbao: Ediciones Mensajero, 1976.

Goldschmidt, G. Arthur. "Commentaires." In Friedrich Nietzsche. *Ainsi parlait Zarathoustra*. Paris: Librairie Générale Française, 1983.

Hitler, Adolf. *Ma Doctrine*. Les grandes études politiques et sociales. Paris: Librairie Arthème Fayard, 1938.

———. *Mein Kampf*. With a preface. Histoire du XXe siècle (2015). At aufildelapensee.blog.

Ibinagabeitia, Andima. "Olerkariarenean." In Jon Mirande, *Poemak 1950–1966*. Donostia: Erein, 1984.

Jaka, Aiora. "Miranderen itzulpen argitarabe batzuk." *Senez* 39 (2010): 247–99.

Jakin 106. 1998. *Mirande arazo*. Special issue (1998).

Larrea, Jose María. *Miranderen lan kritikoak*. Iruña: Pamiela, 1985.

Lopez Adan, Emilio. "Jon Mirande, eskuin muturreko idazlea." *Mirande arazo*, special issue, *Jakin* 106 (1998): 45–58.

Milza, Pierre. *Les fascismes: Notre siècle*. Paris: Imprimerie nationale, 1985.

Mirande, Jon. *24 poema, Miranderen poemak faksimilean*. At http://www.susa-literatura.eus.

———. "Er devobis anmarvoloris." *Ar stourmer gouenn ha glenn, gwad ha glad!* 1 (1962): 8–9.

———. "Dogmennoù nevez." *Ar stourmer gouenn ha glenn, gwad ha glad!* 2 (1962): 19.

———. "Ur sell ouzh bro-spagn franco." *Ar stourmer gouenn ha glenn, gwad ha glad!* 4–5: 51–52.

———. "Niet ierdereen kan heiden zijn-ne hell ket bout pagan pep den René de Clerq, De Noodshoorn, Brezhoneg gant Jon Mirande." *Ar stourmer gouenn ha glenn, gwad ha glad!* 6 (1962): 63.

———. "Hor c'hredenn II: Paris, 25/12/1962." *Ar stourmer gouenn ha glenn, gwad ha glad!* 6 (1962): 70.

———. "Edo traidore edo abertzale (Ou traître ou patriote basque)—Pe vroadelour pe dreitour? Troidigezh gant Jon Mirande . . ." *Ar stourmer, gouenn ha glenn, gwad ha glad!* 6 (1962): 72.

———. "Culture et Folk-lore, 25 janvier 1961." In *Le Devenir Européen, organe ethniste-socialiste de doctrine et d'information: Spécial Euskadi: Hommage à Jon Mirande.* Nantes: Y. Jeanne, 1974.

———. "Ma foi: 25 décembre 1962 (Ar Stourmer n°6)." Translated from Breton by Goulven Pennaod. In *Le Devenir Européen, organe ethniste-socialiste de doctrine et d'information: Spécial Euskadi: Hommage à Jon Mirande.* Nantes: Y. Jeanne, 1974.

———. *Poemak 1950–1966.* Edited by Txema Larrea. Donostia: Erein, 1984.

———. *Claroscuros, Ilhun-argiak.* Translated by Felipe Juaristi. Leioa: UPV-EHU, 1992.

———. *Jon Miranderen gutunak (1948–1972).* Edited by Patri Urkizu. Donostia-Saint-Sebastián: Susa, 1995.

———. *Jon Mirande orhoituz (1925–1972): Antologia.* Edited by Patri Urkizu. KM Kulturunea. Donostia: Gipuzkoako Foru Aldundia-Diputación Foral de Gipuzkoa, 1997.

———. *Jon Mirande, olerkaria (Jon Mirande poète parisien).* Euskaltzainak bilduma. Bilbao: Euskaltzaindia, 2012.

Münster, Arno. *Nietzsche et le nazisme.* Collection Philosophie, épistémologie. Paris: Éd. Kimé, 1998.

Olarra, Xabier. Introduction. Jon Mirande, *24 poema*. Facsimile edition (online). Susa literatura, at http://www.susa-literatura.eus/emailuak/mirande/.

Peillen, Txomin. "Jon Mirande, penseur basque." In *Le Devenir Européen, organe ethniste-socialiste de doctrine et d'information: Spécial Euskadi: Hommage à Jon Mirande*. Nantes: Y. Jeanne, 1974.

———. "Jon Miranderen bizia." In *Jon Mirande-ren idazlan hautatuak. Gero*. Euskal liburuak, Literatura. Bilbao: Ediciones Mensajero, 1976.

———. "Jon Mirande Aiphasorho y su novela 'La ahijada'." *Revista de lenguas y literaturas catalana, gallega y vasca* 2 (1992): 99–116.

———. "Jon Miranderen ordeinua bere lekuan." *Mirande arazo*, special issue, *Jakin* 106 (1998): 11–30.

Saguxarra. Literatur aldizkaria 2 (1981).

Chapter 11

Aerial Assault on Catalonia: Nazi and Fascist Terror Bombings

Joan Villarroya

In 2013, historians Ramon Arnabat and David Iñiguez singled out 1938 as the year of terror in their study of the air raids perpetrated on the districts of Tarragona province and the Terres de l'Ebre region:

> 1938 was a year of genuine terror for most of Catalonia's populace in general, and its southern districts in particular. Nobody knew when an air raid might come: in the morning or evening, at night or at dusk, or perhaps in the middle of the day. Nor could they tell who would strike: heavy bombers, light bombers, fighter aircraft, or seaplanes. Or even whether it would be bombs or shells that fell. What was certain was that, sooner or later, flurries of fire would rain down, in the words of Antoni Rovira i Virgili. All told, this produced not only a swathe of dead and wounded and material destruction, but also a state of permanent distress, particularly among the citizens living in the cities hit most heavily by the fascists, Reus, Tarragona, and Tortosa.[1]

---

1   Ramon Arnavat and David Iñiguez, *Atac i Defensa de la reraguarda. Els bombardeigs franquistes a les comarques de Tarragona i Terres de l'Ebre 1936–1939* (Valls: Cossetània Edicions, 2013), 11–12. For more on the bombardments of Reus, see Ezequiel Gort and Palomar Salvador, *Viure sota les bombes. Els bombardeigs a Reus. 1937–1939* (Reus: Publicacions Municipals de Reus, 2010). For more on the bombardments of Tarragona, see two works by Francisco J. González Huix: *El asedio aéreo de Tarragona 1937–1939* (Tarragona: Institut d'Estudis Tarraconenses Ramon Berenguer IV; Diputació de Tarragona, 1990) and *El puerto y la mar de Tarragona durante la guerra civil, 1936–1939* (Tarragona: Institut d'Estudis Tarraconenses Ramon Berenguer IV, 1995).

Unfortunately, many other cities and villages in Catalonia beyond those in the south suffered the consequences of the Nazi and fascist assault, though perhaps we should put *fascist* before *Nazi*. In terms of the number of bombardments, the air raids carried out by the Italian Legionary Air Force caused greater damage and loss of life. One need only recall the attack on Lleida on November 2, 1937 (with over 300 casualties); Granollers on May 30, 1938 (with nearly 250 casualties); Barcelona, apart from the March bombardments, the air raids of January 15, 19, and 25, 1938 (leaving a total of 600 dead in their wake); Badalona on June 30, 1938 (with over 60 victims), and the late January/early February 1939 air raids against Figueres, which took dozens of lives. Of course, the perpetrators never acknowledged the character of these air raids as acts of terror, but always claimed that the attacks were made on legitimate military targets: a bridge in Lleida, a power plant in Granollers, command centers in Barcelona, and so forth.

Now for all this mayhem to be made possible, and without going into detail on the concept of terror bombing,[2] it is my view that there were two conditions that enabled these air raids to take place. First, the Nazi and fascist air forces had bombers in sufficient numbers to carry them out; and second, they enjoyed overwhelming air superiority from the spring of 1937 until February 1939, when the war ended, militarily speaking, in Catalonia.

For example, the Italian air force sent 197 bomber aircraft: 84 Savoia-Marchetti SM-81s, 100 Savoia-Marchetti SM-79s, and 13 Fiat BR-20s. A quarter of all aircraft sent by the Italians were bombers.[3] Notably, between January 1938 and March 1939, the 8° Stormo (8th Wing)[4] had a fleet of between 22 and 24 Savoia-Marchetti SM-79s with some 15 in service, while the 25th Night Bomber Group had 12 Savoia-Marchetti SM-81s. In total, nearly 40 bombers were dedicated to air raids against the coastline held by the Republic. Nor should we forget the German unit of the Condor Legion AS/88 based in Pollença, which reached a total of 27 Heinkel He-59 seaplanes that would play a key part in the coastal blockade and in the shelling and bombardment of lines of communication, especially railroads. In addition, the Condor

---

2   For a good summary of the terror bombings between 1919 and 1936, see Xabier Irujo, *El Gernika de Richthofen. Un ensayo de bombardeo de terror* (Gernika: Gernikako Bakearen Museoa Fundazioa, 2012), 309.

3   Edoardo Grassia, *L'Aviazione Legionaria da bombardamento* (Rome: IBN Editore, 2009), 87.

4   Arnavat and Iñiguez, *Atac i Defensa de la reraguarda*, 23.

Legion[5] had 62 Junkers Ju-52, a civilian aircraft converted into a bomber; 100 Heinkel He-111s, the most modern plane to ply the Spanish skies, and 29 Dornier Do-17s. At the time of the final campaign against Catalonia, a hundred of these aircraft were operational.

While the first bombardments of villages in Catalonia took place in late 1936 and early 1937, there was a spectacular increase in the number of bombardments and Catalan localities attacked from early 1938 onward. This would remain a constant until the end of the war.

The following pages will look at the most terrifying air raids suffered by the Catalan cities of Lleida and Granollers, examine the bombardments of Barcelona in March 1938, and offer a more detailed analysis of the bombardments between December 23, 1938, the date on which the final offensive was launched, and February 10, 1939, when the campaign in Catalonia officially came to an end.

THE AIR RAIDS ON LLEIDA AND GRANOLLERS

These two air raids were among the cruelest suffered by any Catalan cities. In a single bombardment, each city saw more than two hundred of its inhabitants lose their lives. In both cases the air raids were attributed to the German air force, as if such barbarism could only come at the hands of the Germans, not the Italians. Historical investigations, however, have shown that the German air force was innocent in both cases and the perpetrator of so much death and devastation was, in fact, the Italian Legionary Air Force.

In the case of the capital of Terra Ferma, Lleida, the air raid of November 2, 1937 was not the only one that it suffered. In March 1938, with Francoist troops at its gates, it was once again bombarded. The air raid of November 1937, however, was without doubt the worst to befall any Catalan city that year and it has been immortalized by the photographs of Agustí Centelles and the memory of dozens of dead schoolchildren at the Liceu Escolar,[6] where a bomb leveled the

---

5   See Patrick Laureau and Jose Fernandez, *La Legion Condor* (Boulogne sur Mer: Editions Lela Presse, 1999).

6   The first appearance in print of a list containing the names of 210 people who died in this air raid came in a book by Mercè Barallat i Barés, *La repressió a la postguerra civil a Lleida (1938–1945)* (Barcelona: Publicacions de l'Abadia de Montserrat, 1991). By the same author, see also *Els bombardeigs a Lleida* (Barcelona. Publicacions de l'Abadia de Montserrat, 2013).

school building and left a horrifying death toll among the young. As noted earlier, this air raid was attributed to the planes of the Condor Legion for many years. Early in this century, however, a brief reference[7] noted the participation of nine Savoia-Marchetti SM-79 planes in the bombardment of a bridge over the Segre River in the vicinity of Lleida. In 2011, in fact, Josep Pla Blanch and Antonio Ruiz Mostany[8] settled the matter once and for all: the attack was carried out by nine Savoia-Marchetti SM-79 planes that had taken off in Soria on a mission to bomb the electrochemical plant in the village of Flix, in the district of Ribera d'Ebre. The village, however, was shrouded in clouds and the nine planes turned toward Lleida, where they dropped the seven tons of bombs they were carrying upon the city. Though the Italian records speak of "*bombardamento de ponti e fabricati di Lérida*" ("the bombardment of Lleida's bridges and factories"), the bombs were actually dropped over the most central parts of the city. The attack caught the inhabitants by surprise; the alarm sirens failed to sound, and within minutes Lleida became an inferno. Bombs struck the Liceu Escolar, where more than sixty students between nine and thirteen years of age were buried under the rubble and died. Also damaged were the Sant Lluís market, the Bank of Spain building, and many houses in Major Street and Blondel Avenue. Some elderly residents basking in the sun on the steps of the bridge were killed by the bombs. One bomb fell on a bus full of passengers, leaving no survivors. As noted above, the historian Mercè Barallat compiles a list with the names of more than two hundred victims of the Lleida air raid. This task, however, was not a simple one, because the Francoists made the registry in which the names were recorded disappear, just as they did away with the archives and back issues of daily newspapers from the days following the attack in which the victims were named.

Until May 31, 1938, nearly two years after the outbreak of the Civil War, the city of Granollers had never been subjected to an air raid. Then, at 9:05 a.m. on the morning of that fateful day, suddenly and entirely unexpectedly, five Savoia-Marchetti SM-79 planes (the Republican communiqué mistook them for German Junkers) dropped their deadly cargo over the city center. In theory, the target of the attack was the power plant. In one minute, Granollers experienced the most tragic day of its entire history: forty 100 kg (220 lb) bombs, ten 20

---

7   Josep Mª Solé i Sabaté and Joan Villarroya i Font, *España en Llamas. La guerra civil desde el aire* (Madrid: Temas de Hoy, 2003), 121.
8   Josep Pla Blanch and Antonio Ruiz Mostany, "El bombardeo de Lérida del 2 de noviembre de 1937," *Revista Ares* 22 (November 2011), 24–31.

kg (44 lb), and ten 15 kg (33 lb) bombs rained down on the city.[9] The bombs destroyed some eighty buildings—including the famous Porxada, an open portico built in 1586 as a corn exchange—and left a tragic imprint on the civilian population. Given the time of day, and since the city had not yet been bombarded, residents were going about their daily business as usual. Some people died after taking their children to school. The initial talk was of more than 100 dead and 450 wounded; from there, however, the number of victims rose sharply and only a few days later the city hall spoke of 205 dead. All of the casualties were civilians except for two or three soldiers. Joan Garriga concludes that the death toll was at least 224,[10] because several people succumbed to their wounds between June and October 1938 – a startling number if we bear in mind that Granollers was a small city with 14,053 inhabitants in 1936, and even more startling in view of the fact the attack was carried out by only five planes.

As we have seen, the theoretical target of the Italian planes was the city's power plant, which served the Puigcerdà railroad line: However, the real objective was to bomb the city center. Garriga reproduces the communiqué of the bombardment, in which the attack on Granollers is mentioned alongside the attack on the power plant in Sant Adrià. According to the document in question, both attacks missed their targets.[11] Besides Garriga, David Gesalí and David Iñiguez also think that there was a launch error and the bombs fell a few hundred meters short of their target.

THE AIR RAIDS OF MARCH 1938[12]

In Barcelona, at 10:00 p.m. on March 16, 1938, air-raid sirens warned of the danger of an attack. Then, at exactly 10:08 p.m., a steady stream of

---

9 Joan Garriga Andreu, *Granollers. El bombardeig de Granollers* (Granollers: Àrea de Cultura i Joventut, Ajuntament de Granollers, 2002), 29.
10 Ibid., 17–18.
11 Garriga, *Granollers*, 30–31. David Gesalí and David Iñiguez, *La guerra aèria a Catalunya (1936–1939)* (Barcelona: Rafael Dalmau, 2012), 414–16.
12 For more information on these air raids, see Joan Villarroya i Font, *Els Bombardeigs de Barcelona durant la guerra civil (1936–1939)*, 2nd ed. (Barcelona: Publicacions de l'Abadia de Montserrat, 1999); Joan Villarroya and Enric Juliana, "Mussolini: Machacad Barcelona," *Revista*, suppl., *La Vanguardia*, December 16, 2001, 4; Ferdinando Pedriali, *Guerra di Spagna e Aviacione italiana*, 2nd ed. (Rome: Aeronáutica Militare Italiana, Ufficio Storico, 1992); Paola Lo Cascio and Susanna Oliveira, *Tres dies de Març* (Girona: El Punt, 2008); Gesalí and Iñiguez, *La guerra Aèria a Catalunya*; and Grassia, *L'aviazione Legionaria da bombardamento*.

bombs fell over the city, hitting several streets including València, Casp, Consell de Cent, and Riera Alta and leaving fourteen dead and forty-three wounded. This state of affairs had become increasingly common in the life of the city's inhabitants, particularly since the preceding January: sirens, air raid, end of air raid. And this ritual was being repeated with increasing frequency, though days or even weeks might pass between one air raid and the next. While residents might not have been aware of the ritual this time, it was nevertheless the same, but with one exception: one air raid followed the next with only hours separating them. According to the Italian historian Ferdinando Pedriali,[13] the technique inflicted on Barcelona left a profound impression. Used against a civilian population for the first time, the effect was terrifying. Five minutes after midnight on March 17, the sirens again sounded and the bombs once more rained down. This would be repeated for a total of thirteen times by midday on March 18, resulting in forty-one hours of terror and panic that had never before been seen in the capital of Catalonia. The alarm systems became unworkable, because the constant attacks made it difficult to tell whether the sirens marked the end of one air raid or the start of the next. The result among the populace was panic and total helplessness.

To understand the reason for these brutal air raids, it is necessary to look at the telegram received by the command of the Italian Legionary Air Force in the Balearic Islands on March 16, issuing a very explicit order: "*Iniziare da sta notte azione violenta su Barcellona con martellamento diluito nel tempo*" ("Tonight initiate violent action against Barcelona with shelling spaced out in time"). The telegram was signed by the deputy minister of the Italian Military Air Force, General Giuseppe Valle, but the orders had come directly from Mussolini himself. From this moment forward, a series of air raids were launched against the most populous areas of Barcelona with the aim of disrupting the city's defenses, swamping its passive defense services, and sowing panic and confusion among its civilian population. Between three and five planes took part in each attack, chiefly Savoia-Marchetti SM-79s and Savoia-Marchetti SM-81s. The historical record of the Legionary Air Force of the Balearic Islands gives the following number of planes taking part in the successive air raids on Barcelona: 10 SM-81s on March 16; 16 SM-79s and 9 SM-81s on March 17; and 12 SM-79s on March 18.

In no corner of the city could the populace feel safe. Barcelona's historic center, its Eixample neighborhood, and La Sagrera were all severely

---

13   Pedriali, *Guerra di Spagna e Aviacione italiana*, 353.

battered by the Italian bombs. The list of affected squares and streets is very long: Plaça Catalunya, Plaça Francesc Lairet, and Plaça Universitat, as well as the streets of Còrsega, Entença, Provença, Tallers, Diputació, Riereta, Egipcíaques, Hospital, Ronda Sant Pau, Amàlia, Gran Via de les Corts Catalanes, Consell de Cent, Aragó, Girona, Casp, Nou de la Rambla, and more. Many buildings were leveled, killing or wounding the people who lived inside. Pedestrians were also killed as they waited for the streetcar and even passengers in a bus run by the Roca company were burned alive when their vehicle caught fire. The greatest damage from the March air raids, however, befell the intersection of Gran Via de les Corts Catalanes and Balmes, where one of the forty-four bombs dropped by the five Savoia-Marchetti SM-79s taking part in the air raid at 2:00 p.m. on March 17 struck a truck carrying TNT, multiplying the destructive effects of the bomb. The 23 soldiers in the truck and all the pedestrians in the vicinity lost their lives in the enormous explosion, which raised a column of smoke some 250 meters (820 feet) into the air.

As the hours passed, the number of victims rose. At 5:00 p.m. on March 17, word reached the head of the Spanish government, Juan Negrín, that the total stood at 400 dead. When the Catalan government gave the official total of casualties a few days later, on March 26, the number of dead had risen to 875, of whom 118 were children. In the coming weeks and months, additional wounded would die until the actual figure neared a thousand. The physical destruction was also significant, with forty-eight buildings destroyed and seventy-five seriously damaged.

The international reactions to such barbarism were many, and a number of them were highly critical. The German ambassador to Nationalist Spain himself, Eberhard von Stohrer, remarked on the brutality of the air raids: "I have learned that the aerial attacks carried out on Barcelona a few days ago by Italian bombers were literally terrible. Nearly every neighborhood in the city has suffered. There is no indication that the aim was to hit military targets."[14] On March 24, the Vatican published a note in the Osservatore Romano deploring the air raids and the number of innocent lives they had claimed. Many newspapers and magazines around the world remonstrated against the actions of the Italian air force. The US Secretary of State expressed his condemnation as follows: "On this occasion, when the loss of human lives among the non-combatant civilian population is perhaps the greatest that has ever occurred in history, I believe I speak for all Americans when I express

---

14   Archives Secrètes de la Wilhelmstrasse, Telegram 373, Paris (1956), 510.

a feeling of horror at what has happened in Barcelona, and when I formulate the profound hope that in the future civilian population centers will no longer be the target of military bombardment from the air." [15]Despite all these condemnations and many others, the air raids went on and Barcelona was to be subjected to bombardment until only a few hours before Francoist troops occupied the city.

As mentioned earlier, the order for the air raids was given personally by Mussolini, but the question is why. What was the trigger? Italian historians themselves wonder whether the order to bomb Barcelona was the result of an attack of envy at Hitler's initiative to annex Austria on March 12, 1938, or a warning sign to the French government, which may have been on the verge of authorizing a massive sale of arms to the Republican government. Perhaps a combination of the two factors played a role.

THE AIR RAIDS DURING THE CATALONIA CAMPAIGN

In late 1938, with the outcome of the war a foregone conclusion, the Francoist army launched an offensive against Catalonia. The rebel air force, with total dominion in the air, continued to carry out raids on cities and villages of Catalonia until the final day of the offensive, spreading fear among the populace and preventing any resistance. In fact, some cities suffered the worst air raids of the war only a few days or even hours before being "liberated," as the Francoist war communiqués euphemistically put it.

During the Catalonia campaign, the three branches of the Francoist air force—the German Condor Legion, the Italian Legionary Air Force, and the Spanish Air Force—intensified their attacks on Catalan towns. It is difficult to determine precisely which of the three air forces bore specific responsibility for the air raids. From its base in Majorca, the Italian Legionary Air Force remained in charge of attacking coastal cities. As the Francoist troops occupied them, however, the Italians redirected their air raids toward more northerly villages and their area of operations gradually dwindled. By mid-January, some Italian squadrons had actually ceased flying over Catalonia.

---

15 Hilari Raguer, "La Santa Sede y los bombardeos de Barcelona," *Historia y Vida* 145 (April 1980), 22–35.

A dire precedent for what was to come during the campaign took place a few days before it began. The village of El Perelló was leveled by a series of air raids on November 15, 16, and 17, carried out by the Condor Legion. Given the number and virulence of the attacks, it was a miracle that the death toll was low: some twenty died in total, because most of the populace was living outside the village, precisely out of fear of such bombardments.[16]

In the first two days of the offensive, the Francoist air force took little action against the cities on the Catalan home front. The chief cause of this inactivity, however, lay in the dreadful weather conditions in Catalonia at the time; as the weather improved, the planes again became ever-present and the list of bombed Catalan cities grew sharply.

In 1938, Christmas Day was an especially tragic day for the town of Ponts. An attack by a bomber squadron destroyed numerous buildings and claimed the lives of nearly twenty people as a consequence of wounds caused by the bombs. To the south of Ponts, in the district of Les Garrigues, two other villages were attacked on the same day, Les Borges Blanques and Castelldans, causing damage and claiming lives.

Along the coast of Tarragona, seaplanes engaged in intense activity, bombing and shelling the railroad stations at Tarragona, Sant Vicenç de Calders, and Torredembarra as well as the hospital of Parc de Samà. On December 26, five SM-79 planes from Group 27 bombarded the city of Reus. One bomb fell on the entrance of an air-raid shelter, killing eight women. On December 27, the Italian air force carried out two air raids on Barcelona: in the first, the bombs were dropped on the port and caused little damage, while the second hit the area surrounding the church of Santa Maria del Mar and several people died. In the port, the vessels *Stancroft* and *Lake Neuchatel* registered minor damage. In the latter case, a bomb fell on the ship's hold, but failed to detonate.

On the same day, December 27, Cervera, Tàrrega, Mollerussa, and Cubells in the province of Lleida were attacked. Throughout the night, the seaplanes kept shelling the railroad station at Sant Vicenç de Calders. Then, on December 28, they attacked the localities of Comarruga, Sant Vicenç de Calders, Hospitalet de l'Infant, and Reus. On December 29, they bombed and shelled Vila-seca, Altafulla, Sant Vicenç de Calders, Milà, Cubelles, Vilallonga, and Vallmoll. In the

---

16 Josep Solé i Sabaté and Joan Villarroya i Font, *Catalunya sota les bombes (1936–1939)* (Barcelona: Publicacions de l'Abadia de Montserrat, 1986), 106–7.

first of these Tarragona localities, the bombs fell right in the middle of the village, leveling several houses and claiming a number of lives. For some of these places, the bombings in this period were the first of the entire war.

In the first dozen days of January, several cities in the western districts of Catalonia were bombarded. On New Year's Day, Cervera was hit. On the January 4 and 7, Bellpuig was the target. In the first attack on Bellpuig, a bomb fell on the house of the Roig-Torres family, killing the couple and their four children, six years old, four years old, two years old, and a seven-month-old baby. Vinaixa and Arbeca were bombarded between January 5 and 8; Barbens on January 6; Ciutadilla on January 12, and Maldà on January 15.

The city of Tarragona was continually bombarded in the days prior to the arrival of Francoist troops. On January 4, a squadron of the 2nd Spanish Bomber Brigade, consisting of twelve SM-79 planes, attacked the port and the railroad station in the only air raid carried out against the city by an exclusively Spanish unit.[17]

On the same day, a formation of twenty-three He-111 bombers of the Condor Legion subjected the port and the lower part of the city to a violent bombardment. One of the planes was shot down by a Republican fighter plane and fell into the sea close to the coastline. Two of the plane's crew members, the pilots Walter Fleming and Frank Repke, ejected in parachutes and were taken prisoner, while the other two crew members died.[18] Also on the same day, a patrol of Ju-87 Stukas carried out a dive-bombing of the port.

As the Francoist army approached the city of Tarragona, the bombardment intensified. On January 6, five SM-79s launched an attack on the port, hitting the patrol boat V-11 of the Flotilla de Vigilància de Catalunya, which had arrived in Tarragona from Barcelona in the early hours of the day. The bombs had a direct impact on the vessel, which sank rapidly.[19] On January 9, He-111 planes of the Condor Legion bombarded the railroad station, taking five lives.

---

17 González Huix, *El asedio aéreo de Tarragona 1937–1939*, 130.
18 Ibid., 130–91.
19 Ibid., 136.

On the eve of the Francoist troops' entry into Tarragona, nearly all the planes of the Condor Legion swarmed over the city. Lluís Maria Mezquida[20] describes the air raid thus:

At 2:00 p.m., 96 Nationalist bombers and fighter planes burst into the skies over the Camp de Tarragona region from the west. While the fighter planes harried the lines of communication, the bombers initiated a run over Tarragona dropping projectiles on No. 9, Carrer de la Merceria; No. 22, Carrer Major; and No. 4, Carrer dels Cavallers, "Cal Trip," which also affected the rear of the house at No. 9 in Avinguda de Ramón y Cajal. Bombs were also dropped in the vicinity of a building known as the "Casal dels Vells" (run by the Little Sisters of the Poor), the port area, and particularly along the length of the highways to Valencia, Reus, and Valls, which the Republican forces were using for their retreat. Likewise, bombs again struck the support on the bank opposite the metal bridge over the River Francolí, with some hitting the tobacco factory and a high-caliber bomb landing on the square known as the Plaza de los Artilleros del Sitio, in front of the "La Chartreuse" factory, and causing a major choke point. The planes remained in the skies of our district until 3:00 p.m., when they returned to their bases unharried, as Republican fighters did not appear and the antiaircraft defenses had been evacuated the night before.

Nor would this be the last air raid. In the morning of the same day of January 15, Ju-87 Stukas twice bombarded the port, sinking the vessel *Cabo Cullera*. According to F. J. González Huix:[21] "In the history of military aviation, the *Cabo Cullera* in Tarragona marks the first time that dive-bombers sank a ship in port during wartime." At noon that day, Francoist troops occupied the city.

Tarragona was not the only locality in the southern districts of Catalonia to be bombarded in the first days of January. Reus suffered bombardment on January 4, 5, 6, 12, and 14, while Valls was hit on January 6 and 14. All of these air raids claimed lives. At Espluga de Francolí, seven people died and twenty-two were injured when seven planes dropped their deadly cargo over the village on New Year's Day.

---

20   Lluís Mª Mezquida, *La batalla del Ebro*, vol. 3 (Tarragona: Diputación de Tarragona, 1970), 170.
21   González Huix, *El asedio aéreo de Tarragona 1937–1939*, 147.

Once the regional capital of Tarragona was occupied by the Francoist troops, the air raids were concentrated against the villages between Tarragona and Barcelona. Sitges, Vilanova i la Geltrú, and Vilafranca were bombarded between the days of January 18 and 21.[22] All of these attacks resulted in bloodshed. In Sitges, the heaviest bombardment took place on January 20, 1939. The inhabitants were stricken with panic and the noise of the exploding bombs still lives on in the memory of many who survived those grim hours.

Nearer Barcelona, the city of Martorell was bombarded on January 23, with eight people dying from shrapnel. On January 25, it was the turn of Monistrol de Montserrat. The Francoist *Causa General* sets out a list of bomb-damaged buildings. Curiously, this list appears under "Estado número 3," which corresponds to the "List of tortures, building fires, lootings, destructions of churches and objects of worship, desecrations and other criminal acts that must be considered serious because of their circumstances, alarm or terror, with the exclusion of assassinations committed within the municipality during the Red Domination."[23] The appearance of Monistrol in the eyes of a monk from Montserrat some days after the bombardment was grim indeed. The village looked half-destroyed and the monk wondered what strategic reasons could possibly lay behind such an attack.

The capital of the district of Bages, Manresa, was bombarded on January 19 by the ten planes of the Third Squadron of the Second Spanish Air Brigade that dropped their bombs on the railroad station and the houses located in the vicinity.

Farther north, Vic and Manlleu were bombarded on January 20 and in both cases there were numerous dead. These two air raids were also carried out by the Third Squadron of the Second Spanish Air Brigade. The squadron that bombed the bridge at Manlleu and the railroad lines communicated that they had hit their target.

Between January 23 and 30, various localities were bombarded in the district of Vallés. The capital of Vallés Oriental, Granollers, was attacked on January 24, 25, and 26. The death toll was greater than thirty, but the damage was not as extensive as the damage caused by

---

22 For more on the bombardments of the Penedès region, see Ramon Arnavat and David Iñiguez David, eds., with Adrian Cabezas and David Gesalí, *El Penedès sota les bombes (Alt Penedès, Baix Penedès, Garraf). Crònica d'un setge aeri (1937–1939)* (Valls: Cossetània, 2012).

23 Solé i Sabaté and Villarroya, *España en llamas*, 238.

the savage air raid of May 31, 1938. On January 29, La Garriga was bombarded for a second time. Fourteen people were recorded as victims of the attack. The records in the civil registry specify that their deaths occurred because of the "bombardment suffered on the occasion of the town's liberation by the glorious Nationalist army."[24]

Between January 21 and 26, the air force carried out several air raids in the district of Maresme, located on the coastline to the north of Barcelona. The village that had witnessed the sinking of the vessel *Ciudad de Barcelona* off its coast in May 1937 was bombarded at 1:00 p.m. on January 21. The bombs affected a variety of houses in the town center and killed several people, mostly women. The primary target of the air raid, which was carried out by five SM-79s, was a convoy sailing for Barcelona, while the secondary target was the port of Barcelona itself. As they could not locate the convoy and the port lay under heavy cloud cover, the planes headed toward Malgrat, where they dropped forty-nine 100 kg bombs and twenty 20 kg bombs.

On January 25, it was the turn of Arenys de Mar, and on the following day, while the Francoist troops entered Barcelona, Masnou and Premià de Mar were bombarded, with the air raid against Masnou being particularly deadly.

THE FINAL AIR RAIDS ON BARCELONA

On the last day of December, an air raid over Barcelona city center hit Rambla de Catalunya, the corner of Diputació and Balmes, Enric Granados, and the building of the University of Barcelona. In Enric Granados, various cars caught fire and some people inside them lost their lives. The occupants of one of the vehicles were two members of the Sabadell city council.[25] The number of deaths exceeded fifty and seventeen of the twenty-seven wounded who were brought to the Hospital Clínic died shortly after being admitted.[26] An international commission[27] that investigated the air raid declared the following: "Barcelona (December 31; 44 dead, 66 seriously wounded and 25 with minor injuries): premeditated attack against people, carried out by bombs

---

24 Ibid., 239.
25 *La Vanguardia,* January 3, 1939.
26 *La Vanguardia* mentions 61 dead on January 3.
27 Pablo de Azcárate, *Mi embajada en Londres durante la guerra civil española* (Barcelona: Ariel, 1976), 108.

specially aimed at this goal, at a time when the streets were exceptionally crowded and in a part of the city in which civilians believed they were safe from air raids since March 1938."

Among the people wounded in the air raid was the son of General Riquelme, Augusto Riquelme Ojeda, captain of engineering in the Navy, who succumbed to his injuries a few days later. On January 8, his funeral was reported in the press.[28]

The historian Ferran Soldevila[29] speaks of the air raid in his memoirs, confirming that some of the bombs fell on the Historic Building of the University of Barcelona. By contrast, Tomás Caballé Clos, a contemporary apologist of the Franco regime, says that they were false alarms and that they had been ordered by the Republican authorities to frighten some Catalan parliamentary representatives who were meeting in a residence in Rambla de Catalunya.[30]

As we have seen, the air raid was no false alarm. On that very day the new French ambassador, Jules Henry, had presented his credentials to the president, Manuel Azaña, at a ceremony held in the Palace of Pedralbes. The ambassador had arrived at the palace by car escorted by the presidential guard in full dress uniform. It goes without saying that the retinue had aroused great expectation as it traveled up Diagonal Avenue to the palace.

Twenty-six days remained before the Francoist troops would occupy the capital of Catalonia, but the presence of bombers over the city was constant. Air raids struck the city on January 4, 8, and 9, hitting the port and its surroundings. On January 16, five SM-79s carried out a bombardment of the port of Barcelona. After bombing the port, one of the planes sent a message to Juan Negrín, the prime minister. According to José Luis Alcofar Nassaes:

> One of the groups of fast bombers, under the command of Lieutenant Colonel Seidl, bombarded the port; then it turned toward the upper parts of the city to deliver a message to the prime minister of the Republican government, Juan Negrín. The antiaircraft reaction was very intense when they saw that the planes were leaving the port and turning inland toward the west;

28 *La Vanguardia*, January 7 and 8, 1939.
29 Ferran Soldevila, *Al llarg de la meva vida* (Barcelona: Edicions 62, 1970), 532.
30 Tomás Caballé y Clos, *Barcelona Roja. Dietario de la revolución* (Barcelona: Libreria Argentina, 1939), 252.

Seidl's plane was hit and barely managed to return to its base in Majorca, because the formation was also attacked by enemy fighter planes out to sea. According to Italian information, a 'Mosca' fighter was shot down and two others were hit.[31]

The Diari Històric del 27è Grup de Bombardeigs confirms that the air raid and the message did exist and that the Italians were attacked by Republican fighters that hit some of the planes, but did not shoot them down. Between January 21 and 25, Barcelona firefighters responded to twenty-eight calls for help in different bomb-struck parts of the city – the highest number of responses of any time during the war, with the exception of the month of March 1938. The Condor Legion was the leading player in the January air raids on Barcelona. Between January 21 and 25, the German air force carried out nearly forty bombardments of the city, mostly of the port and the nearby neighborhood of Barceloneta, with some strikes against the old city. Taking part on the first day of the attacks were thirty-four He-111 and three Ju-87 Stukas. Over the same period, the Italian Legionary Air Force carried out three air raids on January 22, 23, and 24, while the Spanish air force carried out a raid on January 21, its only attack against Barcelona recorded throughout the entire war. On January 25, on the eve of the entry of the Francoist troops into Barcelona, the air raids on the city ended. Their intensity in the days prior to occupation had been the greatest of the whole war, although they largely affected the port and nearby neighborhoods. It is difficult to determine exactly the air raids suffered by Barcelona in the final days of January 1939 because there are some inconsistencies in the information provided by the Italians, the summary reports of the Francoist air raids, and the information from the passive defense forces.

In those final days, the spirits of Barcelona's residents were at rock-bottom. According to Caballé Clos:[32]

The repeated air raids had left spirits in despondency. Many, many citizens, who would not quickly give up because of their ideological convictions, would give up expeditiously in order to bring an end once and for all to the mortal danger of the bombs. The part of Barcelona closest to the port, generally all of the old city, presented a complete absence of life that gave it the look of a cemetery. Most of the commercial establishments

31 José Luis Alcofar Nassaes, *La aviación legionària en la guerra española* (Barcelona: Euro Editorial, 1975), 253.
32 Caballé y Clos, *Barcelona Roja*, 254.

closed their doors. The residents of the area abandoned their apartments, moving to the homes of friends and acquaintances. Nobody inhabited Barceloneta. Barcelona practically ended at Plaza Cataluña. On the Paralelo, not a living soul was about.

These lines reinforce the idea of what the air raids represented for the morale of the populace living in the cities on the home front.

THE AIR RAIDS IN THE CLOSING DAYS OF THE CIVIL WAR

After the fall of Barcelona, the war was practically over, from the military point of view. Between Barcelona and the French border, there were no organized Republican military units, only some isolated detachments that tried to slow the advance of the Francoist troops with sporadic resistance in a few specific places. What could be found between Barcelona and the border, however, were men, women and children fleeing toward France in their tens of thousands. The roads and highways were full of terrorized, starving people heading toward an uncertain future on an exodus that was without precedent in the country's history.

It is, therefore, totally unjustifiable in such circumstances that the Francoist air force should continue bombarding and shelling cities and villages in the province of Girona, seeking out supposed military targets, the destruction of which would not change the course of the war but would, by contrast, cause high mortality among the fleeing civilian population. Figueres became the clearest and most tragic example. Franco himself had issued orders to General Kindelán, head of the Francoist air force, saying that "we should not order more bombardments of towns than are strictly necessary." Kindelán informed General Dávila of the order to restrict the bombardments, in theory, and to carry them out only when absolutely necessary and only if there were military targets.[33]

However, was there any military target that justified bombardment when the Republican army was already practically nonexistent? How can hundreds of civilian deaths be explained if only military targets were to be bombarded according to the orders? The response is clear. First, the Francoist air force continued the bombardments until the final moments of the war in Catalonia; and second, the mentioned military

---

33   José María Martínez Bande, *La campaña de Cataluña* (Madrid: Editorial San Martín, 1979), 113.

targets were, in many cases, defenseless urban centers with their streets full of long columns of fugitives fleeing toward France.

The city of Girona had not suffered a serious air raid since the spring of 1938, at least in terms of victims. This situation, however, changed in late January when planes over the city became an increasingly frequent sight. It must be borne in mind that rivers of people were arriving in the city in those days, seeking accommodation in any corner of the place. This was the situation on January 27, the day after the occupation of Barcelona, when bombs began to fall over Girona, as they continued to do on January 28 and 29 and on February 1. The Francoist war communiqués always speak of bombardments of military targets, primarily railroad stations, but the reality was starkly different because the bombs fell on the city center and caused real physical and human destruction. A bomb fell on the cathedral, producing a hole three meters (ten feet) wide and causing damage to the stained-glass windows. Apparently, the air raid of January 28 was carried out by squadrons of He-111s, which would logically be part of the Condor Legion.

The areas of Girona affected by the air raid on February 1 were some houses on the highway to Barcelona and in Plaça del Carril. The building of the Little Sisters of the Poor suffered a direct strike and a number of priests staying there were killed. In total, around thirty local people died in this series of attacks, although witnesses at the time recall that totally unknown people passing through also died, suggesting that the death toll was higher.

On the last day of January 1939, the villages of Sils, Maçanet de la Selva, and Sant Hilari Sacalm in the province of Girona were bombarded. All three villages suffered loss of life. In Sant Hilari, the air raid was carried out by five SM-79s of the 289th squadron based at the Valenzuela airfield (Zaragoza), which dropped sixty 50 kg bombs.

One of the towns that had experienced the anxiety and suffering of the air raids until shortly before the entry of the Francoist troops was La Bisbal. Because La Bisbal contained no military targets, its inhabitants were confident that the war would end without causing damage there. On February 3, however, the situation abruptly changed. Twice the Italian air force strew the streets with ruins and corpses, resulting in one of the worst tragedies in the town's history. The death toll topped twenty, the panic was enormous, and most of the people fled toward the outskirts. The town was left deserted, sorrowful, and silent, without a single living soul on the street; this was how the Italian troops found it as they made their entry on the night of February 5.

More toward the interior of the province of Girona, Ribes de Freser and Sant Quirze de Besora were bombarded on January 23, while Campdevànol suffered the same fate on January 27. The attack on Campdevànol had the most serious consequences, with thirty-five people losing their lives. On the same January 27, seventeen He-111s bombarded the station at Massanes. At 8:20 a.m. on the following morning, another group of He-111s attacked the port of Palamós.

The Italian air force, which had its base at the Valenzuela airfield (Zaragoza), bombarded the ports of Palamós, Roses, and Port de la Selva on January 27. These operations featured fifteen SM-79s dropping 180 50 kg bombs on the targets. The land-based planes again bombarded Palamós on February 1.

Up to the latter part of January, Ripoll and its thousand-year-old monastery had not yet been bombarded. That, however, was about to change. On January 22, 23, and 25, several squadrons of planes bombarded the railroad station. Two days before the entry of the Francoist troops into the city, the air raids grew much more intense and bombs were dropped on the city center. In 1940, here is how the city architect would explain the bombardment to the civil governor of Girona:

> The fourth bombardment was carried out on the morning of the following February 5, two days before liberation, by six planes that dropped some fifty bombs on the city center. The bombing run went from south to north. The bombardment produced great damage in the city, not only the direct damage caused by bombs falling on buildings, but also the effects from the explosion of a truck carrying TNT that was hit by a bomb where it was parked in front of the houses at No. 20 and 22 in Passeig de Ragull. Residents of the neighborhood had been forced to evacuate, leaving their windows and balconies open as in previous bombardments in order to avoid shattered windowpanes. However, when the truck exploded, not only did the windowpanes shatter, but so did the woodwork and interior partitions of the apartments in the lower part of the city. The houses at No. 20 and 22 in Passeig de Ragull were completely razed to the ground. . . . It is also difficult to pin down the precise number of dead and wounded. Such a large

number of Red military personnel in retreat happened to be in the city, making it hard to know how many of them were killed or injured. It is known for certain, however, that there were deaths: three women, two children, and twelve or thirteen soldiers. Some of the victims were in the entrance to air-raid shelter number 1 when the TNT exploded in the last attack. The number of military casualties is presumably much higher, because one of the air raids caused heavy damage to the premises of the Escuelas Nacionales, which had been set up as a hospital, and it also left the Casino building completely destroyed.[34]

According to the campaign communiqués of the Spanish Air Brigade, this bombardment was carried out by its own planes.

As the Francoist troops advanced ever closer to the French border, the bombardment of the villages between the city of Girona and the border intensified. Leaving aside the air raids against Figueres, the ports on the coast of the province of Girona were methodically bombarded. In the last week of the war in Catalonia, the bombardments of Sant Feliu de Guíxols, Roses, and Port de la Selva were relentless. Two air raids were especially deadly: Port de la Selva on February 5 and Roses on February 8. Some authors say that forty-six He-111s, with fighter escorts, attacked Port de la Selva on February 4 in one of the highest concentrations of bombing in the entire war.

In the same district, one of the targets most heavily attacked by the Francoist air force was the airfield on the outskirts of Vilajuïga, because it was the most important and practically the last airfield still in the hands of the Republican air force. These bombardments of military targets outside urban centers did not claim any civilian lives.

The last Francoist war communiqué that speaks of air raids on Catalonia dates from February 9 and says: "Yesterday the military targets of the ports of Roses, La Selva, etc., were bombarded."[35]

Last to be considered here are the air raids suffered by Figueres.[36] First, we will look at the days in January and February 1939 on which the city

---

34 Report from the city architect Señor Riera, submitted on April 6, 1940 to the civil governor of the province, Archive of the Folklore Museum of Ripoll.

35 José María Gárate Córdoba, *Partes oficiales de Guerra, 1936–1939*, vol. 1, *Ejército nacional* (Madrid: Editorial San Martín, 1977), 402.

36 See Solé i Sabaté and Villarroya i Font, *España en Llamas*, 243. *Figueres Sota les Bombes 1936–1939*, texts by Enric Pujol (Figueres: Úrsula Llibres, 2014); and David Garcia Algilaga and Ales Negres i Xampinyons, *Bombardeigs i refugis Figueres 1936–1939* (Viladamat: Gorbs Comunicació, 2015).

was bombarded. On January 26 and 30, the attack was carried out by German planes from the Garrapinillos airfield (Zaragoza). Then again on February 3 and 4, the same planes returned to bomb the capital of the Empordà. The attack on February 3 was carried out by three full squadrons of Heinkel He-111s and the bombs fell on the city and the castle located on its outskirts. On January 27, it was the Italian air force that launched an attack on the railroad station. Five Savoia-Marchetti SM-79s were responsible. Two further air raids, which took place on February 6 and 7, were also the work of the Italian air force.

Given the city's geographical location, the streets of Figueres were silent witnesses to the passage of thousands and thousands of people overflowing the main highway in their flight to France. Some witnesses say that fifty thousand people passed through the city each day. Crossing the street was nearly impossible; bending to pick up a lost shoe was dangerous because of the risk of being crushed. The real peril, however, came from the sky, from which bombs fell mercilessly on that great mass of people. The air raid on February 3 was especially tragic. It claimed the lives of eighty-three people, of which forty-nine remained unidentified, twenty-five were children, and only nine were identified adults. The people seemed numb to the danger of the bombardments as the noise of the air-raid sirens failed to move them.

It is difficult to determine the total number of victims from these air raids. The municipal archive of Figueres has a list of more than two hundred dead. Many of them were found only in later months as the clearing of destroyed buildings proceeded. As late as 1943, seven bodies were found when an air-raid shelter in Plaça de Catalunya was dug out. In addition to the lives they claimed, the bombs also destroyed 520 buildings in the city center. At the close of the war, Figueres seemed a dead city.

What justification can be found for these air raids in the final days of the war? Honestly, none – especially if we consider the chaotic state of the Republican army and the impossibility of halting the Francoist offensive amid the flight of tens of thousands of people. The bombardments were gratuitous acts of terror that in no way changed the course of the war and only contributed to increase the fear, anxiety, and mortality among the civilian population of Figueres and the floods of refugees.

If we take stock of what the air raids in the last month-and-a-half of the war in Catalonia meant, looking only at what the war communiqués of the two sides say, we see that while the Francoist communiqués speak only of bombarding military targets, ports, and railroad stations until the final eve of the entry of the Francoist troops into the corresponding city, the Republican war communiqués speak generally of the bombardments of villages on the home front that took the lives of members of the civilian population, specifying days on which the dead were mostly women and children. Which communiqués are closer to reality, those of the Francoists or those of the Republicans? The list of air raids and local victims offers one response: the cities, towns, and villages of Catalonia were bombarded until the final day of the so-called Catalonia campaign. And the victims? Without a shadow of a doubt, they were civilians, mostly women and children, and if uncertain, one need only look at the list of the Figueres dead for a clear-cut answer.

The air raids ended when the Francoist army occupied the entirety of Catalonia, and not before.

To conclude, I offer a brief personal reflection: many times when we speak of the effect of the air raids and the terror, I have the impression that this effect is conveyed solely in terms of the bombardments that caused a great deal of death and destruction. While such an effect was certainly the case, no less important an effect of those months and months of air raids lay in the impossibility of stopping them and in the panic and demoralization that this ultimately spread among the civilian population living in Catalonia. When fascist planes from Majorca were detected, the air-raid sirens might blare as easily in Barcelona as in Badalona, Gavà, Hospitalet, or elsewhere. Only when the bombs did not fall overhead and were then heard to fall far in the distance had the danger passed. But until that moment, the anxiety and distress and fear were at their peak. In Badalona, bombs fell upon the city for the entirety of the war, at least twenty times in all. However, the sirens sounded practically every night in 1938 and the effect on morale was devastating. The inhabitants of the streets most seriously affected by some of the air raids moved to another part of the city as soon as they could; if they had children, they sent them to the homes of relatives living in areas considered less dangerous. This is what took place in many of the medium-sized and small cities of Catalonia. The examples are manifold. The terror bombings of the Nazis and fascists were not the sole reason for victory, but their contribution was clear and they brought pain and suffering to thousands upon thousands of families.

BIBLIOGRAPHY

Alcofar Nassaes, José Luis. *La aviación legionària en la guerra española.* Barcelona: Euro Editorial, 1975.

Arnavat, Ramon, and David Iñiguez. *Atac i Defensa de la reraguarda. Els bombardeigs franquistes a les comarques de Tarragona i Terres de l'Ebre 1936–1939.* Valls: Cossetània Edicions, 2013.

Arnavat, Ramon, and David Iñiguez David, eds., with Adrian Cabezas and David Gesalí. *El Penedès sota les bombes (Alt Penedès, Baix Penedès, Garraf). Crònica d'un setge aeri (1937–1939).* Valls: Cossetània, 2012.

Azcárate, Pablo de. *Mi embajada en Londres durante la guerra civil española.* Barcelona: Ariel, 1976.

Barallat i Barés, Mercè. *La repressió a la postguerra civil a Lleida (1938–1945).* Barcelona: Publicacions de l'Abadia de Montserrat, 1991.

———. *Els bombardeigs a Lleida.* Barcelona. Publicacions de l'Abadia de Montserrat, 2013.

Caballé y Clos, Tomás. *Barcelona Roja. Dietario de la revolución.* Barcelona: Libreria Argentina, 1939.

Figueres Sota les Bombes 1936–1939. Texts by Enric Pujol. Figueres: Úrsula Llibres, 2014.

Gárate Córdoba, José María. *Partes oficiales de Guerra, 1936–1939,* volume 1, *Ejército nacional.* Madrid: Editorial San Martín, 1977.

Garcia Algilaga, David, and Ales Negres i Xampinyons. *Bombardeigs i refugis Figueres 1936–1939.* Viladamat: Gorbs Comunicació, 2015.

Garriga Andreu, Joan. Granollers. *El bombardeig de Granollers.* Granollers: Àrea de Cultura i Joventut, Ajuntament de Granollers, 2002.

Gesalí, David, and David Iñiguez. *La guerra aèria a Catalunya (1936–1939).* Barcelona: Rafael Dalmau, 2012.

González Huix, Francisco J. *El asedio aéreo de Tarragona 1937–1939.* Tarragona: Institut d'Estudis Tarraconenses Ramon Berenguer IV; Diputació de Tarragona, 1990.

————. *El puerto y la mar de Tarragona durante la guerra civil, 1936–1939.* Tarragona: Institut d'Estudis Tarraconenses Ramon Berenguer IV, 1995.

Gort, Ezequiel, and Palomar Salvador. *Viure sota les bombes. Els bombardeigs a Reus. 1937–1939.* Reus: Publicacions Municipals de Reus, 2010.

Grassia, Edoardo. *L'Aviazione Legionaria da bombardamento.* Rome: IBN Editore, 2009.

Irujo, Xabier. *El Gernika de Richthofen. Un ensayo de bombardeo de terror.* Gernika: Gernikako Bakearen Museoa Fundazioa, 2012.

Laureau, Patrick, and Jose Fernandez. *La Legion Condor.* Boulogne sur Mer: Editions Lela Presse, 1999.

Lo Cascio, Paola, and Susanna Oliveira *Tres dies de Març.* Girona: El Punt, 2008.

Martínez Bande, José María. *La campaña de Cataluña.* Madrid: Editorial San Martín, 1979.

Mezquida, Lluís Mª. *La batalla del Ebro.* Volume 3. Tarragona: Diputación de Tarragona, 1970.

Pedriali, Ferdinando. *Guerra di Spagna e Aviacione italiana.* 2nd ed. Rome: Aeronáutica Militare Italiana, Ufficio Storico, 1992.

Pla Blanch, Josep, and Antonio Ruiz Mostany. "El bombardeo de Lérida del 2 de noviembre de 1937." *Revista Ares* 22 (November 2011): 24–31.

Raguer, Hilari. "La Santa Sede y los bombardeos de Barcelona." *Historia y Vida* 145 (April 1980): 22–35.

Soldevila, Ferran. *Al llarg de la meva vida.* Barcelona: Edicions 62, 1970.

Solé i Sabaté, Josep Mª, and Joan Villarroya i Font. *Catalunya sota les bombes (1936–1939).* Barcelona: Publicacions de l'Abadia de Montserrat, 1986.

————. *España en Llamas. La guerra civil desde el aire.* Madrid: Temas de Hoy, 2003.

Villarroya i Font, Joan. *Els Bombardeigs de Barcelona durant la guerra civil (1936–1939).* 2nd ed. Barcelona: Publicacions de l'Abadia de Montserrat, 1999.

Villarroya, Joan, and Enric Juliana. "Mussolini: Machacad Barcelona." *Revista*, suppl., *La Vanguardia*, December 16, 2001: 4.

Chapter 12

The Port of Barcelona as a Military Target in the Spanish Civil War

Oriol Dueñas Iturbe

Italian fascism drew inspiration from theorists like Giulio Douhet[1] who, after the experience of the World War I, saw the crucial role that air power would play in future conflicts. Aircraft were the weapons needed to cut an army's lines of communication, destroy its manufacturing plants and supply chains, ignite its stockpiles of armaments, and, in short, paralyze a country by engulfing it in everpresent threat and crushing any material and moral resistance.

The Spanish Civil War (1936–1939) can be viewed as a transitional conflict, placed somewhere between the "classic" confrontations of earlier times and modern warfare. This characterization is ascribed to it because the war reached well beyond the frontlines. Locations on the home fronts were bombarded systematically by sea and by air. These attacks had a dual purpose. The first was to sow terror among the civilian populace, which doubtless suffered the most from the new concept of war; air raids on cities and villages claimed innocent victims in the tens of thousands. The second aim of the relentless raids on urban centers was to destroy military targets identified by the warring sides. These targets could be military infrastructure, communication networks, or wartime industries.

Indeed, this second aim was one of the most prominent aspects of the Civil War. The unremitting bombardment of so-called military targets by the Fascist and Nazi air forces and navies went on without let-up throughout nearly three years of warfare. The attacks on Barcelona

---

1   Giulio Douhet, *Il dominio dell'aira* (Milà: Mondadori, 1932).

by air and by sea were especially significant. One of the priority targets of the rebel aircraft was the port of Barcelona; indeed, the rebel authorities justified most of the attacks on the Catalan capital by claiming that they were aimed against the port. As a consequence, the port of Barcelona became one of the most heavily bombed sites in Catalonia throughout the war.

THE FOREIGN PRESENCE IN THE PORT OF BARCELONA: CIVILIAN EVACUATION, MILITARY CONTROL, AND ESPIONAGE

With the failed military uprising and the start of the Civil War, the port of Barcelona emerged as one of the most significant locations on the Catalan home front. Because of its economic and strategic importance, the port became a key place for foreign military personnel. It also turned into one of the leading points of departure for thousands of men and women fleeing the horrors of war, especially the persecutions, and one of the points of entry by sea for products of all kinds arriving from the four corners of the globe. In addition, it became a focus for spies and a primary military target for Franco's side, resulting in its unabated bombardment from mid-1937 onward.

Shortly after the failure of the military uprising of July 19, 1936, foreign ships of all kinds began to arrive in Catalan ports. Summoned by their embassies and consulates, their mission was to observe, protect, and evacuate their citizens. Once they had dropped their gangways, however, the ships began to embark civilians who were the political foes of the Catalan government but were under its protection.[2] Thus, the port of Barcelona became a point of departure for thousands of people fleeing into exile.[3]

---

2   For a detailed study of the flight into exile and the European countries that took part, see: Daniel Díaz i Esculies, *L'exili dels Països Catalans durant la Guerra Civil de 1936–1939* (Barcelona: Publicacions de l'Abadia de Montserrat, 2013); Rubèn Doll-Petit, *Els catalans de Gènova: història de l'èxode i l'adhesió d'una classe dirigent en temps de guerra* (Barcelona: Publicacions de l'Abadia de Montserrat, 2003); Arnau González Vilalta, *Amb ulls estrangers. Quan Catalunya preocupava Europa. Diplomàcia i premsa internacional durant la Guerra Civil* (Barcelona: Editorial Base, 2014); Albert Manent, *De 1936 a 1975. Estudis sobre la guerra civil i el franquisme* (Barcelona: Publicacions de l'Abadia de Montserrat, 1999); and Jordi Rubió, *L'èxode català de 1936 a través dels Pirineus* (Maçanet de la Selva: Editorial Gregal, 2014).

3   It should be recalled that the attempted coup unleashed a wave of violence across Catalonia. Casualties numbered in the thousands. The authorities in Catalonia lost control of public order and until 1937 severe repression was exacted against anyone viewed as an opponent of the Republic itself or of the revolution that some were

At the same time, the port area teemed with spies. Much of the espionage was carried out from Italian and German vessels moored in the port. All of these ships not only protected and evacuated their citizens but also worked to gather information. While evacuating fellow their countrymen and also thousands of foreigners in a gesture of magnanimity, the Italian and German consulates were also busy informing Rome and Berlin about political developments in Catalonia and carrying out studies of the city's military targets. As will be seen below, the lists of ordnance factories, communication hubs, and strategic antiaircraft defenses were very thorough and this information would subsequently be used by the Francoist, Italian, and German air forces and navies to shell Barcelona for much of the war.

The chief aim of the reports prepared by Italian spies was to compile information on the wartime industries that were being organized, military barracks or headquarters of political and labor union organizations, communication services (telephone exchanges, post offices, and telegraph offices), railroad stations, power plants, anything relating to the antiaircraft defenses being set up in Barcelona, and, of course, information on the port of Barcelona itself. There was a steady flow of reports with detailed lists of various types of information sorted by subject area and armed with coordinates to locate the target on different maps of the city. Maps of Barcelona with highly detailed markings have been located, as have handmade drawings prepared by the agents themselves, on which the target in question is pinpointed.

A report filed on September 22, 1936 provided eight pieces of information for consideration by the Italian authorities, including several

---

trying to impose. These events could not be brought under control, but they never received the endorsement of the authorities. From May 1937 to early 1938, they would become the subject of investigation and prosecution.

This repression on the Catalan home front was primarily targeted against the clergy or individuals related to the ecclesiastical or Catholic world, people viewed as right-wing and conservative—especially industrialists and landowners, many of whom had ties to the Regionalist League—and groups connected to the armed forces and the far right, members of the Falange movement, and traditionalists. The violence was extreme and it was carried out by individuals affiliated with the workers' movement who had capitalized on the turmoil caused by the attempted coup and seized arms from the military barracks in order to wrest control of the streets. The repression on the home front in Catalonia was at its most violent and extreme between July 19 and December 31, 1936, and particularly between July and October. The final tally from the repression came to at least 8,360 deaths. See Josep M.Solé i Sabaté and Joan Villarroya, *La repressió a la reraguarda de Catalunya: 1936–1939* (Barcelona: Abadia de Montserrat, 1989).

ordnance factories, the arrival of Russian pilots, the city's inadequate defenses, and the unloading of weaponry in the port by night:

> The chemical manufacturing plant is engaged today in the production of gas for bombs, whose casings have been made in the Elizalde automobile factory. The arrival of Russian pilots at the Barcelona seaplane base is confirmed with certainty.
>
> There are no gun batteries other than the ones at the Castle. Also, these cannons, which are all small or medium-caliber, are nearly all inefficient because of their age and because some lack breechblocks. There is no reinforced concrete shelter level.
>
> There is currently a French steamer in the port unloading weapons at night.
>
> There is a small-caliber battery in the vicinity of the old gasometer. The cannons would appear not to have breechblocks.
>
> The Hispano-Suiza factory is manufacturing armor for tanks.
>
> There is a factory in Barceloneta: it is the Vulcano factory and it assembles tanks.[4]

This is only one example of the reports filed by Italian agents; as can be seen, the information is plentiful and detailed. The reports plainly show that the agents were highly familiar with different parts of the city and with military matters that should have been confidential, such as the issue of defenses and of arms manufacture. It also bolsters the notion that the spies received help from a number of Barcelona residents.

All the compiled data were sent first to Rome and to Majorca, where the Italians had set up their base of operations in the Mediterranean. Later, once the information had been studied, it was relayed to the Francoist authorities in Burgos.

The Italians were not the only ones to engage in spying activities in Barcelona in the early months of the war. The Germans also took advantage of the moment to collect reports on targets of interest in the city, such as the port. In the latter case, photographs and maps of the port's installations have been located bearing various labels to indicate, for example:

---

4   Italian Naval History Office (USMMI), OMS 217, file 1269, "Information on Barcelona targets, communiqué to Count Margottini supported by a map contained in the dossier and directions on page no. 206."

Wasserflugzeugstation: the seaplane base.

Lagerschuppen: storage sheds.

Lagerhäuser: warehouses.

Fort Montjuich: Montjuïc Castle.

Bahnhof: the port's railroad station.

Wharves forming part of the port.[5]

As the records show, the spying carried out by foreign residents in Barcelona was constant in the war's early stages. Indeed, the activity never ceased and would ultimately be crucial for the air raids carried out both on the city and on the port of Barcelona throughout the war.

THE PORT OF BARCELONA AS A MILITARY TARGET

Undoubtedly, one of the most heavily surveilled spots in the city of Barcelona was its port. The port's strategic importance as an entry point for ships carrying goods and ordnance of all kinds made it one of the leading military targets, both for surveillance and for bombardment.

As noted earlier, spies were a constant presence on the wharves from the outbreak of the war. At first, the spying was the work of foreigners. However, the Francoist espionage services also began to operate in the port area to gather information on the wartime industries in the vicinity, on ship arrivals, and on the defenses in place. In both cases, the information collected was sent to the rebel air and naval forces so that they could proceed with the bombardment needed to halt activity in the port. These attacks, as is well known, were not limited to the port and its environs, but affected the entire city.

Clearly, without this information, the repeated bombardment would not have been as effective as it was. Thanks to the detailed reports compiled by Francoist spies, the attacks on the port and other declared military targets were more efficient and destructive.

If there is a military aspect in which the development of the Spanish Civil War made enormous strides, it was in the area of aviation. Both quantitatively and qualitatively, the leap forward was impressive.

---

5   Italian Naval History Office, Military operations in Spain, Information on military targets in Catalonia, folder 33, Spanish War.

The military conflict of 1936 to 1939 became the perfect testing ground for the countries that took part indirectly in the struggle. The experience that they gained would be applied intensively in the world war set to begin only a few months after the Civil War came to end.

The arrival of new technology in the hands of rebel authorities, thanks in large part to the collaboration of their Italian and German allies, gave rise to preparations for the relentless bombardment of population centers both by air and by sea. The excuse given to justify these attacks was that important military targets were clustered in various localities on the Republican home front and that they had to be destroyed to prevent any advantage accruing to the Republican armed forces. Soon, the Francoist authorities began to prepare detailed reports with lists of localities and bombing targets. Once completed, the lists were sent on to the Italian and German forces so that they could initiate the bombardments as they saw fit.

To draw up all these lists, the Francoist authorities had the inestimable assistance of secret services engaged in intelligence gathering and spying, most of which were at work on the Republican home front itself. Espionage was a key element in the air and sea war, because it was responsible for identifying the targets for bombardment.

To obtain additional enemy information, Franco's secret services[6] carried out two further types of covert activities on the Republican home front. First, the military had two branches devoted to information: espionage and counterespionage. These two branches gathered information through observation, electronic eavesdropping, and interrogations of fugitives and prisoners of war. All the information obtained through these mechanisms was studied and analyzed for later transfer to Franco's HQ, where it was included in dispatches sent to the lower echelons.

---

6   For more in-depth information on the subject, see: José Bertran i Musitu, *Experiencias de los Servicios de Información del Nordeste de España (SIFNE) durante la guerra* (Madrid: Espasa-Calpe, 1940); Cristina Badosa, *Josep Pla, biografia del solitari* (Barcelona: Edicions 62, 1996); Borja de Riquer, *L'últim Cambó (1936–1947). La dreta catalanista davant la guerra civil i el primer franquisme* (Vic: Editorial Eumo, 1996); Jordi. Guixé, *La República perseguida. Exilio y represión en la Francia de Franco* (València: Publicacions de la Universitat de València, 2012); Jordi Guixà, *Los espías de Franco. Josep Pla i Francesc Cambó.* (Madrid: Ed. Fórcola, 2014); Morten Heiberg and Manuel Ros Agudo, *La Trama oculta de la guerra civil: los servicios secretos de Franco: 1936–1945* (Barcelona: Crítica, 2006); Domènec Pastor Petit, *Traïdors a Catalunya* (Barcelona: Ed. Base, 2007); and José Ramón Soler Fuensanta and Francisco J. López-Brea Espiau, *Soldados sin rostro. Los servicios de información, espionaje y criptografía en la Guerra Civil española* (Barcelona: Inédita Editores, 2008).

Second, there were the famous fifth columns, which were concentrated in the major cities. These were underground groups that were organized to varying degrees and that mounted passive resistance. Their aim was to undermine morale on the home front and to gather as much information as they could so as to pinpoint military targets for bombardment by the Francoist air force and navy.

These activities were very important for gathering the maximum information on the forces and infrastructure in Republican territory. Catalonia, because of its importance, came under particularly heavy surveillance. It was home to a large number of wartime industries and it enjoyed direct communication with France, from which assistance could arrive. From 1938, it was also home to the Republican authorities and their commanding officers. All these factors meant that data was constantly being collected by military and civilian elements in the Principality from the first day of the war onward. The maximum information had to be gathered in order to act, that is, to begin bombing anything deemed a military target.

One of the most important nonmilitary information services was the network organized by the Catalan lawyer Josep Bertran i Musitu, who had been a minister under Alfonso XIII and was a member of the Regionalist League of Catalonia. The activities of Bertran i Musitu's service were to have a significant impact in the Principality. Operating under the acronym SIFNE (Servicio de Información del Nordeste de España, the Information Services of the Northeast Frontier of Spain), it became an effective and modern spy service which was skillfully organized by its founder and achieved a high degree of influence with the German and Italian information services.

With the assistance of the leader of the Regionalist League Francesc Cambó and other politicians, Bertran i Musitu built up a network of spies from mid-August 1936 onward. The chief mission of his network was to gather all possible information on Republican movements, particularly in the port. Agents engaged in collecting information and sending it to be studied at SIFNE headquarters, which were located first in Biarritz and then in Irun. Upon arrival, the information was sorted into sections: cartography and maps, intercepted enemy radio signals, code breaking, press, general records, radio broadcasts, photographs, and so on, which were analyzed thoroughly for authentication.

From an aspect as apparently innocuous as a reading of the Republican press, for instance, the SIFNE information services succeeded in extracting valuable information on the Republican military and home front. Because censorship was ill-focused, inadequate, and lacking in centralization, the press was an important and free source of secrets. Until May 11, 1937, the enemy could simply read information on matters of paramount importance such as details of wartime industries, internal problems in the Republican zone, activities of law enforcement officials, activities of the "people's courts," an indication of the countries helping the Republic, the arrival of ships from abroad carrying weaponry and supplies, the situation of the columns at the front, and so on. Information on these and other matters should have been kept secret but they were published in the daily press, providing a major source of information for the enemy.[7] This would further account for the detailed reports that were prepared in the Francoist zone on military targets for bombardment.

SIFNE coordinated efforts very closely with Majorca, Burgos, and Seville, and its network of informers was spread over England, the Netherlands, Belgium, France, and Switzerland. Agents had a particular interest in any movements in those countries' ports because they were viewed, despite the nonintervention agreement in force, as potential sources of help to the Republic. Eventually, on February 28, 1938, SIFNE was absorbed into the recently created SIPM (Servicio de Información y Policía Militar, Service of Information and Military Police), the centralized Francoist espionage service.

The port of Barcelona was viewed as a crucial target for destruction because of its strategic importance in the arrival of vessels carrying materials, the transport of goods to other points in the country, the presence of factories producing materiel for the war effort, and so on. This is why it was a focus of constant spying by Francoist informers. The reports on the port that have been located are plentiful and highly precise, featuring detailed documents that explain the location of the wharves, the arrival of vessels carrying goods, the situation of the port's defenses, warehouses, factories, the effects of any bombardments, and so forth. On many occasions, the information also came with maps.

---

7   In the Francoist zone, press censorship was strictly enforced from the very first day. This prevented the leaking of even a single piece of news that might help the Republican authorities. Domènec Pastor Petit, *La cinquena columna a Catalunya (1936–1939)* (Barcelona: Galba, 1978), 2.

BOMBARDMENTS OF THE PORT OF BARCELONA

As noted earlier, the port of Barcelona acquired major strategic importance during the Civil War. In the years of conflict, the port became the infrastructure through which vital supplies arrived and were distributed to support the war effort and maintain the home front, including weaponry, munitions, food, medicine, and so on. To block the arrival of products by sea and to eliminate military targets located within the port, the rebel authorities took the decision to bombard the port systematically, turning it into one of the most heavily punished areas of the Catalan capital.

In the early stages of the war, the air force, like the navy and army, undertook operations within the parameters of a conflict typified by the technology, equipment, and mentality of the early twentieth century. Soon, however, the arrival of new modern military aircraft, mainly from Italy, Germany, and the Soviet Union, upended this situation and turned the aerial war into a modern technological confrontation that would also become one of the key elements in the rebel victory. New aviation technology marked a shift in the mentality of warfare; the battlefronts shifted into the cities, which would now be shelled relentlessly from the sea and, especially, from the air. Many Spanish cities became constant targets of bombardment, in keeping with the publicly stated aim of destroying military objectives and the covert rationale of undermining the resistance and morale of the civilian populace. High on the list of targets was Barcelona, which suffered constant bombardment, first by sea and later by air, throughout almost all the conflict.

From the initial months of the Civil War, the rebel military set out to block any assistance that the government of the Republic might receive from abroad. News of aid arriving in Mediterranean ports from the USSR and other countries accelerated their intention to bomb Republican ports. To carry out the mission, Franco obtained valuable support from Italian and German forces.[8]

Broadly speaking, the Italian air force based in the Balearic Islands, which was known as the Aviazione Legionaria delle Baleari (Legionary Air Force of the Balearic Islands), conducted air raids against a variety of military targets: ports, railroads, highways, factories, industries, arms stockpiles and fuel depots, power plants, places of political power,

---

8   Josep M. Solé i Sabaté and Joan Villarroya, *España en llamas. La Guerra Civil desde el aire* (Madrid: Temas de Hoy, 2003), 257.

military installations, and airports. The Italian contingent operated quite effectively in its maritime blockade of Republican ports. All of this deployment stood in stark contrast to the shortfall in the Republican air force, which would not be redressed until the arrival of Russian materiel.

On November 17, 1936, Franco's *junta* in Burgos sent a telegram to the British government in which, among other things, they informed the UK authorities that their primary ambition was to blockade and shell the port of Barcelona to prevent assistance from reaching the Republican government. The communiqué from the Burgos authorities also requested that British vessels and subjects stay well clear of what was now considered a military target:

> On the 17th of this month [November], the Government of London received the following telegram from the Junta in Burgos: 'We know that materiel has been unloaded and will continue to be unloaded in Barcelona. The ships in question fly various flags, but most of them fly the Soviet or Spanish flag. We the Spanish fascists are determined to stop this traffic by all means. IF IT IS NECESSARY, WE WILL DESTROY THE PORT OF BARCELONA [sic]. We advise foreign vessels located in said port to leave immediately to avoid becoming victims of collateral damage'.[9]

A few conclusions can be drawn from the Burgos communiqué. First, it made clear that the port of Barcelona would soon become a military target for the rebel troops. Second, espionage was now beginning to work toward the aim of obtaining the maximum information from the home front. And third, the fascist government in Burgos wanted to inform British authorities of its plans so as to avoid an international incident with a foreign power that, of course, it wanted to remain neutral. Indeed, sensitivity to the final point would be everpresent throughout the war.

According to Italian sources, General Sperrle, commander of the German Condor Legion, made a proposal to Franco's general staff in late October and early November 1936 concerning an aerial offensive plan

---

9   *La Vanguardia*, November 21, 1936, 6. From November 17 to 26, various pieces of information were published in relation to the responses of the British and French governments to the threats coming from Burgos to blockade and shell Republican ports. In the end, the British authorities requested the creation of a neutral zone in the port of Barcelona. As will be seen, however, this proposal was never put into effect.

against the chief Mediterranean ports under the control of the Republic. The plan provided for Italian bombardment of the port of Barcelona and other places using planes from as far afield as Sardinia. From the very start, Franco agreed with the plan, but the Italians showed little enthusiasm, rejecting the idea of attacking from the island of Sardinia to avoid potential international conflicts.[10]

The approach gained acceptance, however, as the Italian air force, which was made chiefly responsible for the bombardment of the port of Barcelona, relocated aircraft and military infrastructure to the Balearics. The failure of the Republican naval expedition to the island of Majorca[11] had enormous repercussions for the future of the Republic and Catalonia, because it gave the Italian and German air forces the opportunity to secure a formidable base of operations from which to launch air raids against cities on the Republican home front, especially Barcelona. Thus, Majorca was turned into a fantastic natural aircraft carrier that enabled fascist planes to bomb any corner of the Principality.[12] Eventually, Majorca saw the installation of the Legionary Air Force of the Balearic Islands, which had originally been relocated to the island in order to thwart the Republican expedition to the archipelago.

In addition to the Italian forces, Majorca also saw a prominent presence of the German Condor Legion, which was based in Pollença. The Condor Legion was responsible for striking various military targets on the Republican home front. Heinkel He 59 twin-motor seaplanes, operating as part of Jagdgruppe 88, carried out bombing runs on the Catalan coast, particularly the city of Barcelona, throughout 1938.

The German air force was also tasked with enforcing the maritime blockade along the Republican coastline. Seaplanes attacked any vessel (wherever it might be) that was suspected of carrying goods bound for

---

10 Solé i Sabaté and Villarroya, *España en llamas*, 258.
11 The primary purpose of the expedition, under the command of Captain Albert Bayo, was to regain the islands of Ibiza, Formentera, and Majorca for the Republic. The expedition was made up mostly of Catalan volunteers and it set sail on August 7, 1936. Despite some initial successes, the expedition ultimately failed and the retreat began on September 3. For additional information, see Josep Massot, *El desembarcament de Bayo a Mallorca, agost–setembre de 1936* (Barcelona: Publicacions de l'Abadia de Montserrat, 1997).
12 Josep M. Solé i Sabaté and Joan Villarroya, *Catalunya sota les bombes (1936–1939)* (Barcelona: Publicacions de l'Abadia de Montserrat, 1986), 10. The authors cite Joan Maluquer i Wahl to describe Majorca as a natural aircraft carrier: "an enormous unsinkable aircraft carrier, anchored menacingly off the Catalan coast. Its situation was so important because targets both along the coast and in the interior of Catalonia now came within the operational range of the military aircraft of the period."

the Republic. In response to the proposals of the British government after the constant offshore attacks against ships flying the Union Jack, an international agreement was struck specifying that it would only be permissible to fire on cabotage shipping less than three miles from the coast and vessels moored in ports. As a result, the Heinkel seaplanes redirected their efforts, shifting their attacks toward strategic locations and toward harrying the home front by damaging port facilities and other coastal targets and sowing panic among the civilian populace.

Besides the Italian and German air forces, the rebels also had a small contingent of Spanish airmen in the Balearic Islands. The planes in the Spanish air force based on the archipelago formed a specialized unit that contributed quite successfully to the blockade and surveillance of the Mediterranean coastline. The Francoist seaplanes carried out long distance reconnaissance missions to provide air support to offensives led by rebel cruisers and Italian submarines. These planes also played a key role in locating Republican maritime traffic.

Nevertheless, the first bombardments of the Catalan coast (more specifically, of the port of Barcelona) were not carried out from the air, but from the sea. Rebel vessels offshore began the shelling, sometimes seeking to pound military targets, sometimes striking indiscriminately at urban centers. That was the plan on January 15, 1937, when the Italian fascist government had met in Rome with rebel military commanders to set the guidelines for the military support that Franco would receive. In the case of the navy, it was decided to keep up the pressure by cutting off supplies to the Republican forces and carrying out shellings of coastal localities. Over time, the naval attacks would be replaced by more effective, more precise air raids.

According to the daily account prepared by the Directorate of Works and Services for the port's highest authority, the Junta del Port de Barcelona, the first air raid did not take place until April 18, 1937. However, the officials tasked with preparing reports noted that the port had been the target of several offshore artillery attacks prior to that April. The available documents indicate, nevertheless, that none of the earlier attacks had succeeded in seriously damaging the wharves or port services, because the shells had fallen into the sea or into the side of the mountain of Montjuïc.[13]

---

13 Historical Archive of the Port of Barcelona (hereafter, AHPB), folder 1620. *Account of the Bombardments in the Port Services Area up to December 31, 1938.*

As the documents show, these initial attacks against the port and the city of Barcelona were, in fact, conducted by sea. Specifically, the first attack against the port appears to have been launched in November 1936, when the *Canarias* fired a total of twenty-one rounds on the port's installations and on Montjuïc Castle without hitting any of its objectives. This opening attack, however, was not followed up, although mention is made of another attack launched from Francoist vessels.[14]

The first submarine campaign of the Italian navy undertook operations against Republican ports and coastline carried out by surface ships and submarines. In January and February 1937, three attacks were directed against installations in the port of Valencia and four against those in the port of Barcelona. According to the captain of the vessel *Genova*, who was aboard the submarine *Torricelli* as an observer, the shelling by the *Torricelli* on January 18, 1937 was aimed at the port of Barcelona's naphtha depots (naphtha is a hydrocarbon used as an industrial solvent). This attack, as with the earlier shellings, failed to destroy any of its intended targets.[15]

It was three o'clock in the early morning on that January 18 when the submarine *Torricelli* took up position off El Prat de Llobregat and started firing on the port's installations. Republican authorities were later able to confirm that the rounds were fragmentation shells. In total, the Italian submarine discharged some forty projectiles against the wharves and fuel storage facilities, using the green lamp at the harbor entrance as its point of reference. The attack went on for roughly twelve minutes and succeeded in damaging the Sant Bertran wharf and the ships *Betis* and *Campillo*.

Days later, the pressure was stepped up. On February 9 and 10, 1937, the port of Barcelona again came under fire from Italian submarines. It was nearing five in the morning on the ninth when the submersible *Ettore Fieramosca* launched several artillery rounds at the port's installations without causing any damage of note. The targets were the tankers *Campeador* and *Zorroza*, which were ready to unload petroleum and to take on heavy oils. The shells succeeded in damaging

---

14 Specifically, this attack is mentioned in Jesús Salas Larrazabal, *La guerra de España desde el aire* (Barcelona: Ariel, 1972), 140, when the author says that during the night of November 18, 1936 the heavy cruiser *Canarias* and the light cruiser *Almirante Cervera* initiated the blockade of the port of Barcelona with a bombardment.

15 Information cited by José Miguel Campo Rizo, "El Mediterráneo, campo de batalla de la Guerra Civil española: la intervención naval italiana. Una primera aproximación documental," *Cuadernos de Historia Contemporánea* 19 (1997): 55–88.

the defenses of the Ponent wharf, while the tankers suffered very limited damage from shell fragments.

On the following day, the attackers once again trained their guns on the port. On this occasion, the submarine fired on the Campsa fuel storage facilities.[16]

By now, it was more than clear that the port area was being turned into a war zone and that it would be necessary to restrict the public's access, not only for its own safety but because of issues relating to espionage. Republican authorities wanted at all costs to stop the rebels from receiving information about the port that could provide a point of reference for further planned bombardment. For this reason, one of the new measures was to ban photography anywhere in the port area. The leading official of the Services of the Commissariat General for Public Order, the anarchist Dionisio Eroles, appeared before the press on January 4, 1937 to deliver the news: "Considering the entire port and coastline of Barcelona as a war zone, all citizens are advised that it is strictly forbidden to photograph or take any view of said port, on the clear understanding that anyone failing to comply with this order will be stripped of their equipment without recourse."[17]

At 10:00 p.m. on February 13, 1937 came the first bombardment of the city to claim civilian casualties. Whereas previous attacks had only affected specific locations in the port, now the Italian cruiser *Eugenio di Savoia*, operating in the area near the eastern breakwater, fired nine salvos on the city itself, striking various buildings and the Elizalde factory. None of the projectiles inflicted damage on the wharves in the port.

From April 1937 on, the aerial bombardment began in earnest and it would not stop until January 25, 1939, the day before the occupation of Barcelona by Francoist troops. The attacks sought to prevent vessels arriving at Barcelona from unloading their cargo. Beyond trying to sink the vessels, the bombs also sought to destroy the port's railroad station, wharves, warehouses, and other facilities, the Vulcano plant, the naval aviation unit Aeronàutica Naval, and most especially the fuel depots. The aim was to eliminate all of these elements in order to disrupt the smooth functioning of the port and to stop the transport of fuel to the frontline, where it was essential for military operations.

---

16   David Gesalí and David Íñiguez, *La guerra aèria a Catalunya* (Barcelona: Rafael Dalmau, 2012), 88–89.
17   *La Vanguardia*, January 5, 1937, 3.

Altogether, this meant that the port of Barcelona was shelled almost daily, making it one of the most dangerous sites in the city. For the residents of Barceloneta, the neighborhood closest to the port area, and for the port workers, the bombardments became a major threat to their lives. In fact, Barceloneta was officially evacuated during the war and a call was issued for air-raid shelters to protect the port workers.[18]

In 1938, the bombardment of the port of Barcelona increased. The escalation was due to technical advancements in the rebel air force that increased the possibility of longer flights and the development of deadlier weaponry. As the months and years of war dragged on, the destructive power of the bombs continued to rise.

A consultation of various documentary sources shows that there were ninety-five attacks on the port of Barcelona between November 1936 and January 26, 1939. Their highest number was recorded in 1938, but their greatest intensity came in the opening days of January 1939, coinciding with the final military operations for the occupation of the city.

Without doubt, the intensity of the air raids in the closing days of January was the highest of the entire war. The fascist air force, with occasional participation from the Condor Legion, struck the port of Barcelona forcefully and accurately in the days leading up to occupation. Bombing raids whose sole purpose was to demonstrate the aerial superiority of the rebel forces ultimately destroyed the port and also sowed terror among a populace that had already experienced enough of the ravages of war. There is no other way to explain the motives for the Francoist authorities' continued hammering of the port in the closing days of the conflict.

As for the role of the Italian air force in operations against the port and city of Barcelona, it would carry out 113 air raids involving 592 planes over the entire war. Of these raids, 110 involving 572 planes were launched from Majorca by the Legionary Air Force of the Balearic Islands. In total, 556,105 kg of explosives were discharged against the port and city.[19] The German Condor Legion, for its part, dropped a total of 370,000 kg of explosives on the city of Barcelona.[20]

---

18 Witnesses who lived through the bombardment confirm that the Barceloneta neighborhood was left deserted. Some recall that Republican authorities took reprisals against people who took advantage of the situation to loot evacuated flats.
19 Historical Archive of the Air Force, file 91, doc. 34.
20 Gesalí and Íñiguez, *La guerra aèria a Catalunya*, 476.

The constant bombardment of the port forced the port authorities and the officials tasked with public safety in the Government of Catalonia to orchestrate a defensive strategy, which was divided into two types of activities. The first was to organize the passive defense of the port through the construction and fitting out of various air-raid shelters.[21] The second was to equip a variety of sites with antiaircraft defenses whose mission was to stop the air raids and thwart any potential landings on the coast. In both cases, the measures that were taken fell short; they could not keep pace the technological evolution of the bomber planes, which proved vastly superior to the location, detection, and neutralization systems that the city had at its disposal. These active defense systems achieved only occasional and very modest successes in relation to the attacks suffered by the city and the port during the war years.

WAR DAMAGE INFLICTED ON THE PORT OF BARCELONA

Francoist troops occupied the port of Barcelona on January 26, 1939. The image of the port at the close of the conflict was a desolate one: a large number of the buildings were destroyed or damaged, while the dock areas were strewn with sunken vessels.

The heaviest damage affected the wharves and related structures, such as covered areas, warehouses, and repair shops, as well as the port's infrastructure such as railroad lines, cranes, Campsa fuel storage facilities, and ships. All this destruction was identified and described by the Francoist port authorities only a few months after they took over their new positions of responsibility. During the preparation of the report on the port of Barcelona between 1935 and 1942,[22] the port's top authority, the Junta del Port, dedicated a special section to a review of the state of the port at the end of the war. The special section made it clear that the port area was destroyed by rebel bombs:

> Anyone looking over the port of Barcelona when it was liberated could see with the naked eye the regrettable scenes of desolation that appeared everywhere.

---

21   AHPB, folder 1620, *Account of the Bombardments in the Port Services Area up to December 31, 1938.*

22   AHPB, Port of Barcelona Board of Works and Services, Directorate of Works and Services, *Report on the state and progress of port works and services and the vicissitudes occurring in same and important matters during the years 1935–1942, including a review of the various enlargement and improvement works* (12/31/1942).

Over the entire terrestrial portion (99 ha) of the port area as a whole (325 ha), one can observe innumerable ravages, destruction, and ruins of all kinds in the infrastructure, buildings, and installations, both official and private, and in the docks and the outer harbor, one sees numerous damaged vessels of all types.[23]

The Francoist press also bore witness to the destruction befalling the port of Barcelona. In the days following the occupation of the city, accounts began to appear in the print media: "The General Stores, with their enormous floor spaces of splendid installations for automated loading and unloading, the powerful cranes, the nineteen kilometers of railroad inside the port, the sheds, the tugboats, etc. were nearly at a standstill."[24]

Once Barcelona was occupied by the Francoist troops on January 26, 1939, the port was one of the areas of the city that most clearly reflected the destructiveness of the aerial war. This is also apparent from the words of José Gomá: "Terrible was the spectacle offered by the port of Barcelona upon the arrival of the Nationalists. Devastated wharves, destroyed storehouses, overturned railcars. The Campsa fuel storage facilities destroyed. There were a large number of damaged and burned-out ships."[25]

A similar impression was shared by one of the few residents of Barcelona to decide to visit the port a few days after the war's end: "This afternoon we went to the wharf to see the heavy damage caused by the Nationalist Air Force. Everything is smashed. The spectacle is stunning: 'sheds', loading docks, buildings, the port's railroad station, everything is destroyed. Many of the ships are sunk and only their masts are visible. The wharf was a daily target and we can now see that the bombardments were always against Barceloneta."[26]

From observing all this devastation, it becomes clear that the Italian Legionary Air Force and the German Condor Legion achieved one of their main objectives: bringing the port nearly to a standstill. Proof that forcing the port to its knees was a top priority is plain to see in the destruction visited on the port's rail transport, the warehouses in

---

23 Ibid.
24 An article on the rebuilding of the port, titled "La reconstrucción del puerto," *ABC*, 25 February 25, 1939, 17.
25 José Gomá, La guerra en el aire (Barcelona: Editorial AHR, 1958), 304.
26 Joaquim Renart, *Diari 1918–1961. La guerra: volum sisè (1936–1939)* (Barcelona: Proa, 2003), 550. Also cited in Santiago Albertí and Elisenda Albertí Casas, *Perill de bombardeig! Barcelona sota les bombes (1936–1939)* (Barcelona: Albertí Editors, 2005), 352.

which materials of varying kinds could be stored, the machinery such as cranes that made the wharves work effectively, and the fuel storage facilities that held fuel supplies needed by the Republican army. Further evidence can be seen in the paralyzing of industry in the port's vicinity and the objective of attacking ships to preclude the supply of fuel, weaponry, and provisions to the home front. Large numbers of vessels were rendered useless from the shelling, and left foundering along the wharves. According to documentation that has been located, a total of forty vessels were damaged at some point by the bombardment.[27]

The air raids, however, did not only cause material damage to the port's installations. The strategy to sow terror on the home front led to a high number of civilian casualties in the shelling of Barcelona (according to studies by Joan Villarroya, there were 2,718 deaths in total, with 77 occurring in the port). As has been well established, these casualties cannot solely be put down to the fact that Barcelona was the site of various military targets.

The argument that the Italian Legionary Air Force focused only on striking military targets has been a popular feature of the historiography since the end of the Civil War. One of the leading experts in the study of the air raids led by the Italian air force, José Luis Alcofar Nassaes,[28] draws on a series of private letters by Italian airmen engaged in the missions to maintain that the Italian air force exercised great restraint in carrying out their raids, trying to hit only military targets while doing the least damage possible to the cities and their inhabitants. Despite this statement, the claim that the rest of the city did not suffer the ravages of the air raids appears scarcely credible. In fact, this argument was already countered at the time by the historian Joan Villarroya in his study.[29] In the work, Villarroya clearly shows that Barcelona was bombarded systematically between 1937 and early 1939 and residential areas that were not military targets had been hammered mercilessly.

---

27 This information has been taken from the AHPB's *Account of the Bombardments in the Port Services Area up to December 31, 1938* and from daily newspaper accounts of the air raids in 1939. According to information from the Naval Commission for the Salvage of Vessels, twenty-three vessels were sunk, whereas José Luis Infiesta Pérez (Alcofar Nassaes) identifies thirty-six vessels in his research. See José Luis Infiesta Pérez, *Bombardeos del litoral mediterráneo durante la Guerra Civil*, vol. 1 (Valladolid: Quiron, 1998).

28 José Luis Alcofar Nassaes, *La aviación legionaria en la guerra española* (Barcelona: Euros, 1975).

29 Joan Villarroya, Els bombardeigs de Barcelona durant la Guerra Civil (1936–1939), 2nd ed. (Barcelona: Publicacions de l'Abadia de Montserrat, 1999).

This latter point is demonstrated by the terrible raids suffered by the Catalan capital between March 16 and 18, 1938. During these three days, during which the city was systematically bombarded, the port of Barcelona was the object of just one of the thirteen raids carried out over the city. This is proof that the aim of the Italian bombers was not solely to destroy the port and other strategic points, but also to sow terror among the populace.

As Graph 1 shows, the port did not come under systematic attack until June 1938, particularly from September onward, when the Battle of the Ebro had become stabilized and the Francoist troops no longer needed all the planes from Majorca to be at their disposal, as had been the case up until that point. Prior to these dates, there was a big difference between the raids on the port and those on the city. Subsequently, however, there was less difference, disappearing and even reversing by January 1939, when the port finally endured more attacks than the rest of the city. In 1937, the port suffered nine raids compared to the twenty-four inflicted on the rest of the city, that is, 37.5 percent of the total. In 1938, the figures increased sharply thanks to the final four months of the year. During the twelve months of 1938, the rest of the city suffered 107 bombardments, while the port suffered 67,[30] or 62.6 percent. Between January 1 and 26, 1939, the port suffered fifteen raids, whereas the rest of the city suffered eleven. In fact, January represented the period with the greatest frequency of attacks, one every 1.7 days, while the equivalent figure for 1937 was one raid every 40 days and the figure for 1938 was one raid every 5.4 days.

---

30 In this case, the data were recorded by Republican port officials and subsequently found in the AHPB. As a result, the information collected by Infiesta Pérez in his *Bombardeos del litoral mediterráneo durante la Guerra Civil*, which refers to eighty-eight air raids on the port of Barcelona in the year 1938, has not been used.

Graph 1. Bombing raids on Barcelona and its port, by year.

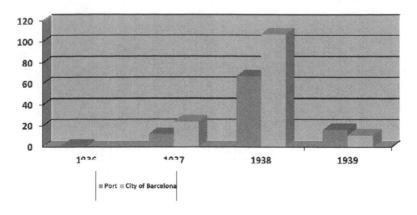

Source: Own elaboration based on data drawn from the Historical Archive of the Port of Barcelona and Joan Villarroya i Font, Els bombardeigs de Barcelona durant la Guerra Civil (1936–1939), 2nd ed. (Barcelona: Publicacions de l'Abadia de Montserrat, 1999).

Graph 2. Evolution of the bombing raids recorded in Barcelona and its port between February 1937 and January 26, 1939, by month.

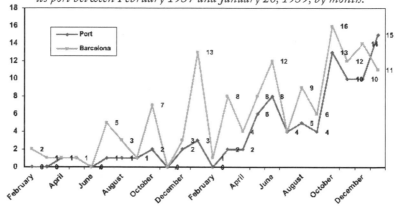

Source: Own elaboration based on data drawn from the Historical Archive of the Port of Barcelona.

Lastly, we should emphasize the lack of vision of the Republican authorities, given the fact that the port of Barcelona was a military target of the highest priority for their enemies. Judging from the results, the defenses that were put into operation were inadequate and the planning for air-raid shelters did not begin until May 1938. As noted earlier, the air-raid shelters were needed to protect port workers, yet they were never built. This lack of protection resulted in seventy-seven deaths according to Republican sources, although the actual figure was almost certainly higher.

Economically speaking, the port was left in ruins and it would not resume full activity until the 1970s; it was only then that it finally recovered the level of goods traffic that it had seen in 1929.[31]

There is no doubt from the documentation of the Republican port authorities that the port was heavily damaged by rebel bombardment. The ninety-five attacks that have been located and explained demonstrate this clearly and help us to understand how the port of Barcelona became one of the most severely damaged pieces of Catalan infrastructure in the Civil War.

BIBLIOGRAPHY

Albertí, Santiago, and Elisenda Albertí Casas. *Perill de bombardeig! Barcelona sota les bombes (1936–1939)*. Barcelona: Albertí Editors, 2005.

Alcofar, Nassaes, José Luís. *La aviación legionaria en la guerra española*. Barcelona: Euros, 1975.

Alcofar, Nassaes, José Luís. *La marina italiana en la guerra de España*. Barcelona: Editorial Euros, 1975.

Alemany, Joan. *El port de Barcelona*. Barcelona: Lunwerg, 1998.

Badosa, Cristina. *Josep Pla, biografia del solitari*. Barcelona: Edicions 62, 1996.

Bertran i Musitu, José. *Experiencias de los Servicios de Información del Nordeste de España (SIFNE) durante la guerra*. Madrid: Espasa-Calpe, 1940.

---

31 Rosa Maria Castejón, "El movimiento comercial del puerto de Barcelona," *Revista de Geografía* 8, nos. 1–2 (1974), 129–57.

Bombardeos aéreos en España. *De la aviación nacional a la retaguardia republicana.* Barcelona: Industrias Gráficas Seix y Barral Hnos, 1940.

Cabezas Sánchez, Adrián. "La defensa de la costa a Catalunya durant la Guerra Civil." PhD diss. University of Barcelona, 2013.

Campo Rizo, José Miguel. "El Mediterráneo, campo de batalla de la Guerra Civil española: la intervención naval italiana. Una primera aproximación documental." *Cuadernos de Historia Contemporánea* 19 (1997): 55–88.

Carreras, Albert, and César Yáñez. "El puerto en la era industrial: una síntesis histórica." In *Economía e Historia del puerto de Barcelona,* edited by Joan Clavera et al. Tres estudiós Civitas, Madrid, 1992.

Castejón, Rosa Maria "El movimiento comercial del puerto de Barcelona." *Revista de Geografía* 8, nos.1–2 (1974): 129–57.

Catalán Vidal, Jordi. *La economía española y la Segunda Guerra Mundial.* Barcelona: Ariel, 1995.

de Riquer, Borja, *L'últim Cambó (1936–1947). La dreta catalanista davant la guerra civil i el primer franquisme.* Vic: Editorial Eumo, 1996.

Díaz i Esculies, Daniel. *L'exili dels Països Catalans durant la Guerra Civil de 1936–1939.* Barcelona: Publicacions de l'Abadia de Montserrat, 2013.

Doll-Petit, Rubèn. *Els catalans de Gènova: història de l'èxode i l'adhesió d'una classe dirigent en temps de guerra.* Barcelona: Publicacions de l'Abadia de Montserrat, 2003.

Douhet, Giulio. *Il dominio dell'aira.* Milà: Mondadori, 1932.

Dueñas Iturbe, Oriol. *La gran destrucció. Els danys de la guerra civil a Catalunya (1936–1957).* Lleida: Pagès Editors, 2016.

———. *El port de Barcelona. objectiu militar durant la Guerra Civil 1936–1939.* Barcelona: Museu Marítim de Barcelona, 2016.

Estado mayor de la Armada. *Comisión para el Salvamento de Buques.* Barcelona, Editorial: Oliva de Vilanova, 1941

Gesalí, David, and David Íñiguez. *La guerra aèria a Catalunya.* Barcelona: Rafael Dalmau, 2012.

Gomá, José. *La guerra en el aire.* Barcelona: Editorial AHR, 1958.

González Echegaray, Rafael. *La Marina Mercante y el tráfico marítimo en la guerra civil.* Madrid: San Martín, 1977.

González Vilalta, Arnau. "Marines de guerra, evacuacions i consolats estrangers al port de Barcelona en guerra (juliol de 1936 – gener de 1937)." Paper presented at the XIII Congrés d'Història de Barcelona, Barcelona, 2013.

———. *Amb ulls estrangers. Quan Catalunya preocupava Europa. Diplomàcia i premsa internacional durant la Guerra Civil.* Barcelona: Editorial Base, 2014.

Guixà, Jordi. *Los espías de Franco. Josep Pla i Francesc Cambó.* Madrid: Ed. Fórcola, 2014.

Guixé, Jordi. *La República perseguida. Exilio y represión en la Francia de Franco.* València: Publicacions de la Universitat de València, 2012.

Heiberg, Morten, and Manuel Ros Agudo. *La Trama oculta de la guerra civil: los servicios secretos de Franco: 1936–1945.* Barcelona: Crítica, 2006.

Ibarz, Jordi. "Col·lectivització i Guerra Civil al port de Barcelona, 1936-1939." In *L'articulació social de la Barcelona contemporània*, edited by Joan Roca i Albert. Barcelona: Proa, Institut Municipal d'Història, 1997.

———. *Treballant el silenci. Les relacions laborals dels estibadors del port de Barcelona durant el primer franquisme, 1939–1947.* Barcelona: Museu Marítim de Barcelona, 2004.

Infiesta Pérez, José Luis. *Bombardeos del litoral mediterráneo durante la Guerra Civil.* Volume 1. Valladolid: Quiron, 1998.

Llaugé, Félix. *Historia mundial de la aviación de guerra.* Barcelona: Ed. De Vecchi, 1973.

Manent, Albert. *De 1936 a 1975. Estudis sobre la guerra civil i el franquisme.* Barcelona: Publicacions de l'Abadia de Montserrat, 1999.

Massot i Muntaner, Josep. *El desembarcament de Bayo a Mallorca, agost–setembre de 1936.* Barcelona: Publicacions de l'Abadia de Montserrat, 1997.

Merino Sánchez, Jacint. *Los militares se sublevan en Barcelona. El general Manuel Goded Llopis y el 19 de julio de 1936.* Barcelona: Ed. Base, 2013.

Pastor Petit, Domènec. *La cinquena columna a Catalunya (1936–1939).* Barcelona: Galba, 1978.

———. *Traïdors a Catalunya.* Barcelona: Ed. Base, 2007.

Pujadó Puigdomènech, Judith. *Oblits de rereguarda: els refugis antiaeris a Barcelona 1936–1939.* Barcelona: Publicacions de l'Abadia de Montserrat, 1998.

Renart, Joaquim. *Diari 1918–1961. La guerra: volum sisè (1936–1939).* Barcelona: Proa, 2003.

Ros Angulo, Manuel. *La trama oculta de la Guerra Civil. Los servicios secretos de Franco.* Barcelona: Crítica, 2006.

Rubió, Jordi. *L'èxode català de 1936 a través dels Pirineus.* Maçanet de la Selva: Editorial Gregal, 2014.

Salas Larrazabal, Jesús. *La guerra de España desde el aire.* Barcelona: Ariel, 1972.

———. *Guerra aérea 1936–1939.* Madrid: Ministerio de Defensa, 1999–2003.

Solé i Sabaté, Josep M., and Joan Villarroya. *Catalunya sota les bombes (1936–1939).* Barcelona: Publicacions de l'Abadia de Montserrat, 1986.

———. *La repressió a la reraguarda de Catalunya: 1936–1939.* Barcelona: Abadia de Montserrat, 1989.

———. *España en llamas. La Guerra Civil desde el aire.* Madrid: Temas de Hoy, 2003.

———, eds. *Breu història de la Guerra Civil a Catalunya.* Barcelona: Edicions 62, 2005.

Soler Fuensanta, José Ramón, and Francisco J. López-Brea Espiau. *Soldados sin rostro. Los servicios de información, espionaje y criptografía en la Guerra Civil española.* Barcelona: Inédita Editores, 2008.

Villarroya, Joan. *Els bombardeigs de Barcelona durant la Guerra Civil (1936–1939).* 2nd edition. Barcelona: Publicacions de l'Abadia de Montserrat, 1999.

———, ed. *Tres dies de març.* Barcelona: El Punt, 2008.

Viñas, Ángel. *El honor de la República. Entre el acoso fascista, la hostilidad britànica y la política de Stalin.* Barcelona: Crítica, 2009.

Chapter 13

The Wounded City: The Traces of the Nazi and Fascist Aerial Bombing of Barcelona

Laia Gallego Vila[1] and Queralt Solé[2]

Between July 17 and 19, 1936 a significant proportion of the Spanish army took part in a military rebellion that aimed to take control of the government of the Spanish Republic. The failure of this attempt resulted in a territorial division of the country between the areas that opposed the rebellion and upheld the legitimacy of the Republic—among them, Catalonia—and those that seconded the rebel military action or had fallen under its control. Thus, what began as an attempted coup led to a bloody Civil War, which was to last until April 1939.

The war severely disrupted everyday life. The advent of armed conflict entailed a recruitment drive, and in the first few days hundreds of volunteers, organized into columns, left Catalonia for the Aragón front. The garrison in the Aragonese capital, Zaragoza, had joined the uprising and the coup had been successful. In addition, at the same time as the military conflict, the ongoing revolutionary process in the Republican zone brought with it profound changes. On the one hand, a fierce repression was directed against those who were considered enemies; and on the other, new forms of organization arose and the

---

1   This chapter was written as part of the master's thesis "Edificis Ferits. Un estudi històrico-arqueològic dels bombardeigs de Barcelona," University of Barcelona.
2   This chapter was written under the auspices of the project "SUBTIERRO: Exhumaciones de fosas comunes derechos humanos en perspectiva histórica, transnacional y comparada," PI Francisco Ferrándiz (CSIC): MINECO CSO2015-66104-R.

people self-managed all aspects of their lives including the economy, leading to the collectivization both of the land and industry: workers took control of the whole agrarian and industrial production.

Despite the instability of the situation, in the early stages cultural and the everyday life continued: cinemas and theaters were kept open and sports events were held. However, over time, the efforts to maintain normality, and the mood at the home front, were affected by shortages, hunger, and above all by aerial bombardments that, for practically the first time in history, brought death raining down from the sky. The main cities of Catalonia were bombarded by Italian and German aircraft, causing damage and death on an unprecedented scale in Lleida, Figueres, Granollers, and Barcelona, in which the bombardments continued relentlessly until the very end of the war.

This chapter provides a new perspective on research into the Nazi and Fascist bombardments during the Spanish Civil War and proposes an interdisciplinary methodological framework for the study of the material remains of the raids that are still visible today in the twenty-first century. The possibilities of dealing with previously unconsidered documentary sources are presented and analyzed, and the study applies a clearly transdisciplinary approach, fundamentally involving history, archaeology, and memory studies.

After a thorough exploration of a range of documentary sources, some of them unpublished, we go on to focus on the analysis of the remains themselves, applying an archaeological methodology to assess the scope of the destruction of the bombings and the meanings of the conservation and interaction with these specific remains, and, above all, to attest to their relevance as painful reminders of a traumatic past.

THE BOMBARDMENT OF BARCELONA: ITS HISTORICAL CONTEXT

The Spanish Civil War saw the implementation of a new military strategy that was tested between 1936 and 1939 and was subsequently consolidated as a key element of modern warfare: the systematic bombing of the civilian population in urban areas. Although bombing raids were used by both Republican and rebel forces during the first few days of conflict, the arrival of Italian bomber aircraft in late July 1936 and, principally, the creation of the German Condor Legion in November of the same year, notably strengthened Franco's air force and were instrumental in deciding the course of the war.[3] In the same month, bombs fell on the Spanish capital Madrid, which thus became the first large European city to undergo mass aerial bombardment.[4] Particularly devastating were the raids on Gernika in April 1937[5] by the German air force; and on Alicante in late May 1938, where in a single day two Italian S-79 aircraft formations dropped 79 bombs of varying weights on the city center, killing more than 230 people and injuring 224.[6]

These actions and many others made evident the appearance of a new form of warfare – aerial warfare, which from that time onward would be waged not only at the front but over the cities as well. With the occupation of Mallorca by the rebels, the Italian Aviazione Legionaria was able to use the island as its base for the intensive bombing raids over the Mediterranean coast, which they carried out with the aim of demoralizing the Republican home front. In fact, these raids are considered among the main causes of the Francoist victory in April 1939. They caused terror among the civilian population in Catalan cities and disrupted production and supplies for the Republican side: cities and villages, industries, transports, hydroelectric power plants, and political centers were devastated by the explosions of the bombs. The death toll ran into the thousands and the city dwellers lived in constant fear of further attack.

Barcelona, capital of Catalonia, was one of the strategic centers of the Republican home front. With a population of over a million according to the 1936 census, the city housed the headquarters of three governments from November 1937 onward – the Catalan *Generalitat*, the Spanish Republican government, and the Basque government, and also most of the war industry in the Republican zone. These circumstances, together with its geostrategic position as a leading Mediterranean port, meant that Barcelona was the major target for the bombing raids in Catalonia, and indeed by the end of the war the city had lost some 2,500 inhabitants in the attacks.[7] On February 13, 1937 Barcelona was

---

3   Josep M. Solé i Sabaté and Joan Villarroya i Font, *España en llamas: la guerra civil desde el aire* (Madrid: Temas de Hoy, 2003), 15–16.
4   Ibid., 46.
5   See the more recent bibliography and critical analysis of previous publications in Xabier Irujo, *Gernika* (Barcelona: Crítica, 2017).
6   Rafael Aracil and Joan Villarroya, *El País Valencià sota les bombes (1936–1939)* (València: Publicacions de la Universitat de València, 2010).
7   Josep M. Solé i Sabaté and Joan Villarroya i Font, *Catalunya sota les bombes: 1936–*

bombarded for the first time by the Italian cruiser *Eugenio de Savoia*, and suffered its first air-raid on March 16. From this point on, the frequency and intensity of the aerial bombardments increased throughout the war. During the months of May, September, and October 1937 the destruction was particularly intense, especially in the area of Barceloneta, the working-class neighborhood near the port. In the early months of 1938 the bombing raids became more frequent and deadlier. The intensity of the attacks increased as the theater of war advanced toward Catalonia (most notably in March, when the rebels' offensive over the Aragón front reached the Ebro River, in western Catalonia) and as the Italian air force incorporated more modern aircraft.

STUDIES OF THE BOMBARDMENTS

The Nazi and Fascist bombardments of Catalonia have been studied in great depth since the 1980s. A broad bibliography has been created with diverse focuses of interest, comprising an exhaustive range of analysis. Without going into specifics, a number of thematic cores can be outlined with regard to the historians who have worked on the topic.

José Luis Infiesta Pérez (who wrote under the pseudonym José Luis Alcofar Nassaes) was the first Spanish author to carry a rigorous study of the bombardments, which was published in 1975 under the title *La aviación legionaria en la guerra Española*.[8] The study is an analysis of the contemporary press and literature, along with testimonies of Italian pilots who participated in the Spanish Civil War. However, the book lacks a further validation of the information provided, due to the limitation of access to original documents; the focus is predominantly military, based on the pilots' testimonies, uncritically accepting the claim that the targets were military (despite the obvious destruction of civilian areas of the city) and justifying the raids. Infiesta's interpretation reproduces the Francoist account imposed since 1940, which would not be challenged until the work of Joan Villarroya. Nevertheless, Infiesta's military and strategic approach continues the work of Italian historians who studied the Italian military archives for information on the organization of the

---

1939 (Barcelona: Abadia de Montserrat, 1986), 235. The authors give a figure of 5,000–5,200 mortal victims of the bombing raids for the whole of Catalonia.

8   José Luis Alcofar Nassaes, *La aviación legionaria en la guerra española* (Barcelona: Euros, 1975).

air force, the wingspans, the amount of bombs dropped, the aircraft involved, and the strategies applied.[9]

After the end of the official narrative of the Franco dictatorship, the first points to be established were the number of bombardments suffered in Catalonia, the sites affected, and the victims caused. The pioneer in this area of study was Professor Joan Villarroya, from the University of Barcelona, whose work focused first on the city of Barcelona and then subsequently broadened out to include the whole of Catalonia.[10] In 2003, together with Josep Maria Solé i Sabaté, professor at the Autonomous University of Barcelona, Villarroya published a comprehensive study on the bombardments in Spain.[11]

Santiago Albertí and Elisenda Albertí Casas extended the study of the bombing raids over Barcelona. Born in 1930, Santiago Albertí was a direct witness of the events, and over the course of his life he compiled a large amount of documentation, personal memories, historical press reports, and testimonies of the bombing. This information was compiled and published by his daughter Elisenda Albertí Casas in *Perill de bombardeig! Barcelona sota les bombes: 1936–1939*.[12] The book presents for the first time the records of the alarms (both those that preceded bombing raids and false alarms) and thus gives a clear picture of the situation of constant alert in which the inhabitants of Barcelona were forced to live. Oriol Dueñas' doctoral dissertation continues the theme of the analysis of the costs of the bombings. Published in 2013 as *La gran destrucció: els danys de guerra i la reconstrucció de Catalunya després de la Guerra Civil 1937–1957*,[13] the book opens up a series of new and unexplored ways of researching the scope of the destruction of the attacks. This work explores in particular the material damage caused by

9   Ferdinando Pedriali, *Guerra di Spagna e aviazione italiana* (Roma: Aeronautica militare italiana; Ufficio storico, 1992).
10 Joan Villarroya i Font, *Els Bombardeigs de Barcelona durant la Guerra Civil* (Barcelona: Abadia de Montserrat, 1981); Solé i Sabaté and Villarroya i Font, *Catalunya sota les bombes*. Both books compile and contrast the existing literature and contemporary press with a series of archive documents that were unknown at the time (records of the bombardments by the Security and Citizen Services, reports by the fire service, and statistics for the dead and wounded from the Hospital Clínic and Hospital General de Catalunya) that allowed the formulation of the first reliable and confirmed figures on the human cost of the bombings.
11 Solé i Sabaté and Villarroya i Font, *España en llamas: la guerra civil desde el aire*.
12 Santiago Albertí and Elisenda Albertí Casas, *Perill de bombardeig! Barcelona sota les bombes: 1936–1939* (Barcelona: Albertí Editors, 2004).
13 Oriol Dueñas Iturbe, *La gran destrucció: els danys de guerra i la reconstrucció de Catalunya després de la Guerra Civil 1937–1957* (Barcelona: Universitat de Barcelona, 2013).

the bombs and the reconstruction of infrastructures and communications such as ports, hydroelectric power plants, railroad systems, bridges, and other military objectives. Hence, despite the brief references noted by Villarroya and Solé,[14] this is the first exhaustive study of the theme that gives an idea of the scope of the destruction, the responsibility, and the postwar situation, as well as the attempts to reconstruct the infrastructure of the territory.

The interpretation of the bombardment of Barcelona is not widely debated. However, while Joan Villarroya and others have focused on analyzing the human and material cost of the bombings, David Gesalí and David Iñíguez apply a slightly different perspective.[15] From a military standpoint and focusing on the analysis of the aerial war, they interpret the role of the bombing raids within the context of the military tactics and their relation to the situation at the front. They aim to emphasize the resistance and the active role of the Republican side; viewing the work of Villarroya and Solé as "victimist," they see the Francoist bombings as a strategy for deterring and distracting the Republican air force in order to advance at the front. Gesalí and Iñíguez stress the role of the mutual reprisals between the two sides in the bombardments of urban areas as military objectives. Focusing especially on the bombing raids of January and May 1938, they interpret them as an escalation of violence against civilians on both sides. Overall, their work follows the military viewpoint of José Luis Infiesta Pérez (Alcofar Nassaes), who, after reading Villarroya's research, rectified his previous interpretations in a new publication: *Bombardeos del litoral mediterráneo durante la Guerra Civil* in 1998.[16] In this book Infiesta retracts his earlier position and, given the exhaustive recordings of attacks on civilians, accepts that the version of the events in which the bombing raids were directed only at military objectives is open to question.

Even though they do not strictly come under the heading of the historiography of the bombardments, passive defense studies are strongly connected to the topic of the active response of the civilians and institutions in the bombed city of Barcelona. The first publication to deal with the air-raid shelters was *Oblits de rereguarda: els refugis antiaeris*

---

14   Solé i Sabaté and Villarroya i Font, *Catalunya sota les bombes*; Villarroya i Font, *Els Bombardeigs de Barcelona durant la Guerra Civil*.

15   David Gesalí Barrera and David Iñíguez Gràcia, *La guerra aèria a Catalunya (1936–1939)* (Barcelona: Rafael Dalmau, 2012).

16   José Luis Infiesta Pérez and Luis Fresno Crespo, *Bombardeos del litoral mediterráneo durante la Guerra Civil* (Valladolid: Quirón, 1998).

a Barcelona, 1936-1939 by Judith Pujadó,[17] which draws attention to their importance and also to the exceptional organizational capacity of the population of Barcelona when faced with this new aerial threat. Following on from this study, Pujadó published a further work;[18] and some more partial studies were also carried out.[19] More recently, the air-raid shelters spread all over the city have become the object of archaeological studies.[20] All the above research has laid the foundations for the production of brief monographs;[21] thorough papers on general aspects of the Civil War in Catalonia;[22] and the inclusion of information on aerial attacks in educational compilations in which maps and statistics provide a comprehensive picture of the death toll and the volume of the bombardment suffered by the Catalan cities.[23]

NEW HISTORICAL RECORDS AND TRANSDISCIPLINARITY

The key areas of research into the bombardments described above are essentially based on two types of accounts: contemporary records of the events and the memories of eyewitnesses. For Barcelona, the focus of our study, we have contemporary records such as newspaper reports,

---

17 Judith Pujadó Puigdomènech, *Oblits de rereguarda: els refugis antiaeris a Barcelona, 1936–1939* (Barcelona: Abadia de Montserrat, 1998).
18 Judith Pujadó Puigdomènech, *El llegat subterrani. Els refugis antiaeris de la Guerra Civil* (Badalona: Ara Llibres, 2008).
19 See for example the study of the air-raid shelters in the neighborhood of Gràcia by Josep M. Contel, *Gràcia, temps de bombes, temps de refugis: el subsòl com a supervivència* (Barcelona: Taller d'Història de Gràcia, 2008).
20 Carme Miró and Jordi Ramos, "Els refugis antiaeris de Barcelona (1936–1937). Una nova visió des de l'arqueologia d'intervenció," *Exnovo* 7 (2011): 55–79 and Carme Miró and Jordi Ramos, "Cronotipologia dels refugis antiaeris de Barcelona," MUHBA documents, no. 6 (2013), 54–66. See also Ramon Arnabat i Mata, *Els refugis antiaeris de Barcelona: criteris d'intervenció patrimonial* (Ajuntament de Barcelona, Institut de Cultura, 2009).
21 Francesc Poblet i Feijoo, *Els bombardeigs a Barcelona durant la Guerra Civil* (Barcelona: Ajuntament de Barcelona, Regidoria de Dona i Drets Civils, 2005); David Íñiguez, *El Vesper de la Gloriosa: L'aviació republicana* (Calafell: Llibres de Matrícula, 2002).
22 Joan Villarroya i Font, "Els bombardeigs durant la guerra civil," in *La guerra civil a Catalunya (1936–1939)*, ed. Josep M. Solé i Sabaté (Barcelona: Edicions 62, 2004), 110–49; Carles Santacana i Torres, "Bombes i lleves: els efectes d'una guerra moderna sobre la població," in *La Segona república a Catalunya: Guerra i revolució 1936–1939*, ed. Jordi Casassas and Joan Villarroya (Barcelona: Edicions 62, 2015) 119–122.
23 Víctor Hurtado, Antoni Segura, and Joan Villarroya i Font, *Atles de la Guerra Civil a Catalunya* (Barcelona: Universitat de Barcelona, 2010); Gabriel Cardona and Manel Esteban i Cano, eds., *Atles de la Guerra Civil a Barcelona* (Barcelona: Edicions 62, 2009); Jordi Barra, *La legión Cóndor* (Barcelona: Dau, 2016).

archives, and audiovisual and photographic materials. Several texts have sought to document the attacks: on the one hand, compilations of the number of bombardments and deaths, such as the protest published by the propaganda commission of the Generalitat de Catalunya entitled *Bombardements et agressions en Espagne*;[24] and *Bombardeos Aéreos en España. Bombardeos de la aviación nacional a la retaguardia republicana*[25] that defended the Nationalist policy; and on the other, newspaper reports during the war by international journalists with a variety of propagandistic aims.[26] There are also other archives that contain interesting information: fire department records;[27] statements and reports concerning the material damage to the buildings;[28] documents of the hospitals and the passive defense council (Junta de Defensa Passiva);[29] and judicial proceedings (including transactions related to the investigations into the deaths and material damage caused by the raids), correspondence, and international reports.[30] Indeed, the contemporary press, both national and international, presents a vast amount of information relating to the bombing raids, although of course their accounts must be read with a critical eye due to the propagandistic objectives of many of these publications.[31] Finally, a vast range of images of the bombing was

---

24 Generalitat de Catalunya, *Bombardements et agressions en Espagne (juillet 1936– juillet 1938)* (Paris: 1938).
25 Generalitat de Catalunya, *Bombardeos Aéreos en España. Bombardeos de la aviación nacional a la retaguardia republicana* (Barcelona: Seix Barral, 1939) presents an account of the bombardment of the Republican army as Franco's troops advanced, and a list of the military objectives of the Republican home front attacked by the Francoist air force.
26 José Sabadell Mercadé, *Historial del Cuerpo de Bomberos y de anteriores organizaciones para combatir los incendios de la misma ciudad, 1379–1939* (Barcelona: Ediciones Técnico Publicitarias, 1943).
27 Solé i Sabaté and Villarroya i Font, *Catalunya sota les bombes.*
28 José María Martino, *Apuntalamiento o derribo de edificios afectados por el bombardeo* (Barcelona: 1938); José María Martino, *Protección de edificios, monumentos artísticos, etc. contra bombardeos* (Barcelona: 1938).
29 Jaume Valentines Álvarez, Antoni Roca Rosell, and Guillermo Lusa Monforte, eds., *El Fons Ramon Perera. Imatges de La Defensa Passiva a Catalunya (1938–1939)* (Barcelona: Universitat Politècnica de Catalunya and Càtedra UNESCO de Tècnica i Cultura, 2008).
30 *Les Archives Secrètes de la Wilhelmstrasse* (Paris: Plon, 1956); *Les Archives Secrètes du Comte Ciano, 1936–1942* (Paris, 1948); Jordi Pons Pujol, *Lliçons de Barcelona: informe britànic sobre el bombardeigs de la ciutat, 1938* (Barcelona: Fundació Carles Pi i Sunyer d'Estudis Autonòmics i Locals, 2004); Ramon Parera, *ARP in Catalonia: Paper read at a meeting of the Institute on Tuesday, December 12, 1939. Discussion* (N.p.: N.d.), 88–117.
31 Without attempting to include the entirety of the articles of the contemporary press, the following are some of the newspapers whose reports have been used by historians: *L'Humanité, Ce Soir, The Times, The Daily Herald, News Chronicle, The Daily Express, La Vanguardia, La Publicitat, Solidaridad Obrera, Les Notícies, Via Libre, Meridià,* and *Primera Plana.*

produced, especially photographic materials that have been compiled in several publications.[32] Of particular interest is the film *Catalunya Màrtir (Le martyre de la Catalogne)*[33] ordered by the propaganda commission of the Generalitat de Catalunya.

Another record used by historiographers are the memories of eyewitnesses of the bombardments published some years after the events, which provide information that is not included in the historical documents and shed light on the civilian perception of the bombardments.[34] These texts, of which we will cite just a sample, contain a wealth of individual and personal perceptions that can enrich the analysis of the social context. Especially interesting are the memories of Marià Manent,[35] which provide a clear view of the conflict and the bombing raids in the fateful days of January 1938. Other kinds of memories have been used for the military study of the bombardments, narrated by the participants in the events on both sides.[36] Many of these records have been used to carry out the core analysis of this paper, along with a variety of archives of largely unstudied materials such as the law proceedings of the Central

32   Rafael Abella, *La vida cotidiana durante la guerra civil. La España Republicana* (Barcelona: Planeta, 1975); Ricardo de la Cierva, *Historia ilustrada de la guerra civil española* (Barcelona: Danae, 1970); Bernardo Gil Mugarza, *España en llamas. 1936* (Barcelona: Acervo, 1968); Tomás Salvador, *La Guerra de España en sus fotografías* (Barcelona: Marte, 1966); Edmon Vallès, *Història gràfica de la Catalunya autònoma. La guerra. 1936–1939* (Barcelona: Edicions 62, 1978); *Visions de guerra i reraguarda. Història gràfica de la Revolució* (Barcelona: Forja, 1937).

33   J. Marsillach, *Catalunya Màrtir (Le martyre de la Catalogne)* (Barcelona: Laya Films, 1938). The film can be seen online at: https://www.youtube.com/watch?v=ExvgQDIn5AU (last accessed September 2017).

34   Claude Gernade Bowers, *Misión en España (1933–1939)* (Mexico City: Grijalbo, 1966); Tomás Caballé Clos, *Barcelona roja. Dietario de la Revolución (julio 1936–enero 1939)* (Barcelona: Librería Argentina, 1939); C. A. Jordana, *Barcelona 1938: La veu de les sirenes* (Barcelona: Edicions de 1984, 2008); Teresa Pàmies, *Quan érem capitans (memòries d'aquella guerra)* (Barcelona: Dopesa, 1974); Carles Pi i Sunyer, *La República y la guerra. Memorias de un político catalán* (Mexico City: Oasis, 1975); Joan Raventós and Jacint Raventós, *Dos infants i la guerra* (Barcelona: El Pi de les Tres Branques, 1974); Joaquim Renart, *Diari 1918–1961*, vol. 6, *La guerra (1936–1939)* (Barcelona: Proa, 2003); Antoni Rovira i Virgili, *Els darrers dies de la Catalunya republicana* (Barcelona: Curial, 1977); Marià Rubió i Tudurí, *Barcelona 1936–1939* (Barcelona: Abadia de Montserrat, 2002); Ferran Soldevila, *Al llarg de la meva vida* (Barcelona: Edicions 62, 1970); Estanislau Torres, *Quasi un dietari (memòries: 1926–1949)* (Barcelona: Abadia de Montserrat, 2003).

35   Marià Manent, *El vel de Maia. Dietari de la guerra civil (1936–1939)* (Barcelona: Edicions Destino, 1975).

36   For example, Andrés García Lacalle, *Mitos y verdades. La aviación de caza en la guerra española* (Mexico City: Oasis, 1973); José Gomá, *La Guerra en el aire* (Barcelona: AHR, 1958); Ignacio Hidalgo de Cisneros, *Cambio de rumbo* (Bucharest: 1964); Alfredo Kinderlán, *Mis cuadernos de guerra* (Madrid: Plantea, 1982); Francisco Tarazona, *Sangre en el cielo* (Mexico: Costa Amic, 1957); and Giuseppe Valle, *Uomini nei cieli. Storia dell'Aeronautica Italiana* (Rome: Centro Edit. Nazionale, 1981)

Archive of the High Court of Justice of Catalonia[37] and the historical archive of the College of Architects of Catalonia, which had not been consulted to date.

The Conceptualization of an "Archaeology of Bombardments"

Twentieth-century aerial bombardment, a strategic attack directed at civilians, had a profound impact on European society and has been debated exhaustively over the years. It is vital to understand the social and moral context that made possible the rapid escalation of the range of destruction and the generalization of the concept of "total war." We believe that, beyond a simple historical reconstruction, this profound understanding should be based on a transdisciplinary approach able to create diverse and collective learning for constructing what is known in Spanish as a "memory of non-repetition"—memory that helps us to avoid repeating the mistakes of history—and a critical understanding of the past and the present. Especially in times like these (when a brutal aggression against the civilian population is taking place in Syria, and the tensions caused by the existence of weapons of mass destruction are growing), history has the task of providing tools for the collective understanding of the historical scope of these events. In this context, here we outline a proposal for an archaeology of bombardments, based on the historical, moral, social, and human impact of the destruction of cities through bombing, aiming to transcend classical disciplinary boundaries and to explore the possibilities for research and dissemination of an approach based on materiality.

Contemporary archaeology has proven to be a useful tool to promote and direct the collective memory through materiality.[38] This

---

37 Arxiu Central del Tribunal Superior de Justícia de Catalunya: 84/1937 del bombardeig de 16 de març de 1937 del Jutjat d'Instrucció 13 de Barcelona; 219/1937 del bombardeig de 29 de maig de 1937 del Jutjat d'Instrucció 12 de Barcelona; 549/1937 del bombardeig de 13 d'octubre de 1937 del Jutjat d'Instrucció 12 de Barcelona; and 6/1938 del bombardeig d'1 de gener de 1938 del Jutjat d'Instrucció 12 de Barcelona.

38 A compilation of some of the most important work on contemporary archaeology in Spain can be found in Queralt Solé i Barjau and Oscar Jané Checa, *L'arqueologia del món modern i contemporani. Noves perspectives 78* (Catarroja: Afers, 2014). Some international accounts are: Victor Buchli and Gavin Lucas, "The Absent Present: Archaeologies of the Contemporary Past," in *Archaeologies of the Contemporary Past* (London: Routledge, 2001), 3–18; Richard A. Gould and Michael B. Schiffer, eds., *Modern Material Culture: The Archaeology of Us* (New York: Academic Press, 1981);

discipline is the starting-point for our analysis of the physical remains of the bombing raids in Barcelona, as a potentially evocative practice able to emphasize the history of the human experience of the destruction. Thus, we will be focusing on the scope of the destruction of the city, the permanence of the ruins, and their role in the postwar city as a potential reminder of the brutal violence inflicted upon it during wartime.

The conceptualization of the archaeology of bombardments arises from the influence of historical, philosophical, and literary studies on the role of the technology of aerial bombing, the appearance and permanence of ruins in the city, collective trauma, and, above all, the social and human causes and consequences of the destruction. In what follows we briefly outline those major influences.

Analyzing the causes of the escalation of violence against civilians, one of the most relevant themes is the technological innovation of deploying bomber planes on the home front – where, in some cases, they were considered to be of greater strategic importance than at the battle front.[39] From the perspective of the history of technology, it has been argued that the implementation of bombers did not imply a crucial advantage in military terms, since they did not entirely replace the artillery used until then.[40] Here, materiality becomes a center of study, given that technology represents the means through which the events could take place. Nonetheless, as David Edgerton notes,[41] the escalation of violence cannot be explained by the internal dynamics of technology but should rather be seen as part of a wider context that transcends the technological and even military field, as outlined below: "Total war" is the concept that represents the rise of a new way of waging war in which "war becomes a matter of turning over the whole of society to the mass production of weapons, to total, industrial war in which civilians in factories are as much combatants, and thus targets, as soldiers on the front."[42] Hence, war is embedded in all dimensions of society and violence penetrates civilian life.

and Alfredo González-Ruibal and Gabriel Moshenska, *Ethics and the Archaeology of Violence* (New York: Springer-Verlag, 2015).

39   See Yuki B. Tanaka and Marilyn B. Young, eds., *Bombing Civilians: A Twentieth-century History* (New York: New Press, 2009) and Thomas J. Misa, *Leonardo to the Internet: Technology and Culture from the Renaissance to the Present* (Baltimore: The Johns Hopkins University Press, 2004).

40   David Edgerton, *Innovación y tradición: historia de la tecnología moderna* (Barcelona: Crítica, 2007), 185–211.

41   Ibid., 186.

42   David Edgerton, *The Shock of the Old: Technology and Global History since 1900* (London: Profile, 2008), 138.

The adoption of aerial bombing is to be explained by a complex conjunction of moral, social, and political causes that imposed a shift in the perception of war and of the threshold of violence, which now admitted the annihilation of the enemy, including the civilian population. Jonathan Glover emphasizes the relevance of mentalities and moral contexts to understand how conventional ethical rules could be shattered.[43] As the main causes for the aggressive shift, he identifies physical distance in the execution of violence[44] (especially patent in the case of aerial bombardments); the existence of precedents;[45] the fragmentation of responsibility; the discourse of excuses; and the calculation of the consequences.[46] Indeed, we are dealing here with the problem of the alienation of violence, facilitated by the use of bomber planes (relatively new technology in the first third of the twentieth century) that used physical distance to deepen the social, political, and identitarian difference of the enemy and hence crush any possibility of empathy. As the Spanish Civil War was the first conflict in which this new form of warfare was used, the experience of Barcelona and of other cities on the Republican home front is especially relevant to a fuller understanding of the process of the adoption of aerial bombardments as a means for modern war and the consequent debilitation of basic ethical rules that Glover mentions.

This change in the perception of violence constitutes a key idea for a new approach to the study of the bombing raids, starting from the

---

43 Glover departs from an analysis of the moral laws underlying European culture in order to understand its breakdown. He establishes the origin and the consolidation of these laws in the Enlightenment and reveals the great contradiction of the twentieth century: "At the start of the century there was optimism, coming from the Enlightenment, that the spread of a humane and scientific outlook would lead to the fading away, not only of war, but also of other forms of cruelty and barbarism." Jonathan Glover, *Humanity: A Moral History of the Twentieth Century* (Yale: Yale Nota Bene, 2001), 6.

44 "When war is conducted at a distance, the psychology is different. The moral resources are not threatened by the ecstasy which overwhelms them in close combat. But, on the other hand, little has to be done to neutralize the inhibitions linked to respect and sympathy. Those running the policy are far away from those killed. Humiliations are not seen. And sympathy is minimal." Moreover, "In long-range war, distance virtually excludes human responses of any strength. It is possible for someone firing a missile to imagine the impact on people at the receiving end, but nothing has the immediacy of actually seeing a man holding up his trousers." Glover, *Humanity*, 64, 79.

45 "Going with the momentum of the established policy is far less troubling to the sense of moral identity than actively starting a new policy. Conscience is protected by a kind of moral inertia." Glover *Humanity*, 114.

46 "A merely foreseen bad effect may be permissible, so long as the badness is not out of proportion to the good being pursued ... moral absolutes limit what can be done to individual people on the basis of calculation of consequences," Glover, *Humanity*, 85.

human and social impact of the experience. The depth of this impact is reflected in the amount of literary references to the bombing itself, the destruction, trauma, and the crisis in morale, and above all in the permanence of the material ruins of the violence. The concept of "moral bombing," conceived by Alexander Kluge,[47] aptly summarizes the effect of this kind of aerial attack: not just death and physical destruction, but moral and psychological debacle. W. G. Sebald also superbly describes the collective psychological impact of bombardment and the ruins of defeat in postwar Germany.[48] The scope of destruction of this new warfare technology appears to civilians as an overwhelming experience: incomprehensible, unassimilable, and unmanageable. Likewise, Jean-Yves Jouannais explores the nature, causes, and consequences of this experience under the name of "obsidional fever," a particular emotional and intellectual collapse suffered after the experience of bombardment.[49] Jouannais also stresses the importance of the material remains of aerial bombing and its political uses as painful reminders of defeat but also as medals for the suffering endured.

In this chapter we maintain the importance of the potential role of material remains of bombardments in cities today, both from a historical and memorial perspective: the potential of materiality for resonance;50 and for revelation;51 because a perceptive engagement with the past and for dealing with traumatic collective memories have already been stressed as a key feature of contemporary archaeology.52 Today, many archaeology projects all over the world are exploring the

---

47 Alexander Kluge, *Ataque aéreo a Halberstadt, el 8 de abril de 1945* (Madrid: Antonio Machado Libros, 2014).
48 W. G. Sebald, *Sobre la historia natural de la destrucción* (Barcelona: Anagrama, 2003).
49 Jean-Yves Jouannais, *El uso de las ruinas* (Barcelona: El Acantilado, 2017).
50 Gabriel Moshenska, "Resonant Materiality and Violent Remembering: Archaeology, Memory and Bombing," *International Journal of Heritage Studies* 15, no. 1 (2009), 51.
51 Alfredo González-Ruibal, "Reclaiming archaeology," in Reclaiming Archaeology: Beyond the Tropes of Modernity, edited by Alfredo González-Ruibal (Milton Park, Abingdon and New York: Routledge, 2013), 1–23.
52 Some relevant examples of archaeology dealing with conflictive memory and ruins are Gabriel Moshenska, "Working with Memory in the Archaeology of Modern Conflict," *Cambridge Archaeological Journal* 20, no. 1 (2010), 33–48; William Logan and Keir Reeves, eds., *Places of Pain and Shame: Dealing with Difficult Heritage* (London and New York: Routledge, 2008); Marion Stone, "A Memory in Ruins?'" *Public Archaeology* 3, no, 3 (2004), 131–44; Caitlin Desilvey and Tim Edensor, "Reckoning with Ruins," *Progress in Human Geography* 37, no. 4 (2012), 465–85; Aloïs Riegl, *El Culto Moderno a Los Monumentos* (Madrid: A. Machado Libros, 2008); and Alfredo González-Ruibal, "Arqueología de la Guerra Civil," *Complutum* 19, no. 2 (2008), 11–20.

remains of warfare and repression, especially in Latin America53 and the United Kingdom. In Spain, battlefields, mass graves, and concentration camp sites from the Spanish Civil War became the subject of study in the second decade of the twenty-first century,54 and the discipline of contemporary and conflict archaeology is playing an increasingly significant role in their study and dissemination.

However, less attention has been paid to the legacy of aerial warfare. Among the few projects carried out to date we should mention the recent archaeological study of Republican aerodromes;[55] and the excavation and recovery of an anti-aircraft battery and several air-raid shelters.[56] In a broader context, the archaeologist Gabriel Moshenska[57] suggests the possibility of an "archaeology of bombardments" to examine the destruction caused by the bomber planes. He argues that, "bombing is by far the most common manifestation or experience of war for the civilian populations of twentieth-century Europe."[58] He also explores the possibilities of the commemorative potential of bombsites in modern cities and the warfare narratives from the perspective of the everyday life of civilians under bombardment. However, Moshenska draws

---

53   A recent compilation of some of the main work on memory and archaeology can be found in Soledad Biasatti and Gonzalo Compañy, *Memorias Sujetadas. Hacia una lectura crítica y situada de los procesos de memorialización* (Madrid: JAS Arqueologia, 2015).

54   Alfredo González-Ruibal, "Arqueología de la Guerra Civil Española." Alfredo González-Ruibal, "Contra La Pospolítica: Arqueología de La Guerra Civil Española," *Revista Chilena de Antropología* (2010), 9–32; Alfredo González-Ruibal, "From the Battlefield to the Labour Camp: Archaeology of Civil War and Dictatorship in Spain," *Antiquity* 86, no. 332 (June 2012), 456–73; Alfredo González-Ruibal, "Making Things Public: Archaeologies of the Spanish Civil War," *Public Archaeology* 6, no. 4 (2007), 203–26; M. Cinta Ramblado-Minero, "Sites of Memory / Sites of Oblivion in Contemporary Spain," *Revista Canadiense de Estudios Hispánicos* 36, no. 1 (2011), 29–42; Xurxo Ayán Vila, "Guerra en la Universidad. Cuando se quebraron las cristaleras de la Facultad," *Arkeogatze* 5 (2015), 27–34; and Jorge Morín and Alicia Torija, eds., *Paisajes de la guerra y la posguerra. Espacios amenazados* (Madrid: Audema, 2017).

55   María del Carmen Rojo Ariza, "¿Arqueología y aviación?: la excavación de aerodrómos de campaña en el Penedés," *Revista Universitaria de Historia Militar* 2 (2013), 85–108; María del Carmen Rojo Ariza and Laia Coma Quintana, "Arqueología y museografía didáctica en los aeródromos de guerra (1936–1939)," *Ebre* 38, no. 4 (2010), 165–77.

56   Miró and Ramos, "Els refugis antiaeris de Barcelona (1936–1937) and "Cronotipologia dels refugis antiaeris de Barcelona."

57   Moshenska, "Resonant Materiality and Violent Remembering;" "Children in Ruins: Bombsites as Playgrounds in Second World War Britain," in *Ruin Memories: Materiality, Aesthetics and the Archaeology of the Recent Past*, ed. Bjørn Olsen and Þóra Pétursdóttir (Abingdon: Routledge, 2014), 230–49, and "Unbuilt Heritage: Conceptualising Absence in the Historical Environment," in *The Good, the Bad and the Unbuilt: Handling the Heritage of the 21st Century*, ed. Sarah May, Hilary Orange, and Sefryn Penrose (Oxford: Archaeopress, 2012), 123–26.

58   Moshenska, "Resonant Materiality and Violent Remembering," 49.

attention specifically to ruined spaces, and does not consider the scars of bombing on buildings.

In contrast to Moshenska's approach, our perspective of a potential archaeology of bombardments specifically addresses buildings and the vestiges of bombing. Remains of this kind have been assessed by the Forensic Architecture group in more recent contexts as part of the evidence for unmasking illegitimate state violence. Paradoxically, bombing scars on buildings are both unseen and common remains at one and the same time. Moshenska himself recognizes that, "we need not dig for ruins; they confront us;"[59] this is central to our purpose, because we are interested in the interactive capacity[60] of the materiality of the violent bombing scars in the current modern cities.

Accordingly, this chapter will deal with the historical and methodological potential of the materiality of the scars of bombardments in the case of the city of Barcelona with the aim of revealing the scope of destruction of the fascist bombardments and the perception of city in ruins. We also explore the successive actions and discourses regarding the material evidence of the bombardments under the Franco dictatorship, and the survival of these remains and their meanings in the twenty-first century.

METHODOLOGY AND TECHNIQUES

Methodologically, this paper explores the possibilities of an archaeology of bombardments based on three case studies described below. As mentioned above, archaeology offers a solid, specialized grounding for the study of materiality, from recording to interpretation.

---

59 Ibid., 46.
60 Eyal Weizman stresses this special agency of materiality: "buildings are thus not just passive elements, receptive sensors on which events are registered. Nor are they just the scenes of a crime, the locations in whichviolence takes place. Rather, built environments are composite assemblies of structures, spaces, infrastructure, services, and technologies with the capacity to act and interact with their surroundings and shape events around them. They structure and condition rather than simply frame human action, they actively—sometimes violently—shape incidents and events." See Eyal Weizman, *Forensic Architecture: Violence at the Threshold of Detectability* (Brooklyn, NY: Zone Books, 2017), 16.

The main methodological framework is based on the transdisciplinary study of the historiography, documentary sources, and, above all, the archaeological study of the traces of the bombing raids in the buildings of the urban landscape of Barcelona. The archaeological record consists of a selection of three cases in the old town of Barcelona that exemplify three different methodological situations and levels of study, in order to contrast their current condition with accounts in the historical documents consulted. The objective is to test the theoretical and methodological potential of the material remains of the fascist bombardments of Barcelona as a field case.

The methodology applied for the basic stratigraphic documentation systems and façade analysis stems from the archaeology of architecture;[61] archaeotecture;[62] and complemented by the use of techniques from forensic architecture.[63] The visual documentation is complemented with a photographic register, sketches, geometric rectification (photoplan) with RDF software from the Università Iuav di Venezia, digitalized drawing, and 3D photogrammetric model building with Agisoft Photoscan software.[64]

The first case is the Plaça de Sant Felip Neri, widely known for its shrapnel impacts and symbolically representative of the memory of the bombardments in Barcelona. The second is the Cinema Coliseum, badly damaged during a well-recorded episode of the bombardments. And the third is a street in the old town named c/Carders (and its prolongation c/Corders), chosen because it was certified as having been affected by the bombing.

---

61 Agustín Azkarate, "La Arqueología de la Arquitectura en el siglo XXI," *Arqueología de la arquitectura* 5 (2008), 11–13; Francesco Doglioni and Marina Ciarocchi, *Stratigrafia e restauro: tra conoscenza e conservazione dell'architettura* (Trieste: Lint Editoriale Associati, 1997); Gian Pietro Brogiolo and Aurora Cagnana, *Archeologia dell'architettura: metodi e interpretazioni* (Fiorentino: All'Insegna del Giglio, 2012); Esther de Vega and Concepción Martín Morales, *Arqueología aplicada al estudio e interpretación de edificios históricos: últimas tendencias metodológicas* (Madrid: Ministerio de Cultura, Subdirección General de Publicaciones, Información y Documentación, 2010).
62 Xurxo M. Ayàn Vila, Rebeca Blanco Rotea, and Patricia Manana Borrazàs, "Arqueotectura 1: Bases teórico-metodológicas para una Arqueología de la Arquitectura," *Tapa. Traballos de arqueoloxía e patrimonio* 25 (2002), 12–101; Xurxo M. Ayàn Vila, Rebeca Blanco Rotea, and Patricia Manana Borrazàs, "Archaeotecture: Seeking a New Archaeological Vision of Architecture," in *Archaeotecture: Archaeology of Architecture*, ed. Xurxo M. Ayàn Vila, Rebeca Blanco Rotea, and Patricia Manana Borrazàs (Oxford: Archaeopress, 2003), p. 1–15.
63 Weizman, *Forensic Architecture.*
64 The photogrammetric model of the facades of the church of Sant Felip Neri can be found at: https://skfb.ly/6rYLM.

CASE STUDIES

Sant Felip Neri

January 30, 1938 was a fateful day for the city of Barcelona. On that day it suffered an unprecedented aerial aggression, which caused the death of more than two hundred people in the area surrounding the Palace of the Generalitat (the Catalan government building) and Sant Felip Neri.[65] The attack was ostensibly carried out to neutralize command posts and management centers.[66] It consisted of two raids performed by two formations of six Savoia S-79s of the Italian Aviazione Legionaria, which dropped thirty-six 250kg bombs and twenty-four 20kg bombs.[67] Forty-two people, most of them children, lost their lives in Sant Felip Neri.[68] The majority died while taking refuge in the sacristy of the church, and others perished in the second attack while attending to the victims.[69] The terrible bombardments were widely reported in the local and international press, prompting new calls for peace and attempts to negotiate the cessation of the air strikes. The eyewitnesses were deeply marked by the atrocity.[70] And the total dehumanization of the war became dramatically apparent.[71]

The façades of the Plaça de Sant Felip Neri still show signs of the bombardments of that January day. The square, which preserves two disfigured walls riddled by the shrapnel of the bombs, has become the most important symbol of the bombarded city, attracting crowds of visitors, and constituting the main site of memory of the Civil War

---

65 Data taken from Villarroya i Font, *Els Bombardeigs de Barcelona durant la Guerra Civil*.
66 Villarroya i Font, "Els bombardeigs durant la guerra civil."
67 Gesalí Barrera and Íñiguez Gràcia, *La guerra aèria a Catalunya (1936–1939)*, 389.
68 "Houses destroyed, many dead and injured, above all in the Sant Felip Neri shelter," *Llibre 73 dels comunicats de Bombers*, in Villarroya i Font, *Els Bombardeigs de Barcelona durant la Guerra Civil*, 50. For a list of the dead, see Villarroya i Font, *Els Bombardeigs de Barcelona durant la Guerra Civil*, 231–35.
69 Albertí and Albertí Casas, *Perill de bombardeig! Barcelona sota les bombes*, 180–81.
70 "I have received and delivered to the Duce an eyewitness account. I have never read a document of such terrifying realism. However, only nine aircraft participated and the raid lasted only a minute and a half," Alcofar Nassaes, *La aviación legionaria en la guerra española*, 229.
71 "On Sunday, Barcelona suffered the cruelest response to our desire to humanize the war. An act of revenge, spurred by impotence, for our victories at the battle front and in the rearguard." An extract from an article in *La Humanitat* of February 1, quoted in Albertí and Albertí Casas, *Perill de bombardeig! Barcelona sota les bombes*, 184. Similarly, "but the assassins of Rome are exerting pressure to ensure that the humanization of the war will be impossible . . . The world has proof of the good will of the Republic in avoiding bombardments of the rearguard," *La Humanitat*, February 4, 1938, 1.

bombardments in Barcelona. Its presence is extraordinarily evocative and moving. The historically empathic potential of this materiality is obvious: but what else might these walls have to tell us?

As we will see, the shrapnel marks provide information not just about the explosion and its effects, but also about the deliberate policy of silence imposed during the Franco dictatorship. The Plaça de Sant Felip Neri shows two preserved facades of the church of the same name with shrapnel scars in the lower section of the walls, at a height of approximately 3.5 m (over 11 feet). In the dispersion pattern (fig. dibuix) three types of marks can be identified—long radial marks around the area detached by the impact waves of shrapnel; short, clean impacts of less than 3 cm in diameter caused by the contents of the explosives; and intermediate marks (fig. tipus impacte)—that reflect the speed and mass of the explosion of the bombs and their subsequent fragmentation. The higher concentration of shorter marks indicates the proximity of the detonation, while the longer marks are more dispersed, due to the greater mass of the fragments of shrapnel.

Equally interesting is the evidence of repair work. Although no major reconstructions on the facades affected are observed, some variations have been documented (see the 3D model in the at https://skfb.ly/6rYLM). The restitution of part of the wall base shows that the left part of the facade of the church was rebuilt after the bombing, during the reconstruction of the square after 1956. In addition, some marks appear to have been filled in with mortar. In any case, there was no clear intention to conceal the evidence of the bombardments.

In contrast to the preservation (whether intentional or contingent) of the church facades, a thorough reconstruction of the other buildings around the Plaça de Sant Felip Neri took place after the bombardments. Today, the other facades of the street show no evidence of shrapnel impacts, and significant rebuilding work is visible. Several records[72] confirm the existence of a series of reconstruction projects in the square that involved the modification of its shape and the complete replacement of the previous buildings devastated by the bombing, except for the church

---

72 Arxiu Municipal Contemporani de Barcelona: Exp. 1266 "Expropiació Finques Núm. 4 C. Montjuïc del Bisbe i Núm. 4 Pl. Sant Felip Neri, Propietat d'Ana Ball-llovera Duster" (1940); Exp. 254 "Projecte Urbanització Provisional Pça. Sant Felip Neri" (1943); Exp. 4962 "Projecte Modificat d'Alineacions de la Pça. de Sant Felip Neri i Carrer en Projecte" (1950–1956); Exp. 6376 "Obres a Sant Felip Neri" (1957); Exp. 6270 "Obres a la Casa dels Gremis de la Plaça de Sant Felip Neri" (1958); Exp. 6.272 "Obres Nova Façana a l'Edifici de la Societat Econòmica d'Amics del País a la Plaça de Sant Felip Neri" (1959).

of Sant Felip Neri. On the whole, the reconstruction project aimed to recreate a fictitious sixteenth-century style.[73] This was also the case in the Born neighborhood.[74] Indeed, it received several ancient facades from other parts of the city.[75] This reenactment project was deliberately organized by the Francoist city council in its attempt to impose a political and identitarian narrative on the country's reconstruction.[76] The result was highly ambiguous, as the scars of the bombing remained fateful vestiges of the war that the rebuilding work would exploit to further its archaizing agenda.

The continued presence of these scars in the twenty-first century, despite the reconstruction, has led to a shift in discourse. In contrast to the ambiguity of the representation of the square during the dictatorship, today the scars have recovered their original evocative potential and have become the most iconic memorial site of the bombardment of Barcelona. Thus, a new stage of memorialization has emerged that calls the public's attention to the bombing. This recent process has served to transmit the historical importance of the bombed city and has drawn attention to the remaining evidence of the aerial aggressions.[77] In 2007, the first commemorative plaque was placed in the square in tribute to the victims of the bombing of January 30, 1938, and six years later another

73 "To bring together the artistic ensemble of the buildings in the square mentioned," Arxiu Municipal Contemporani de Barcelona, Exp. 6.272 "Obres Nova Façana a l'Edifici de la Societat Econòmica d'Amics del País a la Plaça de Sant Felip Neri" (1959): "the square of San Felipe Neri will become one of the most beautiful places in Barcelona, calm and peaceful in its monumentality and connected in a natural way to the *barrio gótico.*" "Crónica de la jornada. La plaza de San Felipe Neri," *La Vanguardia*, December 18, 1958, 23.
74 Joan Ganau Casas, "La recreació del passat: el Barri Gòtic de Barcelona, 1880–1950," *Barcelona quaderns d'història* 8, "El procés urbà i la identitat gòtica de Barcelona" (2003), 257–72.
75 "The square has the flavor of the 'old Barcelona', an impression that has not been erased by the passing of the years," Adolf Florensa i Ferrer, *La plaza de San Felipe Neri: ayer, hoy y mañana* (Barcelona: Ayuntamiento de Barcelona, 1958), 11; Arxiu Municipal Contemporani de Barcelona, Exp. 6.376 "Obres a Sant Felip Neri" (1957).
76 "A plan has been devised to restore to the square of San Felipe Neri its lost charm ... The sixteenth century is a moment of great delicacy in the architecture of our country, but, for various reasons (above all political) it is not well represented in Barcelona; this fact increases the interest in rebuilding these façades in an ideal environment such as the square of San Felip Neri," Florensa i Ferrer, *La plaza de San Felipe Neri*, 9-11; Pedro Voltes, "Otro éxito de la revalorización del Barrio Gótico. Barcelona ha recobrado en la plaza San Felipe Neri, uno de sus rincones más atractivos," *La Vanguardia*, July 23, 1963, 21.
77 "Although many residents of Barcelona today do not know this, the traces of the bombings are still visible in numerous places such as the square of Sant Felip Neri, where the impact of the shrapnel is still to be seen," *La Vanguardia*, February 11, 2007, 2; Daniel Romaní, "Las paredes hablan. Heridas de guerra. Plaza Sant Felip Neri," *La Vanguardia*, June 26, 2002, 5.

plaque bearing more historical information was installed, though some complained that it should have been made more visible. Indeed, there is a striking contrast between the symbolic power of the scars of the Plaça de Sant Felip Neri and the limited effort expended on making its history known.[78]

THE CINEMA COLISEUM

The Cinema Coliseum was hit during one of the largest air raids of the Spanish Civil War. The bombing took place during a particularly harsh period on the home front, known as the bombardments of March 1938. Over three deadly days, March 16, 17, and 18, the Italian air force mercilessly bombarded the center of Barcelona,[79] subjecting the city to a permanent state of alarm. As the British journalist John Langdon-Davies reported,[80] the bombardments were experimental attacks spread over time and dispersed around the city, creating confusion and panic. This programmed experiment was met with immediate international condemnation and was said to have been executed by General Valle on direct orders from Mussolini.[81]

---

78 The wall of Sant Felip Neri recovers the memory of the events. The poet Sam Abrams describes this sad episode thus: "these deathly pock-marks that disfigure the walls were, in other times, the open wounds of war." Romaní.

79 "Barcelona suffered yesterday the worst bombings by the foreign air force. A thousand victims and numerous buildings destroyed. The airmen dropped their bombs over the most central points of the city. At noon, 252 people had been killed and 525 wounded. By nighttime, 400 dead and 600 injured. The attacks began last night at ten o'clock, lasted more than three hours and were repeated this morning at 7:40, at 10:25 and this afternoon at 2 o'clock. The bombs were dropped from a height of more than 5,200 meters [17,000 feet]." Villarroya i Font, *Els Bombardeigs de Barcelona durant la Guerra Civil*, 80.

80 The inability of the defense services to give any warning of the arrival of the bombers meant that the inhabitants lived in a state of permanent alarm. See Albertí and Albertí Casas, *Perill de bombardeig! Barcelona sota les bombes*, 202, and Villarroya i Font, *Els Bombardeigs de Barcelona durant la Guerra Civil*, 82.

81 The US ambassador declared: "Nothing on such a terrifying scale, involving the white race, had been known until then. The bombing did not pursue any military objective. The bombs were deliberately dropped in the center of the city, the most crowded and inhabited part, where people were eating, walking, resting in their beds," Villarroya i Font, *Els Bombardeigs de Barcelona durant la Guerra Civil*, 87. The German ambassador von Stohrer stated: "I have learned that the effects of recent air strikes on Barcelona by Italian bombers have been literally terrible. Almost every neighborhood in the city has suffered. There is no indication that they intended to attack military targets. Hundreds of houses and streets have been destroyed by the bombs," Villarroya i Font, *Els Bombardeigs de Barcelona durant la Guerra Civil*, 88.

The Cinema Coliseum was affected by a major explosion at 2:00 p.m. on March 17 at the crossroads of Gran Via de les Corts and c/ Balmes.[82] One of the bombs dropped by the S-79 in the attack unexpectedly hit a truck full of TNT, which thus exponentially increased the destructive effects:[83] several buildings were razed to the ground.[84] The Damage Assessment Report of the Cinema Coliseum[85] provides a grim idea of the extent of the destruction. The building was not directly affected by the explosions, but it suffered from the shock wave and was seriously damaged by the deflagration.

Although the present-day building does not bear any sign of the explosion, the case is particularly interesting from the perspective of memorialization. As opposed to Sant Felip Neri, where it is the resonance of the material evidence of the bombardments that establishes the church as a site of memory, the Cinema Coliseum is iconic because of the exceptional nature of the events. In the absence[86] of material traces of the destruction of the building and in the context of the emergence of a process of memorialization of the bombardments of Barcelona, in 2003 a monument was placed in front of the building alongside a tribute to the memory of the victims. Thus, once again, materiality, both old (the traces of past events) and modern (monuments and plaques), acts as a vehicle for the transmission and stimulation of memory.

CARRER CARDERS

Carrer Carders, and its prolongation into c/Corders, is a street in Ciutat Vella, the medieval center of the city. Carrer Carders was hit by the bombardment of August 19, 1938. Unlike Sant Felip Neri and the

---

82 Albertí and Albertí Casas, *Perill de bombardeig! Barcelona sota les bombes*, 204.

83 The *New York Times* correspondent H. L. Matthews left a bloody account of the events: "Almost all the windows from Paseo de Gracia to Calle Mallorca were shattered. A little closer to the site of the explosion, lampposts had been ripped out and the trees were burned. A loaded bus, which was near the site of the main explosion, was reduced to a thick mass of scrap metal. Throughout the area there were viscous masses of blood that had once been human beings. A curtain of smoke and dust remained floating for hours in the same way as the acrid smell of gunpowder and other chemicals," Villarroya i Font, *Els Bombardeigs de Barcelona durant la Guerra Civil*, 135.

84 See the fire department's report, recorded in Villarroya i Font, *Els Bombardeigs de Barcelona durant la Guerra Civil*, 91.

85 Arxiu Històric del Col·legi d'Arquitectes de Catalunya, Valoració C456/1129.

86 As Moshenska underlines, absence depends on the social conscience and perceptions of the past, because something absent can only be remembered in somebody's memory. See Moshenska, "Unbuilt Heritage," 123.

Cinema Coliseum, the street is not a major symbol of the bombing of Barcelona. We have selected it as a case study precisely because it is an invisible scenario of the bombardments, in which we can compare and contrast the historical documents with the archaeological investigations in search of any possible remaining evidence.

The bombing raid over c/Carders on August 19, 1938 was one of several recorded that month. In fact, there was a raid practically every three days,[87] and the attack on the 19th was the most severe of the month. It took place at 4:15 a.m., and caused eighteen of the twenty-four deaths recorded in the whole of August.[88] Albertí records two further bombardments on the same day, at 10:00 a.m. and 12:00 a.m., from heights of 3,000 meters (just under 10,000 feet), and releasing thirty explosive bombs that destroyed at least six buildings and affected forty more.[89]

At a documentary level, in addition to the Junta de Defensa Passiva's records of affected sites, a specific damage assessment report issued by the Syndicate of Architects brings to light new information on the material destruction. The report refers expressly to the building at c/Carders 13, adjoining c/Tarrós, and was produced by the National Service of Devastated Regions and Repairs in October 1939 at the request of the owner Isidoro Saló i Pons.[90] It contains a roster of the damage recorded by an architect, and a certificate of validity issued by an architect of the insurance agency, the Sociedad de Seguros Mútuos contra Incendios, responsible for compensation. All this information is presented on a map showing the range of destruction of the bombardments in this specific case.

At an archaeological level, the work comprised a systematic survey of c/Carders and c/Corders, with special attention to the sites affected and shown on the map. On this map the "positive" buildings (the ones that show traces of bombardment), are documented in the form of photographs and drawings.

First, the "positive" buildings are analyzed in order to document the traces of the bombardments and the evidence of repair work in other

---

87 The city was bombed on August 3, 4, 10 13, 14, 17, 19, and 28. Villarroya i Font, *Els Bombardeigs de Barcelona durant la Guerra Civil*, 65; Albertí and Albertí Casas, *Perill de bombardeig! Barcelona sota les bombes*, 280–84.
88 Villarroya i Font, *Els Bombardeigs de Barcelona durant la Guerra Civil*, 65.
89 Albertí and Albertí Casas, *Perill de bombardeig! Barcelona sota les bombes*, 282.
90 Arxiu Històric del Collegi d'Arquitectes de Catalunya, Valoració C1786/17.

buildings. For example, the building on c/Carders 48 appears renovated and no signs of the bombing are visible. At c/Carders 13, according to the document mentioned, the facades show no visible scars, and the building appears to be entirely reconstructed, as one might expect in view of the damage assessment in 1939 and the request for construction.[91] To apply the methodology to an extended area (given the impossibility of an exhaustive register) the "positive" results are photographed, described and located on a map; in this case, the aim is to acquire a global view of the damage of the bombardments in a particular street. The buildings that show scars of the bombardments today are c/Corders 15 and c/Carders 41, 43, 44, and 46.

Comparing the information on the damaged buildings from the historical documents and the current presence of traces of the bombing (see the map fig. mapa carders) allows us to see that around half the sites of the buildings hit in 1939 still bear damage and indicates the extent of the destruction caused by the bombardments in this area of the city. Thus, a significant amount of traces of the bombing is preserved, as opposed to reconstructions and partial renovations. Even though this is also the case of Sant Felip Neri, the example of c/Carders suggests an arbitrary conservation rather than a conscious decision, motivated by practical considerations: the buildings at greatest risk of collapse were restored, while those less affected were not.

Finally, this case is interesting due to the lack of any commemoration or any information regarding the bombardment, despite the visible presence of traces of the attack.

CONSIDERATIONS AND FUTURE OPPORTUNITIES

The archaeology of bombardments constitutes a theoretical and methodological tool for assessing the materiality of bombardments: impacts, scars, and destruction. Even though commonly unnoticed, the city of Barcelona is full of "wounded" buildings that embody traces of the violence of the bombardments. As Xavier Domènech and Laura Zenobi caution, "under the light that daily accompanies the city, an unknown city is hidden, an underground that we have exiled from our background, a city that contains in its entrails the record of our history."[92]

---

91 Ibid.
92 Xavier Domènech and Laura Zenobi, *Quan plovien bombes: els bombardeigs i la*

In fact, these traces are not underground but in front of our very eyes. Beyond the iconic square of Sant Felip Neri, shrapnel pockmarks are spread over the urban fabric, unobserved. Despite their historical value, these scars have not been studied, preserved, or protected as heritage.[93]

This chapter has attempted to examine this particular type of historical remains and to draw attention to their historical and memorial relevance. We contend that the traces of the bombardments are a part of the material heritage of twentieth-century Barcelona, because they have the potential to *reveal*[94] the bombardments to new generations and to bring the experience of these dramatic events closer to a new audience. Their presence leads to profound reflections on preservation, new kinds of heritage, and the role of materiality in memory.

As mentioned above, materiality embodies a key resource because of its *resonance*, that is, its "power to be heard, to be seen, to be felt, and to be responded to through the existence of a physical marker or an evocation of place."[95] This makes it an ideal element for bridging past and present. Materiality preserves and transmits memory by itself; it remembers beyond human memory, silence, and oblivion. As Eyal Weizman says, "architecture could be an access to memory . . . it could work as an entrance to repressed memory."[96] In this way, shrapnel impacts, as fossilized testimony, constitute a palpable expression of the events; they produce an empathetic connection with the past, and at the same time provide new perspectives for the study of the historical, human, and material significance of the bombardments. Here, materiality emerges as a tool for preserving, reinforcing, and transmitting collective memory in order to enrich the historical debate and to raise awareness of the human experiences of bombing. To quote Jonathan Glover: "keeping the past alive may help to prevent atrocities. There can be terrible significance in what some people expect others to forget."[97]

---

ciutat de Barcelona durant la Guerra civil (Barcelona: Museu d'Història de Catalunya, 2007), 13.

93 In fact, there is no cataloguing or recognition of any kind. Its preservation is thus possible owing to coincidence or individual owners. The city council has no legal mechanisms to warrant its preservation.

94 In the sense contended by Alfredo González-Ruibal, "Time to Destroy. An Archaeology of Supermodernity," *Current Anthropology* 49, no. 2 (2008), 247–79.

95 Gabriel Moshenska, "Resonant Materiality and Violent Remembering," 51.

96 In Maruxa Ruiz del Álamo and Douglas Belisario, "Big Data y 3D para denunciar crímenes de Guerra," *El País*, May 23, 2017.

97 Glover, *Humanity*, 412.

On the basis of these convictions, this chapter has explored ways to capitalize on the potential of this materiality, based on a strong dialog with the documentary sources and on its key role in memorialization. On the one hand, the damage assessment reports represent an essential source for the creation of an archaeology of bombardments, given the abundance of descriptive and visual information on material damage. These assessments provided detailed information on the kind and the extent of the destruction and their exhaustive study allowed us to carry out comparisons with the present-day remains. The case study in c/Carders constituted a test for these possibilities, materialized in the comparison of the postwar damage contained in the report and the endurance of the traces of the bombing recorded in the archaeological survey.

On the other, the archaeological analysis of the shrapnel impacts also sheds new light on the bombardments. The register performed at Sant Felip Neri is a methodological experiment at a widely known site. The application of this methodology in other less well-known case studies may be able to provide new historical information. We also foresee a role for archaeology in the study and classification of the traces in reconstructing and discerning impact directions, as well as in subsequent rebuilding and renovation. Given the impossibility of carrying out a wider study, this chapter has taken the first steps on a new path toward applying archaeology to the study of bombardments. In a scientific, as well as heritage, sense we see a need for a thorough study of the evidence of the bombardments preserved today in the buildings of modern cities; as a way to contrast and complete historical discourses and to address the debate on their preservation and the suitability of criteria and procedures designed for intervention.

Finally, we have confirmed the importance of the role of materiality in the memorialization of the bombardments. The shrapnel marks at Sent Felip Neri have become a site of memory in their own right, and the square is now a place of remembrance thanks to their evocative power. Plaques have been the main element used for memorials, consisting in some sentences of a tribute to the victims and bearing a limited amount of historical information. In the case study of the Cinema Coliseum, unlike Sant Felip Neri, memorialization has been based on secondary elements (a plaque of tribute and a sculpture). Despite the potential of the shrapnel scars to create profound sensations among onlookers, sometimes we lack the tools to interpret them.[98] Thus, materiality runs

---

98 Gesalí and Iñíguez note one of the common problems of interpreting this evidence

the risk of becoming incomprehensible. In the field of dissemination and memorialization, several projects have been developed in Catalonia: for example, the Memorial Democràtic has created some itineraries and information panels boards with visual, textual, and documental resources for interpreting memory sites.[99] Recently, Valencia ran a similar initiative under the "València en la memòria" itinerary, with a panel containing explanations of a site with shrapnel impacts. Barcelona, as we have seen, possesses an important heritage as the site of one of the earliest experiences of civilian bombardments. Why not recognize and study them? Why not use their power to catalyze the memory and the historical dissemination of these events toward the construction of a critical understanding of this brutal violence against a civilian population?

BIBLIOGRAPHY

Abella, Rafael. *La vida cotidiana durante la guerra civil. La España Republicana*. Barcelona: Planeta, 1975.

Albertí, Santiago, and Elisenda Albertí Casas, *Perill de bombardeig! Barcelona sota les bombes: 1936–1939*. Barcelona: Albertí Editors, 2004.

Alcofar Nassaes, José Luis. *La aviación legionaria en la guerra española*. Barcelona: Euros, 1975.

Aracil, Rafael, and Joan Villarroya, *El País Valencià sota les bombes (1936–1939)*. València: Publicacions de la Universitat de València, 2010.

Arnabat i Mata, Ramon. *Els refugis antiaeris de Barcelona: criteris d'intervenció patrimonial*. Ajuntament de Barcelona, Institut de Cultura, 2009.

Ayán Vila, Xurxo. "Guerra en la Universidad. Cuando se quebraron las cristaleras de la Facultad." *Arkeogatze* 5 (2015): 27–34.

---

for people: "If you walk through the square, which is very different today, you often see tourists with their backs to the walls, pretending to reenact an execution by firing squad – thinking that the holes in the stone were caused by the bullets of the murders of 1936," Gesalí Barrera and Íñiguez Gràcia, *La guerra aèria a Catalunya (1936–1939)*, 390.

99   "Xarxa d'espais de memòria de Catalunya. Memorial Democràtic," at http://memorialdemocratic.gencat.cat/ca/espais_de_la_memoria/xarxa_espais_catalunya_cat/> (last accessed May 29, 2017).

Ayàn Vila, Xurxo M., Rebeca Blanco Rotea, and Patricia Manana Borrazàs. "Arqueotectura 1: Bases teórico-metodológicas para una Arqueología de la Arquitectura." *Tapa. Traballos de arqueoloxía e patrimonio* 25 (2002): 12–101.

———. "Archaeotecture: Seeking a New Archaeological Vision of Architecture." In *Archaeotecture: Archaeology of Architecture*, edited by Xurxo M. Ayàn Vila, Rebeca Blanco Rotea, and Patricia Manana Borrazàs. Oxford: Archaeopress, 2003.

Azkarate, Agustín. "La Arqueología de la Arquitectura en el siglo XXI." *Arqueología de la arquitectura* 5 (2008), 11–13.

Barra, Jordi. *La legión Cóndor*. Barcelona: Dau, 2016.

Biasatti, Soledad, and Gonzalo Compañy. *Memorias Sujetadas. Hacia una lectura crítica y situada de los procesos de memorialización*. Madrid: JAS Arqueologia, 2015.

Bowers, Claude Gernade. *Misión en España (1933–1939)*. Mexico City: Grijalbo, 1966.

Brogiolo, Gian Pietro, and Aurora Cagnana. *Archeologia dell'architettura: metodi e interpretazioni*. Fiorentino: All'Insegna del Giglio, 2012.

Buchli, Victor, and Gavin Lucas. "The Absent Present: Archaeologies of the Contemporary Past." In *Archaeologies of the Contemporary Past*. London: Routledge, 2001.

Caballé Clos, Tomás. *Barcelona roja. Dietario de la Revolución (julio 1936–enero 1939)*. Barcelona: Librería Argentina, 1939.

Cardona, Gabriel, and Manel Esteban i Cano, eds. *Atles de la Guerra Civil a Barcelona*. Barcelona: Edicions 62, 2009.

Cierva, Ricardo de la. *Historia ilustrada de la guerra civil española*. Barcelona: Danae, 1970.

Contel, Josep M. *Gràcia, temps de bombes, temps de refugis: el subsòl com a supervivència*. Barcelona: Taller d'Història de Gràcia, 2008.

Desilvey, Caitlin, and Tim Edensor. "Reckoning with Ruins." *Progress in Human Geography* 37, no. 4 (2012): 465–85.

Doglioni, Francesco, and Marina Ciarocchi. *Stratigrafia e restauro: tra conoscenza e conservazione dell'architettura*. Trieste: Lint Editoriale Associati, 1997.

Domènech, Xavier, and Laura Zenobi. *Quan plovien bombes: els bombardeigs i la ciutat de Barcelona durant la Guerra civil.* Barcelona: Museu d'Història de Catalunya, 2007.

Dueñas Iturbe, Oriol. *La gran destrucció: els danys de guerra i la reconstrucció de Catalunya després de la Guerra Civil 1937–1957.* Barcelona: Universitat de Barcelona, 2013.

Edgerton, David. *Innovación y tradición: historia de la tecnología moderna.* Barcelona: Crítica, 2007.

———. *The Shock of the Old: Technology and Global History since 1900.* London: Profile, 2008.

Florensa i Ferrer, Adolf. *La plaza de San Felipe Neri: ayer, hoy y mañana.* Barcelona: Ayuntamiento de Barcelona, 1958.

Ganau Casas, Joan. "La recreació del passat: el Barri Gòtic de Barcelona, 1880–1950." *Barcelona quaderns d'història* 8, "El procés urbà i la identitat gòtica de Barcelona" (2003): 257–72.

García Lacalle, Andrés. *Mitos y verdades. La aviación de caza en la guerra española.* Mexico City: Oasis, 1973.

Generalitat de Catalunya. *Bombardements et agressions en Espagne (juillet 1936–juillet 1938).* Paris: 1938.

———. *Bombardeos Aéreos en España. Bombardeos de la aviación nacional a la retaguardia republicana.* Barcelona: Seix Barral, 1939.

Gesalí Barrera, David, and David Íñiguez Gràcia. *La guerra aèria a Catalunya (1936–1939).* Barcelona: Rafael Dalmau, 2012.

Gil Mugarza, Bernardo. *España en llamas. 1936.* Barcelona: Acervo, 1968.

Glover, Jonathan. *Humanity: A Moral History of the Twentieth Century.* Yale: Yale Nota Bene, 2001.

Gomá, José. *La Guerra en el aire.* Barcelona: AHR, 1958.

González-Ruibal, Alfredo. "Making Things Public: Archaeologies of the Spanish Civil War." *Public Archaeology* 6, no. 4 (2007): 203–26.

———. "Arqueología de la Guerra Civil." *Complutum* 19, no. 2 (2008): 11–20.

———. "Time to Destroy. An Archaeology of Supermodernity." *Current Anthropology* 49, no. 2 (2008): 247–79.

————. "Contra La Pospolítica: Arqueología de La Guerra Civil Española." *Revista Chilena de Antropología* (2010): 9–32.

————. "From the Battlefield to the Labour Camp: Archaeology of Civil War and Dictatorship in Spain." *Antiquity* 86, no. 332 (June 2012): 456–73.

————. "Reclaiming Archaeology." In *Reclaiming Archaeology: Beyond the Tropes of Modernity*, edited by Alfredo González-Ruibal (Milton Park, Abingdon and New York: Routledge 2013).

González-Ruibal, Alfredo, and Gabriel Moshenska. *Ethics and the Archaeology of Violence*. New York: Springer-Verlag, 2015.

Gould, Richard A., and Michael B. Schiffer, eds. *Modern Material Culture: The Archaeology of Us*. New York: Academic Press, 1981.

Hidalgo de Cisneros, Ignacio. *Cambio de rumbo*. Bucharest: N.p., 1964.

Hurtado, Victor, Antoni Segura, and Joan Villarroya i Font. *Atles de la Guerra Civil a Catalunya*. Barcelona: Universitat de Barcelona, 2010.

Infiesta Pérez, José Luis, and Luis Fresno Crespo. *Bombardeos del litoral mediterráneo durante la Guerra Civil*. Valladolid: Quirón, 1998.

Íñiguez, David. *El Vesper de la Gloriosa: L'aviació republicana*. Calafell: Llibres de Matrícula, 2002.

Irujo, Xabier. *Gernika*. Barcelona: Crítica, 2017.

Jordana, C. A. *Barcelona 1938: La veu de les sirenes*. Barcelona: Edicions de 1984, 2008.

Jouannais, Jean-Yves. *El uso de las ruinas*. Barcelona: El Acantilado, 2017.

Kinderlán, Alfredo. *Mis cuadernos de guerra*. Madrid: Plantea, 1982.

Kluge, Alexander. *Ataque aéreo a Halberstadt, el 8 de abril de 1945*. Madrid: Antonio Machado Libros, 2014.

Les Archives Secrètes de la Wilhelmstrasse. Paris: Plon, 1956.

Les Archives Secrètes du Comte Ciano, 1936–1942. Paris, 1948.

Logan, William, and Keir Reeves, eds. *Places of Pain and Shame: Dealing with Difficult Heritage*. London and New York: Routledge, 2008.

Manent, Marià. *El vel de Maia. Dietari de la guerra civil (1936–1939)*. Barcelona: Edicions Destino, 1975.

Martino, José María. *Apuntalamiento o derribo de edificios afectados por el bombardeo*. Barcelona: 1938.

———. *Protección de edificios, monumentos artísticos, etc. contra bombardeos*. Barcelona: 1938.

Miró, Carme, and Jordi Ramos. "Els refugis antiaeris de Barcelona (1936–1937). Una nova visió des de l'arqueologia d'intervenció." *Exnovo* 7 (2011): 55–79.

———. "Cronotipologia dels refugis antiaeris de Barcelona." MUHBA documents, no. 6 (2013): 54–66.

Misa, Thomas J. *Leonardo to the Internet: Technology and Culture from the Renaissance to the Present*. Baltimore: The Johns Hopkins University Press, 2004.

Morín, Jorge, and Alicia Torija, eds. *Paisajes de la guerra y la posguerra. Espacios amenazados*. Madrid: Audema, 2017.

Moshenska, Gabriel. "Resonant Materiality and Violent Remembering: Archaeology, Memory and Bombing." *International Journal of Heritage Studies* 15, no. 1 (2009): 44–56.

———. "Working with Memory in the Archaeology of Modern Conflict," *Cambridge Archaeological Journal* 20, no. 1 (2010): 33–48.

———. "Unbuilt Heritage: Conceptualising Absence in the Historical Environment." In *The Good, the Bad and the Unbuilt: Handling the Heritage of the 21st Century*, edited by Sarah May, Hilary Orange, and Sefryn Penrose. Oxford: Archaeopress, 2012.

———. "Children in Ruins: Bombsites as Playgrounds in Second World War Britain." In *Ruin Memories: Materiality, Aesthetics and the Archaeology of the Recent Past*, edited by Bjørn Olsen and Þóra Pétursdóttir. Abingdon: Routledge, 2014.

Pàmies, Teresa. *Quan érem capitans (memòries d'aquella guerra)*. Barcelona: Dopesa, 1974.

Parera, Ramon. *ARP in Catalonia: Paper read at a meeting of the Institute on Tuesday, December 12, 1939. Discussion*. N.p.: N.d.

Pedriali, Ferdinando. *Guerra di Spagna e aviazione italiana*. Roma: Aeronautica militare italiana; Ufficio storico, 1992.

Pi i Sunyer, Carles. *La República y la guerra. Memorias de un político catalán*. Mexico City: Oasis, 1975.

Poblet i Feijoo, Francesc. *Els bombardeigs a Barcelona durant la Guerra Civil*. Barcelona: Ajuntament de Barcelona, Regidoria de Dona i Drets Civils, 2005.

Pons Pujol, Jordi. *Lliçons de Barcelona: informe britànic sobre el bombardeigs de la ciutat, 1938*. Barcelona: Fundació Carles Pi i Sunyer d'Estudis Autonòmics i Locals, 2004.

Pujadó Puigdomènech, Judith. *Oblits de rereguarda: els refugis antiaeris a Barcelona, 1936–1939*. Barcelona: Abadia de Montserrat, 1998.

———. *El llegat subterrani. Els refugis antiaeris de la Guerra Civil*. Badalona: Ara Llibres, 2008.

Ramblado-Minero, M. Cinta. "Sites of Memory / Sites of Oblivion in Contemporary Spain." *Revista Canadiense de Estudios Hispánicos* 36, no. 1 (2011): 29–42.

Raventós, Joan, and Jacint Raventós. *Dos infants i la guerra*. Barcelona: El Pi de les Tres Branques, 1974.

Renart, Joaquim. *Diari 1918–1961*. Volume 6. *La guerra (1936–1939)*. Barcelona: Proa, 2003.

Riegl, Aloïs. *El Culto Moderno a Los Monumentos*. 1903. Madrid: A. Machado Libros, 2008.

Rojo Ariza, María del Carmen. "¿Arqueología y aviación?: la excavación de aerodrómos de campaña en el Penedés." *Revista Universitaria de Historia Militar* 2 (2013): 85–108.

Rojo Ariza, María del Carmen, and Laia Coma Quintana. "Arqueología y museografía didáctica en los aeródromos de guerra (1936–1939)." *Ebre* 38, no. 4 (2010): 165–77.

Rovira i Virgili, Antoni. *Els darrers dies de la Catalunya republicana*. Barcelona: Curial, 1977.

Rubió i Tudurí, Marià. *Barcelona 1936–1939*. Barcelona: Abadia de Montserrat, 2002.

Sabadell Mercadé, José. *Historial del Cuerpo de Bomberos y de anteriores organizaciones para combatir los incendios de la misma ciudad, 1379–1939*. Barcelona: Ediciones Técnico Publicitarias, 1943.

Salvador, Tomás. *La Guerra de España en sus fotografías*. Barcelona: Marte, 1966.

Santacana i Torres, Carles. "Bombes i lleves: els efectes d'una guerra moderna sobre la població." In *La Segona república a Catalunya: Guerra i revolució 1936–1939*, edited by Jordi Casassas and Joan Villarroya. Barcelona: Edicions 62, 2015.

Sebald, W.G. *Sobre la historia natural de la destrucción.* Barcelona: Anagrama, 2003.

Soldevila, Ferran. *Al llarg de la meva vida.* Barcelona: Edicions 62, 1970.

Solé i Barjau, Queralt, and Oscar Jané Checa. *L'arqueologia del món modern i contemporani. Noves perspectives 78.* Catarroja: Afers, 2014.

Solé i Sabaté, Josep M., and Joan Villarroya i Font. *Catalunya sota les bombes: 1936–1939.* Barcelona: Abadia de Montserrat, 1986.

———. *España en llamas: la guerra civil desde el aire.* Madrid: Temas de Hoy, 2003.

Stone, Marion. "A Memory in Ruins?'" *Public Archaeology* 3, no, 3 (2004): 131–44.

Tanaka, Yuki B., and Marilyn B. Young, eds. *Bombing Civilians: A Twentieth-century History.* New York: New Press, 2009.

Tarazona, Francisco. *Sangre en el cielo.* Mexico: Costa Amic, 1957.

Torres, Estanislau. *Quasi un dietari (memòries: 1926–1949).* Barcelona: Abadia de Montserrat, 2003.

Valentines Álvarez, Jaume, Antoni Roca Rosell, and Guillermo Lusa Monforte, eds. *El Fons Ramon Perera. Imatges de La Defensa Passiva a Catalunya (1938–1939).* Barcelona: Universitat Politècnica de Catalunya and Càtedra UNESCO de Tècnica i Cultura, 2008.

Valle, Giuseppe. *Uomini nei cieli. Storia dell'Aeronautica Italiana.* Rome: Centro Edit. Nazionale, 1981.

Vallès, Edmon. *Història gràfica de la Catalunya autònoma. La guerra. 1936–1939.* Barcelona: Edicions 62, 1978.

Vega, Esther de, and Concepción Martín Morales. *Arqueología aplicada al estudio e interpretación de edificios históricos: últimas tendencias metodológicas.* Madrid: Ministerio de Cultura, Subdirección General de Publicaciones, Información y Documentación, 2010.

Villarroya i Font, Joan. *Els Bombardeigs de Barcelona durant la Guerra Civil.* Barcelona: Abadia de Montserrat, 1981.

———. "Els bombardeigs durant la guerra civil." In *La guerra civil a Catalunya (1936–1939)*, edited by Josep M. Solé i Sabaté. Barcelona: Edicions 62, 2004.

Visions de guerra i reraguarda. Història gràfica de la Revolució. Barcelona: Forja, 1937.

Weizman, Eyal. *Forensic Architecture: Violence at the Threshold of Detectability.* Brooklyn, NY: Zone Books, 2017.

Chapter 14

The Vatican Archives and the Civil War

Hilari Raguer i Suñer

THE RELIGIOUS ASPECT OF THE CIVIL WAR

Of the various dimensions of the Civil War—military, social, economic, international, cultural—the religious aspect is one of the most important. Although the uprising of July 1936 was not religiously motivated, Spain became immersed in a religious war almost within a matter of days. In the areas in which the uprising failed, that is, the major cities and the industrial regions, a terrible religious persecution was unleashed; and in the areas in which the insurgents triumphed, they were joined by a great many lay people in the belief that they were fighting in defense of religion. Above all, the new authorities understood that the banner of religion could be particularly useful to them – not just domestically, but also in the eyes of international opinion. For the study of the religious aspect of the Civil War, the most important source is the Vatican Secret Archive.

THE VATICAN SECRET ARCHIVE

Leo XIII, who did so much to help the Church meet the challenges of the contemporary world, issued the *Saepenumero* papal bull in 1883. This bull decreed that the Vatican archives, which had been kept secret over a period of many centuries, should be made available to historians for consultation. It stated that "the first law of history is not to lie; the second, not to be afraid of the truth, and that in its writing one should not give rise to any suspicion of adulation or aversion."[1]

All official archives remain secret for specific periods of time, and in the case of ecclesiastical archives these periods tend to be longer on the grounds that they contain confidential documents, or deal with matters of conscience. The documentation in the Vatican Secret Archive remains inaccessible for seventy-five years, but even when this period has elapsed it does not become available to the public automatically; it is only released with the following change of pontificate. In 2006, for example, Benedict XVI ordered the opening of the documentation referring to the pontificate of Pius XI, which lasted from February 6, 1922 to February 10, 1939.

Currently, access to the documents is governed by the *motu proprio* of John Paul II of March 21, 2005, which introduced a law regarding the archives of the Holy See. This law maintains secrecy on the conclaves for the election of popes,[2] the processes for the appointment of bishops, and matrimonial causes.

During the pontificate of Benedict XVI, the Secretary of State Tarcisio Bertone took out from the Vatican Secret Archive all the documents pertaining to the second section of the secretary of state, formerly called Affari Esteri Straordinari ("Extraordinary Foreign Affairs") and currently titled "Relations with the states," and had it transferred to the secretary of state building.

Of all the documents recently released, the most interesting are probably the notes that the Secretary of State Cardinal Pacelli recorded after his audiences with His Holiness Pius XI. These audiences were held practically every day, even on Sundays. In a very concise style, Pacelli wrote down what the Pope had said to him, for his own personal use: comments on events and people, dispositions taken, and so on. In a sense, these notes are more important than the official documents themselves, because they shed light on the reasons why these documents were prepared and offer a different view of events that is not to be found in the authorized accounts.

---

1   *Acta Sanctae Sedis* 16 (1883), 49–57.
2   However, the Francisco Franco Foundation has published the information that Franco received from two sources (the police and the Falange) regarding the candidates for the episcopate.

I have not been able to see all the new papers that have been made public. In what follows I will discuss what I regard as the most interesting of the documents that I have been able to examine.

THE PROCLAMATION OF THE SPANISH REPUBLIC

Historians have traditionally agreed that the Holy See recognized immediately and unreservedly the Spanish Republic proclaimed on April 14, 1931. However, the new documentation casts some doubt on this claim. In principle, ever since Leo XIII's *ralliement* to the French Republic that had broken with the centuries-old alliance of throne and altar, the general doctrine of the Vatican had been that the Church was not bound *to* any form of political regime. However, ultra-right-wing monarchists in Spain held that the *ralliement* had been a failure, and that, in any case, the situation of Spain was not the same as France.[3]

By order of Pius XI, on April 23, 1931 the Congregation for Extraordinary Affairs met to ratify the Vatican's position with regard to the proclamation of the Republic. All the cardinals, including the secretary of state, were of the opinion that the new government was illegitimate because a municipal election could not lead to a change of regime, and also because the monarchists had obtained more votes and returned more council members than the Republicans;[4] but at the same time everyone believed that the Republic had to be recognized, if not *de jure*, then *de facto*, in order to defend the rights and interests of the Church under the new regime via democratic and parliamentary channels. This had been the Vatican's policy since Leo XIII – a far cry from that of centuries past, when popes had issued patents of legitimacy to kings and rulers. On

---

3   Cf. Eugenio Vegas Latapie, *Catolicismo y República: un episodio de la historia de Francia* (Madrid: Ed. Gráficas Universal, 1932).
4   During the Franco era, this argument was used to discredit the Republic. However, it should be noted that most of the monarchist council members had been elected thanks to the electoral laws in force at the time; if in a municipality only one candidate had stood for election, he would be returned automatically. The *caciquismo* of the period meant that in rural areas no one would dare oppose the local party boss or his candidate. For this reason, the results that mattered were the votes in the major cities, where the republicans won an overwhelming majority. At the meeting of the Congregation of Extraordinary Affairs the cardinals were reminded that Federico Tedeschini's telegram of April 15 noted that although those elections were only administrative, "*assunsero carattere politico, perchè si svolsero con programmi monarchico e republicano.*" Alfonso XIII himself, who left a power vacuum behind him on leaving Spain, recognized sadly that "the elections held on Sunday clearly reveal that I do not enjoy the love of my people."

April 24, reflecting the opinion of the Congregation after its meeting of the previous day, Federico Tedeschini, the nuncio to Spain, sent to each bishop the well-known note stating: "It is the wish of the Holy See that Your Excellency recommend that the priests, other religious members, and worshippers in your diocese should respect the powers constituted and obey them, in the interests both of the maintenance of order and of the common good."[5]

On April 18, after sending Pacelli a few terse telegrams reporting the result of the elections and the fall of the monarchy, the nuncio Tedeschini issued an extensive report that was highly unfavorable toward the fledgling Republic. Apart from the fact, mentioned above, that Monarchist council members had been in the majority, Tedeschini acknowledged that all the parties, on both the Monarchist and the Republican sides, had attributed a great political significance to those elections; but that nobody had expected a set of results so dramatic that they made the holding of elections for the provincial councils and for the central government almost pointless. He went on to say that on the afternoon of Sunday, April 12, the results in Madrid had been such that the government was seized with panic, and that this panic only increased as the news of the Republican triumph in the provinces poured in. The situation in Catalonia was a cause for particular concern; there, said Tedeschini, "the separatist leader had proclaimed the Republic of the State of Catalonia, which he wished to be fully independent" (although in fact President Francesc Macià had proclaimed a Catalan State within a federation of Iberian Republics).

THE BURNING OF CHURCHES ON MAY 11

On May 11, a month after the birth of the Republic, churches were burned in several Spanish cities, above all in Madrid and Malaga. On May 15, Tedeschini informed Pacelli that, "one cannot say for certain that the government has provoked this incendiary movement, but it is easy to show that it did nothing to prevent it." Miguel Maura, minister for home affairs and a Catholic, dedicates a whole chapter to the burning of the churches in his memoirs. When he heard of the first incidents he

---

5   Miquel Batllori and Victor Manuel Arbeloa, eds., *Església i Estat durant la Segona República. 1931–1936* (Scripta et Documenta, 20, 21, 23, 24, 27, 28, 33, 37, and 39), vol. 1 (Barcelona: Publicacions de l'Abadia de Montserrat, 1971), 24.

was convinced that a show of public force would suffice to stop them, and requested authorization from the council of ministers to act; but almost all the ministers voted against him, and as a result he resigned. He only withdrew his resignation, Maura says, when the nuncio, in a long telephone conversation, insisted that he could not renounce his post.[6] Later, however, Tedeschini contradicted the minister's version when speaking of the subject of the insurrection of October 1934: "When I went to protest about these deplorable fires, Mr. Maura, among other things, made the fatuous comment that to defend the convents of Spain not even the entire French army would suffice."[7] If Tedeschini's reference is accurate it would bear some resemblance to the words attributed to Azaña, when, during discussions at the council of ministers, he refused to put the Civil Guard out onto the street: "All the convents of Madrid are not worth the life of a single Republican citizen."

TEDESCHINI AND THE NATIONALIST MOVEMENTS

Both during the monarchy and under the Republic, the archives of the nunciature of Madrid show us a Tedeschini fiercely opposed to both Basque and Catalan nationalism. However, the monarchist ultra-right hated him because, obeying the edicts of the secretary of state and with the collaboration of the Catalan Cardinal Vidal i Barraquer, he obliged the bishops to abide by the new regime. The monarchists made accusations of all kinds against the nuncio, and eventually managed to have him relieved of the post – albeit at the price of having him created cardinal. At the outbreak of the Civil War, now in Rome, Tedeschini repeatedly professed support for the uprising, but the rebels were not convinced and continued to regard him as an enemy. His appointment as Apostolic delegate at the International Eucharistic Congress of Barcelona in 1952 was a serious affront to Franco.

THE PLOTS OF THE MONARCHISTS

Another interesting theme that appears in the new documentation is the strength of the right-wing monarchists in Rome and their intrigues to

---

6   Miguel Maura, *Así cayó Alfonso XIII* (Barcelona: Ariel, 1966), 249–64.
7   Nunciatura de Madrid, fasc. 3, fol. 201–203, report dated October 17, 1934.

prevent an agreement between the Holy See and the Republic. Canon Carles Cardó said that one of the main causes of the Civil War was the refusal of some Spanish Catholics to accept the conciliatory overtures from the Vatican. When the right-wing parties won the Spanish elections of November 1933, the new government tried to negotiate a *modus vivendi* [8] with the Vatican, with the intention of modifying the constitution at a later date and removing the elements that were most offensive to the Church. However, the monarchists, who had powerful contacts in the Vatican, boycotted these negotiations on the grounds that there was no need to reach any agreement with the Republic because it was bound to be short lived; indeed, they did their best to ensure that this would be the case.

The schemes of the monarchists are copiously described in the Vidal i Barraquer Archive during the years of the Republic and are also reflected in the newly available documentation from the Vatican. In fact, the way in which they were filed in the Vatican Archive bears witness to the secretary of state's disapproval. On May 19, 1934, Tedeschini sent a report entitled "The monarchists and the hypothetical restoration of the monarchy," and the archive also contains a dossier bearing the significant title "The importune and inopportune nature of the monarchist intrigues." A letter from Pacelli to Tedeschini dated March 28, 1932, in a folder entitled "Intrigues of Count Rodriguez de San Pedro in Rome," narrates a curious episode. The Spanish Church, which had lost funding under the Republic, was in dire financial straits: the priests continued to be paid, but no new recruits were entering the clergy. The monarchists promised that if the monarchy was restored, the Church would receive part of the money levied from income tax.

Pacelli's letter demonstrates his disapproval of this plan. The letter is interesting because of the economic matters it discusses, but also because Pacelli addresses Tedeschini with the familiar *tu* form and speaks with great familiarity, signing off as "Your affectionate friend E. C. Pacelli," even though the pages bear the secretary of state's letterhead Pacelli and Tedeschini were two very different personalities, but they had been classmates at the Pontifical Ecclesiastical Academy at which the future diplomats of the Holy See were trained, and later they had coincided at the secretary of state. From the context it appears that Tedeschini had complained, or been surprised, that Count Rodríguez de San Pedro (one of the right-wing monarchists) had boasted that he had

---

8   An agreement inferior to a concordate.

had an interview with Pacelli in which they had reached an important agreement. The secretary of state says that they met by chance, and explains that the Church does not favor this type of financing:

> During our conversation, the Count raised the question of the ecclesiastical tax for the expenses of the clergy and of worship, and I told him that this method does not correspond *per se* to the intentions of the Church, which prefers voluntary oblations; in Germany these taxes had to be introduced out of necessity and in view of the particular circumstances in that country, although it must be admitted that they have also had some harmful consequences, and the anticlerical propaganda machine has exploited them to induce the less enthusiastic Catholics officially to leave the Church.

THE INSURRECTION OF OCTOBER 6, 1934

Today, the insurrection of 6 October 1934 arouses enormous interest among historians. Those in the neo-Francoist camp argue that it marked the *de facto* beginning of the Civil War, or at least that it made a powerful contribution to its outbreak. Coinciding with this revisionist trend, in the processes of beatification and canonization of the "martyrs of the Civil War," there have been moves to include the victims of the 1934 uprising in Asturias, so as to be able to speak of an unbroken line of religious persecution from 1931 to 1939.[9] But in fact the priests murdered in Asturias in October 1934 were the victims not of persecution by the Republic, but of a revolutionary insurrection *against* the Republic; indeed, the Republic entrusted the repression of this rebellion—which would prove ferocious—to General Franco. The aim of this historical misrepresentation is to criminalize the Republic and, in the final analysis, to legitimize the uprising of 1936.

All the Republican politicians who propitiated the insurrection of 1934 acknowledged later that it had been a mistake. To launch a rebellion in protest at the presence in the new government of two ministers from the party that had obtained the most votes and the most representatives

---

9   Cf. Vicente Cárcel Ortí, *La persecución religiosa en España durante la segunda República (1931–1939)* (Madrid: Rialp, 1990).

(the right-wing CEDA, led by Gil Robles) was hardly a democratic course of action. The call to arms was followed only in Asturias and Catalonia. In Catalonia, in fact, the unions did not participate and the uprising was over in a single day, thanks to the resolute intervention of General Domingo Batet and also to the response of the Catalan president Lluis Companys. Companys had wanted to join the protest of the Spanish Republicans and expected the coup to be a peaceful one, as had been the case on April 14, 1931; but on seeing that the call had not been followed in the rest of Spain and that the army had swiftly brought the situation in Barcelona under control, he surrendered and over the radio he urged his followers to do the same.

Even though in Asturias the rebellion was longer-lasting and caused many victims, in the eyes of the far right the uprising in Catalonia was far more troubling because Companys had proclaimed a Catalan State—albeit "within a Spanish federal Republic"—and had invited Spanish Republicans to set up the provisional government of the Republic in Catalonia. Franco, who had been entrusted with the repression of the coup by minister of war, Diego Hidalgo, wanted General Batet to enter the Palace of the Generalitat by force, but Batet convinced Hidalgo, the president of the government, Alejandro Lerroux, and the president of the Republic, Azaña, that a night attack on the Generalitat would cause numerous military and also civilian casualties and instead assured them that he would be able to force Companys to surrender at dawn. Companys duly obliged, but the anti-Catalan reaction in the rest of Spain was extremely hostile: José Antonio Primo de Rivera said that Batet's speech, in which he regretted having had to use force, was unworthy of a Spanish general[10] (Spain might see itself portrayed in the figure of Ambrosio de Spínola magnanimously receiving the keys of the city of Breda rendered to him by the mayor, a scene immortalized by Velázquez in *The Spears*; but if the person surrendering was a Catalan, he deserved not the slightest regard). The response of General Sanjurjo, who had been sentenced to death after leading an insurrection in August 1932 but whose punishment had been commuted, is illustrative of this general animosity. Sanjurjo, who had escaped and now lived in Portugal, offered his services to the government to fight – not in Asturias, where the fighting was indeed extremely fierce, but in Catalonia, where the situation was already under control. Similarly, Franco ordered a war

---

10   Cf. Hilari Raguer, *El general Batet* (Barcelona: Publicacions de l'Abadia de Montserrat, 1994), 191.

fleet to head toward Barcelona at top speed carrying a large contingent of the Spanish Legion.

This anti-Catalan atmosphere is worth emphasizing because the reports of the nuncio reflect the same sentiments, always condemning the positions of the nationalists (especially the Catalan nationalists). Significantly, Tedeschini informed Pacelli that at the request of the bishop Irurita he had made arrangements with the government of the Republic to obtain pardons for two Catalan soldiers who had been sentenced to death. Irurita had telegraphed Tedeschini, begging him "to urge the government to pardon two men condemned to death. Bishop Barcelona." He did not name the condemned men, but they were most probably Commandant Pérez Farràs and Captain Escofet, heads of the *mossos d'esquadra* (the Generalitat's body in charge of public order), who had been sentenced to death following a court martial. Tedeschini notes in his own hand: "With my best will and without delay I presented Your Excellency's request to the government in favor of the two condemned men, gladly adding my recommendation and request. Apostolic Nuncio."[11] Finally, the two men were reprieved.

But aside from these humanitarian actions, the important report of October 17 showed that Tedeschini's main concern, like that of the Spanish far right, was not Asturias but Catalonia:

> It was Catalonia, which I have always singled out as the dangerous starting point of a revolutionary movement, that gave the signal for attack, and in the most treacherous way. Anyone who read the newspapers of the early days of this month would have been surprised by the signs of deference that the government of the Generalitat of Catalonia gave to the central government, and of which the new minister of the interior [Eloy Vaquero, a Radical who did much to promote Andalusian nationalism along with Blas Infante] spoke boastfully in public. This only made one suspicious of the insistence with which Companys, president of the Generalitat, warned the Catalans to be on their guard, and of the presence of politicians from Madrid, such as Mr. Azaña, in Barcelona. . . . The army has remained loyal for the moment . . . Later it will be important that the state should not have dealings with the regionalist movements, which foment discord and rebellion. Catalonia—the Catalonia which has made this

---

11   Telegrams dated October 13, 1934. Nunciatura de Madrid, 912, fasc. 3, fol. 191.

nuncio to Spain suffer so much, and which is now showing him to have been so [right] in everything he said then—has done what has long been foreseen. For now, it has been humiliated, but in the north the Basque Country is burning with dangerous political passions, in which, it is painful to say, both the lay and the regular clergy take an extremely active and scandalous part, as I shall say in my next report. If the central government fails to solve these problems, Spain will not have attained the desired hour of salvation, and the bloody days of this October will be repeated and this poor nation will be devastated once more.[12]

The unpleasant experience in 1928 that Tedeschini mentioned was an ecclesiastical dispute that arose at the end of the Primo de Rivera dictatorship, caused by the *do ut des* of the longstanding alliance of the throne and the altar. The government of the monarchy granted the ecclesiastical hierarchy honors and privileges of all kinds, but in return it demanded that the Church should instill respect and obedience toward the monarchy among the faithful. Alfonso XIII sent the Marquis de Magaz as ambassador to the Holy See, bearing a personal letter to the Pope, recalling the favors given to the Church and seeking the collaboration of the Vatican in the repression of Basque and (especially) Catalan nationalism. Moved by false accusations, Pius XI decreed an Apostolic Visit to the Catalan Church, which was accused of fomenting separatism, and entrusted the mission to the nuncio Tedeschini.[13]

In the archive of the Spanish Embassy in the Vatican I found the correspondence between the dictator Primo de Rivera, the Captain General of Barcelona Emilio Barrera, and the ambassador Antonio Magaz, in which they prepared the Apostolic Visit with a rigorous selection of compliant witnesses who would testify to the seditious activity of the Catalan clergy before Tedeschini. Altogether the correspondence runs to seventy-one large folios, single-spaced, under the title *Catalanism.*[14] In one of the letters, Magaz claims that Catalanism would have disappeared were it not because the clergy and the bourgeoisie promoted the Catalan

---

12 Report dated October 17, 1934. Nunciatura de Madrid, 912, fols. 200–203.
13 Cf. Ramon Cortis i Blay, "La Visita Apostòlica de 1928 del Nunci Tedeschini a Barcelona. Un intent de repressió d'una pastoral en català," pmbl., *Analecta Sacra Tarraconensia* 81 (2008), 197–608; Ramon Cortis i Blay, "L'informe final de la Visita Apostòlica de 1928 del Nunci Tedeschini a Catalunya," *Analecta Sacra Tarraconensia* 83 (2010), 485–558; Ramon Cortis i Blay, "La Visita del Nunci Tedeschini de 1928-1929 a Montserrat," *Analecta Sacra Tarraconensia* 84 (2011), 839–970; Hilari Raguer, "La política anticatalanista de la Dictadura de Primo de Rivera, segons una correspondència íntima," *Analecta Sacra Tarraconensia* 84 (2011), 735–838.
14 Historical archive of the Spanish Embassy in the Vatican, Leg. 44, Política 1928.

language, and with their patronage made it possible to publish books that were not commercially viable. Of the nearly 8,000 documents in the archive of Tedeschini's nunciature, the most extensive (almost three hundred pages long), is the final report on this Apostolic Visit, dated June 22, 1928, accompanied by a letter from the nuncio to Cardinal Gasparri, secretary of state. The report concluded that there were two main "exponents and promoters of the Catalan nationalist movement, especially as regards the use of the Catalan language ... who are virtuous and in many other ways meritorious, that is, the Cardinal Archbishop of Tarragona and the Reverend Abbot of Montserrat." He proposes that they be replaced, since a simple admonition would not suffice: "I do not doubt that they would do everything to obey, but I doubt very much that their efforts would be effective. They are, *ab antiquo*, convinced of their so-called *politics* ... If they stayed, they would be two figures who, if not with their words then certainly with their deeds, their silence, and their sympathies, would always preach that the Holy See has been deceived." The upshot of that Apostolic Visit was a set of unfortunate decrees made by some of the Roman congregations. Professors and students allegedly guilty of separatist propaganda were expelled from the seminaries, and priests who in the sacrament of penance refused absolution to those who confessed in Castilian were condemned (this was a totally unfounded accusation: in fact, there had been cases of the opposite, that is, worshippers confessing in Catalan who were denied absolution). These decrees must have been questioned in the Vatican itself because they were not published in the *Acta Apostolicae Sedis*, and when Vidal i Barraquer demonstrated their falsity, they were quietly repealed and the Secretary of State Cardinal Gasparri acknowledged that they had been "an unfortunate error." The whole episode reflected very badly on Tedeschini as the Apostolic Visitor, but it only entrenched his anti-Catalanism still further. This was the unpleasant experience of 1928 that he remembered with such indignation in 1934.

Pius XI and *La Main Tendue*

Faced with the growth of fascist movements in Europe, and in particular with the threat that Hitler posed to Russia, the Comintern changed tactic, and now campaigned in favor of the union of the whole of the Left and the creation of a set of Popular Fronts. The first victorious Popular Front movement was the Spanish one, which won the elections of February

16, 1936; in May, the French Popular Front would come to power. On April 7, nine days before the first round of legislative elections in France, a speech had been broadcast on Radio Paris by the general secretary of the French Communist Party, Maurice Thorez. In this speech, Thorez called for a national reconciliation of all the French people, from the Catholic working-classes to the far right of the Croix-de-Feu (Cross of Fire), against the common enemy of fascism. His closing words astonished everyone: "We reach out to you, Catholic, worker, employee, craftsman, farmer, we who are lay, because you are pour brother . . . We reach out to you, national volunteer, veteran turned member of the Croix-de-Feu, because you are a son of our people."

Prior to the recent opening of the secret archives, it was widely believed that the Vatican had firmly rejected the policy of *la main tendue*, or "the outstretched hand." March 1937 saw what an Italian journalist would call "the Easter of the three encyclicals:" almost simultaneously, Pius XI published an encyclical against communism, another against Nazism and a third on the subject of persecution in Mexico. It defined the Vatican's "third way," opposing both left-wing and right-wing totalitarianism; but for Pius XI communism was far more dangerous than Nazism, which had at least the merit of being radically anticommunist. The Vatican did its best to silence Thorez's call to the French people. Shortly after the triumph of the French Popular Front, the nuncio to Paris, Maglione, sent a "top secret" letter to the secretary of the Assembly of Cardinals and Archbishops of France (the predecessor of the Episcopal Conference, which would be set up after Vatican Council II), expressing the Pope's concern at the communists' tactics of "insinuating themselves among the ranks of the Catholics, and especially of young people under the pretext of pursuing humanitarian ends, such as the struggle against capitalism's exploitation of the working class, greater human dignity, a better distribution of wealth, and so on." "His Holiness," he said, "desires that the Holy See be kept informed of communist action in France under its various guises and in particular of its attempts to found cells of communist infection among the Catholics." In fact, since 1935 a Communist Catholic movement had published its views in the magazine *Terre nouvelle*, whose cover page bore the hammer and sickle superimposed on a cross.

After the triumph of the Popular Front on May 3, 1936, some voices on the Catholic side were raised in support of the *rapprochement*, especially in the magazine *Esprit* run by Emmanuel Mounier, who said:

"We will continue, we will help, we will support everything that is done, in power or alongside it (I am thinking in particular of trade unionism) to fight against war and against misery, to disarm capitalism from within." The Christian daily newspaper *L'Aube*, led by Francisque Gay (a close ally of Unió Democràtica de Catalunya and who during the war in Spain would be fiercely criticized by the Burgos government) spoke approvingly of the reforms undertaken by Léon Blum and was willing to support everything that "might allow coexistence, if not collaboration, with socialists and communists." At an audience with Hungarian pilgrims on May 11, days after the victory of the Popular Front, Pius XI denounced "communism which tries to penetrate everywhere—and unfortunately has managed to do so in so many places—by using either violence or intrigue and trickery, and even appears to be inspired by the best intentions." And on the next day, at the opening of an exhibition of the international Catholic press, the Pope said: "The first danger, the biggest and certainly the most widespread, is communism in all its forms and at all levels: it threatens everything, seizes everything, infiltrates everywhere, either openly or surreptitiously." On May 15, *L'Aube* published an article by Francisque Gay that seemed to play down the importance of the warning of the Pope; and on the May 31, before representatives of Catholic Action from twenty-five countries, the Pope said: "There is a newspaper that calls itself Catholic, which, in referring to our thought, does so in such a way as to suggest that if We had not noticed, or had forgotten, the dangers of Communism for religion; as if there might exist a compromise between the truth of the Holy Catholic Faith and the denial of every human and divine right that Communism contains." Francisque Gay was obliged to publish a retraction in his newspaper.

Aware of these repeated condemnations of the policy of the *main tendue*, when examining the personal notes that Pacelli took after his audiences with the Pope I was very surprised to find a note that reflects a very different attitude. On November 6, 1937, at the height of the Spanish Civil War and a year and a half after Thorez's speech, Pacelli wrote that the Pope had spent a sleepless night thinking about the *main tendue* policy. Pius XI had told him:

> We grasp the hand that you extend to us and we extend our own hand and ask you to receive it, because we do not want one without the other, if it is not to make ours the Word of Our Lord Jesus Christ as is our right and our duty: "Come

unto me, all you who toil and are weary, and I will give you rest." We mean that we take your hand and offer you ours with the intent of doing good. There can be no confusion about the principles of the Catholic Church, which everyone knows and recognizes. Perhaps, since this matter has arisen in France, the French Episcopate should make a similar gesture. If they do so in these or similar terms, it will not be one Episcopate applauding another, but the Holy Father will reply: You have understood very well the thought of the Holy Father, because you have done no more than interpret the thought of Jesus Christ. Jesus Christ came into the world to give salvation and its benefits to all. *Venite ad me omnes.*[15]

As a token of the good will of the Church, the Pope sent the French episcopate a million francs to be devoted to charitable or social work.

When Pacelli informed the nuncio Valeri and the cardinal of Paris, Verdier, of what Pius XI had said, they were quite taken aback; the comments were at odds with his previous manifestations and with the line which, in obedience to him, the Church of France was following. They could hardly reply that his plan was nonsensical. Instead, they bided their time, and no more was said about the outstretched papal hand.

THE MYSTERY OF BISHOP IRASTORZA

Javier Irastorza Loinaz, born in Donostia-San Sebastián, was bishop of Orihuela-Alicante. Like all the priests trained in the seminary of Vitoria-Gasteiz, Irastorza was well versed in the social doctrine of the Church and in Catholic social action and syndicalism. In 1935, the Holy See appointed Juan de Dios Ponce y Pozo as Apostolic Administrator of Orihuela-Alicante, and relieved Irastorza of his obligation to reside there, which was tantamount to asking him to leave. In July 1936 he was in Donostia-San Sebastián, from where he fled to France. He would later spend the whole of the Civil War in England.

Irastorza did not appear among the signatories of the collective letter of the Spanish bishops, although Isidro Gomá, president of the Spanish Episcopal Conference and author of the letter, had his address

---

15 *Affari Esteri Straordinari*, Posiz. 430, fasc 354 1937, fol. 64. Audience of November 6, 1937.

and the two exchanged a number of letters. Perhaps Gomá considered that since Irastorza had been relieved of the governance of the diocese, he should not sign. Another non-signatory of the letter was Cardinal Segura, but he had resigned from his see in Toledo, while Irastorza remained the titular bishop of Orihuela-Alicante. Did Irastorza in fact refuse to sign, like his compatriot Múgica, and like Vidal i Barraquer? In any event, the mere fact that he did not go over to the "national" zone was already significant and was enough for him to be considered as hostile to the regime.

It so happened that Ponce y Pozo was murdered on November 30, 1936. Irastorza must have concluded that as a result he automatically recovered the governance of the diocese. The fact is that, after the war he arrived in Alicante and, to the great surprise of all, took up episcopal authority. He could hardly have done this without the support of the Holy See and, indeed, he appears as bishop of Orihuela-Alicante in the *Annuario Pontificio* for the years 1940 to 1943, when he passed away.

The relations between the Franco government and the Vatican during the war and in the immediate postwar period were extremely tense; the Vatican did not recognize Franco's right to present bishops, and the Holy See probably thought it appropriate to restore Irastorza to his see without negotiating the matter with Franco's government. This reinstatement suggests that there had been no dishonorable reason for his removal and for the appointment of Ponce y Pozo as Apostolic Administrator. During my research, I was told in confidence that the answer lies in the archives of the diocese of Orihuela-Alicante, but that the documents were kept in the strictest secrecy. The Vatican Secret Archive must contain all the documentation on the case, but I have not been able to consult it to date. But in fact, I was able to find the reason for the decision to relieve Irastorza of his post, in the archive of the nunciature of Madrid. Irastorza was accused of sending capital abroad; the Consistorial Congregation, the body that oversees the conduct of bishops, called for his resignation and obliged him to go to Rome. But rather than a misappropriation of funds, the operation was probably an illicit act intended to safeguard the patrimony of the diocese, which had been placed in great danger by the political situation.[16]

---

16 Nunciature of Madrid, título VII, fasc. 2, fols 177–86: he was accused of sending capital abroad; fols. 187–225, stay in Rome.

The Nunciature of Madrid During the War

The monarchist ultra-right—sworn enemies of Tedeschini, whom they could not forgive for seeking a reconciliation between the Church and the Republic—eventually managed to have him removed from the nunciature, albeit at the price of seeing him promoted to the rank of cardinal. On June 4, 1936, Filippo Cortesi was appointed as his substitute. Cortesi had been nuncio to Argentina since 1926, but he was prevented from taking up his new post in Spain by the outbreak of the Civil War. When Tedeschini departed on June 11, the auditor of the nunciature, Mgr Silvio Sericano, remained as *chargé d'affaires*. The nunciature remained open throughout the entire war, protected by the police. When Sericano left on November 4, 1936, he was replaced by a Basque Passionist priest, Máximo Alfonso Ariz Elcarte.

During the first months of the war, the ministry of state treated the nunciature in the same way as the foreign embassies. On September 4, the minister Álvarez del Vayo informed Sericano of the composition of the new government of the Republic, presided over by Largo Caballero, and on September 6 Sericano acknowledged receipt. Another letter, sent to all the embassies and also to the nunciature, asked them to provide descriptions of their automobiles so that the ministry would be able to protect them, or to recover them if they had been requisitioned. In the *Annuario Pontificio* for 1937, prepared at the end of 1936, Sericano still features as *chargé d'affaires ad interim* to the government of Valencia, although he is described as "absent."

When the Vatican agreed to raise diplomatic relations with Franco to the highest level, the foreign minister Jordana announced the government's approval of the new nuncio Cicognani. However, on being informed that the Holy See intended to appoint Sericano as secretary of the nunciature, Jordana expressed "the displeasure caused by this appointment" and his government's view that "it would have been preferable if the post had been taken by a person who had not occupied the position so recently in the nunciature of Madrid."[17] For the Francoist propaganda machine, the suggestion that the nunciature had continued to function as normal in Republican Madrid was intolerable. Sericano remained in Rome, attached to secretary of state for Spanish affairs. Both the Burgos government and Gomá would have preferred

---

17 *Archivo Gomá* 10, 167-168.

Antoniutti as nunciate because, despite the inauspicious start to his mission, he had later earned everyone's admiration; but in the end Gaetano Cicognani was appointed, ostensibly because he had lost the nunciature of Vienna due to the Anschluss, but also, in all likelihood, because the Holy See was keen that the nuncio to Spain should be someone who had experience dealing with an authoritarian regime such as the one imposed by the Nazis in Austria.

Following a visit to the nunciature by the priest Leocadio Lobo, who collaborated with the Republic and had been appointed head of the Section of Confessions and Congregations, Ariz Elcarte wrote to the minister of justice Manuel de Irujo asking him to renew his identity card that accredited his diplomatic status and had become worn out by use. The card was renewed by the ministry of state on October 7 and by the governor's office on October 10.[18] In the letter of September 19, Ariz informed Irujo that during his visit Lobo had told him that "the government of the Republic would gladly send a special mission to the Holy See to discuss the matter of the systemization of public religious worship in Spain."

Pius XI and the Basque Catholics

Pius XI admired the Basque Catholics, and especially their clergy. Although they had supported the Republic, he always refrained from condemning them; he said that they were wrong to do so, but he did not accept the censure of the Bishops Múgica and Olaechea, who were reproached for allying with the Communists in a document written by Gomá and signed by members of the clergy.

In August 1936, the National Defense Council of Burgos, presided over by the freemason Cabanellas, had sent the Marquis de Magaz to the Vatican to request its support in the fight against Basque and Catalan nationalism. Magaz, who had previously been ambassador to the Vatican under the Primo de Rivera dictatorship, now demanded the condemnation of the Basque Catholic nationalists. In vain he tried to prevent the consecration of Bishop Antonio Pildain, a Basque

---

18 Manuel de Irujo, *Un vasco en el Ministerio de Justicia,* Segunda parte (Buenos Aires: Ekin, 1979), 71–72 and 528–30 (facsimile of the letter from Ariz to Irujo and of the identity card accrediting him as a diplomat).

nationalist who had been a member of the Spanish parliament and had been appointed bishop of the Canary Islands in May 1936.

Magaz had been recognized by the Vatican only as an unofficial *chargé d'affaires* (the position Gomá held vis-à-vis the Burgos government) and had been received by Pizzardo and even by Pacelli, whom he bombarded with letters that the papal diplomats left unanswered. He protested strongly when the Pope would not receive him; naturally, the appearance of his name on the list of papal audiences in the *Osservatore romano* would have been significant, as it would have marked the beginning of recognition of the government he represented. On November 23, 1936 he was informed by the secretary of state that he would be received by His Holiness. But the audience did not go as he had expected; the Pope had received information about the Basque priests who had been shot, imprisoned, or exiled, and about the expulsion of Bishop Múgica, and at the very beginning of the audience he snapped: "In Nationalist Spain priests are shot, just as they are in Republican Spain." The exact words of Magaz's reply are unknown, but we do know that the Pope, who had a very strong sense of his own authority, suffered an asthma attack and almost choked to death; servants came with a glass of water and the meeting was terminated. On December 9, Pacelli informed Gomá that the Pope had received the Marquis de Magaz and "had paternally taken up the defense of the innocent priests."[19] After this diplomatic failure, Franco sent Magaz as ambassador to Berlin – much to the latter's surprise and displeasure, since he considered himself to be indispensable to relations with the Vatican.

Another illustration of Pius XI's sympathies for the Basque Catholics, and by no means the least important, was his attempt to persuade Franco to grant favorable conditions for the surrender of Euskadi. On May 6, 1937, Cardinal Gomá received an encrypted telegram from the Holy See asking him to negotiate an honorable surrender of the city of Bilbao.[20] Simultaneously, the secretary of state had communicated the Pope's wish to Magaz, who rushed to transmit it to Franco.

---

19 Anastasio Granados, *El cardenal Gomá* (Madrid: Espasa-Calpe, 1969), 146.
20 See Granados, *El cardenal Gomá*, 158–65; Fernando de Meer, *El Partido Nacionalista Vasco ante la guerra de España (1936–1937)* (Pamplona: Eunsa, 1992), 415–48; Alberto de Onaindia, *Hombre de paz en la guerra* (Buenos Aires: Ekin, 1973), 196–228; and José Antonio de Aguirre y Lecube, *De Guernica a Nueva York pasando por Berlín* (Buenos Aires: Ekin, 1944), 34–39.

In fact, the preparations had begun some months before. On February 13, Pacelli recorded that the Pope had told him: "On the Basque question (the conditions of the Franco government). If Mussolini agreed, he might advise in favor of moderation. There are examples: United States, Canada, Switzerland, etc. He might start, for example, with a short speech, etc., and then things would move on from there."[21] Indeed, Mussolini would soon intervene through the Consul Cavalletti.

After receiving Pacelli's telegram, Gomá met General Mola in Vitoria-Gasteiz on May 7 and agreed on a broad outline for the surrender: the city would remain intact, the Basque leaders could leave, the occupying troops would not commit excesses, the soldiers and militiamen who surrendered their arms (except deserters) would be freed, and any criminal acts such as looting would be submitted to the courts; the leaders of the Basque army would be considered deserters but would be tried by a court that would act benevolently. Mola then telephoned Franco, who was in Salamanca, and told him what they had agreed. Franco not only approved the plan but actually toned down the last point, saying: "I respect the lives and property of those who surrender willingly, even the military chiefs," and added two clauses of a political nature: Bizkaia would have a decentralized government similar to that of other favored regions, and social justice was promised in accordance with the encyclical *Rerum novarum* and with the possibilities of the national economy. But for all these proposals to be carried through, the Basques had to surrender immediately. In order to obtain their agreement Gomá traveled to Donibane Lohizune (Saint-Jean-de-Luz) to meet the Basque nationalist Canon Onaindia, Aguirre's main advisor in ecclesiastical matters, but the latter had gone to Paris.

The Pope's personal interest in the issue is palpable in all of Pacelli's notes. At the audience of May 8, the day of the famous intercepted telegram to Aguirre, in his characteristically concise style Pacelli quotes His Holiness as follows: "Telegram sent to Aguirre. And another to Monsignor Valeri who should act in some way (through the French government or via a special envoy). Money is no object: any expense is authorized, including aviation. Tutto quello che si vuole (Anything that is needed)."[22]

---

21 *Affari Ecclesiastici Straordinari* 1937, Posiz. 430, Fol. 24.
22 Ibid., fol. 45.

Pacelli's telegram to Aguirre, sent on 8 May at 1:40 pm, said:

Your Excellency Aguirre. Bilbao. I have the honor of informing Your Excellency that the Generals Franco and Mola, asked expressly about the matter, have made known to the Holy See their conditions for the immediate surrender of Bilbao. 1. They undertake to keep Bilbao intact. 2. They will facilitate the departure of all the leaders. 3. They fully guarantee that Franco's army will respect people and property. 4. They grant absolute freedom for militia soldiers who surrender with their arms. Perpetrators of acts against common law and looters will be brought before the courts. 6. They guarantee the lives and property of those who surrender in good faith, including the military leaders. 7. As regards the political order, administrative decentralization in the same way as other regions. 8. As regards social order, progressive justice, in accordance with the capacity of the national treasury and in accordance with the principles of the encyclical *Rerum Novarum*. Stop. Trusting in the generous sentiments of Your Excellency and those dear children, the Holy Father exhorts Your Excellency to take these proposals into attentive and solicitous consideration, in the desire that this bloody conflict should finally cease. = Cardinal Pacelli.[23]

This telegram should have been sent from the Vatican via Paris to Bilbao, but in fact it was sent via Paris to Barcelona. Realizing its importance, a telegrapher named Bermúdez stopped it and at 4:35 p.m. he sent it on to Largo Caballero, the president of the government in Valencia, before another telegram explaining that he was retaining the first one until he was expressly authorized to forward it.[24]

The council of ministers was to meet that same afternoon, but Largo Caballero called a meeting in the morning to which the Basque minister, Irujo, and the Catalan minister, Ayguadé, were not summoned. It was decided to keep the document secret and it was not discussed at the council of ministers that afternoon, attended by Irujo and Ayguadé. Largo Caballero wanted to make sure that no more telegrams from the Vatican would reach Aguirre. In fact, the Vatican had tried to resend the telegram. In the Largo Caballero archive at the Pablo Iglesias Foundation, next

---

23 The original is preserved in the historical archive of the Pablo Iglesias Foundation in Madrid, in the Fondo Largo Caballero-LIV-5.
24 Ibid.

to the telegram from Pacelli to Aguirre is another, dated May 12, from Largo Caballero to the head of the Army of the North, General Llano de la Encomienda, ordering him to transmit the following telegram to the chief of telegraphs in Bilbao: "If via London or anywhere else, a message arrives from Rome it should be intercepted and sent encrypted to the General Army North so that he may communicate it to me."The bottom of the telegram bears the following handwritten addition: "All this caused heated arguments in the council of ministers, which gave rise to the letter that follows." On May 12, a telegram from the director-general of telecommunication to Largo Caballero informed him of the second dispatch of Pacelli's telegram to Aguirre, which was also intercepted in Barcelona, and reported that the minister of communications and merchant marine was calling for orders to be sent urgently to the chief of telegraphs in Bilbao so that, if the famous telegram was sent again via Bilbao, it should not be delivered.

Aguirre knew nothing of the telegram until two years later, when he learned of the existence of an article by the Jesuit Jacques Bivort de la Saudée entitled "Les martyrs d'Espagne et l'alliance Basque-Communiste" (The martyrs of Spain and the Basque-communist alliance),[25] in the *Revue des Deux Mondes*.The author condemned the alliance of the Basque nationalists with the communists, the persecutors of the Church, and reproached Aguirre for not having responded to Pacelli's proposal. On April 30, 1940 the *lehendakari* (Basque president) sent a letter to the then secretary of state, Cardinal Maglione, in which he swore under oath that he had not received the telegram from Pacelli (by now Pius XII) or had heard anything from him; if he had received it, he said, he would have made sure to answer it given the political importance of the subject, out of the respect due to the Holy See from a devout Catholic, and because the Basque government had done all it could during the war to establish direct contact with the Vatican and would not have missed an opportunity of this kind. This devout and respectful letter from Aguirre received no response; now, in 1940, with the idyll between Franco and the Church well established, Pius XII probably considered it inconvenient to enter into a relationship with the president of the Basque government-in-exile.

---

25 Jacques Bivort de la Saudée, "Les martyrs d'Espagne et l'alliance Basque-Communiste," *Revue des deux Mondes*, February 15, 1940, 703.

On July 21, 1937 the Pope informed Franco, through Gomá, that he had been very pleased with the "rapid and complete response" to his appeal for favorable conditions for the surrender of the Basques and, "as a new token of paternal benevolence" he was willing to "receive as official *chargé d'affaires*" the current unofficial representative of the government of Burgos.[26]

THE MISSION OF MGR ANTONIUTTI[27]

The Basque nationalists would recall the mission of Mgr Antoniutti with considerable displeasure, and not without reason; but Pius XI's decision to send the archbishop was a further expression of the high esteem in which he held the Basque Catholics.

On June 15, 1937, all attempts at a negotiated surrender having failed, Bilbao fell to Franco's troops. The fear of reprisals was great. On July 21 Pacelli informed Gomá by telegram: "The Holy Father has decided to send Mgr Ildebrando Antoniutti, currently Apostolic Delegate in Albania, to the Basque Country with the task of studying, in agreement with your Eminence, whether, and how, the Basque children might be returned to their families. Stop. I urge you to secure the prelate's free entrance and movement."[28] On July 25, Pablo de Churruca y Dotres, who had been Franco's *chargé d'affaires* to the Vatican since June, announced by telegram that Archbishop Antoniutti would leave for Spain with the mission of aiding the repatriation of Basque children who had been evacuated abroad during the final offensive against Bilbao; but Churruca added: "Undoubtedly, he also has the power to examine other aspects of the situation," and suggested that the border authorities and the civil governor of Donostia-San Sebastián should be warned of his arrival. On August 3, Gomá wrote to his close friend Tomás Muniz, archbishop of Santiago, and described the appointment as a success: "he brings with him two missions: one official, the repatriation of the Basque children; and another unofficial, for the moment secret, which coincides with the instructions that I receive directly from the secretary of state and will probably lead to the recognition of the National government in the

---

26 Archivo Histórico del Ministerio de Asuntos Exteriores, R 1051, exp. 12.
27 Cf. Ildebrando Antoniutti, *Memorie autobiografiche* (Udine: Arti Grafiche Friulane, 1975); Onaindia, *Hombre de paz en la guerra,* 271–302; Hilari Raguer, *La Pólvora y el Incienso* (Barcelona: Península, 2001), 247–51.
28 *Archivo Gomá* 6, 529–30.

near future. My recent efforts seem to have had their effect."²⁹ Gomá's secretary canon Despujol expressed his own opinion in a letter to the cardinal on July 24, a view that Gomá shared and repeatedly stated in private: namely, that the Vatican had misunderstood the situation in Spain and the true nature of the "crusade," and that this incomprehension was due to the nefarious influence that certain Basque and Catalan elements had over the Holy See:

> Let me now tell you frankly what I think. This is another ploy by the rabble that prowls around that holy house. The Vatican has realized that your Eminence speaks his mind; your comments are unwelcome, because the Vatican officials wish to believe the opposite of what you say. For this reason, they have sent a man who, however much he may wish to tell the truth, will not do so because his desire is to stay here as N.[uncio] and of course all his efforts will be devoted to satisfying his *padrone*, alias Mgr P.[izzardo]. Also, you can be sure that the supporters of the new ex-Republic [Euskadi] are doing everything they can to bring him over to their side. And that is the real danger: all the rabble moving around in B.[ilbao] will see this visitor as an element of defense and of accusation: defense against overseas [Rome; in the coded language of the hardline Spanish ecclesiastics, already in use before the war, "overseas" signified Rome or the Vatican], and accusation against F.[ranco]. The reason is not just offensive to F.[ranco] but is completely ridiculous, since all [the evacuated children] have to do is being the journey: no one will do anything to stop them returning to their homes.³⁰

In his memoirs, Antoniutti describes the mission he received from Pizzardo on July 23: "In the Basque Country I was to deal with the question of the prisoners of war and the return of children sent abroad because of the conflict in that region."³¹ Significantly, he mentions the prisoners first. This perspective is confirmed by my examination of the Antoniutti files in the Vatican Secret Archives. The evacuated children are scarcely mentioned; almost all of the voluminous documents are communications with the Francoist authorities in defense of the Basque clergy. Further, in the telegram to Gomá of July 23 announcing the

---

29 Granados, *El cardenal Gomá*, 103.
30 *Archivo Gomá* 6, 546–48.
31 Antoniutti, *Memorie autobiografiche*, 29.

arrival of Antoniutti, Pacelli stated that the visitor would deal with the return of the Basque children "and other similar charitable works."[32]

But let us return to the arrival of Antoniutti. With his passport endorsed by Churruca, he went to Paris, where the nuncio Valeri gave him useful information on both the Nationalist and the Republican zones in Spain, and he then took the train to Hendaia (Hendaye). In the Nationalist zone, however, the feelings that Despujol had expressed in the letter mentioned above were running high; they did not want an Apostolic Delegate residing in the Basque Country, but a full-fledged nuncio in Salamanca. When Antoniutti reached the frontier with Spain, he was refused entry by Commander Troncoso, head of the border police. There were some journalists there, who had been told that a nuncio was coming. Antoniutti was wearing a simple priest's cassock with nothing to indicate his rank or his identity. Antoniutti suggested to the police officers that the journalists would surely be interested in the news that an archbishop representing the Pope had been denied entry to Spain. Cardinal Gomá was in Santiago, where, on July 25, he was to preside over the recently reinstated ceremony of the offering to the Apostle. His secretary, Despujol, who had been sent to receive the Apostolic Delegate, informed him of the incident at the border, and Gomá hastened to resolve the problem. The barely credible excuse proffered later was that Churruca's telegram had been misplaced. Despujol went to the head of the diplomatic service, Sangróniz, and found the allegedly lost telegram. Sangróniz went personally to apologize to Antoniutti but also told him that he should go directly to Pamplona-Iruñea; in other words, his headquarters during his mission should not be the Basque Country. Pamplona-Iruñea was where Gomá resided, even after the liberation of Toledo, and he was the Pope's "unofficial provisional *chargé d'affaires*" to Franco's government. Indeed, Pamplona-Iruñea was the ecclesiastical capital until the end of the war.

On his return from Santiago, Gomá met Antoniutti in Valladolid, and together they went on to Salamanca, where they were received by Franco. Antoniutti later recalled his first contact with the heart of Francoist Spain: "I had the impression that I was on top of a volcano spewing lava, sulfur, and rocks. From the accounts that I received I was able to imagine the atmosphere of violence that dominated Spain at the time and the repugnant atrocities that cast such a shadow over the

---

32 *Archivo Gomá* 6, pp. 538–39.

country."[33] Later, the *chargé d'affaires* to the Vatican, Churruca, told Sangróniz that the incident of the arrival of Antoniutti "had caused an unpleasant impression here."[34] But Antoniutti immediately gained the trust and the appreciation of both the civil authorities and the episcopate; they were pleased when, in September, he was promoted to *chargé d'affaires* and the event at which he presented his credentials was organized as if he were a nuncio, with the accompaniment of Franco's Moorish guard.

So everyone was content – with the exception of the Basques, who had been meant to be the main beneficiaries of his mission. In August 1938 Antoniutti visited the colony of Basque children in Donibane Garazi (Saint-Jean-Pied-de-Port) in France and criticized the Basque nationalists, and he endorsed the Francoist slander of an alleged robbery of jewels and crowns of the Child Jesus and Our Lady of Begoña. When in May 1938 the Vatican raised its representation in Spain to the highest level, both the government and the episcopate hoped strongly that the nuncio would be Antoniutti, but instead Pius XI appointed Gaetano Cicognani, who had been nuncio in Vienna and had lost his post after the Anschluss.

THE BOMBARDMENT OF BARCELONA IN MARCH 1938

In the Spanish war, mass aerial bombardments of the civilian population were carried out for the first time. The bombing of Gernika is the best known, but no less terrible were the attacks on Barcelona between March 17 and 20, 1937. In all, 875 people died and more than 1,500 were injured. Unlike previous and later bombardments, the attacks were not limited to military targets such as railroad stations, ports, gasoline deposits, and industrial areas, but extended to residential neighborhoods. The bombers also used a new tactic: instead of concentrating on massive but brief attacks, the planes now arrived in unceasing, successive waves. These bombardments provoked protests worldwide, and the Vatican also denounced them, although it was at pains to show that it was acting independently and was not part of the international diplomatic campaign.

---

33 Antoniutti, *Memorie autobiografiche*, 36.
34 Churruca to Sangróniz, August 3, 1937. Archivo Histórico del Ministerio de Asuntos Exteriores, R 1051, exp. 12.

As early as February 16, Antoniutti informed Pacelli that the Pope had urged him to tell Franco of the Vatican's displeasure regarding the bombardments.[35] After the terrible events of March, on the 24th of that month the *Osservatore Romano* published a severe condemnation on its front page, under the title "On the subject of aerial bombardments." The article set out to be impartial, as if the bombardments were taking place in both zones. It explained that a month earlier, having heard of "the numerous victims among the civilian population and the destruction of works of art caused by the increasingly frequent bombing of cities, while other powers intervened with the Republican government," the Holy Father "made a heartfelt appeal to the Catholic and noble sentiments of Generalisimo Franco to urge that the Nationalists should also desist from these bombardments. Generalisimo Franco was most receptive to the paternal interest of His Holiness in favor of the innocent victims of the war, and through the *chargé d'affaires* of the Holy See, His Eminence Archbishop Antoniutti, transmitted to the Holy Father filial and reassuring explanations and declarations." But the end of the article adopted a different tone:

> Many victims have now been added, caused this time by the recent aerial bombardments of Barcelona: innocent victims, whose loss the Holy See deplores more than ever, while, faithful to its mission, it continues to send words of moderation and temperance to mitigate as far as possible the horrors of war. And this is why the August Pontiff, acting at all times on his own initiative and independently of the action of other powers, on the 21st commissioned the aforementioned Monsignor Antoniutti to undertake urgent talks with Generalisimo Franco.

The bombardments continued, and on June 10 the *Acta diurna* section in the *Osservatore Romano* carried the following report, which everyone knew came from the secretary of state:

> As the Spanish war enters its third year, the attention of Europe is drawn at this time to the bombardments of civilian populations, which have provoked protests and indignation.
>
> These protests are justified by the fact that the places where the bombs have fallen are of no military interest, nor are they in the vicinity of military centers or public buildings that are of any relevance to the course of the war. The senseless massacre

---

35   Nunciatura de Madrid, fasc. 4, fols. 411–414.

of the civilian population has once again brought to the fore the serious and difficult problem of the "humanization" of war, which is by its very nature destructive and inhumane. Pius XI had recently agreed to raise diplomatic relations with Franco to the highest level. On May 16 he had appointed as nuncio Gaetano Cicognani, who was preparing to present his credentials to Franco. Pacelli ordered Antoniutti to submit a verbal note, dated June 16, announcing that "the Holy See wishes to make a new appeal for measures to ensure that there should be no more innocent victims, which is also in the interests of the Nationalist cause." He suggested, in any case, that the arrival of the nuncio should not coincide with new bombardments.

On June 16 Antoniutti sent the following telegram:

> The Holy See would be unfavorably surprised if new victims were to be lamented in the bombed towns precisely at a time when the nuncio of His Holiness is arriving in Spain and preparing to present his credentials to His Excellency the Head of State. It is easy to foresee the repercussions in the Catholic world if the event were to coincide with bombardments causing innocent victims among the civilian population.

On the same day Antoniutti sent another telegram:

> I have made the arrangements set out in the encrypted telegram 30. – The government authorities have accepted with good grace the new protest regarding the bombings, but at the same time declare that the Nationalist aviation is pursuing military objectives, as demonstrated by the sinking of foreign steamers carrying armaments for the Republicans and the destruction of ammunition depots and of 60,000 tons of gasoline in Barcelona. There is great indignation in these governmental circles at the ever-increasing levels of aid provided by the French to the Red Army, without which aid the Communists in Barcelona would be easily defeated.

In another report, Antoniutti stated that, "Franco says that Barcelona is a military stronghold with some 200 military targets and that the victims would have been caused mainly by the explosion of ammunition depots inside the city."[36]

---

36 Nunciatura de Madrid, fasc. 4, fols. 428 and 431–432.

The Burgos government indignantly rejected the international protests, and still more those of the Holy See. The Nationalists insisted that the objectives pursued were strictly military. But the German ambassador Eberhard Von Stohrer (no doubt recalling the international scandal a year earlier caused by the bombing of Gernika by the Condor Legion) sent the following report to Berlin on March 23:

> I have learned that the effects of recent air strikes on Barcelona by Italian bombers have been literally terrible. Almost every neighborhood in the city has suffered . . . The reports sent by the foreign journalists who have witnessed the outcomes of these bombings to their newspapers reflect the most vivid indignation. They are convinced that these bombardments, carried out indiscriminately on the city of Barcelona, are experiments with new weapons. I am afraid that aerial bombardments that do not target clearly military objectives do not produce the moral effect sought in a Civil War such as the one in Spain; quite the contrary, they create serious dangers for the future. I am convinced that after the war, both in Spain and abroad, the Italians, and we ourselves will be the objects of hatred, on the grounds that, obviously, it is not Spanish planes that have destroyed their own cities, but the planes of the Italian and German allies.[37]

Among the collection of Mussolini's personal documents preserved in the Archivio Centrale dello Stato Italiano are two telegrams signed by him that are especially important. The first, dated December 14, 1937, addressed to General Berti, says: "The Air Force of the Balearics will be reinforced and will have the task of terrorizing the red rearguard and especially the urban centers." In the second telegram, a few days before the March bombings, the Duce says he has learned that celebrations for the anniversary of the Battle of Guadalajara are being prepared in Paris, and that something must be done to counter them.

---

37   Stohrer to Ribbentrop, March 23, 1938, *Documents on German Foreign Policy* (1949; London, H.M. Stationery Office, 1983), 624–26.

A Letter from Cardinal Pacelli on the "Collective Letter"

The collective letter of the Spanish bishops in favor of the uprising is undoubtedly the episcopate's most famous document from the period, and the most controversial. The Vatican's secret documents, recently made available to researchers, reveal some interesting details about how the Vatican received this letter.

Franco was very critical of certain foreign Catholics who, while condemning the religious persecution unleashed in the Republican zone, rejected the title of crusade that Franco's supporters attributed to the insurrection and denounced the severe repression that was taking place in the Nationalist zone. Given that he had the support of all the bishops, on May 10, 1937, he asked Cardinal Gomá to publish "a letter addressed to the episcopate of the whole world, with the request that it be printed in the Catholic press, so that the truth be known." After the failure of the pastoral instruction written by him but signed by the bishops of Pamplona-Iruñea and Vitoria-Gasteiz against the Basque Catholic nationalists who were fighting alongside the Republic, Gomá was firmly against any collective document, but he complied with Franco's request. He consulted Cardinal Pacelli, secretary of state, and all the bishops. The bishops accepted the proposal with enthusiasm, with the exception of Vidal i Barraquer and Múgica, but in his reply to Gomá the secretary of state discussed other matters and did not mention the letter. Gomá continued to write to Pacelli, and Pacelli remained silent. Finally, on July 5 Gomá sent Pacelli the proofs of the definitive text. On July 31, Pacelli wrote to Gomá acknowledging receipt of the proofs, and said:

> It is the opinion of the Secretariat of State that for the publication of a document of such importance as the above-mentioned letter the unanimity of the episcopate would be desirable. Since His Eminence Vidal y Barraquer, as you note in your letter No. 88, does not consider the publication of the document to be appropriate, and since Bishop Múgica and perhaps other Spanish bishops do not wish to sign it, this Secretariat leaves it to Your Eminence's well-known consideration to consider whether it would not be the case to suspend publication for the moment.[38]

---

38 *Affari Esteri Straordinari* 4, vol. 16 Spagna, fasc. 282, fol. 13.

This important letter was not sent. Nor was it destroyed; the original, unsigned, was filed in the secretary of state's archives, with a handwritten note in pencil, enclosed in a circle, saying *sospeso* (suspended).

The collective letter was dated July 1, and this is the date that is usually attributed to it, although in fact it was not published until the end of August. Gomá said that it was necessary to make sure that the bishops, its formal recipients, had received it beforehand; but also, until the very last moment, he tried to persuade Vidal i Barraquer to sign. In his letter to Pacelli accompanying the proofs of the press, responding to Vidal i Barraquer's main objection to the document (namely, that it might provoke reprisals against the clergy and the faithful in the Republican zone), he asserted that "it will be sent to bishops all over the world, so that they can orient the Catholic press in their countries;" but in fact the Francoist propaganda machine was already working frantically on the translation and dissemination of the document. Did someone tell Pacelli that there was no turning back? Vidal i Barraquer had rightly said: "Very suitable for propaganda, but I consider it inappropriate to the condition and character of the people who are to sign it." The director of national propaganda, Conde, would say to a priest who worked with him: "Tell the Cardinal (Gomá) that, with my experience in these matters, I can say that the collective letter has met with more success than the rest of our endeavors."

In the letter, Gomá had omitted all the matters that he knew would displease the Vatican. Although in previous documents he had repeatedly proclaimed that the war was a crusade, in this letter he states expressly that it is not, and also refrains from offering unconditional adherence to the new regime; he says that at the moment the regime is of great benefit to the Church, but that it is impossible to know how it might develop. This is why some bishops had said that the letter did not go far enough. Pla y Deniel, for example, would have approved the project if it said what the bishops had already been affirming (as he had done in his famous pastoral *The Two Cities*, namely, that the war was indeed a crusade). But not even with this moderate stance did Gomá obtain the approval he desired. The Vatican did not prohibit the letter, but did not approve it either; it acknowledged receipt only nine months later, and even then in terms that provoked an energetic protest from the ambassador José de Yanguas Messía.[39]

---

39   Cf. Raguer, *La pólvora y el incienso*, 151–74.

CONCLUSION

This brief summary of the materials in the Vatican Archives which have recently become available for consultation gives a clear idea of their interest to historians. It will take researchers many years to exploit this treasure trove to the full.

BIBLIOGRAPHY

Aguirre y Lecube, José Antonio de. *De Guernica a Nueva York pasando por Berlín*. Buenos Aires: Ekin, 1944.

Antoniutti, Ildebrando. *Memorie autobiografiche*. Udine: Arti Grafiche Friulane, 1975.

Batillori, Miquel, and Victor Manuel Arbeloa, eds. *Església i Estat durant la Segona República. 1931–1936*. (Scripta et Documenta, 20, 21, 23, 24, 27, 28, 33, 37, and 39), volume 1. Barcelona: Publicacions de l'Abadia de Montserrat, 1971.

Bivort de la Saudée, Jacques. "Les martyrs d'Espagne et l'alliance Basque-Communiste." *Revue des deux Mondes*, February 15, 1940, 703.

Cárcel Ortí, Vicente. *La persecución religiosa en España durante la segunda República (1931–1939)*. Madrid: Rialp, 1990.

Cortis i Blay, Ramon. "La Visita Apostòlica de 1928 del Nunci Tedeschini a Barcelona. Un intent de repressió d'una pastoral en català." Preamble in *Analecta Sacra Tarraconensia* 81 (2008): 197–608.

———. "L'informe final de la Visita Apostòlica de 1928 del Nunci Tedeschini a Catalunya." *Analecta Sacra Tarraconensia* 83 (2010): 485–558.

———. "La Visita del Nunci Tedeschini de 1928-1929 a Montserrat." *Analecta Sacra Tarraconensia* 84 (2011), 839–970.

Granados, Anastasio. *El cardenal Gomá*. Madrid: Espasa-Calpe, 1969.

Irujo, Manuel de. *Un vasco en el Ministerio de Justicia*. Buenos Aires: Ekin, 1979.

Maura, Miguel. *Así cayó Alfonso XIII*. Barcelona: Ariel, 1966.

Meer, Fernando de. *El Partido Nacionalista Vasco ante la guerra de España (1936–1937)*. Pamplona: Eunsa, 1992.

Onaindia, Alberto de. *Hombre de paz en la guerra.* Buenos Aires: Ekin, 1973.

Raguer, Hilari. *El general Batet.* Barcelona: Publicacions de l'Abadia de Montserrat, 1994.

———. *La Pólvora y el Incienso.* Barcelona: Península, 2001.

———. "La política anticatalanista de la Dictadura de Primo de Rivera, segons una correspondència íntima." *Analecta Sacra Tarraconensia* 84 (2011): 735–838.

Vegas Latapie, Eugenio. *Catolicismo y República: un episodio de la historia de Francia.* Madrid: Ed. Gráficas Universal, 1932.

Chapter 15

Catalunya del Nord under the Vichy Regime (1940–1944)

Daniel Roig i Sanz

The Vichy regime came into being on July 10, 1940 with the historic vote that granted full constituent powers to Marshal Pétain. At this time, Catalunya del Nord (Northern Catalonia, or to give it its official name, the *département* of the Eastern Pyrenees)[1] had long been living in an exceptional and anomalous situation – due not just to the outbreak of World War II in September 1939 but also to the aftermath of the Spanish Civil War that, since its beginning in 1936, had caused turmoil in the region's social and political life.

The effect of the Spanish war is a key factor in the analysis of the historical period between 1940 and 1944 in Catalunya del Nord, a peripheral and essentially agricultural region situated on the transnational border. After the creation and institutionalization of the Vichy regime, its reception by the population, enthusiastic or otherwise, was indissolubly linked the collective trauma caused by the avalanche of refugees arriving from Spain. In early 1939, the inhabitants of the region and the civilian and military authorities had to face one of the largest civil exoduses in twentieth-century Europe, with almost half a million refugees arriving from the other side of the Pyrenees. After an arduous journey, hundreds of thousands of exiles were redirected to the beaches of Argelès-sur-Mer, Saint-Cyprien, and Barcarès, where they spent the

---

1   Catalunya del Nord is the region in France in which Catalan is traditionally spoken. Annexed by France in 1659 under the Treaty of the Pyrenees, it lies on the other side of the national border from Catalonia proper.

following months sleeping in the open or crowded into impromptu tents and huts built on the sand.

The impact was dramatic: not counting the refugees who had already crossed the border during the conflict itself, within a few weeks of its termination, the arrivals from Spain had doubled the total of the population of the *département*, which, according to the last official census of 1936, amounted to 233,347 inhabitants. As tensions grew in the rest of Europe, French attention to the matter of the Spanish exiles began to wane, but in Catalunya del Nord the issue of the refugees would continue to be urgently debated during that spring and summer of 1939.

This, then, was the background to the outbreak of the World War II, soon to bring with it the worst military disaster in the history of France. The consequence was the étrange défaite (strange defeat), as the historian Marc Bloch would call it four years before he was murdered in Lyon by the Gestapo; and with the signing of the armistice on June 22, 1940 and the division of the country into two halves, the stage was set for the most important political and institutional change since the declaration of the Third Republic in 1870. More than a political change brought about by the circumstances, in fact, the birth of the new French state in 1940 signified the country's radical break with its own republican and democratic tradition and its replacement by another political culture, supported by a highly influential minority that had already turned republican values into its primary scapegoat.

Since the 1970s, historians have worked on many aspects of the Vichy period, and a great many studies have been published. Nevertheless, the deployment of the regime at regional level remains relatively unexplored. In the 1990s, Gérard Bonet's monograph on Catalunya del Nord (published in 1992) and the four volumes by Jean Larrieu and Ramon Gual (published between 1994 and 2000)[2] were important milestones in the historiography of the region, but there are still many gaps in our understanding of the evolution and the actions of the Pétainist authorities in the *département* of the Eastern Pyrenees. Leaving aside other aspects that are no less important, for reasons of space, we aim to examine the following questions: what was the impact of the arrival of Pétain and the *Révolution nationale*? What form would the

---

2   Gérard Bonet, *Les Pyrénées Orientales dans la guerre: les années de plomb, 1939–1944* (Ecully: Horvath, 1992). Jean Larrieu and Ramon Gual, *Catalunya Nord, 1939–1944. Vichy, l'Occupation nazie et la Résistance catalane*, 4 vols. (Prades: Terra Nostra, 1994–2000); the third volume, entitled *La Poste départamentale et la censure*, includes texts by Jean Tubert.

new Pétainist legislation take in Catalunya del Nord? And through what sort of processes would the region become integrated into the new political-administrative order established by Vichy?

FROM THE OUTBREAK OF THE WORLD WAR II
TO THE ARRIVAL OF MARSHAL PÉTAIN

Indeed, when the war broke out in early September 1939, public opinion in Catalunya del Nord was still focused on the issue of the refugees from Spain. The matter had been debated energetically by the two camps: those in favor of welcoming the refugees, and those who advocated their immediate expulsion. Among the latter were the region's far-right organizations, including the newspapers *Le Roussillon*, the local mouthpiece of Charles Maurras's *Action Française* (AF, French Action), *Somatent!*, attached to the Parti Social Français (PSF, French Social Party), and *La Flamme du Midi* of the Parti Populaire Français (PPF, French Popular Party). Their pages fired harsh criticisms at any policy that aimed to accommodate the refugees and blamed the Spaniards for disorder and destruction of all kinds that, they claimed, were a threat to the region's social harmony.[3] Without reaching the same level of verbal violence, the region's main newspaper *L'Indépendant* was clearly hostile toward the Spanish exiles – even though its staff included a fair number of columnists who were close to the Catalan nationalists, like the Perpignan journalist François Francis, who would nevertheless remain pro-Vichy until he was purged in the summer of 1944.[4]

Obviously, these were not the only opinions on the issue. In fact, the Spanish exodus of 1939 generated an enormous civil mobilization. Dozens of welcoming committees and charity organizations were created over the months for the refugees,[5] and hundreds of posters, pamphlets, and flyers denounced the inadequacy of the authorities' official response.

---

3 The study of reference of the far right in Catalunya Nord remains Pierre Hugues, *Naissance et développement des mouvements fascistes en Catalogne-Nord dans les années 30. PSF et PPF* (Perpignan: Universitat de Perpignan, mémoire de maîtrise, 1977).

4 Gérard Bonet, *L'Indépendant des Pyrénées Orientales: un siècle d'histoire d'un quotidien, 1846–1950* (Perpignan: Publications de l'Olivier, 2004), 251–55.

5 On this issue, see Andreu Balent and Nicolas Marty, eds., *Catalans du Nord et languedociens et l'aide à la République espagnole, 1936–1946* (Perpignan: Presses Universitaires de Perpignan, 2009). For an overview of the impact of the Spanish Civil War, see Jean Sagnes and Sylvie Caucanas, eds., *Les Français et la Guerre d'Espagne: actes du colloque de Perpignan* (Perpignan: Presses Universitaires de Perpignan, 2004).

Not surprisingly, many of the posters that proliferated on the streets of the capital Perpignan demanded immediate solutions to this large-scale problem: "Women, children dying of cold and hunger! The evacuations must be stepped up! Let every Catalan family take a child in under its roof," urged a poster produced by the Comité d'Accueil aux Réfugiés d'Espagne (Reception Committee for Refugees from Spain).[6] Others simply noted (sometimes in rather veiled terms) the inconvenience caused by the refugees in their respective towns: for instance, a poster that appeared in Elne in early March 1939 appealed to the public authorities to evacuate the municipal stadium, occupied by Spanish refugees, so that the local youth would be able to play their rugby games. It was proposed that the refugees should be moved elsewhere, basically to the Mediterranean coasts, that their situation should be made legal, or that they should be "sent back to Madrid or Burgos."[7] What is surprising about the request for the evacuation of the stadium is the fact that it was signed by the town's four Communist councilmembers. This example illustrates not only the tensions generated by the presence of the refugees, but also the social polarization that the issue caused, and which would actually anticipate some of the currents of opinion that would emerge from July 1940 onward.

In any case, when mobilization was ordered in early September 1939, the pressure of the refugees had already begun to diminish. There had been a slow but progressive evacuation, and both repatriations to Spain and departures for Latin American countries had helped to relieve the situation in the camps. With the aim of preparing the country in case of war, the Daladier government had created the *Compagnies de Travailleurs Étrangers* (Companies of Foreign Workers, CTE) in April 1939, in which numerous Spanish exiles had enlisted since the spring.[8] This workforce would also serve to replace the manpower lost due to the mobilization itself and later, during the occupation, it would be used both by the Vichy regime and by the German authorities.

However, the outbreak of war implied not just the mobilization of the male population and its replacement by female or foreign labor, but also a whole series of passive defense measures, such as traffic restrictions and limitations on public lighting, shows, and movie theaters that would be implemented during the fall and winter of 1939 and 1940.

---

6   Arxius Departamentals dels Pirineus Orientals (APDO), 4M 799.
7   APDO, 4M 801.
8   According to Xavier Deulonder, by August 18, 1939, 13,758 refugees had left the camps. See Xavier Deulonder, *França i Catalunya* (Barcelona: Bubok, 2017), 486–87.

In fact, the movie theaters also served to finance the war effort: 25 percent of the revenue from ticket sales went directly to the state's coffers. Toward Christmas, some of these restrictions would be lifted and, to an extent, things returned to normal; Perpignan's seven theaters were able to screen movies once more, including the huge box office success *Stagecoach*, the western directed by John Ford that would catapult the young actors John Wayne and Claire Trevor to fame.[9]

The declaration of war on Germany had significant political consequences, especially for the French Communists. In response to the German-Soviet Pact of late August 1939, the dissolution of Communist organizations was decreed on September 26. However, the final step—after weeks of profound disagreements between the minority Communist party and the other parties—would not arrive until January 20, 1940, when a law passed unanimously by the Senate and the House of Representatives dismissed the elected Communist representatives from their posts.[10] Article 2 granted the departmental authorities the power to enforce the law, and so accordingly the prefect of the Eastern Pyrenees, Raoul Didkowski, dismissed more than seventy Communist municipal councilmembers, mayors, and deputy secretaries in Catalunya del Nord. This figure corresponded to slightly more than 0.3 percent of all municipal councilmembers dismissed in France, according to official figures given by the Interior Minister Albert Sarraut in mid-March 1940.[11]

This would be the first wartime purge of the French Communists. Then came Vichy. But the most important point for the matter that concerns us here was the twofold consequence of the new geopolitics, in political and social terms: on the one hand, diplomatic tensions with the USSR would be effectively reflected by repressive measures against the French Communists; on the other, the attempt to isolate Spain from the international conflict would lead to a policy of *rapprochement* (though without offering any concessions) toward Franco's government,

---

9   For an appraisal of this specific period in Catalunya Nord, see Bonet, *Les Pyrénées Orientales dans la guerre*, 50–55. For a more general overview, see Fabrice Grenard, *La drôle de guerre. L'entrée en guerre des Français: setembre 1939–mai 1940* (Paris: Belin, 2015).

10 "Loi prononçant la déchéance de certains élus," *Journal Officiel de la République Française*, January 20–21, 1940, 602.

11 According to the figures presented by Sarraut on March 19, 1940 in the Senate, the Communist representatives removed were: 87 general councilmembers, 70 district councilmembers, 2,500 municipal councilmembers, 60 deputies, and one senator. "Discurs d'Albert Sarraut al Senat," *JOD Sénat*, March 19, 1940. On this issue, see Georges Sentís, *Les communistes et la Résistance dans les Pyrénées-Orientales* (Perpignan: Editions Marxisme, 1992).

much to the detriment of Republican Spain and the refugees. In fact, at the beginning of 1940 many Republicans were still in Catalunya del Nord, despite repatriations and numerous evacuations to other departments. In Barcelona, from where many of these refugees had fled, the censorship exercised by the Franco regime ensured that little was known about this situation; however, the long lists that appeared periodically in the Barcelona press in February 1940 announcing the deaths of 513 refugees in hospitals in the French Midi, most of them in Perpignan, were a chilling illustration of their plight during the *drôle de guerre*.[12]

It was against this background, then, that the Germans launched their offensive against France. The arrival of Pétain to the vice-presidency in mid-May, and to the presidency of the council of ministers on June 16, 1940, would have direct consequences for Catalunya del Nord. Two days later the prefect Didkowski was appointed General Director of National Security. Once again, the point of connection had been the Spanish refugees: Pétain, as French ambassador to Franco's Spain, had met Didkowski in a visit to the refugee camps at the end of July 1939.[13] In the end Didkowski would be dismissed on July 10, 1940. But this episode, along with the claims that some Spanish circles would make on Catalunya del Nord in 1941, placed the *département* at the forefront of Spanish and European geopolitics during World War II.[14]

JULY 10, 1940 AND THE *RÉVOLUTION NATIONALE*

Most of the political representatives of the *département* of the Eastern Pyrenees voted against granting full powers to Pétain. Of the three departmental deputies, only the radical socialist François Delcos voted for constitutional reform, while Louis Noguères and Joseph Rous, deputies of the French Section of the Workers' International for the constituencies of Ceret and Prades, voted against. Of the two senators, only the Socialist Georges Pezières would reject the reform, because Joseph Parayre, a Socialist senator who had come to prominence with

---

12 For the list of refugees that appeared on February 2, 14, 24, and 28, see: "Lista de refugiados españoles fallecidos en los hospitales de Francia" and "Lista de refugiados españoles fallecidos en los hospitales de Perpignan," *La Vanguardia*, February 28, 1940, 4.

13 For the evolution of the relations between Franco and Pétain, see Matthieu Séguéla, *Pétain-Franco: les secrets d'une alliance* (Paris: Albin Michel, 1992).

14 Pere Grau, "La Catalogne française revendiquée par l'Espagne," *Etudes Roussillonnaises* 9 (1989): 159–68.

his determined defense of the Catalan wine sector, was unable to attend the session and in fact would die two months later at the age of forty-six.

In proportional terms, therefore, Catalunya del Nord was one of the *départements* most opposed to the constitutional reform that would usher in the Vichy regime. This was so because its Socialist majority would eventually position itself against the dominant current within the Socialist ranks, something that would also happen in the departments of Var, Gironde, and Finistère. But this dissidence would come at a political cost: a significant gap opened immediately in the French Section of the Workers' International between the eighty or so representatives of the movement who supported Pétain's move to dissolve the Third Republic, and the more than thirty (including the Catalans) who opposed him.

In fact, the story of the deputies of Catalunya del Nord illustrates well the fate of those who rejected Pétain in the vote of July 10 at the Casino of Vichy. The purge was aimed not just at Socialists and Communists but a large number of Republicans of the Left and progressive Christian Democrats as well, who would soon be forced underground. Their position would spark fierce reactions among the population, at a time of unanimous support for Pétain during the summer of 1940. An anecdotal, but by no means insignificant, episode reflects these tensions well. When Joseph Rous returned to Prades, he was shouted down and assaulted by some of the inhabitants of this important town in the geographical center of Catalunya del Nord; Rous went into self-imposed exile in Ariège, where he would live under supervision. Pezières, on the other hand, died of a serious illness in March 1941. At Pezières's burial Louis Noguères publicly criticized Pétain, and as a result was sent into internal exile in various *départements* in the Midi: first to Corrèze, then to La Lozère, and finally to Aveyron, where he joined the Resistance.[15]

Apart from the careers of these politicians, a good example of the initial support that the regime enjoyed among broad sectors of the population was also reflected in the editorial line of the region's leading newspaper, *L'Indépendant*. On July 14, 1940, the editor-in-chief, Georges Brousse, began his leader column by praising the "National Revolution" and blaming the parliamentary regime for "our current disaster." Thus, despite recognizing that the power of Pétain surpassed even that of Napoleon, the only way out of the impasse was to throw oneself into

---

15 Jean Sagnes, "Le refus républicain: les quatre-vingt qui dirent 'non' à Vichy le 10 juillet 1940," *Revue d'histoire moderne et contemporaine* 38 (1991), 555–89. See also Louis Noguères, *Vichy, juillet 1940* (Paris: Fayard, 2000).

the arms of the *Maréchal* and to entrust the country's fate to him. After all, it was no longer a struggle between right and left – "these are the concerns of another era," as Brousse would argue, but now "there is only France . . . she needs the competition of all her sons and not partisan struggles."[16] From that point onward *L'Indépendant* would be fervently Pétainist, and would later become collaborationist. Brousse later changed his position; and was eventually murdered by the Nazis in April 1945, after being deported to Auschwitz and Buchenwald.[17]

The public acceptance of the regime would also find its supporters among the regionalists of Catalunya del Nord. For some of them, Pétain's arrival signified a ray of hope: the new regime seemed to herald the long-awaited political decentralization of the country. An example is Joan Amade, one of the main instigators of regionalism in Catalunya del Nord, and author of *L'Idée regionaliste* (The regionalist idea), published in 1912. His position can be traced in his correspondence: in a letter to the poet and cultural activist Carles Grando in October 1940, he affirmed:

> You are right; the time is favorable for the resumption of our Felibrian [a reference to the Félibrige movement] and regionalist life. You have seen that our governing authorities encourage learning local history, cultivating local dialects. The message of Marshal Pétain to Mrs. Mistral is a strong beautiful thing. I always lead the good fights: for the region, for France, for Latinity; this is the triptych of my faith, as well as of my activity."[18]

Indeed, for many French regionalists, heirs of the Félibrige movement founded by the Provencal writer Frédéric Mistral, the Pétainist revolution represented a window of opportunity for a structural remodeling of the state, which would once and for all abolish the Republican Constitution of 1875 and would restore to the old provinces their true *essence* that Jacobinism had absorbed. It was the promise that the National Revolution represented for the regionalization of the country that led broad regionalist sectors to support the regime and, indeed, quite a few nationalist militants in Brittany, Corsica, and other

---

16 Jean Arago, "La Révolution Nationale," *L'Indépendant*, July 14, 1940, 1.
17 For Brousse's life, see Bonet, *L'Indépendant des Pyrénées Orientales dans la guerre*, 654–55.
18 Letter from J. Amade to C. Grando dated October 18, 1940. Fons Grando, Universitat de Perpinyà. Quoted in Nicolas Berjoan, *L'identité du Roussillon (1780–2000): penser un pays catalan à l'âge des nations* (Perpignan: Éditions Trabucaire, 2011), 217.

peripheral nationalities in France would be ultra-collaborationist between 1940 and 1944.[19] This drift did not occur with the same intensity in Catalunya del Nord, although some nationalists in the region such as Alfons Miàs, founder of the Catalan movement Nostra Terra, remained loyal to Vichy until the very end.[20]

ESTABLISHMENT OF THE VICHY REGIME: LEGISLATION, PUBLIC ADMINISTRATION, AND DAILY LIFE (1940–1942)

Apart from this inevitably limited assessment of some of the reactions to the regime, the new political situation had its consequences in many other areas. It was a gradual process, in which the changes were brought about by remodeled institutions and a purged public administration. Of course, it is impossible now to deal comprehensively with the legislation introduced by Vichy in the area that interests us, but we can at least identify a set some of the most important features of this first constituent phase in Catalunya del Nord, through both the regime's management of the region and the implementation of its new directives.

A good example of this is the first major crisis that the Vichy authorities had to face, apart from the war itself. Just three months after the introduction of the first constitutional acts—and one week before the meeting between Hitler and Pétain at Montoire, at which the foundations for the collaboration between France and Germany would be established—both sides of the Catalan Pyrenees would suffer terrible flooding. In a particularly tragic October, more than fifty people were killed and large areas of Catalunya del Nord were devastated; indeed, the railroad communications with Spain would not be resumed until December 15 of the same year.[21] Five days later, the Fédération Départamentale des groupements et associations des sinistrées des Pyrénées Orientales (Departmental federation of the groups and associations

---

19 Despite the absence of references to Catalunya Nord, see Francis Arzalier, *Les régions du déshonneur: la dérive fasciste des mouvements identitaires au XXe siècle* (Paris: Vuibert, 2014).
20 Andreu Balent, "Alfons Mias (1903–1950). El fundador de Nostra Terra durant la Segona Guerra Mundial," in *Ultralocalisme. D'allò local a l'universal*, ed. Òscar Jané and Xavier Serra (Catarroja: Afers, 2013), 133–74. On the contacts between some Catalan nationalists and the Nazis, see Pere Grau, "Quand les Allemands courtisaient les catalanistes du Nord: un témoignage inédit et son context," *Lengas* 50 (2001), 77–101.
21 "Se reanuda por Cerbere la comunicación ferroviaria con Francia," *La Vanguardia*, November 17, 1940, 2.

of the victims of the Eastern Pyrenees) was set up to provide "mutual help and defense of the interests of the victims" caused by the floods of October 17 and 18. The headquarters was the Chamber of Commerce of Perpignan, and delegations were created immediately throughout the region.[22] The strength of these bodies, which to a certain extent kept alive the notion of solidarity that had characterized the reception given to the Spanish refugees, served to put pressure on the departmental authorities to organize calls for public tenders for the reconstruction or repair of the infrastructure damaged by the floods. On April 18, 1941, for example, a call for tenders was published for the repair of national highway 115, a road that linked the whole of the northern part of the Pyrenees, passing through the towns of Ceret and Prats de Molló and reaching the Spanish border at the Coll d'Ares. The prefecture would allocate 2.08 million francs, 90 percent of which would be paid to the firm that won the tender,[23] but the works were not declared "of public utility and urgent" until August 22. The aim was to reinforce the river banks and to redirect the course of the river by means of channeling systems.[24]

The example of the floods of October 1940 serves to illustrate how, through daily administrative procedures of this kind, the regime spread its tentacles farther and farther. Companies or individuals considered to be unenthusiastic about the regime were removed from public life. In fact, the administration would be one of the first areas in the state that would undergo a thorough-going purge: on July 17, 1940, a law on access to employment in the public administrations was approved that, among other provisions, expelled all magistrates or civil servants whose fathers were not French.

This was not the only legislation of this kind; nor would it be the last. A new law passed on November 16, 1940 introduced a reorganization of the municipalities, in which a great many mayors and municipal councilmembers were relieved of their functions and were replaced by *"délégations spéciales"* that had been in charge of the

---

22 The headquarters of the delegation of Perpignan, created on the following day, December 26, was the café Glacier at no. 87, Àv. de Maréchal Joffre. "Déclarations d'associations," *Journal Officiel de la République Française* 3, January 3, 1941, 48. From that time on, the official bulletin would be renamed the *Journal Officiel de l'État français*.

23 "Prefecture du Département des Pyrénées-Orientales – Avis d'adjudication publique," *Journal Officiel de l'État français* 101, April 11, 1941, 1568 (11).

24 "Communications et Travaux Publics," *Informations Générales* 52, August 26, 1941, 556.

municipal management until the official appointment was made by Vichy. December saw the abolition of the municipal councils of Mosset, Arles-sur-Tech, Perpignan, Taurinya, Fontrabiouse, Banyuls-sur-Mer, and the major town of Thuir, home to Byrrh, the famous aperitif, as well as the dismissal of the mayor of Rigarda on December 11, 1940.[25] During January 1941 it would be the turn of the town halls of Maury, Bages, Vernet, and Catllar,[26] and in the spring those of the communes of Finestret, Font-Romeu, Villelongue-de-la-Salanque, Corsavy, Laroque-des-Albères, Bouleternère, Toulouges, Lesquerde, Caramany, Saint-Paul-de-Fenouillet, Salses, Valmanya, Olette, and Py were officially closed due to the "the impossibility of forming a municipality capable of satisfactorily managing municipal affairs."[27] The purge continued: in the second half of 1941, nine more municipalities would be dissolved, so that by the beginning of 1942 roughly two thirds of the population of Catalunya del Nord were run by the new municipal authorities fully integrated in the structures of the regime.[28]

In the regional capital Perpignan, an order dated March 25, 1941 appointed the new city council, after a three-month period during which Antoine Castillon had acted as temporary mayor. The new council was made up of twenty-one members, among them winemakers, businessmen, and storeowners in the city, as well as representatives of newly created Pétainist organizations such as the Légion Française des Combattants (French Veterans' Legion).[29] This, then, was the social foundation of the new regime, in which all the sectors of French society that had been skeptical or directly hostile toward the Republic during the political upheavals of the previous decade felt entirely at home.

By 1942, then, thousands of people throughout the *département* had been affected by the purging of government offices and municipal

---

25 On these dissolutions, see the gazette of the ministry of the interior *Informations Générales* for December 10, 17, and 31, 1940.

26 Published in *Informations Générales* 22, January 28, 1941.

27 See *Informations Générales*, March 25, April 1, May 6 and 13, and June 6, 10, and 17, 1940.

28 In these towns perhaps the most significant events were the removal of the mayor Joseph Noell in Prats de Molló, and the dissolution of the municipal council of Canet. See *Informations Générales* 47, July 22, 1941 and *Informations Générales* 57, September 30, 1941, 913.

29 For a list of the members, see "Nominations de conseillers municipaux," *Journal Officiel de l'État français* 85, March 26, 1941, 1308. The mew mayor of Perpignan would be the doctor and soldier Ferdinand Coudray (1882–1962), who officially replaced the Socialist Laurent Baudru, mayor since the spring of 1937. See "Nominations de mairies – Pyrénées-Orientales," *Journal Officiel de l'État français* 64, March 5, 1941, 1017.

councils. A lukewarm attitude toward the new regime was enough; in the small town of Sournia in le Fenouillèdes, the only Occitan-speaking region of Catalunya del Nord, a municipal magistrate named Moulenat had, according to the official sources, "adopted a hostile attitude toward the creation of a local Legion branch and thereby failed in the duties of his office."[30] Freemasons and Jews in particular felt the full force of the purge. During 1941 and 1942, numerous lists would regularly appear in the *Journal Officiel de l'État Français* bearing the names of the people who were to be admonished or removed from their posts, or whose property was to be partially or totally confiscated, in accordance with the law of July 22, 1941. In the case of the Jews, the so-called General Commission for Jewish Affairs, led from March 1941 by the ultraconservative Xavier Vallat, and then from May 1942 by the philo-Nazi Louis Darquier de Pellepoix,[31] was responsible for applying anti-Semitic legislation. In Perpignan alone as many as thirty-five firms were taken over between November 1941 and 1942, from small and medium-sized businesses to movie theaters and banking entities such as the Société Bancaire du Sud-Ouest.[32] Many other properties were placed under the charge of a provisional administrator, or in some cases given over directly to the Church.[33]

At another level of government, one of the laws that introduced the greatest changes in the division of political and administrative powers was the creation of the regional prefects on April 22, 1941. The prefects were granted special powers in police matters and also in the running of the economy, as well as the regulation of the production and distribution of food. Therefore, although it was argued that the new law was imposed by the circumstances, the legislation in fact deployed part of the political program of regionalization included in the Pétainist National Revolution. For the French federalists, however, the reform fell far short of their expectations; as the text of the law itself stated: "a certain degree of decentralization can therefore be conceived that will not affect the essential prerogatives of the government but will, on the

---

30 "Révocation de magistrats municipaux," *Informations Générales* 24, February 11, 1941, 14.
31 Among the multiple books on the subject, see Laurent Joly, *Vichy dans la solution finale. Histoire du Comissariat Général aux questions juives, 1941–1944* (Paris: Grasset, 2006).
32 For this bank, see "Comissariat général aux questions juives – Administrateurs provisoires," *Journal Officiel de l'État français* 204, August 26, 1942, 2911.
33 For example, by a decree of May 11, 1943 the diocesan association of Perpignan was granted the land belonging to an old factory in Saint Cyprien. See *Journal Officiel de l'État français* 121, May 21, 1943, 1396.

contrary, enable it to exercise them in their fullness."[34] The *département* of the Eastern Pyrenees was grouped together with Hérault, Lozère, Aveyron, Tarn, and Aude under the region of Montpellier. With the return of Pierre Laval at the head of the government of Vichy in April 1942 the *départements* would recover their previous form, although they continued to function in a corporativist and nondemocratic manner.

The institutionalization of the system at the departmental level would also be reflected in other fields of public life. One example was the organization of sport, which for the Pétainists was the cornerstone for the regeneration of youth. Under Vichy, sports were now regulated by the Sports Charter created on December 20, 1940. In Catalunya del Nord, this move helped to reinstate the cross-border relations with the other side of the Catalan Pyrenees, which had been broken in 1936.[35] To some extent, this was possible thanks to the improvement of Hispanic-French relations during the first stage of the Vichy regime. These relations were regulated by the Spanish consular body in Catalunya del Nord, and especially by the Spanish consul in Perpignan, the Navarrese writer, journalist, and diplomat Román Oyarzun (1882–1968). He was a fervent traditionalist who, in the Spanish elections of February 1936, had been part of the candidacy of José María Gil Robles for Madrid. The Spanish authorities in the province of Girona were also involved in promoting contacts, and the civil governor Francisco J. Díaz visited the prefect of the Eastern Pyrenees on more than one occasion.[36]

After a long period of inactivity, sporting contacts were resumed in the fall of 1941. The Perpignan water polo team the *Enfants de Neptune* met Barcelona clubs in October of that year, and on Friday, December 26, the Barcelona soccer team traveled to Perpignan to play a game against the French champions, Racing Club Catalan.[37] In 1942 the prefect of the Eastern Pyrenees asked town councils to introduce "as much sport as possible . . . in official Labor Day programs." For its part, in early September 1942, the Excursionist and Sports Club of Girona

---

34 "Loi instituant des Préfets régionaux," *Informations Générales* 34, April 22, 1941, 235.

35 On the relations between sports clubs on both sides of the Pyrenees, see Daniel Roig i Sanz, "Mirall trencat: cultura popular i relacions transfrontereres entre el *nord* i el *sud* de Catalunya durant els anys trenta," *Mirmanda* 9 (2014), 110–21.

36 "Gobierno Civil – Secretaria Paticular," *El Pirineo*, August 13, 1943, 4. On the cross-border relations between the French/German and Spanish authorities, the main reference is Josep Clara, *Nazis a la frontera dels Pirineus Orientals* (Barcelona: Rafael Dalmau, 2016).

37 "Los Deportes – La natación," *La Vanguardia*, October 4, 1941, 7; "Los Deportes – Rugby," *La Vanguardia*, December 24, 1941, 6.

visited Perpignan for the first time since May 1936 to play against the *Enfants de Neptune*;[38] the same month, the Perpignan club returned the visit with a game attended by the mayor, Alberto de Quintana, and the French consul in Girona. There was a soccer game on the following day, Sunday, September 13, and Perpignan boxers were invited to a "great evening of boxing" during the St Narcís festivities in Girona.[39] In July 1943, swimmers from Girona would compete in an international meet held in Perpignan.[40]

How, then, should we evaluate the impact of the Vichy government on Catalunya del Nord? Among the multitude of possible explanations, the reports written by some foreign observers, albeit partial, provide an insight into everyday life in the *département*. The correspondent in Perpignan of the Barcelona newspaper *La Vanguardia*, Gustavo Gutiérrez-Gili, was well acquainted with the situation in the region. In December 1941 he described the new appearance of the French countryside as it tried to recover from the floods of the previous year: "As is well known, Roussillon gives the impression of being very similar to Catalonia. To the surprise of many, this important agricultural region is not superabundantly supplied, despite its extensive vine crops, the six million fruit trees planted in recent years, and its varied horticultural produce." Despite the measures applied by the regime and the ruralist rhetoric of the National Revolution, the vineyards and orchards, the principal sources of the *département*'s wealth, had been badly hit.[41] Indeed, on a trip through the countryside of the French Midi in April 1942, Gutiérrez Gili noted that, "although the fields are not barren, they are pale and lack the intense green color that characterizes them." The reporter quoted the French authorities' calls for solidarity and fraternity to prevent hunger and disorder. The shortage of food began to be a real problem.[42]

Despite the precarious situation of the local industry, Gutiérrez-Gili also commented on the speed with which the Vichy directives were put into practice. In September 1942 he would write that "the

---

38 "El G.E. y E.G. de Educación y Descanso, a Perpiñán," *El Pirineo*, September 2, 1942, 4.
39 "Sociedad," *El Pirineo*, September 15, 1942, 2: "Programa oficial de las Ferias y Fiestas de San Narciso," *El Pirineo*, October 29, 1942, 13.
40 "Brillante actuación de los nadadores gerundenses en el encuentro internacional de Perpiñán," *Los sitios de Gerona*, July 29, 1943, 4.
41 Gustavo Gutiérrez-Gili, "La nueva fisonomia rural francesa," *La Vanguardia*, December 21, 1941, 3.
42 For a compilation of his reports, see Gustavo Gutiérrez Gili, *Vichy-París: de la derrota a la liberación* (Barcelona: Castells-Bonet, 1945).

orders issued by Vichy are swiftly carried out." In Perpignan, he noted the presence of the French Legion, recruitment offices for volunteers to fight in Russia, youth organizations, mutual aid centers, centers for ex-prisoners, rural women's training centers, "and even those offices that are springing up in all the cities of France: The German Offices de Placement." Gutiérrez-Gili quoted the testimony of a German officer who had just arrived in Perpignan: "we feel no animosity toward France ... we must learn to understand each other."[43] Two months later, the *département* of the Eastern Pyrenees was occupied by Nazi troops.

CATALUNYA DEL NORD UNDER NAZI OCCUPATION (1942–1944)

On November 11, 1942 Operation Attila was launched – the military operation that would lead to the occupation of all the southern zone of France. The strategy was Berlin's response to the disembarkation of Anglo-American troops in North Africa. The next day, Thursday 12th, shortly before noon, the first German motorized units arrived in Perpignan. The occupation was immediate: the Germans quickly took over the main buildings and strategic sites in the city, as well as the aerodrome, where the first Messerschmitt 109 and Focke-Wulf 190 fighter aircraft were installed. Within a week, the German army already had military units all over the *département*.

The sequence of events has been described by witnesses and historians, some of whom have estimated that the army of occupation deployed up to between twenty and twenty-five thousand troops in the Eastern Pyrenees.[44] A large number of these troops would be billeted in Perpignan and in neighboring villages such as Bompas, but also across the border with Spain and on the Mediterranean coast. The French authorities cooperated fully with the occupation forces, in accordance with article 3 of the Armistice Convention according to which the prefects, as representatives of the Vichy government, were to collaborate and submit to the decisions of the German military commanders. This new situation caused some tension inside the departmental administration, and there were a number of more or less disguised desertions: after all, many officials in the Pétainist administration, without going as far as enlisting in the Resistance, would maintain an ambivalent attitude to-

---

43 Gustavo Gutiérrez-Gili, "Cuando el corazón habla," *La Vanguardia*, September 24, 1942, 5
44 Bonet, *Les Pyrénées Orientales dans la guerre*, 82–85.

ward official collaboration. This was especially so after the introduction of the Relève and then the STO (Service du travail obligatoire), the compulsory labor plan that sent young Frenchmen to work in factories in Germany – measures that, in many circles, would put an end to all loyalty to Vichy.

Indeed, despite the limitations of political sovereignty imposed on Vichy France after November 1942, the program of political and administrative reform continued. The regime simply adapted to the new circumstances. In fact, in the municipal councils at least, the purges seem to have lost the severity of the earlier period. Reports in the regime's official publication indicate that the purges did not disappear completely, but there is no doubt that the repression was less intense.

In this second stage of the occupation, the departmental councils had to be modified in accordance with the law of August 7, 1942. In Catalunya del Nord, the new members would be appointed by an official decree signed by Pierre Laval himself on January 23, 1943 in Vichy. The person responsible for its application was Charles Daupeyroux, who was appointed prefect of the Eastern Pyrenees in September 1942 and knew the German temperament well: he was from the *département* of the Yonne, in which he had been prefect in 1941 and now, in Perpignan, he was tasked with maintaining the collaboration of the French authorities with the German military command. The new general council was made up of the following members: Louis Marassé as president; Georges Clerc and François Laffon as vice-presidents; and François Brunet, Pierre Nöel-Trilles, and René Puig as secretaries. The other sixteen members were representatives of the *communes*: presidents of special delegations, or Pétainist mayors like Camille Augé of Port-Vendres.[45]

In fact, the powers of this general council were limited. The *département* had already lost some of its autonomy, as Daupeyroux's successor as prefect in August 1943, Jacques Henry, would acknowledge at the second ordinary session of the departmental council of the Eastern Pyrenees in autumn 1943: "the largest fraction of our staff, now 'nationalized', is no longer paid by us."[46] Therefore, although the

---

45   The rest of the council comprised Achille Batlle, mayor of Escaro; Marcel Ducassy, deputy mayor of Perpignan; Antoine Garrigue, mayor of Baho; Jacques Illes, mayor of Estoher; Camille Massina, mayor of Oms; Isidore Monceu, president of the special delegation of Mosset; Aimé Peprats, president of the special delegation of Claudies-de-Fenouillèdes; Lucien Piechon, mayor of Sournia; and Marius Sevene, mayor of Mont-Louis. "Conseils départementaux," *Journal Officiel de l'État français* 21, January 24, 1943, 220.

46   *Conseil Départemental du Département des Pyrénées-Orientales – Rapport du Préfet,*

regionalization of the country had begun and had reinforced the role of the regional prefects, it seems clear that the nationalization of the civil service, already approved in November 1940, clashed head on with any attempt to decentralize.

In these circumstances, what powers did the *départements* retain? The report by Jacques Henry identifies the three sectors that formed the basis of the functions of the departmental advisers during this latter stage: finances, public works and agriculture, and medical care and sanitation. The budget submitted for the year 1944 provides some data in this regard: of the 57.6 million francs budgeted, 23.5 million were assigned to maintaining social and medical assistance, of which the *département* only contributed 16.26 percent, while the municipalities provided 28.11 percent and the state 55.63 percent.[47] The distribution of a sector as important as social and medical assistance indicates that basic services continued to depend to a great extent on the state and municipal budgets. In fact, the *département*'s capacity for raising revenue would continue to be extremely low under the Vichy regime, and was limited to the sale or rental of departmental property, the sale of old paper, and the levying of some minor taxes linked to ownership. These revenues were absolutely necessary in order to be able to repair and maintain key infrastructures, water networks, telephone and sewage systems, to subsidize youth organizations, sports activities, and school cafeterias, and to provide essential help for the many families whose sons had been sent (or who had gone as volunteers) to factories in Germany under the STO.

Apart from this budgetary question, the tendency toward centralization would also be reflected in the remodeling of the local police forces, some of which now became part of the national police in the southern zone in June 1943. The new contingent for the whole of the Montpellier region (which included the *département* of the Eastern Pyrenees) comprised seven police secretaries, twelve inspectors of public safety, six brigade members, and seventy-six patrolmen.[48] In terms of public order, the German occupation would also have other consequences that would directly affect dozens of Catalan municipalities. An order issued by the ministry of the interior on February 18, 1943 created a

---

second ordinary session of 1943, Perpignan, 14.

47   For the budget for 1944 see ibid., 17–21. The report contains detailed information on the departmental expenditure for 1943.

48   Among the municipalities with a presence of state police were Rivesaltes and Port-Vendres. See *Journal Officiel de l'État français* 285, November 28, 1943, 3067–3068.

reserved area along the border with Spain, stretching from the French Basque Country to the Catalan coast, and completed the restrictions that had already been imposed on the Mediterranean coastline immediately after the occupation. In practice, therefore, these restrictions prohibited access to the area to anyone of any nationality who had not previously obtained a special permit issued by the police or by the brigades of the *gendarmerie*. Failure to comply could entail penalties of between 200 and 10,000 francs and the application of other administrative measures.[49]

Two months later, the municipalities that would be affected were specified. In Catalunya del Nord, almost all the Ceret district, with thirty-two municipalities, and half of the Prades district, with fifty-one, would be subject to the new special regime.[50] On the coast, the port of Port-Vendres, the eleventh largest port in mainland France in terms of volume of passengers at the outbreak of the war, would be the paradigmatic example of the impact on populations living in places of strategic importance. In fact, since 1940 the activity of Port-Vendres (like that of so many other ports) had already been badly hit, with a notable decrease in both merchandise and (above all) passenger traffic.[51] With the town now under the control of the Wehrmacht, the main goal of the Germans was to turn Port-Vendres into an impregnable fortress able to fight off any attempt by the Allies to disembark. The situation of the townsfolk would only grow worse in early 1944 when, by order of the German authorities, the prefecture decreed the evacuation of all the residents living within 15 km (just under 10 miles) of the coastline.

None of this stopped the regime from trying to push its political project forward. Between the spring and fall of 1943, part of the legislation on the corporative organization of agriculture, already approved on December 2, 1940, would be implemented. For its application at regional and departmental level, a series of measures were approved that radically changed the political and social relations of the French countryside. For instance, the key issue of the health of farming families was regulated in July 1943, with the constitution of the *Fédération de la mutualité agricole des Pyrénées-Orientales* (Mutual insurance federation of the Eastern Pyrenees). Also important were the modifications

---

49 "Zones réservées," *Informations Générales* 130, February 23, 1943, 280.
50 "Zone réservée de la frontière pyrénéenne," *Informations Générales* 143, May 25, 1943, 344–45.
51 Christian Xancho, "L'Occupation allemande de Port-Vendres: 12 novembre 1942 – 19 août 1944," *Domitia* 1 (2001): 85–98.

concerning the designations of origin, which would affect especially the wines of Rivesaltes and those of the whole of the region of Roussillon.[52]

After the purge of the administration, political control would also be extended over institutions and all kinds of smaller organizations. As an example, by order of July 12, 1943 a new board was appointed for the Chamber of Commerce of Perpignan. In fact, while the chamber's headquarters had already been taken over to house the offices of the German civil engineering and military organization Todt on December 27, 1942, a decree had modified its executive council, increasing its members from eighteen to twenty-one representatives. Once again, its composition reflects the support that many Catalan industrialists would give to the regime – among them, Jacques Violet, the producer of the aperitif Byrrh in Thuir, Charles de Lacroix, president of the electricity firm Ecoiffier, Jean Maler, a sandal manufacturer from Ceret, and the builder and metal industrialist René de Chefdebien of Perpignan, owner of the factory in which the first strike had broken out after the electoral victory of the French Popular Front in the hot June of 1936.[53]

From the summer of 1943 onward, the balance would begin to shift in favor of the Resistance. The gunfight at Puy-de-Dôme near Clermont-Ferrand in June 1943 between STO conscripts at a police station triggered a reaction that would affect Catalunya del Nord, and which would again be echoed by the journalist Gutiérrez-Gili, who wrote his first story on Catalunya del Nord in *La Vanguardia* for six months: by decision of the governing council, he reported, the Pyrenean spas were now out of bounds to any men (patients or not) between eighteen and sixty years of age.[54]

In this situation, the first Bastille Day (July 14) after the Nazi occupation of the territory presented a new opportunity to express general discontent. Numerous demonstrations were held simultaneously in cities in southern France, and in Perpignan dozens of protesters congregated in the Place d'Aragon.[55] This would not be the last demonstration: dates of symbolic importance such as the anniversary of the end of World War I inevitably became days of struggle against

52 See "Organismes professionnels de mutualité agrícola," *Journal Officiel de l'État français* 174, July 22, 1943, 1938–1939. On the question of the designation of origin, see *Journal Officiel de l'État français* 174, October 31, 1943, 2822.
53 "Chambres de Commerce," *Journal Officiel de l'État français* 170, July 17, 1943, 1909.
54 Gustavo Gutiérrez-Gili, "Una obligación penosa," *La Vanguardia*, June 17, 1943, 1.
55 Rémi Dalisson, *Les fêtes du Maréchal: propagande et imaginaire dans la France de Vichy* (Paris: Éditions Tallandier, 2007), 359.

the occupation, as manifested in a flyer that appeared in the Catalan town of Estagel: "Catalans, act on November 11, 1943."[56] Finally, after the disembarkation of Allied troops in Provence on August 15, 1944, the Germans announced that the *département* of the Eastern Pyrenees would be evacuated four days later. On the following day, Sunday, August 20, the Vichy regime was history.

Three key ideas emerge from the study of Vichy and its impact in the *département* of the Eastern Pyrenees. First of all, the effects of the traumatic changes that the population of Catalunya del Nord had suffered since 1936, and especially since 1939, with the massive influx of refugees from the Spanish War, should not be underestimated. This factor had an undeniable influence on the population's initial reception of Pétain and the Vichy regime, regardless of the political positions that the Catalan deputies would adopt. Second, despite the hopes that the Pétainist Révolution Nationale represented for the regionalist movement, the evolution of the regime did not satisfy the initial expectations of many of these social sectors. Thus, in spite of the notable structural changes, the decentralization project undertaken by Vichy was a resounding failure. And third, despite the difficulties of the wartime period, especially after the German occupation of the southern zone, Catalunya del Nord was fully integrated into the new political and administrative order restored by Vichy until its demise in the summer of 1944.

BIBLIOGRAPHY

Arzalier, Francis. *Les régions du déshonneur: la dérive fasciste des mouve-ments identitaires au XXe siècle*. Paris: Vuibert, 2014.

Azéma, Jean-Pierre, and François Bédarida, eds. *La France des années noire*, 2 volumes. Paris: Éditions du Seuil, 2000.

Balent, Andreu. "Alfons Mias (1903–1950). El fundador de *Nostra Terra* durant la Segona Guerra Mundial." In *Ultralocalisme. D'allò local a l'universal*, edited by Òscar Jané and Xavier Serra. Catarroja: Editorial Afers, 2013.

Balent, Andreu, and Nicolas Marty, eds. *Catalans du Nord et languedo-ciens et l'aide à la République espagnole (1936–1946)*. Perpignan: Presses Universitaires de Perpignan, 2009.

---

56 Ibid., 377.

Berjoan, Nicolas. *L'identité du Roussillon (1780–2000): penser un pays catalan à l'âge des nations*. Perpignan: Éditions Trabucaire, 2011.

Bonet, Gérard. *Les Pyrénées Orientales dans la guerre: les années de plomb, 1939–1944*. Ecully: Horvath, 1992.

———. *L'Indépendant des Pyrénées Orientales: un siècle d'histoire d'un quotidien, 1846–1950*. Perpignan: Publications de l'Olivier, 2004.

Clara, Josep. *Nazis a la frontera dels Pirineus Orientals (1942–1944)*. Barcelona: Rafael Dalmau, 2016.

Dalisson, Rémi. *Les fêtes du Marechal: propagande et imaginaire dans la France de Vichy*. Paris: Éditions Tallandier, 2007.

Deulonder, Xavier. *França i Catalunya*. Barcelona: Bubok, 2017.

Grau, Pierre. "La Catalogne Française revendiquée par l'Espagne." *Etudes Roussillonnaises*, volume 9 (1989): 159–68.

———. "Quand les Allemands courtisaient les catalanistes du Nord: un témoignage inédit et son contexte." *Lengas* 103 (2001): 77–101.

Grenard, Fabrice. *La drôle de guerre. L'entrée en guerre des Français: setembre 1939–mai 1940*. Paris: Belin, 2015.

Gutiérrez-Gili, Gustavo. *Vichy-París: de la derrota a la liberación*. Barcelona: Castells-Bonet, 1945.

Hugues, Pierre. *Naissance et développement des mouvements fascistes en Catalogne-Nord dans les années 30. PSF et PPF*. Perpignan: Université de Perpignan, mémoire de maîtrise, 1977.

Joly, Laurent. *Vichy dans la solution finale. Histoire du Comissariat Général aux qüestions juives, 1941–1944*. Paris: Grasset, 2006.

Larrieu, Jean, and Ramon Gual. *Catalunya del Nord, 1939–1944. Vichy, l'Occupation nazie et la Résistance catalane*, 4 volumes. Prades: Terra Nostra, 1994–2000.

Noguères, Louis. *Vichy, juillet 40*. Paris: Fayard, 2000.

Roig Sanz, Daniel. "*Mirall trencat:* cultura popular i relacions transfrontereres entre *nord* i *sud* de Catalunya durant els anys trenta." *Mirmanda* 9 (2014): 110–21.

Sagnes, Jean. "Le refus républicain: les quatre-vingts parlamentaires qui dirent 'non' à Vichy le 10 juillet 1940." *Revue d'histoire moderne et contemporaine* 38 (1991): 555–89.

Sagnes, Jean, and Sylvie Caucanas, eds. *Les Français et la Guerre d'Espagne: actes du colloque de Perpignan*. Perpignan: Presse Universitaires de Perpignan, 2004.

Séguéla, Matthieu. *Franco-Pétain: les secrets d'une alliance*. Paris: Albin Michel, 1992.

Sentís, Georges. *Les communistes et la Résistance dans les Pyrénées-Orientales*. Perpignan: Editions Marxisme, 1992.

Xancho, Christian. "L'Occupation allemande de Port-Vendres: 12 novembre 1942 – 19 août 1944." *Domitia* 1 (2001): 85–98.

Chapter 16

The Catalan (and Spanish) Republicans under Nazism[1]

Antoni Segura i Mas

THE END OF THE CIVIL WAR AND EXILE

On February 10, 1939, the Civil War in Catalonia officially came to an end. Some small groups of Republicans held out until February 13; they crossed the French border at the Coll d'Ares (Ripollès), where they suffered more losses because of the sudden fall in the temperature during the night, and via Osséja, in France. Two weeks earlier, Republican Catalonia had set out on the road to exile, as the bombs of Franco's aviation rained down.

On the night of January 27–28, France opened the frontier to allow women and children to cross. Three days later the wounded were admitted, and on February 5 the authorization arrived for the troops. That night alone, 20,000 combatants crossed the border, giving up their arms to the French authorities. The president of the Generalitat, Lluís Companys, and the Basque *lehendakari* José Antonio Aguirre sought refuge in France. Alongside the Catalans, refugees from all over Spain

1   This paper was written under the auspices of the Group of Research and Analysis of the Present-day World (Granma) of the Center for International Historical Studies (CEHI) at the University of Barcelona, Consolidated Research Group of the Generalitat of Catalonia, and the R & D Project of the Ministry of Economy and Competitiveness (HARD2013-41460-P), "La Guerra Civil española y tres décadas de guerra en Europa: herencias y consecuencias (1914–1945)," 2014.

had flocked to Catalonia to escape Franco's occupation: in the middle of 1938, the total number of refugees in Catalonia was 702,000: 121,000 from Asturias and Santander, 50,000 from Euskadi, 39,000 from Aragón, 339,000 from Extremadura and New Castile, and 153,000 from Andalusia. Toward the fall, the figure had reached a million.[2]

In total, Javier Rubio estimates that at the beginning of March 1939 there were some 440,000 Republican refugees in France: 170,000 women, children, and elderly; 220,000 soldiers and militiamen; 40,000 able-bodied male civilians; and 10,000 wounded.[3] Rubio's estimates coincide with the French figures that record the presence of 441,000 Spanish refugees on April 1, 1939. On March 9, the French minister of the interior spoke of 450,000 refugees, but the census of the Légation du Mexique in France raised the figure to 527,843. Subtracting those who migrated to other countries (about 20,000 in all) and those who returned to Spain shortly thereafter (between 30,000 and 40,000 able-bodied men and about 160,000 elderly, women, and children), some 272,000 refugees remained in France.[4]

Joan Villarroya adds around 70,000 who returned to Spain via Irun between February 1 and 19 and subtracts some 45,000 refugees who were already in France before 1939. This gives a total of 470,000 refugees arriving from Catalonia between late January and early February 1939. By the end of the year there were only "182,000 refugees, distributed amoing France, the Soviet Union, other European countries, and the Americas."[5] Jordi Guixé notes that, between February 27 and March 15, some 30,000 Republican soldiers returned.[6]

In conclusion, nearly half a million Republican refugees crossed over from Catalonia to France. Roughly half of these returned to Spain in the following months and others migrated to other countries. In 1940 between 160,000 and 200,000 exiles remained in France. Most were interned in concentration camps: 275,000 in February 1939; 162,932 in June; 95,336 in July; and some 5,000 in November 1940. In addi-

---

2   Joan Villarroya i Font, *Desterrats. L'exili català de 1939* (Barcelona: Editorial Base, 2002), 14.
3   Javier Rubio, *La emigración en la guerra civil de 1936–1939: Historia del éxodo que se produce con el fin de la II República española*, 3 vols. (Madrid: San Martín, 1977).
4   Amicale des Anciens Guérilleros, *Guérilleros en Terre de France. Les Républicains espagnols dans la Résistance française*, preface Léo Figuères (Pantin: Le Temps des Cerises éditeurs, 2000), 17.
5   Villarroya i Font, *Desterrats*, 58.
6   Jordi Guixé Coromines, "El regreso forzado y la persecución contra los exiliados en Francia," *Historia del Presente* 18 (2011), 106.

tion to repatriations, the fall in the number of internees was due to the provision of October 1939 and the offer of employment made by the government and the French army to the workers and farmers.[7] Another point is that it is impossible to determine exactly what percentage of the exiles from Spain were from Catalonia or the Països Catalans.[8] In any case, the percentage appears to have been between 40 percent and 50 percent.

WORLD WAR II

On September 1, 1939 Germany invaded Poland. Two days later, France and the United Kingdom declared war on Germany. On September 17, under a secret clause of the Ribbentrop-Molotov Pact, the USSR invaded Poland and the Polish government was forced into exile. Shortly afterward the USSR attacked Finland, and in June 1940 the Baltic Republics were annexed.

Back in Catalunya Nord,[9] in October 1939 a new regulation transformed the camps of Argelès, Sant Cyprien, Barcarès, Agde, Bram, Gurs, and Septfonds into work centers. The exiles had little option: "they either joined the CTEs [*compagnies de travailleurs étrangers*, or companies of foreign workers], or the French army, or they returned to Spain. Enlisted by force, most were sent to defend the famous [and useless] Maginot Line; others were sent to Yonne, or to the mines of Crevant, to Dunkirk, to the French-Italian Alps, or to Indre."[10] During the battle of France in May–June 1940 the CTEs were militarized and some 60,000 Spanish Republicans aged between twenty and forty-eight

---

7   Villarroya i Font, *Desterrats*, 42–43 and 55–56. On the "reception" of the Republican exiles, see, among others, Alted, *La voz de los vencidos, el exilio republicano de 1939* (Madrid: Aguilar, 2005); Daniel Díaz Esculies, *Entre filferrades: un aspecte de l'emigració republicana dels Països Catalans (1939–1945)* (Barcelona: La Magrana, 1993); Geneviève Dreyfus-Armand, *El exilio de los republicanos españoles en Francia: de la guerra civil a la muerte de Franco* (Barcelona: Crítica, 2000); Jordi Font Agulló, ed., *Reflexionant l'exili. Aproximació a l'exili republicà: entre la història, l'art i el testimoniatge* (Catarroja and Barcelona: Editorial Afers; Museu Memorial de l'Exili, 2010); Dolores Pla Brugat, *Els exiliats catalans a Mèxic. Un estudi de la immigració republicana* (Catarroja and Barcelona: Editorial Afers, 2000); and Villarroya i Font, *Desterrats*.
8   The term Països Catalans refers to a larger territorial entity, covering the areas in which the Catalan language is spoken.
9   The area inside France that corresponds approximately to the modern *département* of the Eastern Pyrenees, historically part of Catalonia.
10   Testimony of Joan Pagès and Joan Surroca in Montserrat Roing, *Els catalans als camps nazis* (Barcelona: Edicions 62, 1977; Barcelona: Edicions 62, 2003), 77–79.

were incorporated into the French Army, fighting in the battles of Dunkirk, the Somme, the Lorraine, and the Loire. Spanish volunteers also joined the French Foreign Legion in Algiers. With the defeat of the French and the British, more than thirty thousand soldiers and officers were taken prisoner; those who managed to avoid capture tried to reach Spain with the help of the first escape networks.[11]

Republican exiles also participated in the Franco-British expedition to Narvik in Norway in May–June 1940. They joined the 13th Demi-Brigade of the Foreign Legion, created in February 1940 and consisting of about 2,000 troops, half of whom were veterans of the Spanish Civil War and the International Brigades. One hundred and twenty of them are buried in the French cemetery.[12] The tombstones bear some thirty names and surnames of Spanish or Catalan ancestry such as sergeant Joan Ramon Pujol from Vilallonga (Tarragonès), captured and shot by the Nazis, and Carles Busquets, who in fact survived and was later decorated for heroism.[13]

On June 17, 1940 France surrendered, and on the 22nd Marshal Pétain signed the armistice with Germany. The country was divided into two: one under full German occupation and the other under the control of the collaborationist regime of Vichy.[14] In total, the French Army had some 80,000 casualties, including about 5,000 Republicans from Spain; between 10,000 and 12,000 Spaniards were captured by the German Army.[15]

---

11   Claude Benet, *Guies, fugitius i espies. Camins de pas per Andorra durant la Segona Guerra Mundial*, 2nd ed. (Andorra la Vella: Editorial Andorra, 2013), 24.

12   The names appear on the tombstones with their rank, company, and date of death: reproduced in Agustín Roa Ventura, "Los españoles en la batalla de Narvik," *Historia y vida* 119 (1978): 120–25.

13   Gonzalo Romero Yáñez-Barnuevo, "Los españoles en la batalla de Narvik, 1940" (2005), in *Paisajes de Guerrilla: Españoles contra el III Reich: Narvik, 1940*, blog, April 3, 2010. At http://paisajesdelaguerrilla.blogspot.com.es/2010/04/espanoles-en-narvik-1940.html; Daniel Arasa, "Españoles en todas las trincheras," *La Vanguardia*, suppl., *Revista*, Sunday, May 1, 2005, 11.

14   See the map of the division of France in Giselher Wirsing, ed., *The War in Maps 1939/40* (New York: German Library of Information, 1941), 53 and Sebastián Agudo Blanco, "Los republicanos españoles en la resistencia francesa de la zona sur: siguiendo el ejemplo de las Brigadas Internacionales," in *Las Brigadas Internacionales: nuevas perspectivas en la historia*, ed. Josep Sánchez Cervelló and Sebastián Agudo (Tarragona: Universitat Rovira i Virgili, 2015), 268.

15   Arasa, "Españoles en todas las trincheras," 11; Amicale des Anciens Guérilleros, *Guérilleros en Terre de France*, 17.

THE REPUBLICAN EXILES IN THE FRENCH RESISTANCE

After the armistice, many exiles joined the French resistance. This meant that, if they were captured, they would be tortured, killed, or deported to a Nazi camp. This was the fate of the brothers Conrad and Josep Miret i Musté, PSUC (Partit Socialista Unificat de Catalunya, Unified Socialist Party of Catalonia) militants,[16] and Joan Martorell, who created the first guerrilla group in the Mauriac area of Auvergne until he was arrested and deported to Dachau.

Through the MOI (the Main d'oeuvre immigrée, immigrant labor, an organization created in 1926 by the French Communist Party to organize foreign workers according to nationality) many Communists and Republicans joined the Franc Tireurs et Partisans Français (French snipers and partisans, FTPF) and other resistance organizations. Along the southern French border, the Spanish Communist Party (Partido Comunista de España, PCE) organized the resistance in a very wide arc covering the whole of the Pyrenees.[17]

In April 1942, the PCE created the Fourteenth Guerrilla Corps, the future military arm of the Unión Nacional Española (Spanish National Union, UNE), which aimed to bring together all the anti-Franco forces to fight the Germans and to "reconquer Spain" (its newspaper was called *Reconquista de España*). Shortly before the Normandy landings, the total of Spanish guerrillas in the resistance rose from 6,000 in early 1944 to 10,000 in May.[18] Jesús Monzón, the leader of the PCE, believed that the time was right for the reconquest of a part of Spain and for an insurrection that would force the Allies to intervene. In the summer and fall of 1944, the UNE organized an invasion of the Val d'Aran in which socialist and anarchist militants also participated, but which eventually ended in failure.[19]

---

16 Jorge Torres Hernández, "Los hermanos Miret i Musté. Los catalanes Conrado y Josep, organizadores de la Résistance en Francia," in *Las Brigadas Internacionales: nuevas perspectivas en la historia*, ed. Josep Sánchez Cervelló and Sebastián Agudo (Tarragona: Universitat Rovira i Virgili, 2015), 364–76.

17 See the map showing communist resistance in the southern zone in Agudo Blanco, "Los republicanos españoles en la resistencia francesa de la zona sur," 270.

18 Jean Ortiz, "La epopeya de los guerrilleros españoles en Francia," in *Las Brigadas Internacionales: nuevas perspectivas en la historia*, ed. Josep Sánchez Cervelló and Sebastián Agudo (Tarragona: Universitat Rovira i Virgili, 2015), 338.

19 Antoni Segura, "La lluita armada: la Guerra Civil continua," in *La guerra civil a Catalunya: l'exili*, ed. J.M. Solé Sabaté, vol. 6 (Barcelona: Edicions 62, 2007). The CNT refused to participate in the invasion, regarding it as a communist ploy that was doomed to failure. Nonetheless, some anarchists and socialists took part on their

Before the end of the Civil War, the CNT (Confederación Nacional del Trabajo, the Spanish confederation of anarcho-syndicalist labor unions) had split into two. The resulting organizations were the General Council of the Libertarian Movement, created in Paris in February 1939 and led by the exiled Catalan leaders Josep Esgleas i Jaume (Germinal Esgleas), Federica Montseny, Joan García Oliver, Francesc Isgleas, and Fidel Miró, and a National Committee that comprised the federations of the Center and the South where the war continued. The CNT was now not only in exile, but divided. The drowning in the Marne River of the Secretary General Mariano Rodríguez Vázquez (*Marianet*), on June 18, 1939, did nothing to encourage the 80,000 exiled CNT members, who were unsure whether to cooperate with other anti-fascist forces or to pursue their libertarian orthodoxy. The differences were accentuated by the creation of the Delegation of the CNT of Spain in Mexico in June 1941, which sought cooperation with all the Republican parties, including the PCE, while the CNT members exiled in North Africa continued to defend the tenets of anarcho-syndicalism.[20] For their part, certain CNT leaders who were considered dangerous by the French authorities were interned in the camps of Saint-Cyprien and Vernet and many of them, including Antoni Ortiz (Barcelona, 1907–1996), were finally deported to Algeria, where they enlisted in the Free French Army.[21]

In short, the anarchists who participated in the resistance often did so in cooperation with groups of the UNE, or alternatively on their own initiative and without any coordination. The exception was in Mauriac in the *département* of Cantal, where in 1942 some six hundred CNT members created a combat group that made contact with other groups of libertarian combatants.[22] Some anarchists who took part in the resistance would later be active in the Catalan *maquis*, such as Francesc Sabaté Llopart, *Quico*, and Ramon Vila Capdevila, *Caracremada*. Anarchists also participated in General Leclerc's army and in the insurrection and liberation of Paris: "the column, of some 160 men, commanded by French captain Dronne, constituted by 146

---

own initiative: Antonio Tellez (Tarragona, 1921–Perpignan, 2005) joined, but left on seeing that the operation had no chance of success. Personal communication with Antonio Tellez, summer 2004.

20 Ángel Herrerín López, "La CNT en el exilio de la organización a la escisión," *Historia Social* 48 (2004): 27–35.

21 See the biography in Juan J. Gallardo and José M. Márquez, *Ortiz, general sin Dios ni amo* (Barcelona: Ed. Hacer, 1999).

22 Quoted in Amicale des Anciens Guérilleros, *Guérilleros en Terre de France*, 200–1.

anti-fascist Spaniards, mostly anarchists. Their tanks bore the names of *Durruti, Ebro, Don Quijote, Teruel, Brunete, Guernica, Guadalajara*, etc."[23]

Spanish and Catalan Republicans could pay a very high price for their participation in the resistance: jail sentences, executions, and deportation to the Nazi extermination camps. In February 1944, there was a revolt at the prison in Eysses (Lot-et-Garonne), between Bordeaux and Toulouse, in which the Vichy government had incarcerated the most dangerous *résistants* since 1943. Inside the prison a resistance group had got hold of some weapons; on the night of February 19–20, the inmates took the prefect, a subprefect, and several dozen prison guards hostage, but the help they were expecting from outside never materialized; with the help of the Germans, the French authorities regained control. The reprisals were ferocious: twelve prisoners were executed, among them the Catalans Jaume Serot, an anarchist from a town near Lleida, and Domènec Serveto Bertran, probably a PSUC member. Among other Catalans involved in the revolt were Jaume Ballester (L'Ampolla), Ramon Buj Ferrer (Barcelona), Lluís Canadell (Barcelona), Joaquim and Modest Canet (Girona), Josep Capella (L'Ametlla de Mar), Josep Comabella (Ponts), Rafael Laborda (Girona), Joan Martorell (Barcelona), Amadeu Pons (Borges Blanques), and César Zayuelas (Barcelona) as well as the Valencians Josep Cardona, Guardia Fernández, Miguel Portolés, and Antoni Turiel. On May 30, 1944, 1,200 prisoners were handed over to the Gestapo and deported to Dachau.[24]

The Nazi repression of the population and the exiles also includes episodes that were not related to the resistance. Four days after the Normandy landings, a unit of the SS Division Das Reich carried out a punitive operation against the French town of Oradour-sur-Glane, near Limoges. Just after two o'clock in the afternoon, a column of soldiers entered the town and divided the population into two groups: the men were shot, and the women and children were locked in the church, which was then set on fire. More than six hundred people died, 38 percent of them women and 32 percent children. The list included nineteen refugees of Spanish or Catalan descent. Entire families were murdered, like the family of Juan Telles from Zaragoza and Maria Domínguez from Barcelona and their three children, two of them born in Barcelona and the youngest born already in exile in Limoges; the family of José Serrano de

---

23 Ortiz, "La epopeya de los guerrilleros españoles en Francia," 339–40.
24 Daniel Arasa, *50 Històries catalanes de la segona guerra mundial* (Barcelona: Laia, 1998) and Montserrat Roig, *Els catalans als camps nazis* (Barcelona: Edicions 62, 1977; Barcelona: Edicions 62, 2003).

Purchena (Almeria), a teacher, and Maria Pardo from Murcia and their three children (two of them twins) born in Limoges; the Gil-Espinosa family from Alcañiz, with two twin daughters; Antonia Pardo from Murcia and her nine-year-old daughter Núria, born in Barcelona; and the Massachs sisters from Sabadell.[25]

REPUBLICAN EXILES IN THE NAZI EXTERMINATION CAMPS

The majority of Republican exiles taken prisoner in the battle of France or as members of the resistance faced a particularly grim fate. As the Franco regime did not recognize them as Spaniards, they were considered stateless and were transferred to concentration camps. Seven thousand were sent to Mauthausen. The brutality of their treatment in the Mauthausen-Gusen complex is reflected by Joaquim Amat-Piniella in the autobiographical novel *K.L. Reich* (1968) and by the photographs of Francesc Boix.[26] The first Spanish prisoners arrived on August 6, 1940; the commemorative gravestone in the camp memorial indicates that, in all, some seven thousand Spaniards were sent there. Just over two thousand survived. In total, around ten thousand Republican exiles were deported to the Nazi camps.

This figure for the number of deportees is given by Ramiro Santisteban Castillo, President of the Spanish Federation of deportees and political internees in Mauthausen, in the preface to *Libro-memorial de los deportados españoles en los campos nazis (1940–1945)* by Benito Bermejo and Sandra Checa (2006). It is confirmed by Joaquim Amat-Piniella, who recalls that, "At Mauthausen and its satellite camps along the Danube some 70 percent of the 7,500 exiled Catalans and Spaniards who were interned fell victim to hunger, work, and ill-treatment."[27]

After decades of silence and oblivion, it is not easy today to reconstruct the lists of the Republican deportees in the Nazi camps. So

---

25 The Town Hall of Oradour sur Glane has an incomplete list, with some additions from the families of the victims: http://static.blog4ever.com/2006/01/63466/artfichier_63466_75116_201004121714651.pdf.
26 On Francesc Boix, the only Catalan (and the only Spaniard) to testify against the Nazi regime in the Nuremberg Judgment (1945–46) see Benito Bermejo, *Francesc Boix, el fotògraf de Mauthausen* (Barcelona: RBA La Magrana, 2002) and the documentary by Llorenç Soler, *Francisco Boix: un fotógrafo en el infierno* (Área de Televisión and Canal+, 2000). At https://www.youtube.com/watch?v=-04d6olo-EU.
27 Joaquim Amat-Piniella, *K.L. Reich (Els catalans en els camps d'extermini de Hitler)*. 2nd ed. (Barcelona: Club Editor, 1968), author's note, 7.

far, four studies have attempted to do so. In chronological order of appearance, *Triangulo azul. Los republicanos españoles en Mauthausen* (1969; 1979) by Manuel Razola and Mariano C. Campo, originally published in French in 1969, includes the name and surnames, the place of birth, and the place and date of death of the 4,074 Spanish Republicans who died and of the 136 who disappeared between August 6, 1940 and May 5, 1945. *Els catalans als camps nazis* (1977; 2003) by Montserrat Roig, is based on interviews, documents, and personal accounts and includes an appendix according to *comarca* (a Spanish territorial division corresponding roughly to "county") with the name and surnames, the place and date of birth, dates of the transfers (and their number in the Stalag of origin),[28] the closest living relative located, and the date of the death of citizens born or resident in the Països Catalans who died in Mauthausen or its satellite camps. The four volumes of the *Livre-mémorial des déportés de France* (2004), with its database (http://www.bddm.org/liv/index_liv. php), includes data on 89,390 deportees (ten percent of them women) in the various camps, distributed in 363 lists including four (lists III.1 to III.4) of Spanish Republicans transferred from various Stalags to Mauthausen between August 1940 and August 1942. The lists indicate the names and surnames, the place and date of birth, the date of death or liberation, and the Stalag of origin. Finally, the aforementioned work by Bermejo and Checa (2006) contains a database (http://pares.mcu.es/ Deportados/servlets/ServletController) that provides deportees' names, surnames, date of birth, and date of death or of liberation.

Montserrat Roig takes as her reference the lists of the Republican deportees to Mauthausen copied by Casimir Climent i Sarrion, who worked in the camp office, and are now preserved at the Amicale de Mauthausen in Paris. The account is highly detailed:

> The first group transport of Republicans arrived at Mauthausen on August 6, 1940. They numbered 392, and very few would survive: among those who did were the Catalans Joan de Diego and Salvador Ginestà, who would remain in the camp for exactly four years and nine months. 1940 and 1941 were the years that Mauthausen devoured the greatest number of Republicans. On November 26, 1940, the 47 Republicans in the group recorded by Casimir Climent were registered in the camp office, among them around twenty Catalans: only seven would come out

---

28 *Stalags:* German prisoner of war camps – not for civilians, in accordance with the Geneva Convention of 1929.

alive. From August 6, 1940 to June 6, 1941, 5,998 Republicans would arrive. A year later, a thousand more and, from then on, the newcomers would be the NNs. By April 16, 1945, 7,189 Republicans had been sent to Mauthausen. Two thirds died.[29]

According to Joan Villarroya i Font, "The first Catalan to lose his life in this sinister concentration camp was Miquel Maydeu Pallerola, from Albiol, Baix Camp, who died at age twenty-seven on September 13, 1940."[30] According to Roig, the total number of deportees was 10,000; 7,189 at Mauthausen and its *kommandos*; 1,000 to Dachau, Buchenwald, and so on. In all, 6,015 died in the camps or as a result of deportation: 477 (153 Catalans) in Mauthausen; 3,839 (1,582 Catalans) in Gusen; 499 gassed in the castle of Hartheim; 200 in other camps; and 1,000 in transport, in the Gestapo prisons, or in bombardments.[31]

Overall, according to Roig, around 60 percent of the Republican deportees in Nazi camps did not survive. Bermejo and Checa give a similar figure.[32] The high mortality is due to the fact that the bulk of deportees who arrived in Mauthausen between August 1940 and the middle of 1942 were considered to be stateless (Franco was indifferent to their fate), and their treatment was worse than that meted out to other nationalities.[33] The inclusion of more than four hundred missing

---

29 Roig, *Els catalans als camps nazis*, 183–84. The term NN is a reference to the order of the supreme commander of the Wehrmacht, Marshal Wilhelm Keitel, *Nacht und Nebel* (Night and Fog, or NN) of December 12, 1941, which laid down a double punishment for those who opposed the Germans. On the one hand, internment in concentration camps until the end of the war; on the other, consignment to oblivion and invisibility. "According to the law, then, the NN had disappeared from the world of the living ... Another term used was *Meerschaum*, which means "sea foam"; like the ephemeral life of the bubbles that form on the liquid, the deportees thus classified were destined to disappear without leaving any trace ... In Mauthausen there were 33 NN Republicans [among them some Catalans] and 31 *Meerschaum*." Roig, *Els catalans als camps nazis*, 196–97.

30 Villarroya i Font, *Desterrats*, 90.

31 Roig, *Els catalans als camps nazis*, 200–1.

32 Benito Bermejo and Sandra Checa, *Libro-memorial de los deportados españoles en los campos nazis (1940–1945)* (Madrid: Ministerio de Educación, Cultura y Deporte, 2006), 21.

33 On September 25, 1940, a Gestapo circular stated that Spanish Republicans and International Brigade members captured in the Battle of France were not prisoners of war and were to be sent to concentration camps. At that time, Ramón Serrano Suñer, Franco's Minister of Foreign Affairs, visited Germany and was received by the Nazi authorities, including Hitler. Between August 20 and October 3, 1940, the Spanish government received four requests from the German embassy to take charge of 2,000 "reds" interned in Angoulême in France. There was no response, except for a handwritten note of April 23, 1941: "it seems inappropriate to do anything in favor of these internees: to be filed." At the beginning of September 1940, a train with 907 deportees arrived in Mauthausen, where the males aged over thirteen were interned and the women and children repatriated. Only 13 percent

increases the figure of victims still further: in any case, it was well above the mortality rate among the French, which was between 39.9 percent and 43.3 percent.[34]

The *Livre-Mémorial* database reproduces the four lists of the names of the 6,692 Republicans (including members of the International Brigades) transferred from the Stalags to Mauthausen between August 1940 and the end of 1941.

---

of the 470 internees survived. Bermejo and Checa, *Libro-memorial de los deportados españoles*, 19–20; Montse Armengou, *El comboi dels 927*, TV documentary (TV3-30 minuts, 2004); Fundación Acción Pro Derechos Humanos, at http://www.derechoshumanos.net/lesahumanidad/denuncia-convoy-de-angulema.htm.

34 This figure depends on whether the missing are included. See *Livre-Mémorial des déportés de France arrêtés par mesure de répression et dans certains cas par mesure de persécution 1940–1945*, vol. 1 (Paris: Fondation pour la Mémoire de la Déportation-Éditions Tirésias, 2004), 52. At http://www.bddm.org/liv/index_liv.php.

SPANISH REPUBLICANS DEPORTED TO MAUTHAUSEN, AUGUST 1940–AUGUST 1942

Date of arrival in Mauthausen	Total	Spanish	%	Deaths	%	Liberated	%	Situation unknown	%	Released by Germans	%
Aug. 1940	1.054	1.054	100.0	756	71.4	204	19.3	93	8.8	1	0.1
Sep. 1940– Jan 1941	3.386	3.347	98.5	2.335	68.7	815	24.0	202	6.0	34	1.0
Feb– Apr. 1941	1.311	1.310	99.4	725	55.0	487	37.0	99	7.5	-	-
May 1941– Aug.1942	990	981	94.4	513	49.4	400	38.5	69	6.6	8	0.8
TOTALS	6.741	6.692	99.3	4.329	64.7	1.906	28.5	463	6.9	43	0.6

Fondation pour la Mémoire de la Déportation, Banque de Donnes, *Livre Mémorial*:
http://www.bddm.org/liv/index_liv.php

The database includes 79 deportees who arrived in Mauthausen after 1942. This gives a total of 6,771 deportees, a slightly lower figure than that provided by Roig. The total number of deaths coincides, since Roig gives the figure of 4,316. The *Livre-Mémorial* shows that the real mortality rate (that is, of identified deportees) stands at 65 percent and may reach 72 percent if the calculation includes deportees whose fate is unknown; thus, only a quarter of the Republicans deported to Mauthausen between 1940 and 1942 survived. They were militants and political leaders who had participated in the Civil War, fought with the French Army, or who had been involved in the resistance. The figures indicate that the Republican deportees endured worse treatment than other nationalities (with the exception of the Jews and, perhaps, Soviet soldiers). By way of example, of the 4,864 deportees arriving from France (95.1 percent of them French) between the spring of 1943 and April 1944, 2,614 survived – that is, a mortality rate of 46.3 percent. Consequently, the probabilities of survival were inversely proportional to the time spent in the camp. In the case of the Republicans the death rate falls with shorter time periods. The mortality rate of the Republican deportees in Mauthausen coincides with the figure given by the *Amicale des anciens guerrilleros*, which raises the figure to 9,067, of whom 6,748 would have been killed (4,200 in Gusen); this gives a mortality rate of 70 percent.[35] From the middle of 1942 onward, captured resistance members began to arrive, either in Mauthausen or in other camps such as Dachau and Buchenwald. Republicans accounted for around 10 percent of the total number of deportees from France during World War II.

Finally, we need to determine how many of the deported Republicans came from Catalonia and the Països Catalans. However, four decades after Roig's study in 1977, very little can be added today since we face a methodological problem that is difficult to solve. It is true that the most important sources include lists of names of deportees and indicate their place and date of birth, but only an individualized study of each one would tell us whether they were living in their place of origin when the Civil War broke out or whether they had emigrated to Catalonia, which is where they pursued their political activities and where they found themselves in July 1936. Indeed, Roig considers both citizens born in the Països Catalans and those who were born elsewhere in Spain and migrated to Catalonia as Catalan deportees.

---

35 Amicale des Anciens Guérilleros, *Guérilleros en Terre de France*, 245.

According to Bermejo and Checa, 21 percent of deported Republicans were from Catalonia, and 31 percent from the Països Catalans.[36] However, if we apply Roig's criteria, the representation of Andalusia, Aragon, Valencia, and other regions falls, and that of Catalonia rises. Let us look at some examples of the internees killed in Mauthausen who had lived in Catalonia but were classified by Bermejo and Checa under their regions of origin: Francesc Cortés Borrás and Josep Cortés Garcia, father and son, born respectively in Huécija and Pechina in Andalusia; Antoni Blanco Blanch, a native of the Aragón borderlands, whose brother lived in Barcelona, according to Roig; Didac Lozano Ribera, from Alavia, Andalusia, European boxing champion and a member of Estat Català (Catalan State, the pro-independence party), whose father lived in Terrassa (Roig); Josep Iglesias Rivera, from Extremadura, a member of the PSUC, a cork factory worker in Palafrugell (Roig); and Joaquim Alegría, from Castellón, a tram driver in Barcelona affiliated with the CNT. We also find brothers like Manuel and Francesc Cazorla Zamora, the former born in Mojácar, Andalusia in 1916 and the latter in Súria in Catalonia in 1919, where their father, Francesc Cazorla Martínez, now lived.

We can provide a more precise comparison between the list of thirty-nine residents of Badalona killed in the Nazi camps, first published by Joan Villarroya i Font in 1985,[37] and the list given by Bermejo and Checa. We find a correspondence in the ten cases of people born in Badalona and in the six people born in Catalonia but not in Badalona; but there is a discrepancy in nineteen people born outside Catalonia (a difference of 49 percent), whom Bermejo and Checa do not classify as Catalans or residents in Catalonia. This difference rises to 64 percent if we refer to the Països Catalans. Finally, Bermejo and Checa cite one person who is not on Villarroya's list, and Villarroya four who are not on Bermejo and Checa's list.

These considerations—and assuming, as seems reasonable, that there is a correlation between deportees and exiles—indicate again that the proportion of Catalans among the exiled would be closer to 50 or 60 percent than to 40 or 50 percent, and that the exiles from the Països Catalans would represent around 60 percent of the total.

---

36 Bermejo and Checa, *Libro-memorial de los deportados españoles*, 35.
37 Joan Villarroya i Font, *Revolució i guerra civil a Badalona 1936–1939*, 2nd ed. (Badalona: Àrea de Cultura, Joventut i Esports, Ajuntament de Badalona, 1986), 217–18.

The living conditions in Mauthausen and Gusen were subhuman. The work was exhausting; prisoners had to carry large stones up the 186 steps that came to be known as the stairway to death. The food was totally inadequate and the clothing and footwear were practically useless in the harsh climatic conditions of the region. Prisoners suffered malnutrition, physical punishment, a lack of hygiene and health care, overcrowding in barracks, executions, fuel injections in the heart, deadly beatings, and gassings at the castle of Hartheim. At Gusen, in November 1941 alone, nine hundred Spaniards died, and of the figure of nearly four thousand deportees barely 10 percent survived. Two-thirds of the Spanish deportees in Mauthausen and Gusen died.[38]

Mauthausen was liberated on May 5, 1945. The presence of Spanish Republicans was clear for all to see when, four days later, a crowd of prisoners greeted the US troops and hung a banner above the main door of the camp in Spanish that read "The Spanish antifascists greet the forces of liberation." This poster and others bearing the same words in different languages were painted by the Catalan deportee Francesc Teix.[39]

Montserrat Roig offers a portrait of the kind of people the deportees were:

> men and women of the CNT, the PSUC, Esquerra Republicana of Catalonia, Estat Català, trade unionists, socialists, anarchists, communists, nationalists, and others who simply held the Republic dear; men and women of the popular classes who never regretted having chosen the side of the Republic . . . Catalans from the countryside abounded, rather than those from the big city . . . on July 19, many of them were working in trades: painters, carpenters, waiters, bricklayers, or in skilled work; they downed tools to volunteer for the defense of the threatened Republic . . . They were the most disadvantaged, the ones who received no help to avoid the French concentration camps. The

---

38 Bermejo and Checa, *Libro-memorial de los deportados españoles*, 16–17.
39 Roig, *Els catalans als camps nazis*, photo no. 13. Dachau also held many Republican deportees, and so "even before the camp was liberated, the Republican and Austrian flags of the International Brigades were already flying at the entrance to Dachau." Both were made by the Catalan Lluís Sunyer, who worked in the camp's clothing workshop. Sunyer also hoisted the *Senyera*, the Catalan flag. See Josep Sánchez Cervelló, "Les brigades internacionals: de la seva retirada a la glòria," in *Las Brigadas Internacionales: nuevas perspectivas en la historia*, ed. Josep Sánchez Cervelló and Sebastián Agudo (Tarragona: Universitat Rovira i Virgili, 2015), 242 and Roig, *Els catalans als camps nazis*, 547.

intellectuals, the liberal professions, the people with contacts in France, the high-ranking members of the parties all managed to escape. The ones that stayed behind were the ones who could not find a way out: the ones who had nobody.[40]

There were workers and farmers and "some from the middle classes": there were social strata in exile too. Around 1,200 Catalans died in the Mauthausen complex alone, and around 1,700 from the Països Catalans as a whole. And, given the ideological complicity of Franco's government with Nazism, these dead should be included in the calculation of the Franco's victims; it pushes up the total of 3,385 executed between 1938 and 1953 estimated by Josep Maria Solé i Sabaté by more than 35 percent.[41]

Franco's repression and the deportation of Spanish Republicans to Mauthausen and other Nazi camps not only aimed to eliminate the most active Republican militants but also to *socialize* terror. That is to say, although one might have expected the repression to be a response to the implantation of leftist or nationalist labor organizations, in fact it was often a consequence of local dynamics, or simply of the large-scale presence of countryfolk among the Republican combatants. In fact, if we relate the terror to the Catalan demographics of 1936, we see that it was not the "working-class" industrial regions that suffered the most (with the exception of Baix Llobregat), in which the proportion of those executed was higher than the mean), but we find rural regions (Baix Empordà, Garrotxa, Alt Camp, Alt Penedès, Baix Penedès, Baix Camp, Conca de Barberà, Priorat, Ribera d'Ebre, Baix Ebre, Montsià, Terra Alta, Berguedà, Solsonès, and Les Garrigues) in which the percentages that correspond to the Francoist repression and the deaths in Mauthausen were higher than would be expected on the basis of their population. The death rate in Mauthausen of people from other rural regions (Garraf, La Segarra, Segrià, Urgell, Alt Urgell, Pallars Jussà, and Pallars Sobirà) was also clearly above the average.[42]

After the occupation of France, Republican politicians and military were arrested and repatriated as a result of the collaboration between Franco's government and the Nazi regime. Antonio Vilanova gives the following list:

---

40 Roig, *Els catalans als camps nazis*, 35–36.
41 Josep M. Solé i Sabaté, *La repressió franquista a Catalunya, 1938–1953* (Barcelona: Edicions 62, 2003), 249.
42 Tarragonès and El Garraf form part of the first and second groups respectively, but they are not areas of a markedly rural character.

Francisco Cruz Salido; Teodomiro Menéndez, member of parliament; Carlos Montilla; Miguel Salvador; Cipriano Rivas Cherif; Luis Companys, President of the Catalan government; J. Fernández Vera; former ministers Julián Zugazagoitia and Juan Peiró; Manuel Muñoz member of parliament, director-general of security; Colonel Antonio Puig Petrolani; Lieutenant Col. Eleuterio Díaz Tendero, Chief of Staff at the Ministry of War; Lieutenant Colonel León Luengo Muñoz; Colonel José Villalba; division commissioner Máximo de Gracia; José Flores; Captain Manuel Martínez Garry, and one hundred more.[43]

The institutionalization of terror had obvious consequences, especially when Germany occupied southern France for fear of an Allied offensive. Thus, from 1942 onward many Republicans returned to Spain (either in secret or otherwise) due to the fear of falling into the hands of the Germans and being sent to an extermination camp. In addition, the full force of the Francoist repression had begun to wane (two thirds of all the executions took place in 1939) and a Spanish jail was clearly to be preferred to a Nazi extermination camp.

Josep Carrió, for example, had been a captain in the 26th Division that had crossed the border at Osséja on the way to exile on February 13, 1939.[44] After passing through the Bram concentration camp (with 100 huts for 100 men each, in total 10,000 men), in October 1939, he began working in a car parts firm in Toulouse. In January 1940, the French government ordered the arrest of all refugees without an employment contract and residence permit: "Those who were caught without papers were arrested and no more was heard of them . . . The idea was to stop the uncontrolled flow of Spanish refugees, many of them from the CNT-FAI, or Communists." The occupation of Belgium caused a flood of Belgian refugees in Toulouse; there were Polish refugees as well.

---

43 Antonio Vilanova, *Los olvidados. Los exiliados españoles en la segunda guerra mundial* (Paris: Ruedo Ibérico, 1969), 18. All those mentioned were repatriated and executed, except Menéndez, Salvador, Montilla, and de Gracia, who were pardoned. The military men were deported to Nazi camps: Puig Petrolani to Mauthausen, where he was released on May 5, 1945; Luengo Muñoz died in Flossenburg on November 18, 1944 and Eleuterio Díaz in Dachau on February 13, 1945. Villalba was able to remain in exile and José Flores survived. Nothing is known of the fate of Martínez Garry. For the collaboration between the Vichy regime, the Franco government, and the Nazi authorities in France in the persecution of Republican exiles, see Jordi Guixé Coromines, *La república perseguida, 1937–1951: exilio y represión en la Francia de Franco* (València: Publicacions de la Universitat de València, 2012).

44 Manuscript 5,080 in the Biblioteca de Catalunya. I thank my friend Joan Villarroya i Font for referring me to it. It bears the title *Memòries de la guerra civil i de l'exili del 1936 al 1943,* and was written fifty years later by Josep Carrió.

With the German occupation of the city in November 1942, Carrió decided to return to Barcelona: "By that time, the repression had become much less severe than in the first three years." In Toulouse, on the other hand, the situation went from bad to worse: "A few days after I left, my friend Gisbert was captured by the Germans in one of the round-ups and sent to Germany. We never saw each other again." In December 1943, Carrió returned in secret to Catalonia.

THE ESCAPE NETWORKS

The Republican exiles (and especially the Catalans, due to their local knowledge of the land) played a key role in the escape networks in the Pyrenees. After the Civil War, these networks allowed militants who had not been able to leave in February 1939 and who were in danger of being executed to cross the border. The networks were often short-lived, but they rarely took long to reemerge in some other form.

After the occupation of France, evacuation networks across the Pyrenees were organized. Jews, Allied soldiers (including the Poles who had fled via Romania), French politicians (including some *Gaullistes*), young Frenchmen who wanted to join the Free French Army, and Allied pilots who had been shot down but had survived and avoided capture – all had to be moved to Spain. Between 1940 and 1942, the Vichy government excluded Jews from French society, and many tried to escape; and from February 1943 onward, many young Frenchmen fled the STO (*service du travail obligatoire*, compulsory work service), the forced enlistment system that sent thousands of French workers to Germany to work for the war industry.

The escape networks in the Catalan Pyrenees started in the towns of the French *départements* of Haute Garonne, Ariège, and the Eastern Pyrenees, in which the fugitives arrived by train, bus, and car. From there the approach toward the border crossings began. It was done at night and on foot, along roads with very little traffic to avoid police checkpoints because a French or German safe conduct was required to approach the Pyrenees. There were also thousands of members of the Vichy security forces patrolling the border, reinforced, from November 1942 onward, by six thousand German soldiers with trained dogs. On the Spanish side, the border was secured by the civil guard, the national police, and the army, and anyone arrested without papers within five kilometers (three miles) of the border was in danger of being handed over to the Germans.[45] The fugitives, with the help of guides (*passeurs*), crossed the mountain passes that led to Catalonia or Andorra. They went on to Manresa, Ripoll, or Lleida to take the train to Barcelona in the hope of reaching the British consulate or the French Red Cross. The pilots and the soldiers returned to Britain via Gibraltar or Lisbon, the Jews sought escape routes to countries in which they were not persecuted, and the exiled Republicans tried to obtain papers or continued the fight against the Franco regime in the underground.

Josep Calvet mentions six routes or passes in the *comarques* of Lleida and fifteen in the *comarques* of Girona. The difference in number is due to the terrain: in the Alt Empordà the altitudes of the passes range between 395 meters (1,300 feet) in Banyuls to 990 meters (3,250 feet) in La Carbassera, while in the Pyrenees in Lleida all the passes are at altitudes of more than 2,000 meters (6,560 feet), reaching 2,406 meters (7,894 feet) in the Port dera Horqueta in the Vall d'Aran.[46] Judging from the number of arrests, the most commonly used routes were those in the Alt Empordà.[47]

Joan Carrió used the Cerdanya route to return to Barcelona in December 1943.[48] He arrived in the border town of La Tour de Carol by train from Toulouse, and from La Tour went on to a farmhouse in Osséja. He crossed the border into Cerdanya in the company of another exile (a Barcelona-based pharmacist and Estat Català member) and the guide, a seventy-year-old shepherd from Balsareny who charged them 500 francs each to take them to within twenty kilometers (twelve miles) of Manresa. They spent the night in a farmhouse in Castellar de N'Hug. Then, always moving at night, they passed through Guardiola de Berguedà, Berga, Gironella, Puig-reig, and Balsareny to take the bus to Manresa and from there they went on to Barcelona by train.

Andorra, in the exceptional situation of being a neutral country in the middle of the border between occupied France and a Spain allied with Germany, was a place of passage and, often, a refuge. Shortly after

---

45   Ferran Sànchez Agustí, *Espías, contrabando, maquis y evasión. La II Guerra Mundial en los Pirineos* (Lleida: Editorial Milenio, 2010), 56–57. About the German presence on the border see also Josep Clarà, *Nazis a la frontera dels Pirineus Orientals (1942-1944)* (Barcelona: Rafael Dalmau, Editor, 2016).

46   Josep Calvet, *Les muntanyes de la llibertat. El pas del evadits pels Pirineus durant la Segona Guerra Mundial* (Barcelona: L'Avenç, 2008), 27–29.

47   Josep Calvet, interview by Xevi Camprubí in *El Temps*, August 11, 2009, 36.

48   Biblioteca de Catalunya, *Memòries de la guerra civil i de l'exili del 1936 al 1943*, manuscript 5,080.

the end of World War II, in his book completed in Sant Julià de Lòria in December 1950, Francesc Viadu stresses the importance of the Alexis network organized by the British MI6, which smuggled 2,800 people (Belgians, Jews, Poles, Gaullists, *résistants*, and Allied aviators) across the border. The Alexis network picked up the fugitives in Toulouse, Foix, Tarascon sur Ariège, and Les Cabannes and led them through the mountain passes to El Serrat or Ordino in Andorra. From there, they went to the Hotel Palanques in La Massana (in which, on September 29, 1943, a Gestapo round-up captured the Andorran Eduard Molné, who died in August 2013, and five Poles), or the Hotel Mirador in Andorra La Vella to reach Sant Julià de Lòria, and then over the border into La Seu d'Urgell. They might also go to Encamp and Grau Roig and from there to Alp and Manresa.[49]

Although the most important escape networks are known— Ponzán,[50] Alexis, Pat O'Leary—due to their clandestine nature, it is difficult to establish the precise number of networks and the number of evasions successfully completed. The estimates range from a minimum of 30,000 to a maximum of 50,000.[51] As for the number of networks, Ferran Sánchez Agustí believes that there were at least 250, among which 100 were very large.[52] On the other hand, Claude Benet offers a list of the ones active in Andorra: the Ponzán group worked for the French, British, and American intelligence services and collaborated with the Anglo-American Pat O'Leary group, the Belgian-Dutch Sabot, and the French Counterespionage TR. The Pat O'Leary was the most important, and was dismantled by the Germans at the end of 1943 and replaced by the Françoise. The others were the British Marie Claire; the Polish EWA or EVA; Bourgogne or Burgundy, created by De Gaulle's secret services; the Organisation Juive de Combat (Jewish Combat Organization); the Polish F2; Paris Bruxelles; the British Bret Morton; the French Mouvements Unis de Résistance (Unified movements of the resistance, Mur); Buckmaster; Combat; Wisigoth-Lorraine; and the American Quakers and Wi-Wi. Networks were also set up by the

---

49   Francesc Viadu, *Entre el torb i la Gestapo*, 2nd ed. (Barcelona: Editorial Nova Terra, 1975) and "Camina, Quimet, camina" and "L'últim del Palanques," *El Periòdic d'Andorra*, January 3, 2012 and August, 27, 2013.

50   Pilar Ponzán, *Lucha y muerte por la libertad 1936–1945. Francisco Ponzán Vidal y la Red de evasión Pat O'Leary 1940–1944* (Barcelona: Tot Editorial, 1996) and Antonio Tellez Solà, *La red de evasión del Grupo Ponzán: Anarquistas en la guerra secreta contra el franquismo y el nazismo (1936–1944)* (Barcelona: Virus, 1996).

51   Sánchez Agustí, *Espías, contrabando, maquis y evasión*, 47 and Benet, *Guies, fugitius i espies*, 47–48.

52   Sánchez Agustí, *Espías, contrabando, maquis y evasión*, 48.

POUM (Partido Obrero de Unificación Marxista, Workers' Party of Marxist Unification), which created the Martin group, an evacuation network for Spanish refugees, and by Estat Català.[53]

In short, although many of the escape networks had their origins in the Allied secret services and although many worked together and shared contacts and *passeurs*, in the truly decisive moments they were heavily dependent on local people who knew the mountain passages well and were familiar with the movements of the German, French, and Spanish patrols. Catalans, Andorrans, and Spaniards who, motivated by altruism, ideology, or financial gain, were willing to risk their lives by providing coordination, guidance, and shelter. On the French side of the border, Spanish Republican exiles combined these tasks with their participation in the Resistance: for example, the commanders Joan Amer Vendrell and Teodoro Marin Masdemont, the lieutenant colonels Ferran Salavera Camps and José Mª García-Miranda Esteban-Infantes, the colonels Jesús Velasco Echave, César Blasco Sasero, and Carlos Redondo Flores (a member of the PSUC) and General Mariano Gamir Ulibarri. These men joined the Combat group, which was both an escape network and a resistance group in Vernet les Bains, led by Pierre Vidal, head of the Resistance of Vernet and Canigou. On December 9, 1943, they were arrested along with Vidal and handed over to the Gestapo in Perpignan. Shortly after the Allied landing of Normandy they were sent to Dachau, where they arrived after several months; Joan Amer died there on November 21, 1944; Ferran Salavera on January 30, 1945; Carlos Redondo, on March 9, 1945; Jesús Velasco, date unknown; and no data are available for either Teodoro Marín or César Blasco. José Mª García-Miranda survived Dachau, and Mariano Gamir was not deported to the Nazi camp because he was admitted to the Hospital of Perpignan.[54]

53   Benet, *Guies, fugitius i espies*, 60–77.
54   E. Bella, 2014; X. Bella, 2015.

BIBLIOGRAPHY

Agudo Blanco, Sebastián. "Los republicanos españoles en la resistencia francesa de la zona sur: siguiendo el ejemplo de las Brigadas Internacionales." In *Las Brigadas Internacionales: nuevas perspectivas en la historia,* edited by Josep Sánchez Cervelló and Sebastián Agudo. Tarragona: Universitat Rovira i Virgili, 2015.

Alted, Alicia. *La voz de los vencidos, el exilio republicano de 1939.* Madrid: Aguilar, 2005.

Amat-Piniella, Joaquim. *K.L. Reich (Els catalans en els camps d'extermini de Hitler).* 2nd edition. Barcelona: Club Editor, 1968.

Amicale des Anciens Guérilleros. *Guérilleros en Terre de France. Les Républicains espagnols dans la Résistance française.* Preface by Léo Figuères. Pantin: Le Temps des Cerises éditeurs, 2000.

Arasa, Daniel. *50 Històries catalanes de la segona guerra mundial.* Barcelona: Laia, 1998.

———. "Españoles en todas las trincheras." *La Vanguardia,* supplement, *Revista,* Sunday, May 1, 2005, 10–11.

Armengou, Montse. *El comboi dels 927.* TV documentary. TV3-30 minuts, 2004.

Bella, Emili. "Percebo un avenir paorós." *El Punt Avui,* March 13, 2014.

Bella Redondo, Xavier. "Vides paral·leles. Nous aspectes en la biografia de Carlos Redondo." Master's thesis, University of Barcelona/ Open University of Catalonia, 2015.

Benet, Claude. *Guies, fugitius i espies. Camins de pas per Andorra durant la Segona Guerra Mundial,* segona reimpressió. Andorra la Vella: Editorial Andorra, 2013.

Bermejo, Benito. *Francesc Boix, el fotògraf de Mauthausen.* Barcelona: RBA La Magrana, 2002.

Bermejo, Benito, and Sandra Checa. *Libro-memorial de los deportados españoles en los campos nazis (1940–1945).* Madrid: Ministerio de Educación, Cultura y Deporte, 2006.

Gobierno de España, Ministerio de Educación. *Españoles deportados a Campos de Concentración Nazis.* At http://pares.mcu.es/Deportados/servlets/ServletController.

Calvet, Josep. *Les muntanyes de la llibertat. El pas del evadits pels Pirineus durant la Segona Guerra Mundial.* Barcelona: L'Avenç, 2008.

Clarà, Josep. *Nazis a la frontera dels Pirineus Orientals (1942-1944).* Barcelona: Rafael Dalmau, Editor, 2016.

Díaz Esculies, Daniel. *Entre filferrades: un aspecte de l'emigració republicana dels Països Catalans (1939–1945).* Barcelona: La Magrana, 1993.

Dreyfus-Armand, Geneviève. *El exilio de los republicanos españoles en Francia: de la guerra civil a la muerte de Franco.* Barcelona: Crítica, 2000.

Font Agulló, Jordi, ed. *Reflexionant l'exili. Aproximació a l'exili republicà: entre la història, l'art i el testimoniatge.* Catarroja and Barcelona: Editorial Afers; Museu Memorial de l'Exili, 2010.

Gallardo, Juan J., and José M. Márquez. *Ortiz, general sin Dios ni amo.* Barcelona: Ed. Hacer, 1999.

Guixé Coromines, Jordi. "El regreso forzado y la persecución contra los exiliados en Francia." *Historia del Presente* 18 (2011): 101–12.

———. *La república perseguida, 1937–1951: exilio y represión en la Francia de Franco.* València: Publicacions de la Universitat de València, 2012.

Herrerín López, Ángel. "La CNT en el exilio de la organización a la escisión." *Historia Social* 48 (2004): 27–46.

Livre-Mémorial des déportés de France arrêtés par mesure de répression et dans certains cas par mesure de persécution 1940–1945. 4 volumes. Paris: Fondation pour la Mémoire de la Déportation-Éditions Tirésias, 2004. At http://www.bddm.org/liv/index_liv.php.

Mairie d'Oradour sur Glane -liste incomplète- et ajouts des familles des victims. At http://static.blog4ever.com/2006/01/63466/artfichier_63466_75116_201004121714651.pdf.

Ortiz, Jean. "La epopeya de los guerrilleros españoles en Francia." In *Las Brigadas Internacionales: nuevas perspectivas en la historia*, edited by Josep Sánchez Cervelló and Sebastián Agudo. Tarragona: Universitat Rovira i Virgili, 2015.

Pla Brugat, Dolores. *Els exiliats catalans a Mèxic. Un estudi de la immigració republicana.* Catarroja and Barcelona: Editorial Afers, 2000.

Ponzán, Pilar. *Lucha y muerte por la libertad 1936–1945. Francisco Ponzán Vidal y la Red de evasión Pat O'Leary 1940–1944*. Barcelona: Tot Editorial, 1996.

Razola, Manuel, and Mariano C. [Constante] Campo. *Triangulo azul. Los republicanos españoles en Mauthausen*. Paris: Gallimard, 1969; Barcelona: Península, 1979.

Roa Ventura, Agustín. "Los españoles en la batalla de Narvik." *Historia y vida* 119 (1978): 120–25.

Roig, Montserrat. *Els catalans als camps nazis*. Barcelona: Edicions 62, 1977; Barcelona: Edicions 62, 2003.

Romero Yáñez-Barnuevo, Gonzalo. "Los españoles en la batalla de Narvik, 1940" (2005). In *Paisajes de Guerrilla: Españoles contra el III Reich: Narvik, 1940*. Blog, April 3, 2010. At http://paisajesdelaguerrilla.blogspot.com.es/2010/04/espanoles-en-narvik-1940.html.

Rubio, Javier. *La emigración en la guerra civil de 1936–1939: Historia del éxodo que se produce con el fin de la II República española*. 3 volumes. Madrid: San Martín, 1977.

Rubio Cabeceran, Josep. *Camp definitiu: diari d'un exiliat al Barcarès*. Edited by Elisenda Barbé i Pou. Prologue by Antoni Segura i Mas. Valls, Tarragona: Cossetània Editorial, 2010.

Sànchez Agustí, Ferran. *Espías, contrabando, maquis y evasión. La II Guerra Mundial en los Pirineos*. Lleida: Editorial Milenio, 2010.

Sánchez Cervelló, Josep. "Les brigades internacionals: de la seva retirada a la glòria." In *Las Brigadas Internacionales: nuevas perspectivas en la historia*, edited by Josep Sánchez Cervelló and Sebastián Agudo. Tarragona: Universitat Rovira i Virgili, 2015.

Sánchez Cervelló, Josep, and Sebastián Agudo, eds. *Las Brigadas Internacionales: nuevas perspectivas en la historia*. Tarragona: Universitat Rovira i Virgili, 2015.

Segura, Antoni. "La lluita armada: la Guerra Civil continua." In *La guerra civil a Catalunya: l'exili*, edited by J.M. Solé Sabaté. Volume 6. Barcelona: Edicions 62, 2007.

Solé i Sabaté, Josep M. *La repressió franquista a Catalunya, 1938–1953*. Barcelona: Edicions 62, 2003.

Soler, Llorenç, director and scriptwriter. *Francisco Boix: un fotógrafo en el infierno.* Documentary. Área de Televisión and Canal⁺, 2000: https://www.youtube.com/watch?v=-04d60l0-EU.

Tellez Solà, Antonio. *La red de evasión del Grupo Ponzán: Anarquistas en la guerra secreta contra el franquismo y el nazismo (1936–1944).* Barcelona: Virus, 1996.

Torres Hernández, Jorge. "Los hermanos Miret i Musté. Los catalanes Conrado y Josep, organizadores de la *Résistance* en Francia." In *Las Brigadas Internacionales: nuevas perspectivas en la historia,* edited by Josep Sánchez Cervelló and Sebastián Agudo. Tarragona: Universitat Rovira i Virgili, 2015.

Viadu, Francesc. *Entre el torb i la Gestapo.* 2nd edition. Barcelona: Editorial Nova Terra, 1975.

Vilanova, Antonio. *Los olvidados. Los exiliados españoles en la segunda guerra mundial.* París: Ruedo Ibérico, 1969.

Villarroya i Font, Joan. *Revolució i guerra civil a Badalona 1936–1939.* 2nd edition. Badalona: Àrea de Cultura, Joventut i Esports, Ajuntament de Badalona, 1986.

———. *Desterrats. L'exili català de 1939.* Barcelona: Editorial Base, 2002.

Wirsing, Giselher, ed. *The War in Maps 1939/40.* New York: German Library of Information, 1941.

Chapter 17

The Long Shadow of Nazism in Catalonia (1933–1947)

J. M. Solé i Sabaté

It is not easy to trace the development and influence of Nazism in Catalonia;[1] indeed, the literature on the subject is relatively scarce.[2]

At the time when Hitler came to power in 1933, Spain was a republic, intent on implementing the ideas of the social and political left and inspired by the hope of transforming a backward, corrupt state into one of the world's most advanced countries in terms of social progress, justice, and modernity.

In Catalonia, power was in the hands of the popular classes. The people had been the spearhead of a movement that had brought down and banished the Bourbon dynasty in April 1931 and laid the foundations of a progressive, democratic state to match any in Europe. The president of the Generalitat, Francesc Macià, proclaimed the Catalan Republic an hour after Lluís Companys, later to succeed him

---

1   On November 24, 1923, in *La Veu de Catalunya*, Eugeni Xammar published a column entitled "Adolf Hitler o la ximpleria desencadenada" (Adolf Hitler or stupidity unleashed), the result of an alleged interview that he and Josep Pla had with Hitler, during the latter's imprisonment after the Beer Hall putsch of November 8–9, 1923.

2   Xavier Deulonder, *Els nazis a Catalunya* (Barcelona: Llibres de l'Índex, 2007); Toni Orensanz, *El nazi de Siurana* (Barcelona: Ara Llibres, 2016); Josep Clara, *Nazis a la frontera dels Pirineus Orientals (1942–1944)* (Barcelona: Rafael Dalmau Editor, 2016); Mireia Capdevila and Francesc Vilanova, *Nazis a Barcelona. L'esplendor feixista de postguerra (1939–1945)* (Barcelona: L'Avenç Ed. Barcelona, 2017); Rosa Sala and Plàcid García-Planas, *El marqués y la esvástica. César González-Ruano y los judíos en el París ocupado* (Barcelona: Edit. Anagrama, 2016).

as president, had made a generic proclamation of the Republic at the City Hall of Barcelona.

As for the Catalan right wing, it was democratic and more advanced than its Spanish counterpart. The only faction of the Catalan political scenery to celebrate the triumph of the Nazis was the miniscule extreme right wing, which was fervently pro-Spanish, antidemocratic, and anti-Catalan. In addition to the Spanish far right, the other group in Catalonia that would identify with Hitler's Germany was the large group of German expatriates.

At the end of the nineteenth century, coinciding with the rapid process of industrialization in Catalonia and the return of capital from Spain's former colonies of Cuba, Puerto Rico, and the Philippines,[3] German investment began to flow into a wide range of sectors, especially the metallurgical, chemical, electrochemical, steel, and equipment industries. At the end of World War I, in late 1918, the influx of German capital into Catalonia rose steadily in the wake of the country's military defeat and due to the need to avoid expropriations by the Allies and economic punishment in the form of war reparations. The trend would increase as the German economy faced crisis after crisis in the 1920s and many industrialists and businessmen fled the financial disaster of their home country—exacerbated by the punitive conditions imposed by the Allies—to settle in Catalonia and Spain.

THE REPUBLIC

In the early 1930s, the German Johannes Bernhardt created a financial empire of about 350 companies that, as José Maria Irujo explains,[4] would have a dramatic and definitive bearing on our story. Bernhardt was instrumental in obtaining Hitler's support for Franco and had major interests in Deutsche Bank, the pharmaceutical industry, and finance.

Part of this migratory trend represented by Bernhardt and others, with its economic power and efficient management, would meet a sympathetic welcome (if not yet complicity) in sections of Catalan

---

3   These colonies were freed by the actions of indigenous emancipation movements, and thanks to military aid from the United States, which was beginning to show an undeniably imperialist streak.

4   Jose María Irujo, "La lista negra. Los espías nazis en España," *El Correo Digital*, February 17, 2003.

society that admired German science, technology, and culture. The solid reputation of all things German was an important factor in the spread of the Nazi influence in Catalonia.

Approximately 10,000 people of German origin were resident in Catalonia, most of whom were wealthy and enjoyed substantial social prestige. Hitler's rise to power increased the migratory flow of Germans, both loyalists and opponents. His direct supporters numbered between 400 and 500 people, and sympathizers around 100. Counting their families, these figures suggest the presence of a group of influence of a few thousand people, mainly resident in Barcelona and in industrial centers funded by German capital.

The anti-fascists, people who were openly opposed to Nazism and who felt welcomed and protected in Catalonia, were of course much fewer in number. Examples were the militants of the German anarcho-syndicalist movement DAS (Deutsche Anarchosyndikalisten), who, on July 19, 1936, acted decisively to bring down the Nazi network run by the German Consulate in the Catalan capital.[5]

Incidentally, the anarchist affiliations of these Germans would make them the propitiatory victims of the communists during the bloody events of May 1937 (known as the civil war within the Civil War) in the Catalan rearguard. It was the direct armed confrontation between communists and anarchists that gave rise to political and military hegemony of the Catalan and Spanish communist parties in the Republican zone. The influence on them of Stalinism would be almost total.

German expatriates in Catalonia voting in the Reichstag elections of 1933 did so on the ship *Halle*, moored in the port of Barcelona. Sixty-five per cent voted for Hitler – a far higher share of the vote than in Germany itself.

In Catalonia, in the brief period between Hitler's triumph and the outbreak of the Spanish Civil War in 1936, only extremist minority groups expressed any sympathy for the Nazi leader. The Falange, more fascist than Nazi, had fewer than a thousand militants. The Juntas de Ofensiva Nacional-Sindicalista (Councils of the National-Syndicalist Offensive, JONS), strongly influenced by national socialism, were a

---

5   Dieter Nelles, *Deutsche Anarchosyndikalisten: DAS. Cronología 1933–1939* (Heidelberg: Verlag Graswurzelrevolution, 2013). See also *El Nazismo al desnudo. Su intervención y ayuda a los facciosos españoles puesta al descubierto por sus propios documentos* (Barcelona: CNT, 1938).

small group of militants who joined forces with the Falange in 1934 but later they severed links; despite their common penchant for violent totalitarianism, the differences between the two groups were very clear.

The data show that the distribution of pamphlets and articles against the Jews began in Portugal. Political relations were promoted by a businessman, Walter Zuchristian, a high-ranking employee of the Siemens company. As the Second Republic did nothing to facilitate the activities of the Nazis, in Catalonia especially it was the business, economic, and cultural worlds that acted as instruments of propaganda under the watchful eye of the government.

The military coup of July 19, 1936 ended in failure in Catalonia. Barcelona was the only city in Spain in which the rebel army was defeated in open combat on the street by the forces of order (the assault guard, *Mossos d'Esquadra* or Catalan police force, and the civil guard) with the courageous support of a multitude of armed militiamen. This defiance gave rise to an unprecedented revolution, one of the most profound and unusual in the history of humankind; its influence spread wherever the columns of armed militiamen fought to defend the Republic, both in Catalonia and on the Aragonese front.

The German consulate, businesses, and schools, and others suspected of Nazi sympathies sought refuge in their status as foreigners. Hitler's immediate dispatch of military aid to Franco's rebels put an end to all the Nazis' relations and activities in Catalonia.

THE CIVIL WAR

The Nazis' immediate response in support of the military coup had one very important collateral effect.[6] The first radio station in Spain was Ràdio Associació de Catalunya, which had had an enormous social impact. The station attracted listeners in their thousands and had gained real prestige, and by the mid-1930s it was planning to expand its coverage. In early 1936 it bought a new 25 KW transmitter from the German

---

6   Nevertheless, on August 29, 1936, Josep Tarradellas, minister of economics and public services of the Generalitat, was ordered by the president, Lluís Companys, to receive a German admiral on the cruiser *Nürnberg*, which was anchored in the port of Barcelona.

company Telefunken which would have turned it into the most powerful broadcaster in Spain.[7]

At the outbreak of war on July 18, the equipment had been dispatched and was awaiting the corresponding import permits on the French side of the border with Spain. However, the Nazi regime seized the transmitter and handed it over to Franco's side, which now had at its disposal the perfect instrument for launching the Spanish National Radio broadcasts. For decades the radio would be the mouthpiece of the Franco regime and the long dictatorship.

The effects of the German military intervention in the Spanish Civil War are well known.[8] In Catalonia, the most important manifestation of the Nazis' support for Franco was the aerial campaign and bombing raids, and the installation of a Condor Legion air base in early 1938 in La Sènia,[9] a town in southern Catalonia that became a key support base during the Battle of the Ebro between July and November 1938. During this campaign, the effects of new types of air raids were tested.[10]

The first German bombing raid in Catalonia took place on February 23, 1937, in Flix, in the Ribera d'Ebre. The target was a factory that produced chlorine, which was used in the manufacture of explosives. The raid destroyed a field hospital and part of the town center.

The Nazi bombing raids continued until the last days of Republican Catalonia, in early February 1939. The raids ranged from attempts to paralyze the energy sources located in the headwaters of rivers and the hydroelectric plants in the Pyrenees to the bombings of Barcelona and other cities with the intention of weakening the morale of the population. The mass bombing of civilians and the machine gunning of thousands of refugees fleeing toward the French borders were examples of sheer indiscriminate terror. As for the Condor Legion, it was the

7   Teodor Garriga, *La meva vida i Ràdio Associació de Catalunya* (Barcelona: Ed. Proa., 1998).
8   The Spanish and Catalan archives contain little information about Nazi activities in Spain, and the Nazi archives were confiscated by the Allies during the occupation of Berlin. We thus have to rely on the documentation in the National Archives in Washington, DC. Jeff Hemmer has studied them in great detail, and provides a classification from before the Civil War to the end of World War II.
9   Heribert García i Esteller, *La aviación republicana y la Legión Condor en el aeródromo de La Sénia* (Valladolid: Edit. Galland, 2015). See also the Centre d'Interpretació del Camp d'Aviació de la Sénia (http://www.campaviaciolasenia.cat/) and Generalitat de Catalunya, "Memòria," at http://memoria.gencat.cat/ca/inici.
10   Ramon Arnabat and David Iñiguez, *Atac i defensa de la reraguarda: els bombardeigs franquistes a les comarques de Tarragona i Terres de l'Ebre (1936–1939)* (Tarragona: Cossetània Edicions, 2013).

merciless, unrelenting scourge of Republican Catalonia, decimating the population and destroying neighborhoods and entire towns.[11]

The Republican period in Catalonia coincided with a radical and unique revolution throughout Spain.[12] During this time, the propaganda poster truly came into its own. With the ideological and political mobilization of illustrators, acknowledged artists, to artisans, the walls of the streets of towns and cities were replete with posters preaching revolutionary, Republican, and anti-fascist commitment. The poet Agustí Bartra wrote that the "walls screamed," so strong was the call to the population to create a new society that would clear away the oppressive and exploitative past and replace it with a just and egalitarian present.

This spontaneous outburst of creativity was overseen by the Generalitat's Commissariat of Propaganda, which promoted a revolutionary social pluralism and a republicanism that was both Catalanist and internationalist.[13] An icon and model of the influence of political propaganda over the population of its time, the Commissariat used all the means at its disposal to criticize and denigrate Nazism. Newspaper and magazine articles, posters, books, and *auques* (a characteristically Catalan form of proto-comic), visual media such as photography[14] and the cinema, artistic events such as competitions, fairs, and exhibitions, and the spoken word, either on the radio or in conferences, rallies and songs – all these media played their part in the struggle.

The Republic also worked hard to promote sport. It saw sport as physical culture, an egalitarian alternative to Nazi racism. In opposition to Hitler's monumental Berlin Olympics of 1936, the Republic organized the Popular Olympiad of Barcelona,[15] which was to be inaugurated on July 19. The attempted *coup d'état* in Barcelona on that same day meant that the event had to be abandoned.

---

11 The Nazis provided Franco's side with some 600 aircraft during the war: 136 Messerschmitt Bf 109s, 125 Heinkel He 51s, 93 Heinkel He 111s, and 63 Junkers Ju 52s. There were also 33 Heinkel He 45s, 20 Heinkel He 46s, 31 Dornier Do 17s, and five Junkers Ju 87s (the *Stuka).*

12 See historians of note such as Pierre Vilar, Paul Preston, Pierre Broué, Emile Témine, Gabriel Jackson, and Hugh Thomas.

13 Josep M. Solé i Sabaté and Joan Villarroya, *Guerra i propaganda. Fotografies del Comissariat de Propaganda de la Generalitat de Catalunya (1936–1939)* (Barcelona: Ed. Viena, 2006).

14 Pere Català Pic's photograph entitled "Crush Fascism," the image of a Catalan espadrille breaking a swastika on a pavement floor, has been considered one of the finest political icons of the first third of the twentieth century. See photograph in Appendix.

15 Xavier Pujadas and Carles Santacana, *L'altra Olimpíada, Barcelona'36. Esport, societat i política a Catalunya (1900-1936)* (Barcelona: Llibres de l'Índex, 2006).

Republican Spain attracted some 60,000 thousand young people from all over the world, of whom some 36,000 were combatants, in its struggle against international and Spanish fascism. Their courage, enthusiasm, and support for the Republic is the lasting memory of the International Brigades in the Spanish Civil War. This international volunteer movement was an idea proposed by the Third International in the USSR and channeled by the French Communist Party in Paris. Not all the volunteers were communists; the Brigades represented a broad church of left-wing, progressive, and revolutionary sentiment.

Among the German anti-fascists in Catalonia during the Civil War we should mention the Thaelmann Brigade, also known as the 11th International Brigade. This was the first brigade to be formed, on October 22, 1936 in Albacete. One of its battalions was the Edgar André battalion, which was involved in fierce combats from the very beginning, and later at the Casa de Campo and the Ciudad Universitaria in the Siege of Madrid. Later, at the battles of Jarama, Belchite, and Teruel, the German anti-fascists suffered many casualties and were replaced by Spanish soldiers. As the hostilities advanced into Catalonia the group was massacred once more at the Battle of the Ebro, from July 25 to November 16, 1938, and renamed the 11th Mixed Brigade.

POST-CIVIL WAR

The first years of the Franco regime are best defined as the Post-Civil War period. At this time, the new regime tried to create a totalitarian state by mobilizing the population in a vaguely defined political movement that would eventually fail for internal and external reasons. The most important of the internal reasons were the economic crisis aggravated by the attempt to impose an economic policy based on autarky[16] and the refusal of large sectors of the population to accept a regime based on militarism, extreme Spanish nationalism, and what became known as *national Catholicism.* Among the external reasons, the most important

---

16 [16] In 1938 the SOFINDUS (Financial and Industrial Society) consortium was founded in order to implement the strategic and economic plans of the Third Reich in Spain. It was structured in three areas: agricultural products, with eight large trusts; transport and services; and mining and related trade, with twenty companies. When the company was created, the *Financial Times* claimed that the Nazis controlled 900 of the 4,800 companies involved.

was the course of World War II that, as the decade wore on, gradually turned the way of the Allies.

In the end, Francoism survived for thirty-seven years – not as a totalitarian state, due to the defeat of Nazism and its own economic failures, but as a bloody dictatorship maintained in place by the army, the clergy, and social sectors of the extreme right under a single party, the Falange. The regime that emerged from the military triumph of the Civil War of 1936–1939, with the inestimable support of the Italian fascists and the Nazis, evolved over time but never ceased to be a repressive dictatorship from its beginnings until its very last days.

Francoist Barcelona declared itself pro-Nazi at the outbreak of World War II.[17] From an initial stance of "non-belligerence" that did little to hide a pro-Nazi public mood, the Franco regime would be forced toward neutrality by the course of the war. It is no coincidence that exchanges of prisoners of war were carried out in the "neutral" port of Barcelona.[18] The Nazis soon made their presence felt in the immediate post-Civil War period. Records of the British Foreign Office show that shortly after the entrance of the Francoist troops into Barcelona, Gestapo agents stormed the synagogue, destroying the ritual objects used for prayer and perpetrating desecrations of all kinds.

With the intention of consolidating their position in Catalan society, the Germans paid particular attention to educational and cultural institutions. One of their main centers of activity was the Colegio Alemán (German School), which lasted until the Nazi defeat in 1945, when it was forced to close. The school had some two thousand students divided into two streams, one for the children of German parents and the other for the rest of the students. The young Germans of military age living in Catalonia were under great pressure to go to the frontline to fight for their homeland. Those who did so were praised to the skies, and those who sought to avoid this destiny were treated with contempt. No figures are available, but the German community maintained a silent, complicit memory of the war dead and the survivors.

The residence of the majority of the German population in Catalonia also shows a clear pattern. With the exception of specific

---

17 In her book *Habíamos ganado la guerra* (Barcelona: Edit. Bruguera, 2007) Esther Tusquets describes how her uncle would lovingly trace the advance of the Nazi troops on the battle front by placing needles with swastikas on a map of Europe. He even had a small museum with Nazi iconography; he saw Hitler as a mythical hero.
18 From October 27, 1943 to May 18, 1944.

geographical areas in which technicians and industrialists obliged to reside (for example, Flix, or areas in the Pyrenees with large hydraulic installations), the majority lived in or around the modern center of the city of Barcelona, in the upper-middle class area built as part of the revolutionary Pla Cerdà in the mid-nineteenth century that descends from the mountain of the Tibidabo toward the Eixample. The Germans had their cultural centers, bars, and restaurants, as well as political and official institutions, between Plaza Molina and its surroundings next to Balmes Street, Paseo de Gracia, Via Laietana, and the Gran Vía de las Cortes Catalanas (renamed after José Antonio Primo de Rivera, the Falangist leader shot during the Civil War). Among the leisure activities offered to the Nazi leaders were bullfights, an entertainment that they accepted enthusiastically; they spent their summers in a Germanic home-from-home stretching from Sitges to the Costa Brava.[19]

Another important body under Nazi influence was the German Institute of Culture, which made no attempt to hide its ideology. The institute promoted cultural exhibitions on architecture, technology, the German press and books, the inauguration of academic years, courses, and ideological events as well such as celebrations of key dates in the Nazi calendar—the day of Hitler's accession to power, the day of the Fallen for National Socialism, and Hitler's birthday—together with conferences, art displays, and official ceremonies at the University of Barcelona and the Palau de la Música.

The Nazis' scorn for Catalonia is reflected in a photograph taken at what was (and remains today) the Parliament of Catalonia. The photograph shows four colossal Nazi flags hanging in front of part of the main façade of the building to celebrate an Exhibition of Modern German Architecture held in October 1942.

NAZI VISITS AND PROPAGANDA EVENTS

The activities of the Nazis in Catalonia are not well documented; very little is kept in official or administrative archives and libraries. As far

---

19   Juan-Ramón Capella, a member of a notorious Francoist family, remembers that, "Clarita Stauffer . . . had set up companies in Morocco that provided cover for Hitler's aid to Franco. At the end of the war she helped the Nazi leaders to flee to South America . . . Sitges was a place of discreet encounters. And Clarita, if her contacts failed her, had no qualms about hiding the runaway Nazis in our house." See *Sin Itaca. Memorias 1940–1975* (Madrid: Edit. Trotta, 2011), 37.

as Nazism and fascism are concerned, propaganda was always more important than facts. On October 23, 1940, the leader of the SS, Heinrich Himmler, paid a lightning visit to Catalonia. The Nazi delegation stayed for a few hours at the Ritz, the city's most luxurious hotel; they watched a military parade and visited Montserrat, the mountain that is a religious symbol of the country.

Accompanying the SS Reichsführer was his chief of staff General Wolff, the consulting surgeon of the SS Colonel Gebhardt, Lieutenant-Colonel Hartmann, and the then Captain General of Catalonia, Luis Orgaz.

In the Benedictine monastery they were not received by Father Abad Escarré, as the Vatican had already expressed its unease with Nazism – but by Father Ripol,[20] who spoke excellent German and acted as the visitors' guide. They greeted each other by shaking hands, not with a Nazi salute; the Germans visited the basilica, the library, the museum, and finally took the Sant Jeroni cable car up to the top of the mountain.

Together with Father Ripol was Father Gregori Estrada, who had also learned German during his time as a refugee during the Civil War at the German Benedictine abbey of Maria Laach. Estrada was a musicologist, composer, and for many years choir director at Monserrat. When he suggested to a military member of the group that they should visit the basilica, the curt reply was: "This does not interest the minister. What he wants to see is the outside."

In any case they visited the entire building. In the library, Himmler asked to see the documents that Montserrat "must have" regarding Parsifal and the Holy Grail, the vessel that Jesus is believed to have used at the last supper. When Father Ripol said that the abbey did not possess the documents in question, Himmler replied "What do you mean? You must have it; in Germany everyone knows that the Holy Grail is in Montserrat."

The Nazi leader was unimpressed by Father Ripol's explanation that all the documents in the archive had been burned during the Napoleonic invasions between 1808 and 1814, and that in any case there had never been any documentary evidence that the Holy Grail was hidden in Montserrat. Himmler was not convinced. But the most awkward moment of this tense visit was still to come, in the Museum.

---

20   The references that follow are taken from Jordi Finestres and Queralt Solé, "1940. Nazis a Montserrat," *Sàpiens* 3 (January 2003), 22–27.

In front of a sepulcher from the time of the Iberians, a pre-Roman people who lived some seven centuries before Christ, Himmler affirmed that it would have held the corpse of a Norseman. When corrected by Father Ripol, Himmler insisted "Yes, but they were descendants of the Norsemen, who came south to these lands." The cultural and personal differences came to a head when Himmler asked all those present to look at the reproduction of the Temple of Jerusalem, which he described emphatically as *"Die erste Bank"* (The first bank). At this attack on the Jews and also on Christ, Father Ripol remained silent, as, he said, he always did in the face of such ignorance.

The Nazis were fêted by the local authorities in several places in Catalonia,[21] and at numerous events in Barcelona, Bisbal del Penedès, Mollet del Vallès, Sabadell, Terrassa, and Martorelles, where a tombstone was laid in tribute to the fallen pilots of the Condor Legion. In Barcelona a similar monument was placed in front of the residence of officers of the Francoist Army on Avenida Diagonal. In Caldes de Montbui the municipal corporation issued an official tribute "to the 5 / F.88 Anti-aircraft Battery of the Condor Legion that was the guest of our town liberated from the Marxist hordes by the victorious troops of our undefeated Caudillo Franco. In proof of our gratitude and affection for the comrades of the sister Nation, to which we are united by unforgettable bonds, we dedicate this humble memorial."[22]

We should also mention the summer camps of the Hitler youth in Sant Pol de Mar, Palamós, Núria, and Sant Feliu de Guíxols. The writer Josep Pla recalled how the participants would strut arrogantly around the restaurants of Figueres and Portbou on visits from neighboring France. In the Spanish police stations, the photos of Franco and José Antonio would hang alongside Hitler, and in some cases, Mussolini and the Portuguese dictator Oliveira Salazar.[23]

The testimonies of Jews at the time affirm that the Gestapo had its own office in the Central Police station in Barcelona. There were

---

21　In the fall of 1942, coinciding with the supposed fall of Stalingrad to the Sixth Army Corps of General von Paulus, a group of Falangists dressed in full regalia and gleaming boots took the children out of the schools of Badalona and instructed them to repeat the slogan "We have taken Stalingrad, We have taken Stalingrad," which they then had to repeat in the main streets of the city, passing in front of the town hall and ending at the Rambla, parallel to the sea.

22　Arxiu Municipal Caldes de Montbui, *Llibre d'Actes* (January 1939). Later, the townsfolk recalled the arrogance of the officers who sometimes visited the town's renowned thermal spas.

23　Capdevila and Vilanova, *Nazis a Barcelona*, 20.

also regular German radio broadcasts. In Andorra, the small Pyrenean state between France and Catalonia, Gestapo members walked around freely without respecting any official norms, and on occasion even came to make arrests.

In the field of propaganda, we find the main Nazi supporters, with a continuous publication of maps that justified a particular geopolitical organization of the world[24] – the territorial hegemony of Germany for economic, political, and cultural reasons.

The comic also emerged at this time. These early forms combined humor and fierce criticism of communism, while at the same time promoting the idea of a supposed Aryan superiority.

THE NAZIS AND THE EXILED CATALAN REPUBLICANS

The Francoist persecution of Spanish Republicans in France received substantial logistical support from the Germans. The Spanish ambassador in Paris, José Félix de Lequerica, asked the German authorities and the collaborationist regime of Vichy to extradite 636 ex-Republican leaders, among them the president of the Generalitat, Lluís Companys, Josep Tarradellas, secretary of the ERC (Esquerra Republicana de Catalunya, Republican Left of Catalonia) in exile, the anarchist and former health minister Federica Montseny, the anarcho-syndicalist leader and also former minister Joan Peiró,[25] and the Catalan Republicans Jaume Aiguader and Ventura Gassol.

Finally, 47 of the initial list of 636 leaders were extradited to Spain.[26] The others underwent an odyssey of their own; but the Vichy regime, in charge of the so-called free zone, did not grant the extraditions on the grounds that the charges would be related to political activities. After pretrial detentions in which they feared for their lives, the prisoners were released.

---

24 In 1940, the historian Jaume Vicens Vives, a modernizer of Catalan and Spanish historiography, published *España. Geopolítica del Estado y del Imperio* (N.p.: Ed. Anvil., 1940), in which he praised Hitler. All the indications are that he was being blackmailed because of his Republican past.
25 Peiró was handed over to the Spanish authorities by the Nazis. He refused to act as a puppet organizing the Francoist unions, and was shot in Paterna (Valencia), on July 24, 1942.
26 Enric Canals and Josep Maria Ràfols, *Tarradellas, el guardià de la memoria* (Barcelona: Pòrtic Ediciones, 2017), 107.

In the zone occupied by the Nazis, the situation was quite different. The fugitives wanted by the Franco regime were arrested by the German authorities and handed over to the Spanish police with whom the Nazi regime had established formal agreements of mutual aid. Two of these fugitives were Lluís Companys and Joan Peiró, the epitome of the honest anarcho-syndicalist worker.[27]

When the German military machine occupied France after encountering hardly any opposition, the Catalan and Spanish Republicans refused to accept defeat and continued their fight against fascism. They were not deterred by the chilling images of Adolf Hitler making his quasi-imperial visit to Paris on June 23, 1940, the day after the signature of the Franco-German armistice – images that broke the hearts of many Frenchmen. Indeed, the morale of the French collapsed on seeing the Nazi leader arrive in Paris by train and, in a three-hour visit, take in the Opera, the Champs Élysées, the Arc de Triomphe, the Eiffel Tower, the Basilica of the Sacré Cœur, and the tomb of Napoleon: the seemingly invincible Führer with the symbolic heart of France at his feet.

The military and moral defeat of France was absolute. This period has been largely forgotten in the French collective imaginary and has still not been studied in depth by the French historiography, which is anchored in the past. This relative silence may be attributed to the shameful collusion, both political and ideological, of a significant sector of the French population with the victorious Germans and with fascism.

It is estimated that between 50,000 and 60,000 Spanish refugees who left the concentration camps in France were enlisted in the CTE (Compagnies de Travailleurs Étrangers, Companies of Foreign Workers).[28] Sometimes the French called them Compagnies de Travailleurs Espagnols (Companies of Spanish Workers) because of the high proportion of Spaniards, and indeed some companies had their own translators. Around 25 percent of the Spaniards were Catalans. When the war broke out they were sent to the Maginot line, the great French defensive fortification designed to stop the German military machine. The Spanish signed up with the CTE in order to leave the hated concentration camps and because they refused to enlist in the Legion or in the Compagnies de Marche, in which they were no longer prisoners but nor were they totally

---

27   See, among others, Josep Benet, *Joan Peiró, Afusellat* (Barcelona: Edicions 62, 2009) and Joan Peiró, *Escrits 1917–1939* (Barcelona: Edicions 62, 1975).
28   Diego Gaspar, "Palabras de un exilio particular: de las Compañías de Trabajadores Extranjeros a los campos nazis," *Hispania Nova* 14 (2016), 229–45.

free. On the Maginot line, they worked in their thousands in tasks of construction, reinforcement, and defense, dressed in uniforms from World War I. They enlisted in the belief that they would be continuing the struggle against the Franco dictatorship. As is well known, the German army bypassed the Maginot line, and its defenders, along with the French military, suffered the consequences of the defeat.

Awaiting the Spanish Republicans in France who resisted the Germans was the worst of all possible scenarios: the Nazi concentration and extermination camps. The Franco regime abandoned the Spaniards taken prisoner by the Nazis to their fate, and as a result some seven thousand Catalan and Spanish Republicans were transported to Mauthausen in Austria, called Ostmark until 1942 and then renamed Alpen-Donau-Reichsgaue until the definitive Nazi defeat.

On January 27, 1941 a group of deportees arrived at the Mauthausen concentration camp, a hell on earth that—lest we forget—was the product of the human mind. A third of the deportees were from the Països Catalans, as Montserrat Roig's pioneering study makes clear. Roig's work opened up a new line of research and is essential reading for all those interested in the subject. Of the more than 7,000 Republican deportees, over two-thirds (4,667) were killed in the camps and satellites, in which they were exploited mercilessly as slave labor in conditions that pushed human resistance to its limits.

There is a little-known story of an illustrious exile who, though not directly involved in politics, gave a universal lesson in democracy that has transcended generations. Pau Casals, the great cellist, conductor, and musical composer, abhorred Francoism and Nazi totalitarianism and all those who connived with them. Casals was in Paris when the Spanish Civil War broke out, and never returned to his homeland. At the end of the Civil War he remained fully committed to helping refugees, visiting concentration camps in France and performing concerts to raise money for the cause and to care for orphaned children. He set up home in Prades de Conflent, a Catalan town in southern France at the foot of Mount Canigó. In late 1942, when France was fully occupied, the Nazis invited him to perform a gala concert in Berlin in the presence of Hitler. Casals replied: "I do not know if you know this, but I have decided not to perform in any dictatorship," and even added, "Not in Germany or in Russia."[29] The German generals who had brought the invitation,

---

29 Canals and Ràfols, *Tarradellas, el guardià de la memoria*, 145.

educated men, took offense and the visit ended in an atmosphere of cold formality. The next morning at 7 o'clock, officers in command of a platoon of soldiers made a meticulous search of Casals' home, looking for documentary evidence of the rumor that Pau Casals and his father had connections with the *maquis* and the Resistance.

LLUÍS COMPANYS, PRESIDENT OF THE GENERALITAT

The exile of Lluís Companys on February 5, 1939 coincided with the most graphic representation of the exodus of a people: almost a biblical image. About 470,000 people out of a population of some three million fled the terror of war and fascism on the road to an uncertain future in France. In its thousand years of history Catalonia had experienced nothing like it.

Not even at this dramatic moment did the presidents of Catalonia, Lluís Companys, and Euskadi, José Antonio Aguirre, receive the political, moral, and personal support of the president of the Spanish Republic, Manuel Azaña. Without informing them, Azaña crossed the frontier ahead of them – as, he believed, was his prerogative. It was a sad presage of the little political understanding there would be between the exiles from Spain in the long years of the diaspora.

The Generalitat had no material or economic resources, but Companys tried to help the many thousands of Catalans held in French concentration camps. He worked hard to keep the presence of the Catalan Republic alive, but the outbreak of World War II, the German occupation of France, the armistice, and the desire not to abandon his sick son led him to take refuge in La Baule-les Pins in Brittany (Ar Baol, in Breton). There, he was arrested on August 13, 1940 by four members of the German military police, assisted by two members of the French fascist militias. His captors stole what little he had.

Transferred to the Santé Prison in Paris, without any form of identification, he was handed over to the Spanish police and taken illegally to Spain.[30] On August 29 he arrived in the prison of the Directorate General of Security in Madrid. On October 3 he was transferred to

---

30 In an event at the Palau de la Generalitat on September 29, 2008, the consuls general of Germany and France, Frau Christine Gläser and M. Pascal Brice, presented formal apologies for the involvement of their countries' governments in the execution of Lluís Companys by the Francoist dictatorship.

Barcelona to be court-martialed. Presenting his own defense, Companys added with dignity and pride that he was being judged for having been president of the Generalitat.[31]

At 6:30 a.m. on October 15, 1940, Companys was shot by firing squad. He died facing his executioners, refusing to be blindfolded; he removed his shoes so as to die with his feet touching Catalan soil. Companys is the only president of a democratic country to have been executed by the totalitarian dictatorships in Europe during World War II. His execution is unanimously regarded as a state crime.

THE BLUE DIVISION

There are several thorough-going studies of the Blue Division, the Spanish military unit that fought with the Nazis on the Eastern front, and of its associations with Catalonia.[32]

The Division comprised 18,104 soldiers, of whom 2,612 were officers. It is estimated that around 46,000 men passed through its ranks. Catalonia accounted for about 10 percent of the total. With 4,954 men killed, 8,700 wounded, and 372 taken prisoner, the Blue Division shed "blood, pain, enthusiasm and disappointment," to quote the writer Luis Romero. As a young man, Romero's experiences in the Civil War had filled him with passion for the cause and he enlisted in the Blue Division to fight "against communism." But not all the "volunteers" were there of their own free will. Many young men were under pressure to enlist, either due to their family origin or to the need to erase a Republican political past; others were coerced, or given false promises.

The Blue Division left a legacy that the Franco regime tried hard to hide, even to forget. Nevertheless, on April 2, 1954 the return of 286 prisoners from the Soviet Union who were thought to have died or disappeared in the campaign on the Eastern Front was met with a huge propaganda fanfare. The captives were able to return fifteen years after the end of the Civil War thanks to Stalin's death the previous year and to the effective and decisive intervention of the French Red Cross.

---

31   Josep M. Solé i Sabaté, *Consell de guerra i condemna a mort de Lluís Companys* (Barcelona: Generalitat de Catalunya, 1999).

32   See Xavier Moreno Julià, *La División Azul: sangre española en Rusia, 1941–1945* (Barcelona: Crítica, 2006); Carme Agustí, *Rússia és culpable! Memòria i record de la División Azul* (Lleida: Pagès editors. 2003); and Albert Royo Campo, "Les terres de Lleida i la División azul," *Shikar* 2 (2015), 56–62.

The Greek ship *Semiramis* set out from the port of Odessa with 229 volunteers of the Blue Division on board, 19 deserters, 7 members of the Blue Legion, 21 members of the SS, and one airman, four "children of the war" sent as refugees in 1937, 19 sailors of the Second Republic's merchant navy confined by the Soviet authorities in 1939, and 15 trainee airmen of the Republican air force who were at the flight school of Kirovabad at the end of the Civil War and who, for various reasons, had been in the gulag since 1941.

Archbishop Monsignor Gregorio Modrego y Casaus presided over the ceremony in the port of Barcelona to mark their return. Among those awaiting them was the minister of the army, Agustin Muñoz Grandes. His presence demonstrates how confident the regime was of its position by 1954, because this was a man who had been the General of the Blue Division, Division 250 of the Wehrmacht, and had been awarded the Iron Cross. In 1953 the Franco regime had entered into firm military and economic agreements with the US and had signed the Concordat with the Vatican. The return of the prisoners allowed the Franco regime to depict itself as a visionary crusader in the fight against communism long before the world split into two polar opposites during the Cold War.

Volunteer Workers in the German War Economy

Spain, a poor country impoverished still further by the war, offered the Axis powers a source of cheap labor to replace the hundreds of thousands of German workers who had been mobilized for battle.

The agreements began in the spring of 1941, and responded to the interests of both countries. For Spain the supply of workers represented a way of paying part of its debt to Nazi Germany for the military aid provided during the Civil War. There was also a great deal of ideological support for the Nazi regimes, at least as long as Hitler's armies appeared invincible on the battlefields. In August, the economic, social, and logistical terms of the agreement were sanctioned by both sides.

An intense propaganda campaign was launched in Spain, with the creation of the Permanent Interministerial Commission for the sending of workers to Germany (Spanish acronym CIPETA). This commission was overseen directly by Ramón Serrano Suñer, minister of foreign affairs.[33]

However, the numbers of workers sent to Germany never met the quota requested by the Germans. The Barcelona contingent, which came from all over Catalonia, comprised the following numbers: November 27, 1941: 608; December 5, 1941: 568; December 11, 1941: 272; June 9, 1942: 494; and March 16, 1943: 400.[34]

Besides volunteers,[35] prisoners of war and political prisoners on "probation" were sent to work in Germany, as were others who had returned from exile in France and were now forced to join. The definitive return to Spain of the workers in Germany would be comic if it were not tragic.[36] With the fall of the Third Reich, on June 15, 1945, a train from Geneva arrived at the French station of Chambery carrying 460 Spanish citizens, among them, according to the French press, some former members of the Blue Division. The Spanish press reported that they were mostly Spanish volunteer workers in Hitler's Germany, and that there were also officials from the Spanish embassies[37] in Germany and in countries under Nazi rule.

The train was assaulted by an unarmed crowd shouting "Death to Franco and the traitors!" who then proceeded to beat the passengers and strip them naked. The French police, who according to press reports did little to intervene, shunted the train back into the hands of the Swiss authorities. In order to return this group of at best half-clothed compatriots to their homeland, the Spanish consul in Geneva contacted some anti-Franco knitwear manufacturers, originally from Canet de Mar, who had been exiled at the beginning of the Civil War and had set up a small factory in Switzerland; in return for a visa, they agreed to provide clothing for the train's passengers.

---

33 Capdevila and Vilanova, *Nazis a Barcelona*, 149.
34 José Luis Rodríguez Jiménez, *Los esclavos de Hitler* (Barcelona: Edit. Planeta, 2002), 107–8.
35 It was under this system that the impostor Enric Marco was hired by the Deutsche Werke Werft company of Kiel. He lied about his role in the Civil War, about his arrest in Nazi Germany, and his time at the concentration camp of Flossenburg in Bavaria. Marco was finally unmasked in 2005. He had been a leader of the anarcho-syndicalist union CNT (Confederación Nacional del Trabajo, National Confederation of Labor) during the Transition, 1976–1979, vice-president of FAPAC (Federació d'Associacions de Pares d'Alumnes de Catalunya, Federation of Parents' Associations of Catalonia) in 1998, and the Associació Amical de Mauthausen (Mauthausen Amical Association), 2003–2005.
36 Francesc Cabana, *37 anys de franquisme a Catalunya. Una visió econòmica* (Barcelona: Edic. Pòrtic., 2000), 99.
37 Also present was the flamenco dancer Nati Morales and her guitarist.

Under Nazi Rule in France

The nature of the collaboration between Spanish refugees and the German military authorities has never been made sufficiently clear. We should mention Josep Antoni Trabal[38] and a few lesser known individuals such as Antoni Alberola, alias Erich, who collaborated with the Gestapo and was believed to be a Gestapo agent, as well as the photographer Josep Argelés, who devoted such efforts to forging passports, and Benet Comas, a former Generalitat policeman.

In Andorra, with its continuous border traffic, Joan Grau was accused in May 1944 of helping the Gestapo to uncover an escape network based at the Hotel Palancas in the key enclave of La Massana, along with Jaime López, Justo Mina, and Aurelio Fernández. This network cooperated with the Allies to allow Jews to flee Nazi rule, and was made up of members of the POUM (Partit Obrer d'Unificació Marxista, Workers' Party of Marxist Unification) exiled in Andorra such as Josep Forné, and members of the ERC like the former member of parliament Francesc Viadiu.

Many murky deals were made to enable fugitives to cross the border to safety. Smuggling of all kinds was rife: trafficking of currency and works of art, money laundering, denunciations, and exchanges. There were also deaths that were never explained, many of them merely murders spurred by greed.

The fate of the Catalans who worked in the German defensive line known as the Todt organization remains a mystery.[39] We do not know how many they were, where they were stationed, or what became of them later.

In occupied Paris, according to the stark testimony of the internationally acclaimed poster artist Carles Fontseré,[40] not everyone turned their backs on the Nazis. The subject is particularly delicate. There were spies, collaborators, actors, musicians, and artists; there were parties, celebrations, and cultural performances given by very different people from all over the world, including Catalan and Spanish Republicans who were ready and able to adapt to the new setting of the occupation.

---

38 Ex-member of the ERC.
39 In the area of the English Channel that was under German control, a fortified line was built containing some 15,000 bunkers, trenches, and tunnels.
40 Carles Fontseré, *Un exiliat de tercera. A París durant la Segona Guerra Mundial* (Barcelona: Proa, 1999).

Another story is the presence of Catalan refugees in the Resistance and the *maquis*. In many places in France, the Spanish refugees fought against the occupiers from the very beginning, and in fact Spanish units were among the first to march into Paris on the day of the city's liberation.

HUNTED AND SAVED

Persecuted by the Nazis, around twenty thousand fugitives managed to flee to Spain via a series of escape routes that stretched across the entire range of the Pyrenees. Their experiences in the area of the Catalan Pyrenees have been the subject of many thorough studies.[41]

The fugitives sought to escape via the mountains or by sea.[42] The mountains were the preferred route, as surveillance was much more difficult. Guides, *résistants*, smugglers, and escape networks provided logistical support, and local people responded with great kindness on seeing the drama of elderly people, children, and entire families attempting to reach mountain passes at heights above 2000 meters (6,500 feet) in the middle of winter and without suitable clothing or equipment.

Certain studies have stressed the importance of these escape routes to the Allies, who were desperate to recover pilots who had been shot down in France in order to be able to continue the aerial war against Nazism. For their part, thousands of Jews of French, Dutch, German, Polish, and Belgian origin crossed the Pyrenees via the provinces of Lleida and Girona with the hope of reaching the British consulate in Barcelona and the Allied agents involved in the clandestine Jewish network in the same city.[43]

---

41   See two studies by Josep Calvet: *Les muntanyes de la llibertat* (Barcelona: Edit. L'Avenç, 2008) and *Huyendo del holocausto: judíos evadidos del nazismo a través del Pirineo de Lleida* (Lleida: Edit. Milenio, 2015).

42   In the mountainous area of Portbou, where the Pyrenees meet the Mediterranean, the German Jewish philosopher Walter Benjamin sought refuge from Nazism; he died there, in unclear circumstances. Dani Karavan erected a monument in his honor in the town of Portbou in 1994.

43   These little-known events in Lleida are commemorated by the IEI (Institut d'Estudis Ilerdencs, Institute of Lleida Studies) in the series "Perseguits i salvats," which narrates the drama of the thousands of people who endured subhuman conditions and lived in constant fear of arrest by the German border patrols. As regards Girona, see Clara, *Nazis a la frontera dels Pirineus Orientals* and Eduardo Martín de Pozuelo, *El Franquismo, cómplice del holocausto* (Barcelona: Ed. Libros de Vanguardia, 2012).

A key figure in this network was Samuel Sequerra,[44] a Jew who arrived in Barcelona in 1941 as a representative of the Red Cross. Sequerra was also an agent of the Portuguese government.[45] In cooperation with the Joint Distribution Committee (JDC), an aid organization for Jewish refugees funded by American Jews, he managed to save thousands of lives The JDC's headquarters in the Hotel Bristol in Plaza Catalonia in Barcelona was always under surveillance by the Francoist police, and was attacked by a group of Falangists on July 18, 1944. Many of the fugitives crossed the Catalan Pyrenees hoping to travel through Spain toward Gibraltar or Lisbon, from where they might catch a ship to Palestine, the US, or other any destination in an Allied country safe from the clutches of the Nazis.[46] This gives the lie to one of Francoism's later myths, which claimed that the regime had welcomed and protected the Jews of Sephardic origin.[47]

Those arrested at the border crossing were initially returned to the French or German authorities under an agreement made between the Francoist and the German police forces on July 31, 1938. From there, they were transferred as detainees to the eighteenth-century building of the Universitat de Cervera, to Sort, Tremp, Lleida, or Barcelona, or the Miranda de Ebro concentration camp in the province of Burgos.

SPAIN AS A NAZI REFUGE

The solid social and cultural support for Nazism in Spain suffered a devastating blow when the atrocities committed by the Third Reich came to be known. Spanish sympathizers had no inkling of the existence of the final solution and the Holocaust or of the presence of concentration and extermination camps. But it is no less true that they were well aware of the basic tenets of Nazism, and so they were not just innocent dupes; by lending their support to the movement they were, to use Hannah Arendt's term, participants in the "banality of evil."

At the end of August 1944, the liberation of the south of France forced hundreds of German officers and soldiers to flee toward Spain.[48]

---

44   See pirineosenguerra.blogspot.com/.../samuel-sequerra-.
45   Bernd Rother, *Franco y el holocausto* (Madrid: Edit. Marcial Pons, 2005), 151.
46   Calvet, *Les muntanyes de la llibertat* and *Huyendo del holocausto*.
47   Martín de Pozuelo, *El Franquismo, cómplice del holocausto*.
48   Capdevila and Vilanova describe the arrival of 436 in Les (Val d'Aran); 250 in the Alt Empordà; and 402 in Puigcerdà, Cerdanya. Nine train carriages were intervened.

Studies carried out in the mid-1980s recall the unusually large presence of Germans in Caldes de Malavella, a spa town in the province of Girona, 83 km (just over 50 miles) from the border with France. Between the fall of 1944 and 1946, a figure of 85 leading Nazis took refuge here. The plan was to find accommodation for 225, all of whom would otherwise have been handed over to the Allies.

This period of relaxed confinement was punctuated by walks and parties, in some cases in the company of relatives. A message issued by the ministry of the interior dated February 24, 1945 stated: "In view of the category of the subjects confined, the majority of whom have been of service to us, the desire is not to establish an excessively rigorous regime."[49] It was Spanish fascism's last favor to German national socialism.[50]

Nazism and fascism had been defeated; Francoism, their ally, now sought to erase them as if they had not existed. The Nazi period is one of the most shameful periods in the history of humankind. Its imprint is not always easy to bring into focus, but it must be studied in depth; historiography must ensure that the *banality of evil* is not forgotten.

BIBLIOGRAPHY

Agustí, Carme. *Rússia és culpable! Memòria i record de la División Azul.* Lleida: Pagès editors., 2003.

Arnabat, Ramon, and David Iñiguez. *Atac i defensa de la rereguarda: els bombardeigs franquistes a les comarques de Tarragona i Terres de l'Ebre (1936–1939).* Tarragona: Cossetània Edicions, 2013.

Benet, Josep. *Joan Peiró, Afusellat.* Barcelona: Edicions 62, 2009.

Cabana, Francesc. *37 anys de franquisme a Catalunya. Una visió económica.* Barcelona: Edic. Pòrtic., 2000.

Calvet, Josep. *Les muntanyes de la llibertat.* Barcelona: Edit. L'Avenç, 2008.

Of all those who passed over the Pyrenees, 1,230 subalterns and 23 officers reached Miranda de Ebro. See *Nazis a Barcelona,* 24.

49 The restrictions imposed were that they should not leave the town without authorization, nor make phone calls outside the town, or receive more visits than strictly necessary. Some were provided with a new identity so as to evade international justice.

50 See Jordi Finestres, "Caldes de Malavella, refugi nazi," *Sàpiens* 36 (October 2005), 21–29.

————. *Huyendo del holocausto: judíos evadidos del nazismo a través del Pirineo de Lleida.* Lleida: Edit. Milenio, 2015.

Canals, Enric, and Josep Maria Ràfols. *Tarradellas, el guardià de la memoria.* Barcelona: Pòrtic Ediciones, 2017.

Capdevila, Mireia, and Francesc Vilanova. *Nazis a Barcelona. L'esplendor feixista de postguerra (1939–1945).* Barcelona: L'Avenç Ed. Barcelona, 2017.

Clara, Josep. *Nazis a la frontera dels Pirineus Orientals (1942–1944).* Barcelona: Rafael Dalmau Editor, 2016.

Deulonder, Xavier. *Els nazis a Catalunya.* Barcelona: Llibres de l'Índex, 2007.

El Nazismo al desnudo. Su intervención y ayuda a los facciosos españoles puesta al descubierto por sus propios documentos. Barcelona: CNT, 1938.

Finestres, Jordi. "Caldes de Malavella, refugi nazi." *Sàpiens* 36 (October 2005): 21–29.

Finestres, Jordi and Queralt Solé. "1940. Nazis a Montserrat." Sàpiens 3 (January 2003): 22–27.

Fontseré, Carles. *Un exiliat de tercera. A París durant la Segona Guerra Mundial.* Barcelona: Proa, 1999.

Garriga, Teodor. *La meva vida i Ràdio Associació de Catalunya.* Barcelona: Ed. Proa., 1998.

Gaspar, Diego. "Palabras de un exilio particular: de las Compañías de Trabajadores Extranjeros a los campos nazis." Hispania Nova 14 (2016): 229–45.

Irujo, Jose María. "La lista negra. Los espías nazis en España." *El Correo Digital*, February 17, 2003.

Martín de Pozuelo, Eduardo. *El Franquismo, cómplice del holocausto.* Barcelona: Ed. Libros de Vanguardia, 2012.

Moreno Julià, Xavier. *La División Azul: sangre española en Rusia, 1941–1945.* Barcelona: Crítica, 2006.

Nelles, Dieter. *Deutsche Anarchosyndikalisten: DAS. Cronología 1933–1939.* Heidelberg: Verlag Graswurzelrevolution, 2013.

Orensanz, Toni. *El nazi de Siurana.* Barcelona: Ara Llibres, 2016.

Peiró, Joan. *Escrits 1917–1939.* Barcelona: Edicions 62, 1975.

Pujadas, Xavier, and Carles Santacana. *L'altra Olimpíada, Barcelona'36. Esport, societat i política a Catalunya (1900-1936)* (Barcelona: Llibres de l'Índex, 2006).

Rodríguez Jiménez, José Luis. *Los esclavos de Hitler*. Barcelona: Edit. Planeta, 2002.

Rother, Bernd. *Franco y el holocausto*. Madrid: Edit. Marcial Pons, 2005.

Royo Campo, Albert. "Les terres de Lleida i la División azul." *Shikar* 2 (2015): 56–62.

Sala, Rosa, and Plàcid García-Planas. *El marqués y la esvástica. César González-Ruano y los judíos en el París ocupado*. Barcelona: Edit. Anagrama, 2016.

Solé i Sabaté, Josep M. *Consell de guerra i condemna a mort de Lluís Companys*. Barcelona: Generalitat de Catalunya, 1999.

Solé i Sabaté, Josep M., and Joan Villarroya. *Guerra i propaganda. Fotografies del Comissariat de Propaganda de la Generalitat de Catalunya (1936–1939)*. Barcelona: Ed. Viena, 2006.

Tusquets, Esther. *Habíamos ganado la guerra*. Barcelona: Edit. Bruguera, 2007.

Vicens Vives, Jaume. *España. Geopolítica del Estado y del Imperio*. N.p.: Ed. Anvil, 1940.

Index

Page numbers in italics indicate illustrations.

A

anti-Semitism, 155
Antoniutti, Ildebrando, 384–87, 389–90
ANV (Acción Nacionalista Vasca, Basque Nationalist Action), 220*n*5
Araba province, Basque powers in, 217*n*1
Arbeca, bombing attacks on, 290
archaeology: of bombardments, 338–43; case studies of bombings,
	344–51; methodology and techniques of, 343–44; range of
	destruction and, 338; remains of warfare and, 342
archaeotecture techniques, 344
architecture, materiality of, 352–54
Arenys de Mar, bombing of, 293
Aresti, Gabriel, 251–52, 254, 254*n*24
Argelès, Josep, 461
Argelés-sur-Mer, 14
Ariz Elcarte, Máximo Alfonso, 378
Armée Secrète, 127
Arnabar, Ramon, 281
Arranz, Francisco, 10, 141
Arrizbalaga, Antonio Múgica, 231
Arrue, Antonio, 252
Artetxe, Aurelio, 49
Art of War, The (Sun Tzu), 144
Aryanization, economic, 164, 166, 167
Aryan superiority, 454
Asistencia social (Social welfare), 94–95, 101
assault landing craft (ALC), 146
Asturias, uprising in, 369–73
asylum for children: Basque children, 93; in Belgium, 99–100; in
	Britain, 101–4; in Denmark, 105; destination country break-
	down, 98; in France, 98–99; in Mexico, 106–7; statistics,
	100–101; in Switzerland, 104–5; temporary host countries,
	96; in USSR, 106
Atlantikwall (Atlantic Wall), 19, 137, 147, 149, 217
Aturri River, 145, 152
Atxaga, Bernardo, 243
Aur besoetakoa (The Foster Daughter) (Mirande), 253–54
Auslands-Organisation der NSDAP, 9
aviación legionaria en la guerra Española, La (Alcofar Nassaes), 332
avurnave, 198
Axis powers, 26, 31

C

Made in the USA
San Bernardino, CA
16 February 2020